WESLEY HOHFELD A CENTURY LATER

Wesley Hohfeld is known the world over as the legal theorist who famously developed a taxonomy of legal concepts. His contributions to legal thinking have stood the test of time, remaining relevant nearly a century after they were first published. Yet, little systematic attention has been devoted to exploring the full significance of his work. Beginning with a lucid, annotated version of Hohfeld's most important article, this volume is the first to offer a comprehensive look at the scope, significance, reach, intricacies, and shortcomings of Hohfeld's work. Featuring insights from leading legal thinkers, the book also contains many of Hohfeld's previously unseen personal papers, shedding new light on the complex motivations behind Hohfeld's projects. Together, these selected papers and original essays reveal a portrait of a multifaceted and ambitious intellectual who did not live long enough to see the impact of his ideas on the study of law.

Shyamkrishna Balganesh is the Sol Goldman Professor of Law at Columbia Law School.

Ted M. Sichelman is a Professor of Law at the University of San Diego School of Law, where he founded and directs the Center for Computation, Mathematics & the Law and directs the Center for Intellectual Property Law & Markets.

Henry E. Smith is the Fessenden Professor of Law at Harvard Law School, where he directs the Project on the Foundations of Private Law. Smith served as the President of the Society for Institutional and Organizational Economics and is the Reporter for the American Law Institute's Fourth Restatement of Property.

Wesley Hohfeld A Century Later

EDITED WORK, SELECT PERSONAL PAPERS, AND ORIGINAL COMMENTARIES

Edited by

SHYAMKRISHNA BALGANESH

Columbia Law School

TED M. SICHELMAN

University of San Diego School of Law

HENRY E. SMITH

Harvard Law School

CAMBRIDGE
UNIVERSITY PRESS

CAMBRIDGE
UNIVERSITY PRESS

University Printing House, Cambridge CB2 8BS, United Kingdom

One Liberty Plaza, 20th Floor, New York, NY 10006, USA

477 Williamstown Road, Port Melbourne, VIC 3207, Australia

314–321, 3rd Floor, Plot 3, Splendor Forum, Jasola District Centre, New Delhi – 110025, India

103 Penang Road, #05–06/07, Visioncrest Commercial, Singapore 238467

Cambridge University Press is part of the University of Cambridge.

It furthers the University's mission by disseminating knowledge in the pursuit of education, learning, and research at the highest international levels of excellence.

www.cambridge.org
Information on this title: www.cambridge.org/9781107192881
DOI: 10.1017/9781108131742

First published 2022

A catalogue record for this publication is available from the British Library.

Library of Congress Cataloging-in-Publication Data
NAMES: Balganesh, Shyamkrishna, editor. | Sichelman, Ted M., 1971– editor. | Smith, Henry E., editor.
TITLE: Wesley Hohfeld a century later : edited work, select personal papers, and original commentaries / edited by Shyamkrishna Balganesh, Columbia Law School; Ted M. Sichelman, University of San Diego School of Law; Henry E. Smith, Harvard Law School.
DESCRIPTION: Cambridge, United Kingdom ; New York, NY : Cambridge University Press, 2022. | Includes bibliographical references and index.
IDENTIFIERS: LCCN 2021027186 (print) | LCCN 2021027187 (ebook) | ISBN 9781107192881 (hardback) | ISBN 9781108131742 (ebook)
SUBJECTS: LCSH: Hohfeld, Wesley Newcomb, 1879–1918 – Influence. | Law – United States. | Law teachers – United States.
CLASSIFICATION: LCC KF373.H574 W47 2022 (print) | LCC KF373.H574 (ebook) | DDC 340.092–dc23
LC record available at https://lccn.loc.gov/2021027186
LC ebook record available at https://lccn.loc.gov/2021027187

ISBN 978-1-107-19288-1 Hardback

Contents

Figures

Tables

Contributors

The Editor-Contributors

Shyamkrishna Balganesh is the Sol Goldman Professor of Law at Columbia Law School. His work examines the connection between intellectual property and private law theory, including ideas and concepts from the common law. His publication, *Foreseeability and Copyright Incentives*, 122 HARV. L. REV. 1569 (2009), is among the most-cited intellectual property law articles over the last decade. His other publications include: *Legal Internalism in Modern Histories of Copyright*, 134 HARV. L. REV. 1066 (2021) (with Taisu Zhang); *The Genius of Common Law Intellectual Property*, 49 J. LEGAL STUD. S91 (2021); *Privative Copyright*, 73 VAND. L. REV. 1 (2020); *Copyright as Legal Process: The Transformation of American Copyright Law*, 168 U. PA. L. REV. 1101 (2020); *Copyright as Market Prospect*, 166 U. PA. L. REV. 443 (2018); *Causing Copyright*, 117 COLUM. L. REV. 1 (2017); *The Questionable Origins of the Copyright Infringement Analysis*, 68 STAN. L. REV. 791 (2016); *Copyright and Good Faith Purchasers*, 104 CAL. L. REV. 269 (2016); *Structure and Value in the Common Law*, 163 U. PA. L. REV. 1241 (2015) (with Gideon Parchomovsky); *Codifying the Common Law of Property in India: Crystallization and Standardization as Strategies of Constraint*, 63 AM. J. COMP. L. 33 (2015); *Unplanned Coauthorship*, 100 VA. L. REV. 1683 (2014); Judging Similarity, 100 IOWA L. REV. 267 (2014) (with Irina D. Manta & Tess Wilkinson-Ryan); *Copyright Infringement Markets*, 113 COLUM. L. REV. 2277 (2013); *Gandhi and Copyright Pragmatism*, 101 CAL. L. REV. 1705 (2013); *The Uneasy Case Against Copyright Trolls*, 86 S. CAL. L. REV. 723 (2013); *The Normativity of Copying in Copyright Law*, 62 DUKE L.J. 203 (2012); *The Obligatory Structure of Copyright Law: Unbundling the Wrong of Copying*, 125 HARV. L. REV. 1664 (2012); *Quasi-Property: Like, But Not Quite Property*, 160 U. PA. L. REV. 1889 (2012); *"Hot News": The Enduring Myth of Property in News*, 111 COLUM. L. REV. 419 (2011); *The Pragmatic Incrementalism of Common Law Intellectual Property*, 63 VAND. L. REV. 1543 (2010); and *Debunking Blackstonian Copyright*, 118 YALE L.J. 1126 (2009).

Ted Sichelman is a Professor of Law and Director of the Center for Computation, Law, and Mathematics at the University of San Diego School of Law. Several of his publications are among the most-cited intellectual property law articles over the last ten years. His selected works include: *Quantifying Legal Entropy*, 9 FRONTIERS IN PHYSICS 665054 (2021); *An Economic Model of Patent Exhaustion*, 29 J. ECON. & MGMT. STRATEGY 816 (2020) (with Olena Ivus & Edwin Lai); *The Case for Noncompetes*, 86 U. CHI. L. REV. 953 (2020) (with Jonathan Barnett); *Cycles of Obviousness*, 105 IOWA L. REV. 107 (2019) (with Ryan Holte); *Ranking the Academic Reputation of 100 American Law Schools*, 60 JURIMETRICS 1 (2019) (with Paul Heald); *Why Do Startups Use Trades Secrets?*, 94 NOTRE DAME L. REV. 751 (2018) (with David Levine); *Patents, Prizes, and Property*, 30 HARV. J.L. & TECH. 279 (2017); *Data-Generating Patents*, 111 NW. U. L. REV. (2017); *Do Economic Downturns Dampen Patent Litigation?*, 12 J. EMPIRICAL LEGAL STUD. 481 (2015) (with Alan Marco & Shawn Miller); *Purging Patent Law of "Private Law" Remedies*, 92 TEX. L. REV. 516 (2014); *The Vonage Trilogy: A Case Study in "Patent Bullying"*, 90 NOTRE DAME L. REV. 543 (2014); *Enforcement as Substance in Tax Compliance*, 70 WASH. & LEE L. REV. 1679 (2013) (with Leandra Lederman); *Patents as Promoters of Competition: The Guild Origins of Patent Law in the Venetian Republic*, 49 SAN DIEGO L. REV. 1267 (2012) (with Sean O'Connor); *Life After Bilski*, 63 STAN. L. REV. 1315 (2011) (with Mark Lemley, Michael Risch, & R. Polk Wagner); *Commercializing Patents*, 62 STAN. L. REV. 341 (2010); *Patenting by Entrepreneurs: An Empirical Study*, 17 MICH. TELECOMM. & TECH. L. REV. 111 (2010) (with Stuart Graham); and *High Technology Entrepreneurs and the Patent System: Results of the 2008 Berkeley Patent Survey*, 24 BERKELEY TECH. L.J. 255 (2009).

Henry E. Smith is Fessenden Professor of Law and the Director of the Project on the Foundations of Private Law at Harvard Law School. Individually and with coauthors he has published some of the most widely cited articles in the law, economics, and philosophy of property and its relation to remedies and private law more generally. Among his published articles are: *Equity as Meta-Law*, 130 YALE L.J. 1050 (2021); *The Economics of Property Law, in* THE OXFORD HANDBOOK OF LAW AND ECONOMICS, VOLUME 2: PRIVATE AND COMMERCIAL LAW 148 (Francesco Parisi ed., Oxford University Press 2017); *On the Economy of Concepts in Property*, 160 U. PA. L. REV. 2097 (2012); *Property as the Law of Things*, 125 HARV. L. REV. 169 (2012); *Intellectual Property as Property: Delineating Entitlements in Information*, 116 YALE L.J. 1742 (2007); *The Language of Property: Form, Context, and Audience*, 55 STAN. L. REV. 1105 (2003); *Exclusion versus Governance: Two Strategies for Delineating Property Rights*, 31 J. LEGAL STUD. S453 (2002); and *Semicommon Property Rights and Scattering in the Open Fields*, 29 J. LEGAL STUD. 131 (2000). With Professor Thomas Merrill of Columbia Law School he is the coauthor of THE OXFORD INTRODUCTIONS TO U.S. LAW: PROPERTY (Oxford University Press

2010) and PROPERTY: PRINCIPLES AND POLICIES (Foundation Press 3rd ed. 2017) and the landmark papers *What Happened to Property in Law and Economics?*, 111 YALE L.J. 357 (2001); *The Property/Contract Interface*, 101 COLUM. L. REV. 773 (2001); and *Optimal Standardization in the Law of Property: The* Numerus Clausus *Principle*, 110 YALE L.J. 1 (2000). In 2015–2016, Smith served as the President of the Society for Institutional and Organizational Economics and, in 2014, the American Law Institute named him Reporter for the Fourth Restatement of Property.

The Contributors

Aditi Bagchi is Professor of Law at Fordham University School of Law, where she teaches Contracts and Labor Law. She writes about the nature of contractual obligation, contract interpretation, and questions in political and moral philosophy as they arise in contract. She has a related interest in the comparative political economy of contract, labor, and corporate law. Professor Bagchi has been a visiting professor at Columbia Law School and Yale Law School and, prior to joining Fordham, she taught at the University of Pennsylvania Law School. Before teaching, she clerked on the Third Circuit Court of Appeals and was a litigation associate at Cravath, Swaine & Moore LLP. She obtained her JD from Yale Law School, an MSc in Economic and Social History from Oxford University, and an AB in Government and Philosophy from Harvard College.

Scott Brewer is a Professor of Law at Harvard Law School. He specializes in Contract Law, Evidence Law, Jurisprudence, eudaimonistic ethics, and the philosophical analysis of arguments. His work on the theory of argument is his Logocratic Method, which is the subject of his contribution to this Hohfeld volume and focuses on the epistemic, logical, and axiological structures of arguments, including – but not limited to – legal arguments. He is cofounder and coadministrator of the annual Summer School on Law and Logic, jointly sponsored by Harvard Law School and the European University Institute, in Fiesole, Italy. He delivered the Walter F. Murphy Lecture in the James Madison Program, Princeton University ("Arguing Excellence: A Logocratic Approach to Measures of Virtue," December 2021), was the Kwa Geok Choo Distinguished Visitor, National University of Singapore (lecture, "Arguing the World: A Logocratic Explanation of 'Post-Truth' Law and Politics," August 2018), and will be the Astor Visiting Lecturer at Oxford University in 2022. He has taught courses and workshops around the world, including Brazil, Singapore, Austria, Italy, Germany, Spain, and France. His writings include: *The Logics of Precedent: A Logocratic Analysis*, in PHILOSOPHICAL FOUNDATIONS OF PRECEDENT (forthcoming Oxford University Press); *First Among Equals: Abduction in Legal Argument from a Logocratic Point of View, in* NEW ESSAYS ON THE NATURE OF LEGAL REASONING (M. McBride & J. Penner eds., Hart 2022); *Interactive Virtue and Vice in Systems of Arguments: A Logocratic Analysis*, 28 ARTIFICIAL INTELLIGENCE & L. 151 (2020); *Indefeasible Analogical Argument*, *in* ANALOGY AND EXEMPLARY REASONING IN LEGAL DISCOURSE

(H. Kaptein & B. van der Velden eds., Amsterdam University Press 2018); EVIDENCE CASES AND MATERIALS (Foundation 10th ed. 2017) (coauthored with Judge Jack Weinstein, Norman Abrams, & Daniel Medwed); *Agonophobia (Fear of Contest) in the Theory of Argument?: The Case of Gary Lawson's* Evidence of the Law, 97 B.U. L. REV. 2303 (2017); *Using Propositional Deductive Logic as an Aid to Teaching American Contract Law: The Logocratic Approach*, in LAW AND LOGIC: CONTEMPORARY ISSUES (D. Krimphove & G. M. Lentner eds., Duncker & Humblot 2017); *Law, Logic and Leibniz: A Contemporary Perspective*, in LEIBNIZ: PHILOSOPHICAL QUESTIONS AND PERPLEXING CASES IN THE LAW (A. Artosi, B. Pieri, & G. Sartor eds. and trans., Springer 2013); *Logocratic Method and the Analysis of Arguments in Evidence Law*, 10 LAW, PROBABILITY & RISK 175 (2011); *On the Possibility of Necessity in Legal Argument: A Dilemma for Holmes and Dewey*, 34 J. MARSHALL L. REV. 9 (2000); *Traversing Holmes' Path Toward a Jurisprudence of Logical Form*, in THE PATH OF THE LAW AND ITS INFLUENCE: THE LEGACY OF OLIVER WENDELL HOLMES, JR. (S. Burton, ed., Cambridge University Press 2000); *Scientific Expert Testimony and Intellectual Due Process*, 107 YALE L.J. 1535 (1998); THE PHILOSOPHY OF LEGAL REASONING (5 Volumes) (S. Brewer ed. and Introduction, Routledge 1998); *Exemplary Reasoning: Semantics, Pragmatics, and the Rational Force of Legal Argument by Analogy, Harvard Law Review*, 109 HARV. L. REV. 923 (1996); *Justice Marshall's Justice Martial*, 71 TEX. L. REV. 1121 (1993); *Quelques raisonnements theoriques sur des raisonnements pratiques a propos du raisonnement theorique*, in FONDEMENTS NATURELS DE L'ETHIQUE (Jacob Odile trans., O. Jacob 1993); *Choosing Sides in the* Racial Critiques *Debate*, 103 HARVARD LAW REV. 1844 (1990); *Pragmatism, Oppression, and the Flight to Substance*, 63 S. CAL. L. REV. 1753 (1990); *Figuring the Law: Holism and Tropological Structure in Legal Interpretation*, 97 YALE L.J. 823 (1988); *DuBois' Talented Tenth: Its Role in 1984 and Beyond*, PROCEEDINGS OF THE THIRD ANNUAL W. E. B. DUBOIS GRADUATE COLLOQUIUM (1984).

David Frydrych is a Lecturer (Assistant Professor) at Monash University's Faculty of Law in Melbourne, Australia, where he teaches legal philosophy, property, and trusts. His jurisprudential scholarship to date mostly focuses on rights and legal realism. David's monograph, THE ARCHITECTURE OF RIGHTS: MODELS AND THEORIES, was published by Palgrave in 2021. Other representative publications include: *Down the Methodological Rabbit Hole*, 49 CRÍTICA 41 (2017); *Hohfeld vs. the Legal Realists*, 24 LEGAL THEORY 291 (2018); *The Case Against the Theories of Rights*, 40 OXFORD J. LEGAL STUD. 320 (2020); *Legal Realism and "Working" Rules*, 35(2) CAN. J.L. & JURIS. (forthcoming 2022); and *Realism and Positivism*, Juris: Int'l J.L. & Pol. Thought (forthcoming 2022). Before joining Monash, David was a postdoctoral fellow at both the University of Singapore Faculty of Law and New York University School of Law. He earned an Honours BA with Distinction and LLM from the University of Toronto, a JD from the Benjamin N. Cardozo School of Law, and a DPhil in Law from the University of Oxford. A Canadian, he is admitted to practice in New York and Victoria, Australia.

Andrew Gold is Professor of Law at Brooklyn Law School. His primary research interests address private law theory, fiduciary law, and the law of corporations. His recent book, *The Right of Redress* (Oxford University Press 2020), offers a new theory of private law. His work has appeared in the *Michigan Law Review, Northwestern University Law Review, University of Toronto Law Journal, Law and Philosophy*, and *American Journal of Jurisprudence*, among others. He is a coeditor of multiple books on fiduciary theory, including Fiduciary Government (Cambridge University Press 2018), Contract, Status, and Fiduciary Law (Oxford University Press 2017), and Philosophical Foundations of Fiduciary Law (Oxford University Press 2014). He is also a coeditor of The Oxford Handbook of The New Private Law (Oxford University Press 2020) (with John Goldberg, Dan Kelly, Emily Sherwin, & Henry Smith eds.). Professor Gold previously was the Bruce W. Nichols Visiting Professor at Harvard Law School; an H. L. A. Hart Visiting Fellow at the University of Oxford; and a Fulbright Visiting Research Chair at McGill University. He is a co-founder of the North American Workshop on Private Law Theory.

John Goldberg is Deputy Dean and Carter Professor of General Jurisprudence at Harvard Law School. A leading scholar of tort law, and of tort and private law theory, he is the coauthor, with Professor Benjamin Zipursky, of Recognizing Wrongs (Harvard University Press 2020) and The Oxford Introductions to U.S. Law: Torts (Oxford University Press 2010)). He is also the coauthor of a leading Torts casebook, coeditor of anthologies on private law theory and on law and equity, and author or coauthor of dozens of book chapters, articles, and essays. Representative articles are: *Inexcusable Wrongs*, 103 Cal. L. Rev. 467–512 (2015); *Torts and Estates: Remedying Wrongful Interference with Inheritance*, 65 Stan. L. Rev. 335 (2013) (with Robert Sitkoff); *Introduction: Pragmatism and Private Law*, 125 Harv. L. Rev. 1640 (2012); and *The Constitutional Status of Tort Law: Due Process and the Right to a Law for the Redress of Wrongs*, 115 Yale L.J. 524–627 (2005).

Andrew Halpin is formerly a Professor of Law and Director of the Centre for Legal Theory in the Faculty of Law at the National University of Singapore. His research interests fall mainly within legal theory, broadly conceived. Previous work related to Hohfeld is found in his book, Rights and Law: Analysis and Theory (Hart 1997); a number of articles – *Hohfeld's Conceptions: From Eight to Two*, 44 Cambridge L.J. 435 (1985); *More Comments on Rights and Claims*, 10 Law & Phil. 271 (1991); *The Concept of a Legal Power*, 16 Oxford J. Legal Stud. 129 (1996); *Fundamental Legal Conceptions Reconsidered*, 16 Can. J.L. & Juris. 41

(2003); *Rights, Duties, Liabilities, and Hohfeld*, 13 LEGAL THEORY 23 (2007); and a contribution, *Bentham's Limits and Hohfeld*, *in* THE LEGAL PHILOSOPHY AND INFLUENCE OF JEREMY BENTHAM: ESSAYS ON "*OF THE LIMITS OF THE PENAL BRANCH OF JURISPRUDENCE*" (Guillaume Tusseau ed., Routledge 2014). Other indicative publications include: *Disproving the Coase Theorem?* 23 ECON. & PHIL. 321 (2007); *Austin's Methodology? His Bequest to Jurisprudence*, 70 CAMBRIDGE L.J. 175 (2011); *Questioning a Uniform Concept of Public Law*, 16 JUS POLITICUM 91 (2016); *The Applications of Bivalent Logic, and the Misapplication of Multivalent Logic to Law*, *in* LAW AND THE NEW LOGICS (H. Patrick Glenn & Lionel Smith eds., Cambridge University Press 2017). More recent research has engaged with the logic of correlativity and its implications for the status of Hohfeldian normative positions, notably of liberty and no-right.

John Harrison is the James Madison Distinguished Professor of Law at the University of Virginia School of Law, following a distinguished career with the U.S. Department of Justice. His publications include: *The Original Meaning of the Habeas Corpus Suspension Clause, the Right of Natural Liberty, and Executive Discretion*, 29 WM. & MARY BILL RTS. J. 649 (2021); *Public Rights, Private Privileges, and Article III*, 54 GA. L. REV. 143–216 (2019); *The Constitution and the Law of Nations*, 106 GEO. L.J. 1659–1705 (2018); *The Political Questions Doctrines*, 67 AM. U. L. REV. 457–528 (2017); *Public Choice and Judicial Virtue*, 10 J.L. ECON. & POL'Y 633 (2014); *Severability, Remedies, and Constitutional Adjudication*, 83 GEO. WASH. L. REV. 56 (2014); *Power, Duty, and Facial Invalidity*, 16 U. PA. J. CONST. L. 501 (2013); *Enumerated Federal Power and the Necessary and Proper Clause*, 78 U. CHI. L. REV. 1101 (2011) (reviewing GARY LAWSON ET AL., THE ORIGINS OF THE NECESSARY AND PROPER CLAUSE (Cambridge University Press 2010)); *The State Action Principle and its Critics*, 96 VA. L. REV. 1767 (2010) (with Lillian Bevier); *On the Hypotheses That Lie at the Foundations of Originalism*, 31 Harv. J.L. & PUB. POL'Y 473 (2008); *New Property, Entrenchment, and the Fiscal Constitution*, *in* FISCAL CHALLENGES: AN INTERDISCIPLINARY APPROACH TO BUDGET POLICY (Elizabeth Garrett et al. eds., Cambridge University Press 2008); *Ex Parte Young*, 60 STAN. L. REV. 989 (2008); *The Relationship between Limitations on and Requirements of Article III Adjudication*, 95 CAL. L. REV. 1367 (2007); *Addition by Subtraction*, 92 VA. L. REV. 1853 (2006); *The Power of Congress over the Terms of Justices of the Supreme Court*, *in* REFORMING THE COURT: TERM LIMITS FOR SUPREME COURT JUSTICES (Roger C. Cramton & Paul D. Carrington eds., Carolina Academic Press 2006); *Time, Change, and the Constitution*, 90 VA. L. REV. 1601 (2004); *The Lawfulness of the Reconstruction Amendments*, 68 U. CHI. L. REV. 375 (2001); *The Power of Congress Over the Rules of Precedent*, 50 DUKE L.J. 503 (2000); *Jurisdiction, Congressional Power, and Constitutional Remedies*, 86 GEO. L.J. 2513 (1998); *Substantive Due Process and the Constitutional Text*, 83 VA. L. REV. 493

(1997); *The Power of Congress to Limit the Jurisdiction of Federal Courts and the Text of Article III*, 64 U. CHI. L. REV. 203 (1997); *Reconstructing the Privileges or Immunities Clause*, 101 YALE L.J. 1385 (1992).

Leo Katz is the Frank Carano Professor of Law at the University of Pennsylvania Law School. His work focuses on criminal law and legal theory more generally. By connecting criminal law, moral philosophy, and the theory of social choice, he tries to shed light on some of the most basic building block notions of the law – coercion, deception, consent, and the use and abuse of legal stratagems, among others. Katz is the author of several books: BAD ACTS AND GUILTY MINDS: CONUNDRUMS OF THE CRIMINAL LAW (University of Chicago Press 1987); ILL-GOTTEN GAINS: EVASION, BLACKMAIL, FRAUD AND KINDRED PUZZLES OF THE LAW (University of Chicago Press 1996); and, most recently, WHY THE LAW IS SO PERVERSE (University of Chicago Press 2011), which he researched with the support of a Guggenheim Fellowship. Together with Stephen Morse and Michael Moore, he edited FOUNDATIONS OF THE CRIMINAL LAW (Oxford University Press 1999).

Ben McFarlane is Professor of English Law at the University of Oxford and a Fellow of St John's College, Oxford. He was formerly Professor of Law at University College London. He is the author of THE LAW OF PROPRIETARY ESTOPPEL (Oxford University Press 1st ed, 2014; Oxford University Press 2nd ed. 2020) and THE STRUCTURE OF PROPERTY LAW (Hart 2009), is one of the authors of LAND LAW: TEXT, CASES AND MATERIALS (Oxford University Press 1st ed. 2009; Oxford University Press 5th ed. 2021), and is one of the contributing editors of *Snell's Equity*. He is an Honorary Senior Fellow of the Melbourne Law School and a Visiting Professor at the Université Panthéon-Assas Paris II.

Chris Newman is an Associate Professor of Law at George Mason University School of Law whose scholarship focuses on the relationship of property theory to intellectual property. His key papers in this area include: *A License Is Not A "Contract Not To Sue": Disentangling Property and Contract in the Law of Copyright Licenses*, 98 IOWA L. REV. 1101 (2013); *Transformation in Property and Copyright*, 56 VILL. L. REV. 251 (2011); and *An Exclusive License is Not An Assignment: Disentangling Divisibility and Transferability of Ownership in Copyright*, 74 LA. L. REV. 59 (2013) (selected as one of year's best by *Intellectual Property Law Review*).

James Penner is Kwa Geok Choo Professor of Property Law at the National University of Singapore. He is one of the world's leading experts in the law of trusts and the philosophy of property, and writes more widely in the areas of private law and the philosophy of law. He has been a visiting professor in China, Canada, Belgium, and Australia, and most recently at Harvard Law School in the autumn semester of 2019. His numerous publications include: THE IDEA OF PROPERTY IN LAW (Oxford University Press 1997); PROPERTY RIGHTS: A RE-EXAMINATION

(Oxford University Press 2020); and THE LAW OF TRUSTS (Oxford University Press 12th ed. 2022).

Anna di Robilant is Professor of Law at Boston University School of Law. She is a property law scholar trained in both Europe and the United States. She writes and teaches in the areas of property law, property theory, legal history, and comparative law. Di Robilant's scholarship focuses on two main themes. The first theme is to question the idea, long shared by comparative law experts, that property law in Europe and the United States is fundamentally different. By contrast, di Robilant's work suggests that modern Western property is the product of a "transatlantic dialogue" shaped by intellectual, professional, social, and economic factors. For example, in her article, *Abuse of Rights. The Continental Drug and the Common Law*, 61 HASTINGS L.J. 687 (2010), Professor di Robilant challenges the idea that the doctrine of "abuse of rights" is a peculiarity of civil law systems, absent in the common law, and explores the reasons for the parallel, yet different, development of the doctrine in the two systems. Similarly, in *Property: A Bundle of Sticks or a Tree?*, 66 VAND. L. REV. 86 (2013), Professor di Robilant questions the idea that the "bundle of sticks" image of property is an American invention and examines the intellectual, political, and economic concerns that led European jurists, in the first half of the twentieth century, to develop a new conceptualization of property as a "tree" that shares many of the intuitions of the "bundle of rights" approach and yet differs from it in significant ways. The second theme in di Robilant's property scholarship is designing property law institutions that reflect the values of a free and democratic society, committed to making access to fundamental resources, such as housing, water, cultural, or natural resources, more equitable. In *Common Property and Equality of Autonomy*, 58 MCGILL L.J. 263 (2012), di Robilant analyzes the challenges involved in the design of common ownership institutions, such as conservation land trusts, affordable-housing cooperatives, community gardens, neighborhood-managed parks, and proposes refocusing the design work on promoting greater "equality of autonomy." Similarly, in *Property and Democratic Deliberation: The* Numerus Clausus *Principle and Democratic Experimentalism in Property Law*, 62 AM. J. COMP. L. 367–416 (2014), di Robilant examines a selection of recently created property forms which establish mechanisms of democratic and deliberative governance for resources as diverse as natural resources, scarce urban land, historic landmarks, or cultural institutions. Professor di Robilant is the chair of the Property section of the "Common Core of European Private Law," a project that has brought together more than 200 legal scholars and practitioners to analyze and map the connections and underlying similarities in contract, property, and torts laws across Europe. She received her JD from the University of Torino, Italy; her PhD in Comparative Private Law from the University of Trento, Italy, and her LLM and SJD from Harvard Law School.

Frederick Schauer has been David and Mary Harrison Distinguished Professor of Law at the University of Virginia since 2008. Previously he was Frank Stanton Professor of the First Amendment at Harvard University, and, earlier, Professor of Law at the

University of Michigan. A Fellow of the British Academy and the American Academy of Arts and Sciences, a recipient of a Guggenheim Fellowship, and the holder of an honorary Doctor of Laws from Wirtschaftsuniversität Vienna, Schauer is the author of THE LAW OF OBSCENITY (Bureau of National Affairs 1976), FREE SPEECH: A PHILOSOPHICAL ENQUIRY (Cambridge University Press 1982), PLAYING BY THE RULES: A PHILOSOPHICAL EXAMINATION OF RULE-BASED DECISION-MAKING IN LAW AND IN LIFE (Oxford University Press 1991), PROFILES, PROBABILITIES, AND STEREOTYPES (Harvard University Press 2003), THINKING LIKE A LAWYER: A NEW INTRODUCTION TO LEGAL REASONING (Harvard University Press 2009), THE FORCE OF LAW (Harvard University Press 2015), and PROOF: THE USES OF EVIDENCE IN LAW, POLITICS, AND EVERYTHING ELSE (Harvard University Press 2022). The editor of KARL LLEWELLYN, THE THEORY OF RULES (University of Chicago Press 2011), and a founding editor of *Legal Theory*, he has chaired the Section on Constitutional Law of the Association of American Law Schools and the Committee on Philosophy and Law of the American Philosophical Association. He has written widely on freedom of speech, constitutional interpretation, evidence, legal reasoning, and the philosophy of law. He is the coeditor of CONSTITUTIONAL LAW: CASES, COMMENTS, AND QUESTIONS (West Academic 2019) (with Jesse Choper, Michael Dorf, and Richard Fallon), the editor of *The First Amendment* (West Academic 2019), and, in 2006, wrote the "Foreword" for the *Harvard Law Review*'s annual Supreme Court issue.

Pierre Schlag is University Distinguished Professor and Byron R. White Professor at the University of Colorado Law School. A broad-ranging legal theorist, his most recent works include: *How to Do Things with Hohfeld*, 78 LAW & CONTEMP. PROBS. 185 (2015); *L'Autonomie des Avocats (Une Conception Problématique Parmi Des Développements Démoralisants), in* L'AUTONOMIE DES AVOCATS (Jean Louis Assier ed., Dalloz 2015); and *Coase Minus the Coase Theorem: Some Problems with Chicago Transaction Cost Analysis*, 99 IOWA L. REV. 175 (2013). His other works include: *The Dedifferentiation Problem*, 42 CONTINENTAL PHIL. REV. 35 (2009); *The Aesthetics of American Law*, 115 HARV. L. REV. 1047 (2002); *Formalism and Realism in Ruins (Mapping the Logics of Collapse)*, 95 IOWA L. REV. 195 (2009); THE ENCHANTMENT OF REASON (Duke University Press 1998); *Law and Phrenology*, 110 HARV. L. REV. 877 (1997); and *The Empty Circles of Liberal Justification*, 96 MICH. L. REV. 1 (1997). His works have been translated into French, Russian, Ukrainian, Italian, and Spanish.

John Henry Schlegel is the U.B. Distinguished Professor and Floyd H. and Hilda L. Hurst Faculty Scholar at the University at Buffalo School of Law. He joined the SUNY Buffalo Law faculty in 1973 where he teaches courses in corporate finance, commercial law and regional economic development. For over twenty years, Schlegel's scholarship was focused on the history of legal education, legal theory, and the activities in the 1920s and 1930s of a group of scholars at Columbia, Yale, and

Johns Hopkins universities known as the American Legal Realists. These efforts resulted in a book entitled AMERICAN LEGAL REALISM AND EMPIRICAL SOCIAL SCIENCE (University of North Carolina Press 1995), which described and analyzed Wesley Hohfeld's life and work. While he continues to publish regularly on these topics, his most recent project is a book titled WHILE WAITING FOR RAIN: COMMUNITY, ECONOMY AND LAW IN A TIME OF CHANGE (forthcoming from the University of Michigan Press in 2022). This book focuses on changes in the U.S. economy and in the local, Buffalo one since the Civil War. It attempts to explain the decline in both and, using the economic theory of the urbanist Jane Jacobs, tries to suggest what communities might sensibly do that might make them as attractive to economic actors today as they were in the years after that war.

Emily Sherwin is Professor of Law at Cornell Law School. She specializes in jurisprudence, property, and remedies. She is the author of four books: AMES, CHAFEE, AND RE ON REMEDIES (West Academic 2019) (with Samuel Bray); ADVANCED INTRODUCTION TO LEGAL REASONING (Edward Elgar 2021) (with Larry Alexander); DEMYSTIFYING LEGAL REASONING (Cambridge University Press 2008) (with Larry Alexander); and THE RULE OF RULES: MORALITY, RULES, AND THE DILEMMAS OF LAW (Duke University Press 2001) (with Larry Alexander). She is also an editor of THE OXFORD HANDBOOK OF THE NEW PRIVATE LAW (Oxford University Press 2020) (with Andrew Gold, John Goldberg, Daniel Kelly & Henry Smith). She has published numerous book chapters, articles, and reviews in her subjects of specialty. She was a member of the advisory committee for the ALI's Restatement (Third) of Restitution and Unjust Enrichment, and is currently a member of the advisory committee for the Restatement (Third) of Torts (Remedies). She continues to be a regular participant in the Analytical Legal Philosophy Conference.

Joseph Singer has been a Professor of Law at Harvard Law School since 1992. He was appointed Bussey Professor of Law in 2006. He began teaching at Boston University School of Law in 1984. Singer received a BA from Williams College in 1976, an AM in political science from Harvard in 1978, and a JD from Harvard Law School in 1981. He clerked for Justice Morris Pashman on the Supreme Court of New Jersey from 1981 to 1982 and was an associate at the law firm of Palmer & Dodge in Boston, focusing on municipal law, from 1982 to 1984. He teaches and writes about property law, conflict of laws, and federal Indian law. He also writes about legal theory with an emphasis on moral and political philosophy. He has published more than eighty law review articles. He is one of the executive editors of the 2012 edition of COHEN'S HANDBOOK OF FEDERAL INDIAN LAW (with 2015 Supplement; LexisNexis). He has written a casebook and a treatise on property law, as well as: PERSUASION: GETTING TO THE OTHER SIDE (Carolina Academic Press 2020); CHOICE OF LAW: PATTERNS, ARGUMENTS, PRACTICES (Carolina Academic Press 2020); NO FREEDOM WITHOUT REGULATION: THE HIDDEN LESSON OF THE SUBPRIME

CRISIS (Yale University Press 2015); ENTITLEMENT: THE PARADOXES OF PROPERTY (Yale University Press 2000); and THE EDGES OF THE FIELD: LESSONS ON THE OBLIGATIONS OF OWNERSHIP (Beacon Press 2000).

Talha Syed teaches at the University of California, Berkeley School of Law. His research focuses on law and political economy, with applications to intellectual property, property, torts, antitrust, and theories of distributive justice. His principal publications include: *Reconstructing Patent Eligibility*, 70 AM. U. L. REV. 1937 (2021); *Educational Accommodation and Distributive Equity: The Principle of Proportionate Progress*, 50 CONN. L. REV. 485 (2018); *The Wrongs of Copyright's Statutory Damages*, 98 TEX. L. REV. 1219 (2020) (with Oren Bracha); *The Continuum of Excludability and the Limits of Patents*, 122 YALE L.J. 1900 (2013) (with Amy Kapczynski); *Beyond Efficiency? Consequence-Sensitive Theories of Copyright*, 29 BERKELEY TECH. L.J. 229 (2014) (with Oren Bracha); *Beyond the Incentive-Access Paradigm? Product Differentiation and Copyright Revisited*, 92 TEX. L. REV. 1841 (2014) (with Oren Bracha); A *Prize Alternative as a Partial Solution to the Health Crisis in the Developing World*, *in* INCENTIVES FOR GLOBAL HEALTH (Thomas Pogge et al. eds., 2009) (with William W. Fisher III); and *Global Justice in Healthcare: Developing Drugs for the Developing World*, 40 U.C. DAVIS L. REV. 581 (2007) (with William W. Fisher III). He has two forthcoming books: FROM PATENTS TO PUBLIC UTILITY: PHARMACEUTICAL INNOVATION POLICY; and A WAR NOT EASILY WON: CURBING INFECTIOUS DISEASES IN DEVELOPING COUNTRIES (with William W. Fisher III). He received his JD from the University of Victoria, Canada, where he graduated as the Gold Medalist, and an LLM from Harvard University. He is a fellow at the Institute for New Economic Thinking and his academic honors include a fellowship at the Harvard Petrie-Flom Center for Health Law, Biotechnology, and Bioethics; the Canadian Bar Association's national Viscount Bennett Fellowship; and a Social Sciences and Humanities Research Council of Canada fellowship.

Benjamin C. Zipursky is Professor of Law at Fordham Law School, where he holds the James H. Quinn '49 Chair in Legal Ethics. A member of the Fordham faculty since 1995, he has taught as a visitor at Columbia Law School, Harvard Law School, University of Pittsburgh Law School, and Vanderbilt Law School, and in the Department of Philosophy at New York University. Professor Zipursky is a leading scholar in torts, jurisprudence, and legal ethics, and has published more than eighty articles and chapters on subjects ranging from punitive damages and conflicts of interest in mass tort litigation to the varieties of pragmatism within legal philosophy. He has lectured extensively in the United States and abroad and is the coauthor of a leading casebook, TORT LAW: RESPONSIBILITIES AND REDRESS (Wolters Kluwer 5th ed. 2021) as well as THE OXFORD INTRODUCTIONS TO U.S. LAW: TORTS (Oxford University Press 2010). His most recent book – RECOGNIZING WRONGS (Harvard University Press 2020) (coauthored with John Goldberg) – is a sustained defense of civil recourse theory in the law of torts.

Introduction: Hohfeld at the Crossroads

Shyamkrishna Balganesh, Ted M. Sichelman, and Henry E. Smith

In the century or so after the untimely death of Wesley Newcomb Hohfeld, his ideas have been a source of inspiration for widely divergent streams of legal scholarship. More generally, the nature of his ideas and the circumstances of his life have placed him at the crossroads of many currents of legal and social thought, making him a – somewhat fortuitously – pivotal figure in legal theory. And, after all the many explications and applications of his framework, it is as fresh and in many ways as enigmatic as on the day he left it in its unfinished state.

Hohfeld wrote at a time when the natural rights paradigm was beginning to become hollowed out and increasingly – if not entirely accurately – regarded as empty formalism. Hohfeld himself was a conceptualist, and he meant his scheme of jural relations as a rational reconstruction of concepts on a more articulated basis. Building on predecessors like Ernst Bierling and John Salmond, in his landmark work, "Some Fundamental Legal Conceptions as Applied in Judicial Reasoning,"[1] Hohfeld pushed the elegance of symmetry further. Specifically, he posited four pairs of jural correlatives (right-duty, privilege-no right, power-liability, and immunity-disability) and opposites across pairs of relations (right-no right, privilege-duty, power-disability, and immunity-liability). Notions like a corporation, a contract, a tort, and property could be broken down into collections of such relations. Further, all such relations would avail between pairs of persons. For instance, what was conventionally thought of as an "*in rem*" right was not treated as a one-on-one "thing" relative to legal persons, but instead as a group of similar rights availing between the holder of the right and numerous mostly unidentified others – each such right was "multital."[2] Hohfeld believed that his scheme was complete: it could

[1] Wesley N. Hohfeld, *Some Fundamental Legal Conceptions as Applied in Judicial Reasoning*, 23 YALE L.J. 16 (1913), *reproduced in* WESLEY N. HOHFELD, FUNDAMENTAL LEGAL CONCEPTIONS AS APPLIED IN JUDICIAL REASONING AND OTHER LEGAL ESSAYS 23 (Walter Wheeler Cook ed., 1923). An annotated version of this article appears in this volume in the introductory chapter "Some Fundamental Legal Conceptions as Applied in Judicial Reasoning."

[2] Wesley N. Hohfeld, *Fundamental Legal Conceptions as Applied in Judicial Reasoning*, 26 YALE L.J. 710 (1917), *reproduced in* WESLEY N. HOHFELD, FUNDAMENTAL LEGAL CONCEPTIONS AS APPLIED IN JUDICIAL REASONING AND OTHER LEGAL ESSAYS 65 (Walter Wheeler Cook ed., 1923).

capture all the legally relevant relationships holding between members of society, both inside and outside the legal system and its machinery.

Hohfeld's conceptualism, robust as it was, was not an exercise in pure logic, and, at least, Hohfeld's stated aim was practical rather than philosophical. In most of his work, Hohfeld does not overtly discuss his motivations or where he stood on moral, social, or political questions. In a famous 1914 speech, Hohfeld laid out his aspirations for legal education and the study of law more generally.[3] Consistent with a reformist optimism, if not the progressivism, of the era, Hohfeld believed that attaining greater clarity and fit in the deployment of legal concepts and their associated linguistic formulations would lead to better law from a policy point of view. This assumption may be the source of one of the most fascinating and most frustrating aspects of Hohfeld's applications of his own framework: in deploying his scheme, he treated judges' and jurists' use of terminology and existing concepts and doctrines as logical fallacies stemming from improperly failing to conform to what he viewed as a framework of legal relations that partook of necessary truth. To some, this endeavor of Hohfeld was a needed debunking of pervasive legal false consciousness and presumptuous category mistakes. To others, it is the obverse of the "crossroads" that Hohfeld's work primarily occupies, and, in this regard, perhaps Hohfeld relied too heavily on terminological usage to infer conceptual error. These divergent perspectives are reflected in some of the chapters in this volume. Nevertheless, there may be some common ground between these seemingly disparate views. Perhaps Hohfeld can, in a somewhat timeless fashion, occupy that central position precisely because of the close relation of his conceptual scheme and normative desirability, even if the precise contours of this relation could not be completely delineated at the time (or now, for that matter).

This close relation between normativity and conceptual precision would before long become implausible to the Realists, who were on guard against any reintroduction of "natural rights" such as liberty and property where sound policy should hold sway. Optimism along these lines would soon run into the buzz saw of Legal Realism. Because Hohfeld died right on the eve of the Realist era, and his concepts were orthogonal to those the Realists deconstructed, we can never know whether Hohfeld would have been swept up and carried by the Realist tide or would have charted a different course. Hohfeld's scheme itself was taken in certain directions by those primarily interested in his conceptualism and in very different directions by those who saw in it a solvent for traditional legal categories, as the first step toward a more policy-oriented overhaul. Hohfeld never had to make these choices, and his scheme hovers out there in between the concerns of many of his successors. And if

3 Wesley N. Hohfeld, *A Vital School of Jurisprudence and Law: Have American Universities Awakened to the Enlarged Opportunities and Responsibilities of the Present Day?*, *in* PROCEEDINGS OF THE FOURTEENTH ANNUAL MEETING OF THE ASSOCIATION OF AMERICAN LAW SCHOOLS 76 (1914), reproduced in WESLEY N. HOHFELD, *FUNDAMENTAL LEGAL CONCEPTIONS AS APPLIED IN JUDICIAL REASONING AND OTHER LEGAL ESSAYS* 332 (Walter Wheeler Cook ed., 1923).

Hohfeld's scheme, in the end, is too loose for philosophers and yet too procrustean for many jurists, we might chalk this up to Hohfeld's assumption – his optimism – that conceptual clarity and good legal policy go hand in hand.

As progressivism and sociological jurisprudence gave way to Legal Realism, some of these tensions in Hohfeld's work would have called for development by Hohfeld himself. Even without the changing state of the world and legal theory, Hohfeld left hints that he planned to address aspects of his scheme that were left open or ambiguous. Notably, he acknowledged the need for a theory of aggregate relations. What form would that take? Would it be a reductionist one in which the aggregates are a collection of the contributing parts, and the features of aggregate relations are the additive sum of the features of the constituent relations? Or would the theory of aggregates allow for some connections to be more important or tighter than others, and for aggregates of legal relations to be interestingly different from a heap of the "atomic" relations? We cannot know, but there is no question that many – and not just legal realists – have taken Hohfeld in a reductionist direction. And while we, along with some of the authors in this collection, would argue that a less reductionist view is compatible with much of Hohfeld's thought, we think that the outpouring of new work on Hohfeld, including all of the chapters in this volume, suggests that once again Hohfeld at the crossroads has set up the problems so that those coming after him may tackle them with greater precision and insight.

To shed new light on Hohfeld's legacy, this volume begins with an annotated and slightly edited version of his most famous article, "Some Fundamental Legal Conceptions as Applied in Judicial Reasoning," originally published in 1913 in the *Yale Law Journal* and then later as part of a collection edited by Walter Wheeler Cook. The excerpt offered here presents the bulk of Hohfeld's theory. Ted Sichelman's extensive commentary clarifies Hohfeld's article, illustrates its connections to and implications for legal theory and philosophy, and offers friendly critique, realigning Hohfeld's landmark typology more with the formalist tradition than the bulk of previous accounts. There follows a brief sketch of Hohfeld's life with accompanying pictures and documents. These documents were assembled by Hohfeld's brother, Edward Hohfeld, and have been graciously made available to editor Ted Sichelman by the late Jane Hohfeld Galante. These materials help illuminate the context in which Hohfeld wrote as well as some of his motivations for pursuing his program. Along with the annotation, these papers set the stage for the chapters that form the main body of this volume.

The contributions to this volume reflect the richness of the framework and diversity of the strands emanating from it. There is Hohfeld the legal philosopher, Hohfeld the proto-Realist, Hohfeld the theorist of equity and property, Hohfeld the denier and student of legal complexity, and Hohfeld the inspiration for many applications throughout law and beyond.

Hohfeld focused on the theory of jural relations, and his analysis has captured the attention of philosophers. One place to begin in an examination of Hohfeld's thought and its influence is legal language itself. Hohfeld was famously interested in legal language and the use of terminology. In Chapter 1, Frederick Schauer examines Hohfeld's program as addressing the nature of legal language and its relation to everyday language. Hohfeld lamented the loose use of terms like "right" and "property," and his scheme of jural relations was meant to bring some clarity to legal reasoning by the more precise use of legal language. Even Hohfeld's insistence on the distinction between legal relations and the facts that give rise to them reflects a concern with how legal language works. In contrast to legal fictions and terms of art, legal language seems to partake simultaneously of ordinary language and a technical code which can then deceive lawyers and judges who miss the distinction. Hohfeld's worry echoes Oliver Wendell Holmes, Jr.'s earlier concern about moral notions in the law. Both Holmes and Hohfeld were not fully Realist in that they thought that legal concepts were real and operative and could be improved by dispelling the confusion between ordinary and technical legal language. The overlap between these kinds of language would later motivate Edwin Patterson and Lon Fuller to suggest the development of more purely legal language. Being of a more practical bent, Hohfeld eschewed the creation of a legal language in favor of devising a scheme of jural relations that would promote clear thinking and close analysis – and thus better law. The problem of technical language as explored by philosophers such as Charles Caton and Friedrich Waismann provides a lens on why Hohfeld thought clarification of legal language was necessary in the first place, and Hohfeld's sometimes cryptic writing can serve as a prompt to thinking about this philosophical problem.

A little ironic for a tool aimed to disambiguate legal analysis, in his chapter on rights correlativity (Chapter 2), David Frydrych pulls apart the different senses of correlativity that feature in Hohfeld's work. To begin with, when legal relations are said to correlate, does this mean that the two "ends" of a legal relation – right and duty, for example – are mirror images of each other? Or can one of the connected normative positions have features the other one does not? And if the positions are mirror images of each other, is it because they are identical or because they mutually entail each other? The former is erroneous and the latter requires elaboration. When it comes to a Hohfeldian claim, is it merely a passive entitlement or a capacity to hold another to account? Frydrych also explores the notion of existential correlativity, which holds that certain normative positions must co-obtain, and justificational correlativity, according to which one normative position justifies the existence of others. These different kinds of correlativity introduce some ambiguities into Hohfeld's scheme of jural relations in some of its most well-known aspects: strict bilateralism of legal relations as holding between pairs of persons and his reconstruction of *in personam/in rem* as collections of bilateral rights. Frydrych also questions the credibility of arguing, on Hohfeldian grounds, that others (e.g., judges) are making erroneous moves under the guise of plausible-sounding fallacies. The difficulties in the notion of correlativity call for further elaboration of the framework in terms of the ideas it rests upon, rather than pure application.

Hohfeld's framework of legal conceptions has generated a good deal of controversy and disagreement among scholars, despite remaining a foundational contribution to conceptual thinking in the law. In his assessment of Hohfeld in this volume (Chapter 3), Andrew Halpin unpacks the possible reasons for this. Halpin readily acknowledges that Hohfeld's contribution belongs to a small category of scholarly works that have the power to illuminate an entire field of inquiry, even when one disagrees with the details of their core ideas. These works are seen as "opening up a perspective" in the field and Hohfeld's jural relations did precisely that. All the same, Hohfeld's untimely death rendered his grand conceptual project incomplete and unfinished in an important sense. This, according to Halpin, interacted with the former attribute of the work to convert it into a rich source of analytical and normative disagreement in the field. The incompleteness is seen to lie in Hohfeld's failure to offer a fuller explanation of aggregate legal positions and the manner in which individual legal relations can be bundled together to generate rules. Critics of Hohfeld treat a perceived reductivism as antithetical to the very idea of rules in the law. Halpin attempts to refute this criticism, pointing to Hohfeld's own reliance on rules in his arguments and highlighting the misunderstanding of Hohfeld by his critics. Halpin concludes by noting that a closer (and potentially more charitable) reading of Hohfeld's work would have been more measured in its criticism of his analysis of legal relations since it was necessarily incomplete; and that a fuller reading incorporating an aggregate level analysis might have enabled his framework to be treated more expansively and envisioned in a less controversial light.

Despite being widely acclaimed as a novel and rigorous mode of legal analysis, Hohfeld's classification of jural relations is far from being widely adopted by scholars today. Nor, indeed, is it a staple of the legal curriculum. In his contribution to this volume (Chapter 4), Scott Brewer attempts to solve the mystery behind this puzzle by using as an explanatory tool the Logocratic Method he has developed. This method provides an explanation of the nature of argument, including legal argument, and identifies both shared structures of argument and distinctive forms of arguments in different domains, such as in philosophical argument and doctrinal legal argument. According to Brewer, the solution to the puzzle of the combination of Hohfeldian influence and nondeployment of his complex system by legal scholars and professors lies in understanding the precise nature of, and mechanism underlying Hohfeld's overall project as a distinct type of philosophical argument. Brewer explains Hohfeld's project as a type of logical inference, familiar to philosophers and argument theorists, known as "abduction" or "inference to the best explanation." Whereas traditional legal analysis represents a type of *legal* abduction, in which applicable legal norms are identified and applied to the facts of cases, Hohfeld's project is a form of unique *philosophical* abduction that is heavily dependent on a prior legal abduction. Only when one performs and uses a prior legal abduction to identify operative facts can one then apply the Hohfeldian jural relation analysis. Brewer further argues that Hohfeld himself adopted a form of analogical reasoning in constructing his system of jural relations, a process that partakes of the method identified by Nelson Goodman and popularized by John Rawls under the title of "reflective equilibrium." Brewer maintains that many of the interpretive debates that are today seen in the application of Hohfeld's jural relations to different problems – reflected by the variety of essays in this volume – were likely encountered by Hohfeld himself and resolved through the process of reflective equilibrium. Brewer concludes that, in light of the basic Logocratic explanations his essay offers, the solution to the puzzle about Hohfeld's influence is straightforward: since Hohfeld's analogically abduced axioms are parasitic on standard legal abductions that form the staple of modern legal reasoning, little appears to be gained by going one step further to add an extra layer of Hohfeldian philosophical abduction, and most law professors, even those who have mastered Hohfeldian abductions, choose not to go that extra step.

Hohfeld's scheme is especially well known to property theorists, both as a precursor of the "bundle of rights" and for his reanalysis of *in rem* rights. In Chapter 5, Anna di Robilant and Talha Syed take issue with the idea that Hohfeld's view is best labeled as a "bundle of rights" conception of property, a conception that has generated a good deal of controversy and criticism in the years since. They argue instead that more central to Hohfeld's theory is an understanding of property as a "social relation," and hence that the more apt label for his view is that of a "relational" conception of property. Taking on the critics of Hohfeld, who they see as attempting to counter the disintegration of Hohfeld's conception of property by "rethingifying" it, they argue that the answer to disintegration is a process of reintegration, wherein property takes meaning and shape as a contextual and resource-specific entitlement and through an architectural analysis of the core components of that entitlement. To substantiate their claims on each of these fronts, they draw on conceptual arguments as well as rich and detailed comparative sources, where they see such a reintegration at work. In developing a new approach to the architectural analysis of property, they consciously reject a thick, substantive conception of such an architecture. In its place, they advance what they call a "focal points approach" to it. In this approach, they identify four salient entitlements that they see as essential to the architecture of property: use-privilege, exclusion-right, expropriation-immunity, and transfer-power. These four entitlements integrate together to form the concept of property in this social relations view, which is generative in nature and thus capable of application to different resources.

In their contribution to the volume (Chapter 6), Shyamkrishna Balganesh and Leo Katz focus on the distinction between multital and paucital legal relations that formed the basis of Hohfeld's framework advanced in the second of his foundational pieces. They argue that Hohfeld's focus on numerosity and indefiniteness does not adequately capture the nature of the distinction that exists between what the law describes as *in rem* and *in personam* relationships, and advance the idea that the distinction instead additionally embodies a feature best described as "persistence." The persistent right in their framework is a right that the law allows to subsist across context and relationship, for varying normative considerations, and is in contrast to symmetrical rights that are nonpersistent and context/identity dependent. *In rem* rights, to Balganesh and Katz, embody the idea of persistence thus defined. The chapter then uses the idea of persistent rights to explain why the law embodies a few previously identified paradoxes, such as the paradox of cycling (or Arrovian circularity), which they see as driven by the effort to accord primacy to a persistent right. They see similar machinations at work in the common law doctrines of libel, negligence, and tortious interference – each of which, they argue, embodies features that have been difficult to account for because they miss the notion of persistence and the law's intuitive preference for partitioning relationships by according priority to persistent rights. While primarily an analytical contribution, the chapter nevertheless ends with a few normative ideas including the recognition that the law's choice of partitioning approach is not immutable and that future discussions of the *in rem/in personam* distinction would do well to consider the implicit role of persistence in the framing of the rights and their ordering within a doctrinal setting.

Likewise focusing on the *in rem* aspect of property rights, Christopher Newman in Chapter 7 seeks to reconcile the traditional and highly persistent use of the concept of an *in rem* right and the related concept of a "right to a thing" with Hohfeld's attempted replacement of these notions. Hohfeld thought the notion of an *in rem* legal relation was not ambiguous but wrong. All legal relations hold between persons, *not* between persons and things and *not* running from one person to many persons. Thus, whereas an *in rem* right is traditionally taken to be a right availing against others generally (the duty holders are people in general), Hohfeld's scheme posits instead a large set of similar one-to-one right-duty pairs (between the right holder and each of the many and possibly unknown individuals in the set of "people in general"). Newman points out that "*in rem* right" and "right to a thing" are shorthand for a higher-level normative characterization. In a sense, Hohfeld by fiat rules that talking about extensions – who gets to do what to whom in the normative system – is the only way to talk, thus excluding the more abstract way of talking, including how the rights are set up and experienced. This other way, "intensional" or "conceptual," picks out these sets in the world but does so in a useful way: we can think about and navigate the world on the basis of such concepts like general rights and duties couched in terms of things ("stay out unless you have permission"). Newman shows that both modes of characterizing interests and relations have their uses and they stand in a productive relationship with each other.

Besides property, the area Hohfeld is most famous for theorizing is equity. James Penner (Chapter 8) places Hohfeld's treatment of equity within the overall Hohfeldian framework and argues that it exhibits its characteristic limits. Hohfeld was keen to refute Maitland's thesis that law and equity do not conflict. At the same time, Hohfeld harbored an unorthodox view of what a conflict between equity and law would look like. Unlike equity purists, Hohfeld did not argue that equity reflected a special unique brand of morally grounded substantive law or a peculiar mode of reasoning. Like equity pragmatists, he was inclined to see equity as an outgrowth of history. He adopted the controversial tripartite division of equitable jurisdiction into exclusive, concurrent, and auxiliary. Yet, where conventionally the exclusive jurisdiction is seen as involving no conflict (there is, simply, no corresponding law) and auxiliary jurisdiction is seen as not much in conflict (equity aids the law), Hohfeld saw these areas as conflicting because legal and equitable rules would deliver, on their own, different results, and so, according to him, they therefore conflicted. But with respect to the concurrent jurisdiction, Hohfeld saw no conflict because in his view the concurrent jurisdiction obtains wherever law and equity exist side by side. Here, Hohfeld saw no conflict because to him law that is "overridden" by equity is not "genuine" law but more akin to a repealed statute. Ultimately, Penner argues, Hohfeld's view of equity's relation to law is indefensible, yet it interestingly reflects his approach to jural relations while at the same time stands in some tension with it. If, in the concurrent jurisdiction, superseded law does not exist there is no purchase for the substantive rights that equity presupposed. Law as a prerequisite for equity is missing in this approach.

Equity's most famous innovation is the trust, which like equity has spawned endless analyses of its nature. This problem is the occasion for Ben McFarlane in his chapter (Chapter 9) to demonstrate how Hohfeldian analysis can help clear up some confusion in judicial treatment of equitable interests and, at the same time, show a slight weakness of Hohfeld's work on the relations between common law and equity. In keeping with Hohfeld's admonition not to oversimplify legal relations but rather find the "right kind of simplicity," more recent analyses have transcended the perennial *in rem* versus *in personam* debate to emphasize the two-tier structure of equitable rights. The trustee has the full package of legal rights against others but is subject to a further set of legal relations with respect to the beneficiary to use those rights and powers for the latter's benefit. McFarlane then shows how this distinction matters in the areas of the assignment of claims, standing to sue third party trespassers, and the liability of a third party recipient of trust property. While jurisdictions may differ in their approach in such areas, a Hohfeldian analysis exposes the flaws in some arguments and sharpens the stakes by revealing the consequences of liability, for example, as to information costs. Notwithstanding those important benefits, Hohfeld's approach to equity contains seeds of later confusion. McFarlane argues that Hohfeld's insistence on focusing on bottom line results and on regarding law and equity as two complete and parallel systems, even if the former would not be "genuine" in the case of override by the latter, might imply that all relations are pre-carved into legal and equitable aspects. Hence the missing half cheer.

Equity is often associated with exceptions to legal rules. In Chapter 10, Emily Sherwin reconstructs what the Hohfeldian project has to say – or would have had to say if it had been completed – on the subject of legal rules and the exceptions to them. Contrary to his image as a precursor of Legal Realism, Hohfeld apparently believed that legal rules were not hopelessly indeterminate, and his project was a positive rather than a mainly deconstructive one. In Anglo-American legal systems, exceptions to general rules often originated in the courts of equity. Sherwin argues that rules are always in danger of second-guessing, and good rules – those which produce better results on average if followed consistently – can easily unravel through ex post overrides and difficult applications. According to Sherwin, in the days of separate equity, the unraveling might have been prevented by keeping the equitable exceptions relatively obscure to the public. With the rise of Legal Realism, rule skepticism swept aside this bifurcated structure so that judges would be encouraged to use situation sense and particularized analysis, which left little room for equity as exceptional. By contrast, Hohfeld's take on equity was that both law and equity consisted in part of rules and that their rules did sometimes conflict. And yet, in any given situation, there could be only one genuine rule. When an equitable rule conflicted with a legal rule, it was the dominant rule. However, because both systems are public and the question of when equity should override the law remains a problem, Hohfeld framed –but failed to solve – the central dilemma about rules and how to maintain them in the face of exception-making judges.

Hohfeld's framework is notable both for the complexities it captures and those it left largely unaddressed. Before his untimely death, Hohfeld left tantalizing hints about his plans to extend his framework to provide a theory of "aggregate" legal relations. Taking up this thread in his chapter (Chapter 11), Ted Sichelman shows how in a Hohfeldian spirit one can isolate complex jural relations consisting of tightly conjoined more basic relations. Extending a common analogy of Hohfeldian legal relations to physics and chemistry, Sichelman points out that certain legal relations might be like atoms, standing in between basic particles like quarks and larger structures like molecules. Among the "compact" complex legal relations that are made up of more basic relations but that function as a unit or module are: common rights and protected privileges, in which a privilege is protected by a right against interference; common liberties and freedoms, in which the performance of some action is protected by a claim right; claim rights that comprise both a (narrow) right and the contingent remedial power to bring an action for the violation of the duty; and constitutional rights, which are clusters of Hohfeldian relations. Some of the supposed logical errors identified by Hohfeld and later the Realists, such as the failure to distinguish privileges and rights, are really the operation of a complex relation like a common right or protected privilege. By recognizing that fundamental legal relations combine tightly in certain ways, we can be reductionists in principle, but we can capture the patterns and the practical value of focusing on those parts of the module of legal relations that are near the boundary, whether inside or outside. By doing so, the bundle picture of property is put in proper perspective.

On its face, Hohfeld's typology and classification of jural relations focus on their analytical – as opposed to normative content. This has, in turn, allowed critics of its facially anti-normative position to argue that it *ignores* important questions about the normative connections between different pairs of relations. In Chapter 12, John Goldberg and Benjamin Zipursky explore this theme further, focusing on how certain domains of private law evince a deep normative link between legal rights and powers. They begin by showing the lengths to which Hohfeld went in maintaining the distinction between rights and powers, a distinction deliberately elided by prominent subsequent rights theorists, including Joel Feinberg and H. L. A. Hart. While defending Hohfeld's insistence on this sharp analytic separation, Goldberg and Zipursky nevertheless criticize Hohfeld for downplaying or overlooking possible normative connections. This they attribute to instrumentalist tendencies in his approach to normative reasoning and, with those, an emphasis on legislation over adjudication. Goldberg and Zipursky then argue that Hohfeld's focus on analytic separation, combined with his inclination toward instrumentalism, has caused some courts and scholars to take separation to an undesirable extreme. They illustrate this move through an examination of the California Supreme Court's well-known decision in *Rowland v. Christian*, which seemingly endorses the idea of granting injury victims a legal power to obtain compensatory damages when doing so would serve societal goals, irrespective of the presence or absence of a duty-right relation between injurer and victim. In this instance and others, they argue, Hohfeld's insistence on analytic separation, combined with strongly instrumentalist notions of normative reasoning, have obscured substantive connections between rights and powers that Hohfeld himself may well have appreciated.

Many have noticed that the framework of liability rules, property rules, and inalienability rules in Guido Calabresi and A. Douglas Melamed's 1972 "Cathedral" article is reminiscent of Hohfeld's scheme of jural relations. In his chapter on immunity rules (Chapter 13), John Harrison employs the Hohfeldian framework to critique Calabresi and Melamed's notion of liability rules. In Hohfeldian terms, Calabresi and Melamed's liability rules encompass Hohfeldian duties of compensation and powers to acquire rights. So, when A negligently damages B's land and the government takes it by eminent domain, in both situations A's entitlement receives only liability rule protection: B need only pay an officially determined "price." In contrast, where entitlements are protected by injunctions and other robust remedies, they enjoy property rule protection. Harrison then shows how duties of compensation and powers to acquire title are so different as not to belong together. Duties of compensation in negligence act as sanctions, unlike the prices in eminent domain. Further, in eminent domain the monetary liability is determined at the time of taking with further risk shifted to the taker. By contrast, duties of compensation do not shift risk, and a defendant can be exposed to increased liability for post-tort developments, including lost profits. Further, one with an entitlement protected only by a liability rule typically still enjoys the Hohfeldian privilege of self-help, unlike those on the receiving end of an exercise of eminent domain. Even from a "bottom line" point of view, the position of one protected by a duty of compensation and one protected by an immunity – protection against private and many public attempts to change entitlements – is quite different. In the area of property, what matters is the strength of protection, and it is the Hohfeldian immunity that is the most important and most ubiquitous kind of protection.

The possibility of complex relations and the distinctiveness of relations like powers that are second order point to yet another problem with the "aggregative" interpretation of Hohfeld's scheme of legal relations. The question of how local legal relations scale up and what properties emerge at higher levels of social organization is the theme of Andrew Gold and Henry Smith's chapter on the scaling up of legal relations (Chapter 14). Both the jural relations and the analysis of *in rem* rights have often been taken to support a reductionism that leaves no role for complex interactions between relations to give rise to emergent properties. Whether he fully intended it or not, Hohfeld paved the way for a flat view of the law in which the local elements would combine additively, thereby building a gap between the micro and the macro into subsequent American theorizing about the law. This gap can be better understood by paying attention to how legal relations are delineated and structured. Sometimes, they are grouped into modules that require far less delineation than an extensionally equivalent list of additive relations. Similarly, many aspects of the law may take the form of second-order adjustments; these include *pace* Hohfeld, much of equity, and the much-derided natural rights style of analysis in nuisance law. Finally, a more articulated (and combinatorially rich) but locally simple set of legal relations has dynamic potential. As in airplane overflights, courts may be called upon to specify what earlier did not need full specification. These analytical, but less reductionist, formulations "scale up" better than the conventional picture and can inspire new theories that explain more of the emergent properties of the legal system.

In Hohfeld's spirit of addressing the legal system in concrete terms, commentators have found his work to be a source of inspiration and a foil for analysis of problems in the legal system as it is situated in society. In his chapter in this volume, Pierre Schlag examines the various nascent tensions that exist between Hohfeld's "platform" of conceptual legal relationships and the legal commitments of liberalism (Chapter 15). The first such tension, in Schlag's account, is between the demands of analytical/conceptual precision and the role of judicial reasoning in adjudication. Adopting an overtly Realist position, Schlag argues that endemic to the judicial function is the need to legitimate and rationalize legal decisions, for which Hohfeld's conceptual precision becomes an unaffordable luxury or even an annoyance in all but a very limited number of cases. In this respect, and contrary to Hohfeld's hopes and ambitions, Schlag sees Hohfeld's platform as more appealing to legal analysts and legal scholars than to contemporary judges. Second, Schlag argues that Hohfeld's basic taxonomy entailed the identification of symmetrical legal relations, a "double entry bookkeeping" approach to legal analysis. Yet, as Schlag argues, much legal reasoning and adjudication abjure such symmetrical reasoning, often focusing attention (almost) solely on the entitlements of the victim or instead (almost) solely on the responsibility of the perpetrator. For Schlag, a third tension originates in what he calls "Hohfeld's residuum" – the broad array of legal relations not (or not yet) fully specified by legal officials. Schlag argues that in any legal system, a number of high-order principles or commitments serve as guides or even defaults for identifying the likely Hohfeldian character of this residuum (i.e., privileges in citizens in the case of liberal democracy, duty of citizens to the state in the case of communism and fascism, and so on). Last, Schlag sees a fourth tension, in a Hohfeldian exposition of the failure of liberalism to distinguish cogently between the vertical and horizontal dimensions of the law. Specifically, Schlag sees the erroneous invocation of "law-free zones," as critical to the character of liberal legalism yet incoherent from a Hohfeldian perspective. Schlag concludes, suggesting that the magisterial indifference of Hohfeldian analysis to existing legal systems is precisely what gives it such power in excavating the political or moral orientations and occasional ambivalences, ambiguities, or outright errors of legal systems.

For reasons that are hard to pinpoint with precision, Hohfeld's approach to analytical jurisprudence has long been considered to reflect his affinity for the ideas of the early Legal Realists. Some of this is perhaps explained by his friendship with several prominent Legal Realists including Arthur Corbin and Walter Wheeler Cook. In Chapter 16, Aditi Bagchi argues that Hohfeld's principal contributions in *Fundamental Legal Conceptions as Applied in Judicial Reasoning* nevertheless undermine the potential for an "egalitarian private law structure." Much of her argument derives from what she describes as the hyper-individuation which is a central feature of Hohfeld's scheme: it is at the level of the individual that Hohfeld attempts to disaggregate individual legal relations and then examine and isolate their analytical features. In Bagchi's account, this introduces three problems. The first is what she calls the absence of lateral references, or the belief that each pair of individual relations is capable of being appreciated without reference to any others. Second, she argues that, by denying imperfect rights and duties any legal status, Hohfeld's structure does not adequately accommodate private rights and duties that may derive from the demands of distributive justice. Third, Bagchi claims that Hohfeld does not fully allow for the possibility that rights within a legal scheme could conflict, such that recognition of one entitlement precludes recognition of another. His framework thus acknowledges no cause for what she calls "system regret." Bagchi's aim is not to offer an alternative framework to Hohfeld's but to show that Hohfeld's formalism does not avoid a set of normative commitments as it might have aspired to do.

In his contribution to the volume (Chapter 17), Joseph Singer applies Hohfeld's conceptual taxonomy to examining the conflict between religious liberty and public accommodations, an issue that has generated a great deal of recent jurisprudence. Singer begins the analysis by identifying three central problems characterizing the conflict: participants' portrayal of their actions as entirely "self-regarding," their treatment of their rights as absolute, and their use of a shifting analysis that oscillates between notions of right, privilege, and power – each of which, he argues, Hohfeld implicitly rejected. While Singer sees in Hohfeld's use of the *in rem/in personam* distinction a commitment to the idea of property as a bundle of rights, he argues that Hohfeld sought to "undermine" this conception himself by allowing for considerations of "justice and policy" to enable the disaggregation of the bundle contextually. In Singer's view, this committed Hohfeldian analysis to a mechanism of mediating many of the conflicting claims underlying the claims of religious liberty and public accommodations. A second, important, lesson that Singer sees as relevant to the conflict lies in Hohfeld's conception of liberty. By revealing that liberties – much like other jural relations – have a correlative, a no-right, Singer sees in Hohfeld's framework a commitment to a relational conception of liberty, in turn, antithetical to liberties as entirely self-regarding actions. Relatedly, Singer also takes Hohfeld's efforts to disentangle liberties from rights and extol their independence as being of deep relevance to the religious liberty debate, where the two are routinely conflated. In the end, Singer's core message is that, while Hohfeld's framework may not have had direct normative lessons for the debate about religious liberty and public accommodations, adopting its conceptual clarity allows for a more direct focus on the normative issues at stake, without the analytical base of the debate becoming a needless distraction.

In Chapter 18, John Schlegel gives Hohfeld's work a distinctively human dimension. Schlegel's contribution traces Hohfeld's difficulties in acculturating to the life of a law professor, first at Stanford and then at Yale. Using Hohfeld's correspondence with Roscoe Pound as its focus, the chapter reveals Hohfeld's own insecurities about his role in the academy and the ways in which he constructed a narrative around them over the course of his career. Constantly worried about the inadequacy of his salary – both objectively and in comparison to his peers at other schools – Hohfeld is portrayed as a thinker distinctly unsure of his place in the legal academy but unwilling to abandon his pretensions about his intellectual abilities. Schlegel portrays Hohfeld's friendship with Pound as driven by elements of sycophancy, self-interest, and genuine scholarly regard for the latter's contributions to legal thinking. In so doing, Schlegel reveals Hohfeld to have been significantly less confident about the value of his work during his own lifetime, something that a bare reading of his foundational papers does not reveal. A particularly intriguing theme in Schlegel's chapter, which captures some of the controversy around Hohfeld's characterization as part-formalist and part-Realist, is the extent to which Hohfeld saw himself doing something fundamentally different from attempting to develop a legal science of juridical ideas, in the vein of Christopher Columbus Langdell. Schlegel documents how Hohfeld – despite being a graduate of Harvard Law School – never fully embraced the ideas of Ames, Langdell, and Beale but situated himself more in the vein of a scholar attempting to engage the world of lawyers and judges more directly. Schlegel's narrative captures these ambiguities in Hohfeld's professional life, best summarized by his characterization of Hohfeld as a "Westerner" attempting to assimilate within the world of the East Coast legal academy.

Hohfeld and his thought occupy a uniquely evocative and provocative place in legal thought. This generative aspect of Hohfeld is on full display in the breadth and depth of the contributions to this volume.

The genesis of this book was a conference at Yale Law School on Wesley Hohfeld graciously hosted by Daniel Markovits and organized by Sadie Blanchard. We are immensely grateful that the coauthors of this volume were able to present and discuss their chapters in the place Hohfeld considered his intellectual home.

As we noted, the release of this volume is the first time Hohfeld's extant personal papers have been published, and we would not have been able to do so without the gracious cooperation from Wesley Hohfeld's niece, the late Jane Hohfeld Galante.

Of course, we greatly appreciate the laboring work of our research assistants. Nikta Shahbaz was invaluable on numerous fronts, from coordinating the submission of manuscripts to providing detailed edits to every chapter and section to cataloguing every document in Hohfeld's personal papers. Madelyn Chen, Casey Corcoran, Connor Haaland, Dylan Hosmer-Quint, Alexander Schwennicke, Millicent Whitemore, and Marianne Xiong also provided superb editing work on the chapters. Jessica McCurdy Crooks painstakingly constructed a valuable index. Josh Kleinfeld and Silva Kleinfeld were gracious in photographing Hohfeld-related material in the special collections at the Yale Law School Library.

We are ever thankful to Cambridge University Press, particularly Matt Gallaway, for their receptivity to the project and especially for allowing us to publish the entirety of every section and chapter that we submitted. Our final thank you is for the final person to read this very line before this book went to print, Benjamin Johnson, for his tireless dedication and outstanding work in editing the volume.

And with that, we very much hope you enjoy and benefit from reading this volume as we have.

Some Fundamental Legal Conceptions as Applied in Judicial Reasoning

Edited and Annotated by Ted M. Sichelman[*]

EDITOR'S INTRODUCTION

This annotated version of Hohfeld's most well-known and cited work is structured to provide important context and explanation both to law students and others seeking to better understand the core of Hohfeld's typology, as well as to those well-versed in the Hohfeldian typology.[1] The text has been condensed (the Editor's deletions of the original text are indicated by ellipses,[2] while Hohfeld's deletions of quoted material are indicated by three asterisks) and annotated (in square brackets) with the law student and Hohfeld novice in mind. For this reason, all footnotes in the original work (that have not been deleted) appear in the text itself (in small type in triangle brackets), following the footnote number in the original article (which appears in normal type). The actual footnotes that appear in this annotated version (with a footnote number in superscript), on the other hand, contain extended discussion and background material, and are written for those already well-versed in the Hohfeldian scheme. Finally, in just a handful of spots, pronouns have been replaced with proper names to improve clarity; in several places, minor typographical edits have been made to spelling, punctuation (dashes, quotation marks, commas, and indentations), and citation formats have been edited to improve readability – none change the meaning of the text.

* Professor, University of San Diego School of Law. I thank Nikta Shahbaz, Henry Smith, and Horacio Spector for their outstanding suggestions to an earlier draft.

1 Other useful introductory works on the Hohfeldian typology include John Finnis, *Some Professorial Fallacies about Rights*, 4 ADELAIDE L. REV. 377 (1971); Curtis Nyquist, *Reaching Wesley Hohfeld's Theory of Legal Relations*, 52 J. LEGAL EDUC. 238 (2002); Pierre Schlag, *How To Do Things With Hohfeld*, 78 LAW & CONTEMP. PROBS. 185 (2015).

2 There is often no indication for original footnote text deleted by the editor. The vast majority of the deleted footnotes are extended citations that are unimportant for all but Hohfeld aficionados, which have been removed given limited space in this volume.

Some Fundamental Legal Conceptions as Applied in Judicial Reasoning[3,4]

From very early days down to the present time the essential nature of trusts and other equitable interests has formed a favorite subject for analysis and disputation. . . . That the subject has had a peculiar fascination for modern legal thinkers is abundantly evidenced by the well-known articles of Langdell and Ames, by the oft-repeated [*17] observations of Maitland in his *Lectures on Equity*, by the very divergent treatment of Austin in his *Lectures on Jurisprudence*, by the still bolder thesis of Salmond in his volume on *Jurisprudence*,[5] . . .

3 This work originally appeared in 23 YALE L.J. 16 (1913) and is signed Wesley Newcomb Hohfeld, Stanford University, California. There is some dispute over whether the article was solicited by the *Yale Law Journal*, or whether Hohfeld submitted it. *See* Chapter 18. In 1919, Hohfeld's close friend and colleague at Yale, Walter Wheeler Cook, published a revised version of the article in a pamphlet (along with an introduction and Hohfeld's 1917 *Yale Law Journal* article), which contains some additions to the footnotes and minor changes to the text that apparently derived from a version of the article that Hohfeld had edited, though it remains unclear whether Cook made additional edits on his own. *See* Chapter 2. The annotated version presented here contains the vast majority of typographical edits appearing in the 1919 work, though the pagination of the text (indicated by a single asterisk) follows that of the original 1913 article.

4 The title of the work is notable in two respects. First, although Hohfeld essentially argued that the "fundamental legal conceptions" introduced in the article could be used to frame the "jural relations" involved in any legal "problem," the qualifier "some" indicates that there may, in Hohfeld's mind, be other "fundamental" legal relations. However, Hohfeld never introduced any other such relations. On the other hand, one can read "conceptions" as broader than "relations," and to the extent that Hohfeld did not intend to exhaust the universe of fundamental legal "conceptions" in this article, perhaps the qualifier is apt. Notably, the 1919 volume edited by Cook is simply titled *Fundamental Legal Conceptions as Applied in Judicial Reasoning: and Other Legal Essays*. Second, as Hohfeld notes throughout the article, he viewed his endeavor as one with a great practical import, especially for judicial reasoning in cases. Although Hohfeld made great attempts to instill his typology into the minds of his students – and many of his colleagues and other law professors did the same for a short period just before and after his untimely death – today, the schema is generally of more interest to legal theorists than those interested in judicial reasoning per se. On the other hand, the Hohfeldian typology is of substantial interest to those designing artificially intelligent machines to "understand" judicial reasoning, a burgeoning field.

5 Hohfeld cites the second edition of John Salmond's JURISPRUDENCE (1907). As David Frydrych notes in Chapter 2, in the first (1902) edition of his JURISPRUDENCE, Salmond had essentially described seven of the eight "fundamental" jural relations, the "no-right" being the sole exception, and even then Salmond used the term "liability" (albeit, confusingly) to stand in for "no-right." Salmond, in turn, had drawn on Bentham and others in his formulation. Terry had also expressed similar formulations. Nonetheless, other than Salmond, no previous scholar had described the "no-right," and even Salmond was relatively unclear in his formulation of it (and, perhaps more importantly, abandoned a complete set of jural relations in his second and later editions). Thus, Hohfeld's primary theoretical contribution was not to introduce what has become known as the Hohfeldian typology, but instead to clearly describe the typology, particularly how it can be applied to a variety of legal "problems," in Hohfeld's words. This is especially so for the "no-right," which was a major innovation – yet largely unrecognized as such by Salmond – because it brought into the fold of legal relations that for which no legal action could lie. In other words, as Hohfeld recounts later in the article, "It is difficult to see, however, why . . . the 'privilege + no-right' situation is not just as real a jural relation as the precisely opposite 'duty + right' relation." *See generally* Walter Wheeler Cook, *Hohfeld's Contributions to the*

It is believed that all of the discussions and analyses referred to are inadequate.[6] . . .

> **Editor's Note:** Hohfeld begins the article with a lengthier discussion of trust law that confuses many readers. The major takeaway is that previous works by leading scholars in the area were, in Hohfeld's view, flawed in one respect or another, because they failed to carefully delineate the legal interests of concern.

But, quite apart from the presumably practical consideration of endeavoring to "think straight" in relation to all legal problems, it is apparent that the true analysis of trusts and other equitable interests is a matter that should appeal to even the most extreme pragmatists of the law. It may well be that one's view as to the correct analysis of such interests would control the decision of a number of specific questions.[7] This is obviously true as regards the solution of many difficult and delicate problems in constitutional law and in the conflict of laws. . . . So on indefinitely.

> **Editor's Note:** Although Hohfeld today is mainly of interest to legal theorists and philosophers, his sincere belief was that the typology he introduced in this article is of great practical importance to clearly understanding legal issues and adjudicating particular disputes.

But all this may seem like misplaced emphasis; for the suggestions last made are not peculiarly applicable to equitable interests: the same points and the same examples seem valid in relation to all possible kinds of jural interests, legal as well as equitable – and that too, whether we are concerned with "property," "contracts," "torts," or any other title of the law.[8]

Science of Law, 28 YALE L.J. 721 (1919). It is this aspect of his approach – namely, that every human action is essentially subject to law (even if nobody has a right to prevent the action) – that was one of the most controversial, and remains so today. *See, e.g.*, Joseph William Singer, *The Legal Rights Debate in Analytical Jurisprudence From Bentham to Hohfeld*, 1982 WIS. L. REV. 975, 985 (1982)(discussing these issues, particularly in the context of the *damnum absque injuria*, roughly, harmful actions for which the law provides no relief).

6 Because this article has garnered over 5,000 citations, there is a vast secondary literature regarding it. Given space limitations, the vast share of (what typically would be routine) citations to this literature have been omitted. For those interested, Singer, *supra* note 5, does an excellent job citing the early secondary literature, and Schlag, *supra* note 1, the same for the more recent secondary literature.

7 Hohfeld has often been termed a proto-realist and has been heavily relied upon by Critical Legal Studies theorists to support a view that policy plays a fundamental role in adjudication. *See, e.g.*, DUNCAN KENNEDY, A CRITIQUE OF ADJUDICATION 82–92, 276 (1997). However, these and other portions of Hohfeld's article indicate that there were at least a class of cases for Hohfeld that sounded more in the formalist problem-and-solution approach. Namely, to the extent that "the correct analysis" of the case could be ascertained, assuming the evidential facts sufficient for the analysis were available, *see infra* notes 51 and 52 and accompanying text, the analysis would yield a unique "solution" to the "problem" presented by the case. *See generally* David Frydrych, *Hohfeld vs. The Legal Realists*, 24 LEGAL THEORY 291 (2018) (arguing that Hohfeld was not a legal realist).

8 Hohfeld's typology is often viewed as one applying solely to private law interests. Although Hohfeld solely offered private law examples in this article, his phrases "or any other title of law," "all types of

> **Editor's Note:** Hohfeld uses the term "jural" to refer to both "legal" and "equitable" interests or relations. However, given the fusion of equity and law, many commentators today simply term the Hohfeldian relations, "legal relations." Technically, "jural" is more precise.

Special reference has therefore been made to the subject of trusts and other equitable interests only for the reason that the striking divergence of opinion relating thereto conspicuously exemplifies the need for dealing somewhat more intensively and systematically than is usual with the nature and analysis of all types of jural interests. Indeed, it would be virtually impossible to consider the subject of trusts at all adequately without, at the very threshold, analyzing and discriminating the various fundamental conceptions that are involved in practically every legal problem. In this connection the suggestion may be ventured that the usual discussions of trusts and other jural interests seem inadequate (and at times misleading) for the very reason that they are not founded on a sufficiently comprehensive and discriminating analysis of jural relations in general.

> **Editor's Note:** Hohfeld published a separate article on the relation between law and equity earlier in 1913, which was published in the *Michigan Law Review*.[9] As other chapters in this volume contended, thorny questions remain as to whether Hohfeld's own representation of equity using his typology was in fact accurate.[10] But Hohfeld's fundamental point – that prior analyses of equity were inadequate as an analytical matter – and that the typology that he introduced assists in reaching the "correct analysis" (or at least a clearer understanding) of trusts and many (if not all) other areas of the law – is fairly well-accepted. Of course, some contended that the labor to reach this clearer understanding using the typology is not worth the candle, but that is a separate issue from whether his analysis is ultimately illuminating.

Putting the matter in another way, the tendency – and the fallacy – has been to treat the specific problem as if it were far less complex than it really is; and this commendable effort to treat as simple that which is really complex has, it is believed,

jural interests," and "practically every legal problem" indicate that he believed that it could apply much more broadly than private law. Nonetheless, Hohfeld directly applied it solely to private law issues. Later scholars have applied the schema to constitutional law, but this application remains controversial because the State must be considered as a single legal actor akin to an individual actor within the legal system, in tension with the Hohfeldian view that the only actors in a legal system are actual persons. *See, e.g.*, Wesley N. Hohfeld, *The Nature of Stockholders' Individual Liability for Corporation Debts*, 9 COLUM. L. REV. 285 (1909). In any event, clearly it is private law scholars who have found the most use for Hohfeld's scheme.

9 Wesley N. Hohfeld, *The Relations Between Equity and Law*, 11 MICH. L. REV. 537 (1913). Interestingly, in the *Michigan Law Review* article, Hohfeld disclosed – though did not explain – all eight of the fundamental legal relations described here. In much earlier work on corporations, Hohfeld briefly described all of the relations other than "no-right." *See* Wesley N. Hohfeld, *The Nature of Stockholders' Individual Liability for Corporation Debts*, 9 COLUM. L. REV. 285 (1909).

10 Specifically, in his *Michigan Law Review* article, Hohfeld contended that there was, at least for many legal relations, a direct "conflict" between law and equity, countering the essentially contrary thesis of Maitland and others. Many of the footnotes (e.g., to Maitland, Langdell, and Ames) at the beginning of Hohfeld's 1913 *Yale Law Journal* article (i.e., the one presented here) pertain to this specific issue. Given that Hohfeld did not directly refer to this issue in the text or the notes, even today's sophisticated readers are unlikely to glean its import. Hence, all of these footnotes have been deleted from this edited version. Interested readers should peruse the *Michigan Law Review* article.

furnished a serious obstacle to the clear understanding, the orderly statement, and the correct solution of legal problems.[11] In short, it is submitted that the [*20] right kind of simplicity can result only from more searching and more discriminating analysis.

Editor's Note: That scholars and judges have been too facile and superficial in their treatment of legal "problems" relative to the complexity needed to clearly understand and "solve" the problems is a recurring theme in this article, and also one that has had notable influence on legal thought more generally.

If, therefore, the title of this article suggests a merely philosophical inquiry as to the nature of law and legal relations – a discussion regarded more or less as an end in itself – the writer may be pardoned for repudiating such a connotation in advance. On the contrary, in response to the invitation of the editor of this journal, the main purpose of the writer is to emphasize certain oft-neglected matters that may aid in the understanding and in the solution of practical, every-day problems of the law. With this end in view, the present article and another soon to follow will discuss, as of chief concern, the basic conceptions of the law – the legal elements that enter into all types of jural interests.[12] A later article will deal specially with the analysis of certain typical and important interests of a complex character – more particularly trusts and other equitable interests.[13]

In passing, it seems necessary to state that both of these articles are intended more for law school students than for any other class of readers. For that reason, it is hoped that the more learned reader may pardon certain parts of the discussion that might otherwise seem unnecessarily elementary and detailed. On the other hand, the limits of space inherent in a periodical article must furnish the excuse for as great a brevity of treatment as is consistent with clearness, and for a comparatively meager discussion – or even a total neglect – of certain matters the intrinsic importance of which might otherwise merit greater attention. In short, the emphasis is to be placed on those points believed to have the greatest practical value.

11 Hohfeld is often viewed as an early realist, but his view that there could be "correct solution[s] of legal problems," plus his exacting formulation of the legal relations and the logical relations between them at the very least shows his formalist roots. Ultimately, whether the Hohfeldian project sounds more in formalism or realism is a difficult question to answer. This annotation attempts to show that at least certain aspects of Hohfeld's critique that have been understood in a realist vein can be reinterpreted in more of a formalist one. *See infra* pages *34–*38.

12 The article "soon to follow" is Wesley N. Hohfeld, *Fundamental Legal Conceptions as Applied in Judicial Reasoning*, 26 YALE L.J. 710 (1917).

13 Unfortunately, Hohfeld never published this later article. A few of the chapters in this volume speculate as to how such "complex interests" would have been formed under the Hohfeldian typology. See Chapters 5, 9, 11, and 14.

Editor's Note: Although Hohfeld was correct to point out that many important implications of his discussion are omitted or discussed quite briefly, for all but the most expert of Hohfeldian scholars, nothing in the article is "unnecessarily elementary." Although the article is certainly "detailed," perhaps to a fault in parts, much of the detail does little to help most readers fully understand the concepts Hohfeld presents. Thus, this article has been an enigma for now over a century to not only law students, but legal scholars alike, resulting in misunderstandings that have been regularly replicated in the literature.

Editor's Note: The next section in the article entitled, "Legal Conceptions Contrasted with Non-Legal Conceptions" has been moved closer to the end of the article (pp. 62–70). Although Hohfeld believed it was "necessary to emphasize" the difference between "purely legal relations from the physical and mental facts that call such relations into being" "at the very outset" of the article, the complexity of the issue actually obscures the pedagogical treatment of the fundamental legal relations proper. Indeed, understanding the nature of legal powers is essentially necessary to comprehend the full import of Hohfeld's discussion, which forms the basis of the "bundle of sticks" view so common in property law today.

...

Editor's Note: The next section in the original article entitled, "Operative Facts Contrasted with Evidential Facts" has been moved to the middle of the article (pp. 47–52). Like the previous section, the complexity of these issues obscure the pedagogical treatment of the fundamental legal relations proper, and the section is better understood after Hohfeld's introductory description of his typology.

...

FUNDAMENTAL JURAL RELATIONS CONTRASTED WITH ONE ANOTHER.

One of the greatest hindrances to the clear understanding, the incisive statement, and the true solution of legal problems frequently arises from the express or tacit assumption that all legal relations may be reduced to "rights" and "duties," and that these latter categories are therefore adequate for the purpose of analyzing even the most complex legal interests, such as trusts, options, escrows, "future" interests, corporate interests, etc.

Editor's Note: In actuality, sophisticated scholars in the late nineteenth and early twentieth centuries had been using schemes quite similar to the one propounded by Hohfeld here. For instance, John W. Salmond described jural privileges, powers, immunities, liabilities, and disabilities in 1902 in his first edition of his *Jurisprudence* treatise. Nonetheless, Hohfeld correctly asserts that the reduction of all legal relations to "rights" and "duties" (or "obligations") occurred (and still occurs) in legal reasoning all too often. Hohfeld explains why this reduction is problematic in the following passages.

Even if the difficulty related merely to inadequacy and ambiguity of [*29] terminology, its seriousness would nevertheless be worthy of definite recognition and persistent effort toward improvement; for in any closely reasoned problem, whether legal or non-legal, chameleon-hued words are a peril both to clear thought and to lucid expression. As a matter of fact, however, the above mentioned inadequacy and ambiguity of terms unfortunately reflect, all too often, corresponding paucity and confusion as regards actual legal conceptions. That this is so may appear in some measure from the discussion to follow.

Editor's Note: Hohfeld's goal in this article was both to introduce a clearer conceptual typology than those offered by previous scholars and also to introduce specific terms that uniquely describe one of the eight concepts in his typology. Although Hohfeld has been quite successful in his former goal, his latter goal has mainly been a failure. In other words, all but the most meticulous scholars continue to use "chameleon-hued" terms that obscure the precision of the underlying, "fundamental" conceptions at-issue. However, this shortcoming – contrary to many who have argued against the Hohfeldian enterprise – is not fatal, for Hohfeld could have called his concepts "rose," "tulip," "daisy," and so forth, and they would have held the same meaning. It is this underlying meaning, and the logical structure and implications of which it partakes, that is of import to legal reasoning, theory, and the practical problems that concern adjudication and legal practice more generally.

[*30] The strictly fundamental legal relations are, after all, *sui generis*; and thus it is that attempts at formal definition are always unsatisfactory, if not altogether useless. Accordingly, the most promising line of procedure seems to consist in exhibiting all of the various relations in a scheme of "opposites" and "correlatives," and then proceeding to exemplify their individual scope and application in concrete cases.[14]

Editor's Note: In other words, instead of trying to define the "fundamental legal relations" that follow on their own terms ("sui generis"), they are defined in relation to one another by logical relationships.[15]

14 Earlier and later scholars – especially in the legal realist vein – have defined "duty" as a shorthand for which actions would subject a legal actor to liability. *See, e.g.*, Arthur L. Corbin, *Jural Relations and Their Classification*, 30 YALE L.J. 226 (1921). Specifically, the violation of a duty is a necessary condition for the imposition of liability by the State. Here, "liability" refers not to a Hohfeldian liability per se, but rather to the performance (or refraining of performance) of some action otherwise against the will of the legal actor, and typically includes payment of money, imprisonment, or the performance of certain "services" to the community-at-large. Once "duty" is defined in this sense, the other first-order legal relations follow as a matter of logic. The second-order legal relations concern the ability of legal actors, including the State, to change first-order legal relations. On this view, Hohfeld's "fundamental legal relations" are not "fundamental," but rather function more as a bookkeeping method to more easily keep track of those actions that may lead to liability than a mere list of "if-then" statements. This "modularization" of the law serves important purposes in reducing the information costs of actors within the legal system. Hohfeld, and many others, of course, view "duty" and the corresponding relations as "fundamental" in the deontic sense that they have meaning beyond "punishment" or the lack thereof. On this view, the violation of a "duty" has meaning – in the *legal* sense – even absent some form of liability. In other words, following the *positive* law takes on significance regardless of the State's ability to impose liability. This distinction is too often lost – or, at least, blurred – in discussions of Hohfeld, and is addressed in a few chapters of this volume. See Chapters 11 and 12.

15 *See generally* Jack Balkin, *The Hohfeldian Approach to Law and Semiotics*, 44 U. MIAMI L. REV. 1119 (1990).

An effort will be made to pursue this method:[16]

Jural Opposites	right	privilege	power	immunity
	no-right	duty	disability	liability

Jural Correlatives	right	privilege	power	immunity
	duty	no-right	liability	disability

Editor's Note: At this point in the article, it is not necessary for the reader to attempt to understand the relationships displayed in the tables above. Rather, the remainder of the article does as much.

Rights and Duties. As already intimated, the term "rights" tends to be used indiscriminately to cover what in a given case may be a privilege, a power, or an immunity, rather than a right in the strictest sense; and this looseness of usage is occasionally recognized by the authorities.

Editor's Note: Thus, for Hohfeld the generic term "right" can refer to four different fundamental legal relations: a "right in the strictest sense," "a privilege," "a power," or "an immunity." In what immediately follows, Hohfeld defines and explains a "right in the strictest sense" (also known as a "claim-right" (or in some earlier scholars' terminology, a "strict right") and a privilege. Later in the article, Hohfeld defines and explains a power and an immunity.

As said by Mr. Justice Strong in *People v. Dikeman*: <FN. 26: 7 How. Pr. 124, 130 (N.Y. Sup. Ct. 1852).>

> The word "right" is defined by lexicographers to denote, among other things, *property, interest, power, prerogative, immunity, privilege* (Walker's Dict, word 'Right'). In law it is most frequently applied to property in its restricted sense, but it is often used to designate *power, prerogative,* and *privilege,* * * *.

[16] In logical terms, jural "opposites" are logical negations. Once this is recognized the table of "jural" opposites can be aligned with the deontic square of opposition, which includes specific logical connectors: contraries, contradictories, subalterns, and subcontraries. A Hohfeldian duty to do some action is equivalent to a deontic obligation to do some action. Once Hohfeldian duty is defined as a deontic obligation, it becomes readily apparent that a Hohfeldian privilege is precisely a standard deontic permission (assuming that that one can be simultaneously subject to a duty not to do X and a duty to do X, a topic examined further below). With these definitions in place, it is clear that the Hohfeldian first-order duty-privilege relations are identical to the deontic relations, both conceptually and logically. Thus, a "privilege" and a "duty" both to do some action A are more precisely logical subalterns. However, Hohfeld's table of "opposites" concerns a privilege to do some action A and a duty to do some action *not* A. Because a duty to do some action not A is equivalent to a deontic impermissibility to do A, it becomes readily apparent that a privilege and obligation in the sense of "opposites" are logical contradictories. Note that because the deontic scheme is wholly devoid of the concepts of "right" or "no-right," there is no deontic equivalent of these relations. Hohfeld's system provides a richer account of deontic relations in the sense of taking account of the legal person to whom a deontic obligation is owed.

> **Editor's Note:** In this New York Supreme Court (i.e., trial court) opinion from the mid-nineteenth century, the judge cites an ordinary, non-legal dictionary to show the many senses of the term "right." This list extends well beyond Hohfeld's earlier list of a strict-right, privilege, power, and immunity, to encompass "property," "interest," and "prerogative." Given these numerous meanings of the term "right," Hohfeld will focus on just one of these meanings – that of the "claim-right" – as a "right in the strictest sense." The other senses of "right" will either be related to the "claim-right" in some logical or structural fashion (e.g., the privilege), or will be a collection of more fundamental legal relations (e.g., property), as explained further herein.

Recognition of this ambiguity is also found in the language of Mr. Justice [Howell Edmunds] Jackson,[17] in *United States v. Patrick*: <FN. 27: 54 F. 338, 348 (M.D. Tenn. 1893).>

> The words "right" or "privilege" have, of course, a variety of meanings, according to the connection or context in which they are used. Their definition, as given by standard lexicographers, include "that which one has a *legal claim to do*," "*legal power*," "*authority*," "*immunity* granted by authority," "the investiture with special or peculiar rights."

... It is interesting to observe, also, that a tendency toward discrimination may be found in a number of important constitutional and statutory provisions. Just how accurate the distinctions in the mind of the draftsman may have been it is, of course, impossible to say. <FN. 30: *See* ... Tenn. Const. of 1834, Art. 9, sec. 7 ("The legislature shall have no power to pass any law granting to any individual or individuals, rights, privileges and immunities or exemptions, other than * * *").>

> **Editor's Note:** Generally, Hohfeld's typology has been understood to apply to private law relations, namely those jural relations inhering between two individual legal persons, such as those occurring in tort, property, and contract law. However, here Hohfeld notes the use of such terms in "constitutional and statutory provisions" that restrict the power of the State in enacting certain statutory or regulatory provisions.[18] For instance, Hohfeld's citation to the Tennessee Constitution concerns the state legislature's "power to pass any law granting to any individual ... rights, privileges and immunities." So much might seem to indicate that Hohfeld believed his system extends to public law. However, this application of the Hohfeldian typology to constitutional and administrative law could be read in one of two ways. First, a narrow reading, in which the role of the typology is merely to discern whether and which "rights, privileges and immunities" have been placed at-issue by State action. Second, a broader reading, in which the typology also concerns the "power" (or lack thereof) held by the State vis-à-vis an individual. Unfortunately, Hohfeld never clarified his position. Later scholars have extended the Hohfeldian typology to public law, including constitutional law, by assuming the State is a legal actor that can be subject to legal relations, but this extension remains controversial.

17 At the time of this opinion, Justice Howell Edmunds Jackson was a judge for the Sixth Circuit, but was shortly thereafter appointed to the US Supreme Court. *See* Federal Judicial Center, *History of the Federal Judiciary*, www.fjc.gov/history/judges/jackson-howell-edmunds.

18 Similarly, earlier in the article, Hohfeld states (at *18): "It may well be that one's view as to the correct analysis of such [jural] interests would control the decision of a number of specific questions. This is obviously true as regards the solution of many difficult and delicate problems in constitutional law."

Recognizing, as we must, the very broad and indiscriminate use of the term, "right," what clue do we find, in ordinary legal discourse, toward limiting the word in question to a definite and appropriate meaning. That clue lies in the correlative "duty," for it is certain that even those who use the word and the conception "right" in the broadest possible way are accustomed to thinking of "duty" as the invariable correlative.

Editor's Note: In other words, given all of the various meanings of "right," it is better in Hohfeld's view to examine the legal relation, "duty," which is used in much a narrower and more precise sense. Because a "duty" and a "claim-right" (or "strict-right") are related logically, once "duty" is understood, then a "right" will be understood.

As said in *Lake Shore & M.S.R. Co. v. Kurtz*: <FN. 31: 10 Ind. App. 60 (1894).>

> [*32] A duty or a legal obligation is that which one ought or ought not to do. "Duty" and "right" are correlative terms. When a right is invaded, a duty is violated.

In other words, if X has a right against Y that he shall stay off the former's land, the correlative (and equivalent) is that Y is under a duty toward X to stay off the place.[19]

Editor's note: Thus, in the Hohfeldian terminology, a "right" – in the narrow sense used in his typology – is a mere legal entitlement that some other legal actor engage (a "positive" right) or refrain from engaging (a "negative" right) in some action. A Hohfeldian right (i.e., a "right in the strictest sense") *never provides the legal actor holding it* the ability to engage (or refrain from engaging) in some action lawfully. Thus, the phrases "right to walk down the sidewalk," "right to drive 50 miles per hour," the "right to remain silent" are not proper statements in the Hohfeldian system. Rather, it is the Hohfeldian "privilege," discussed in detail in the following section, that provides the ability for legal actors to engage in certain actions lawfully. Perhaps the most common mistake by students in the use of the Hohfeldian typology is to continue the common usage of right to indicate an entitlement to perform (or not perform) some action. It is critical to understand that a Hohfeldian right is strictly narrow and only concerns whether the actor holding it has some legal entitlement that *another legal actor* perform or not perform some action.[20]

19 Interestingly, although Hohfeld quotes the deontic definition of obligation – namely, "that which one ought or ought not to do" – he does not consider what is essentially a "*sui generis*" definition to be sufficient to define duty, but instead resorts to defining "duty" in terms of "right," and "right" in terms of "duty." However, it seems one could start with the deontic definition "that which one ought or ought not to do" from the perspective of the legal system. This definition could link "ought" to potential liability (in the broader sense of some form of criminal or civil punishment, see *supra* note 14, rather than the narrower meaning of "liability" in the Hohfeldian sense), or simply to the violation of a legal rule (i.e., some action that is contrary to the prescriptive force of the law, even absent liability). From this starting point, the other relations may be constructed.

20 One can define a "common right" as the coupling of a privilege to engage some action X, plus a Hohfeldian strict-right against interference from third-parties with the performance of the action, at least against bodily interference broadly speaking (e.g., through rights against assault, battery, and the like). Properly understood, the phrase "right to walk down the street" is a "common right," i.e., the coupling of a privilege with a right against interference. Since a vast swathe of privileges are coupled with general rights against bodily interference, the use of "right" in place of "privilege" is sensible as long as it understood that this is a compound relation. *See* Chapter 11.

Editor's Note: In the Hohfeldian scheme, as made clearer below, legal relations hold between two legal actors.[21] Thus, X may have a Hohfeldian right against Y that Y not enter X's land, but X may not have a right against Z (X's gardener) that Z not enter X's land. Thus, every relation must be examined with respect to those who hold and are subject to the legal relation.[22] Hohfeld's follow-up piece to this article more fully examines how legal relations function relative to various sets of actors; for instance, X's collection of rights against many undefined persons not to enter X's land, against a small set of defined persons to provide lateral support to X's land, and so forth.

If, as seems desirable, we should seek a synonym for the term "right" in this limited and proper meaning, perhaps the word "claim" would prove the best. The latter has the advantage of being a monosyllable. . . .

Editor's Note: Although the term "claim" may have been helpful at the time Hohfeld wrote this article, it is much less useful today. Specifically, a common contemporary meaning of "claim" is a valid cause of action in court, which (as described further below) typically involves a Hohfeldian power on the part of the claim-holder and a corresponding liability of the defendant to undertake specific remedial action or pay damages. A Hohfeldian right is thus different from the modern usage of claim, because Hohfeld's usage merely refers to some general claim under law that another person engage or not engage in an action, rather than the narrow claim a legal actor may hold to force another person via judicial process to undertake remedial action for violation of a Hohfeldian right. In this sense, Hohfeld's system leaves open the possibility that the violation of a Hohfeldian right could be without a remedy – namely, while the violation of a right is *necessary* to pursue legal action against the third party that breached the correlative Hohfeldian duty, it is not always *sufficient* to bring such action. In other words, the Hohfeldian system allows for "naked" rights – i.e., rights not protected by remedies.[23] Of course, a legal system may impose an external constraint precluding naked

[21] As noted earlier, Hohfeld seemed to posit that the two actors must be individuals, not entities, yet the schema has been applied when one legal actor (e.g., the State, a corporation, etc.) is an entity. Indeed, at times, Hohfeld seems to contemplate as much, though his exposition is somewhat ambiguous on this score. *See supra* note 5.

[22] This requirement has been an important ground for scholars to reject the Hohfeldian scheme, at least as he specified it. For instance, some scholars contended that certain legal relations have no subject, such that a right exists absent a corresponding duty. *See, e.g.*, Neil MacCormick, *Rights in Legislation*, *in* Law, Morality and Society 200 (P. M. S. Hacker & Joseph Raz eds., 1977). However, the "rights" adduced as evidence of such by these scholars are usually "interests" (i.e., reasons for rights or the like), "inchoate" rights (i.e., rights contingent upon some other fact to come into being), rights against the State (i.e., rights that inhere not against an individual person, but against the government), and other types of "rights" that are either not part of the Hohfeldian scheme per se, or can be modeled with a more complex form of the scheme.

[23] Unfortunately, many Hohfeldian scholars have wrongly assumed that a Hohfeldian "claim-right," perhaps largely because of its terminology, is sufficient for the holder to bring an action in the event of breach. As the chapter in this volume by Goldberg and Zipursky makes clear, rights can certainly be uncoupled to remedies, resulting in so-called naked rights. *See* Chapter 12. In other words, rights – at least in the Hohfeldian sense – may stand on their own. One can perhaps partly save the "claim-right as claim" view of the Hohfeldian right by specifying a defeasible sufficiency – in other words, breach of a Hohfeldian claim-right is sufficient to bring an action, but such action may be barred in the event the breaching party holds a Hohfeldian immunity to such an action. In this case, the natural and logical consequences of a breach of Hohfeldian right would be in effect stemmed by the higher-order immunity. In other words, rights can only be "naked" to first-order; a more precise formulation would couple breached claim-rights to an applicable second-order relation: either to a power to initial suit (i.e., a liability of the breaching party) or a disability to do so (i.e., an immunity of the breaching party).

rights, but there is nothing in the Hohfeldian scheme that requires as much. Given these concerns, probably a better term for a Hohfeldian right – and one used by Bentham and Salmond – is "strict right," which clearly indicates the narrowness of the Hohfeldian right.

Privileges and "No-Rights." As indicated in the above scheme of jural relations, a privilege is the opposite of a duty, and the correlative of a "no-right." In the example last put, whereas X has a *right* or *claim* that Y, the other man, should stay off the land, he himself [i.e., X] has the *privilege* of entering on the land; or, in equivalent words, X does not have a duty to stay off.

Editor's Note: Importantly, X's privilege to enter his own land is not entailed by X's right that Y stay off X's land. Rather, the incidents of X's ownership include both X's right that third parties such as Y not trespass as well as X's privilege that X can enter his own land. The privilege of an owner to enter his own land may seem self-evident, but compare patents, for which the owner of the patent is only afforded a negative right that others not make, use, or sell the patented invention. In other words, a patent does not afford any privileges to the owner to make, use, or sell the patented invention – to the extent such privileges exist, they do so regardless of the owner's patent rights. In other words, a mere right to prevent trespass (or infringement) does not logically entail a privilege to use one's own property (or patented invention). Similarly, a privilege to enter one's land (or use a patented invention) does not logically entail a right to prevent others to do so.

The privilege of entering is the negation of a duty to stay off. As indicated by this case, some caution is necessary at this point; for, always, when it is said that a given privilege is the mere negation of a *duty*, what is meant, of course, is a duty having a content or tenor precisely *opposite* to that of the privilege in question.

Editor's Note: Importantly, the negation of a duty *not* to do some action X is equivalent to a privilege to do X. As Hohfeld notes, the absence of a duty *not* to enter X's land is equivalent to a privilege to enter X's land. Conversely, the absence of a duty to do some action X is equivalent to a privilege *not* to do X. Thus, the absence of a duty to rescue an injured person is equivalent to a privilege *not* to rescue an injured person.[24]

Yet, even still, a breach of a Hohfeldian right in the most general sense would still only remain a *necessary*, not a sufficient, condition to bring an action in court for a remedy.

24 Some commentators have regarded this "flipping" of the action as somehow destroying the symmetry in the Hohfeldian relations. Such views are incorrect as a matter of logic. Indeed, as noted earlier, one can easily show that the Hohfeldian privilege to do some action A is equivalent to deontic logic's permission to perform A, and the Hohfeldian duty not to do some action A is equivalent deontic logic's obligation not to perform A. In deontic logic the negation of an obligation not to perform A, i.e., $\sim O(\sim A)$, is equivalent to a permission to perform A, i.e., PE(A). In other words, $\sim O(\sim A) \leftrightarrow PE(A)$. This equivalence in deontic logic is equivalent to the Hohfeldian correspondence between the privilege to do A and the negation of a duty not to do A. Thus, the Hohfeldian typology exhibits the same logical structure as that of deontic obligation and permission operators. Indeed, one can show that the first-order Hohfeldian relations of duties and privileges fully replicate the traditional definitional scheme (TDS) that underlies standard deontic logic. In this sense, the Hohfeldian system antedated even Mally's attempts to formulate a deontic logic. Commentators have generally appreciated some connection between the Hohfeldian system and deontic logic, but few have noted the identity between the first-order Hohfeldian typology and the TDS of deontic logic. With that said, Hohfeld proposed no axioms of normative relations like those in deontic logic, which are needed to fully specify a deontic system.

Thus, if, for some special reason, X has contracted with Y to go on the former's own land, it is obvious that X has, as regards Y, both the privilege of entering and *the duty of entering*.

> **Editor's Note:** This sentence is not a typographical error. Here, Hohfeld's example is the owner, X, contracting with another party, Y, so that X is now contractually obligated to enter her own land. For instance, perhaps X is an absentee owner of a house adjacent to Y's, and weeds have overtaken X's front yard, which X agrees to clear in a contract with Y. Because X already had a privilege to enter her own land, the contract merely changes the owner X's privilege to stay off her land to a duty to enter her own land – resulting in both a privilege and a duty to enter her own land.

The privilege is perfectly consistent with this sort of duty – [*33] for the latter is of the *same* content or tenor as the privilege – but it still holds good that, as regards Y, X's privilege of entering is the precise negation of a duty to *stay off*.

> **Editor's Note:** In addition to explaining the previous point, Hohfeld shows that a duty to do A and a privilege to do A are consistent with one another. Thus, merely having a Hohfeldian privilege to do A does not imply that *one may not do A*. For instance, modifying Hohfeld's example, suppose there are two entirely separate public parks, A and B, and that Y has a privilege to enter A and also a privilege to enter B at some particular day and time. Because Y can choose to enter B instead of A, Y has a privilege not to enter A. However, if Y contracts with X to enter A at that day and time, then Y now holds both a privilege to enter A and is subject to a duty to enter A. Y's duty to enter A implies that Y must have lost the privilege *not* to enter A (at least vis-à-vis X). In other words, Y can no longer enter B at that day and time, at least not without violating a duty owed to X to enter A at that day and time. Thus, a Hohfeldian privilege to do some action A – although this implies no duty *not to do A* – is entirely consistent with having a duty *to do A*. At the same time, "privilege" sometimes connotes a complete absence of duty – i.e., no duty to do A and no duty not to do A. This more expanded "two-sided" privilege is much broader than the "one-sided" Hohfeldian privilege, and for this reason perhaps the term "permission" is a more apt label for Hohfeld's one-sided privilege.[25] In other words, X's privilege to do A – like a permission – simply means that X is not under a duty *not* to do A. As for doing A itself, X may have a duty to do A, or X may not have a duty to do A. Thus, X's privilege to do A tells us nothing per se about whether X has a duty to do A – she may have one, she may not. (Hohfeld and other commentators have also suggested the term "liberty" for privilege, but "liberty" is often used in a two-sided way – i.e., to refer to the complete absence of *both* a duty to do A and not to do A.) As such, the Hohfeldian privilege is, like the Hohfeldian right, very narrow in meaning, much narrower than some of the standard usages.[26]

25 For instance, deontic logic uses the term "permission" and is equivalent to the Hohfeldian privilege (*see supra* note 10). A deontic "option" is the coupling of a positive permission (i.e., permission to do A) and a negative permission (i.e., permission not to do A).

26 A more subtle question arises as to whether all duties to perform (or refrain from) some action A must be coupled with a privilege to perform (or refrain from) the action A. Suppose instead of Hohfeld's example of the owner, X, contracting with Y for X to enter her own land, X contracts with Y such that Y has a duty to enter X's land. Prior to the contract, Y has a privilege not to enter the land and Y has a duty not to enter the land. In order for the contract to create both a privilege and a duty to enter the land, two legal relations must be changed. First, Y's privilege not to enter the land must be changed to duty to enter the land (a contractually imposed duty); second, Y's duty not to enter the land must be changed to a privilege to enter the land (a license). In this regard, consistent with the earlier discussion, note that when a privilege to do some action A is changed via contract to a duty, it becomes a duty *not* to do A. But suppose the contract simply changed Y's privilege not to enter the land to a duty to enter the land, but left intact Y's duty not to

Similarly, if A has not contracted with B to perform certain work for the latter, A's privilege of not doing so is the very negation of a duty of *doing so*. Here again the duty contrasted is of a content or tenor exactly opposite to that of the privilege.

> **Editor's Note:** This sentence just reiterates previous points. For instance, if A is not under any contract with B – say, to paint B's house – then A has a privilege not to paint B's house, which corresponds to no duty of A to paint B's house.

Passing now to the question of "correlatives," it will be remembered, of course, that a duty is the invariable correlative of that legal relation which is most properly called a right or claim. That being so, if further evidence be needed as to the fundamental and important difference between a right (or claim) and a privilege, surely it is found in the fact that the correlative of the latter relation is a "no-right," there being no single term available to express the latter conception. Thus, the correlative of X's right that Y shall not enter on the land is Y's duty not to enter; but the correlative of X's privilege of entering himself is manifestly Y's "no-right" that X shall not enter.

> **Editor's Note:** Much ink has been spilled regarding Hohfeld's "no-right," but in essence it refers to the absence of a right in the narrow Hohfeldian sense.[27] As Hohfeld notes, if X holds a privilege to enter his own land, then Y does not hold a right (i.e., has a "no-right") that X shall not enter. Note again the change in "tenor" of the action subject to the relation when shifting between privilege (enter the land) and no-right (not enter the land). Thus, more specifically, a privilege to do A is correlative of no-right not to do A. Yet, a duty not to do A is correlative of a right not to do A.[28] For instance, X's privilege of self-defense against Y implies no-right of Y that X *not* use self-defense. However, if X has no privilege of self-defense, this means X has a duty *not* to use self-defense, which implies a right on Y's part that X *not* use self-defense.

enter the land – in other words, the contract imposed a duty to enter without any license that creates a privilege to enter. Thus, the situation would be one in which Y had a duty to enter without a corresponding privilege to enter. In that instance, Y would be subject to conflicting duties, and no matter what Y chose, Y would have a violated a duty to X. Importantly, nothing in the Hohfeldian scheme *logically* restricts a single legal actor from holding conflicting duties *vis-à-vis the same actor*. In order to prevent such Kafkaesque schemes, it is necessary to impose an internal consistency constraint – namely, that a single actor cannot hold conflicting duties to another single actor without violating the constraint. But note that such a constraint would simply be based on a matter of policy or morality, not logic. Indeed, deontic logic imposes such a constraint as an axiom. Although many descriptions of deontic logic assume that an obligation to perform A implies a permission to perform A *even absent such an axiom*, these descriptions are incorrect. (A related issue in the Hohfeldian system is whether a single legal actor may hold conflicting duties vis-à-vis different legal actors. Of course, absent such a consistency constraint, the previous discussion implies that such conflicting duties are also logically possible.)

27 As noted earlier, Salmond had introduced the notion of "liability" in the first sense that was homologous in a structural sense to Hohfeld's "no-right," yet Hohfeld arguably recognized much broader and deeper implications of this legal relation. *See supra* note 4.

28 Again, that the tenor of the action changes is entirely consistent with standard deontic logic and does not somehow violate any symmetry that is seemingly required by the system. On the other hand, in specifying his "opposites" and "correlatives," Hohfeld did not generalize the underlying action to which a jural relation applies as a generic concept, which – at least absent a careful read of his article – could certainly cause confusion for some readers. Also, his term "opposite" is somewhat vague. As noted earlier, the jural relations that are "opposites" are technical logical contradictories. *See supra* note 13.

In view of the considerations thus far emphasized, the importance of keeping the conception of a right (or claim) and the conception of a privilege quite distinct from each other seems evident; and, more than that, it is equally clear that there should be a separate term to represent the latter relation. No doubt, as already indicated, it is very common to use the term "right" indiscriminately, even when the relation designated is really that of privilege; and only too often this identity of terms has involved for the particular speaker or writer a confusion or blurring of ideas. Good instances of this may be found even in unexpected places. Thus Professor [Thomas Erskine] Holland, in his work on *Jurisprudence*, referring to a different and well known sort of ambiguity inherent in the Latin "*Ius*," the German "*Recht*," the Italian "*Diritto*," and the French "*Droit*" – terms used to express "not only 'a right,' but also 'Law' in the abstract"[29] – very aptly observes:

> If the expression of widely different ideas by one and the same term resulted only in the necessity for * * * clumsy [*34] paraphrases, or obviously inaccurate paraphrases, no great harm would be done: but unfortunately the identity of terms seems irresistibly to suggest an identity between the ideas expressed by them. <FN. 35: THE ELEMENTS OF JURISPRUDENCE 83–84 (11th ed. 1910).[30]>

Editor's Note: A major thrust of Hohfeld's analytical work was to disambiguate concepts in the law so as to distinguish related, but very different, concepts in order to show weaknesses in previous scholarly analytical treatments as well as judicial reasoning. Thus, when scholars, lawyers, and judges use the word "right," if they do not specify which form of "right" they are using, inferential errors can easily be made. In this regard, Hohfeld believed that analytical reasoning was often central to determining the outcome of judicial opinions.[31]

29 In addition to the term "right" being used to refer to Hohfeldian privileges, powers, and immunities, as Hohfeld notes, it is used in some systems to refer to "law" more generally. Indeed, the term "right" is also used to refer to interests, moral claims, "natural" rights, and the like (particularly as inputs to legal rules – e.g., in Dworkin's usage "taking rights seriously"); certain combinations of Hohfeldian rights, privileges, powers, and immunities; generalized legal principles (e.g., "right to free speech"); and so forth.

30 Based on the pin cites in this section, it appears Hohfeld was working with both the 10th and 11th editions of Holland's treatise, which are identical with respect to the quoted passages. All cites herein are to the 11th edition, published in 1910.

31 For this reason, Hohfeld was to a substantial degree a formalist. Although the legal realists heavily relied on Hohfeld for two important critiques of classical formalism – namely, one, that facial judicial reasoning often masked underlying policy decisions, and two, that certain legal concepts assumed as natural were in actuality bundles of underlying relations tied together for policy reasons – Hohfeld would not likely have agreed that policy plays a fundamental role in deciding the bulk of judicial decisions. Rather, in Hohfeld's system, it seems fairly clear that many legal rules (and even standards) result in fully determinate legal relations that uniquely determine the outcome of a case. On the other hand, contrary to at least standard accounts of nineteenth-century formalism, Hohfeld would certainly agree that at least in some cases, the legal relations would be insufficient to determine an outcome, necessitating the use of policy, justice, or morality to reach a decision. *See infra* at page *36. In this sense, Hohfeld was at least a proto-realist – how many cases, and hence how much of a realist he would have become, remains unanswered by his extant writings.

Curiously enough, however, in the very chapter where this appears – the chapter on "Rights" – the notions of right, privilege and power seem to be blended, and that, too, although the learned author states that "the correlative of * * * legal right is legal duty," and that "these pairs of terms express * * * in each case the same state of facts viewed from opposite sides."[32] While the whole chapter must be read in order to appreciate the seriousness of this lack of discrimination a single passage must suffice by way of example:

> If * * * the power of the State will protect him in so carrying out his wishes, and will compel such acts or forbearances on the part of other people as may be necessary in order that his wishes may be so carried out, then he has a "legal right" so to carry out his wishes. <FN. 36: *Id.* at 85.>

The first part of this passage suggests privileges, the middle part rights (or claims), and the last part privileges.

Editor's Note: Specifically, the first part of the passage refers to "carrying out his wishes," which suggests a Hohfeldian privilege to perform some action. The second part refers to "compel such acts or forbearances on the part of other people," which suggests to Hohfeldian rights. When the third part refers to "'legal right' so to carry out his wishes," Hohfeld assumes that this refers to privileges. However, Hohfeld's interpretation of the third part is likely incomplete and, hence, ultimately incorrect. As Hohfeld notes, Holland recognized that "the correlative of * * * legal right is legal duty." Thus, in using the term "legal right," Holland must be referring, at least in part, to the duty on the part of the others that follows from the State's ability to "compel" actions by others to protect the person's "carrying out his wishes." At the same time, Hohfeld is correct in asserting that the "right" to carry out his wishes seemingly refers to privileges, particularly because a "right" in the narrow Hohfeldian sense only restricts third parties, and never provides justification to the first party (i.e., the person holding it) to engage in certain action. So does Holland's ultimate phrase "right so to carry out his wishes" refer to Hohfeldian rights or Hohfeldian privileges? Hohfeld's faulty assumption is that it refers to one or the other, but not both. A seemingly better interpretation is that the term "right" in "right so to carry out his wishes" is a "complex" Hohfeldian relation that is a *combination* of a privilege to carry out his wishes *and* a Hohfeldian right to compel acts or forbearances on the part of others "as may be necessary in order that his wishes may be so carried out."[33] Thus, rather than "blending" legal concepts, arguably Holland is conjoining them. Nonetheless, Hohfeld stands correct that the indiscriminate use of the

[32] The Elements of Jurisprudence 86 (11th ed. 1910) ("Where such furtherance is merely expected by the public opinion of the society in which they live, it is their 'moral duty.' Where it will be enforced by the power of the State to which they are amenable, it is their 'legal duty.' The correlative of might is necessity, or susceptibility to force; of moral right is moral duty; of legal right is legal duty. These pairs of correlative terms express, it will be observed, in each case, the same state of facts viewed from opposite side.").

[33] This view is further supported by Holland's statement a few sentences thereafter: "If it is a question of legal right [to carry out his wishes], all depends upon the readiness of the State to exert force on his behalf." *Id.* In other words, the focus of Holland is on the strict-right against non-interference, with an implicit assumption that there is – absent some specified duty otherwise – a privilege to carry it out. As noted earlier, the coupling of a privilege and a right to non-interference with performance of the privilege can be termed a "common right," because a very common legal usage of "right" is to refer to this combination of more fundamental relations, as well as to distinguish "common right" from the even more complex "constitutional right." *See* Chapter 11.

term "right" often leads to confusion and error in legal reasoning. In this respect, Holland's usage could certainly be more precise.[34]

Similar difficulties seem to exist in Professor [John Chipman] Gray's able and entertaining work on *The Nature and Sources of Law*. In his chapter on "Legal Rights and Duties" the distinguished author takes the position that a right always has a duty as its correlative; <FN. 37: *See* NATURE AND SOURCES OF LAW §§ 45, 184 (1909).> and he seems to define the former relation substantially according to the more limited meaning of "claim."

Editor's Note: As recounted earlier, the usage of the term "claim" to refer to a Hohfeldian right is likely to cause confusion given today's usage of "claim" to refer to a legal action. *See supra* at 25–26.

Legal privileges, powers, and immunities are prima facie ignored, and the impression conveyed [is] that all legal relations can be comprehended under the conceptions, "right" and "duty." But, with the greatest hesitation and deference,[35] the suggestion may be ventured that a number of his examples seem to show the inadequacy of such mode of treatment. Thus, for example, he says:

> The eating of shrimp salad is an interest of mine, and, if I can pay for it, the law will protect that interest, and it is therefore a right of mine to eat shrimp salad which I have paid for, although I know that shrimp salad always gives me the colic. <FN. 38: *Id.* § 48.>

This passage seems to suggest primarily two classes of relations: *first*, the party's respective privileges, as against A, B, C, [*35] D and others in relation to eating the salad, or, correlatively, the respective "no-rights" of A, B, C, D and others that the party should not eat the salad; *second*, the party's respective rights (or claims) as against A, B, C, D and others that they should not interfere with the physical act of eating the salad, or, correlatively, the respective duties of A, B, C, D and others that they should not interfere.

These two groups of relations seem perfectly distinct; and the privileges could, in a given case, exist even though the rights mentioned did not.

[34] Nonetheless, because most actions are indeed privileged – i.e., not subject to a duty to refrain from performing the action – in stating that an actor has a "right" to engage in some activity, the locus of interest is on the duties placed on third parties not to interfere with the performance of the privileged act. In other words, when examining whether there are "rights" to protect carrying out one's wishes, there is arguably an implicit assumption that such rights will only protect actions one wishes to perform that are not otherwise precluded (i.e., are privileged in the Hohfeldian sense). Thus, to the extent Holland's and similar discussion fail to refer to a "privilege," there is some justification for as much.

[35] Hohfeld was Gray's assistant while a student at Harvard Law School, which could explain the "hesitation and deference" qualifier. *See* Chapter 18.

Editor's Note: At this point in the article, it is very clear that the failure of prior scholars to delineate rights from privileges is a recurring theme, and this aspect of Hohfeld's work became an important component of realist critiques of so-called formalism. As Hohfeld properly notes, Gray seems to refer to a privilege of his to eat the salad, as well as a right against interference in his exercise of his privilege. Such a constellation of legal relations is clearly different from a Hohfeldian "right." Yet, as my chapter in this volume contended,[36] it seems more appropriate to infer that Gray – like Holland in the previous quoted passage – used "right" as a "complex relation," namely, one that referred both to rights and privileges. Indeed, the usage of "right" to refer to a privilege to engage in some activity, plus a strict Hohfeldian right against non-interference, remains common legal parlance. With that said, again like Holland, Gray's treatment certainly could have been clearer if he had referred to the fundamental relations, namely, a "right" and a "privilege," rather than referring only to the less precise term "right."

A, B, C, and D, being the owners of the salad, might say to X: "Eat the salad, if you can; you have our license to do so, but we don't agree not to interfere with you." In such a case the privileges exist, so that if X succeeds in eating the salad, he has violated no rights of any of the parties. But it is equally clear that if A had succeeded in holding so fast to the dish that X couldn't eat the contents, no right of X would have been violated.

Editor's Note: This is an unusual example, because typically a license from an owner of real or personal property to another to enter or use that property implies that the owner will not interfere with such entry or use. For instance, imagine an owner of land stating to a neighbor, "Why don't you come over for tea this afternoon?," then when the neighbor arrives, the owner shoves him into the street. In this instance, the owner would very likely be liable for the tort of battery, particularly because the neighbor was under no duty not to enter (i.e., had a Hohfeldian privilege to enter the owner's land). More generally, as this chapter noted earlier, a privilege to do some action is usually accompanied – at least indirectly by the torts of assault, battery, trespass, and the like – by some right against non-interference to do the action. Thus, if A, B, C, and D had said to X, "Go ahead, eat the salad, you have our license to do so," then subsequently interfered with X's eating the salad, they could very well be liable in tort.[37] Here, however, A, B, C, and D said more, "If you can ... we don't agree not to interfere with you." These qualifiers make X's eating of the salad more like a game or sport. Consider a boxing contest, A and B both have a license to punch each other (privilege to punch) and yet are under no duty not to interfere with each other's punching (privilege to block). Like a game or sport, Hohfeld importantly shows that it is always logically possible to decouple a privilege to do some action from a duty on others not to interfere with such an action. Further, as explained below, Hohfeld critically shows that any such coupling must be a matter of policy, justice, or the like, not a matter of logic. However, Hohfeld's criticism of Gray – who was not referring to a game, but rather the ordinary transaction of purchasing a salad – obscures the fact that most privileges are accompanied by rights to non-interference and that this complex jural relation is often termed a "right" (what can be termed a "common right").[38] Again, Hohfeld is right to point out Gray's looseness of usage, but this is a different criticism than accusing Gray of conceptual error.

36 *See* Chapter 11.

37 *See id.*

38 In a footnote (n.39), Hohfeld provides similar examples in which Gray conflates privileges with potential and actual "rights" in the broader sense (i.e., one or more of strict-rights, powers, privileges,

Perhaps the essential character and importance of the distinction can be shown by a slight variation of the facts. Suppose that X, being already the legal owner of the salad, contracts with Y that he (X) will never eat this particular food. With A, B, [*36] C, D and others no such contract has been made. One of the relations now existing between X and Y is, as a consequence, fundamentally different from the relation between X and A. As regards Y, X has no privilege of eating the salad; but as regards either A or any of the others, X has such a privilege. It is to be observed incidentally that X's right that Y should not eat the food persists even though X's own privilege of doing so has been extinguished.[39]

Editor's Note: In this example, Hohfeld shows that the legal relations inhere between specific legal actors. For instance, suppose Y owns and is the only occupier of a piece of land, and X is a neighbor who wants absolute privacy for one week. Subsequently, Y contracts with X not to enter her (Y's) own land for a week. In this instance, Y has a duty to X, but not to third parties, A, B, C, and D. Similarly, if Y owns a salad and contracts with X not to eat it, Y only owes the duty to X, not to A, B, C, and D. Thus, Y has no privilege to eat the salad with respect to X, but has a privilege to eat it with respect to A, B, C, and D. However, this point is fundamentally different from Hohfeld's prior assertion that a privilege is conceptually distinct from a right to non-interference, i.e., *even with respect to the same legal actor*. As such, Hohfeld's example arguably does not illustrate "the essential character and importance of the distinction" between privileges and rights to non-interference. At the same time, the example is important to show that legal relations always inhere between determinate legal actors, and that specific sets of relations may vary across actors (including privileges with respect to some actors and duties with respect to others concerning the same action).[40]

and immunities). One example is "If there is an ordinance that the town constable may kill all dogs without collars, the constable may have the legal right to kill such dogs." *Id.* (quoting Gray, *supra*, at § 102). Hohfeld contended that "what the ordinance did was to create a privilege – the absence of a duty not to fill which otherwise would have existed in favor of the owner of the dog. . . . The latter doesn't except very remotely, call up the idea of the constable's accompanying rights against all others that they shouldn't interfere with his actual killing of the dog." However, as noted earlier, the right to non-interference that typically accompanies a privilege need not be expressly stated, because the non-interference right is typically a background right protected by general tort obligations. Absent some exemption from these general obligations (e.g., as in a game or sport), a privilege will always be coupled with a right, yielding a "common right." Like the salad example, Gray presumably is referring to such a common right when he states "the constable may have the legal right to kill such dogs."

39 Immediately after this paragraph, Hohfeld writes in a footnote: "It may be noted incidentally that a statute depriving a party of privileges as such may raise serious constitutional questions under the Fourteenth Amendment. *Compare, e.g., Lindsley* v. *Nat. Carbonic Gas Co.*, 220 U.S. 61 (1910)." In *Lindsley*, the Court considered, inter alia, whether a New York statute preventing a landowner from removing excess carbonic gas from underground natural mineral springs was a substantive due process violation. The *Lochner*-era Court decided it was not, though of course other decisions from that era struck down prescriptions on Hohfeldian privileges as unconstitutional, specifically those dealing with "liberty of contract." *See, e.g., Allgeyer* v. *Louisiana*, 165 U.S. 578 (1897).

40 This reflection applies to active legal relations. Inchoate relations – i.e., that are contingent upon some additional fact to become active – will not often inhere between determinate legal actors until they actually become active. For instance, the "right of a child to appropriate care from his or her parents or guardians" is not an active, determinate relation until a specific child is born and is owed a duty from his or her specific parents or guardians. Future interests in the field of real property would constitute another class of inchoate relations. *See, e.g., Hagan* v. *Transportation Cabinet*, 559 S.W.3d

On grounds already emphasized, it would seem that the line of reasoning pursued by Lord Lindley in the great case of *Quinn v. Leathem* <FN. 41: [1901] AC 495, 534.> is deserving of comment:

> **Editor's Note:** *Quinn v. Leathem* is an important early twentieth century British labor law case that involved the propriety of a secondary boycott (i.e., of the customer) of the plaintiff, Leathem, a butcher. Specifically, a trade union with workers at Leathem's butcher shop requested that one of Leathem's customers, Munce, refuse to do business with Leathem in order to pressure Leathem to agree to the trade union's demands. The trade union stated that if Munce refused to do so, they would call a strike among Munce's own workers. Leathem sued Quinn, who was the treasurer of the trade union, and other officers.

> The plaintiff [Leathem, the butcher] had the ordinary *rights* of the British subject. He was at *liberty* to earn his living in his own way, provided he did not violate some special law prohibiting him from so doing, and provided he did not infringe the rights of other people. This *liberty* involved the *liberty* to deal with other persons [such as Munce] who were willing to deal with him. This *liberty* is a *right* recognized by law; its *correlative* is the general duty of everyone not to prevent the free exercise of this *liberty* except so far as his own liberty of action may justify him in so doing. But a person's *liberty* or *right* to deal with others is nugatory unless they are at liberty to deal with him if they choose to do so. Any interference with their liberty to deal with him affects him.

A "liberty" considered as a legal relation (or "right" in the loose and generic sense of that term) must mean, if it have any definite content at all, precisely the same thing as *privilege*, and certainly that is the fair connotation of the term as used the first three times in the passage quoted.

> **Editor's Note:** Here, Hohfeld asserts that "liberty" to do some action is the "same thing" as a Hohfeldian privilege to do some action, that is, the absence of a duty not to do the action. However, as this chapter noted earlier, the term "liberty" often refers to a legal actor holding *both* a Hohfeldian privilege to do A *and* a privilege not to do A. For example, suppose X has a privilege to do A, but lacks a privilege not to do A. In this case, X must do A (i.e., has a duty to do A). It would be odd to state that one with a duty to do A has a "liberty" to do A simply because the duty is coupled with a privilege to do A. Rather, the connotation of liberty is that a choice exists as to whether to do some act. A privilege is a mere exemption from a duty. Thus, and contrary to Hohfeld's assertion, the typical usage of "liberty" is often not synonymous with a Hohfeldian privilege.

783, 784 (Ky. 2018) ("Edward's interest is an inchoate right, an expectancy of an interest or a future interest contingent upon his surviving Rose"); *McArthur* v. *Franklin*, 15 Ohio St. 485, 496 (1864) ("Before the death of the husband, the wife has no estate in his lands – nothing but an inchoate or imperfect right – a possible future interest").

> **Editor's Note:** Even if one ignores this concern about the term "liberty," this also does not agree with Hohfeld that the term "liberty" as it is used the first three times in the passage means "precisely the same as privilege, and certainly that is the fair connotation of the term." Rather, as noted earlier, a privilege is often coupled with a right against non-interference, at least a general right against assault, battery, trespass, and other torts. In this instance, Lord Lindley's use of "liberty" was arguably that of a complex relation, namely, a Hohfeldian privilege plus a right against non-interference with exercise of that privilege.

It is equally clear, as already indicated, that such a privilege or liberty to deal with others at will might very conceivably exist without any peculiar concomitant rights against "third parties" as regards certain kinds of interference. Whether there should be such concomitant rights (or claims) is ultimately a question of justice and policy; and it should be considered, as such, on its merits. The only correlative logically implied by the privileges or liberties in question are the "no-rights" of "third parties." It would therefore be a *non* [*37] *sequitur* to conclude from the mere existence of such liberties that "third parties" are under a *duty* not to interfere, etc.

> **Editor's Note:** Hohfeld is correct that if one starts with a mere Hohfeldian privilege, there is no concomitant right against non-interference. Rather, like Hohfeld's shrimp salad "game," it is possible that a privilege to do some action may be met by interference from others that violates no duty. Yet, as just noted, privileges are typically coupled with rights against non-interference. Because Lord Lindley very likely used liberty to refer to a complex aggregate of a privilege plus a right against non-interference, it would not (as Hohfeld contended) be a logical error – i.e., "non sequitur" – "to conclude from the mere existence of such liberties that 'third parties' are under a duty not to interfere."

> **Editor's Note:** At the same time, Hohfeld is correct that there is no logical reason to couple privileges to rights against non-interference. Rather, such a coupling is as Hohfeld explains, a "question of justice and policy." That Lord Lindley began his analysis with a "liberty" that assumed a right against non-interference, one could argue that he assumed his conclusion that Quinn was under a duty not to interfere with Leathem's business. However, as my later chapter in this volume explains, Lord Lindley did provide at least some policy reasons to support his conclusion later in the opinion.[41] Thus, Hohfeld's contention that Lord Lindley obscured what should have been a policy determination in conceptual analysis is somewhat misplaced.[42] With that said, Lord Lindley's language – like that of Holland and Gray – is not

[41] *See* Chapter 11. Specifically, Lord Lindley determined that the defendants' conduct was not justified as a normative matter. First, Lord Lindley recounted how the defendants' threat to strike Leathem's customer in the event Leathem did not fire his non-union employees was determined by the jury to be "wrongful and malicious." Second, Lord Lindley found that the defendants' conduct "was the more reprehensible" because Leathem had offered to pay for his non-union employees to join the defendant's union. Third, unlike earlier cases, there was no dispute in this case between Leathem and his employees or his customer, or his customer and his employees. For these and other reasons, he found that the action of the defendants amounted to a "form of coercion, intimidation, molestation, or annoyance . . . very difficult to resist, [that] to say the least, requir[ed] justification" [1901] AC 495 (HL) (Lindley, LJ).

[42] Hohfeld's critique of *Quinn* v. *Leathem* has been an exemplar for many in the realist camp who claim that so-called formalist judges were surreptitiously importing policy into their opinions under the veneer of seemingly plausible, but ultimately illegitimate, reasoning. However, given the above

crystal clear, and that more precise usage in these situations would certainly be preferable. But lack of clarity is distinct from logical or conceptual error.

Yet in the middle of the above passage from Lord Lindley's opinion there is a sudden and question-begging shift in the use of terms. First, the "liberty" in question is transmuted into a "right," and then, possibly under the seductive influence of the latter word, it is assumed that the "correlative" must be "the general duty of every one not to prevent," etc.

Editor's Note: If Hohfeld had been correct that Lord Lindley used "liberty" (at least "the first three times in the passage" to mean "privilege," he would be correct in asserting that Lord Lindley wrongly "transmuted" a privilege into a right against non-interference, begging the question of the issue under decision. Yet, for the reasons noted, it seems much more plausible that Lord Lindley used "liberty" to mean the coupling of a privilege to a right against non-interference.

Another interesting and instructive example may be taken from Lord Bowen's oft-quoted opinion in *Mogul Steamship Co. v. McGregor*. <FN. 44: 23 QBD 59 (1889).>

Editor's Note: Like *Quinn v. Leathem*, this case also involves the tort of "conspiracy to injure." In *Mogul Steamship*, a group of shipowners essentially formed a cartel via a trade association that excluded the Mogul Steamship Company. When Mogul attempted to compete with the cartel, the association threatened to punish anyone who dealt with Mogul. The Queen's Bench and on appeal, the House of Lords, held the actions of the association to be lawful.

> We are presented in this case with an apparent conflict or antinomy between two rights that are equally regarded by the law – the right of the plaintiffs to be protected in the legitimate exercise of their trade, and the right of the defendants to carry on their business as seems best to them, provided they commit no wrong to others.

Editor's Note: The opinion continues in relevant part as follows:

[The] right to trade freely is a right that the law recognises and encourages but it is one which places him at no special advantage as compared with others. No man, whether trader or not, can, however, justify damaging another in his commercial business by fraud or misrepresentation. Intimidation, obstruction and molestation are forbidden; so is the intentional procurement or violation of individual rights, contractual or other, assuming always that there is no just cause for it ... [but] the defendants have been guilty of none of these acts. They have done nothing more against the plaintiffs than pursue to the bitter end a war of competition waged in the interest of their own trade.

analysis of this and other examples in this article, this line of critique is largely unfounded. *See also* Thomas D. Perry, *Reply in Defense of Hohfeld*, 37 PHIL. STUD. 203 (1980).

As the learned judge states, the conflict or antinomy is only apparent; but this fact seems to be obscured by the very indefinite and rapidly shifting meanings with which the term "right" is used in the above quoted language. Construing the passage as a whole, it seems plain enough that by "the right of the plaintiffs" in relation to the defendants a legal right or claim in the strict sense must be meant; whereas by "the right of the defendants" in relation to the plaintiffs a legal privilege must be intended. That being so, the "two rights" mentioned in the beginning of the passage, being respectively claim and privilege, could not be in conflict with each other. To the extent that the defendants have privileges the plaintiffs have no rights; and conversely, to the extent that the plaintiffs have rights the defendants have no privileges ("no-privilege" equals duty of opposite tenor).

Editor's Note: As may be apparent from our prior discussion, by the "right" of the defendants to carry on their business very likely meant a Hohfeldian privilege coupled with a strict-right against non-interference, i.e., a "common right" as this chapter uses that term. Nonetheless, Hohfeld is correct that this case turns on whether the defendants have a privilege (to suppress competition) or the plaintiffs have a strict-right to be "protected" from such action. However, in contrast to Hohfeld's contention, there is at least an "apparent conflict" between the privilege and strict-right given the background law, which both protected the "legitimate exercise" of one's trade as well as carrying on one's business as he pleases. In other words, because Mogul has sued the association, the court must specifically decide whether the association's actions to prevent competition are either lawful, (i.e., privileged) or violate a duty owed to Mogul. On the surface, there was no clear to answer to the court – hence, the "apparent" conflict. Ultimately, although the court held that certain actions can certainly wrongly interfere with the carrying out of one's business (e.g., "fraud or misrepresentation"), reviewing the relevant case law, the association's formation of a cartel and its contractual actions to prevent competition did not violate any right of Mogul's. (Not long after the decision, the legislature passed an act proscribing actions like the association's.) Like the earlier discussion, while Lord Bowen certainly could have been clearer in his allegation of an "apparent conflict of rights," he did not commit any conceptual or logical error.

[*38] Thus far it has been assumed that the term "privilege" is the most appropriate and satisfactory to designate the mere negation of duty. Is there good warrant for this?

Editor's Note: In what follows, Hohfeld examines whether the term "privilege" is used to represent the negation of a duty. Note that this question is different from whether, as a conceptual matter, what Hohfeld means by the term "privilege" is the negation of a duty. Rather, the question addressed in what follows is purely terminological.

In Mackeldey's *Roman Law* <FN. 46: Ferdinand Mackeldey, Handbook of the Roman Law §§ 196–97 (Moses A. Dropsie trans., ed., 1883).> it is said:

> Positive laws either contain general principles embodied in the rules of law * * * or for especial reasons they establish something that differs from those general principles. In the first case they contain a common law (*jus commune*), in the second a special law (*jus singulare s. exorbitans*). The latter is either favorable or

> unfavorable * * * according as it enlarges or restricts, in opposition to the common rule, the rights of those for whom it is established. The favorable special law (*jus singulare*) as also the right created by it * * * in the Roman law is termed benefit of the law (*beneficium juris*) or privilege (*privilegium*) * * *

Editor's Note: This reference continues in relevant part, "[A] privilege is either an especial advantage conferred on the privileged person over others . . . or in exempting him from a duty incumbent on others."

First a special law, and then by association of ideas, a special advantage conferred by such a law. With such antecedents, it is not surprising that the English word "privilege" is not infrequently used, even at the present time, in the sense of a special or peculiar legal advantage (whether right, privilege, power or immunity) belonging either to some individual or to some particular class of persons.[43]

Editor's Note: Hohfeld properly recognizes here that the term "privilege" often refers to some special or unique legal advantage relative to other legal actors. This is consistent with the definition of privilege in Roman law in which it is exemption from a "duty incumbent on others."

There are, indeed, a number of judicial opinions [*39] recognizing this as one of the meanings of the term in question.

Editor's Note: However, Hohfeld's view is that the term "privilege" has a broader meaning, namely, the mere negation of duty, as in Hohfeld's typology. This claim has been more controversial, because there are many actions that are not subject to duties (e.g., breathing the air, scratching one's nose, and the like). The terminological question becomes whether the absence of a law governing these actions should be described by the word "privilege." A more difficult question, and one that is conceptual, is whether these actions should be classified by a legal relation whatsoever, whether it is named "privilege," "permission," or otherwise.

That the word has a wider signification even in ordinary nontechnical usage is sufficiently indicated, however, by the fact that the term "*special* privileges" is so often used to indicate a contrast to ordinary or general privileges. More than this, the

[43] Of interest, footnote 48 in the original article states, in part:

> According to an older usage, the term "privilege" was frequently employed to indicate a "franchise," the latter being really a miscellaneous complex of special rights, privileges, powers, or immunities, etc. Thus, in an early book, *Termes de la Ley*, there is the following definition: "'Privileges' are liberties and franchises granted to an office, place, towne, or manor by the King's great charter, letters patent, or Act of Parliament, as toll, sake, socke, infangstheefe, outfangstheefe, turne, or delfe, and divers such like." [John Rastell & William Rastell, Les Termes de la Ley 322 (1812).]

Hohfeld's recognition of the definition of privilege as a "franchise" is consistent with the Roman "privileged person over others," for which MacKeldey's Roman Law provides a legal "monopoly" as an example. MacKeldey's, *supra*, § 197.

dominant specific connotation of the term as used in popular speech seems to be more *negation of duty*. This is manifest, in the terse and oft-repeated expression, "That is your privilege," meaning, of course, "You are under no duty to do otherwise."

Editor's Note: Hohfeld's position is that a "privilege," as that term is used in the law, simply represents the mere "negation of duty." In other words, Hohfeld asserts that *any time* any person has no duty to perform an action – *including breathing the air, scratching one's nose, etc.* – this constitutes a legal "privilege," both terminologically and conceptually. This view was (and still is) controversial, because it assumes that law, in effect, applies (e.g., in loose terms, "has a say") to any action a legal person may ever undertake. Such a view was popular among the legal realists.[44] A different and more traditional view is that law only concerns those actions to which its rules possibly apply, and a "privilege" (or "permission") is a mere exemption from those rules. For instance, even the statement, "That is your privilege . . . You are under no duty to do otherwise," typically implies that there is some possibility that the action of interest is subject to a duty. For instance, someone would not typically say, "go ahead and scratch your nose . . . this is your privilege . . . you are no under no duty to do otherwise" unless it is a non-legal situation, such as a doctor telling a patient who just received a nose job that doing so would cause no harm.[45] Whether the term "privilege," both terminologically and conceptually, captures all behavior not subject to a duty remains a contentious issue.

Such being the case, it is not surprising to find, from a wide survey of judicial precedents, that the *dominant* technical meaning of the term is, similarly, negation of *legal duty*.[46] There are two very common examples of this, relating respectively to

44 For popular realist accounts of Hohfeld's approach, see Arthur L. Corbin, *Legal Analysis and Terminology*, 29 YALE L.J. 163 (1919); Arthur L. Corbin, *Jural Relations and Their Classification*, 30 YALE L.J. 226 (1921); Max Radin, A *Restatement of Hohfeld*, 51 HARV. L. REV. 1141, 1164 (1938).

45 Even Hohfeld's contention that "special" privileges contrasted with "general" privileges in our view does not support his argument. For instance, in the same MacKeldey's *Roman Law* (§ 197) that Hohfeld quotes earlier, it states: "Such privilege may be either by conferred by a general law on all persons who are capable of it . . . or it may be specially conferred by the government on a certain designated person or thing, in which case it is a privilege in its narrow sense." Read in the context of the relevant sections of the treatise, the privilege in either case is still a benefit or exemption from duty conferred upon some subclass of persons otherwise lacking such benefit or under such duty. *See id.* at §§ 196–97. Thus, while a "special" privilege may be narrower than a "general" privilege, it is not the case that a "general" privilege indicates any and all exemptions from duty, including scratching one's nose. With that said, as a conceptual matter, it is possible to extend the notion of privilege in such a manner. In other words, since the State can hypothetically regulate every manner and aspect of life, as a theoretical matter, one may define a Hohfeldian privilege as applying to any action not subject to a duty. But as noted in the text, such a position is fairly controversial, because it brings within the sweep of law, actions that many would consider to simply be outside the law's scope. For instance, Albert Kocourek, a well-known contemporary of Hohfeld's, vigorously criticized Hohfeld's notion of "privilege" on precisely these grounds. Albert Kocourek, *The Hohfeld System of Fundamental Legal Concepts*, 15 ILL. L. REV. 24, 36 (1920).

46 However, in the footnote in the article to this sentence (n.50), Hohfeld cites an opinion stating: "([T]he term privilege) is a special right belonging to an individual or class; *properly*, an *exemption* from some duty." Contrary to Hohfeld's assertion, this statement is consistent with the view that a privilege is an exemption from some *pre-existing* duty that applies to a certain subset of persons, rather than the general negation of duty – that is, regardless of whether there is some pre-existing legal duty.

"privileged communications" in the law of libel and to "privileges against self-[in]crimination" in the law of evidence ... It must be evident also, that whenever the [first] privilege does exist, it is not special in the sense of arising from a special law, or of being conferred as a special favor on a particular individual. The same privilege would exist, by virtue of general rules, for any person whatever under similar circumstances. So, also, in the law of evidence, the privilege against self-[in]crimination signifies the mere negation of a duty, to testify – a duty which rests upon a witness in relation to all ordinary matters; and, quite obviously, such privilege arises, if at all, only by virtue of general laws.[47]

Editor's Note: Here, Hohfeld argues that because certain "privileges" are afforded by "general" (as opposed to "special") laws, the term privilege must generally mean "negation of a duty." In other words, in Hohfeld's view, a "privilege" extends beyond a mere "special" exception from some already existing duty. However, even though general laws may create "privileged communications" and "privileges against self-incrimination," these privileges are still exemptions from legal duties that would ordinarily apply. For instance, the privilege against self-incrimination is an exception to the ordinary rule that witnesses subject to the jurisdiction of the court must testify. So, while the term "privilege" may be viewed as the negation of a *pre-existing* duty, i.e., one that would ordinarily apply, it is not so broad as to encompass the mere absence of a duty, i.e., with respect to any action whatsoever. At the same time, Hohfeld's *conception* of "privilege" in his typology goes well beyond the usual understanding of the term "privilege" so as to capture the mere absence of a duty. But it should be understood that Hohfeld's usage of the term is atypical. Perhaps more importantly, his conception subsumes within the ambit of the law any action that may be undertaken by a legal actor whatsoever. This chapter returns to this controversial position shortly.

As already intimated, while both the conception and the term "privilege" find conspicuous exemplification under the law of libel and the law of evidence, they nevertheless have a much wider significance and utility as a matter of judicial usage ...

[47] In a footnote in the article to this sentence (n.52), Hohfeld explains the distinction between "substantive" and "adjective" relations, which likely derived from earlier work by Austin and Bentham. Specifically, Hohfeld states:

> The subject of witnesses is usually thought of as a branch of the so-called *adjective* law, as distinguished, from the so-called *substantive law*. But, as the writer has had occasion to emphasize on another occasion (*The Relations between Equity and Law*, 11 Mich. L. Rev. 537, 554, 556, 569 (1913)), there seems to be no intrinsic or essential difference between those jural relations that relate to the "substantive" law and those that relate to the "adjective" law. This matter will be considered more fully in a later part of the discussion.

Hohfeld had intended to discuss these distinctions "more fully" in his 1917 follow-up article to this one, but he never did, instead focusing on his reconception of *in personam* and *in rem* relations. Thus, his earlier article remains the only discussion on the subject. As one commentator has lamented, "Hohfeld's great influence might have been enough to prevent the concepts of procedure and substance from being cut adrift from all dependable content by the realists in the 1920s and 1930s, but his observations were too fragmentary to have much impact. Indeed, I have never seen them cited." D. Michael Risinger, *"Substance" and "Procedure" Revisited with Some Afterthoughts on the Constitutional Problems of "Irrebuttable Presumptions,"* 30 UCLA L. Rev. 189, 216 n.49 (1982).

In the great case of *Allen v. Flood* <FN. 54: AC 1, 19 (1898).> the opinion of Mr. Justice Hawkins furnishes a useful passage for the purpose now in view:

> **Editor's Note:** *Allen v. Flood* is the third well-known English labor law case that Hohfeld discusses in this article. In this case, a trade union pressured an employer to terminate non-union workers. After the employer refused to retain the non-union workers, the non-union workers sued the trade union. Hohfeld quotes from the lower court opinion, where Justice Hawkins stated in relevant part:

> [*41] Every person has a privilege * * * in the interests of public justice to put the criminal law in motion against another whom he *bona fide*, and upon reasonable and probable cause, believes to have been guilty of a crime. * * * It must not, however, be supposed that hatred and ill-will existing in the mind of a prosecutor must of necessity *destroy* the *privilege*, for it is not impossible that such hatred and ill-will may have very natural and pardonable reasons for existing.

As a final example in the present connection, the language of Baron Alderson in *Hilton v. Eckersley* <FN. 56: 6 E. & B. 47, 74 (1856).> may be noticed:

> *Prima facie* it is the privilege of a trader in a free country, in all matters not contrary to law, to regulate his own mode of carrying them on according to his discretion and choice.

> **Editor's Note:** Like the earlier uses of "privilege," both of these examples reaffirm that the term "privilege" is an exemption from a pre-existing duty, rather than some general absence of a duty. In the first example, Justice Hawkins describes the privilege of "putting the criminal law in motion" in contrast to an duty not to engage in "malicious prosecution."[48] In the latter example, the "privilege of a trader in a free country" is in contrast to the numerous obligations of traders in countries that are not "free," again signifying some exemption from ordinarily imposed duties.[49]

The closest synonym of legal "privilege" seems to be legal "liberty" or legal "freedom." This is sufficiently indicated by an unusually discriminating and instructive passage in Mr. Justice Cave's opinion in *Allen v. Flood*: <FN. 58: AC 1, 29 (1898).>

> The personal rights with which we are most familiar are: 1. Rights of reputation; 2. Rights of bodily safety and freedom; 3. Rights of property; or, in other words, rights relating to mind, body and estate * * * In my subsequent remarks the word 'right' will, as far as possible, always be used in the above sense; and it is the more [*42] necessary to insist on this as during the argument at your Lordship's bar it was frequently used in a much wider and more indefinite sense. Thus it was said that a man has a perfect right to fire off a gun, when all that was meant, apparently, was

48 Specifically, Justice Hawkins had previously described the difference between the "bona fide" or good faith belief compared to a "mala fide" or bad faith undertaking in the context of slander. *Id.* at 19. He then remarked, "The ordinary action for malicious prosecution affords a good illustration of what I desire to convey," followed by the quoted passage. *Id.*

49 *Hilton* v. *Eckersley* is yet another English case dealing with restraints of trade, which was later cited in Lord Esher's opinion in *Mogul S.S.*

that a man has a *freedom* or *liberty* to fire off a gun, so long as he does not violate or infringe any one's rights in doing so, which is a very different thing from a right, the violation or disturbance of which can be remedied or prevented by legal process." <FN. 59 [*Reproduced below the following Editor's Note*].>

Editor's Note: In contrast to the term "privilege," the term "liberty" often denotes a general absence of duty, that is, even without exemption from some pre-existing duty. Thus, in the passage above, "liberty to fire off a gun" is used in a manner akin to "liberty to scratch one's nose." Rather than being some exemption for a generally imposed duty, "liberty" in this sense concerns actions entirely free of legal restraint. However, as noted earlier, this "freedom" from legal restraint typically implies not a simple Hohfeldian privilege, but the coupling of a "positive" Hohfeldian privilege (i.e., to do some action) and a "negative" Hohfeldian privilege (i.e., not to do some action). Suppose, for instance, that the person in the example had both a privilege *and* a duty to fire off the gun. (Recall that privilege and duty can both apply to the same underlying action. It is just the case a privilege *to do some action* implies the absence of the duty *not to do the action*, but such a privilege does not entail the absence of a duty to do the action.) If the person is under such a duty, the term "freedom to fire off a gun" seems inapt. In other words, "freedom" in this situation presumably implies that the person has a choice whether to fire the gun. This can only occur if the person holds both a privilege to fire the gun *and* a privilege not to fire the gun. Thus, the typical meaning of "liberty" (a two-sided relation) synonymous with the narrow (one-sided) Hohfeldian definition of "privilege."

Editor's Note: In what follows, a large portion of perhaps the most important footnote in the article is reproduced.

<FN. 59: … Sir Frederick Pollock … seems in effect to deny that legal liberty represents any true legal relation as such. JURISPRUDENCE 62 (2d ed. 1904). Thus, he says, *inter alia*: "The act may be right in the popular and rudimentary sense of not being forbidden, but freedom has not the character of legal right until we consider the risk of unauthorized interference. It is the duty of all of us not to interfere with our neighbors' lawful freedom. This brings the so-called primitive rights into the sphere of legal rule and protection. *Sometimes it is thought that lawful power or liberty is different from the right not to be interfered with; but for the reason just given this opinion, though plausible, does not seem correct.*" …

It is difficult to see, however, why, as between X and Y, the "privilege + no-right" situation is not just as real a jural relation as the precisely opposite "duty + right" relation between any two parties. Perhaps the habit of recognizing exclusively the latter as a jural relation springs more or less from the traditional tendency to think of the law as consisting of "commands," or imperative rules. This, however, seems fallacious. A rule of law that *permits* is just as real as a rule of law that *forbids*; and, similarly saying that the law permits a given act to X as between himself and Y predicates just as genuine a legal relation as saying that the law *forbids* a certain act to X as between himself and Y. That this is so seems, in some measure, to be confirmed by the fact that the first sort of act would ordinarily be pronounced "lawful," and the second "unlawful."[50]>

Editor's Note: In this footnote, Hohfeld makes explicit the controversial point that otherwise is implied by Hohfeld's definition of privilege as a mere absence of duty – namely, that "the 'privilege + no-right' situation is ... just as real a jural relation as the precisely opposite 'duty + right' relation ..." Besides the typology itself, this is one of the most important contributions to legal theory made by this article. Prior to Hohfeld, the standard view was that exemplified by Pollock in the quoted passage; namely, that a "legal" relation only inheres when there is "legal rule and protection." Thus, as noted earlier, the absence of a duty in "scratching one's nose" does not – on this traditional view – partake of a legal relation per se. As Pollock notes, once "we consider the risk of unauthorized interference," and the background strict-rights that protect our ability to scratch our nose – such as assault, battery, and the like – then we have entered the "sphere of legal rule and protection." In other words, privileges coupled with rights to non-interference – a complex relation that can be termed "common rights" – are of a "legal" nature. Additionally, "true" privileges – i.e., exemptions from commonly imposed legal duties – are of a "legal" nature. But mere unprotected privileges considered alone – i.e., if we solely examine the action of scratching one's nose without considering any rights to non-interference – would on this view not be of a "legal" nature, because no legal rule concerns the action.

On Hohfeld's view, such a "command"-centric view of the legal world is far too narrow. Rather, for Hohfeld, any action that is permitted by the legal system – express rule or not – and that entails a privilege (in the Hohfeldian sense) concerns a "legal" relation. Hohfeld argues as much in two steps. First, he states that "A rule of law that permits is just as real as a rule of law that forbids." So much is uncontroversial, at least to the extent that an *express* rule of law that permits is only necessary when there is some background rule of law that forbids. This is the typical "privilege" that exempts a subset of legal actors from some generally imposed duty. In other words, if an action is simply not subject to law *ab initio* (e.g., scratching one's nose), there is no need for a rule of law to state as much.

Rather, it is Hohfeld's second step, at least interpreted broadly, that is controversial. From the first step, he infers "saying that the law permits a given act to X as between himself and Y predicates just as genuine a legal relation as saying that the law forbids a certain act to X as between himself and Y." One could interpret this statement narrowly to mean 'saying that because the law *expressly* permits a given act predicates a genuine legal relation.' But even Pollock would agree with such a statement because this is simply the traditional "privilege," again, an exemption from a generally imposed duty, at least broadly speaking. Thus, it appears Hohfeld intended a more expansive meaning; namely, that even when the

[50] In the previous portion of the same footnote (n.59) to the article, Hohfeld references Salmond's JURISPRUDENCE. He states: "For the reference to Mr. Justice Cave's opinion, the present writer is indebted to Salmond's work on Jurisprudence. Citing this case and one other ... the learned author adopts and uses exclusively the term 'liberty' to indicate the opposite of 'duty,' and apparently overlooks the importance of privilege in the present connection." As noted earlier, Salmond had introduced close to the entirety of Hohfeld's typology, particularly in the first edition of his treatise. *See supra* note 4. The main conceptual difference is that Salmond did not fully appreciate the concept of "no-right." Here, Hohfeld identifies a terminological difference regarding the term "privilege."

law *implicitly* permits a given act – i.e., in the absence of any express legal rule – predicates a genuine legal relation. Although such an act is technically "lawful," Pollock and others would reply that this is so only in a philosophical or a popular sense, but not in a legal sense. The legal realists, on the other hand, fully adopted the Hohfeldian position, arguing that "law" and the "legal system" more generally play a role with respect to all human behavior, whether explicitly or implicitly. Today, the realist view has largely won out, though debates surrounding this contentious point persist.

While there are numerous other instances of the apt use of the term "liberty," both in judicial opinions and in conveyancing [*43] documents, it is by no means so common or definite a word as "privilege." The former term is far more likely to be used in the sense of physical or personal freedom (i.e., absence of physical restraint), as distinguished from a legal relation; and very frequently there is the connotation of *general* political liberty, as distinguished from a particular relation between two definite individuals. Besides all this, the term "privilege" has the advantage of giving us, as a variable, the adjective "privileged." Thus, it is frequently convenient to speak of a privileged act, a privileged transaction, a privileged conveyance, etc.

. . .

Editor's Note: Although neither the "privilege" or "liberty" precisely capture the Hohfeldian privilege, this does not diminish from the conceptual, logical, and analytical importance of the Hohfeldian privilege. As noted earlier, the label for the concept of the Hohfeldian privilege is less important than the concept, and as long as the label is used precisely and consistently, it serves a valuable theoretical and practical role. With that said, it is important not to casually impute a meaning that is identical to the Hohfeldian notion to the terms "privilege," "liberty," (and "right" for that matter) in legal opinions, statutes, and other documents. Indeed, this chapter has asserted that Hohfeld himself is guilty of such a transgression, and despite the clarity and analytical force of his scheme, it shows the importance of clearly delineating and disambiguating the meanings of legal terms of art.

Editor's Note: Hohfeld concludes this section with a discussion of licenses, which has been moved below (to p. 67) to improve overall readability.

[*44] *Powers and Liabilities.* As indicated in the preliminary scheme of jural relations, a legal power (as distinguished, of course, from a mental or physical power) is the opposite of legal disability, and the correlative of legal liability.

Editor's Note: By "mental power," Hohfeld refers earlier in the article (at *24) to the "mental capacity to do a thing" – in other words, mental intent and whatever apparatus translates mental intent into action. By "physical power," Hohfeld refers to the "physical . . . capacity to do a thing" – in other words, the capacity of the physical structure to carry out some action. Although mental and physical power are surely interests of the law, they are quite different from Hohfeld's usage of "legal power."

But what is the intrinsic nature of a legal power as such? Is it possible to analyze the conception represented by this constantly employed and very important term of legal discourse? Too close an analysis might seem metaphysical rather than useful; so that what is presented here is intended only as an approximate explanation sufficient for all practical purposes.

Editor's Note: This annotation attempts to note briefly what Hohfeld may have meant by the metaphysical aspects of his understanding of "power" below, but it is difficult to have any certainty on this issue given Hohfeld's treatment of power here and in other works.

A change in a given legal relation may result (1) from some superadded fact or group of facts not under the volitional control of a human being (or human beings); or (2) from some superadded fact or group of facts which are under the volitional control of one or more human beings. As regards the second class of cases, the person (or persons) whose volitional control is paramount may be said to have the (legal) power to effect the particular change of legal relations that is involved in the problem.

Editor's Note: In the previous discussion of rights, duties, privileges, and no-rights, Hohfeld implicitly assumed that these "first-order" legal relations were static in that they didn't change. Of course, legal relations may change. For instance, it is a common doctrine that a contractual duty may be effectively discharged in the case of impossibility. For instance, suppose that a house that a painter has contracted with a homeowner to paint is destroyed by an earthquake. In that case, the previous duty of the painter and right of the homeowner then become a privilege and no-right, respectively, from, as Hohfeld explains, "some superadded fact or group of facts not under the volitional control of a human being." This is in contrast to, for instance, the rescission (i.e., cancellation) of the agreement between the homeowner and the painter. In this case, the painter's duty and homeowner's right also become a privilege and no-right, respectively, but from, in Hohfeld's words, "some superadded fact or group of facts which are under the volitional control of one or more human beings." Changes of legal relations under such volitional control of legal actors are "legal powers" in the Hohfeldian sense.[51]

[51] Hohfeld asserts that only human beings can exercise legal powers. This raises the question of whether legal entities, such as corporations, associations, the State, and so forth, can exercise legal powers. Because Hohfeld viewed all legal entities essentially as legal fictions that, as a theoretical matter, solely depended upon legal relations between human beings, Hohfeld's view was that legal entities were never truly subject to any legal relations. Although Hohfeld's view regarding entities may be technically correct – though, it is disputed among legal scholars – it is usually possible without loss of accuracy to treat legal entities as directly holding and being subject to legal relations, including powers. Indeed, the information costs in doing otherwise would be unbearably high. *See generally* James Y. Stern, *Property, Exclusivity, and Jurisdiction*, 100 Va. L. Rev. 111, 178–79 (2014).

> **Editor's Note:** Legal powers must be effectuated through some type of action on the part of the powerholder (e.g., signing a contract), and these actions will typically be subject to privilege (though not always). In other words, the breach of a duty may still be an exercise of a power. For instance, in Hohfeld's view, when a legal actor commits a battery – which breaches a duty – that battery may give rise to a privilege of self-defense on the part of the victim, thereby changing what had previously been a duty on the part of the victim not to strike the aggressor into a privilege to do so.[52]

The second class of cases – powers in the technical sense – [*45] must now be further considered. The nearest synonym for any ordinary case seems to be (legal) "ability" – the latter being obviously the opposite of "inability," or "disability." The term "right," so frequently and loosely used in the present connection, is an unfortunate term for the purpose – a not unusual result being confusion of thought as well as ambiguity of expression. The term "capacity" is equally unfortunate; for, as we have already seen, when used with discrimination, this word denotes a particular group of operative facts, and not a legal relation of any kind.

> **Editor's Note:** In other words, a legal power is the "ability" to change some legal relation subject to the power. For instance, two parties to a contract typically possess the ability to alter the contract through an amendment. A landowner usually possesses the ability to sell or gift land, immediately changing a host of legal relations of the landowner and the buyer (or donee) with respect to the land. And so forth. Unfortunately, as Hohfeld notes, often judges, scholars, and others refer to powers as "rights." Like Hohfeld's distinction between "right" and "privilege," it is important to distinguish between "power" and "right."

> **Editor's Note:** Next, Hohfeld asserts that "capacity" is a poor designator for "power," because technically speaking, capacity refers to what he terms a group of "operative facts," namely a set of facts that is sufficient to change, create, or extinguish a legal relation. For instance, in his view, the parties to a contract have the "capacity" to enter into an amendment – i.e., undertake the mental and physical acts necessary to effectuate the

52 Yet, it seems awkward to characterize an aggressor's use of force in breach of a duty as an exercise of a "legal power." Rather, a better definition might be to characterize a legal power as "some superadded fact or group of facts which are under the volitional control" of a legal actor (or actors) *in which the actors intend, expressly or impliedly, to change a legal relation*. Thus, the acts of passing laws, creating contracts, legal judgments, and so forth would constitute the exercise of a legal power as an express intention to change a legal relation. The abandonment of property, although sometimes constituting the express intention to change a legal relation, would likely more often be an implicit intention to change a legal relation – namely, the implicit desire on the part of the previous owner to create a power in third-parties to take ownership of the property, among other changes in legal relations. In contrast, it seems difficult to contemplate that one committing battery desires to change legal relations, explicitly or implicitly, so as to create a privilege of self-defense in a victim. Such actions – although under the volitional control of a legal actor – seem better characterized as an external event that changes legal relations. Thus, beyond volition, intent seems an important component of the exercise of legal powers. *See generally* H. L. A. Hart, The Concept of Law 92–96 (2d ed. 1994). Ultimately, however, the distinction between "external" and "internal" changes in legal relations is perhaps all too often philosophical. From a legal perspective, frequently a "change is a change" regardless of the cause – in other words, the ultimate effect on the legal relations being changed is typically the same irrespective of whether such change was caused by the volitional, intentional acts of a legal actor or some external event.

amendment – which is precisely the set of facts that provides the parties the "ability," i.e., "legal power" to change their relations. Hohfeld describes such "operative facts" in more detail earlier in the article. However, this discussion flows better after a brief discussion of powers, and instead this chapter inserts an abbreviated version of this section here before turning to Hohfeld's continued discussion of legal powers (leaving the original page and footnote numbers, where reproduced, intact).

OPERATIVE FACTS CONTRASTED WITH EVIDENTIAL FACTS.

. . . [I]t seems necessary at this point to lay emphasis upon another important distinction inherent in the very nature of things. The facts important in relation to a given jural transaction may be either *operative* facts or *evidential* facts. Operative, constitutive, causal, or dispositive facts are those which, under the general legal rules that are applicable, suffice to change legal relations, that is, either to create a new relation, or to extinguish an old one, or to perform both of these functions simultaneously.[53]

Editor's Note: Thus, on Hohfeld's view, operative facts are those facts that either (1) are not under the volitional control of a legal actor, but nonetheless change, extinguish, or terminate legal relations; or (2) are under the volitional control of a legal actor, and constitute the exercise of a legal power that changes, extinguishes, or terminates legal relations.

For [*26] example, in the creation of a contractual obligation between A and B, the *affirmative* operative facts are, *inter alia*, that each of the parties is a human being,

53 There is an important distinction between the "change" of legal relations with respect to given legal actors and a particular action, the "creation" of new relations when a new legal person is recognized under a legal system, and "termination" of existing relations when an existing legal person is no longer recognized under a legal system. In the first scenario, A and B are legal actors within the system, and a "change" of relation between A and B concerning some action (e.g., B's entry onto A's land) simply converts a pre-existing relation to its Hohfeldian "opposite" (e.g., duty to privilege). In the second scenario, a new legal actor comes into being (e.g., by being born, entering the country, etc.), and now partakes of all the Hohfeldian relations that other actors subject to the legal system would. In other words, legal relations are "created." In the third scenario, a legal actor no longer is in existence (e.g., upon death) and relations that otherwise applied to this actor completely "extinguish." Hohfeld, on the other hand, referred to the "creation" of a new relation as that relation now in effect upon a "change" of legal relations, and the "extinguishing" of a previous relation as that relation previously in effect upon a "change" of legal relations. For instance, a change from a duty to privilege "extinguishes" the duty and "creates" the privilege in Hohfeld's view. However, reserving the terms "create" and "extinguish" for the creation and extinguishing of legal relations upon the occasions of a new legal actor coming into being and terminating, respectively, serves a more useful and apt role. In other words, when a pre-existing legal relation "changes" it is relatively easy to keep track of the old and new relation without the use of the terms "creation" and "extinguishment," whereas these terms do play a much more central role for the creation and termination of legal actors per se the concomitant creation and termination of legal relations that accompanies these circumstances. *See generally* James Penner, *On the Very Idea of Transmissible Rights*, *in* PHILOSOPHICAL FOUNDATIONS OF PROPERTY LAW 244 (James Penner & Henry E. Smith eds., 2013).

that each of them has lived for not less than a certain period of time (is not "under age"), that A has made an "offer," that B has "accepted" it, etc.

> **Editor's Note:** In other words, these are some of the operative facts (note that Hohfeld's list is prominently missing "consideration") necessary for a contract to be formed so as to change the underlying legal relations of the contracting parties – e.g., from privileges to duties.

It is sometimes necessary to consider, also, what may, from a particular point of view, be regarded as *negative* operative facts. Thus, for example, the fact that A did not willfully misrepresent an important matter to B, and the fact that A had not "revoked" his offer, must really be included as parts of the totality of operative facts in the case already put.

> **Editor's Note:** In other words, for legal relations to change, sometimes it is necessary that certain facts do not occur, which Hohfeld terms "negative operative facts."

Taking another example – this time from the general field of torts – if X commits an assault on Y by putting the latter in fear of bodily harm, this particular group of facts immediately create in Y the privilege of self-defense – that is, the privilege of using sufficient force to repel X's attack; or, correlatively, the otherwise existing duty of Y to refrain from the application of force to the person of X is, by virtue of the special operative facts, immediately terminated or extinguished.

> **Editor's Note:** On the strict Hohfeldian view, because X's assault on Y is under the "volitional control" of X, then X's assault is technically the exercise of a "legal power" that, inter alia, changes Y's duty not to use force against X to a privilege of self-defense. Yet, it seems somewhat odd to place the legal power of private parties to amend a contract or the legal power of a legislature to enact a law in the same category as the "legal power" to change a relation by committing an assault. Rather, an assault more akin to some change in legal relations from an external event, instead of an exercise of a legal power proper. With that said, whether a change in legal relations is effectuated by a legal power or an external set of circumstances, both mechanisms rely upon what Hohfeld terms "operative facts" to do so.

In passing, it may not be amiss to notice that the term, "facts in issue," is sometimes used in the present connection. If, as is usual, the term means "facts put in issue by the *pleadings*," the expression is an unfortunate one. The operative facts alleged by the pleadings are more or less *generic* in character; and if the pleadings be sufficient, only such *generic* operative facts are "put in issue." The operative facts of real life are, on the other hand, very specific. That being so, it is clear that the *real* and *specific* facts finally relied on are comparatively seldom put in issue by the pleadings.

> **Editor's Note:** Specifically, and particularly under so-called code pleading, a complaint will often state the elements of a particular claim in a fairly generalized, "generic" manner,

without stating with particularity why such elements are met in the specific case. However, there are exceptions to such generic pleading, such as when fraud is plead, which generally requires some particularized set of facts to support such an allegation in a complaint. Yet, whether a complaint is ultimately successful will turn on the plaintiff adducing specific facts to show each and every element of the claims at issue are satisfied subject to the applicable pleading standard. So while, technically speaking, the "real and specific facts finally relied on" to prove a claim are not "put in issue by the pleadings" (i.e., the complaint); the complaint will delineate the "generic" elements that must be shown by the "specific" facts for the plaintiff to win their case. Once the elements of the complaint are sufficiently proven, then the court is vested with a Hohfeldian power to change the applicable status of the defendant.[54] For example, in a civil case for ordinary contractual damages, the defendant's privilege of not paying the plaintiff becomes an obligation to pay. Indeed, the court is under a duty itself to exercise such a power.

Thus, if, in an action of tort, the declaration of A alleges that he was, through the carelessness, etc., of B, bitten by the latter's dog, the fact alleged is generic in character, and it matters not whether it was dog Jim or dog Dick that did the biting ... [*27] ... A common fallacy in this connection is to regard the *specific* operative facts established in a given case as being but "evidence" of the *generic* (or "ultimate") operative facts alleged in the pleadings.

Editor's Note: Per the earlier comment, for plaintiff A to win, he must introduce evidence specifically showing that B's dog bit him. To the extent that Jim is B's dog and Dick is C's dog, the identity of the dog that bit A will ultimately matter to A winning the case. Thus, while the complaint can allege a generic cause of action, the plaintiff must adduce "specific operative facts" prior to judgment. These specific operative facts must demonstrate that each and every element of the cause of action is met to whatever standard is applicable (e.g., clear and convincing evidence). Hohfeld is correct in that the "generic" facts alleged in the pleading are not operative facts per se. However, the specific operative facts that a plaintiff must show in order for the court to exercise its power to change the defendant's status amount to, in essence, particularized evidence demonstrating the generic facts pled in the complaint. Thus, it is excusable that these "generic" or "ultimate" facts are sometimes referred to as "operative" facts. As with the Hohfeldian relations proper, as long as the term is used in a context in which its more precise meaning can be easily understood or used in a context that has no effect on the ultimate outcome, often such usage is more linguistically and cognitively efficient than using the full Hohfeldian machinery. Yet, in other cases, such machinery is essential to comprehending the precise nature of the legal concepts at issue. These cases are ones in which the use of terms is so ambiguous or vague that conceptual or logical errors can easily be made. While the Hohfeldian analysis is useful as a *theoretical* lens in all cases, it is arguably only useful as a *practical* matter in this latter set of cases.

An evidential fact is one which, on being ascertained, affords some logical basis – not conclusive – for inferring some other fact ... Of all the facts to be ascertained by the tribunal, the operative are, of course, of primary importance; the evidential are subsidiary in their functions.

[54] *See generally* Chapter 12.

Editor's Note: In a dispute subject to adjudication, as noted earlier, the plaintiff (or prosecutor) must adduce evidence sufficient to demonstrate operative facts in order for the court to exercise its power to change the legal status of the defendant. Any fact that is not an operative one is "evidential"; that is, it affords some basis for inferring another fact in a chain that ultimately leads (or not) to the operative facts at issue in the case.

As a rule, there is little danger of confusing evidential facts with operative facts. But there is one type of case that not infrequently gives rise to this sort of error. Suppose that in January last a contractual obligation was created by written agreement passing between A and B.

Editor's Note: In this hypothetical, in the previous January, A and B entered into a written agreement exercising their powers to change their legal status, changing what were previously privileges to duties (which Hohfeld treats synonymously with "obligations").[55]

In an action now pending between these parties, the physical *instrument* is offered for inspection by the tribunal. If one were thoughtless, he would be apt to say that this is a case where part of the operative facts creating the original obligation are directly presented to the senses of the tribunal. Yet a moment's reflection will show that such is not the case. The document, in its [*28] then existing shape, had, as regards its operative effect, spent its force as soon as it was delivered in January last. If, therefore, the unaltered document is produced for inspection, the facts thus ascertained must, as regards the alleged contractual agreement, be purely evidential in character. That is to say, the present existence of the piece of paper, its specific tenor, etc., may, along with other evidential facts (relating to absence of change) tend to prove the various operative facts of last January – to wit, that such paper existed at that time; that its tenor was then the same as it now is; that it was delivered by A to B, and so forth.

Editor's Note: Hohfeld's point in many ways may appear to be pedantic. For instance, suppose it is undisputed between the parties, as is typically the case, that the "physical instrument" being offered in evidence is indeed the contract that the parties signed, and that the obligations remain binding. In this case, the instrument is not an evidential fact needed to prove that "such [a] paper existed at that time, ... that is was delivered by A to B, and so forth." Rather, the physical instrument is direct evidence of the operative facts present at signing. On the other hand, if the parties dispute that a contractual agreement existed, or at least dispute that a contract imposed the obligations currently under dispute, then the original instrument is merely an evidential fact from which the tribunal must infer (or not) whether operative facts were present so as to generate obligations in the first instance. Nonetheless, Hohfeld is correct in stating that it is not the case that operative facts are directly presented to the tribunal when the physical instrument is produced. In this

55 As noted previously, the deontic obligation is precisely the same concept as the Hohfeldian duty. Although some previous scholars have argued that the Hohfeldian duty exhibits an asymmetry between a duty not to do some action A and its Hohfeldian opposite, i.e., a privilege to do so some action A, this is the same asymmetry that exists between the deontic obligation and permission. In other words, a deontic obligation not to do some action A is precisely the contradiction of a permission to do some action A.

regard, there is an important, unpedantic point that Hohfeld makes here and in other portions of the article (reproduced below): that the legal relations generated by underlying facts, and the concepts upon which those relations rest, are typically abstract in nature compared to the tangible nature of facts per se. Thus, a piece of paper evidencing a contract is different from the collection of abstract legal relations embodied in the contract even at the time of contracting. Similarly, physical property is different from the collection of abstract legal relations related to the property. And so forth. Hohfeld's view was important in the genesis of the so-called "bundle of rights" view of property, which this chapter returns to later.[56]

It now remains to observe that in many situations a single convenient term is employed to designate (generically) certain miscellaneous groups of operative facts which, though differing widely as to their individual "ingredients," have, as regards a given matter, the same *net* force and effect. When employed with discrimination, the term "possession" is a word of this character; so also the term "capacity," the term "domicile," etc.

Editor's Note: Like a "contract," which at the time it takes effect is a "group of operative facts" given rise to a change in legal relations among the parties to the agreement (and, sometimes, third-party beneficiaries), there are similar groups of operative facts in other legal relations. For instance, when a person takes "possession" of real or personal property, a host of legal relations changes with respect to the person possessing the property. When a legal actor changes her domicile to a new location, that actor typically becomes subject to a large number of new legal relations: not only obligations, but also rights, powers, privileges, immunities, and the like. As with a "contract," Hohfeld's major point is that these legal concepts are not irreducible, but rather represent "groups of operative facts" that may "differ widely as to their individual 'ingredients.'" For instance, "possession" is not a unitary, indivisible notion, but rather an aggregation of attributes that may differ depending on the circumstances.

But the general tendency to confuse legal and non-legal quantities is manifest here as elsewhere; so that only too frequently these words are used rather nebulously to indicate legal relations as such.

Editor's Note: The term "possession," for instance, can refer to the *physical* possession of an object or the *legal* possession of an object, among other meanings. The physical possession of an object by a person is a "non-legal quantity" in the sense that the physical possession may or may not correspond to the legal possession of the object by a person. For instance, the fact someone is driving a car does not necessarily mean that person has legal possession of the car. There is a tendency, even among lawyers and judges, in Hohfeld's view to use terms such as "possession" nebulously – that is, in a manner in which it is unclear whether the term is being used in a legal or non-legal manner, or both. Such nebulous usage leads to a lack of clarity that makes it difficult to determine exactly which legal relations are encompassed by use of the term. A more discriminating and accurate usage, according to Hohfeld, would more precisely identify

[56] *See generally* Thomas W. Merrill & Henry E. Smith, *Why Restate the Bundle?: The Disintegration of the Restatement of Property*, 79 Brook. L. Rev. 681 (2014); Thomas W. Merrill & Henry E. Smith, *What Happened to Property in Law and Economics?*, 111 Yale L.J. 357, 365 (2001). Hohfeld's abstraction of legal relations away from the underlying tangible constituents generating or at least concerning the legal relations had less of an impact in the areas of tort and contract law than in property law.

those legal relations applicable when using such terms (or not). Again, such a view affirms the notion of legal concepts as aggregates or "bundles" of more fundamental constituents.

Editor's Note: Here, the chapter returns to the original text of the article on legal powers (at [*45]).

Many examples of legal powers may readily be given. Thus, X, the owner of ordinary personal property "in a tangible object" has the power to extinguish his own legal interest (rights, powers, immunities, etc.) through that totality of operative facts known as abandonment; and – simultaneously and correlatively – to create in other persons privileges and powers relating to the abandoned object – *e.g.*, the power to acquire title to the latter by appropriating it. <FN. 66: It is to be noted that abandonment would leave X himself with precisely the same sort of privileges and powers as any other person.> *Similarly*, X has the power to transfer his interest to Y – that is, to extinguish his own interest and concomitantly create in Y a new and corresponding interest.[57]

Editor's Note: A very common example of a power is the ability to transfer property. In Hohfeld's example, suppose X owns personal property, e.g., a book. X can sell or gift the book to Y, which transfers ownership from X to Y. In so doing, X has exercised a power and Y is subject to liability for Y's legal relations relative to the book to immediately change upon transfer. For instance, X's prior privilege to read the book immediately changes to an obligation not to read the book absent permission from Y. Similarly, X may abandon the book by leaving it in the street. As of the moment of abandonment, any person – including X – may pick up ("appropriate") the book and thereby gain ownership ("title") to the book. The act of appropriation is thus an exercise of both a privilege (to pick up the book) and a power (acquire title to the book). Once ownership is acquired, the acquiror is in the same position as X was as regards the acquiror's legal relations with respect to the book. For instance, the acquiror has a privilege to read the book; a strict-right to keep others from reading it; powers to transfer, abandon, or destroy it, and so forth.

[57] In a footnote (n.67) to the article, Hohfeld states in part: "Since the power of alienation is frequently one of the fundamental elements of a complex legal interest (or property aggregate), it is obvious that a statute extinguishing such power may, in a given case be unconstitutional as depriving the owner of property without due process of law." Complex legal interests are aggregates of legal relations. Here, Hohfeld states that "property" is such an interest – namely, an aggregation of more fundamental legal relations. Property typically includes a right against trespass, a privilege to use, a power to alienate, a power to abandon, a power to destroy, and others. *See generally* A. M. Honore, *Ownership, in* Oxford Essays in Jurisprudence 107, 112–24 (A. G. Guest ed., 1961). For instance, Hohfeld notes that property may include a constitutional immunity to a purported exercise of power by the State to eliminate the power of alienation. Hohfeld's view is a precursor to the modern "bundle of rights" view of property. Arthur Linton Corbin, *Taxation of Seats on the Stock Exchange*, 31 Yale L.J. 429, 429 (1922) ("Our concept of property has shifted . . . '[P]roperty' has ceased to describe any *res*, or object of sense, at all, and has become merely a bundle of legal relations – rights, powers, privileges, immunities."); Max Radin, A *Restatement of Hohfeld*, 51 Harv. L. Rev. 1141 (1938) (interpreting the Hohfeldian scheme from a legal realist's point of view). *See generally* Thomas W. Merrill & Henry E. Smith, *What Happened to Property in Law and Economics?* 111 Yale L.J. 357 (2001).

So [*46] also X has the power to create contractual obligations of various kinds.

> **Editor's Note:** As discussed in the section regarding operative facts, legal actors generally have the power to impose duties upon themselves and other legal actors via contractual agreements.

Agency cases are likewise instructive. By the use of some *metaphorical* expression such as the Latin, *qui facit per alium, facit per se*, the true nature of agency relations is only too frequently obscured. The creation of an agency relation involves, *inter alia*, the grant of legal powers to the so-called agent, and the creation of correlative liabilities in the principal. That is to say, one party P has the power to create agency powers in another party A – for example, the power to convey X's property, the power to impose (so-called) contractual obligations on P, the power to discharge a debt, owing to P, the power to "receive" title to property so that it shall vest in P, and so forth.

> **Editor's Note:** Hohfeld continues to delineate the meaning of somewhat vague legal concepts. For instance, the expression *qui facit per alium, facit per se* roughly means "He who acts through another does the act himself." As Hohfeld explains, the key aspect of an agency relationship is the power of the agent to change legal relations with respect to the principal. This susceptibility of the principal is a Hohfeldian "liability," which is the correlative to a Hohfeldian power. When the agent undertakes some action that binds the principal, the principal's legal relations change. For instance, if an agent "receives" title to property, through such receipt, the agent in essence exercises a power that in turn vests title in the principal, after which the principal is the owner of the property along with all the incidents of ownership.

In passing, it may be well to observe that the term "authority," so frequently used in agency cases, is very ambiguous and slippery in its connotation. Properly employed in the present connection, the word seems to be an abstract or qualitative term corresponding to the concrete "authorization" – the latter consisting of a particular group of operative facts taking place between the principal and the agent. All too often, however, the term in question is so used as to blend and confuse these operative facts with the [*47] powers and privileges thereby created in the agent. A careful discrimination in these particulars would, it is submitted, go far toward clearing up certain problems in the law of agency.

> **Editor's Note:** Like the terms "domicile" and "possession," the term "authority" is better understood as a general category of operative facts that relate to the principal-agent relationship. Specifically, when there are facts showing the agent's "authority" with respect to a particular action, these facts are "operative" in the sense that the action is an exercise of the agent's privilege and power to bind the principal. When the agent acts outside of the scope of its authority, then there are no such operative facts, and no power is exercised (and the agent may have simultaneously breached a duty to the principal). As with domicile and possession, the tendency among lawyers and judges is to confuse general legal concepts with the legal relations that the concepts may call into being. In Hohfeld's view, this confusion creates problems in properly discerning the underlying

nature of legal issues and, hence, leads to poorly reasoned judicial decisions and unjustified outcomes.

. . .

There are, on the other hand, cases where the true nature of the relations involved has not, perhaps, been so clearly recognized. Thus, in the case of a conditional sale of personalty, assuming [*48] the vendee's agreement has been fully performed except as to the payment of the last installment and the time for the latter has arrived, what is the interest of such vendee as regards the property? Has he, as so often assumed, merely a contractual *right* to have title passed to him by consent of the vendor, on final payment being made; or has he, irrespective of the consent of the vendor the power to divest the title of the latter and to acquire a perfect title for himself? Though the language of the cases is not always so clear as it might be, the vendee seems to have precisely that sort of power.

Editor's Note: Here, Hohfeld addresses the example of a conditional sale of personalty (i.e., personal, moveable property). The vendee (i.e., buyer) purchases a product on an installment basis from the vendor (i.e., the seller), and the due date for the last payment has arrived. In this case, Hohfeld seeks to determine the legal interest of the buyer just prior to the final payment. If the buyer simply has a strict-right that the vendor pass title to the product upon final payment, then the seller's decision not to deliver the product would merely result in money damages for contractual breach (barring the product being so unique as to justify injunctive relief forcing the seller to deliver the object). On the other hand, if the buyer has a legal power, then they may force the seller via court order to deliver the product upon final payment. Thus, determining whether the buyer has a Hohfeldian right, power, or both entitlements, is critical to determining the appropriate remedy in the event of breach by the buyer. According to Hohfeld, the cases indicate the buyer has a power to divest the seller of the product – unlike an ordinary, non-installment purchase, in which case the buyer typically can only receive money damages in the event of breach (again, barring a sufficiently unique product). Understanding the difference between a strict-right and power helps to discern the nature of the possible remedies.

Fundamentally considered, the typical escrow transaction in which the performance of conditions is within the volitional control of the grantee, is somewhat similar to the conditional sale of personalty; and, when reduced to its lowest terms, the problem seems easily to be solved in terms of legal powers. Once the "escrow" is formed, the grantor still has the legal title; but the grantee has an irrevocable power to divest that title by performance of certain conditions (i.e., the addition of various operative facts), and concomitantly to vest title in himself. While such power is outstanding, the grantor is, [*49] of course, subject to a correlative liability to have his title divested. <FN. 74: . . . It is hardly necessary to add that the courts, instead of analyzing the problem of the escrow in terms of powers, as here indicated, are accustomed to stating the question and deciding it in terms of "delivery," "relation back," "performance of conditions," etc.>

> **Editor's Note:** Judges and lawyers often analyze the notion of escrow in terms of generalized legal concepts, such as "delivery," "relation back," "performance of conditions," and the like. At its root, in Hohfeld's view, escrow sounds in powers and liabilities. Take, for example, the typical sale of a house. Once a house is under contract, the parties will generally use a third-party escrow service. By placing the house and funds into escrow, this ensures that if the conditions are performed, the transaction is consummated and the house is delivered. If the conditions are not performed, then each party receives back whatever it put into the escrow (possibly, less some payment of a penalty for non-performance). Of course, this description sounds in the same generalities that Hohfeld criticized. A more accurate description of the escrow is one that describes the transaction in terms of powers and liabilities. Specifically, upon the addition of certain operative facts (namely, the performance of certain conditions), the buyer has the power to divest title from the seller. The seller is subject to a correlative Hohfeldian liability for title to transfer to the buyer upon the performance of those certain conditions. The buyer also has a Hohfeldian privilege – at least vis-à-vis the contract – to perform the conditions necessary to effectuate the transfer. In the event the conditions are not performed, there is no exercise of power. By analyzing the transaction in terms of powers, liabilities, privileges, and no-rights, one can understand what Hohfeld understood to be the essential nature of legal transactions.

Similarly, in the case of a conveyance of land in fee simple subject to condition subsequent, after the condition has been performed, the original grantor is commonly said to have a "*right* of entry." If, however, the problem is analyzed, it will be seen that, as of primary importance, the grantor has two legal quantities, (1) the privilege of entering, and (2) the power, by means of such entry, to divest the estate of the grantee. The latter's estate endures, subject to the correlative liability of being divested, until such power is actually exercised.

> **Editor's Note:** When land is conveyed in fee simple subject to a condition subsequent – e.g., "upon express condition that" – the grantee may lose the property if the condition is breached. For instance, grantor O sells grantee A Blackacre in fee simple "but upon condition that no alcohol is served on the premises." Suppose A then builds a bar on the property and starts serving alcohol. When land is conveyed fee simple determinable, a condition that is breached automatically transfers the property back to the grantor. However, with a fee simple subject to a condition subsequent, the grantor retains a "right of re-entry" that allows the grantor the option to re-enter the property and terminate the estate so that ownership reverts to the grantor. Like the escrow situation, it is possible to more precisely characterize a fee simple subject to a condition subsequent in which the condition is breached using the Hohfeldian relations. First, the grantor has a privilege of entering the property (and also a privilege of not entering, which Hohfeld doesn't mention in the passage above) because the grantor has the option of deciding whether to enter the property (or not). Second, the grantor has the power to divest the estate of the grantee when the grantor re-enters the land following the breached condition. The grantee who breached the condition has the liability of being divested when the grantor's power is exercised. Thus, the term "right of entry" refers to the complex relation of a power plus a privilege to enter and a privilege not to enter. By decoupling the "right of entry" into its constituent components, one can more clearly comprehend this and other estates in real property.

Passing now to the field of contracts, suppose A mails a letter to B offering to sell the former's land, Whiteacre, to the latter for ten thousand dollars, such letter being duly received. The operative facts thus far mentioned have created a power as regards

B and a correlative liability as regards A. B, by dropping a letter of acceptance in the box, has the power to impose a potential or inchoate obligation *ex contractu* on A and himself; and, assuming that the land is worth fifteen thousand dollars, that particular legal quantity – the "power *plus* liability" relation between A and B – seems to be worth about five thousand dollars to B.

Editor's Note: Offer and acceptance can be understood in terms of powers and liabilities. Specifically, when an offer is made, the offeree has a power to accept the offer, subjecting the offeror to a liability of acceptance. A "potential" or "inchoate" obligation is one that is not owed immediately, but at some future time, potentially subject to triggering conditions. Specifically, when the conditions necessary to transfer land – including payment directly to the offeror (or to some escrow) – are satisfied, then the obligation for the offeror to transfer becomes actual and owing at that time.[58]

The liability of A will continue for a reasonable time unless, in exercise of his power to do so, A previously extinguishes it by that series of operative facts known as "revocation." These last matters are usually described by saying that A's "offer" will "continue" [*50] or "remain open" for a reasonable time, or for the definite time actually specified, unless A previously "withdraws" or "revokes" such offer. While no doubt, in the great majority of cases no harm results from the use of such expressions, yet these forms of statement seem to represent a blending of non-legal and legal quantities which, in any problem requiring careful reasoning, should preferably be kept distinct. An offer, considered as a series of physical and mental operative facts, has spent its force as soon as such series has been completed by the "offeree's receipt." The real question is therefore as to the *legal effect*, if any, "at that moment of time. If the latter consist of B's power and A's correlative liability, manifestly it is those *legal relations* that "continue" or "remain open" until modified by revocation or other operative facts.

Editor's Note: Hohfeld again describes more accurately the loose usage regarding a contractual offer and revocation. Typically, it is stated that an offer will remain open until the time it is revoked or expires. Technically, as a factual matter, the facts underlying the offer (e.g., a letter stating product, price, quantity for sale, and delivery terms) are only relevant up until the time of the offeree's receipt of the offer. These physical and mental facts are operative upon receipt, creating a power in the offeree to accept and a correlative liability in the offeror. To be precise, it is the power and liability that continue – not the facts creating them – until the offer is revoked or expired. Although it is often harmless to blend the facts underlying the offer with such facts' legal effect, in some situations, such blending leads to mistakes in legal reasoning. Thus, besides shedding light on the nature of legal concepts, the Hohfeldian

[58] In a footnote within this passage in the article (n.77), Hohfeld cites the English case of *Frost* v. *Knight*, LR 7 Exch 111 (1872), in which the appeals court remarked on a agreement that required the defendant to marry the plaintiff upon the death of the defendant's father. The court stated in relevant part: "The promisee has an inchoate right to the performance of the bargain, which becomes complete when the time for performance has arrived."

typology can be used for judges and lawyers to more carefully reason about legal issues at-hand.

What has thus far been said concerning contracts completed by mail would seem to apply, *mutatis mutandis*, to every type of contract. Even where the parties are in the presence of each other, the offer creates a liability against the offeror, together with a correlative power in favor of the offeree. The only distinction for present purposes would be in the fact that such power and such liability would expire within a very short period of time.

Editor's Note: As Hohfeld notes, every type of offer and acceptance will fit the mold of power and liability. Moreover, not only does the offeree's acceptance of a contract change the privileges of the offeror to duties, but also changes the offeree's own privileges to duties. In this sense, the liability of the offeror to contractual acceptance is not a unilateral detriment in which only the offeree benefits, but an exchange of bilateral benefits and detriments.

[*51] In connection with the powers and liabilities created respectively by an ordinary offer ... it is interesting to consider the liabilities of a person engaged in a "public calling" ... [*52] It has indeed been usual to assert that such a party is (generally speaking) under a present *duty* to all other parties; but this is believed to be erroneous.

Editor's Note: A "public calling" is a business or profession that is sufficiently "public" in nature that it becomes subject to laws and regulations beyond those that apply to an ordinary, "private" business or profession. For instance, common carriers (e.g., an airline) and innkeepers (e.g., a hotel) are sometimes subject to duties to protect and assist passengers and guests that would not ordinarily apply.

Thus, Professor Wyman, in his work on *Public Service Companies* <FN. 82: 1 Bruce Wyman, The Special Law Governing Public Service Corporations and All Others Engaged in Public Employment §§ 330–33 (1911).> says:

> The duty placed upon every one exercising a public calling is primarily a *duty* to serve every man who is a member of the public. * * * It is somewhat difficult to place this exceptional duty in our legal system. * * * The truth of the matter is that the obligation resting upon one who has undertaken the performance of public duty is *sui generis*.[59]

It is submitted that the learned writer's difficulties arise primarily from a failure to see that the innkeeper, the common carrier and others similarly "holding out" are under present *liabilities* rather than present *duties*. Correlatively to those liabilities are the respective powers of the various members of the public. Thus, for example, a travelling member of the public has the legal power, by making proper application

59 Like John Chipman Gray, Bruce Wyman was a professor of Hohfeld's at Harvard Law School. As explained in Chapter 18 of this volume, Hohfeld reportedly refused to attend Wyman's classes.

and sufficient tender, to impose a duty on the innkeeper to receive him as a guest. For breach of the duty thus created an action would of course lie. It would therefore seem that the innkeeper is, to some extent, like one who had given an option to every travelling member of the public. He differs, as regards net legal effect, only because he can extinguish his present liabilities and the correlative powers of the travelling members of the public *by going out of business*. Yet, on the other hand, his liabilities are more onerous than that of an ordinary contractual offerer, for he cannot extinguish his liabilities by any simple performance akin to revocation of offer.

Editor's Note: To be sure, businesses and professions classified as a "public calling" are subject to additional duties in the Hohfeldian sense, such as the duty to protect and assist. However, in some cases, these businesses and professions are sometimes subject to Hohfeldian liabilities, not duties, at least until a power is exercised subject to the business or profession or a correlative liability. For instance, an innkeeper (e.g., a hotel) is often said to be under a "duty to receive guests" – in other words, to provide lodging, if available, to anyone who properly applies, subject to certain exceptions. However, Hohfeld rightly recognizes that this so-called duty is in actuality a Hohfeldian liability. Namely, a traveler has the power (and privilege) of requesting lodging, which – if exercised properly and is not subject to exceptions – changes the innkeeper's privilege not to house the traveler to a duty to house the traveler. Moreover, unlike the power to accept a contractual offer, the innkeeper cannot revoke the traveler's power, absent going out of business. Thus, like the blurring of right and power, there is sometimes a blurring of duty and liability. Although this blurring need not lead to faulty legal reasoning, sometimes it may, necessitating the proper, technical usage described by Hohfeld.

As regards all the "legal powers" thus far considered, some caution may be necessary. If, for example, we consider the ordinary property owner's power of alienation, it is necessary to distinguish carefully between the *legal* power, the *physical* power to do the things necessary for the "exercise" of the legal power, and, finally, the *privilege* of doing these things – that is, if such privilege does really exist. It may or may not.

Editor's Note: As explained earlier, there is a distinction between a legal power, the acts necessary to effectuate the legal power, and the privilege of undertaking those acts. The legal power per se changes some other legal relations. The acts necessary to effectuate the legal power are physical and mental – for instance, those physical and mental acts necessary to enter into a contractual agreement. The privilege concerns whether the party or parties undertaking the acts can do so without violating a duty. For instance, a wholesaler may validly contract to sell a restaurant a case of vodka, but unbeknownst to the wholesaler, the restaurant may only be licensed by the state to purchase and sell beer and wine, resulting in the restaurant's violation of a duty.

Thus, if X, a landowner, has contracted with Y that the former will not alienate to Z, the acts of X necessary to exercise the power of alienating to Z are privileged as between X and every party other than Y; but, obviously, as between X and Y, the former has no [*53] privilege of doing the necessary acts; or conversely; he is under a duty to Y not to do what is necessary to exercise the power.

> **Editor's Note:** Hohfeld provides another example illustrating these distinctions. Suppose X, a landowner, has agreed with Y not to transfer the land to Z. In this instance, X still has the legal power to sell the land to Z by providing a deed to Z and following the usual requirements the transfer land. Thus, X can engage in the physical and mental acts necessary to effectuate the legal power to transfer. At the same time, X has violated a duty to Y, which would likely result in some form of contractual damages owed by X to Y. In other words, the ability to exercise a legal power may not be coupled with an unfettered privilege to do so.[60]

In view of what has already been said, very little may suffice concerning a *liability* as such. The latter, as we have seen, is the correlative of power, and the opposite of immunity (or exemption). While no doubt the term "liability" is often loosely used as a synonym for "duty," or "obligation," it is believed, from an extensive survey of judicial precedents, that the connotation already adopted as most appropriate to the word in question is fully justified.

. . .

> **Editor's Note:** Hohfeld describes a number of references and cases to justify his usage of "liability." However, the more common meaning of "liability" is narrower than Hohfeld's. Specifically, "liability" more typically refers to responsibility for one's acts or omissions that violate some duty, which result in potential criminal, civil, or regulatory penalties. To be certain, a breach of a duty gives rise to a power on the part of the State or a private party to bring a (valid) action and impose, through the power of the State, some form of sanction on the offender, making the offender "liable." However, a Hohfeldian "liability" is much broader, because it refers to susceptibility with respect to *any change* in legal relations. Thus, contractual agreements, the transfer of property, the power of a trustee, and even constitutions, involve powers and thus Hohfeldian "liabilities." In other words, when there is a valid effectuation of a legal power, the actors subject to that power are under a "liability" to have their corresponding legal relations altered. Because traditional "liability" is one of the few areas where this susceptibility to legal power actually has a conceptual label, it is perhaps the best term, but one that certainly does not denote the breadth of Hohfeld's conception.

60 This is a useful example of how conflicting, yet enforceable, duties may arise in law. Specifically, X first contracts with Y that he shall not sell land to Z. Thus, X is under a duty not to sell to Z. Next, suppose X contracts with Z to sell the land in 30 days. As noted in the text, notwithstanding X's agreement with Y, X's agreement with Z is, barring unusual circumstances, fully enforceable. In other words, X's obligation to Y has no bearing on X's ability to effectuate X's legal power both to: (1) entering into a contractual duty to transfer the land at some future time; and (2) actually transfer the land to Z at that time. A court will also enforce X's contract with Y in the event of breach. Thus, X is under a simultaneous obligation both to Y and Z that is conflicting in the sense that there is no action that X may undertake that satisfies both obligations. Standard deontic logic makes the assumption that an actor cannot be subject to conflicting obligations. This, and many other similar examples, shows this assumption to be incorrect, at least with respect to two different legal actors. (Query whether this can arise even with respect to one legal actor.) Importantly, unlike standard deontic logic, one cannot in the Hohfeldian scheme infer a privilege to do some action A from a duty to do that action A. Rather, a duty to do an action A in Hohfeld's scheme only implies that there is no privilege *not* to do the action A. Mandating that a duty to do implies a privilege to do in Hohfeld's scheme, as in deontic logic, requires an additional assumption that is not mandated by the definitions of the original relations (or operators in deontic logic) or by logic.

> **Editor's Note:** The difference in Hohfeld's conception of liability and its ordinary meaning is strikingly evident in footnote 90 of the article, which appears at about this point in the original article, and states in relevant part as follows:

<FN. 90: We are apt to think of liability as exclusively an onerous relation of one party to another. But, in its broad technical significance, this is not necessarily so. Thus X, the owner of a watch, has the power to abandon his property – that is, to extinguish his existing rights, powers, and immunities relating thereto (not, however, his privileges, for until someone else has acquired title to the abandoned watch, X would have the same privileges as before); and correlatively to X's power of abandonment there is a liability in every other person. But such a liability instead of being onerous or unwelcome, is quite the opposite. As regards another person M, for example, it is a liability to have created in his favor (*though against his will*) a *privilege* and a power relating to the watch – that is, the privilege of taking possession and the power, by doing so, to vest a title in himself. Contrast with this agreeable form of liability the liability to have a duty created – for example the liability of one who has made or given an option in a case where the value of the property has greatly risen.>

> **Editor's Note:** Because a liability in the Hohfeldian typology is simply a susceptibility to a change in relations, this change may be positive in nature – for instance, a change from a duty to a privilege, or from an immunity to a power. This is quite unlike the ordinary meaning of liability, which typically represents the susceptibility to a remedy for breach of a duty and, hence, some "onerous" relation.

[*55] *Immunities and Disabilities.* As already brought out, immunity is the correlative of disability ("no-power"), and the opposite, or negation, of liability.

> **Editor's Note:** A legal actor may attempt to change legal relations by undertaking the physical and mental acts that typically effectuate a power. But suppose that the legal actor does not have the legal power to do so. For instance, suppose legal actor A doesn't own a particular piece of land, but fraudulently enters into an agreement with unsuspecting buyers to sell the land. In this example, A has no legal power to transfer the land, and the buyers are immune from any purported attempt by A to transfer the land. Hohfeld terms the lack of power in this and similar instances "disabilities." Another example is a breach of a criminal duty by a foreign diplomat who has diplomatic "immunity." In this case, the diplomat's actions are not privileged (because they violated a duty), but the State is disabled from prosecuting the diplomat. As this example shows, in practical effect, an immunity may often result in the same outcome as a privilege, but it is often important to distinguish the two to avoid errors in legal reasoning.

Perhaps it will also be plain, from the preliminary outline and from the discussion down to this point, that a power bears the same general contrast to an immunity that a right does to a privilege. A right is one's affirmative claim against another, and a privilege is one's freedom from the right or claim of another. Similarly, a power is one's affirmative "control" over a given legal relation as against another; whereas an immunity is one's freedom from the legal power or "control" of another as regards some legal relation.

> **Editor's Note:** A legal power usually changes of the "first-order" legal relations (rights, privileges, duties, and no-rights),[61] but is there any relationship or similarity of a power to one or more of these relations? Hohfeld posits that powers and rights are similar with respect to the "control" a legal actor may hold when it holds these entitlements. Specifically, Hohfeld alleges that a right provides an "affirmative claim" against another, while a power involves "affirmative 'control' against another. As we saw earlier, "claim," at least as it used today in the sense of the ability to sue another, sounds more in power than right. So what does Hohfeld mean by claim here? Arguably, the term "control," the same one Hohfeld uses for power, is more applicable. Specifically, if A owes some obligation to B, then in essence B may control A's behavior (as a legal matter). The legal control is a substitute for B's potential physical and mental control over A, because given a legal obligation, B generally will have a strong incentive to abide by the obligation even absent physical and mental control by A.[62] In the case of a power, a legal actor may control a given legal relation of others by changing that relation. So a right allows for control over behavior, while a power allows for control over those relations that control behavior.[63] Correlatively, a privilege is the absence of control over potential behavior and an immunity is the absence of control over potential changes in legal relations.

A few examples may serve to make this clear. X, a landowner, has, as we have seen, power to alienate to Y or to any other ordinary party. On the other hand, X has also various immunities as against Y, and all other ordinary parties. For Y is under a disability (i.e., has no power) so far as shifting the legal interest either to himself or to a third party is concerned; and what is true of Y applies similarly to everyone else who has not by virtue of special operative facts acquired a power to alienate X's property. If, indeed, a sheriff has been duly empowered by a writ of execution to sell X's interest, that is a very different matter: correlative to such sheriff's power would be the *liability* of X – the very opposite of immunity (or exemption). It is elementary, too, that as against the sheriff, X might be immune or exempt in relation to certain parcels of property, and be liable as to others. Similarly, if an agent has been duly appointed by X to sell a given piece of property, then, as to the latter, X has, in relation to such agent, a liability rather than an immunity.

> **Editor's Note:** Like rights, powers are possessed by specific legal actors relative to specific sets of legal relations. Ordinarily, X is immune from attempts by Y and other third parties to sell land X owns. However, suppose that X is held liable for the tort of battery far in excess of his liquid assets and the State is empowered to sell some of X's land so that the tort defendant can

61 Higher-order powers may also change powers, liabilities, immunities, and disabilities. For instance, the State may use a higher-order power to abridge private parties' lower-order contractual powers. The constitutional amendment power is an example of a potentially even higher-order power (e.g., the constitution may abridge a state's higher-order power to abridge private parties' lower-order powers).

62 This incentive to follow obligations is of course generally strongest when there is a non-trivial possibility of a remedy in the event of breach, but even the pure force of law (i.e., in the absence of a realistic remedy) often serves as material incentive to obey obligations.

63 Specifically, second-order powers control relations that relate to the control of behavior. Third- and higher-order powers control lower-order powers. *See supra* note 61.

be paid. In this case, X is now liable to the State in the exercise of its power with respect to the applicable land (but still immune with respect to the land over which the State has no power to sell). Similarly, if X appoints an agent Z to sell land X owns, then X is liable in the event of Z's exercise of a power, which is just a general statement of agency law discussed earlier.

Editor's Note: As examples, Hohfeld then discusses two cases concerning immunity from taxation, which have been removed for readability.

[*57] So far as immunities are concerned, the two judicial discussions last quoted concern respectively problems of interpretation and problems of alienability. In many other cases difficult constitutional questions have arisen as the result of statutes impairing or extending various kinds of immunities. Litigants have, from time to time, had occasion to appeal both to the clause against impairment of the obligation of contracts and to the provision against depriving a person of property without due process of law.

Editor's Note: As noted earlier, Hohfeld envisioned his typology as applying to all legal problems. Here, Hohfeld notes the relevance of immunities to constitutional issues. For instance, the Contract Clause prohibits states (and the federal government, via a similar rule implied from the 5th Amendment's Due Process Clause) from passing laws that interfere with private and public contracts under applicable tests. Rather than placing a duty on state legislatures and the U.S. Congress from passing these laws, they instead disable legislatures and Congress by stripping them of power. Correlatively, individuals hold immunities against the passage of these laws (under certain circumstances). Thus, any purported legislative action by state legislatures or Congress that violates the Contract Clause is beyond the scope of Congress's authority and, hence, null and void (at least when declared so by a court). Similarly, the Due Process Clauses of the 5th and 14th Amendments, which protect against deprivations of "life, liberty, or property without due process of law" typically provide immunities (not strict-rights) to individuals to effectively negate the ostensible passage of (otherwise unconstitutional) laws and other actions by the federal and state governments, respectively. Generally, most constitutional "rights" are in actuality Hohfeldian immunities, often coupled with other Hohfeldian relations to ensure enforcement in the event of breach.[64]

Editor's Note: Here, the chapter returns to material that originally appeared closer to the beginning of the article, which has been moved here to improve readability.

[*20] LEGAL CONCEPTIONS CONTRASTED WITH NON-LEGAL CONCEPTIONS.

At the very outset it seems necessary to emphasize the importance of differentiating purely legal relations from the physical and mental facts that call such relations into being. Obvious as this initial suggestion may seem to be, the arguments that one may hear in court almost any day, and likewise a considerable number of judicial

64 *See generally* John C. Harrison, *Power, Duty, and Facial Invalidity*, 16 U. Pa. J. Const. L. 501 (2013). *See infra* Chapter 11 and Chapter 13.

opinions, afford ample evidence of the inveterate and unfortunate tendency to confuse and blend the legal and the non-legal quantities in a given problem.

Editor's Note: As discussed earlier, there is a difference between a legal power and the physical and mental actions that create, terminate, and change legal relations. For instance, when there is a "meeting of the minds" as documented in a written legal agreement, the mental and physical agreement are operative facts that trigger a legal power. Thus, the contractual document, the very moment after it is signed, is but documentary evidence of the exercise of legal powers, which exist abstractly. This separation of abstract legal relations from the physical and mental facts that call such legal relations into being was one of Hohfeld's major theoretical goals in this and related work, and it has had a long-lasting effect not only in legal theory, but doctrine more broadly.

There are at least two special reasons for this.

[*21] For one thing, the association of ideas involved in the two sets of relations – the physical and the mental on the one hand, and the purely legal on the other – is in the very nature of the case, extremely close. This fact has necessarily had a marked influence upon the general doctrines and the specific rules of early systems of law.

Editor's Note: As we saw earlier in the article, when we say "the parties are under contract," we often think of the physical contract itself and the mental act of agreement between the parties. In reality, the "contract" is the collection of legal relations called into being by the physical contract and associated mental acts. Similarly, a legal transfer of personal property is not the physical transfer of the thing, but the change in legal relations effectuated by the acts leading to the physical transfer. Because we tend to think in physical and mental terms, it becomes easy to slip into sloppy thinking about legal relations. Although it is often possible to speak of contracts and property in terms of "things" without committing errors in legal reasoning, a complete understanding in Hohfeld's opinion requires analysis of the legal relations associated with these things.

Thus, we are told by Pollock and Maitland:

> Ancient German law, like ancient Roman law, sees great difficulties in the way of an assignment of a debt or other benefit of a contract * * * men do not see how there can be a transfer of a right unless that right is embodied in some corporeal thing. The history of the incorporeal things has shown us this; they are not completely transferred until the transferee has obtained seisin, has turned his beasts onto the pasture, presented a clerk to the church or hanged a thief upon the gallows . . . <FN. 13: 2 F. Pollock & F. Maitland, History of English Law 226 (2d ed. 1905).>

Editor's Note: These examples show that jurists and scholars alike often tend to speak of legal relations in terms of physical "things." This "physicalist" approach to law is in contrast to Hohfeld's "abstract" approach to law, in which there is a clear separation between the legal relations, the subjects of those relations (i.e., legal actors), and the objects that the legal relations concern (i.e., actions, physical things, etc.).

In another connection, the same learned authors observe:

> ... The layman who wishes to convey the advowson of a church will say that he conveys the church; it is for Bracton to explain to him that what he means to transfer is not that structure of wood and stone which belongs to God and the saints but a thing incorporeal, as incorporeal as his own soul or the anima mundi. <FN. 14: *Id.* at 224.>

> **Editor's Note:** Again, this is an example of loose usage regarding the transfer of property. Of course, not only laymen, but often lawyers and judges use similar wording. But as just noted, there is no danger in using such a shorthand as long as one keeps in mind what it represents at a more fundamental level.[65]

A second reason for the tendency to confuse or blend non-legal and legal conceptions consists in the ambiguity and looseness of our legal terminology. The word "property" furnishes a striking example. Both with lawyers and with laymen this term has no definite or stable connotation. Sometimes it is employed to indicate the physical object to which various legal rights, privileges, etc., relate; then again – with far greater discrimination and accuracy – the word is used to denote the legal interest (or aggregate of legal relations) appertaining to such physical object. Frequently there is a rapid and fallacious shift from the one [*22] meaning to the other. At times, also, the term is used in such a "blended" sense as to convey no definite meaning whatever.

For the purpose of exemplifying the looser usage just referred to, we may quote from *Wilson v. Ward Lumber Co.*: <FN. 15: 67 F. 674, 677 (C.C.E.D. Mo. 1895).>

> The term "property," as commonly used denotes any external object *over which* the *right* of property is exercised. In this sense it is a very wide term, and includes every class of acquisitions which a man can own or have an interest in.

> **Editor's Note:** As Hohfeld explains, in this passage, the term "property" refers not to abstract relations, but the "external object" that the relations concern.

Perhaps the ablest statement to exemplify the opposite and more accurate usage is that of Professor Jeremiah Smith (then Mr. Justice Smith) in the leading case of *Eaton v. B., C. & M.R.R. Co.*: <FN. 16: 51 N.H. 504, 511 (1872).>

[65] There is a deeper jurisprudential issue lurking underneath this statement – namely, whether by reducing property, contracts, wills, etc., to aggregates of legal relations, one obscures "emergent" properties of the aggregate that are better captured by simply referring to these legal objects as "things." In other words, if the various attributes of a thing (which might correspond to use privileges or not) contain many synergies, the things as a whole may exhibit emergent properties – properties not traceable in practice to those components taken individually. Moreover, thinghood becomes more important if such clusters of attributes interact relatively less with attributes outside the cluster. *See generally* Henry E. Smith, *The Economics of Property Law*, *in* 2 THE OXFORD HANDBOOK OF LAW AND ECONOMICS 148–77 (Francesco Parisi ed., 2017).

> In a strict legal sense, land is not "property," but the subject of property. The term "property," although in common parlance frequently applied to a tract of land or a chattel, in its legal signification "means only the rights of the owner in relation to it." "It denotes a right over a determinate thing." "Property is the right of any person to possess, use, enjoy, and dispose of a thing." Selden, J., in *Wynehamer v. People*, 13 N. Y., 378, p. 433; 1 Blackstone's com., 138; 2 Austin's *Jurisprudence*, 3rd ed., 817, 818. * * * The right of indefinite user (or of using indefinitely) is an essential quality of absolute property, without which absolute property can have no existence. * * * This right of user necessarily includes the right and power of excluding others from using the land. See 2 *Austin on Jurisprudence*, 3rd ed. 836 . . .

Another useful passage is to be found in the opinion of Sherwood, J., in *St. Louis v. Hall*: <FN. 17: (1893) 116 Mo. 527, 533–534 (1893).>

> Sometimes the term is applied to the thing itself, as a horse, or a tract of land; these things, however, though the subjects of [*23] property, are, when coupled with possession, but the *indicia*, the visible manifestation of invisible rights, "the evidence of things not seen."
>
> Property, then, in a determinate object, is composed of certain constituent elements, to wit: The unrestricted right of use, enjoyment, and disposal, of that object.

Editor's Note: These passages illustrate Hohfeld's view – and that of several before him – that "property" ultimately is an aggregate of legal relations, such as the privilege to use, the power and privilege to dispose, the right to exclude, and so forth. These views ultimately coalesced in the "bundle of rights" view of property pervasive today and especially popular among the legal realists.

In connection with the ambiguities latent in the term "property," it seems well to observe that similar looseness of thought and expression lurks in the supposed (but false) contrast between "corporeal" and "incorporeal" property. . . . For further striking illustration, reference may be made to Blackstone's well-known discussion of corporeal and incorporeal hereditaments. Thus, the great commentator tells us:

> But an hereditament, says Sir Edward Coke, is by much the largest and most comprehensive expression; for it includes not only lands and tenements, but whatsoever *may be inherited*, be it corporeal or incorporeal, real, personal, or mixed. <FN. 18: 2 William Blackstone, Commentaries 16–43 (1765).>

It is clear that only *legal interests* as such can be inherited; yet in the foregoing quotation there is inextricable confusion between the physical or "corporeal" objects and the corresponding legal interests, all of which latter must necessarily be "incorporeal," or "invisible," to use the expression of Mr. Justice Sherwood.

Editor's Note: Consistent with Hohfeld's immediately preceding discussion, the transfer of property, including via inheritance, is a transfer of abstract legal interests. Thus, whether the "objects" of these legal interests are corporeal (e.g., land) or incorporeal (e.g., patents) is irrelevant to whether "property" per is "incorporeal" or "corporeal," because property is always an abstract (i.e., "incorporeal") interest. In other words, on Hohfeld's view, it is only the "object" of the aggregate of legal relations identified as "property" that is incorporeal or corporeal.

[*24] Since all legal interests are "incorporeal" – consisting, as they do, of more or less limited aggregates of *abstract* legal relations – such a supposed contrast as that sought to be drawn by Blackstone can but serve to mislead the unwary. The legal interest of the fee simple owner of land and the comparatively limited interest of the owner of a "right of way" over such land are alike so far as "incorporeality" is concerned; the true contrast consists, of course, primarily in the fact that the fee simple owner's aggregate of legal relations is far more extensive than the aggregate of the easement owner.

Editor's Note: Hohfeld reiterates that Blackstone's supposed distinction between "incorporeal" and "corporeal" can be misleading with respect to the actual nature of legal interests, including "aggregates" of legal interests, such as "property." Whether the interest is a mere easement (such as a right of way) or fee simple absolute, both are incorporeal – the only difference is that fee simple absolute is a more extensive set of legal relations than the easement.

Editor's Note: Yet, like Hohfeld's discussion of "right" earlier, to the extent lawyers, judges, and scholars use "property" to refer to an aggregate of legal relations *and* the object to which the aggregate pertains, as long as the referent of the term is clear, arguably, such "loose" usage does not always mislead, particularly to knowledgeable speakers. Indeed, like the term "right," it may be more efficient to use a single term to simultaneously denote multiple concepts, as long as the speaker and listener understand that the term can be further delineated. Thus, what seem to be Hohfeldian errors may in actuality be perfectly proper usage.

Much of the difficulty, as regards legal terminology, arises from the fact that many of our words were originally applicable only to physical things; so that their use in connection with legal relations is, strictly speaking, figurative or fictional. The term "transfer" is a good example. If X says that he has transferred his watch to Y, he may conceivably mean, quite literally, that he has physically handed over the watch to Y; or, more likely, that he has "transferred" his *legal interest*, without any delivery of possession – the latter, of course, being a relatively figurative use of the term.

Editor's Note: Because of the conflation of physical and mental acts and the legal relations that concern these acts, in Hohfeld's view, not only laymen, but also jurists and lawyers have imported physical and mental terms into the law that further this confusion. For instance, lawyers and judges use the term "transfer" of a legal interest, when technically, the "transfer" is a change in a host of legal relations. In a sense, if A "transfers" Blackacre to B, then A's strict-right against trespass with respect to Blackacre "transfers" to A, but more fundamental, A's strict-right simply becomes a no-right and B's no-right becomes a strict-right. Properly understood, there is no actual "movement" of A's legal interest to B.

As another instance of this essentially metaphorical use of a term borrowed from the physical world, the word "power" may be mentioned. In legal discourse, as in daily life, it may frequently be used in the sense of physical or mental capacity to do a thing; but, more usually and aptly, it is used to indicate a "*legal* power," the connotation of which latter term is fundamentally different. The same observations apply, *mutatis mutandis*, to the term "liberty."

Editor's Note: As Hohfeld explained earlier (in this annotated version), it is important to distinguish between the physical and mental power to effectuate some physical or mental act and the legal power to change legal relations. Legal power may depend upon physical and mental power, but they are not one and the same. Thus, the physical power one may possess to sign a contract is separate from the legal power one may possess to alter legal relations via the contract. Similarly, physical liberty and legal liberty are fundamentally different concepts – one may be able to drive at 100 miles per hour physically, but doing so would in most circumstances violate a legal duty.

Editor's Note: The following section has been moved from pages *43–*44 in the original article, again, to improve readability, as it tracks Hohfeld's argument in the preceding passages.

The term "license," sometimes used as if it were synonymous with "privilege," is not strictly appropriate. This is simply another of those innumerable cases in which the mental and physical facts are so frequently confused with the legal relation which [*44] they create. Accurately used, "license" is a generic term to indicate a group of operative facts required to create a particular privilege – this being especially evident when the word is used in the common phrase "leave and license." This point is brought out by a passage from Mr. Justice Adams' opinion in *Clifford v. O'Neill*: <FN. 62: 12 App. Div. 17; 42 N.Y.S. 607, 609 (App. Div. 1896).>

> A license is merely a permission to do an act which, *without such permission*, would amount to a trespass * * * nor will the continuous enjoyment of the *privilege conferred*, for any period of time cause it to ripen into a tangible interest in the land affected.

Editor's Note: In Hohfeld's view, the term "license" merely refers to the operative facts that effectuate a legal power to change an obligation to a privilege, rather than the privilege itself. Again, as long as the meaning is sufficiently clear, the term "license" can be used to refer both to operative facts and the legal privilege effectuated by those operative facts. Of course, if the meaning is not clear, Hohfeld is certainly justified in asserting that such usage can lead to confusion.

Passing to the field of contracts, we soon discover a similar inveterate tendency to confuse and blur legal discussions by failing to discriminate between the mental and physical facts involved in the so-called "agreement" of the parties, and the legal "contractual obligation" to which those facts give rise. Such [*25] ambiguity and confusion are peculiarly incident to the use of the term "contract." One moment the word may mean *the agreement* of the parties; and then, with a rapid and unexpected shift, the writer or speaker may use the term to indicate the *contractual obligation* created by law as a result of the agreement.

> **Editor's Note:** This simply reiterates the main point discussed for the last several paragraphs. However, recall that Hohfeld had included the last several paragraphs very early on in the original article, even before his discussion of rights and duties. By moving them *after* Hohfeld's discussion of legal powers, his points are much easier to understand.

> **Editor's Note:** The chapter now returns to the original end of the article.

[*58] In the ... preceding discussion, eight conceptions of the law have been analyzed and compared in some detail, the purpose having been to exhibit not only their intrinsic meaning and scope, but also their relations to one another and the methods by which they are applied, in judicial reasoning, to the solution of concrete problems of litigation. Before concluding this branch of the discussion a general suggestion may be ventured as to the great practical importance of a clear appreciation of the distinctions and discriminations set forth. If a homely metaphor be permitted, these eight conceptions – rights and duties, privileges and no-rights, powers and liabilities, immunities and disabilities – seem to be what may be called "the lowest common denominators of the law." Ten fractions (1–3, 2–5, etc.) may, *superficially*, seem so different from one another as to defy comparison. If, however, they are expressed in terms of their lowest common denominators (5–15, 6–15, etc.), comparison becomes easy, and fundamental similarity may be discovered. The same thing is [*59] of course true as regards the lowest generic conceptions to which any and all "legal quantities" may be reduced.

> **Editor's Note:** A similar, but perhaps a more apt, metaphor is to compare legal relations to a set of fundamental physical particles, like quarks, which cannot be further reduced. Quarks combine with one another to form different "complex" particles that may seem to have no commonalities until it is understood that they are composed of the same fundamental constituents. Similarly, fundamental legal relations may be combined to form "complex" legal conceptions – such as property, contracts, trusts, etc. – that seem fundamentally different until analyzed in terms of their constituent parts.[66]

[66] As at least one commentator has recognized, because the first-order set of legal relations are all logically related and the second-order set, similarly related, the fundamental relations can be reduced

Reverting, for example, to the subject powers, it might be difficult at first glance to discover any essential and fundamental similarity between conditional sales of personalty, escrow transactions, option agreements, agency relations, powers of appointment, etc. But if all these relations are reduced to their lowest generic terms, the conceptions of legal power and legal liability are seen to be dominantly, though not exclusively, applicable throughout the series.

Editor's Note: In other words, while the "object" of laws and related legal concepts may differ – for instance, real property generally relates to land and structures built on land while contracts relate to performance obligations – the legal relations describing these laws and concepts are always the same eight Hohfeldian relations. Thus, sales of personal property, options to purchase real property, powers of appointment in a trust, and a contract all concern legal powers and liabilities to some degree. By understanding these seemingly different concepts in terms of their constituent legal relations, it becomes possible to compare and contrast in a manner that would be exceedingly difficult otherwise.

By such a process it becomes possible not only to discover essential similarities and illuminating analogies in the midst of what appears superficially to be infinite and hopeless variety, but also to discern common principles of justice and policy underlying the various jural problems involved. An indirect, yet very practical, consequence is that it frequently becomes feasible, by virtue of such analysis, to use as persuasive authorities judicial precedents that might otherwise seem altogether irrelevant. If this point be valid with respect to powers, it would seem to be equally so as regards all of the other basic conceptions of the law. In short, the deeper the analysis, the greater become one's perception of fundamental unity and harmony in the law.

Editor's Note: Like "unified" theories of physics, Hohfeld's typology assists in perceiving "fundamental unity and harmony in the law" in the sense that all legal circumstances – and changes in those circumstances – can be described in terms of Hohfeldian legal relations, the subjects of those relations (i.e., the legal actors to whom the relations apply), and the objects of those relations (the actions and items that the relations concern). This universal structure of the law also lends itself, in Hohfeld's view, to "discern common principles of . . . policy" across various fields of law, making it possible to cite judicial precedents in one field for use in another. For instance, determining whether a Hohfeldian privilege should be coupled to a right of non-interference may follow a similar analysis whether in the field of torts, antitrust, or labor law.

<FN. 100: The next article in the present series will discuss the distinctions between legal and equitable jural relations; also the contrast between rights, etc., *in rem*, and

to any one of the first-order and any one of the second-order sets, e.g., to rights and powers. *See, e.g.*, A. K. W. Halpin, *Hohfeld's Conceptions: From Eight to Two*, 44 Cambridge L.J. 435 (1985). Unpublished work of the editor indicates that a strict-right can be mathematically formalized as a lower-order power, consistent with Hohfeld's analogical treatment comparing powers to rights. Thus, ultimately, one can start with one relation (e.g., right or power) and derive all of the remaining relations in a generalized mathematical formalism.

rights, etc., *in personam*. The supposed distinctions between substantive and adjective jural relations will also be considered – chiefly with the purpose of showing that, so far as the intrinsic and essential nature of those relations is concerned, the distinctions commonly assumed to exist are imaginary rather than real. Finally, some attention will be given to the nature and analysis of complex legal interests, or aggregates of jural relations.>

> **Editor's Note:** Unfortunately, as Walter Wheeler Cook explained, Hohfeld's "'next article' deals chiefly with rights, etc., *in personam* and rights, etc., *in rem*. The author's untimely death prevented the carrying out of the remainder of the plan" set forth in this footnote.[67] Although Hohfeld left hints as to how his typology could be expanded beyond his published work, it became the labor of those who followed in his footsteps to do so. Some of those efforts can be found later in this volume.

[67] Wesley N. Hohfeld, Some Fundamental Legal Conceptions As Applied in Judicial Reasoning 64 n.100 (1920).

Selected Personal Papers of Wesley Newcomb Hohfeld

Edited by Ted M. Sichelman

Following Wesley Newcomb Hohfeld's untimely death, he bequeathed nearly all of his academic papers to his colleague and friend, Walter Wheeler Cook, his law books to the Yale Law Library, and his personal letters and effects to his family. Unfortunately, other than one set of Hohfeld's class notes deposited by Cook at Johns Hopkins, Hohfeld's academic papers have been irretrievably lost or discarded. Hohfeld's law books have been available at the Yale Law Library (indeed, mainly in the general collection) since his death. However, despite many requests for his family to release Hohfeld's personal papers, it was not until fairly recently that one of the editors (Sichelman) was able to acquire the entire collection of papers, including additions by his extended family, notably by his brother, Edward. Totaling about 650 pages of personal letters, photos, press clippings, family trees, and other memorabilia – as well as a lightly annotated version of Oliver Wendell Holmes's, *The Path of the Law* – the papers are an invaluable resource, of which we reproduce a small selection from the papers, accompanied by short descriptions of Hohfeld's life and the material.[1]

HOHFELD'S CHILDHOOD

Hohfeld was born to Edward (Sr.) and Rosa (née Hillebrand) Hohfeld in Oakland, California, on August 15, 1879 (the same year as Albert Einstein). His father, Edward, was born in Germany and was a musician and music teacher at Mills College in Oakland. His mother, Rosa, was born in San Francisco, and Rosa's father was a Professor at the University of California (Berkeley). Wesley had five siblings, one of whom died at a young age. The others were his brother, Edward (Jr.), who was one the founders of what evolved into the law firm of Morrison & Foerster, and his twin sisters, Rose and Lily, who graduated from UC Berkeley first and second in the class

[1] The plan is for the entire set of papers to be deposited in the Yale Law Library; in the meantime, interested historians and others should contact Professor Ted Sichelman for access.

in 1899, just before Wesley graduated, at a time when relatively few women attended college. Indeed, the sisters were passed over for Phi Beta Kappa upon graduation, only to be admitted 51 years later. Finally, there was his brother, Clarence, about whom we have less information.

According to his brother Edward:

> In his boyhood, Wesley was of a quiet, thoughtful disposition and had a very sensitive nature – qualities which were pronounced throughout his life. He graduated from the Valencia Grammar School in San Francisco in 1894 and stood at the head of his class. . . . His principal and teachers in this school all remarked about the originality of his mind and his independence of thought and judgment. He entered the Boys' High School [now the renowned Lowell High School] in San Francisco in 1894 and graduated therefrom in 1897 at the head of his class. He took the classical course which at that time concentrated on Greek, Latin and mathematics.

Pictured below is a photograph of Hohfeld, aged 11.

Pictured below are Hohfeld's twin sisters, Rose and Lily, upon graduation from UC Berkeley in 1899.

Pictured below is Hohfeld's brother, Clarence, at approximately 28 years old.

Pictured below is Hohfeld's brother, Edward, Jr., circa 1960.

Pictured below is Hohfeld's father, Edward, Sr., circa 1890.

Pictured below is Hohfeld's mother, Rosa (Hillebrand), circa 1890.

HOHFELD'S COLLEGE YEARS

Hohfeld attended the University of California (Berkeley) from 1897 to 1901, graduating first in his class and being elected to Phi Beta Kappa. He was awarded the California Gold Medal for outstanding scholarship. His coursework included ancient and modern languages, history, political economy, logic, philosophy, science, jurisprudence, and a course in "elementary" law. He was an active member of the College Debating Society and the University's chess team. According to his brother Edward, "he was always a hard working, serious minded student. He did not seem to care for, nor did he take part to any great extent, in social activities."

Pictured below is the University of California Chess Team, 1899–1900. Hohfeld is in the back row, third from the right.

Pictured below is an excerpt describing the Chess Club from the University of California 1901 yearbook, the "Blue and Gold."

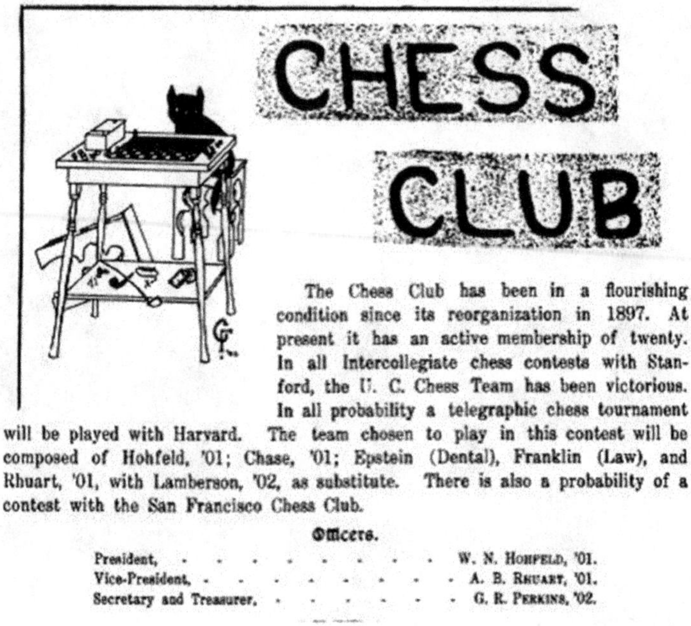

CHESS CLUB

The Chess Club has been in a flourishing condition since its reorganization in 1897. At present it has an active membership of twenty. In all Intercollegiate chess contests with Stanford, the U. C. Chess Team has been victorious. In all probability a telegraphic chess tournament will be played with Harvard. The team chosen to play in this contest will be composed of Hohfeld, '01; Chase, '01; Epstein (Dental), Franklin (Law), and Rhuart, '01, with Lamberson, '02, as substitute. There is also a probability of a contest with the San Francisco Chess Club.

Officers.

President, ... W. N. Hohfeld, '01.
Vice-President, ... A. B. Rhuart, '01.
Secretary and Treasurer, ... G. R. Perkins, '02.

Pictured below is a humorous excerpt from the same yearbook, indicating that Hohfeld was already well on his way to formulating his logical treatment of the law.

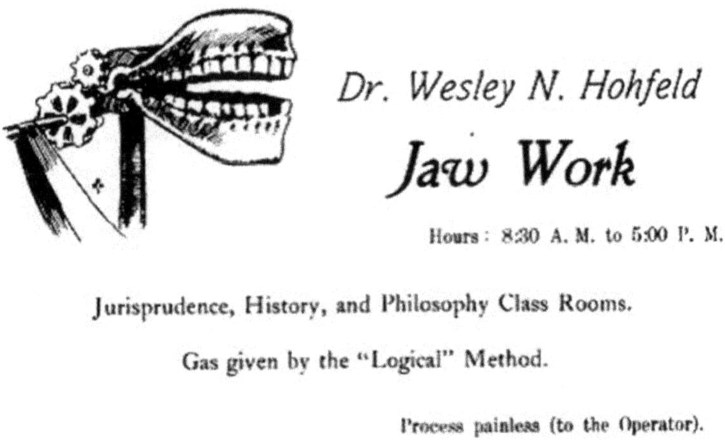

Dr. Wesley N. Hohfeld

Jaw Work

Hours: 8:30 A. M. to 5:00 P. M.

Jurisprudence, History, and Philosophy Class Rooms.

Gas given by the "Logical" Method.

Process painless (to the Operator).

HOHFELD'S LAW SCHOOL YEARS

After graduating from the University of California, Hohfeld enrolled in Harvard Law School in the fall of 1901, graduating in 1904. He assisted Professor John Chipman Gray, a well-known property scholar, with legal work at Ropes & Gray, now a very large, multinational firm. According to his brother Edward, "Wesley always took an active part in the class discussions of the law cases, and often disagreed with his teachers in some of their fundamental theories in regard to the law." He served on the editorial board of the *Harvard Law Review*, but according to Arthur Corbin, his later colleague at Yale Law School, he resigned (apparently because of an editorial disagreement).

Pictured below is a photograph of Hohfeld, circa 1902.

Pictured below is Hohfeld's class photo from Harvard Law School, circa 1904. Hohfeld is in the second row from the front, second to the left.

HOHFELD AT STANFORD LAW SCHOOL

Upon graduation, Hohfeld practiced for one year at Morrison, Cope & Brobeck in San Francisco, which later evolved into the two firms Morrison & Cope (which further evolved into the multinational firm, Morrison & Foerster) and Brobeck Phleger & Harrison (once a major law firm, but now defunct). At Morrison & Cope, Hohfeld briefed a complex question regarding conflict of laws and California's law regarding shareholder liability. This work later formed the basis for Hohfeld's series of articles on the topic in the *Columbia Law Review*,[2] which caught the interest of Justice Oliver Wendell Holmes. Justice Holmes contacted Hohfeld regarding the work and the two remained friends until Hohfeld's death.

In 1905, despite Morrison's proclamations that Hohfeld would earn a lucrative partnership at the firm within a few years, he became an instructor briefly at the Hastings College of Law (University of California) and soon thereafter joined the

[2] Wesley N. Hohfeld, *The Nature of Stockholders' Individual Liability for Corporation Debts*, 9 COLUM. L. REV. 285 (1909); Wesley N. Hohfeld, *The Individual Liability of Stockholders and the Conflict of Laws*, 9 COLUM. L. REV. 492 (1909), 10 COLUM. L. REV. 283, 520 (1910).

faculty at Stanford Law School. Hohfeld eventually became a full-time professor and taught at Stanford until 1914, when he moved to Yale Law School. During this period at Stanford, he also consulted on various litigation matters for Morrison & Cope, including the division of the estate of California sugar magnate Claus Spreckels.

While at Stanford, Hohfeld was active in summer workshops at the University of California, Michigan, Chicago, and Columbia, where he became friendly with several other law professors, including Roscoe Pound and Walter Wheeler Cook. A few summers, Hohfeld traveled to Europe.

Pictured below is Hohfeld's business card from when he worked at Morrison & Cope, located in the now torn-down Crocker Building at the corner of Market, Montgomery, and Post Streets in San Francisco.

Pictured below is the Stanford Law School faculty as of 1907 (today, the faculty numbers 93). Hohfeld is in the back row on the right.

Pictured below is the University of Chicago Law School summer workshop faculty from 1908. Hohfeld is on the left and Pound on the right in the back row.

Pictured below is postcard from Hohfeld to his brother Edward from Paris, dated July 3, 1912.

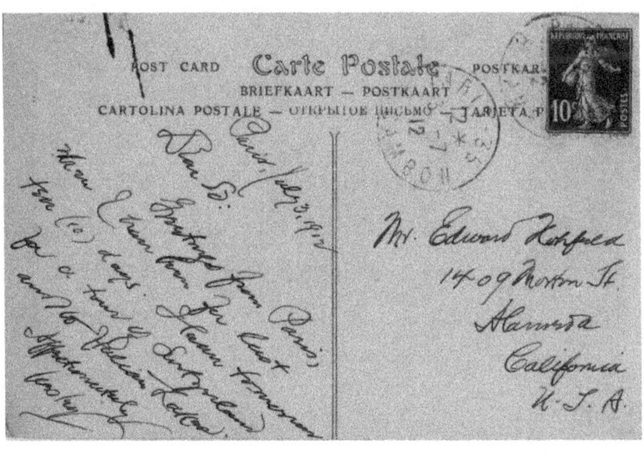

Pictured below is a letter from Justice Oliver Wendell Holmes to Hohfeld, dated March 21, 1914.

Supreme Court of the United States
Washington, D. C.

Private March 21, 1914.

Dear Sir:

Your kind compliance with my request should have received my thanks before this. My excuse must be that I have been so very busy that I have had no time to read or even to write (anything but decisions). From a rapid glance I should imagine that you would agree with the decision in Thomas v. Matthiesen Feb. 2, 1914, and the general mode of reasoning therein followed. I have not yet grasped the extent of your hostility to the fiction theory of the corporation. I always have been a little suspicious of the effect upon Semi-Enlightenment of the discovery that only human beings really have rights (of course you understand that I am not hitting at one of your knowledge, and thoughtful ability) or putting on side - which I should not dream of. I ventured a restraining word, early, in E. Remington & Son v. Samana Bay Co. 140 Mass. 494, 501. I don't know that I have got any farther. The only meaning of the fiction (or whatever you call it) is that you should act as you would if it were true.

As to Eq. & Law also I haven't time yet to do more than fire a snap shot - If, as I understand, you think it only a school master's question whether the Eq. Doctrines shall be taught under Contract & & or separately, under the genl. head Equity for historical reasons, but also think it rather a piece of quibbling to say that Eq. is consistent with the law, all my prejudices are with you – nor have I ever been able to see anything better than a quibble in the passage from Longdell you quote at p. 7. In an article on Early English Equity I endeavored to show this origin as the only substantial doctrine of any scope Contributed by Equity Uses – and to those, how far it was from being a product of Eq. procedure. Maitland et al I believe adopted my views. But I do not feel it is a very burning question whether you shall say that Eq. overrides or supplements the law when you agree what it does. I thought however that Ames got a straddle of a hobby on that theme. He and I were very good friends but he always had a whack at me when he could, perhaps because there was a light touch of irony in my sincere appreciation of his adored Longdell.

Sincerely yours,

O. W. Holmes

Prof. W. N. Hohfeld

I shall have your pamphlets bound together forthwith unless you tell me to expect another soon.

Pictured below is a page from Hohfeld's notes inscribed on Holmes's "Path of the Law," *Harvard Law Review* (1897).

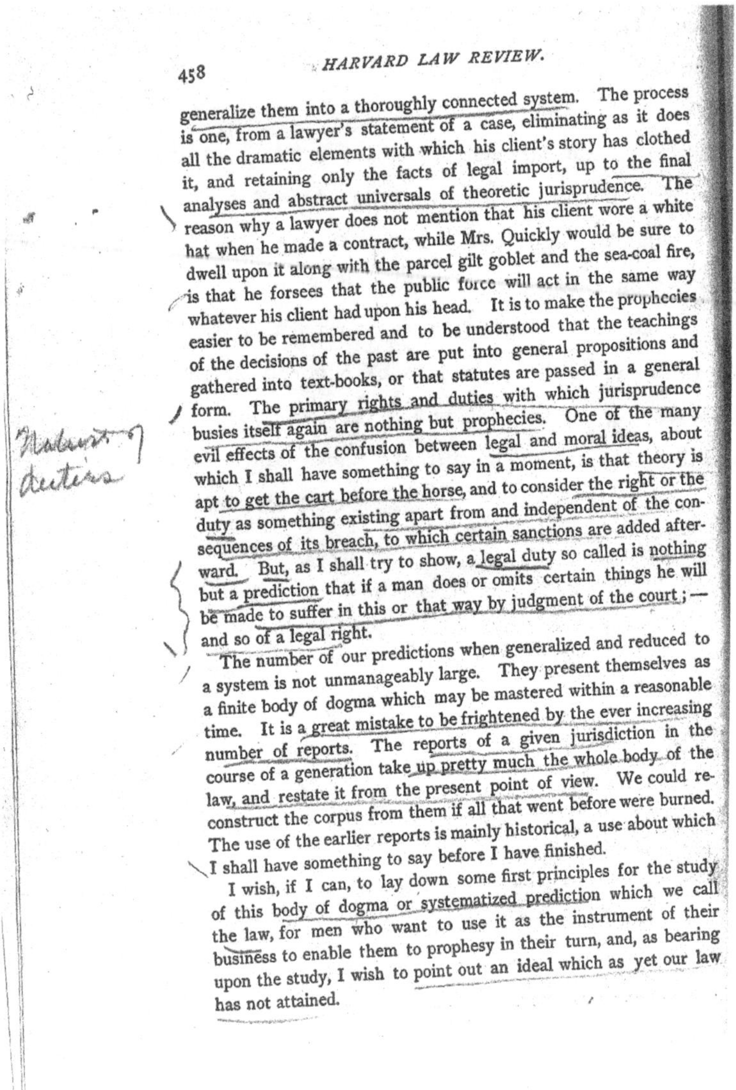

458 HARVARD LAW REVIEW.

generalize them into a thoroughly connected system. The process is one, from a lawyer's statement of a case, eliminating as it does all the dramatic elements with which his client's story has clothed it, and retaining only the facts of legal import, up to the final analyses and abstract universals of theoretic jurisprudence. The reason why a lawyer does not mention that his client wore a white hat when he made a contract, while Mrs. Quickly would be sure to dwell upon it along with the parcel gilt goblet and the sea-coal fire, is that he forsees that the public force will act in the same way whatever his client had upon his head. It is to make the prophecies easier to be remembered and to be understood that the teachings of the decisions of the past are put into general propositions and gathered into text-books, or that statutes are passed in a general form. The primary rights and duties with which jurisprudence busies itself again are nothing but prophecies. One of the many evil effects of the confusion between legal and moral ideas, about which I shall have something to say in a moment, is that theory is apt to get the cart before the horse, and to consider the right or the duty as something existing apart from and independent of the consequences of its breach, to which certain sanctions are added afterward. But, as I shall try to show, a legal duty so called is nothing but a prediction that if a man does or omits certain things he will be made to suffer in this or that way by judgment of the court; — and so of a legal right.

The number of our predictions when generalized and reduced to a system is not unmanageably large. They present themselves as a finite body of dogma which may be mastered within a reasonable time. It is a great mistake to be frightened by the ever increasing number of reports. The reports of a given jurisdiction in the course of a generation take up pretty much the whole body of the law, and restate it from the present point of view. We could reconstruct the corpus from them if all that went before were burned. The use of the earlier reports is mainly historical, a use about which I shall have something to say before I have finished.

I wish, if I can, to lay down some first principles for the study of this body of dogma or systematized prediction which we call the law, for men who want to use it as the instrument of their business to enable them to prophesy in their turn, and, as bearing upon the study, I wish to point out an ideal which as yet our law has not attained.

HOHFELD AT YALE LAW SCHOOL

According to Corbin, Hohfeld was offered a professorship at Yale "[l]argely because of [his landmark] article," "Some Fundamental Legal Conceptions as Applied in Judicial Reasoning," published in the *Yale Law Journal* in 1913. As Corbin explained, Hohfeld made good use of his scheme in moving from Stanford to Yale. Specifically, Yale agreed that Hohfeld would have a (Hohfeldian) "right" to a permanent appointment and also a (Hohfeldian) "privilege" of returning to Stanford at the end of the academic year; correspondingly, Stanford agreed to give him a privilege of leave for one year or longer with the right to return to his permanent position at Stanford at the end of the academic year. Hohfeld eventually effectuated his right to an appointment at Yale. There, Hohfeld taught Equity, Trusts, and Evidence, among other courses, and required his students to learn his typology, often to their chagrin.

Also while at Yale, Hohfeld delivered the 1914 plenary address at the annual meeting of the Association of American Law Schools (AALS), later published as "A Vital School of Jurisprudence and Law: Have American Universities Awakened to the Enlarged Opportunities and Responsibilities of the Present Day?" In it, he describes a monumental classification of jurisprudence and legal thought more generally, including teleological jurisprudence, analytical jurisprudence, sociological jurisprudence, and others. In so doing, he set out an ambitious vision to reorganize legal education in a manner more focused on jurisprudence, analytical reasoning, and policy, informed by an understanding of politics, sociology, and related subjects, in order to reform the law and legal system according to sound principles. Arguably, Yale Law School and other top law schools molded themselves to a large degree in such a fashion in the following years – how much can be traced to Hohfeld is difficult to discern.

Pictured below is a photo of Hohfeld from around 1916.

Pictured below is the cover of a reprint of "A Vital School of Jurisprudence and Law," addressed to Roscoe Pound.

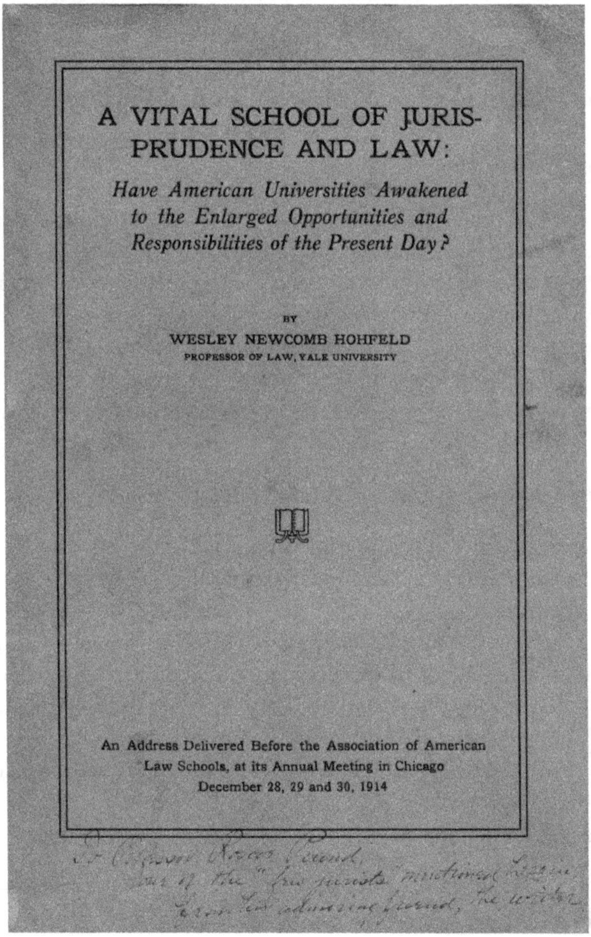

A VITAL SCHOOL OF JURISPRUDENCE AND LAW:

Have American Universities Awakened to the Enlarged Opportunities and Responsibilities of the Present Day?

BY

WESLEY NEWCOMB HOHFELD

PROFESSOR OF LAW, YALE UNIVERSITY

An Address Delivered Before the Association of American Law Schools, at its Annual Meeting in Chicago December 28, 29 and 30, 1914

HOHFELD'S ILLNESS AND UNTIMELY DEATH

Hohfeld died on October 21, 1918, from endocarditis induced by a severe infection from the 1918 flu pandemic. Following his death, colleagues and students sent many condolence letters to the family. One of those students was Karl Llewellyn, then Editor-in-Chief of the *Yale Law Journal*, who also penned a moving tribute to Hohfeld in a commemorative issue, which featured articles on Hohfeld and his work by Walter Wheeler Cook, Arthur Corbin, Albert Galloway Keller, and Thomas Swan.

Llewellyn poetically wrote:

> When a master-craftsman has laid down his tools for the last time, there falls upon those who have worked with him and under him a heavy loss – a loss too heavy to be realized at once. With increasing realization comes a need for expression, for some tribute, however inadequate, to the memory and to the work of the master who is gone. . . . To have the vision lifted beyond the little point at hand, out of the single "field" staked off as "Bills and Notes" or "Equity" – carried up into high places, to look out over the whole land, hills and valleys, ploughed land and fallow, spread out in its wonder – this was the inspiration to be had in Hohfeld's classes.

Llewellyn closed with a glowing portrait of Hohfeld in the classroom:

> But welcome as a student was who came into his office, it is not in his office that one's memory pictures "Hoh"; but in his class-room, there behind the desk–in his class-room when some man had interposed a question. There he sits, crouched somewhat forward on the desk; his black-haired eagle-face seems set with anticipation of the clash of views, his heavy shoulders tense, for all their student's stoop, – there he sits, silent through several seconds. You too grow tense for the struggle; but as you watch his eyes, you thrill with a dawning wonder, almost awe-slowly, alone, you see him climbing up into the mountain, to see this little question set out against the background of the whole, to look again upon the body of the Law as one, – and signal down to you the way to join him.[3]

Additionally, in November 1918, the *California Law Review* published reflections by Professor Orrin McMurray, in which he stated:

> Hohfeld's mind was of that sensitive logical temper, almost Greek in its character, that a fallacy was to it as ugly as a deliberate falsehood. It had no patience with the so-called legal reasoning that hides behind metaphors and takes refuge in ambiguous phrases. It had the courage to attempt the Herculean task of stripping off the masks from legal commonplaces and showing their true nature, as distinguished from the accidental costumes which they wore, the legacy of history. Such work is comparable to that of the mathematician or the pure physicist or the philosopher. It is not of the sort which the mass of mankind appreciates, yet the entire structure of modern life rests upon the results of such workers' devotion.

[3] Karl N. Llewellyn, *Wesley Newcomb Hohfeld: Teacher*, 28 YALE L.J. 795, 797 (1919).

In 1958, Edward Hohfeld, Jr., as trustee of the May Treat Morrison Foundation, endowed a chaired professorship at Yale Law School, the Wesley Newcomb Hohfeld Professorship of Jurisprudence, currently occupied by Gideon Yaffe.

Pictured below is the cover of the *Yale Law Journal* issue in memory of Hohfeld.

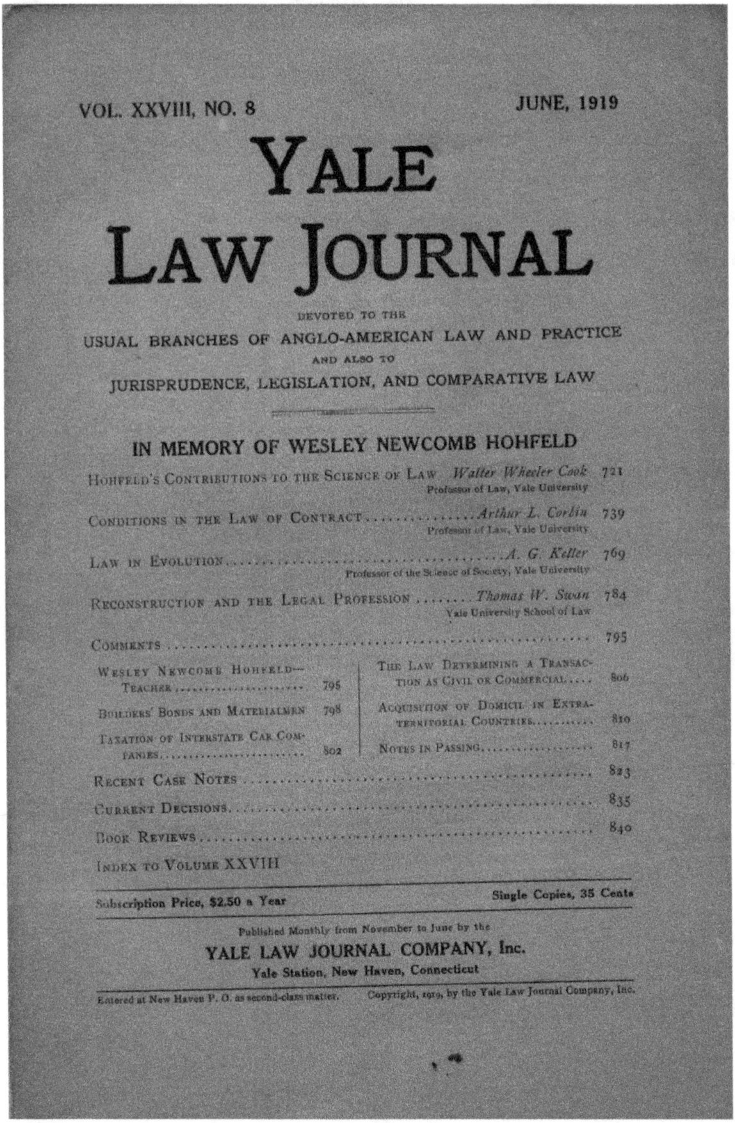

VOL. XXVIII, NO. 8 JUNE, 1919

YALE

LAW JOURNAL

DEVOTED TO THE

USUAL BRANCHES OF ANGLO-AMERICAN LAW AND PRACTICE

AND ALSO TO

JURISPRUDENCE, LEGISLATION, AND COMPARATIVE LAW

IN MEMORY OF WESLEY NEWCOMB HOHFELD

Subscription Price, $2.50 a Year Single Copies, 35 Cents

Published Monthly from November to June by the

YALE LAW JOURNAL COMPANY, Inc.

Yale Station, New Haven, Connecticut

Entered at New Haven P. O. as second-class matter.

Pictured below is a typed copy of a condolence letter from Karl Llewellyn to Hohfeld's mother.

YALE UNIVERSITY

SCHOOL OF LAW

New Haven, Connecticut

My dear Mrs. Hohfeld:

On behalf of the student body of the School we have just written to Mr. Edward Hohfeld, trusting that the letter would in due time reach you as well. Professor Hohfeld was a friend and a master among masters of the law; and that was a thing that might best be said to a man and to a lawyer.

But as men who with each year that passes come to realize more, that boys mean to mothers all that mothers mean to boys - with a sense of all that our mothers are to us - we wish to let you know our personal sympathy for you in your loss.

For the student body,

Karl N. Llewellyn

Wm. A. Kelly 2nd

Charles H. Harrison

Oct. 24, 1918.

Pictured below is a typed copy of a letter upon Hohfeld's death from Pound to Thomas Swan, then-Dean of Yale Law School.

COPY

Law School of Harvard University,

Cambridge, Mass.

28th October, 1918.

Thomas W. Swan, Esq.,
Dean of the Law School, Yale University,
New Haven, Conn.

Dear Swan:-

The news of Professor Hohfeld's death came as a great shock to me. I had heard that he had returned to New Haven to go on with his work and had supposed and hoped that he was fully recovered.

His death is an irreparable loss to American legal scholarship. I came to know him at Chicago ten years ago when we were both teaching in the summer quarter. A community of interest in Jurisprudence brought us together, and after I came to Harvard I used to look forward to the visit which he was in the habit of making each year. He had a truly wonderful mind and his tireless industry, severely critical analysis and power of thinking down into the bottom of things which would have been certain in the end to make him a leader among the teachers of law in this country.

I know of no one else to whom to write, and cannot repress this which may be the only tribute I shall be able to make to the memory of a true scholar and a true friend.

Yours very truly,

(signed) Roscoe Pound.

HOHFELD'S UNFINISHED MANUSCRIPT?

As noted earlier, Hohfeld left his academic papers to Walter Wheeler Cook. Edward, Hohfeld's brother, had inquired earlier of Cook whether Hohfeld had left an unfinished manuscript. In a January 1919 letter from Cook to Edward, Cook notes, "[I] gathered every scrap of notes which I found in Wesley's office, outside of his desk. I found no uncompleted manuscript of any kind; merely notes or isolated cases which obviously he intended to put into a case book." The contents of Hohfeld's desk was shipped to the family, but they found no manuscript. (However, the desk did contain Hohfeld's corrections to his first article on the "Fundamental Legal Conceptions," which Cook used in the republication of Hohfeld's article in 1920.)

Years later, Llewellyn claimed that the ideas for Cook's most well-known article, "The Logical and Legal Bases of the Conflict of Laws," were derived from Hohfeld's annotations and notecards in his copy of Joseph Beale's treatise on the conflict of laws. Although Hohfeld left all of his law books to the Yale Law Library, notably, Beale's treatise never made its way to the stacks.[4] Llewellyn's claim remains to be fully examined. In any event, whatever academic papers, notecards, and the like that Cook collected from Hohfeld's office never surfaced, other than one set of class notes deposited at Johns Hopkins University.[5]

4 Hohfeld's books on logic, ethics, psychology, and miscellaneous subjects were left to Arthur Corbin. It does not appear these books were ultimately deposited in the Yale Law Library.

5 A substantial body of academic letters and related materials on Hohfeld is available in a variety of law library special collections, at Yale, Northwestern, Harvard, and otherwise. Excellent articles and books recounting Hohfeld's life and works include George W. Goble, *Wesley Newcomb Hohfeld, in* DICTIONARY OF AMERICAN BIOGRAPHY (1932); N. E. Hull, *Vital Schools of Jurisprudence: Roscoe Pound, Wesley Newcomb Hohfeld, and the Promotion of an Academic Jurisprudential Agenda, 1910–1919*, 45 J. LEGAL EDUC. 235, 273 (1995); John Henry Schlegel, AMERICAN LEGAL REALISM AND EMPIRICAL SOCIAL SCIENCE (1995); N. E. Hull, ROSCOE POUND AND KARL LLEWELLYN: SEARCHING FOR AN AMERICAN JURISPRUDENCE (1997). *See also* Chapter 18.

Pictured below is the letter from Cook to Edward:

YALE UNIVERSITY
SCHOOL OF LAW
New Haven, Connecticut

Walter W. Cook
Professor of Law

January 20, 1919.

Mr. Edward Hohfeld,
Crocker Building,
San Francisco, Calif.

Dear Mr. Hohfeld:

I have been intending to write you for many weeks but we have been so busy trying to do some of the things which we knew Wesley would have wanted done that time has been lacking, especially as we have been without adequate stenographic assistance for a considerable part of the period.

I gathered together every scrap of notes which I found in Wesley's office, outside of his desk. I found no uncompleted manuscript of any kind; merely notes or isolated cases which obviously he intended to put into a case book. The latter were not, however, arranged in order and did not constitute a complete collection.

I hope that when you examine the contents of his desk, you will find some uncompleted manuscript which perhaps I can put into shape for publication, but I am not very hopeful upon that point. However, the main outlines of the structure he intended to build he had already sketched in the things which he had published, and when everything is gathered together in one book I believe the importance of his work will become more generally recognized.

We are planning some time during the current year to issue a memorial number of the Journal which will contain his portrait, an article attempting to indicate the main outlines of his contributions, and probably two or three articles (by Professor Corbin, myself and perhaps some other member of the Faculty) - articles which will apply to the analysis of concrete legal problems the fundamental legal conceptions so clearly worked out by Wesley.

We are trying to make plans for the future of the school which will carry out his ideas. Of course we can not fill his place, and his absence will make it harder to make the Yale Law School all that he would have wished it to be. Nevertheless we are determined to push on and do our best in that respect.

Mr. Edward Hohfeld, 2.

I think you will find among the papers from the desk an annotated copy of his first article on Fundamental Legal Conceptions, containing corrections which he made. I am, of course, extremely anxious to have everything of that kind in hand before I undertake the work of editing his works for publication.

Sincerely yours,

WWC:G WALTER W. COOK.

PART I

Philosophy of Jural Relations

1

Hohfeld on Legal Language

Frederick Schauer[*]

1.1 INTRODUCTION

Wesley Newcomb Hohfeld is well-known for maintaining that various terms in law – "rights," most prominently – confusingly designate a number of quite different legal relationships. But what is the source of the confusion? Is it that the terms themselves are vague or ambiguous, thus making them susceptible to multiple meanings? Or is it that the lawyers, judges, and commentators who use such terms are loose thinkers, needing careful analysis in order to clear their minds and their thoughts? Or is it something else?

My goal in this chapter is to examine one possible "something else" – a "something else" identified by Hohfeld, and discussed earlier by Oliver Wendell Holmes and later by Lon Fuller and Edwin Patterson, among others. This "something else" is the tendency of law and lawyers to use for legal purposes terms that are also used by ordinary people in their ordinary language. The fact that many legal terms have both nonlegal and legal aspects was thus, for Hohfeld, at least one source of the confusion that he sought to remedy. The aim of this chapter is, first, to explore Hohfeld's suggestive thoughts on legal language as technical language; and then to relate Hohfeld's thinking on legal technical language to those of others who have worried about the same problem; and, finally, to go beyond or around Hohfeld to discuss more generally the problem of technical language as it applies, in particular, to law.

[*] David and Mary Harrison Distinguished Professor of Law, University of Virginia. This chapter was prepared for the Symposium on the Work of Wesley Newcomb Hohfeld, held at the Yale Law School, October 14–15, 2016. An earlier version of Section 1.4 of the chapter was presented at the University of Vienna on September 16, 2016, as a keynote lecture at the conference on Friedrich Waismann's Legacy and Presence, and I am grateful for audience comments and questions on that occasion, as well as for the support of Centre Themis (Geneva) and the Hans Kelsen Institut (Vienna).

1.2 HOHFELD'S PROBLEM AND HOHFELD'S DIAGNOSIS

Hohfeld described the goal of his two now-prominent articles as, in part, helping people to "'think straight' in relation to all legal problems."[1] Of course, Hohfeld would not have thought that helping people, particularly lawyers, to think straight was his goal were it not for his implicit belief that the lack of straight thinking was widespread and in need of a remedy – a remedy that Hohfeld sought in his writings to provide.

Hohfeld not only aimed to offer a remedy for the lack of straight thinking in law but he also had views about the source of the problem. And one source, he argued, was the failure to recognize "the importance of differentiating purely legal relations from the physical and mental facts that call such relations into being."[2] Here, Hohfeld might be understood as implicitly recognizing a distinction later drawn by H. L. A. Hart[3] and then by the philosopher John Searle[4] – the distinction between, to use Searle's terminology, law in its *constitutive* mode and law in its *regulative* mode. With respect to the former, we know that law often creates or constitutes relations, powers, and behavior that could not exist at all without the law. Just as it is impossible to hit a home run without the rules of baseball, or to place someone in check without the rules of chess, so too does law often constitute behavior that has no pre-legal (in the logical and not only the temporal sense) existence. Without law there would be, for example, no trusts, nor corporations, nor habeas corpus. In creating and labeling such behavior, law is operating in its constitutive mode by creating the rule-based framework that provides the conceptual foundation for such activities.

By contrast, law sometimes regulates or otherwise operates on[5] behavior whose existence is conceptually antecedent to and independent of law. It is possible, for example, to drive a car at eighty miles per hour without the law, and thus the

1 Wesley N. Hohfeld, *Some Fundamental Legal Conceptions as Applied in Judicial Reasoning*, 23 YALE L.J. 16 (1913), as published in WESLEY N. HOHFELD, FUNDAMENTAL LEGAL CONCEPTIONS AS APPLIED IN JUDICIAL REASONING 23, 25 (Walter Wheeler Cook ed., 1919).

2 *Id.* at 27.

3 *See* H. L. A. Hart, *Definition and Theory in Jurisprudence*, *in* ESSAYS IN JURISPRUDENCE AND PHILOSOPHY 21 (1983). *See also* M. Black, *The Analysis of Rules*, *in* MODELS AND METAPHORS 95, 123–25 (1962); B. J. Diggs, *Rules and Utilitarianism*, 1 AM. PHIL. Q. 32, 40 (1964); John Rawls, *Two Concepts of Rules*, 64 PHIL. REV. 3 (1955).

4 JOHN R. SEARLE, SPEECH ACTS: AN ESSAY IN THE PHILOSOPHY OF LANGUAGE 33–42 (1969). Searle couched his analysis as one about *rules*, but his distinction is equally applicable to language and to law. Indeed, it is possible that the distinction is not between types of rules but (and especially relevant here) between types of (or usages of) language. *See* JOSEPH RAZ, PRACTICAL REASON AND NORMS 108–13 (2d ed. 1990) (1975); FREDERICK SCHAUER, PLAYING BY THE RULES: A PHILOSOPHICAL ANALYSIS OF RULE-BASED DECISION-MAKING IN LAW AND IN LIFE 7 n.13 (1991).

5 "Operates on" is infelicitous, but the idea is that law has the ability to authorize, empower, facilitate, and encourage as well as to constrain and to prohibit. In the broad sense, all of these deontic modalities may be thought of as forms of regulation, and although the terminology is not important, it is useful to understand that there are many things other than restricting or prohibiting that law can do with respect to antecedently defined and antecedently existing behavior.

legally-imposed speed limit regulates behavior whose very existence is analytically, conceptually, and empirically independent of the law. Similarly, people killed each other before the law even existed, and although "murder" may have a technical legal meaning (about which much more will be said presently), the laws against murder provide another example of law regulating conceptually antecedent behavior.

Against this background of the distinction between constitutive and regulatory law, Hohfeld's articles can be understood, at least with respect to the quotation above, as focusing largely on regulatory law. When Hohfeld refers to "the physical and mental facts that call such relations into being," he appears to be describing some state of affairs – we should not take the idea of "physical and mental facts" too literally – that pre-exists the law, and on which law then applies its rules and procedures. At the outset of his analysis, therefore, we see Hohfeld's recognition of the distinction between antecedent behavior, on the one hand, and the law's regulation of it, on the other.[6]

But what would lead Hohfeld to suppose that people would fail to recognize this distinction? For him, one source of the confusion was the similarity between the physical and mental facts, on the one hand, and the legal relationship between the two, on the other. In identifying this seeming similarity between two phenomena which he believed to be fundamentally different, Hohfeld might be understood as suggesting something closer to the realm of the constitutive, at least insofar as he appears to be implying that what law creates is different from that which exists without law. But here Hohfeld is hardly clear about what he has in mind, and his quotations from Pollock and Maitland do not help very much in clarifying the matter.[7]

Thus, Hohfeld is more than a bit opaque when he discusses the "extremely close" but apparently misleading "association" of the physical and mental relations with the legal relation, but he becomes considerably clearer when he turns to the other possible cause of the confusion – "the ambiguity and looseness of our legal terminology."[8] An especially good example, and one that Hohfeld himself uses, is the word "property." That word, he suggests, is used in one way in ordinary talk, where people tend to understand the word "property" as referring to something concrete, or tangible, as for example a piece of land or a physical object. But when the legal system talks of property, Hohfeld insists, it is referring not to something

[6] See also Hohfeld's observation that failing to distinguish "license" from "privilege" is "simply another of those innumerable cases in which the mental and physical facts are so frequently confused with the legal relation which they create." *See* Hohfeld, *supra* note 1, at 49–50. Hohfeld's use of the word "create" is curious, because it is not at all clear what it is for a pre-legal physical or mental fact to "create" a legal relation. Charitably, we might best understand Hohfeld as referring simply to the physical and mental facts that are the object of legal relations when law is operating in its regulative mode.

[7] Hohfeld, *supra* note 1, at 27–28.

[8] *Id.* at 28.

physical, but instead to a collection of rights, responsibilities, duties, and relations, the collection of abstractions that we now often understand by use of the classic "bundle of sticks" metaphor.[9] The problem, Hohfeld suggests, is that the same word – "property" – is used both to refer to the ordinary and pre-legal facts – the object or the piece of land – and to the decidedly nonordinary and legally created relationships that law tends to group under the heading of "property." Failing to recognize this distinction, Hohfeld says, is a substantial cause of unclear thinking about law and about legal relations.

After developing the property example with an array of quotations from Coke, Blackstone, and many American judicial opinions, Hohfeld then argues that this confusion between the pre-legal entity and the relations that the law attaches to that entity (or to the physical and mental facts about it) is further exacerbated by the way in which the language that refers to both was originally used to refer only to the physical things, with the legal usage consequently being in some way "figurative or fictional."[10] And although "property" provides a particularly good example of Hohfeld's point,[11] one can see many other manifestations of the same phenomenon. Consider, for example, the idea of a sale. In Hohfeld's sense of the physical (a term which is itself a bit figurative or metaphorical in this context), a "sale" might be a physical – that is, pre-legal – act, as when someone transfers possession of some object in exchange for money. But a "sale" according to the Uniform Commercial Code (UCC) is something else, such that there might be sales in the pre-legal sense that are not sales according to the UCC,[12] and there might be sales under the UCC that people would not think of as sales in their ordinary pre-legal discourse.[13] So too with "security," where the definition of a security under, say, the Securities Act of 1933 is both under- and over-inclusive vis-à-vis the ordinary nontechnical sense of security that people might use in everyday discourse.[14] Or consider the idea of a "cause," where the legal understanding, in both the law of torts and the criminal law, varies from the pre-legal

9 *See* Benjamin N. Cardozo, The Paradoxes of Legal Science 129 (1928); Anna di Robilant, *Property: A Bundle of Sticks or a Tree?* 66 Vand. L. Rev. 869 (2013); William R. Vance, *The Quest for Tenure in the United States*, 33 Yale L.J. 248, 270 (1924). Hohfeld is often credited with creating the metaphor, but there seems little evidence to support that view. *See* Pierre Schlag, *How to Do Things with Hohfeld*, 78 Law & Contemp. Probs. 185, 190 n.17 (2015).

10 Hohfeld, *supra* note 1, at 30.

11 It is of some interest – or irony – that those who object these days to the enforcement of intellectual property rights by way of copyright law, especially, often trade on the same confusion, arguing that the very phrase "intellectual property" falsely suggests that words and images are similar to land and physical objects. *See, e.g.*, Lawrence Lessig, *The Law of the Horse: What Cyberlaw Might Teach*, 113 Harv. L. Rev. 501, 539 (1999).

12 *See Leake* v. *Meredith*, 267 S.E.2d 93 (Va. 1980) (alleged sale was under the UCC a non-sale lease transaction).

13 *See Ebrahimi* v. *Rahmanan*, 566 N.Y.S.2d 26 (App. Div. 1991) (seeming partnership was, in fact, a sale).

14 *See, e.g.*, S.E.C. v. *W.J. Howey Co.*, 328 U.S. 293 (1946) (share in an orange grove was a security for purposes of the Securities Act of 1933).

understanding and usage.[15] And the same applies to the conceptions of "search,"[16] "seizure,"[17] and "speech," for example, in constitutional law, where each of these words has a legal meaning that is again both under- and over-inclusive when compared to the ordinary nontechnical meaning. There are, for example, activities that are "speech" in ordinary language that are not "speech" under the First Amendment, as with the words of an oral contract or the words used to fix prices in violation of the Sherman Act.[18] And there are activities that are not "speech" in a pre-legal sense but are considered as "speech" for free speech purposes,[19] such as wearing an armband,[20] waving or burning a flag,[21] or dancing in the nude in an "adult" theater.[22]

Although Hohfeld uses the term "fictional" to describe legal usages that depart from ordinary usages, it is important to distinguish these legal technical usages from the classic idea of legal fiction. Although the term "legal fiction" is now, unfortunately, often used to refer to an assertion of fact, typically in a judicial opinion, with which some commentator disagrees,[23] the narrower and more traditional usage is different. Traditionally, what is described as a legal fiction is the knowing deployment of a false factual conclusion in order to bring some set of facts within the ambit of a legal rule, or to exclude some facts from the ambit of some legal rule, in either case for the purpose of avoiding the poor outcome that would ensue from accurately placing the actual facts within the operative rule.[24] In the famous instance of *Mostyn v. Fabrigas*,[25] for example, Lord Mansfield determined that the island of Minorca was in London, which it is not, in order to provide otherwise unavailable relief for an aggrieved individual who without the fiction would have had no remedy for his politically inspired and plainly unjust imprisonment.[26]

15 *See* H. L. A. HART & TONY HONORÉ, CAUSATION IN THE LAW 26–61 (2d ed. 1985) (distinguishing legal and "common sense" notions of causation).

16 *See United States* v. *York*, 895 F.2d 1026 (5th Cir. 1990) ("search" in the ordinary sense might not be a search for Fourth Amendment purposes); *United States* v. *Andreas*, 1998 WL 42261 (N.D. Ill., Jan. 30, 1998) (same).

17 *See Dillingham* v. *Millsaps*, 809 F. Supp. 2d 820, 836 (W.D. Tenn. 2015) (restriction on movement is a seizure for Fourth Amendment purposes even if no person or no property is actually taken).

18 *See* Frederick Schauer, *The Boundaries of the First Amendment: A Preliminary Exploration of Constitutional Salience*, 117 HARV. L. REV. 1765 (2004).

19 *See* Mary Jane Morrison, *Excursions into the Nature of Legal Language*, 37 CLEVE ST. L. REV. 271 (1989).

20 *See Tinker* v. *Des Moines Independent School Dist.*, 393 U.S. 503 (1969).

21 *See Stromberg* v. *California*, 283 U.S. 359 (1931); *Texas* v. *Johnson*, 491 U.S. 397 (1989).

22 *See Barnes* v. *Glen Theatre, Inc.*, 501 U.S. 560 (1991); *Erie* v. *Pap's A.M.*, 529 U.S. 277 (2000).

23 *See, e.g.*, Peter J. Smith, *New Legal Fictions*, 95 GEO. L.J. 1435 (2007).

24 *See* LON L. FULLER, LEGAL FICTIONS (1967); Roderick Munday, *The Bridge that Choked a Watercourse, or Repetitive Dictionary Disorder*, 29 STATUTE L. REV. 26 (2008).

25 [1774] 1 Cowper 180 (K.B.).

26 *See* Frederick Schauer, *Legal Fictions Revisited*, *in* LEGAL FICTIONS IN THEORY AND PRACTICE 113 (Maksymilian Del Mar & William Twining eds., 2015). *See also* Sidney T. Miller, *The Reasons for Some Legal Fictions*, 8 MICH. L. REV. 623 (1910).

Legal fictions in this narrow and traditional sense are important, but Hohfeld's usage is different. He assumes that, as a linguistic matter, the ordinary usage is in some sense primary, making the legal usage figurative or fictional by virtue of its divergence from ordinary use. And here, Hohfeld's understanding of what it is for a usage to be figurative or fictional is similar to that which we see in Jeremy Bentham's writings a century earlier.[27] In excoriating the common law for its use of fictions (and, of course, for much else),[28] Bentham was thinking of the common law's presumption of legitimacy, in which a child born to a married woman is presumed to be the child of the husband, even though that might not in fact (biologically) be the case, or in which a corporation is treated as a natural person for certain purposes, even though a corporation is not a natural person in ordinary pre-legal understanding.[29]

It is also important to distinguish Hohfeld's broader claim from a more trivial point about the pervasive presence of terms of art in law. It is well known that law contains countless terms of art – terms whose definitions are context specific, and in law, serve as the labels for complex areas of legal doctrine.[30] Sometimes, such terms of art announce their character by being in Latin, or in some other way by having no everyday language counterpart. Ordinary people simply do not use terms like "assumpsit," or "covenants running with the land," and so the very presence of such expressions warns the reader or hearer that the phrases are to be understood as covering terms for vast swaths of doctrine. And at other times, some terms are so well understood as terms of art that much the same applies even if they are written in language that appears on the surface to be ordinary. In 2022, for example, "freedom of speech" might have that status, even if it did not earlier, and even if that status might not be fully understood by those outside of the legal or constitutional culture.

Hohfeld's point goes beyond the conventional idea of terms of art in part because his writings are addressed to lawyers and not lay people. It might be an interesting and important exercise to explain to nonlawyers that many legal terms have

[27] *See* C. K. Ogden, Bentham's Theory of Fictions (1932).

[28] *See* 7 Jeremy Bentham, Works 283 (1843).

[29] The example is timely, because many of the complaints about the Supreme Court's *Citizens United* decision (*Citizens United* v. *Federal Elections Commission*, 588 U.S. 310) take the Court to task for fictionally believing that corporations are the same as natural persons for free speech purposes. But even if that was what the Court decided, which is not exactly the case (*see* Frederick Schauer, *Constitutions of Hope and Fear*, 124 Yale L.J. 528 (2014)), the best understanding of what transpired is that corporations, labor unions, and other collectivities were *deemed* to be persons for free speech purposes, in much the same way as the child of a married woman was deemed to be the legitimate child of the marriage for inheritance and other purposes, even though the child might not be so deemed for other purposes. The complaints notwithstanding, therefore, *Citizens United* did not hold that corporations *are* natural persons. Rather, the Court held that corporations and other collectivities would be treated the same as natural persons for First Amendment purposes. Whether this conclusion is correct or incorrect is a matter of free speech theory, but is not dependent on any claim that corporations simply *are* natural persons.

[30] *See* Caleb Nelson, Statutory *Interpretation* 84–86 (2011); Robert Fugate, *Defining Terms of Art in Legal Writing*, 72 Texas B.J. 748 (2009).

meanings that depart from what nonlawyers think those terms mean, but this is not Hohfeld's agenda. Rather, Hohfeld appears to believe that even lawyers are deceived by the two-faced nature of much of legal language, looking in one way at legal usage and in another at the pre-legal ideas that the law intends to regulate. And so although Hohfeld believes that this aspect of language is by no means the only cause of the problem he aims to remedy, he believes that it is at least one of the causes. As such, it may be valuable to say more about this aspect of legal language, without claiming that it is the only, or perhaps, even the primary source of the kind of conceptual confusion that prompted Hohfeld's analysis.

1.3 PREDECESSORS AND SUCCESSORS

Not many years before Hohfeld published the first of his "Fundamental Legal Conceptions" articles, Oliver Wendell Holmes had expressed a similar worry in "The Path of the Law."[31] Concerned that a seeming identity in "phraseology" would encourage people, mistakenly, to move from the moral domain to the legal, Holmes speculated that it might be preferable if all words with moral connotations were to be removed from the law, in order that such confusion might be avoided. Holmes writes: "For my own part, I often doubt whether it would not be a gain if every word of moral significance could be banished from the law altogether, and other words adopted which should convey legal ideas uncolored by anything outside the law."[32]

Plainly, Holmes did not intend that his suggestion be taken too seriously. He obviously knew that it was too late in the legal day to expect such a linguistic purge to take place in law, and he recognized that any gain would be more than offset by the loss of legal language's historical usages and associations. Nevertheless, Holmes's earlier warning resonates with Hohfeld's later one. Both of them believed that legal language and legal concepts were well-designed, in the normal run of things, to serve important purposes, and thus both feared that failing to recognize legal language for its context-specific function would detract from the ability of law to do what law was designed to do. Indeed, Holmes's concern surfaces even more notably in another part of the "Path of the Law," where he recounts the almost certainly apocryphal story of the Vermont justice of the peace and the churn:

> There is a story of a Vermont justice of the peace before whom a suit was brought by one farmer against another for breaking a churn. The justice took time to consider, and then said that he had looked through the statutes and could find nothing about churns, and gave judgment for the defendant.[33]

[31] Oliver Wendell Holmes, Jr., *The Path of the Law*, 10 HARV. L. REV. 457 (1897).

[32] *Id.* at 463.

[33] *Id.* at 474–75. For my commentary on and analysis of the story and its importance, *see* Frederick Schauer, *Law's Boundaries*, 130 HARV. L. REV. 2434 (2017); Frederick Schauer, *Prediction and Particularity*, 78 B.U. L. REV. 773 (1998).

Holmes's goals in telling this story were surely multiple. One, we suspect, was making fun of rural and unsophisticated Vermont and Vermonters, a favorite pastime of well-bred Bostonians in Holmes's era. Another was disparaging those without legal training, which was what Holmes had in mind with the image of the country justice of the peace – typically a person with no formal legal training and no experience in the actual practice of law. But the point of mocking those without legal training or sophistication was to emphasize that legal knowledge, however obtained, was necessary for the comprehension of legal language and legal categories. The "master" of law would have recognized the claim as one for conversion under the law of bailments, and would have recognized that the appropriate category for the action was thus conversion and not churns. Thus:

> The same state of mind is shown in all our common digests and textbooks. Applications of rudimentary rules of contract or tort are tucked away under the head of Railroads or Telegraphs or go to swell treatises on historical subdivisions, such as shipping or equity, or are gathered under an arbitrary title which is thought likely to appeal to the practical mind, such as Mercantile Law. If a man goes into law it pays to be a master of it, and to be a master if it means to look straight through all the dramatic incidents and to discern the true basis for prophecy.[34]

In this addendum to the churn story, Holmes makes clear that he thinks that judges actually do make decisions according to the categories of law, and that predicting judicial decisions accordingly requires deep knowledge of the legal categories that judges will genuinely use. And one interpretation of Hohfeld follows the same line of thought. Hohfeld's concern with the contamination of legal language by erroneous associations with the physical objects that the legal language is about represents an implicit endorsement, in the same vein as Holmes, of law's use of law-specific categories. It is not, after all, as if Hohfeld believed that the different jural relations designated by his four categories of rights[35] were relations that did not already exist in law. Rather, he believed that these various jural relations existed in law, and that they existed for a good purpose. It was just for Hohfeld that the language that law used to designate these relations was insufficiently precise, which, when coupled with the fact that the language – and the label of "rights" – possessed an antecedent nonlegal meaning. And it was the existence of this antecedent lay meaning that Hohfeld believed led, even for lawyers, to the confusion that he was attempting to alleviate.

[34] *See* Holmes, *supra* note 31, at 475.

[35] *See* Hohfeld, *supra* note 1. Hohfeld's four categories and the relations among them have generated an industry of commentary, sometimes expository, sometimes appreciative, and sometimes critical. Some noteworthy representatives are JULIUS STONE, LEGAL SYSTEMS AND LAWYERS' REASONINGS 137–61 (1964); J. W. Salmond, JURISPRUDENCE, ch. 7 (P. J. Fitzgerald ed., 7th ed., 1966); Arthur L. Corbin, *Legal Analysis and Terminology*, 29 YALE L.J. 163 (1919); Roscoe Pound, *Fifty Years of Jurisprudence*, 50 HARV. L. REV. 557, 571–76 (1937); Max Radin, *A Restatement of Hohfeld*, 51 HARV. L. REV. 1141 (1938); Roy L. Stone, *An Analysis of Hohfeld*, 48 MINN. L. REV. 313 (1963).

This interpretation of Holmes and Hohfeld casts some doubt on the claim that both are best understood as close allies of 1920s and 1930s Legal Realists such as Jerome Frank,[36] Joseph Hutcheson,[37] and Karl Llewellyn.[38] Arguments about who is or is not a Realist are often pointless, partly because it is not clear and still contested as to just what Legal Realism is,[39] and partly because it is often uncertain about what views particular candidates for the Realist label actually held.[40] Still, insofar as one strand of Realism holds that judges actually decide cases according to the situations (hence Llewellyn's idea of "situation sense"[41]) and categories of the pre-legal world,[42] and another that this state of affairs is both inevitable and normatively desirable, the sympathy that both Holmes and Hohfeld held for law's own law-created categories consequently emerges as having a decidedly non-Realist cast.

Hohfeld's and Holmes's Realist credentials aside, it is plain that Holmes anticipated Hohfeld's concerns about the confusions that would be created when the legal and nonlegal worlds shared the same language. The concern was echoed later when Edwin Patterson, in his never-completed treatise on contract law,[43] suggested that the basic operative words of contract law – "offer," "acceptance," and "contract" itself, among others – be replaced with new law-specific terminology (as in "spikbond" for an acceptance) in order to keep people from thinking, for example, that the legal idea of an offer was satisfied just because some behavior had taken place that ordinary people using ordinary language would have described as an "offer."[44]

[36] *See* JEROME FRANK, LAW AND THE MODERN MIND (1930).

[37] *See* Joseph C. Hutcheson, Jr., *The Judgment Intuitive: The Function of the "Hunch" in Judicial Decision*, 14 CORNELL L.Q. 274 (1929).

[38] *See* KARL N. LLEWELLYN, THE BRAMBLE BUSH: ON OUR LAW AND ITS STUDY (1930); KARL N. LLEWELLYN, THE THEORY OF RULES (Frederick Schauer ed., 2011); WILLIAM TWINING, KARL LLEWELLYN AND THE REALIST MOVEMENT (2d ed. 2012).

[39] Valuable analyses of Realism include: HANOCH DAGAN, RECONSTRUCTING AMERICAN LEGAL REALISM AND RETHINKING PRIVATE LAW THEORY (2013); BRIAN LEITER, NATURALIZING JURISPRUDENCE: ESSAYS ON AMERICAN LEGAL REALISM AND NATURALISM IN LEGAL PHILOSOPHY (2007); TWINING, *supra* note 38. *See also* FREDERICK SCHAUER, THINKING LIKE A LAWYER: A NEW INTRODUCTION TO LEGAL REASONING 124–47 (2009); Frederick Schauer, *Legal Realism Untamed*, 91 TEXAS L. REV. 749 (2013).

[40] Indeed, these were Llewellyn's complaints as far back as 1931. *See* Karl N. Llewellyn, *Some Realism about Realism: Responding to Dean Pound*, 44 HARV. L. REV. 1222 (1931).

[41] *See* TWINING, *supra* note 38, at 216–27.

[42] *See* Brian Leiter, *Legal Realism*, *in* A COMPANION TO THE PHILOSOPHY OF LAW AND LEGAL THEORY 261 (Dennis Patterson ed., 1996); Brian Leiter, *Positivism, Formalism, Realism*, 99 COLUM. L. REV. 1138 (1999). This Realist theme of reliance on pre-legal or extra-legal categories is most obvious in Leon Green's Realist-era torts casebook (LEON GREEN, THE JUDICIAL PROCESS IN TORTS CASES (1931)), which was organized not around traditional and traditionally legal torts categories as such as negligence, causation, and strict liability, but instead around pre-legal categories such as Transportation, Animals, and (!) Women, Green believing that an event falling within (or without) such categories was more outcome-determinative than how the event would be treated according to the traditional categories and doctrines of tort law.

[43] *See* Edwin L. Patterson, Treatise on the Law of Contracts 1 (unpublished manuscript available at the Columbia Law School Library).

[44] For Patterson's earlier ideas on legal language as technical language, see EDWIN L. PATTERSON, JURISPRUDENCE: MEN AND IDEAS OF THE LAW 252–58 (1953).

As with Holmes, there is no indication that Patterson seriously intended to implement his idea of replacing law's two-faced terminology with new law-specific words and phrases. But as with Hohfeld, Patterson offered his nonserious suggestion as a way of pointing out the confusions that could occur when there was insufficient attention paid to the use by and in law of language that referred to pre-legal or extra-legal ideas, objects, relations, and behavior.

Writing at more or less the same time as Patterson, Lon Fuller also lamented the confusions arising out of law's use of nonlegal language to convey distinctively legal ideas and relationships.[45] Fuller, however, was even more normative (or prescriptive), arguing that law advances to the extent that it develops its own language – language that would reflect law's deeper purposes and the methods that those purposes generated.[46] Fuller, too, recognized the practical limitations of his proposal, but, like Hohfeld, Holmes, and Patterson, he believed that the use by law of language that the legal system shared with the nonlegal world would stand as an impediment to the advancement of law as a form of social organization.

An interesting contrast is thus presented. Although Holmes, Hohfeld, Patterson, and Fuller all identified more or less the same problem and the same source of confusion, the solution for Holmes, Patterson, and Fuller, even if one offered in a plainly utopian voice, was to create language that would accurately reflect law's categories and concepts. Hohfeld, however, was more practical. Creating entirely new words and phrases – new law-specific language – was, we suspect he thought or would have thought, both unnecessary and impractical. Better simply to have lawyers and judges understand the multiple relationships lurking behind simple words with nonlegal associations. Were this to transpire, we interpret him as believing that creating a new language would have been unnecessary. Thus, we might understand Hohfeld's dissection of jural relationships, and his division of them into separate groups, as an attempt to alert lawyers to a problem that could be solved more easily by clear thinking and close analysis than by the creation of new legal language.

1.4 THE PROBLEM OF TECHNICAL LANGUAGE, IN LAW AND ELSEWHERE

The problem with which Hohfeld and the others just mentioned were wrestling is, more broadly, the problem of technical language – a problem hardly exclusive to law. Interestingly, and perhaps ironically, the problem was most explicitly identified and discussed during the heyday of so-called ordinary language philosophy. The philosopher Charles Caton, for example, noted that many disciplines used technical language, but that technical language was at the same time both different from and

[45] *See* FULLER, *supra* note 24. *See also* Kenneth Campbell, *Fuller on Legal Fictions*, 2 LAW & PHIL. 339 (1983).

[46] FULLER, *supra* note 24, at 23–27.

related to (or parasitic on) ordinary language.[47] The technical English of physics, of literary criticism, and of automobile mechanics, for example, is related to ordinary English in ways that it is not related to ordinary Bulgarian or Swahili, but, in other ways, it differs in fundamental ways from the ordinary English of "the man on the Clapham omnibus."[48]

Even earlier than Caton, the philosopher Friedrich Waismann devoted considerable attention to what he called "language strata."[49] Different enterprises within a larger linguistic community, he suggested, had in many respects different languages, and not just in the different meanings they attached to various nouns, verbs, adjectives, etc. Rather, different enterprises and different contexts generated languages with different deep structures – structures reflecting the role that language served within that particular enterprise.

Waismann's suggestion, although at best loosely worked out by Waismann himself and even more loosely by others, seems especially applicable to legal language. To the extent that the language of the law reflects law-specific ideas of separation of powers (in the nontechnical sense), of burden of proof, and of defeasibility,[50] for example, then the comprehension and interpretation of that language will differ from that of other languages or other uses of what appear to be the same words and phrases. Thus, if Waismann's lead is to be followed, the problem of technical language is not only the problem of discerning the meaning of specific nouns, verbs, adverbs, and adjectives but also the problem of the meaning of the entire linguistic structure of law. When Lon Fuller, for example, suggested that what we think of as a vehicle in ordinary language might not be a vehicle at all when applied to a certain object of a certain legal regulation,[51] he was positing that the entire meaning of legal language, syntax and all, might be such as to incorporate all of the goals of law itself. For Fuller, the very reference of the word "vehicle" was different

47 Charles Caton, *Introduction*, *in* PHILOSOPHY AND ORDINARY LANGUAGE v, viii–xii (Charles Caton ed., 1963).

48 *See* PETER M. TIERSMA, PARCHMENT, PAPER, PIXELS: LAW AND THE TECHNOLOGIES OF COMMUNICATION 120 (2010); Frederick Schauer, *Is Law a Technical Language?* 52 SAN DIEGO L. REV. 1 (2015); Frederick Schauer, *On the Relationship Between Legal and Ordinary Language*, *in* SPEAKING OF LANGUAGE AND LAW (Lawrence M. Solan et al. eds., 2015).

49 The idea appears at numerous points in Waismann's writings, but the most concentrated treatment can be found in F. Waismann, *Language Strata*, *in* LOGIC AND LANGUAGE (SECOND SERIES) 11 (Antony Flew ed., 1953). *See also* F. WAISMANN, THE PRINCIPLES OF LINGUISTIC PHILOSOPHY 252–56 (R. Harré trans., 1965); F. WAISMANN, HOW I SEE PHILOSOPHY 172–207 (R. Harré trans. 1968); F. Waismann, *The Linguistic Technique*, *in* PHILOSOPHICAL PAPERS 150 (Brian McGuinness ed., 1977).

50 That is, of the idea that legal rules (necessarily, according to some writers, and contingently, according to others) can be set aside when following them would lead to absurd, morally wrong, or otherwise suboptimal results. On the topic generally, see THE LOGIC OF LEGAL REQUIREMENTS: ESSAYS ON DEFEASIBILITY (Jordi Ferrer Beltran & Giovanni Battista Ratti eds., 2012); LUIS DUARTE D'ALMEIDA, ALLOWING FOR EXCEPTIONS: A THEORY OF DEFENCES AND DEFEASIBILITY IN LAW (2015); Frederick Schauer, *On the Open Texture of Law*, 87 GRAZER PHILOSOPHISCHE STUDIEN 195 (2013).

51 Lon L. Fuller, *Positivism and Fidelity to Law: A Reply to Professor Hart*, 71 HARV. L. REV. 630 (1958). On this specific point, see Frederick Schauer, *A Critical Guide to Vehicles in the Park*, 83 N.Y.U. L. REV. 1109 (2008).

when that word appeared in a legal regulation than when the same word appeared in a different context, and thus a "vehicle" designated by a legal regulation prohibiting vehicles in this or that location was only that object whose prohibition would be consistent not only with the purpose of the particular legal regulation at issue, but also of the legal system in its entirety.

Fuller's suggestion was extreme, and reflected his own ideas about the obligation of all interpreters of legal language to interpret the language so as to produce all-things-considered reasonable results in accordance with the largest purposes of the entire legal order. But one of the things that makes Fuller's ideas about legal meaning extreme, and that makes his views about the development of legal technical language with no affinities with ordinary language extreme as well, is that law does not only speak to lawyers and judges. Law speaks as well to its subjects, and it often does so without the intermediation of legal experts. Indeed, when Jeremy Bentham in all seriousness suggested that perhaps it ought to be illegal to give legal advice for money,[52] it was his way of arguing that law at its best would avoid the unnecessary complexities that made most lawyers and most judges necessary, and that prohibiting the profit-motivated provision of legal advice would eliminate what Bentham thought was the chief reason that laws were drafted with such inordinate complexity and obscurity as to make the intervention of "Judge and Co." necessary. Were law simpler and more accessible to the ordinary person, Bentham believed, law would operate more transparently, more efficiently, and more to the overall benefit of society at large.

Bentham's suggestions were, of course, no more realistic than Fuller's. Law often does need to speak directly to its subjects, but as law develops, it often takes on and creates more complex relationships that need complex language and categories to perform satisfactorily. Perhaps this is what Hohfeld recognized. In a complex society, there is a genuine need for each of the Hohfeldian concepts – claim-rights, privileges (liberties), powers, and immunities – and it would be a step backwards to think otherwise. But law is an institution of and dependent on language, and embodying, reflecting, and operationalizing these different relationships is, in part, the job of legal language. If we were to follow Bentham and try to explain and embody all of this in simple ordinary language, the value of the different relationships might be lost. But if we were to follow Fuller and Patterson and accordingly attempt to have new and distinct terms for each of these ideas, the ability of law to speak to its subjects might then be lost. Negotiating these conflicting goals – determining the extent to which legal language should be ordinary or technical, and should or should not track the categories of what Hohfeld called the "physical" world – is no easy task. Nevertheless, one way of understanding Hohfeld's concern with the confusion between the physical world and the law's

[52] *See* Jeremy Bentham, *Scotch Reform, in* 5 THE WORKS OF JEREMY BENTHAM 1 (John Bowring ed., 1843).

imprint on it is as an initial attempt to at least identify the relationships that law's use of nontechnical language often obscures.

1.5 CONCLUSION

Vast amounts have been written about Hohfeld's disaggregation of legal rights into claim-rights, privileges, powers, and immunities, and about his related ideas of the jural opposites and jural correlatives for each of these categories.[53] But one question, and one about which less has been written, is why Hohfeld thought that clarification was necessary, and another, about which still less yet has been written, is what Hohfeld thought was the cause of the confusion he set out to remedy. Hohfeld's writings suggest that he believed the confusion to emerge from multiple sources, but there is little doubt that he thought that one source – not the only source, to be sure – was the failure to differentiate between the ordinary and the technical connotations of the words that appear in law, and of the words that are used to describe the law. By scrutinizing Hohfeld's scant but suggestive ideas about the law-specific dimension of legal language, we may learn a great deal about the still under-studied topic of the technical (or not) language of the law.

[53] *See supra* note 35 and accompanying text.

2

Rights Correlativity

David Frydych[*]

2.1 INTRODUCTION

Philosophers and jurists have long argued that there are different senses of the term "a right" in legal, moral, and political discourses and that these senses, in turn, reflect distinct concepts. Accordingly, they developed models of rights to make sense of this diversity.[1] Models provide a typology of fundamental types of rights,[2] explain how rights and other kinds of normative positions (e.g., duties, liabilities, etc.) relate to one another,[3] and show if, and how, they can be combined into larger constructs.[4]

For example, in Wesley Hohfeld's *schema of jural relations*, there are four conceptually basic types of rights: a claim, privilege,[5] power, and immunity.[6] Each of those four types is said to correlate with one – only one, and always the

* Faculty of Law, Monash University.

1 *See, e.g.*, Roscoe Pound, *Rights*, *in* 4 JURISPRUDENCE (1959) [hereinafter Pound (1959)]; David Frydych, *Rights Modelling*, 30 CANADIAN J. L. JURISPRUDENCE 125 (2017) [hereinafter Frydych (2017)].

2 "Fundamental" here is used in the sense of being conceptually basic or simple, as opposed to marking a judgment about which rights are morally or politically essential for persons, justice, a legal order, etc. A popular idea in analytic philosophy is that concepts are (often) complex and decomposable into more basic ones. I take no stance on whether this is true of most concepts and will simply use "fundamental" and "conceptually basic" as a description of certain features of rights models.

3 The philosophy of rights literature often refers to rights and some related concepts (e.g., duties, liabilities, etc.) as "normative positions." This suggests peoples' and institutions' identities and/or statuses within a normative system or domain: a legal system, a community's positive morality, a corporation, etc. It is also a slightly controversial term, as some philosophers deny that certain positions (e.g., liberties and powers) constitute norms on the grounds that they do not guide or regulate behavior. *See, e.g.*, CARL WELLMAN, REAL RIGHTS 8 (1995).

4 Most lawyers and the general public have nevertheless ignored these jurisprudential distinctions and continue to speak as though "a right" is a univocal term.

5 While Hohfeld uses the term "a privilege," it has become commonplace in the literature (for better or worse) to use "a liberty" instead.

6 A fifth type, a right complex, is a larger construct composed of any number of tokens of the four fundamental types, e.g., a claim + a power + a privilege, etc. That Hohfeld sees certain aggregations of the more fundamental positions as being what lawyers and judges call "rights," and not just larger legal concepts (e.g., "property," etc.), *see* Wesley N. Hohfeld, *Some Fundamental Legal Conceptions as Applied in Judicial Reasoning*, 23 YALE L.J. 16, 28–30, 35 n.39, 38 n.48 (1913) [hereinafter *FLC 1*]. *See*

same type of one – normative position: a duty, no-right, liability, and disability.[7] For want of a better term, these other four fundamental positions can be called "ligations."[8]

There is a legion of scholarship explicating and debating the various conceptions[9] of A RIGHT,[10] Hohfeld's particularly. To the best of my knowledge, though, no one has yet attempted a comprehensive treatment of all the various concepts of RIGHTS CORRELATIVITY and the issues they raise.[11] Indeed, some of the issues have

also HENRY TERRY, SOME LEADING PRINCIPLES OF ANGLO-AMERICAN LAW EXPOUNDED WITH A VIEW TO ITS ARRANGEMENT AND CODIFICATION 386 (Philadelphia, T. & J.W. Johnson & Co. 1884).

7 The change in title from Hohfeld's first to second rights articles involved dropping the word "some." In 1920, William Page lampooned Hohfeld for adopting certain conceptions produced at least a couple of generations earlier and then dubbing them "the" fundamental legal conceptions, "the" lowest common denominators to which *all* legal problems could be reduced. *See* William Herbert Page, *Terminology and Classification in Fundamental Jural Relations Terminology and Classification in Fundamental Jural Relations – A Symposium*, 4 AM. L. SCH. REV. 616 (1921). *But cf.* Ernst Bierling on *Juristische Grundbegriffe*: "juristic fundamental concepts." *See* ERNST BIERLING, ZUR KRITIK DER JURISTISCHEN GRUNDBEGRIFFE 2 (Gotha, F.A. Perthes 1877). One ought to add that Hohfeld never even really tried to show whether legal standards and principles could be explained in terms of normative positions.

8 The term "ligation" comes from Albert Kocourek, *Wanted: Phrase for Legal Capabilities and Restraints*, 9 A.B.A. J. 25, 26 (1923). Years before Hohfeld, Salmond noted the lack of a generic term for these four, but failed to coin one. *See* JOHN SALMOND, JURISPRUDENCE, OR THE THEORY OF THE LAW 236 (1st ed. 1902) [hereinafter SALMOND (1902)]. While there is no common term, "ligation" is the least bad option. Pavlos Eleftheriadis calls them "legal negations." *See* PAVLOS ELEFTHERIADIS, LEGAL RIGHTS 123 (2008). However, this seems to miss some of the four positions' affirmative qualities, e.g., the requirement to act in a duty, to have one's position changed in a liability, etc. The same problem applies to Pierre Schlag's distinction between "entitlements" and "disablements." *See* Pierre Schlag, *How to Do Things with Hohfeld*, 78 LAW & CONTEMP PROBS. 185, 188 (2015). Other scholars divide Hohfeld's eight terms into four "advantages" and four "burdens," but Hohfeld himself shows why many liabilities are actually desirable and even sometimes advantageous. See *FLC 1*, *supra* note 6, at 54 n.90.

Kocourek was an Imperatival theorist, holding that all jural relations involve some form of legal constraint. However, one can employ "ligation" as a technical term that excises that element: not all ligations are obligations, borne of legal officials' commands, let alone ones that are subject to sanction for nonconformity. Kocourek's terminology of "dominant" and "servient" parties (*dominus* and *servus*) may also be a good way to distinguish right-holders and ligation-bearers. *See* Albert Kocourek, *Plurality of Advantage and Disadvantage in Jural Relations*, 19 MICH. L. REV. 47, 49 (1920).

9 Some philosophers employ a concept/conception distinction. A *concept* is said to refer to either a "thin" idea or an entire field of enquiry (e.g., the concept of justice), while a *conception* refers to particular viewpoints about that concept, such as different theorists' "rational reconstructions" or analyses of it. For example, Hohfeld's claim, H. L. A. Hart's *private law* right-correlative-to-an-obligation, and Joseph Raz's right might be said to be different conceptions of the kind of right that correlates with a duty. *See FLC 1*, *supra* note 6, at 30–2; H. L. A. Hart, ESSAYS ON BENTHAM: JURISPRUDENCE AND POLITICAL THEORY 183–86 (1982) [hereinafter HART (1982)]; *cf.* JOSEPH RAZ, THE MORALITY OF FREEDOM 166 (1986) [hereinafter RAZ (1986)]. Hart and Raz see their conceptions as criticisms of, and improvements upon, Hohfeld's. *See* HART (1982), *id.* at 162; JOSEPH RAZ, ETHICS IN THE PUBLIC DOMAIN 254, 255 (Revised ed. 1996) [hereinafter RAZ (1996)]; *cf.* JOSEPH RAZ, THE CONCEPT OF A LEGAL SYSTEM: AN INTRODUCTION TO THE THEORY OF LEGAL SYSTEM 178–80 (2d ed. 1980).

10 The contemporary philosophical convention is to use all capitals to mark concepts. This, to distinguish them from denotations of words, phrases, and terms, for which quotation marks are used instead.

11 For some partial treatments, *see, e.g.*, Max Radin, *Correlation*, 29 COLUM. L. REV. 901 (1929) [hereinafter Radin (1929)]; David Lyons, *The Correlativity of Rights and Duties*, 4 NOUS 45 (1970);

hitherto gone unnoticed. As they are indispensable to all rights models (let alone for assessing their merits), including Hohfeld's, it is vital to address them.

There are actually three core disputes about correlativity in the philosophy of rights literature – though the first and third tend to be implicit. The first concerns the conceptual structures of the tethered normative positions: does correlativity mean that rights and duties must be *symmetrical*? Are correlatives the "mirror images" of each other, or not? A second dispute is over "existential" correlativity: must the correlated normative positions invariably co-obtain, or can one exist without the other(s)? For example, can there be a right without a correlative duty, or vice versa? The third regards "justificational" correlativity: *must* all correlative relationships be explained in terms of one position grounding the other(s)? Is it necessarily the case that, when a right and a duty correlate, the right was the reason for the duty, the basis for imposing a duty on its bearer in the first place?

The chapter proceeds as follows. Section 2.2 explicates and assesses those three issues and the various concepts. Section 2.3 demonstrates how Hohfeld's understanding of the concept(s) motivated all of the novel features in his *schema* and defends some of them from criticisms. Section 2.4 then presents some worries about Hohfeld's conceptions and their use in analyses.

2.2 DISAGREEMENTS ABOUT CORRELATIVITY

2.2.1 *Symmetrical versus Asymmetrical Views of Correlativity*

Is CORRELATIVITY best understood as a relationship wherein (View A) two or more connected normative positions are the "mirror images" of one another, or (View B) as a relationship wherein one or more of the positions bears features that are not reflected in the other(s)? While scholars have discerned the difference between these two before,[12] no one seems to have noticed that A and B are in fact ranges of views.

Commencing with View A, it is often said that correlatives are "two sides of the same coin,"[13] or, again, mirror images of one another.[14] I will style this the "symmetrical view" of correlativity. It actually admits of different versions because adherents (implicitly)

Jack Donnelly, *How are Rights and Duties Correlative?* 16 J. VALUE INQUIRY 287 (1982); Matthew Kramer, *Rights Without Trimmings, in* A DEBATE OVER RIGHTS: PHILOSOPHICAL ENQUIRIES (Matthew Kramer ed., 1998) [hereinafter Kramer (1998)]; JONATHAN GORMAN, RIGHTS AND REASON: AN INTRODUCTION TO THE PHILOSOPHY OF RIGHTS 83–99 (2003).

12 *See, e.g.*, Radin (1929), *supra* note 11, at 901; A. R. Anderson, *Logic, Norms, and Roles*, 4 RATIO 36, 43 n.3 (1962).

13 JOEL FEINBERG, RIGHTS, JUSTICE, AND THE BOUNDS OF LIBERTY: ESSAYS IN SOCIAL PHILOSOPHY 148–49 (1980); Donnelly, *supra* note 11, at 290. Both scholars deny that the metaphor fully covers matters, though. In part, this is because they seem to hold that rights are perforce claimable. *See* FEINBERG, *id.* at 149; Donnelly, *supra* note 11, at 290. They nonetheless fail to see that, if A DUTY includes the feature of being subject to claims of right, then the metaphor remains apt – as far as the claimability charge is concerned at any rate.

14 *See, e.g.*, Radin (1929), *supra* note 11, at 903.

disagree about whether it denotes: an *identity* or *logical equivalency*[15] of the connected positions; a relationship of *mutual entailment*; one of *logical converses*;[16] or something else.

For example, Max Radin endorses an *identity version* of the symmetrical view. He rejects the idea that a Hohfeldian claim and duty constitute two united but distinct positions. Instead, they are said to be merely two names that express the same thing: "a relation."[17] "They are not even two aspects of the same thing. They are two absolutely equivalent statements of the same thing."[18] In part, Matthew Kramer's account of Hohfeld also reflects that stance:

> [Hohfeld] posited the correlativity for rights and duties as a definitional fundament of his theory, by explicating the concepts of 'right' and 'duty' in such a way that each *entails* the other; each *is* the other from a different perspective, in much the same way that an upward slope viewed from below is a downward slope viewed from above.[19]

The identity version is nevertheless erroneous. The normative positions in a correlative relationship are not the same, so it is a mistake to deny that they constitute distinct components of a jural relation. My requirement to act or forbear vis-à-vis you is not the same thing as your entitlement to my action or forbearance; that I must do something for you is not the same thing as your being entitled to my action. My power to make you a trustee is not the same thing as your being liable to being designated as such. Take "parent" and "child" as a further example of correlatives. One cannot be a parent without the existence of a child and (at least till now, technologically speaking) vice versa. This pair does not involve identical concepts, and nor is one of the pair reducible to the other; being a parent is neither the same thing as, nor reducible to, being a child, simply viewed from the vantage of one position rather than the other.[20]

15 *See, e.g.*, Philip Mullock, *The Hohfeldian Jural Opposite*, 13 RATIO 158, 159 (1971).

16 *See, e.g.*, Frederick Fitch, A *Revision of Hohfeld's Theory of Legal Concepts*, 10 LOGIQUE ET ANALYSE 269 (1967).

17 Radin (1929), *supra* note 11, at 903–04. The word "relation" invites confusion because Hohfeld uses it to refer to: (i) a singular normative position, such as a claim; (ii) the relationship between two normative positions, such as that between a claim and a duty; and (iii) the larger construct: a jural relation composed of a claim plus a duty, say.

18 Max Radin, *A Restatement of Hohfeld*, 51 HARV. L. REV. 1141, 1149–50 (1938) [hereinafter Radin (1938)]. While acknowledging that Hohfeld's own view is of a relationship between two united "things," Radin believes he was wrong to think thus. Radin prefers to instead construe rights and duties as being logical converses, on the grounds that that better explains what happens when one term is replaced with the other in a given proposition. *See* Radin (1929), *supra* note 11, at 904–5. Hohfeld himself says the two positions are mere "phases" of one jural relation, as viewed from two different angles. *See* Wesley N. Hohfeld, *Fundamental Legal Conceptions as Applied in Judicial Reasoning*, 26 YALE L.J. 710, 719 (1917) [hereinafter *FLC* 2]. *Cf. id.* at 749–50.

19 Kramer (1998), *supra* note 11, at 24 (emphasis added). *Cf. id.* at 33, 39, 43. Kramer conflates different possible understandings of correlativity here: mutual entailment and identity.

20 *See* Markus Stepanians, Rights as Relational Properties: In Defense of Right/Duty-Correlativity 68–69 (Habilitation Thesis, 2005) (on file with author). *Cf. id.* at 53.

Many rights scholars also ignore (potential) differences between: (1) logical equivalency and entailment; and (2) mutual (two-way) and one-way entailment. From X's entailing Y it neither follows that X is strictly identical with Y nor that Y in turn necessarily entails X. For example, many jurists acknowledge the existence of "absolute" duties: duties that do not correlate with rights, such as self-regarding ones. The existence of such duties undermines the *mutual equivalence* version of the symmetrical view of correlativity, because they show that a duty is not necessarily equivalent with, or identical to, a right. Absolute duties also serve as a counterexample to the idea that duties and rights must mutually entail one another; a right may entail a duty, but not necessarily vice versa.[21] As a second example, people are sometimes susceptible to having their legal positions changed by operations of law, rather than because someone used a legal power to do so. Regardless of what Hohfeld thought of the matter, someone might believe that his conception, A LIABILITY, is apt here, but deny that the position bears a correlate in such circumstances. Hence, a power entails a liability, but not necessarily vice versa.[22]

View B, by contrast, holds that correlatives can bear distinct features. In other words, the connected positions are neither equivalent nor identical because one or more of them might include features not borne by the other(s); they therefore need not "mirror" each other in structure. For simplicity's sake, this will be styled the "asymmetrical view" of correlativity.

Joseph Raz's account of normative positions is a good example of the asymmetrical view. For Raz, rights are reasons, ones that are sufficient but unnecessary grounds for imposing duties and other normative positions on (the right-holder and) others.[23] In contrast to Hohfeld, Raz also believes that a right can correlate with any number of, and different types of, normative positions, e.g., with duties, liabilities, disabilities, etc.[24] These correlatives, however, are not the same reasons. Further, Raz's A DUTY is not equivalent to A RIGHT in either its content or structure. For one thing, a duty is a reason to act or forbear, rather than a reason *for another party to bear* a normative position in the first place. For another, a Razian duty is an *exclusionary* reason: in addition to the first-order normative requirement to act or forbear, it also includes a second-order normative requirement to exclude from consideration certain matters that would weigh against fulfilling the duty's

21 Carl Wellman, A Theory of Rights: Persons Under Laws, Institutions, and Morals 57 (1985) [hereinafter Wellman (1985)]. Wellman treats the bi-conditional stance and its rejection as "weak" versus "strong" correlativity theses. *Id.*

22 Absolute duties and any liabilities triggered solely by operation of law (and thus not by powers) also serve as counterexamples to the idea that jural positions perforce bear correlatives, thus marking a deficit in the *schema*.

23 *See* Raz (1986), *supra* note 9, at 176, 180–81, 183–84, 188, 192–93, 202, 249; Raz (1996), *supra* note 9, at 3, 41. Raz thinks rights are merely sufficient grounds because other sorts of reasons can also ground duties, e.g., those which ground absolute ones. *See* Raz (1986), *supra* note 9, at 170, 183–84, 186, 201.

24 Raz (1986), *supra* note 9, at 167–68, 170–71; Raz (1996), *supra* note 9, at 31, 46, 268. He therefore rejects what I call the strict bilaterality thesis below in Section 2.3.2.

requirements.[25] This (purported) exclusionary feature of a duty, however, is not reflected in a Razian right.[26]

Albert Kocourek's work provides a second example of the asymmetrical view of correlativity. He lambastes Hohfeld's AN IMMUNITY on the grounds that it is insusceptibility from nothing: it merely marks someone else's lack of power.[27] Wittingly or otherwise, Kocourek is hereby criticizing a symmetrical view of immunities and disabilities. It is a separate question whether his criticism is actually on the mark; that will depend on whether you think it accurately captures Hohfeld's view. For, as discussed below, one possible asymmetrical view conception of AN IMMUNITY is as a trump over someone else's power.[28]

The nature of the relationship between Hohfeldian claims and duties, which is contested in the philosophy of rights literature, also serves as a good example for contrasting the symmetrical and asymmetrical views of correlativity. On one symmetrical view, a claim can be understood as an entitlement to a second party's required action or forbearance, while a duty is a normatively required action or forbearance owed to the entitled first party. There is nothing more to A CLAIM than the idea of being entitled to another's duty-bound action or forbearance; you need not, and do not, "do" anything *qua* claim-holder in order to possess a bona fide claim.[29]

On an asymmetrical view, by contrast, in addition to its being an entitlement to another party's action or forbearance, a claim authorizes *claiming* the required action or forbearance from the duty-bearer. However, even if claimability is a necessary feature of A CLAIM, the liability to being claimed, through some means or other, might not be a feature of A DUTY. Instead, that susceptibility is the function of separate liabilities (e.g., to compelled participation in dispute resolution processes). In other words, under this view, the capacity to claim is a feature of A CLAIM, while liabilities to being claimed are exogenous to A DUTY. Hence, claims and duties are asymmetrical in structure.

25 Raz (1986), *supra* note 9, at 168. Exclusionary reasons are nevertheless said to have scope: they only exclude some, but perhaps not all, countervailing considerations. *See* Joseph Raz, Practical Reason and Norms 46–47 (2d ed. 1999).

26 Some Razians might disagree with this interpretation, since Raz claims that rights possess a special force, one that is reflected in the fact that they are sometimes the grounds of duties, which are peremptory reasons for action. *See* Raz (1986), *supra* note 9, at 249. However, Raz himself cannot really believe this about *legal* or *institutional* rights because he thinks there are: trivial ones, ones granted by officials by mistake, rights that are the product of corruption, morally invalid ones, etc. *See* Raz (1986), *supra* note 9, at 170, 186, 261–62; Raz (1996), *supra* note 9, at 45–48, 269–74; David Frydrych, *The Case Against the Theory of Rights*, 40 Oxf. J. Leg. Stud. 320, 332–33 (2020).

27 Albert Kocourek, *The Hohfeld System of Fundamental Legal Concepts*, 15 Ill. L. Rev. 24, 32 (1920) [hereinafter Kocourek (1920)].

28 *See infra* Section 2.3.1.

29 *See, e.g.*, Finnis (1972), *infra* note 85; Williams, *infra* note 86.

Now, some people hold that the liability to being claimed is a feature of A DUTY itself.[30] True or not, if this is coupled with the idea that a Hohfeldian claim itself bears the capacity to make claims, then that is an example of a symmetrical view. It also entails that claims and duties are not conceptually basic: for each position then bears at least two features. Specifically, A CLAIM would be composed of (i) being entitled to another's duty-based action or forbearance and (ii) a (set of) capacity(ies) by which to make claims of right. In turn, A DUTY would include (i) the requirement to undertake a particular action or forbearance and (ii) a (set of) liability(ies) to having the required activity or forbearance claimed of the duty-bearer in some manner.

The consequences of giving preference to one of these two vying views of correlativity are substantial. As will be shown in Section 3: (i) picking either the symmetrical or asymmetrical views, and (ii) deciding whether the conceptions of the normative positions can bear one or more features (i.e., whether they are "fundamental" or not) leads to significantly different interpretations of Hohfeld's *schema* – and, more generally, of A RIGHT and A DUTY.

2.2.2 *Existential Correlativity*

A second scholarly disagreement concerns "existential" correlativity. This is the view that certain normative positions perforce co-obtain.[31] As already seen in terms of duties and liabilities, scholars dispute which basic normative positions must bear correlatives (i.e., which must form parts of a jural relation) and which positions, if any, are capable of being freestanding.

The strongest interpretation of existential correlativity is that rights are always tied to duties *and* vice versa. Few scholars actually adhere to that bi-conditional stance, though. Most, including some contemporary Hohfeldians, happily acknowledge that certain duties do not correlate with rights.[32] This leaves a narrower, or "weaker," view of existential correlativity: that all rights correlate with duties, but not vice versa.[33]

A handful of scholars nevertheless dissent even from that narrower stance. Neil MacCormick, for example, argues that rights are "logically," and sometimes also temporally, prior to duties. For him, rights not only ground duties but can also exist

30 *See, e.g.*, HART (1982), *supra* note 9, at 159–60, 266. *Cf. id.* at 183–84; Nigel Simmonds, *Rights at the Cutting Edge*, *in* A DEBATE OVER RIGHTS: PHILOSOPHICAL ENQUIRIES 223 (Matthew Kramer ed., 1998); JOHN STUART MILL, UTILITARIANISM 71 (London, Parker, Son, and Bourn 1863) ("It is part of the notion of duty in every one of its forms that a person may rightfully be compelled to fulfil it. Duty is a thing which may be exacted from a person, as one exacts a debt. Unless we think it can be exacted from him, we do not call it his duty.").

31 The terms "existential" and "justificational" in reference to rights correlativity (the latter of which is discussed below in Section 2.2.3) are taken from Kramer (1998), *supra* note 11, at 40.

32 John Salmond and Kramer are notable exceptions. By rejecting the idea of absolute duties, Kramer suggests that all troublesome cases, wherein a duty-bearer is discernible but a correlative right-holder is hard to find, can be explained in terms of a *collective* right held by the state or the community. *See* Kramer (1998), *supra* note 11, at 58–59. *Cf.* SALMOND (1902), *supra* note 8, at 224.

33 WELLMAN (1985), *supra* note 21, at 57.

without them.[34] (He nevertheless seems to believe that: (i) a second party must eventually be assigned the role of duty-bearer; and (ii) unenforceable legal rights constitute "imperfect" cases).[35]

Inspired by Raz and Hohfeld, Pavlos Eleftheriadis distinguishes between "rights" and "legal relations." The former are general weighty reasons that figure in practical (including legal) reasoning, while the latter, identified with Hohfeld's eight fundamental normative positions, are what help to protect and effectuate a right.[36] Eleftheriadis does not himself seem to say so, but it could be thought that, *qua* general reasons, rights lack correlatives.[37]

While the case may still be out on "uncorrelated" rights, the bases for subscription to the notion are quite weak. For example, MacCormick's particular efforts to provide examples are unsuccessful. One of his most important is of a Scottish intestate statute affirming a child's right to inherit under it. The child, he holds, has the right even without a correlative duty-bearer to provide what is owed; and there is no such duty-bearer till an executor is appointed.[38] Kramer nevertheless shows that the case in question does in fact include correlative rights.[39] I, in turn, think MacCormick's example fails to establish the lack of a correlative position because the child's right is really *to the status of being an heir* (which entails a claim to a share of the estate, and not to any specific quantum of funds per se – if there is anything in the estate, that is), which includes, amongst other things, an immunity from being divested of that status (to which other parties bear correlative Hohfeldian disabilities).[40]

Raz and Eleftheriadis' bases for deeming general reasons to be rights, rather than *reasons for* rights, are also debatable. It is furthermore difficult to make sense of a Razian right *qua* legal position. For once the weighty reason adopted by legal

34 *See, e.g.*, Neil MacCormick, *Rights in Legislation*, *in* LAW, MORALITY AND SOCIETY: ESSAYS IN HONOUR OF H. L. A. HART 200–1 (P. M. S. Hacker & J. Raz eds., 1977) [hereinafter MacCormick (1977)].

35 NEIL MACCORMICK, INSTITUTIONS OF LAW: AN ESSAY IN LEGAL THEORY 129 (2008). The idea of rights grounding duties does not necessarily entail a given conceptual or "logical" priority between the two concepts thereof. For example, Joseph Raz's view of a right as a sufficient but unnecessary ground for duties entails that, while rights are *justificationally* prior to some duties, conceptually speaking, A DUTY is prior to A RIGHT. *See* RAZ (1986) *supra* note 9, at 170–71, 180–81, 196; RAZ (1996), *supra* note 9, at 33, 35–36. In other words, because in Raz's view a right is a sufficient reason for grounding duties, one must first have the concept A DUTY in order to even understand the concept A RIGHT.

36 ELEFTHERIADIS, *supra* note 8at 1, 123–28, 168. For Raz on rights as reasons, see, e.g., RAZ (1986), *supra* note 9, at 169, 181; RAZ (1996), *supra* note 9, at 46.

37 Raz himself would reject that idea (along with Eleftheriadis' right/relation distinction). "Nothing, however, can legitimize the notion of rights against oneself. The very idea is self-contradictory, for rights are essentially interpersonal. Their existence entails consequences to others." *See* Raz (1996), *supra* note 9, at 33.

38 MacCormick (1977), *supra* note 34, at 200–01.

39 The first being an immediate *in rem* right against interference with the proper distribution of the estate, and a second *in personam* right once an executor is appointed. *See* Kramer (1998), *supra* note 11, at 27–29. *Cf. id.* at 23–24.

40 Almost all Hohfeldians, moreover, reject the notion of uncorrelated rights on conceptual grounds. *See, e.g.*, Kramer (1998), *supra* note 11, at 22, 31.

officials is not, or, is no longer, merely a reason for grounding a duty (per Raz's analytic definition). Following August Thon and Ernst Bierling (who criticize Rudolph von Jhering's conception, which deems a legal right to be a protected interest), Roscoe Pound notes the importance of distinguishing between an interest and something conferred by law which makes that interest effective.[41] That "something" is an entitlement, a normative position – over and above the typical modes of protection (e.g., court enforcement).

2.2.3 *Justificational Correlativity*

A third – implicit – disagreement in the philosophy of rights literature is over "justificational" correlativity. This is the idea that one normative position justifies another's existence. For example, A's right is the reason for, the ground of, *B*'s duty; it is the reason why the duty was imposed upon *B* in the first place. The implied disagreement is this: is justificational correlativity a *conceptually/logically necessary* feature of: any right-duty relationship, all jural relations, and any sound model of rights?

According to Raz, it is – *if* rights are involved, that is (for, again, he thinks there are absolute duties). While Raz deems a right to be a reason that is a sufficient but unnecessary ground for a duty,[42] he seems to deny that justificational correlativity ever obtains without existential correlativity.[43] Thus, my right can be the basis for your duty (and liability, and disability, etc.) even if both normative positions are (and must be) generated at the same time.

Here, then, are the various possible relationships between existential and justificational correlativity. Option A: existential correlativity can obtain without justificational correlativity and vice versa.[44] Option B: no existential correlativity without justificational correlativity. Option C: no justificational correlativity

[41] *See* Pound (1959), *supra* note 1, at 70. Hohfeld agrees: *see FLC 2*, *supra* note 18, at 726 n.34. On Jhering's view of a legal right being composed of a core (the interest) plus a protective shell (*die klage*, entitlement to sue), see 3 RUDOLPH VON JHERING, DER GEIST DES RÖMISCHEN RECHTS AUF DEN VERSCHIDENN STUFEN SEINER ENTWICKLUNG 316–17 (1st ed. 1865); Stepanians (2005), *supra* note 21, at 72 n.38, 144–50.

Joel Feinberg, who otherwise seems to think that a right is an invariably enforceable and invocable claim, nevertheless extends an olive branch to what he calls "manifesto" rights: cases where people invoke morally valid concerns about human needs that nonetheless cannot (yet) suffice to practically ground (legal?) duties in anyone. Feinberg deems this to be acceptable "rhetorical license": people who invoke such matters are not really talking about "rights," but merely saying that there *ought to be* rights. *See* FEINBERG, *supra* note 13, at 153.

[42] RAZ (1986), *supra* note 9, at 166–68.

[43] RAZ (1996), *supra* note 9, at 33–35. Further, the right may later ground new positions in either the existing duty-holder or other parties. *See* RAZ (1986), *supra* note 9, at 171.

[44] MacCormick's view, restated, allows for the possibility of justificational correlativity without existential correlativity: my already-existing right can come to serve as the grounds for imposing a duty on someone at some point.

without existential correlativity. Option D: no existential correlativity without justificational correlativity and vice versa.[45]

To my mind, justificational correlativity is not a necessary feature of normative (e.g., jural) relations. Here is an example to that effect: a vehicle's right-of-way at a traffic intersection. When two roads intersect there are four ways by which a vehicle might approach the intersection. In most technologically and legally advanced countries, such intersections are governed by streetlights or stop signs. This example concerns those instances governed by the latter. The general rule at such intersections is that, if multiple vehicles are approaching the intersection, the one that arrives first has the right-of-way. This means that other vehicles must let the first one to arrive traverse the intersection before they themselves may start to do so (in some legally governed sequence). There is also another common legal rule that, if two cars arrive at this sort of intersection at the same time, the one that approaches from the right side of the other has the right-of-way. Let us concern ourselves with this latter, more specific right-of-way. This rule solves a simple coordination problem. The legal right and duty created by it are temporally and justificatorily equal: one position does not ground the other. While it might be said that the duty-bearers have reason to comply with their duties because of the other parties' rights of way, the reason for their duties' creation or existence is not due to the other drivers' rights. No drivers have personal interests in having such rights. While you may prefer to be able to go first in order to expedite your own journey, your arrival at the intersection from the right (direction) relative to [the] other driver is merely a coincidence. (Nor is it a role-based or kind-based right: what is the role of the "accidentally-arriving-first-at-an-intersection-vehicle-driver"?)[46]

2.3 CORRELATIVITY AND THE SCHEMA OF JURAL RELATIONS

Each one of Hohfeld's *schema of jural relations*' novel features is borne out of, or driven by, his views about CORRELATIVITY. These include: (1) what I shall call the strict bilaterality thesis – the proposition that jural relations only ever obtain between two persons; (2) adding A NO-RIGHT; (3) delimiting A LIABILITY; and (4) calls for replacing the *in rem/in personam* distinction with a paucital/multital

[45] Kramer convincingly argues that existential and justificational correlativity are wholly compatible. *See* Kramer (1998), *supra* note 11, at 38–44.

[46] It is also not the case that this right is grounded in the driver's *personal* interest (itself insufficient to do the grounding) as *buttressed by* the community's interest in the driver having that right. For, again, there is no personal interest in this case that requires or warrants buttressing. On personal interests being buttressed by group or communal interests in order to ground individual rights, see RAZ (1986), *supra* note 9, at 247–49; RAZ (1996), *supra* note 9, at 49–51. Raz's buttressing approach has been deemed fatal to his Interest theory of rights. *See* Gopal Sreenivasan, *A Hybrid Theory of Claim-Rights*, 25 OXFORD J. L. STUD. 257, 265–67 (2005); Leif Wenar, *The Analysis of Rights*, *in* THE LEGACY OF H. L. A. HART: LEGAL, POLITICAL, AND MORAL PHILOSOPHY 255 (Matthew Kramer et al. eds., 2008). On the Interest and Will theories of rights, see David Frydrych, *The Theories of Rights Debate*, 9 JURIS.: INT'L J. L. & POL. THOUGHT 566 (2018).

TABLE 2.1 *Jural correlatives*

Jural correlatives	Right	Liberty	Power	Immunity
	Duty	Liability	Liability	Disability

TABLE 2.2 *Jural absences*

Jural absences	Right	Liberty	Power	Immunity
	Liability	Duty	Disability	Liability

alternative. Additionally, in no small part due to his equivocations and ambiguity regarding CORRELATIVITY (and certain other matters), Hohfeld left us with a contested concept: A CLAIM.[47]

Without recounting the history of the philosophy of rights, it is worthwhile to show why only these features are new with Hohfeld. The *schema* relies heavily upon its predecessors. Here, for example, is John Salmond's model (with which Hohfeld was familiar) and its tables of "correlatives" (see Table 2.1) and "absences" (see Table 2.2).[48]

2.3.1 *Symmetry and Asymmetry in the Schema*

In his first "Fundamental Legal Conceptions" article, Hohfeld states that the basic rights and ligations are incapable of formal definition. Instead, each is to be comprehended via its relationships with its specific correlative and "opposite" (i.e., logical contradictory) positions.[49] Despite this methodological proclamation, he nevertheless proceeds to define the four basic rights:

> A right is one's affirmative claim against another, and a privilege is one's freedom from the right or claim of another. Similarly, a power is one's affirmative "control" over a given legal relation as against another; whereas an immunity is one's

[47] While CORRELATIVITY also drives Hohfeld's deeming a unilateral privilege to form part of a jural relation, some of his predecessors had already established this idea.

[48] SALMOND (1902), *supra* note 8, at 217–38, esp. 236, 238. *Cf.* Roscoe Pound, *Legal Rights*, 26 INT'L J. ETHICS 92 (1915) [hereinafter Pound (1915)]; Frydrych (2017), *supra* note 1, App. Hohfeld cites to the second edition of Salmond's work, wherein Salmond relegates immunities from the body (where it had been in the first edition) to a footnote; JOHN SALMOND, JURISPRUDENCE, OR THE THEORY OF THE LAW 194 n.2 (2d ed. 1907); *FLC* 1, *supra* note 6, at 17. Salmond also cites to his English and German rights modelling predecessors (*see* SALMOND (1907), *supra* note 8, at 197). Hohfeld cites to his English predecessors as foils for their understandings of *in rem* rights, but not for their analyses of the various senses of "a right." *See, e.g.*, *FLC* 2, *supra* note 18, at 728–29, 740–41, 750–51.

[49] *See FLC* 1, *supra* note 6, at 36.

freedom from the legal power or "control" of another as regards some legal relation.[50]

Notice Hohfeld's slippage between symmetrical and asymmetrical views of correlativity here. (These definitions should also be contrasted with his explications of the various correlative and "opposite" relationships.)

Considering A PRIVILEGE, is it: (A) the nonexistence of a duty (not) to φ and a second party's lack of a claim to that effect, or (B) a permission to (not do) φ that outweighs, or trumps, a second party's claim that the privilege-holder must (not) φ? In *FLC* 1, Hohfeld tells us that the privilege of entering some land is the "negation" of a duty to stay off.[51] It is one thing to say that A has a claim but *B* is nonetheless free from it (for some reason or other), and quite another to say that A has no claim whatsoever vis-à-vis *B*. The former (suggested by Hohfeld's definition, quoted above) means that the privilege surmounts the duty; the latter is that there is no duty the privilege-holder requires "freedom from" in the first place.

As another example, Hohfeld also tells us that an immunity is the opposite, or "negation" of, a liability,[52] and that a disability is the equivalent of the negation of a power.[53] On one symmetrical view, a Hohfeldian liability simply means susceptibility to another party's power, and an immunity is not "freedom from" a power: the correlative disability simply marks the absence of any such power. On an asymmetrical view, by contrast, a liability-bearer may have an immunity that is nevertheless surmounted or trumped by the other party's power.

Further, Hohfeld never clarifies what the modifier "affirmative" does vis-à-vis a claim or power in his definitions. For example, can you (performatively) *make a claim* using a Hohfeldian claim,[54] or is the position instead simply an inert one that marks its holder as the recipient of another party's duty-required act or forbearance?[55]

Such conflicts do not only arise from the clash between Hohfeld's definitions and his elucidations of his conceptions elsewhere. The *FLC* articles present other inconsistencies about the intension and implications of CORRELATIVITY – particularly concerning claim-duty jural relations, discussed below. The consequent impact upon the *schema*, and how it can be understood, is therefore considerable.

50 *Id.* at 55.
51 *See FLC* 1, *supra* note 6, at 32.
52 *Id.* at 55.
53 *Id.* at 58 n.99.
54 Elsewhere, Hohfeld explains "affirmative" in contrast to "negative" as being the distinction between an act and a forbearance. *See FLC* 2, *supra* note 18, at 719. However, that cannot be what he means in this context.
55 Here is another example: "In other words, if X has a right against Y that he shall stay off the former's land, the correlative (and equivalent) is that Y is under a duty toward X to stay off the place." *See FLC* 1, *supra* note 6, at 32.

2.3.2 *Strict Bilaterality*

Hohfeld appears committed to the idea that rights and ligations only obtain as parts of jural relations.[56] (I will style this the exclusively jural relations thesis.) He also deems jural relationships to be solely *interpersonal* relations, thus rejecting the possibility of person-object relationships.[57] Both of these propositions had been defended and attacked in the rights literature for nearly a century prior.[58] What appears to be novel with the *schema*, though, is Hohfeld's commitment to what I shall call the strict bilaterality thesis: the idea that all jural relations only ever obtain between two parties, never more.

Strict bilaterality adds a further specification to CORRELATIVITY. It requires that any given right (or ligation) have a determinate normative position tethered to it, wielded by a determinate, or potentially determinable, second party.[59] While Hohfeld never explicitly articulates the thesis in these terms, strict bilaterality is implicit in the *FLC* articles. For example, his arguments that *A*'s contracting with *B* does not affect the (formerly) analogous jural relations of A with parties *C*, *D*, *E*, etc., respectively, relies on such relations being exclusively bilateral in character.[60] Arthur Corbin (correctly, I think) explicates Hohfeld's view thus:

> The term "legal relation" should always be used with reference to two persons, neither more nor less. One does not have a legal relation to himself. Nor does one have a legal relation with two others; he has separate legal relations with each. A so-called legal relation to the State or to a corporation may always be reduced to many legal relations with the individuals composing the State or the corporation, even though for convenient discussion they may be grouped. There can be no such thing as a legal relation between a person and a thing. The relation of A to his house is a physical relation; but A has many legal relations to other persons with respect to his house.[61]

56 *FLC* 2, *supra* note 18, at 722 n.30 could be interpreted as Hohfeld's rejection of absolute duties. He is certainly not unaware of the concept. *Id.* at 744 n.71.

57 *Id.* at 720–33.

58 The idea of a jural relation can be traced back to von Savigny, at least. *See* FRIEDRICH CARL VON SAVIGNY, SYSTEM OF THE MODERN ROMAN LAW 6–7, 269–280 (William Holloway trans., 1867). Pound claims that Savigny got the idea from medieval works. *See* Pound (1959), *supra* note 1, at 65–66.

59 *See FLC* 2, *supra* note 18, at 718, 742–45. *Cf.* Radin (1938), *supra* note 18, at 1155–56; Kramer (1998), *supra* note 11, at 10 n.1.

60 *See FLC* 1, *supra* note 6, at 32–33, 35–36, 52; *FLC* 2, *supra* note 18, at 742, 747.

61 Arthur Corbin, *Legal Analysis and Terminology*, 29 YALE L.J. 163, 165 (1919). *Cf.* Walter Wheeler Cook, *Hohfeld's Contributions to the Science of Law*, 28 YALE L.J. 721, 727 n.12 (1919) ("[S]ince the concept involved is of the legal relation of *one person to another person*. A lead-pencil must have two ends; so must a legal relation."); Pound (1959), *supra* note 1, at 78.

Note that it is possible to retain strict bilaterality without endorsing Hohfeld's call for a reduction of all groups and legal persons to natural persons, i.e., analyzing all jural relations as being between two humans. *See* Wesley N. Hohfeld, *Nature of Stockholders' Individual Liability for Corporation Debts*, 9 COLUM. L. REV. 285, 289, 290–91 n.14 (1909) [hereinafter Hohfeld (1909)]. *See* Kramer (1998), *supra* note 11, at 49–60, *pace* Hohfeld on this point.

Both Hohfeld's detractors and even some of his defenders reject strict bilaterality.[62] Why can a right not correlate with more than one ligation?[63] Why could three or more terms or normative positions not be equivalences? Here are two different ways by which a Hohfeldian might dissent. First, while Kramer is a Hohfeldian who supports the symmetrical view of correlativity, he nevertheless believes that a claim may correlate with multiple token duties (but not tokens of a different type of ligation).[64] Second, Nigel Simmonds supports the asymmetrical view. For him, a claim can, in a sense, correlate with both a duty and a liability.[65]

Interestingly, Kramer provides a strong reason for rejecting his own divergence. He holds that, on Hohfeld's view, correlatives must be specified by reference to the actions or activities they concern.[66] John Finnis styles this as an "axiom" of Hohfeld's: "*Each Hohfeldian relation (e.g. of claim-right: duty, or of privilege: no-right) concerns only one activity of one person.*"[67] A jural relation is therefore to be understood as three-termed: it contains two persons and one action (or forbearance, incompetency to act, etc.). If it is indeed an axiom, and if my claim is to be understood vis-à-vis *your* duty to φ, then how can we say that *B* and *C*'s duties to undertake φ for A refer to the same claim? Something has to give here.

2.3.3 *The Paucital/Multital Distinction*

Again, Hohfeld thinks that: (i) normative positions are always (and only ever) components of a jural relation and (ii) that a jural relation only ever concerns two people.[68] However, if the content of my right is to be understood in part vis-à-vis *your* ligation, then IN REM and IN PERSONAM are fractured. For if one is committed to the exclusively jural relations and strict bilaterality theses, then A's right that *B* stay off Blackacre must be distinct from A's right that C stay off Blackacre.[69]

I have no desire to defend the *multital/paucital* distinction here. Instead, a Hohfeldian *critique* of it may be worth making. Hohfeld defines paucital and

62 The debate over strict bilaterality was not included as one of the core disputes in Section 2 because both that thesis and the bases for rejecting it are themselves dependent upon particular views about CORRELATIVITY.

63 *See, e.g.*, RAZ (1986) and (1996), *supra* note 9 and accompanying text.

64 Kramer (1998), *supra* note 11, at 10 n.2.

65 Simmonds, *supra* note 30, at 222–23 n.137.

66 *See, e.g.*, Kramer (1998), *supra* note 11, at 14.

67 John Finnis, *Some Professorial Fallacies About Rights* (1972) 4 ADELAIDE L. REV. 377, 379 (1972) [hereinafter Finnis (1972)]. The discussion of the active/passive distinction below in Section 2.3.5 nevertheless casts doubt on the soundness of correlative jural relations always concerning "an" action.

68 Right (and ligation) complexes are packages of (one half of) such jural relations.

69 "[I]nstead of there being as single right with a single correlative duty resting on all the persons against whom the right avails, there are many separate and distinct rights, actual and potential, each one of which has a correlative duty resting upon some one person." *See FLC 2, supra* note 18, at 742.

multital rights as being "one of" a few, or a large, class of fundamentally similar but separate rights:

> A paucital right . . . is either a **unique** right residing in a person (or group of persons) and availing against a single person (or single group of persons); or else it is **one** of a *few* fundamentally similar yet separate, rights availing respectively against a few definite persons. [While the word "paucital" is suggested as the generic term to cover all rights *in personam*, the word "**unital**" would be available to denote that particular kind of right *in personam* that is "unique" and "unaccompanied."] A multital right . . . is always **one** of a large *class* of *fundamentally similar* yet separate rights, actual and potential, residing in a *single* person (or single group of persons) but availing *respectively* against persons constituting a very large and indefinite class of people.[70]

He later says:

> It is therefore to be hoped that, instead of continuing to be used to indicate the entire multiplicity of separate and independent rights, or claims, that a person may have against many others, the term right *in rem* may gradually come to be used to represent one, and only one, of this multiplicity of distinct rights.[71]

What, though, is the difference between a *singular* multital right and a singular paucital one? Hohfeld suggests there is none. There are just questions of a right: being a member of a small versus a large class; availing against definite versus indefinite classes of persons; and of (a multital) position being either a potential or actual one.[72]

Hohfeld therefore appears to have erred here by confusing the component with the aggregate. Multitality and paucitality (insofar as the latter concerns more than one basic position, i.e., is not unital) would make more sense if they instead operate at the level of a right *complex*, rather than the individual basic normative position. (That is, at least if one rejects the strict bilaterality thesis, so that A's right complex can correlate with *B*'s, *C*'s, *D*'s, etc., respective ligations). Alternatively, we could construe the *sets* of similar but distinct basic rights to be multital or paucital, rather than the individual basic positions making up the sets. Either way, the qualities of few versus large, definite versus indefinite, are cogent at *those* levels of analysis, not at that of the constituent/singular positions.

Two additional points about the distinction are worth (re-)making. First, this unique feature of the *schema* is logically entailed from Hohfeldian theses and commitments, themselves predicated upon particular understandings of CORRELATIVITY. Second, and as a corollary, most Hohfeldians ignore or reject the multital/paucital distinction out of hand in favor of the traditional *in rem*/*in*

[70] *Id.* at 718 (bold emphasis added). The sentence in square brackets incorporates Hohfeld's remarks on "unital" rights from the corresponding footnote. *Id.* at 718 n.18.

[71] *Id.* at 745.

[72] He states that the actual/potential distinction must be "discussed at a later time." *Id.* at 718 n.19.

personam one (under which, for example, A's right can be said to hold against multiple parties). Being able to do so without impacting upon other Hohfeldian beliefs, including the exclusively jural relations and strict bilaterality theses, is nonetheless questionable.

2.3.4 *A New Correlative*

Despite the absence of a sophisticated methodology or meta-theory justifying it, Hohfeld is committed to the exclusively jural relations thesis: rights and ligations must always be components of jural relations, never alone without correlatives. He follows Salmond (however inconsistently) in suggesting that normative positions are to be comprehended in terms of their respective correlatives and "opposites," i.e., logical contradictories.[73] These commitments, in addition to others a outlined above, are probably what led him to see the need to add more technical terms and concepts than his predecessors.

For example, if one adopts (consciously or otherwise) the symmetrical view of correlativity and additionally commits to the strict bilaterality thesis, then it is dubious to treat a liability as being the correlative of two fundamental kinds of rights (as Salmond had done). It would also be simpler and clearer to have distinct positions correlate with those two rights, rather than have "a liability" denote two different technical senses (over and above that term's regular senses employed by lawyers and others) – especially when the very raison d'être for one's account is to clarify ambiguities in certain terms and concepts. Hence, A NO-RIGHT.

Now, following Joseph Singer, one might think it would be explanatorily inadequate to explicate A PRIVILEGE without considering the ramifications of its usage on other persons – especially if one is inclined toward socioeconomic-political theorization about legal systems.[74] Doubtless, Hohfeld shared some such concerns, as evidenced by his analysis of *Quinn v. Leathem*. *Pace* Singer, though, it is rather unlikely that they have played much of a role for rights modellers generally.[75] The simpler explanation for the genesis of A NO-RIGHT is this: if rights and ligations are to be understood vis-à-vis their correlatives and logical contradictories, and if a duty is the contradictory of a privilege, then (i) a claim ought also to have a contradictory, and (ii) a privilege ought to have a correlative.

Serious criticisms were nevertheless levied against some of Hohfeld's (and Salmond's) novel conceptions and the reasoning that gave rise to them. Soon after *FLC 1* was published, Pound argued that liberties, powers, and immunities do not

73 SALMOND (1902), *supra* note 8, at 236, 238.

74 Joseph Singer, *The Legal Rights Debate from Bentham to Hohfeld*, 1982 WIS. L. REV. 975 (1982).

75 *FLC 1*, *supra* note 6, at 36–37. I have argued elsewhere that, *pace* certain philosophers and historians' assertions to the contrary, Hohfeld was not a legal realist: he has nothing to do with theories about alternative drivers of official decision-making (e.g., "extra-legal" factors, "working" rules, "situation-types", etc.) and nor must his *schema* advance a "realist" political agenda. *See* David Frydrych, *Hohfeld vs. the Legal Realists*, 24 LEGAL THEORY 291 (2018) [hereinafter Frydrych (2018)].

actually bear correlatives, and that no-rights and disabilities are not genuine jural positions.[76] Hohfeld (and Salmond), he claimed, had constructed terms and concepts out of mere absences. You lack a right, therefore you *have* "a no-right." You lack a power; thus, you *have* a disability. Kocourek went further. What need have we for AN IMMUNITY or A DISABILITY when we can just say there was no power? What need have we for A NO-RIGHT when it suffices to simply note the lack of a claim? Furthermore, if you deny that normative positions must be components within, or be understood in terms of, a jural relation, then there is no need to posit correlatives.[77] Hence, the impetus for constructing A NO RIGHT and certain other "fundamental" conceptions disappears. Pound and Kocourek's charge here is not just that these conceptions are redundant, but that they are spurious. If these arguments are sound, they might only serve to show that some of the *schema*'s conceptions are reducible to others, rather than being entirely bogus conceptions. If so, then some of Hohfeld's conceptions are more fundamental than others.[78]

2.3.5 *What Is a Hohfeldian Claim?*

In no small part due to his inconsistency about CORRELATIVITY and how it shapes jural positions, Hohfeld left us with a contested concept of A CLAIM. To this day, Hohfeldians disagree whether it is an inert entitlement to another party's action or forbearance, or if it additionally authorizes its holder to *make* claims of right. Sometimes Hohfeld seems to support a symmetrical view, at other times an asymmetrical one. Compounding the problem, some of the two *FLC* articles' examples of claims are quotations from judges and scholars. Whether Hohfeld actually endorses what each person states or is instead using it as an example of what he considers to be fallacious reasoning, is often debatable.[79]

To better understand this interpretive dispute, it will help to introduce a common heuristic in the philosophy of rights: the active/passive distinction.[80] (This is not the same thing as the difference between symmetrical and asymmetrical views of correlativity.) The distinction carves up the various fundamental types of rights and ligations as being either "active" or "passive." More specifically, it identifies a position as: (1) authorizing or requiring a certain action, or the forbearance from an

76 Pound (1915), *supra* note 48, at 97–100; Pound (1959), *supra* note 1, at 77–81.

77 Kocourek (1920), *supra* note 27, at 26–29, 33–39.

78 Albert Kocourek, *Reply to Paper of Professor Corbin, Terminology and Classification in Fundamental Jural Relations Terminology and Classification in Fundamental Jural Relations – A Symposium*, 4 Am. L. Sch. Rev. 614, 615 (1921) [hereinafter Kocourek (1921)] (the jural relations are reducible to claim-duty and power-liability); Thompson G. Marsh, *The Legal Continuum*, 64 Nw. U. L. Rev. 459, 466 (1969) (the eight positions are reducible to duty and power). These problems also raise the following issue: how can deontic logic account for AN IMMUNITY, A NO-RIGHT, or (a "passive" interpretation, explained below, of) A CLAIM?

79 *See, e.g.*, *infra* note 83 and accompanying text for some of the relevant quotations.

80 Whatever its true provenance, the distinction certainly predates the twentieth century. *See, e.g.*, Salmond (1902), *supra* note 8, at 225, who cites to earlier authors discussing it.

action; (2) the (in)competency to act; or (3) as marking its holder as the person toward whom a different person's action or forbearance is to be directed or to affect.

Bear in mind that "active" and "passive" are misleading labels. Normative positions mark out what each party is entitled to, able to do, required to do, unable to do, etc. An active right, though, is neither an action, nor the physical basis by which, or through which, someone acts. Rights may authorize actions, but the physical acts thereby authorized are events, not normative positions. Take the right to self-defense as an example. The act of kicking an attacker is not itself a right; a right is rather what entitles you to kick the attacker.

Scholars also dispute which basic kinds of normative positions are active or passive. Regarding Hohfeld's *schema*, for example, the majority interpretation is that privileges and powers are active, while claims and immunities are passive.[81] The minority holds that claims and/or immunities are, or can also be, active.[82] (All would probably agree, though, that a duty-to-act is the only active kind of ligation.)

Hohfeldians particularly disagree about claims. On the active interpretation, a claim not only entitles its holder to another party's duty-based action or forbearance, it also enables the holder to *make* a claim of right – where "claiming" usually means being able to initiate legal proceedings.[83] Those who interpret a claim thus

81 *See, e.g.*, Kocourek (1920), *supra* note 27, at 25; Glanville Williams, *The Concept of Legal Liberty*, 56 COLUM. L. REV. 1129 (1956); WELLMAN (1985), *supra* note 21, at 70–71 (but *cf. id.* at 39); Andrew Halpin, *More Comments on Rights and Claims*, 10 L. & PHIL. 271, 293 (1991) (two senses of "a claim": as an assertion and as a justified restraint); Kramer (1998), *supra* note 11, at 13–14, 22 n.8; Vivienne Brown, *Rights, Liberties, and Duties: Reformulating Hohfeld's Scheme of Jural Relations?*, 58 CURRENT L. PROBS. 343 (2005); GEORGE RAINBOLT, THE CONCEPT OF RIGHTS 32–33 (2006).

82 *See, e.g.*, Simmonds, *supra* note 30, at 223, 223 n.137; ELEFTHERIADIS, *supra* note 8. The American legal realists interpreted Hohfeldian claims as not only active, but also as being invariably enforceable. *See* Frydrych (2018), *supra* note 75, at 315–22.

83 The most conspicuous active view examples in Hohfeld's works are probably the quotes from Justices Jackson and Sneed in *FLC 1*, *supra* note 6, at 30–31 ("a legal claim to do"; "whatever may be lawfully claimed"), from Justice Stayton in *FLC 2*, *supra* note 18, at 717 n.16 (an "enforceable claim"), and from the book edition edited by Cook: ["Compare the following passage from Holmes, *The Common Law*, 214: 'A legal right is nothing but a permission to exercise certain natural powers, and upon certain conditions to obtain protection, restitution, or compensation by the aid of the public force.'"] *See* WESLEY N. HOHFELD, FUNDAMENTAL LEGAL CONCEPTIONS AS APPLIED IN JUDICIAL REASONING AND OTHER ESSAYS 42 n.39 (Walter W. Cook ed., 1919) (square brackets in the original book version) [hereinafter HOHFELD (1919)].

At least some of the relevant quotes and text, such as the one just provided, are not found in Hohfeld's essays as originally published. They made their way into the posthumously published book versions. Whether they are all really Hohfeld's own amendments (ones based upon recommendations for changes derived from his notes: he was planning to publish the essays in a book), or instead unscrupulous insertions by his editor, Walter Wheeler Cook, may be impossible to discover. The 1919 book's first *FLC* chapter notes that it is reprinted with permission from the *Yale Law Journal* and "with manuscript changes by the author." (HOHFELD (1919) at 23.) The 1923 version includes a preface noting that all of the changes and additions to the text, aside from some purely typographical ones, are indicated in Hohfeld's manuscript notes. This new material, the preface states, is noted in the text either by being enclosed in square brackets or, in the case of a new footnote, indicated by the letter "a," e.g., "32a." *See* WESLEY N. HOHFELD, *Preface*, *in* FUNDAMENTAL LEGAL CONCEPTIONS AS APPLIED IN

sometimes deem it to be a species of power.[84] On the passive interpretation, by contrast, a claim simply marks a party as the intended recipient of a duty-required action or forbearance. Hohfeldian claims do not entitle or authorize their holders to act. You, therefore, cannot make claims using a claim. Finnis' and Glanville Williams' understandings reflect the passive view:

> *A Hohfeldian claim-right can never be to do or omit something: it always is a claim that somebody else do or omit something*: A's claim-right is always to B's action or omission, never to A's.[85]
>
> No one ever has a [claim-] right to do something; he only has a right that some one else shall do (or refrain from doing) something. In other words, every right in the strict sense relates to the conduct of another, while a liberty and a power relate to the conduct of the holder of the liberty or power.[86]

It may be tempting to interpret these scholars as suggesting here that, while the content of a claim is the duty-based action, the claim nevertheless authorizes the making of a claim of right. For example, *B* owes *A* ten dollars. While *B* must transfer the funds, *A* may also claim the money from *B*. On the passive view, this suggestion is erroneous. Claiming a right is a normatively governed act. Yet, a Hohfeldian claim, interpreted as a passive position, concerns a second party's conduct: the duty-bearer's requirement to act or forbear from action (here, to transfer the ten dollars).

The dispute between the active and passive interpretations is not merely terminological. The use of the term "a claim" for a (kind of a) right, and its active interpretation, has roots in the nineteenth-century German jurisprudential concept *ANSPRUCH*, which was often taken to mean both an entitlement to another's

JUDICIAL REASONING AND OTHER ESSAYS (Walter W. Cook ed., 1923). However, there may be reason to doubt that all of the square bracketed material originates with Hohfeld rather than Cook. Unfortunately, the preface's caveat and/or the letters marking new footnotes and the square brackets were dropped in some of the later editions. *See, e.g.*, WESLEY N. HOHFELD, FUNDAMENTAL LEGAL CONCEPTIONS AS APPLIED IN JUDICIAL REASONING AND OTHER ESSAYS (Walter W. Cook ed., 1964); WESLEY N. HOHFELD, FUNDAMENTAL LEGAL CONCEPTIONS AS APPLIED IN JUDICIAL REASONING (David Campbell & Philip Thomas eds., 2001). Ted Sichelman suggested to me that the book manuscript was just an annotated copy of the 1913 paper, which is mentioned in a letter sent by Cook and Dean Swan to Edward Hohfeld, Wesley's brother. However, square bracket additions are also to be found in the second *FLC* chapter, *e.g.*, HOHFELD (1919) at 73 n.22a. These additions influenced certain scholars' "active" interpretations of a claim and their endorsement of the Will theory of rights. *See, e.g.*, WELLMAN (1985), *supra* note 21, at 35, 39; Hillel Steiner, *Working Rights*, *in* A DEBATE OVER RIGHTS: PHILOSOPHICAL ENQUIRIES 244 n.19 (Matthew Kramer ed., 1998).

84 *See, e.g.*, Simmonds, *supra* note 30, at 223.

85 *See* Finnis (1972), *supra* note 67, at 380. Finnis also states that "[a] claim-right is always either, positively, a right to be given something (or assisted in a certain way) by someone else, or, negatively, a right *not* to be interfered with or dealt with or treated in a certain way, by someone else. When the subject matter of one's claim of right is one's own act(s), forbearance(s), or omission(s), that claim cannot be to a claim-right, but can only be to a liberty or, in the case of juridical acts, to a power." *See* JOHN FINNIS, NATURAL LAW AND NATURAL RIGHTS 200 (2d ed. 2011).

86 Williams, *supra* note 81, at 1145.

duty and the capacity to claim, if not still older ideas.[87] However, the dispute about whether A RIGHT is necessarily self-enforceable, and hence an active normative position, dates back – at least – to the middle ages.[88]

As noted in Section 2.2.1, were the ability to claim a feature of a *Hohfeldian* claim, then the latter would not be conceptually basic – a meta-theoretical desideratum Hohfeld believes his conceptions ought to meet.[89] That, I think, is the best reason to endorse the passive interpretation over the active one. Adding the capacity to claim as a feature of A CLAIM renders the concept subject to decomposition into more basic components. On the active interpretation, it is: (i) an entitlement to someone else's act or forbearance and (ii) a normative capacity or permission, or set of them, to act oneself, i.e., to performatively claim. Furthermore, the capacity to claim is better explained in terms of other normative positions, i.e., privileges, powers, and complexes thereof.

The same holds for AN IMMUNITY. It is better understood as marking a disability-bearer's powerlessness (incompetence) to alter certain of the immunity-holder's other normative positions. On the passive interpretation, in other words, you do not "exercise" an immunity either. Again, on the active interpretation, an immunity is a trump over another's power that is somehow utilized by its holder. However, the capacity (and permission) to utilize the position would not only make AN IMMUNITY conceptually complex, but also any such "utilization" would be better explained in terms of other positions (i.e., a power, privilege, etc.).[90]

Notice, however, that the same argument cannot be used to champion a *symmetrical* view of AN IMMUNITY over an *asymmetrical* rival; for it need not be the case that, on the latter interpretation, one must utilize or exercise the immunity in order for it to trump another party's power. In other words, on an

87 *See, e.g.*, ALOIS VON BRINZ, LEHRBUCH DER PANDEKTEN 49–50, 52 (1st ed. 1857); BIERLING, *supra* note 7, at 39–40; AUGUST THON, RECHTSNORM UND SUBJEKTIVES RECHT: UNTERSUCHUNGEN ZUR ALLGEMEINEN RECHTSLEHRE chs 5–7 (Weimar, H. Böhlau 1878). See Pound (1915), *supra* note 48, at 105–11 and Pound (1959), *supra* note 1, at 62–6, 69–70 on the views of rights of nineteenth-century German legal scholars such as Alois Brinz, Bernhard Windscheid, August Thon, and Ernst Bierling. *Cf.* HART (1982), *supra* note 9, at 159–60, 183–84, 188, 194, 266.

88 *See, e.g.*, BRIAN TIERNEY, THE IDEA OF NATURAL RIGHTS: STUDIES ON NATURAL RIGHTS, NATURAL LAW AND CHURCH LAW 1150–1625 36, 55–68, 117–18, 189 (1997).

89 *See, e.g.*, *FLC* 1, *supra* note 6, at 30.

90 While it is valuable for flagging the fact that normatively authorized, entitled, or required actions are features of many if not all rights and ligations, the active/passive distinction cannot accurately or fully account for what normative positions do and require. Indeed, passive understandings of immunity/disability relations and claim/duty-to-forbear relations mark the breakdown of the distinction's soundness and utility. For where is the relevant "action"? Further, how are we to understand duties of the following sort: the duty to obey a commander's orders? (This, rather than the duty to obey a commander's particular order, e.g., to go over the trench). Is a duty to adhere to a state of affairs (e.g., an authoritative command structure), or to adhere to future orders, really best described as a normative requirement to act or forbear? Third, powers affect *both* the power-holder and liability-bearer's positions concurrently. A's gift-giving to *B* changes both parties' statuses vis-à-vis the chattel. Is the power-holder's position *both* active and passive, then? Does the power correlate with liabilities in both a second party and the power-holder?

asymmetrical view, AN IMMUNITY could trump another's power without the immunity-holder having to act to make it do so. Thus, the position need not be conceptually complex.

2.3.5.1 Imperatival and Sanction Theories of Law

That is not the end of the story in terms of determining how best to understand A CLAIM. Further textual evidence about Hohfeld's views about rights and law more generally must also be addressed. Particularly germane are his stances regarding Imperatival and Sanction theories of law, rights, and duties.[91] *Imperatival* theories hold that all laws are, or are predicated upon, commands issued by officials; essentially, all laws take the form "thou shall (not)" and constrain a subject's behavior and actions.[92] *Sanction* theories posit that all (unexcused) breaches of legal duties will be met with system-imposed liabilities (e.g., court-ordered remedies) or punishments.[93] (A Sanction theory need not also be an Imperatival one: it does not require that all laws take the form of commands.) Over time, Sanction theories have expanded the relevant sort of "liabilities" to include mere susceptibility to litigation and comparable legal processes.[94] These – often complementary – theories were dominant in English analytic jurisprudence from John Austin's time till H. L. A. Hart.

Sanction theories present at least three ways by which to understand A RIGHT and A DUTY. Option A: some versions analytically reduce A CLAIM to A POWER, because they treat claims as powers by which to enforce duty compliance or to pursue remedies for breaches. A DUTY, in turn, is reduced to A LIABILITY: susceptibility to such enforcement efforts. Adherents therefore tend to identify legal rights with secondary or tertiary ones.[95] Option B: other versions present

91 The following subsection builds on Frydrych (2018), *supra* note 75, at 298–99, 307–8.

92 *See, e.g.*, Kocourek (1920), *supra* note 27, at 35 n.28 ("The real difficulty lies in the failure to understand the nature of a jural relation. A jural relation involves the idea of constraint; so, also, does a legal rule"). *Cf.* Kocourek (1921), *supra* note 78, at 615 ("Do legal rules always constrain? My answer is that the concept of constraint is involved in every rule whether legal or not").

93 *See* Anthony Woozley, *Legal Duties, Offences, and Sanctions*, 77 Mind 461 (1968); P. M. S. Hacker, *Sanction Theories of Duty*, *in* Oxford Essays in Jurisprudence, Second Series (A. W. B. Simpson ed., 1973).

94 *See, e.g.*, Albert Kocourek, Jural Relations 345 (2d ed. 1928). *Cf.* Joseph Raz, *Hart on Moral Rights and Legal Duties*, 4 Oxford J. Legal Stud. 123, 131 (1984) on H. L. A. Hart's supposed "Kelsenian twist"; Thomas Grey, *Holmes and Legal Pragmatism*, 41 Stanford L. Rev. 787, 830–31 (1989).

95 The primary/secondary/tertiary rights distinction is commonplace in jurisprudence. *Primary* rights are substantive entitlements, e.g., to engage in free speech, to purchase some land, etc. *Secondary* rights do several things. Some authorize their holders to initiate dispute resolution proceedings (litigation, arbitration, mediation, etc.) when primary rights seem to have been, or are threatened to be, violated. They also authorize right-holders to waive such processes. Other secondary rights are those afforded and used within official proceedings, e.g., to file certain motions. Still others are employed outside of institutional settings, e.g., entitlements to undertake self-help remedies. *Tertiary* rights are (i) the "remedial" entitlements provided in official dispute resolution mechanisms such as courts and, some argue, (ii) the means by which to enforce or waive those too. *Cf.* Hart (1982), *supra* note 9, at 183–86.

enforcement capacities and correlative liabilities as being necessary, but nonexclusive, features of A CLAIM and A DUTY, respectively. Option C: *primary* rights and duties are only rendered real via an official's say-so in a decision or decree.

Sanction theories stand in contrast to understanding A RIGHT as a passive entitlement to another's required action or forbearance and A DUTY as being a normative requirement (which is meant to guide its bearer's reasoning) to so act or forbear from so acting. On such nonsanction theory accounts of duties, moreover, enforcement capacities and liabilities to them must be analyzed in terms of distinct concepts, i.e., as "secondary" and "tertiary" rights and duties. Whether the relationship between primary, secondary, and tertiary rights is merely a contingent one, conceptually speaking, is heavily debated.

Sanction theories are said to go awry by ignoring the distinct role of legal duties as requirements to act or forbear. For they reduce A DUTY to either A LIABILITY to a sanction, remedy, etc., issued by authorities, or at least to the legal proceedings that might give rise to them. They also tend to reduce or replace the normative sense of duty (a belief in the requirement to comply) with motivations to conform out of fear of punishment or other undesirable repercussions.[96]

Long before H. L. A. Hart's masterful criticisms of them in *The Concept of Law*, but not prior to Salmond and several other dissident English analytic jurists having done so too, Hohfeld also rejected *Imperatival* theories of law. Like Salmond, Hohfeld held that privileges and powers are genuine features of legal systems despite not necessarily being (tethered to) commands. Further, the negative

Hohfeld also styles "primary," "secondary," and "tertiary" positions as "antecedent," "remedial," and "adjective" jural relations respectively. *See* Wesley N. Hohfeld, *The Relations Between Equity and Law*, 11 MICH. L. REV. 537, 553–58, esp. 569 n.32 (1913) [hereinafter Hohfeld, *Equity*]. *Cf. FLC 1*, *supra* note 6, at 40 n.52; *FLC 2*, *supra* note 18, at 712. However, some may object to this rendering of matters because his "adjective" category covers the initiation of legal proceedings, actions parties can undertake therein, and matters that obtain after a court judgment is rendered. I suggest that the last case ought to fall under a separate category of (what should be called) "quaternary rights": legal norms by which to enforce tertiary positions, e.g., judgment creditors' rights to secure liens in furtherance of court orders. But see also *FLC 2*, *supra* note 18, at 714 on a distinction between "primary" and "secondary" stages of judicial proceedings (which Hohfeld nevertheless deems to be somewhat flawed). Hohfeld also denies that there is an "intrinsic" difference between substantive and adjective jural relations. *See FLC 1*, *supra* note 6, at 40 n.52; Hohfeld, *Equity* at 569 n.32. I have also argued elsewhere that the label "remedial" is inapt for all secondary rights because their holders may not actually gain a remedy, need not necessarily win a lawsuit, etc. DAVID FRYDRYCH, THE ARCHITECTURE OF RIGHTS: MODELS AND THEORIES 100 (2021).

Hohfeld's analyses of secondary and tertiary rights' structures are also inconsistent across his works. Most importantly for our purposes is when he identifies a claim as being but one of the components therein (*FLC 1*, *supra* note 6, at 35 n.39) and when he instead identifies them exclusively with a claim (*FLC 2*, *supra* note 18, at 753, 760). The latter may be another example of a textual basis for an active interpretation of A CLAIM. *Cf.* Hohfeld (1909), *supra* note 61, at 293–94; Wesley N. Hohfeld, *Review of Charles Huston's* The Enforcement of Decrees in Equity, 25 YALE L.J. 166, 170 (1915) [hereinafter Hohfeld (1915)]. His *Equity* article also suggests that there can be secondary and tertiary claims, privileges, and powers. *See* Hohfeld, *Equity* at 550, 554, 556.

96 *See* H. L. A. HART, THE CONCEPT OF LAW chs 2–4 (2d ed. 1994).

character of no-rights, disabilities, liabilities, and immunities, he thinks, does not disqualify them from constituting bona fide jural positions:

> It is difficult to see, however, why, as between X and Y, the "privilege + no-right" situation is not just as real a jural relation as the precisely opposite "duty + right" relation between any two parties. Perhaps the habit of recognizing exclusively the latter as a jural relation springs more or less from the traditional tendency to think of the law as consisting of "commands," or imperative rules. This, however, seems fallacious. A rule of law that *permits* is just as real as a rule of law that *forbids*; and, similarly, saying that the law *permits* a given act to X as between himself and Y predicates just as genuine a legal relation as saying that the law *forbids* a certain act to X as between himself and Y. That this is so seems, in some measure, to be confirmed by the fact that the first sort of act would ordinarily be pronounced "lawful," and the second "unlawful."[97]

The last sentence leads us to the explanatory and normative significance of Hohfeld's conceptions. Against the charge that mere absences fail to constitute bona fide legal positions (per Pound and Kocourek), Hohfeld and his defenders noted that if *B* sues A, mistakenly thinking that A owed him a duty under a contract, the court *vindicates* A's privilege (i.e., entitlement not to have so acted); Hohfeld and some of his defenders actually went further and said that A's privilege is *a ground* for assigning *B* costs for the vexatious litigation.[98] (One can imagine this sort of thing transpiring in the moral realm as well.) As another example, if the US Congress passes a law *ultra vires* its constitutional competency (i.e., it is constitutionally disabled from passing a certain law but goes through the motions anyway), then that is a basis for chastising it, for seeking a legal remedy, and for the courts or other bodies to grant one and/or to strike down the law.

Hohfeld's stance on Sanction theories is more complicated. While he fails to provide analyses of A CLAIM and A DUTY,[99] most of the time he appears to endorse the juridical reality of primary rights and duties.[100] He also provides examples of primary rights' violations giving rise to "new" jural positions: secondary claims or powers and correlative secondary duties and liabilities which, in turn, may give rise to tertiary rights and power, etc.[101]

97 *FLC 1*, *supra* note 6, at 42 n.59.

98 Hohfeld, *Equity*, *supra* note 95, at 553; George Goble, *Affirmative and Negative Legal Relations* 4 Ill. L.Q. 94, 105 (1921–22). (Goble, nonetheless, mistakenly believes that a court's imposing costs demonstrates that this sort of jural relation contains an element of constraint after all.)

99 The analysis *should have been* at *FLC 1*, *supra* note 6, at 30–32. Compare these pages to the analyses provided for the other three kinds of jural relations.

100 *See, e.g.*, Hohfeld, *Equity*, *supra* note 95, at 553, 555.

101 *See, e.g.*, Hohfeld (1909), *supra* note 61, at 293–94; Hohfeld, *Equity*, *supra* note 96, at 553–57; Hohfeld (1915), *supra* note 95, at 170; *FLC 2*, *supra* note 18, at 752, 760. One might also interpret Hohfeld's remarks about "jural realism" regarding legal and equitable rules as endorsing a sort of *metaphysical* realism about law. *See FLC 2*, *supra* note 18, at 768.

However, buried in the thirteenth page of the supplemental notes to an article on the relationship between the Common Law and Equity, Hohfeld posits that the existence of primary and secondary normative positions can only be ascertained through court proceedings:

> As regards both law and equity, all primary, or antecedent, relations and all secondary, or remedial, relations can, in general, be ascertained only by inference from the purely adjective juridical processes, that is, by inference from either affirmative or negative action regularly to be had from the particular courts from which a judgment or decree may be sought. As said by Maitland, in relation, more particularly, to the early law: "*De Natura Brevium*, Of the Nature of Writs, – such is the title of more than one well known text-book of our mediaeval law. Legal Remedies, Legal Procedure, these are the all-important topics for the student. These being mastered, a knowledge of substantive law will come of itself. Not the nature of rights, but the nature of writs must be his theme."[102]

Although this may be an obtuse reading, technically Hohfeld is not necessarily saying that primary and secondary rights can only be determined *post hoc* via a court's decree or decision; this, as he seems to allow for their discernibility simply by virtue of juridical processes (regularly) having been initiated. If so, then he does not necessarily believe that you only have a real legal right if you can (have) *successfully* enforce(d) it. Regardless, this should be deemed a dubious metric, as people can commence and prosecute legal actions on spurious grounds.

Even so, the quote above on the grounds for ascertaining the reality of primary jural positions has implications for: (1) whether or not A PRIMARY CLAIM necessarily includes enforcement powers and A PRIMARY DUTY includes liabilities to being subjected to institutional dispute resolution processes; (2) whether only tertiary/adjective rights are real (making the active interpretation of A CLAIM the superior/only option); and (3) whether Hohfeld's account constitutes a Sanction theory. As the passage quoted above is out of step with the rest of Hohfeld's corpus, and because most of his work is unoriginal anyway, I am inclined to think it can be discounted, but not ignored.

2.4 ASSESSMENTS AND COMPARATIVE EVALUATIONS

One might want to challenge the idea that Hohfeld (and his predecessors) provided neutral, objective, and uncontested/incontestable conceptions and forms of analysis. For example, he famously criticizes *Quinn v. Leathem*, stating that the decision erroneously treats – what he calls – a privilege as a correlative of a duty.[103] Privileges, he insists, only correlate with no-rights. Hence, the House of Lords got it wrong.

102 Hohfeld, *Equity*, *supra* note 95, at 569 n.34, quoting Frederic Maitland, *The History of the Register of Original Writs*, 3 Harv. L. Rev. 97 (1889).

103 FLC 1, *supra* note 6, at 36–37, discussing *Quinn* v. *Leathem* (1901) AC 495 (UKHL).

Critics, however, are free to reject his analysis. On certain asymmetrical views of correlativity, for example, there is nothing problematic about a privilege correlating with a duty.[104] Was *Quinn* wrongly decided simply because it does not track Hohfeld's preferred conceptualizations? Why does the case not instead count as a counterexample to Hohfeld's reckoning?

This raises a larger concern about how to compare and evaluate (i) competing views of CORRELATIVITY and (ii) rival conceptions of rights and ligations. Hohfeld's *schema* is an analytical work, i.e., it is a rational reconstruction of concepts used by lawyers, judges, if not also ordinary people. It is thus a corrective to "everyday" linguistic practices.[105] However, not only are the *schema*'s construction methods heavily disputed, so are its work products: its components (i.e., A CLAIM, A NO-RIGHT, etc.) are *themselves* contested conceptions. In fact, they are doubly contested; for not only do there exist various conceptions of A RIGHT, A POWER, etc., in the marketplace of the philosophy of rights (Hohfeld's, H. L. A. Hart's, Joseph Raz's, etc., in addition to lawyers, judges, and others' commonplace conceptions),[106] but Hohfeldians also have interpretive disputes about Hohfeld's own conceptions.

Further, while some scholars believe that an Hohfeldian analysis can help to expose "normative" (in the sense of being morally and politically evaluative) and other sorts of commitments and assumptions embedded in legal concepts, rules, and definitions – especially of a certain politics or ideology that the analyst disfavors[107] – they fail (or choose not) to see that this is true of Hohfeld's very conceptions too. Using the *schema* to "expose" crypto-normative assumptions and beliefs in legal rules, principles, and decisions may itself simply be a function of using a partisan tool, or at least of employing the tool in a partisan (and perhaps disingenuous) way. Less nefariously, such analyses may all simply beg the question by using "loaded" (rationally reconstructed) conceptions.[108]

104 Leaving aside the question of how it is that a jurist is meant to definitively determine whether that was the only normative position the plaintiff in *Quinn* actually possessed.

105 *See* Kramer (1998), *supra* note 11, at 22–23. However, one may dispute Kramer's claim that the *schema* is not subject to empirical refutation.

106 For example, correctly or otherwise, some scholars dispute Hohfeld's A PRIVILEGE on analytic grounds: can there really be a unilateral privilege, or must it instead be bilateral, i.e., must the position contain both a permission to do φ *and* a permission not to do φ? Can there be a genuine privilege without the protection of a claim, or not? Must a genuine privilege be an express permission, or can it also be the mere lack of a duty? *See, e.g.*, R. E. Robinson et al., *The Logic of Rights*, 33 U. Toronto L.J. 267, 269 (1983); Hart (1982), *supra* note 9, at 172. *Cf. FLC 1*, *supra* note 6, at 32–33, 42 n.59.

107 *See, e.g.*, Walter Wheeler Cook, *Privileges of Labor Unions in the Struggle for Life*, 27 Yale L.J. 779 (1918); Walter Wheeler Cook, *Comment – The Associated Press Case*, 28 Yale L.J. 387 (1919).

108 For further discussion of this point, see Frydrych (2018), *supra* note 75, at 322–26, 337–43.

2.5 CONCLUSION

This chapter raised three related issues concerning rights correlativity. Some of these are, in turn, the bases for all of the novel elements in Hohfeld's *schema of jural relations*. However, Hohfeld does not explicitly explore any of them. Furthermore, the issues surrounding them have either been insufficiently addressed or gone wholly unnoticed by those interested in providing rigor to our understanding of rights and related normative positions. This chapter therefore provides a starting point for those interested in exploring some of the fundamental ideas upon which Hohfeld's *schema* and other philosophical accounts of rights turn. This is nonetheless an area where more research is required.

3

Hohfeld and Rules

Andrew Halpin[*]

3.1 AN UNFINISHED STORY

To some extent, the story of the reception of Hohfeld's analytical scheme[1] over the past hundred years has been a story of conflict between the ardent supporters of Hohfeld's work and its harsh critics. To the former, the genius of Hohfeld was to provide (or gather together[2]) seminal insights regarding the operation of law, which

* Professor of Law and Director of the Centre for Legal Theory, Faculty of Law, National University of Singapore. I gratefully acknowledge the financial assistance of the National University of Singapore research fund (R-241–000–107–133) in supporting the research for this chapter. I have benefited greatly from the discussion of an earlier draft of this chapter at the Yale Hohfeld Centennial Conference in October 2016, particularly the comments of Jack Schlegel and Ben Zipursky; prior to the conference, from Ted Sichelman's generous provision of access to the archival material; and from subsequent helpful discussion with Henry Smith. Related work on Hohfeld (referred to in note 6 *infra*) from which the present chapter draws has benefited from discussions with a number of colleagues at NUS Law, notably James Penner, Mark McBride, and David Frydrych. More widely still, I have benefited from discussions over the years with William Twining on Hohfeld and Realism, and with Peter Sparkes on property in the law.

1 Wesley N. Hohfeld, *Some Fundamental Legal Conceptions as Applied in Judicial Reasoning*, 23 YALE L.J. 16 (1913). This article was sufficient to establish Hohfeld's analytical scheme regarding his arrangement of fundamental legal conceptions (or legal relations – to introduce a preference we shall adopt). His subsequent article, expanding on certain points introduced in the first, Wesley N. Hohfeld, *Fundamental Legal Conceptions as Applied in Judicial Reasoning*, 26 YALE L.J. 710 (1917), was then republished with the first in book form after Hohfeld's death. *See* WESLEY N. HOHFELD, FUNDAMENTAL LEGAL CONCEPTIONS AS APPLIED IN JUDICIAL REASONING (Walter Wheeler Cook ed., 1919). Page references throughout this chapter are to the book version of Hohfeld's work [hereinafter FLC].

2 The precise degree of originality of Hohfeld's analytical scheme is open to discussion. Similarities can be found with earlier efforts by Terry and Salmond. What is undoubtedly the case is that Hohfeld's systematic exposition and illustrated applications of the scheme gave it a far wider prominence than the analytical schemes attempted by his predecessors. *See* Walter Wheeler Cook, *Hohfeld's Contributions to the Science of Law*, 28 YALE L.J. 721, 728–29 (1919). Interestingly, Arthur Corbin, in his 1957 letter providing an account of Hohfeld to the then Dean of Yale, Eugene Rostow (Thomas Swan Papers, Yale University Library at p. 9), in emphasizing the originality of Hohfeld's analysis states that he "know[s] of no connection between Salmond and Hoh." Corbin makes this statement despite being aware of Hohfeld's personal copy of Salmond's *Jurisprudence*, which was left to the Yale Law Library.

are fundamental to any clear understanding of law. To his detractors, Hohfeld's analytical scheme, at best, imposes a distorted understanding on our appreciation of law's operations by falsely exaggerating the value of his terminological distinctions, displayed in the form of fundamental conceptions linked together within legal relations, as capable of producing an exhaustive understanding of law. At worst, Hohfeld's attempt to provide terminological and conceptual clarity is denigrated as creating obscurity and confusion.

The story cannot, however, be related as a simple narrative of opposing viewpoints regarding the value of Hohfeld's work. Had that been the case, we might reasonably have expected an ending of sorts. Initial confusion caused by the complexity of his analysis might have given way to widespread appreciation of its merits (as reportedly occurred in the case of some of his first Yale students). Or the failure of his analysis to command general respect might have reduced its study to an idiosyncratic pastime of a dwindling number of scholars. The existence of a contemporary engagement with Hohfeld that remains both vibrant and disputatious suggests the lack of an ending to this story[3] and calls for some explanation.

I suggest two factors can assist by way of explanation. The first may be regarded as common to a number of works with an enduring significance, which are nevertheless accompanied by controversy and have a tendency to promote unresolved debate. The key characteristic of such works lies in their ability to provoke beyond a grasp of their own tenets and ideas a wider discussion of central issues within the subject matter that they attempt to illuminate. Take an author you regard as influential on the discipline you study and the chances are that the value of that author's work lies less in providing an accessible and definitive statement of the author's own ideas but that the process of your attempting to work out those ideas brings with it a richer sense of the subject that the ideas themselves may fail to fully capture.

If this phenomenon is recognized, then a peculiar talent needs to be attributed to the authors of these works. The talent is found in opening up a perspective upon a subject that has been previously overlooked but which becomes crucial to any full understanding of the subject. It is manifested in the opening up of new and fruitful lines of inquiry rather than simply contributing to existing disputes. The presence of this talent is, accordingly, perfectly compatible with protracted controversy, even with exciting fresh controversies. I shall indicate below why I think that Hohfeld qualifies for the accolade of possessing this talent, but in Hohfeld's case, there is another explanatory factor for the lengthy and unresolved controversy over his work.

The second factor is readily apparent, irrespective of how the first factor I suggested is taken, although I shall point out the potential for some interaction between the two. This other factor, while not unique to Hohfeld, marks his work

[3] One indicator of Hohfeld's enduring significance is that in a recent collection of essays on rights, RIGHTS: CONCEPTS AND CONTEXTS (Brian Bix and Horacio Spector eds., 2012), discussion of Hohfeld features in 14 of the 25 essays, in quite disparate ways.

with a particular poignancy. His untimely death left his work in an unfinished state, its readers bereft of a mature development of its ideas from their author.[4] Consequently, there was greater opportunity for diverse understandings of Hohfeld to emerge and controversy to ensue, in the absence of a completed body of authoritative source material.

Obviously, a merely unfinished work is not capable of stimulating the depth and volume of interest that Hohfeld's work has received; additionally, its unfinished state must have already attained some remarkable level of achievement. In part, this attainment could be equated with the skill demonstrated by Hohfeld in his extant work of opening up one or more perspectives that are crucial to the understanding of law (in the manner I have just referred to), but there is a more specific connection between the achievement present in Hohfeld's extant analytical scheme and the incomplete state of his work, which, I will argue, can account for the unfinished story of its reception together with the dynamic controversy that it continues to attract.

3.2 THE ARGUMENT OF THE PRESENT ESSAY

What is undeniably present, even in the first of Hohfeld's two *Yale Law Journal* articles is a fully worked out scheme of legal conceptions arranged in both correlative and opposing relations. It is this analytical framework that represents a major achievement,[5] notwithstanding that the fuller analytical scheme that Hohfeld proposed to construct around this framework remained uncompleted. In other recent work, I have argued that there is evidence to show that Hohfeld anticipated providing within his completed scheme of analysis as significant a role for an aggregate level of analysis as that already delivered within his extant work for a legal relations level of analysis. The currency of legal relations as expressing the basic correlative settings for Hohfeld's fundamental legal conceptions is naturally associated with Hohfeld's acclaimed analytical framework, but has wrongly been used to represent the limits of Hohfeld's analytical scheme – so I argue in that project.[6]

I further argue there that the neglect of the aggregate level analysis, in Hohfeld's extant work and in its subsequent reception, has encouraged misrepresentations of Hohfeld (notably as supporting the reductionist bundle of sticks/rights approach to property[7]) and has fuelled further controversy over his work and the value of its

[4] As Brian Simpson put it, in his Biographical Dictionary of the Common Law (1984), "He never lived to complete the analytical work of which these articles were to be the basis . . . an adequate study of his difficult and at times strange ideas, some lurking in footnotes, has not yet been published." I am grateful to William Twining for drawing this assessment to my attention.

[5] It is credited as an informal precursor of deontic logic by Philip Mullock, *The Hohfeldian Jural Opposite*, 13 Ratio 158, 160 (1971).

[6] The project is being pursued as a book with the provisional title, "Hohfeld Reconsidered: A Century of Misunderstanding." The present chapter draws significantly from that broader project.

[7] Thomas W. Merrill & Henry E. Smith, *What Happened to Property in Law and Economics?* 111 Yale L. J. 357, 365 (2001), regard Hohfeld as providing the "intellectual justification" for the bundles approach.

practical application. A specific illustration employed in that project takes the two dominant positions in property theory as relying on impoverished understandings of Hohfeld limited to an appreciation of the legal relations level of analysis (either as a platform or as a target) so as to promote a disagreement with no prospect of resolution. In that particular case, the basic point is that since the limited legal relations level of analysis is inadequate (without being supplemented by the aggregate level of analysis) there can be no constructive dialogue between opposing viewpoints, where one seeks to take the limited level of analysis as fully adequate, and the other rejects the adequacy of that level of analysis and then downgrades any role it might perform. In short, constructive dialogue within property theory can only emerge once the appropriate place of the legal relations level of analysis is viewed within a completed scheme of analysis, which may be described as a dual-level scheme of analysis in that it also incorporates the aggregate level.

However, to speak in terms of levels would be misleading if that were taken to mean that each level offers a self-contained mode of analysis for its own discrete purposes. The image is not of different levels of a building on which independent activities could be observed. Nor is it of different levels of perception from which cruder or finer details could be detected. (Taking a view through the microscope to discover the microbes responsible for the symptoms displayed by our illness.) Nor, importantly, should the two levels be understood as combining in a relationship of supervenience, with the supervenient level providing greater information than that found at the subvenient level while being regarded as being determined by it. (Diamonds sparkle but are composed of atoms of carbon, which do not sparkle.)

As we shall see, the relationship between the two levels within a completed Hohfeldian scheme of analysis is far more complex than any of these understandings of levels would suggest. For one thing, it is mutually dynamic, such that data deliverable at one level of analysis can inform and be informed by the data provided at the other level. For another thing, it is organic, in that change may occur at one level so as to effect a development at the other level. And although one level of analysis has its own particular part to play (that is to say, an essential part) in providing a full understanding of the operation of law, neither part can be fully played without some reference to the other. Ultimately, the relationship between the two levels of analysis is a reflection of the nature of the analysandum: the actual operation of the law.

More generally, then, the thesis is that the failure to grasp the role for an aggregate-level analysis in Hohfeld's thinking, compounded by the incomplete state of his work, has distorted a fuller understanding of his analysis of legal relations beyond the basic framework setting out the correlative and opposing relationships between the eight fundamental legal conceptions. And furthermore, that this serious

This justification was transmitted through the realist perception of his work by Hohfeld's colleagues, which, as indicated in Section 3.4.2, could be at variance with his own understanding.

misunderstanding of Hohfeld has sustained an environment of controversy and uncertainty surrounding the discussion of his work, while the work itself retains a strong sense of significance. That significance is largely due to the recognition of the importance of his analytical framework of legal relations, that I have mentioned, but is also assisted, I suggest, by the feature of his work I have referred to as opening up a perspective on law that is crucial to our understanding of the subject. The precise ways in which Hohfeld's work exhibits this feature is a topic that can best be addressed in the concluding reflections of this chapter, once a fuller appreciation of his work has been delivered. For now, we can note that protracted controversy found in the reception of Hohfeld's work fits a reading of his work as both seminal and misunderstood.

The present chapter relates to the broader project I have been working on, with its suggestion that a preoccupation with a legal relations level analysis misrepresents the full intentions Hohfeld had for his analytical scheme, and its finding that a reductionist character has been falsely attributed to Hohfeld's analytical scheme, being incompatible with his own extant writings. This chapter focuses on what can be regarded as an offshoot of the critique of (conventionally understood) Hohfeldian reductionism, the view that Hohfeldian analysis is destructive of efforts to represent the law in the form of rules. James Penner and Henry Smith are significant proponents of this view in arguing, respectively, that Hohfeldian analysis is incapable of supporting the normative guidance that law provides, and that it is incompatible with legal generalizations.

The core argument of this chapter proceeds by first demonstrating the general position that Hohfeld was not analytically hostile to legal rules. Three key points are used in evidence here: (i) Hohfeld himself deals with legal rules in a routine way in his writing when applying his analysis; (ii) Hohfeld's analytical scheme was employed for the crafting of legal rules in the American Restatements; and (iii) Arthur Corbin reveals that Hohfeld's general understanding of law was to see it as consisting of positive, formal rules, contrary to Corbin's own realist viewpoint. More particularly, the chapter then considers how it is possible to reconcile Hohfeld's analytical recognition of rules with Penner's and Smith's concerns. Partly, it is suggested, there is a misunderstanding of Hohfeld, and partly a misunderstanding (or imperfect representation) of the operations of law, affecting their concerns. Once the deficiencies contributing to their portrayals of Hohfeld and rules are taken into account, as well as any residual legitimacy in their concerns, the need for embracing a dual-level Hohfeldian scheme of analysis is reinforced.

The structure of the chapter frames this core argument within a preliminary sketch of the understanding of Hohfeld's analytical scheme and his unfulfilled objectives for a dual-level analysis (which I discuss in greater detail in the broader project I have referred to), and a concluding reflection which draws on the specific discussion of Hohfeld and rules and the importance of a dual-level analysis in order to better appreciate the way Hohfeld's work has contributed a perspective that is crucial to our understanding of the subject of law.

3.3 PRELIMINARY MATTERS

There are four features of the understanding of Hohfeld's work that I develop more fully elsewhere which form the setting for the present discussion of Hohfeld and rules. These are:

(1) the practical focus of Hohfeld's analysis on matters arising in legal disputes;
(2) the importance of legal relations, as expressing both correlative and opposing legal positions, in providing the analytical tools to present the cutting edge of legal disputes;
(3) the nonreductionist insistence on the equal importance of an aggregate-level analysis to complement the legal relations level of analysis; and
(4) the essential contributions made by the aggregate level in its interaction with a legal relations level of analysis.

As for the first of these features, the practical focus of his analysis on legal disputes arising before a court could not be more clearly spelled out by Hohfeld in his two *Yale Law Journal* articles. His concern with "practical, everyday problems of the law" was accompanied by an express rejection of "a merely philosophical inquiry,"[8] and reinforced by other statements stressing an emphasis on "those points believed to have the greatest practical value" and on "the solution of concrete problems of litigation."[9] Nor should it be forgotten that Hohfeld's fundamental conceptions were given a primary location by their author "in judicial reasoning."[10]

Overlooking this first feature has diverted much of contemporary discussion of Hohfeldian analysis into the type of philosophical inquiry that he himself denigrated. This is notably so in the debates over will and interest theories of rights. Without wishing to suggest that such philosophical inquiry is without value, there is a danger that insights are being neglected that might be gleaned from a practical application of Hohfeldian analysis to the operations of law and, in turn, inform grander philosophical inquiry.[11]

The second feature naturally follows from the first. If a legal dispute is the focus, then it will involve two parties and the legal outcome will necessarily affect both

[8] FLC, 26.

[9] *Id.* at 27, 66.

[10] Evident in the titles of his articles and reinforced in the opening paragraphs of the second article, previously cited: "actually applied *in judicial reasoning* to the solution of concrete problems of litigation": *id.* at 66.

[11] I pursue this suggestion in *The Value of Hohfeldian Neutrality when Theorising about Legal Rights*, *in* NEW ESSAYS ON LEGAL RIGHTS (Mark McBride ed., 2017).

together, in mutual relation to each other.[12] Hohfeld differentiated four types of rights to assist in clarifying the practical legal positions of the parties to a legal dispute, which otherwise fell to be asserted with no clear understanding of what precisely was at stake between the parties.[13] The four types of rights then had to be linked with the subordinate positions of the parties over which they are exercised, within a legal relation, constituted by the correlative relationship formed from a dominant position (one of the four types of right) together with its subordinate position.

This provides us with four fundamental legal relations:

(A) X has a *right* to the conduct of Y and Y is under a *duty* to perform that conduct.
(B) X has a *liberty* to engage in conduct and Y has *no-right* that X refrain from it.
(C) X has a *power* to change a legal relation of Y and Y is under a *liability* to have that legal relation changed.
(D) X has an *immunity* against having a legal relation changed by Y and Y has a *disability* to change it.

The full capacity of Hohfeld's scheme to clarify what is at stake in a legal dispute depends also on another relationship he identified between his fundamental legal conceptions (or the relational legal positions they represent). One of the four correlative relations – (A), (B), (C), or (D) – may be used to express precisely what is being claimed by one party in a legal dispute, but if it is a dispute we also need to know what is being denied by the other party. This requirement could have been met by placing simple negations of the first party's claims in the mouth of the opposing party. X claims a right over Y's conduct; i.e., that Y owes X a duty. Y responds by denying X's claim: X has no-right over Y's conduct; i.e., Y owes no-duty to X. Hohfeld's scheme became a little more elaborate at this point in talking of relationships of "opposites" between the legal positions.[14]

Considering the precise nature of a Hohfeldian opposite or negation[15] would take us into one of the more technical aspects of Hohfeld's scheme, which happily need not detain us here.[16] The key point being made by Hohfeld is that if one party to a legal

[12] Hohfeld's preoccupation was with private law issues, and the application of his analysis to public law and criminal law issues is less straightforward, but that is not to say irrelevant or unhelpful. *See* Matthew Kramer, *Rights without Trimmings*, *in* MATTHEW KRAMER ET AL., A DEBATE OVER RIGHTS: PHILOSOPHICAL ENQUIRIES 58 (1998): "As this essay seeks to extend the Correlativity Axiom into the domains of public duties and the criminal law, it moves into territories which Hohfeld left largely unexamined." For present purposes, we can restrict the discussion within Hohfeld's chosen emphasis on private law.

[13] FLC, 35–36 ("inadequacy and ambiguity of terms unfortunately reflect, all too often, corresponding paucity and confusion as regards actual legal conceptions"), 43 ("obscured by the very indefinite and rapidly shifting meanings with which the term 'right' is used").

[14] *Id.* at 36.

[15] *Id.* at 39, Hohfeld casts his opposite as a "mere negation."

[16] The issue is not pertinent to our present concerns as it does not affect the common understanding that a Hohfeldian liberty involves the negation of a duty, which is enough in order to proceed with the elementary application of his scheme.

dispute is claiming what can be represented by one of the four correlative relations, (A), (B), (C), or (D), then the position of the opposing party can be represented by an alternative from these relations, described as its opposite or negation. Specifically, a claim in the form of (A) will be denied by making a claim in the form of (B), with due adjustment for the party who is now dominant; and similarly for (C) and (D). Although Hohfeld himself describes the relationship of opposite as occurring between the fundamental legal conceptions or individual positions (a liberty is the opposite of a duty, etc.),[17] since these cannot exist outside of their correlative relationships, a fuller representation, as given here with (A)–(D), requires the legal relations to be mentioned.[18]

As the first two features are closely connected, so too are the third and fourth. The distinctive move in this understanding of Hohfeld's scheme of analysis occurs between the second and the third features. That is to say, contrary to the conventional understanding of Hohfeld which equates the analytical clarity achieved by his scheme with breaking down complex legal materials into the different kinds of legal relations, so adopting a reductionist approach, the portrayal of Hohfeldian analysis I have promoted in the broader project takes seriously the insistence by Hohfeld himself that full analytical clarity cannot be attained by a legal relations level analysis alone, without taking into account an aggregate-level analysis.

The conventional view of Hohfeld, which finds perhaps its most important expression in linking Hohfeld with the bundle of sticks approach to property, can be detected within the earliest assessments of his work provided in tribute to Hohfeld in the 1919 *Yale Law Journal*. There, Arthur Corbin states:[19]

> Furthermore, the legal relations of any two persons are frequently numerous and complex, and it is of great service to analyze them into their simplest forms. Such terms of the law as "contract," "trust," "property" and "marriage" do not represent a single legal relation; they describe and represent complex and variable aggregates of legal relations. For clear thinking and for just and correct decision it is necessary to analyze these complex concepts into their simpler and invariable elements.

From this perspective, the complex aggregates are seen as completely accounted for once reduced into their component legal relations.

Any matter that might arise regarding our understanding ("clear thinking") of a contract, trust, etc.; any matter that might be of interest regarding the deeper policy or justification ("just decision") for a contract, trust, etc.; any matter affecting

[17] FLC, 38–39.

[18] Hohfeld referred to the conceptions themselves as "the lowest common denominators" (*id.* at 63–64) but no single conception could exist for Hohfeld without the presence of its correlative within a legal relation, so that it is the relations and not the conceptions that are truly fundamental and form the atomic particles of law in the Hohfeldian scheme (to employ another metaphor), with the two correlative conceptions in each relation amounting to subatomic particles (to extend the image further).

[19] Arthur Corbin, *Legal Analysis and Terminology*, 29 Yale L.J. 163, 165 (1919).

a dispute ("correct decision") over a contract, trust, etc. – is to be apprehended at the legal relations level alone. This view has repercussions both for the aggregate and for the legal relations. The aggregate becomes of no significance, and the legal relations are then seen as self-standing elements which derive no significant feature from their aggregate location. The final inference to draw from this line of reasoning is that the aggregate, having no significance in itself or for the legal relations, is random and superfluous for practical legal understanding. Notably, this has led to the conclusion that a reductionist Hohfeldian analysis supports a finding of no special significance for an aggregate identified as property, and also to the corollary that any aggregate may count as property.[20] This then leaves no essential part for an aggregate-level analysis to play.

In the broader project, I rebut the view that Hohfeld was himself a reductionist, drawing on several indications to the contrary in his work. For our present interests it is sufficient to mention the clearest expression of Hohfeld's nonreductionist position, which appears in a comment he makes on property in his second article:[21]

> It is important, in order to have an adequate analytical view of property, to see all these various elements in the aggregate. It is equally important, for many reasons, that the different classes of jural relations should not be loosely confused with one another.

Although the subsequent passages in that article reflect Hohfeld's preoccupation with the second of his analytical imperatives quoted here, emphasizing the value of an analysis that breaks property down into distinct types of legal relations, this should not distract us from recognizing the equal importance Hohfeld attached to an analysis taking in a view of the aggregate. Hohfeld states quite starkly here that an analysis of legal relations without an analysis of the aggregate would produce an inadequate view of property.

Accepting the equal importance of an aggregate-level analysis to complement a legal relations level of analysis, the question arises as to where the essential contributions are to be found from the aggregate-level analysis, in its interaction with a legal relations level of analysis. Hohfeld himself in his published work did not pursue this question. Elsewhere, I speculate on why this might have been so, and aim to fill out the missing picture in some detail. Again, present interests can be satisfied with a more cursory answer.

[20] As Hanoch Dagan, Property: Values and Institutions 30 (2011), puts it, the independent legal relations may be combined in "a limitless number of permutations." For more radical implications, see Joseph William Singer, *Democratic Estates: Property Law in a Free and Democratic Society*, 94 Cornell L. Rev. 1009, 1032 (2009) ("property has no meaning whatsoever as a legal category"); Thomas C. Grey, *The Disintegration of Property*, in Nomos XXII: Property 81 (J. Roland Pennock and John W. Chapman eds., 1980) ("[P]roperty ceases to be an important category in legal and political thought").

[21] FLC, 97.

There is a fairly obvious way in which an aggregate-level understanding provides something absent from a legal relations level of analysis alone which is essential in order to represent the operation of law, particularly as occurs in dealing with legal disputes. If, as has been suggested, the cutting edge of a legal dispute can be represented as opposing legal relations, the complete picture of a particular dispute, that has to be taken into account in order to reach a resolution of that dispute, requires information only obtainable at the aggregate level. This holds irrespective of whether a more formalist (doctrinal dependent) or more realist (reliance on extra-legal normative factors) approach is taken to how legal disputes are resolved.

In order to illustrate the essential contribution of the aggregate level, consider the case of *Craft*.[22] The legal issue in *Craft* was whether the husband possessed property in a particular Grand Rapids property[23] held with his wife under a tenancy by the entirety so as to make it subject to a federal tax lien which operated against "all property and rights to property" held by him.[24] This is resolved by recognizing either that the husband and wife have an immunity against the Internal Revenue Service thus placing that body under a disability to exercise a lien against the Grand Rapids property (a (D) relation), or the Internal Revenue Service has the power to exercise a lien against that property thus placing the husband and wife under a liability (a (C) relation). The cutting edge of the dispute both when it is still active (in terms of opposing Hohfeldian relations), and as a matter of outcome when it is resolved by judgment (in terms of a favored Hohfeldian relation), revolves around accepting or dismissing a particular legal relation.

In *Craft*, there are indications that the majority and dissent were swayed by different normative considerations: respectively, a concern that the Grand Rapids property would escape the claims of the IRS entirely;[25] and the rejection of that concern[26] accompanied by a concern that protection should be given to the wife against her husband's indebtedness.[27] The normative argument for providing the IRS with an effective revenue stream is not made by baldly asserting a power to exercise a lien, but through a consideration of the normative significance of the aggregate position of the IRS with respect to the source of this particular revenue, including the past default of payment by the husband, and any prospective revenue that might be forthcoming from the Grand Rapids property. Similarly, the normative argument for securing independent financial security for the wife is not made by baldly asserting an immunity against the IRS, but through a consideration of the

22 *United States* v. *Craft*, 535 U.S. 274 (2002).

23 The term "property" here (where the report uses "a piece of real property") is unavoidably confusing when "property" is employed for both the object held and the legal interest over that object. I occasionally use "Grand Rapids property" or "matrimonial property" to make it clear that it is the piece of property that is being referred to at that point.

24 Under 26 U.S.C. § 6321.

25 535 U.S. 274, 285 (2002).

26 *Id.* at 301.

27 *Id.* at 289–90.

normative significance of her aggregate position, including the expectations present when the tenancy by the entirety was set up, and the wider social importance of providing her with financial security in this way.

However, even if the legal issue in *Craft* were to be regarded in formalist doctrinal terms, the dispute is not over the immunity-disability or power-liability relation, but whether one of those relations attaches to the tenancy by the entirety, which expresses the aggregate legal position of the property interest held by the husband. For legal argument to take place we need to consider the legal significance of the Crafts holding the Grand Rapids property under a tenancy by the entirety, as opposed to, say, the property being in the sole name of the husband with the wife being in residence, with or without a beneficial interest. This sort of doctrinal inquiry and the argument that follows can only be commenced at the aggregate level. Without the doctrinal purposive identification of the appropriate property interest available at the aggregate level, it would be impossible to identify which collective (or "bundle") of legal relations were relevant. A tenancy by the entirety, a beneficial interest in the matrimonial home, etc., are not fundamental legal conceptions and appear nowhere in Hohfeld's set of fundamental legal relations, (A)–(D).

Beyond the setting of practical legal argument, there are other concerns about a party's legal position that cannot be expressed within statements of legal relations. For example, one may want to investigate the principles of justice or policy that produced a particular legal position, from a historical or sociological or normative inquiry. This it will be possible to do only by working at the aggregate level. Individual legal relations cannot be the subject of such inquiries. One does not ask whether an individual right-duty relation to pay a sum of money is just, or accords with a particular policy. The question would be meaningless. One asks whether the duty of the tenant to pay the landlord a sum of money as rent is just, or in accordance with a particular policy, regarding fair rent, etc. The question can only become meaningful when the aggregate positions of landlord and tenant are brought into the picture, and the political, social, and normative aspects[28] of the parties' conflicting interests are explored, as landlord or tenant, spouse or creditor, etc.

We can now revisit the view of Corbin excerpted above.[29] It turns out that his view of "clear thinking," "just decision," and "correct decision" depending upon a reductionist analysis into legal relations is simply false. For all of these inquiries an aggregate analysis is essential. That is not to say that an analysis of legal relations has no part to play, as our example has illustrated. The relationship observed here between an aggregate-level analysis and a legal relations level analysis can be briefly

[28] I use this triple expression loosely here to indicate that nondoctrinal (extra-legal) factors may encompass policies and values of different kinds.

[29] Text at n 19 above.

generalized,[30] within what can be described as a Hohfeldian dual-level analysis, as capable of representing three crucial features of any form of property:

(a) its known contours – as a configuration or tentative aggregate of legal relations;
(b) any disputed aspect – as a dispute over opposing legal relations;
(c) the setting in which that disputed aspect will be resolved – in terms of assimilating the contentious legal relation into a putative aggregate position (on normative or doctrinal grounds), and then advancing to an established aggregate position.

Reflecting the organic aspect of the relationship between the two levels, the established aggregate eventually reached at (c) will then become the new (a), possibly awaiting the emergence of another disputed aspect of the proprietary interest at a new (b).

3.4 RULES

3.4.1 *The Incompatibility of Rules and Reductionist Legal Relations*

For some time now, James Penner has been pointing out that a reductionist analysis into Hohfeldian legal relations misses out on the ordinary role of the law to normatively guide behavior. His famous example of the car park was used to point out that in order to behave in a law-abiding way in a car park, among other things, one complies with the general prohibition not to take somebody else's car, and does so without knowing who owns all the cars in the car park.[31] Such everyday and significant normative guidance provided by the law does not require, and cannot be generated by, a statement of (innumerable) individual legal relations. It is both impersonal and general.[32] Penner continues to advance this argument in recent work,[33] and in doing so treats it as a clear refutation of Hohfeldian reductionism.[34]

Penner's insistence on recognizing the general, impersonal guidance provided by the law amounts to the recognition of general legal rules having a vital existence apart from the set of instantiations that fall under them. In drawing an analogy with the arithmetical rule of addition, he points out, "we do not conceive of rules as being the sum of the occasions for their application."[35]

[30] Discussed more fully in Halpin, *supra* note 6.
[31] James Penner, The Idea of Property in Law 75 (1997).
[32] James Penner, *On the Very Idea of Transmissible Rights*, *in* Philosophical Foundations of Property Law 258 (James Penner & Henry E. Smith eds., 2013).
[33] *Id.*
[34] *Id.* at 251 ("the constellation of jural relations, which, for a Hohfeldian, define the right as the right that it is"). It appears that Penner is now prepared to distinguish between reductionist Hohfeldians and a nonreductionist Hohfeld. *See* J.E. Penner, Property Rights: A Re-Examination (2020).
[35] Penner, *supra* note 32, at 259.

Henry Smith has also written extensively on the importance of legal generalizations, and continues to do so. Although his motivation in combating Hohfeldian reductionism is shared with Penner, Smith has his own particular concern in employing the significance of legal generalizations in order to expound his modular concept of property. I shall concentrate here on one of his essays, in which he takes up the idea of a generalized concept of property as satisfying the need for economy of information.[36] Clearly, expressing something as a general rule does provide for economy of information when contrasted with an exhaustive list of all the possible instantiations of that rule. Interestingly, where Penner looks to the rules of arithmetic to obtain his analogy, Smith looks to the rules of language.

One rule regarding all verbs is that they can take the past tense.[37] This is portrayed by Smith as an example of generalization which produces economy of information by the simple device of expressing a rule that applies to all members of a particular category and so avoids giving the information multiple times to cover every instance of the category. Smith then introduces the complication of adding exceptions to a general rule. The general rule is that verbs form the past tense by adding the suffix -ed, but there are exceptions to this rule, such as "rang" and "was." Smith covers the complication by invoking the "specific-over-general" principle.[38] However, there is an important point to note here. The strategy of applying a general rule with exceptions only works to produce economy of information if all the exceptions are mastered first. Otherwise, without an authoritative grasp of the exceptions (as in the case of a young child or a nonnative speaker of the language), we would not know if the general rule was applicable to an unfamiliar instance of a verb. Economy of information would degenerate into ignorance.

Nevertheless, we can agree with Smith – and Penner – that general statements or rules of law are regularly relied on both for economy of information and for normative guidance. We can also agree that a reductionist dogma on only portraying legal materials as individuated legal relations would have the effect of denying the possibility of these valuable practices. The significant question is whether the reductionist dogma is all that can be said about Hohfeldian legal relations.[39] Or, to put it another way, whether Hohfeldian legal relations are compatible with these uses of legal rules. We can start that inquiry by looking first at Hohfeld himself.

[36] Henry E. Smith, *On the Economy of Concepts in Property*, 160 U. PA. L. REV. 2097 (2012). For a more recent elaboration of Smith's position, see Chapter 14.

[37] Smith, *supra* note 36, at 2109–11. (Even without the exceptions for formation, below, the generality of the rule might be stretched to cover "can" and "must.")

[38] *Id.* at 2110–11.

[39] Penner, *supra* note 32, at 258–59, leaves some space for bilateral legal relations. Smith, in promoting his modular approach to property, with its asymmetry of information challenging the need for correlative legal relations, is less accommodating. See Henry E. Smith, *Property as the Law of Things*, 125 HARV. L. REV. 1691 (2012), and the approach of Simon Douglas & Ben McFarlane, *Defining Property Rights*, *in* PHILOSOPHICAL FOUNDATIONS OF PROPERTY LAW (James Penner & Henry E. Smith eds., 2013), which follows this line.

3.4.2 *The Compatibility of Hohfeld and Rules*

There really is no question that Hohfeld himself was utterly comfortable with legal rules, too comfortable in the view of some of his contemporaries. More pointedly, Hohfeld routinely expressed the analytical distinctions conveyed by his legal relations in the form of legal rules. The examples are so copious as not to excite particular attention. So, we find mention of a general rule regarding the power of an owner of personal property to extinguish his own legal interest by abandonment; of a general rule regarding the creation of agency by the grant of legal powers; of a general rule regarding the power of a sheriff to sell property under a writ of execution; etc., etc.[40]

It is also common knowledge that Hohfeld's analytical scheme was invoked in order to assist with the drafting of legal rules in the American Restatements, in order to attain greater clarity. In an interview with William Twining, Arthur Corbin mentions his own role in ensuring that "Hohfeld's classification of concepts" informed the drafting of *Contracts*,[41] and elsewhere Corbin points to Hohfeld's influence on *The Restatement of the Law of Property*.[42] Twining also refers to the influence of Hohfeld's analysis on Karl Llewellyn's work on the *Uniform Commercial Code*.[43]

We can – uncontroversially – conclude that both in his own work, and in legal expository work that he influenced, Hohfeld's analytical scheme of legal relations was no threat to the economy of information or the expression of normative guidance effected by legal rules. Moreover, from a purely theoretical perspective, Hohfeld was, if anything, too enamored with legal rules. At least, that was the view of his realist colleagues. Corbin's recollection of Hohfeld draws attention to Hohfeld's attachment to "the positive law," which provoked the astonishment of Corbin and Cook at a Yale faculty meeting, and to his own disagreement with Hohfeld on the importance Hohfeld gave to legal rules.[44] If a formalist streak in Hohfeld's understanding of law is evident in Corbin's reminiscence, so making law open to logical deduction from general rules,[45] in his own writing Hohfeld hints at a more ambitious view of a perfectionist formalism. This is not simply regarded as compatible

[40] FLC, 51–53. It is significant that in these passages Hohfeld refers in the singular to the power to extinguish by abandonment, the power of an agent to convey property, and the power of a sheriff to sell property, when all these singular powers represent collectives of multital powers, according to a rigorous Hohfeldian analysis. So Hohfeld's insistence on a multital analysis does not get in the way of expressing law in the form of rules for effective communication, any more than his insistence on recognizing individual legal relations that are general in character obstructs their expression in the form of a general rule.

[41] William Twining, Karl Llewellyn and the Realist Movement 35, n.31 (2d ed. 2012).

[42] Arthur Corbin, *Foreword*, *in* FLC, xiii. For a wider critique of the value of Hohfeld's analytical approach here, see Thomas W. Merrill & Henry E. Smith, *Why Restate the Bundle?: The Disintegration of the Restatement of Property*, 79 Brook. L. Rev. 681 (2014).

[43] Twining, *supra* note 41, at 35 n.32.

[44] Corbin, *supra* note 2, at 3, 7.

[45] *Id.* at 7.

with his fundamental legal relations but is believed to be accessible through grasping them:[46]

> But if all these relations are reduced to their lowest generic terms ... [b]y such a process it becomes possible not only to discover essential similarities and illuminating analogies in the midst of what appears superficially to be infinite and hopeless variety, but also to discern common principles of justice and policy underlying the various jural problems involved.

The grounds for asserting this ambitious outcome for Hohfeld's analytical scheme can be doubted.[47] What cannot be doubted is Hohfeld's own view of the compatibility of his analysis of legal relations with legal generalizations or rules. Nor can it be doubted that an analysis into legal relations is capable of finding practical expression in the form of legal rules.

3.4.3 *Making Sense of Rules from a Dual-Level Analysis*

A simple way of showing the compatibility of Hohfeld's scheme of analysis with legal rules is to concentrate on the objective of terminological clarity that was an important incentive for Hohfeld.[48] Take a legal rule (actual or proposed) otherwise using the vocabulary of rights and then substitute the more precise Hohfeldian terminology in that rule. This effectively was the point in drawing upon Hohfeld when drafting the *Restatements*.[49] However, that is not to say the doctrinal articulation of legal rules involving rights can be expressed purely in the terminology of Hohfeldian legal relations. In order to make sense, even at a doctrinal level, there must be additional reference to the aggregate positions to which those rights adhere.[50]

More than that, in addressing the concerns of Penner and Smith, we need to be sensitive to the possibility that legal rules or generalizations may be found in different forms, outside of a doctrinal setting. Penner's concern is that the legal normative guidance offered to the law-abiding citizen produces a legal rule that cannot exist if Hohfeldian reductionism into legal relations is maintained. Since such guidance is impersonal, it has no involvement with individual legal relations. The refutation of Hohfeldian reductionism promoted here goes some way to answering Penner, in that the nonreductionist allowance for the significance of aggregate positions in Hohfeld's scheme fits with Penner's guidance rules, expressed as generalizations involving aggregate legal positions. The prohibition not to take a car owned by someone else relies upon the aggregate legal position of ownership (of a car). But it does not meet Penner's concerns entirely, in that he is not insisting

46 FLC, 64.

47 I provide an extensive criticism in Halpin, *supra* note 6.

48 See passages cited *supra* note 13 and the title of Corbin's article, *supra* note 19. Similarly, George W. Goble, A *Redefinition of Basic Legal Terms*, 35 COLUM. L. REV. 535 (1935).

49 TWINING *supra*, note 41; Corbin, *supra* note 42.

50 See *supra* note 27 and accompanying text.

only on a form of legal rule that requires something other than legal relations. Penner's legal rule does not require legal relations at all.

However, the redundancy of legal relations in general legal guidance pertains to the particular setting in which that guidance is offered. The modest needs of the law-abiding citizen entering a car park related by Penner can be contrasted with the needs for legal guidance of the citizen who bumps his car into another car while parking, or of the citizen who smashes open the window of a parked car to release a dog that is suffocating inside. In these cases, individual legal relations will be pertinent, as Penner seems to acknowledge.[51] Given the specific concern of Hohfeld's scheme of analysis with legal disputes before the courts, and taking into account the nonreductionist view of Hohfeld in allowing for the significance of aggregate legal positions, there is then no challenge to Hohfeld from Penner's particular concerns.

The concerns of Smith differ in that the setting for his generalization lies in establishing a concept of property based on exclusion. The modularity of his concept requires a generalization of the exclusion of others from the property without specifying the particular ways in which the property holder can enjoy the property. As he puts it, "property is like a black box, a module where the type of use is simply irrelevant to the duty of abstention."[52] In one sense, Smith's modular concept of property is the converse of Penner's general guidance to the law-abiding citizen. Indeed, Smith cites Penner's car park case approvingly, immediately before the passage just quoted. Law-abiding citizens just keep off others' property, without knowing who owns it; property owners then get to do what they want with their property, without anybody else needing to know what they do with it.

The argument directed against Penner above could be run again to show that with Hohfeld's concern with legal disputes before the courts, and accepting the non-reductionist allowance for the significance of aggregate legal positions, there is no challenge to Hohfeld from Smith's particular concerns. Nevertheless, Smith's concerns pose an additional challenge to Hohfeld's analytical scheme, in that if he has identified a legal concept of property that leaves no room for legal relations, this threatens a Hohfeldian dual-level analytical scheme in which legal relations play a significant role. The conceptual claim cannot be discarded so easily as Penner's claim, by being relegated to a specific location of legal guidance.

The real issue then with Smith is whether he has accurately identified a legal concept of property. On this point he is vulnerable precisely because his concept relegates legal relations, and closes off the corresponding interplay between parties'

[51] *See supra* note 39. More fully, the role of legal relations is twofold: (1) specific instantiation to the two parties involved; (2) terminological clarity as to the particular circumstances involving the two parties (as in the examples given here), in a type-(A) duty not to cause damage to the car, or a type-(B) liberty to break the car window.

[52] Smith, *supra* note 36, at 2116. Smith's approach is amplified in his *Emergent Property*, *in* Philosophical Foundations of Property Law (James Penner & Henry E. Smith eds., 2013) and discussed more fully in Halpin, *supra* note 6.

interests that are apparent in legal cases before the courts. The pressing requirement of the legal context is that a common norm governs the conduct and expectations of both parties to a dispute brought before the courts. The correlativity in Hohfeld's scheme provides exemplary recognition of this point. This basic requirement of the operation of law is denied by Smith's modularity, where the position of one party, the duty bearer, is (loosely) established by the concept of property, but the position of the other party, the right holder, is left unspecified by that concept (on the grounds of informational economy).

It is possible that the property holder's position could be portrayed in such an unspecified way that is of relevance to some other appreciation of the value of property, outside of the law. For example, the holding of property might provide social status: the property holder is respected for enjoying exclusive use and control of the thing owned. However, such a social perception of property and the legal perception of property are not dealing with quite the same thing. The social aspirations of property holders to have exclusive enjoyment of the thing owned are sometimes defeated by the legal subordination of those aspirations to the interests of other members of the community. For example, when a private beach club is required to allow members of the public across its land to reach the wet sand beach.[53]

For the provision of general normative guidance, or the expression of the general social status of property, in terms of rules, a nonreductionist awareness of aggregate positions is necessary. Regarding the aggregate within a dual-level analysis as interrelated to a legal relations level of analysis is additionally necessary in order to provide a full legal analysis of property. That fuller analysis can also be informative about the limited settings or qualified uses of the rules which may be articulated without reference to a legal relations level of analysis.

3.5 CONCLUSION

One way to demonstrate that Hohfeld's work has opened up a perspective that is crucial to our understanding of the subject of law is to point to our need to move beyond a perception of legal materials (maybe as rules, or even, as rules and principles) in arriving at an understanding of how legal materials impact upon the specific situations involving parties before the courts. At the very least, clarificatory work is required on the different types of legal relations involved in legal disputes. But much more is required in working through the contested understandings of how exactly legal materials are used in order to produce an outcome to legal disputes. More still, if the organic nature of law is recognized, in that the derivation of outcomes from legal materials is not regarded as rigid, stable, or stagnant.

[53] *Raleigh Ave. Beach Ass'n* v. *Atlantis Beach Club*, 879 A.2d (N.J. 2005), discussed in GREGORY S. ALEXANDER & EDUARDO M. PEÑALVER, AN INTRODUCTION TO PROPERTY THEORY 133–34 (2012).

Hohfeld's contribution to the clarificatory aspect is valuable in itself, but his insistence on a rigorous examination of law at the level of legal relations provokes deeper inquiries across contested but core territory for our understanding of law. He himself never really pursued those deeper inquiries,[54] and the incomplete attention he had given to the aggregate level of analysis encouraged greater controversy to attach to the reception of his work and its perceived significance or insignificance in addressing those deeper inquiries.

However, if we are to take seriously the importance Hohfeld himself stressed for the aggregate level of analysis, this suggests that Hohfeld's completed analytical scheme would have involved a dual-level analysis, providing a nonreductionist interaction between aggregate and legal relations levels. This, in turn, offers a reassessment of the potential influence and contribution of a Hohfeldian scheme of analysis, in not merely opening up a perspective that is crucial to our understanding of the subject of law but in also developing an analytical framework that can advance the deeper inquiries that follow from opening up that crucial perspective. As an example, toward the end of Section 3.3, I sketched just how the interaction between aggregate and legal relations levels might produce a clearer representation of standard features of any form of property in the law, and so assist with the fuller inquiries that can be undertaken over our understanding of property in the law.

I have also alluded in Section 3.4.3 to the limitations of rules of general normative guidance or rules expressing broad social perceptions of property, in their preoccupation with an aggregate level alone. That is not to say that rules here, as in the case of technical doctrinal rules, have no role to play. Just that their roles are limited and need supplementing by further investigation involving the legal relations level.

It is worth pointing out, briefly, another implication of the insistence on a nonreductionist view of legal relations, which creates a dynamic playing between but capable of escaping beyond the interaction between aggregate and legal relations levels: embracing normative considerations that may relate to the aggregate position (as of a property holder) yet which do not bother with the technical legal concerns found at a level of legal relations. We may accordingly recognize at a third level of analysis what can be referred to as ideology or grand theory[55] that may influence the socio-political (normative) aspects of the legal aggregate and through that the doctrinal aspect of the aggregate, despite being unconcerned with the precise outworking of those

[54] *Cf.* John Henry Schlegel, American Legal Realism and Empirical Social Science 55 n.196 (1995) (doubting Hohfeld contemplated the "use of his grand analytic engine" for making inquiries into social and economic policy).

[55] Alexander & Peñalver, *supra* note 53, devote approximately half an introductory book to such grand theory. In their Introduction, Penner & Smith (*supra* note 32, at xix) observe: "Locke, Hume, Grotius, Kant, and Hegel and their views of the nature of property . . . remain a continuing source of inspiration and puzzlement."

socio-political values at the legal relations level.[56] I provide a diagrammatic representation in Figure 3.1 of a triple-level analytical scheme.[57]

I am now far from bringing an end to the story of Hohfeld's analytical scheme. Yet I hope to have shown that the story of its reception might have taken a different path with the recognition of the importance of the aggregate level of analysis. Possibly a less controversial path. Arguably delivering a more fruitful yield for Hohfeld's work than he himself lived to anticipate.

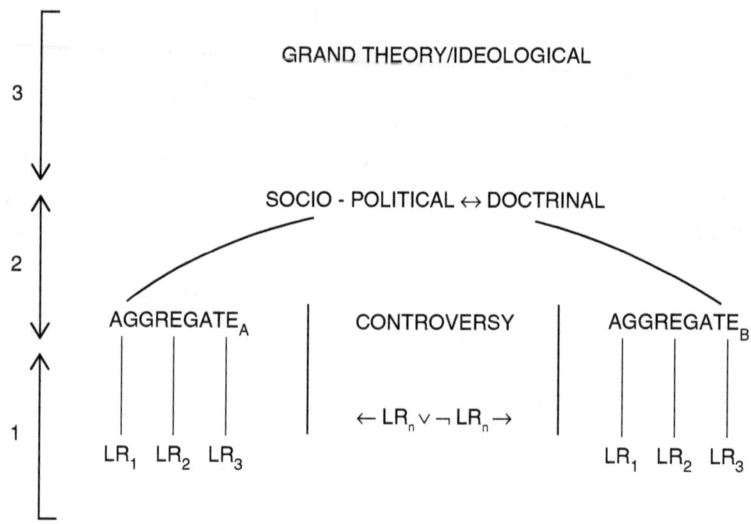

FIGURE 3.1 A triple-level analytical scheme

Note that the central column of controversy expresses the difference between two putative views of an aggregate, as described in (b) & (c) at the end of Section 3.3, with the cutting edge of that controversy manifested as opposing legal relations, either LR_n or $\neg LR_n$.

[56] This suggests a demarcation between legal and nonlegal theoretical concerns dependent on attention to the legal relations level. *Cf.* AMNON LEHAVI, THE CONSTRUCTION OF PROPERTY: NORMS, INSTITUTIONS, CHALLENGES, ch. 1 (2013), for the view that legal renderings of property are distinct from those portrayed in other disciplines (including philosophy).

[57] Expounded more fully in Halpin, *supra* note 6.

4

Logic and the Life of the Law (Professor): A Logocratic Lesson from Hohfeld

Scott Brewer[*]

4.1 PROEM: A PUZZLE ABOUT HOHFELD'S LEGAL-PEDAG(L)OGICAL ACCOMPLISHMENTS

This chapter is an essay, literally an attempt, to present and solve a puzzle about Wesley Newcomb Hohfeld. In addition to being a doctrinal legal scholar, he was – and is justly renowned for his work as – a legal theorist, legal philosopher, and logician operating without, but anticipating, the formal grammar of logic (deontic logic, specifically[1]). Given the huge influence of his work, he had surprisingly few publications, resulting in a high yield of impact per page – and, indeed, per year of his short life.[2] Wesley Hohfeld was also a law professor who had difficulty getting his students to see the value of his method as a tool for learning and mastering legal argument. (Some can sympathize.) Thus, reports Arthur Corbin, his Yale Law School colleague, admirer, booster, and astute interpreter:[3]

> Hohfeld's teaching at Yale began in the autumn of 1914. He was a severe taskmaster, requiring his students to master his classification of "fundamental conceptions" and to use accurately the set of terms by which they were expressed. They found this, in the light of the usage of the other professors, almost impossible. There is no more

* Harvard Law School. Thanks for extremely helpful comments from Ted Sichelman, to the participants in the Hohfeld centennial conference, and students in classes in which I have taught Hohfeld at Harvard Law School and the European University Institute-Harvard Law School 2018 Summer School on Law and Logic. Thanks also to my cofounder and coadministrator of the Summer School, Professor Giovanni Sartor, for many illuminating discussions of Hohfeld's logic over the years.

1 "*[I]t appears that Hohfeld devised nearly half a century ago what is essentially a system of deontic logic.* Hohfeld outlined his analytical system in English prose, without using symbols and without relating his terms to any precise system of logic. So, by comparison with modern deontic logic, his system is sometimes unclear and confusing. This does not in the least detract from the greatness of Hohfeld's accomplishment, but it does suggest ways for carrying on with his work." Alan Cullison, *Logical Analysis of Legal Doctrine: The Normative Structure of Positive Law*, 53 Iowa L. Rev. 1209, 1221 (1968) (emphasis in original).

2 The 38-year-old Hohfeld died in 1918, five years after publication of his most important article, namely: Wesley N. Hohfeld, *Some Fundamental Conceptions as Applied in Legal Reasoning*, 23 Yale L.J. 16 (1913).

3 *See, e.g.*, Arthur L. Corbin, *Jural Relations and Their Classification*, 30 Yale L.J. 226 (1921).

> difficult job for any teacher. All people resent the criticism of their usage and the effort to reform it. Not realizing the benefit to be obtained, they regard the effort as unnecessary. "We are getting along well enough with the good old English language as it is." They are much like the orthodox but untutored "fundamentalists" in theology who resent tampering with their accustomed King James version of the Bible and assert that "God's language is good enough for us." The students called him bad names and complained bitterly. I once saw Dean Henry Wade Rogers (himself a Prussian taskmaster) put a fatherly hand on Hohfeld's shoulder and heard him say: "Be kinder to them, Hohfeld."[4]

This narrative from Hohfeld's life illustrates a problem that I seek to solve in this chapter. While writing this chapter, I asked a few colleagues who are experts on Hohfeld and who also teach areas of substantive private law whether they teach Hohfeld relations in those courses. Each replied in the negative.[5] Why not? Close student-scholars of Hohfeld's work hail it as "a landmark of legal thought,"[6] and Hohfeld himself as "the most important obscure figure in American legal thought" whose "pathbreaking article" and other related work "has become part of the fabric of American law."[7] It is not difficult to find similar sentiments. As the conference that occasions this volume attests, for more than a century, Hohfeld's work has been taken quite seriously by scholars of substantive law doctrine[8] and by varying types of

4 Arthur Corbin, *Foreword* to WESLEY N. HOHFELD, FUNDAMENTAL LEGAL CONCEPTIONS AS APPLIED IN JUDICIAL REASONING (Walter Wheeler Cook ed., 1964). Hohfeld was visiting Yale Law School from Stanford Law School and was eligible to accept an offer of tenure from Yale (toward Yale Law School or its agents Hohfeld had a privilege and a power to accept "its" offer). Corbin goes on to note: "The seniors in the courses on trusts and conflict of laws became truly fearful that they could not satisfy Hohfeld's requirements and would fail in his examinations. Rumors of the terms of his contract with Yale reached them and led to the belief that he had only a one-year appointment. Most of them signed a petition addressed to President Hadley asking that his appointment be not extended ... [T]he President had called Hohfeld to his office and informed him of the petition. Hohfeld was severely shocked and grieved. Without making any argument, on leaving the President's office he went straight to Western Union and sent a final resignation to Stanford." That is, he resigned Stanford and exercised his Hohfeldian *power* to acquire a tenured position at Yale. One wonders whether the pained, bold, young professor Hohfeld had an attitude toward his students like that of the New York City guru-stand-up-nihilist Brother Theodore, who intoned to his audiences, "Now, I'm afraid I can detect, I can detect symptoms of idiocy in the audience ... It is obvious you haven't the vaguest idea of what I am talking about. And that fills me with pride and satisfaction." Notes taken from performance by Brother Theodore, 13th St. Theater, NYC (December 26, 1992).

5 Curtis Nyquist is one admirable exception to (that proves?) the rule, if it is a rule, that even doctrinal professorial scholars who know Hohfeld well do not teach his system in their doctrinal classes. *See* Curtis Nyquist, *Teaching Wesley Hohfeld's Theory of Legal Relations*, 52 J. LEGAL EDUC. 238, 238 (2002) ("[I]n law schools today Hohfeld is relatively unknown and, I suspect, seldom mentioned in the classroom. For the past several years I have taught a Hohfeldian component in all of my courses.").

6 Joseph Singer, *The Legal Rights Debate in Analytical Jurisprudence from Bentham to Hohfeld*, 1982 WIS. L. REV. 975, 979 (1982).

7 Nyquist, *supra* note 5, at 238.

8 A tiny-fraction sample: Walter Wheeler Cook, *Privileges of Labor Unions in the Struggle for Life*, 27 YALE L.J. 779, 785 (1918); Henry E. Smith, *Property as the Law of Things*, 125 HARV. L. REV. 1691, 1696 (2012); Thomas C. Grey, *The Disintegration of Property*, *in* NOMOS: XXII 69, 85 n.40

legal theorists,[9] jurisprudes, moral and political philosophers,[10] and logicians.[11] If Hohfeld's work is all that, why not teach it in basic courses in law? I seek to solve this puzzle and offer my answer in the chapter's concluding remarks.

I arrive at my solution by a journey rich with detail and explanation. My rudely anecdotal survey of expert Hohfeldian but non-Hohfeld-teaching colleagues reinforced my interest in two overarching questions that I address here. First, what exactly is Hohfeld's enterprise? Second, how does his enterprise relate to the enterprise of doctrinal legal analysis? My generic answer to these two questions is that both Hohfeld's enterprise and that of standard legal analysis (by which I mean,

(J. Roland Pennock & John W. Chapman eds., 1980); Hohfeld's scheme was important for the *Restatement of Property*, *see, e.g.*, John P. Maloney, *Restatement of the Law of Property* 12 ST. JOHN'S L. REV. 1 (1937), and sometimes makes its way into judicial opinions, *see, e.g.*, *Flast* v. *Cohen*, 392 U.S. 83, 119 n.5 (Harlan, J., dissenting) ("I have here employed the phrases 'Hohfeldian' and 'non-Hohfeldian' plaintiffs to mark the distinction between the personal and proprietary interests of the traditional plaintiff, and the representative and public interests of the plaintiff in a public action. I am aware that we are confronted here by a spectrum of interests of varying intensities, but the distinction is sufficiently accurate, and convenient, to warrant its use at least for purposes of discussion.").

9 *See, e.g.*, Frank Michelman, *There Have to Be Four*, 64 MD. L. REV. 136 (2005) (Symposium: *Calabresi's The Costs of Accidents: A Generation of Impact on Law and Scholarship*); DUNCAN KENNEDY, LEGAL REASONING (COLLECTED ESSAYS) 96–101 (2008); Jack Balkin, *The Hohfeldian Approach to Law and Semiotics*, 44 U. MIAMI L. REV. 1119, 1121–22 (1990); Pierre Schlag, *How To Do Things With Hohfeld*, 78 LAW & CONTEMP. PROBS. 185 (2015); Singer, *supra* note 6; Eric Engel, *Taking the Right Seriously, Hohfeldian Semiotics and Rights Discourse*, 3 THE CRIT: CRITICAL STUD. J. 84 (2010).

10 Hohfeld is widely recognized as an important exponent of analytical jurisprudence. Three of its leading contemporary thinkers clearly take Hohfeld seriously, though with differing valences. H. L. A. Hart regards Hohfeld as a precursor, and he and John Finnis both offer analyses of rights that are complimentary, complementary, supplementary, and corrective to Hohfeld's. *See* H. L. A. HART, ESSAYS ON BENTHAM, STUDIES IN JURISPRUDENCE AND POLITICAL THEORY, chs. VII, VIII (1982); H. L. A. Hart, *Definition and Theory in Jurisprudence*, 70 LAW Q. REV. 37, 54 (1954); H. L. A. Hart, *Analytical Jurisprudence in Mid-Twentieth Century: A Reply to Professor Bodenheimer*, 105 U. PA. L. REV. 953, 956–57, 959, 970 (1957); John Finnis, *Some Professorial Fallacies About Rights*, 4 ADEL. L. REV. 377 (1971–1972); JOHN FINNIS, NATURAL LAW AND NATURAL RIGHTS § VIII.2 (2d ed. 2011). While engaging with Hohfeld, Joseph Raz is more critical and perhaps unforgiving. *See* JOSEPH RAZ, THE CONCEPT OF A LEGAL SYSTEM 178–80 (2d ed. 1970). There is an abundance of discussion of Hohfeld by philosophers. A few that I have found particularly helpful for this chapter are: Walter Sinnott-Armstrong, *Moral Dilemmas and Rights*, *in* MORAL DILEMMAS AND MORAL THEORY 48–65 (H. E. Mason ed., 1996); the collection of articles in A DEBATE OVER RIGHTS, PHILOSOPHICAL INQUIRIES (Matthew Kramer et al. eds., 1998); James B. Brady, *Language and Logic, The Legal Philosophy of Wesley Newcomb Hohfeld*, 8 TRANSACTIONS OF THE CHARLES S. PEIRCE SOC'Y 246 (1972); Thomas D. Perry, A *Paradigm of Philosophy: Hohfeld on Legal Rights*, 14 AM. PHIL. Q. 41 (1977); Andrew Halpin, *Hohfeld's Conceptions: From Eight to Two*, 44 CAMBRIDGE L.J. 435 (1985).

11 Hohfeld's reception among logicians, and the interpretation of Hohfeld relations *as a scheme of logical relations*, is of central interest to me in this chapter, as I shall explain. A small sample of logicians' interpretations of Hohfeld's system as a system of logical relations includes: Alan Ross Anderson, *The Logic of Hohfeldian Propositions*, 13 LOGIQUE ET ANALYSE 231 (1970) (this publication contains interesting colloquies with other scholars; one of them, Chaim Perelman, complains of the inutility of the logical analysis of Hohfeld that Anderson offers for lawyers); Frederick B. Fitch, A *Revision of Hohfeld's Theory of Legal Concepts*, 10 LOGIQUE ET ANALYSE 269 (1967); Sinnott-Armstrong, *supra* note 10; Giovanni Sartor, *Fundamental Legal Concepts: A Formal and Teleological Characterization*, 14 A.I. & L. 101 (2006); Mark Andrews, *Hohfeld's Cube*, 16 AKRON L. REV. 471 (1983).

applying sets of potentially applicable legal rules to actual or hypothetical patterns of fact) are instances of the mode of logical inference (a term I define in upcoming discussion) referred to as *abduction* or as *inference to the best explanation*. As such, they share the invariant structure of all abductions. But they also differ in the type, the *logical species* of abduction that they instantiate. Standard legal analysis, as defined above, is what I shall call *legal abduction*. Hohfeld's enterprise is philosophical: his system, his "platform,"[12] is a type of *philosophical abduction* that is both distinct and influential enough to earn its own brand: *Hohfeld abduction*. Although it is correct, and not uncommon, to see Hohfeld referred to as a legal philosopher, it is far from common to *explain* Hohfeld's project specifically, in detail, as a type of abduction, as I do here. Moreover, I shall argue that Hohfeld abductions are logically parasitic on legal abductions (but parasites have gotten an undeservedly bad rap). One cannot, for example, know that any particular person A has a claim-right against person B unless and until one determines, by a process of abductive reasoning (which I explain later and refer to as *legal abduction*) that A and B have a transaction whose "operative facts"[13] justify the conclusion that A has made an enforceable promise to B.[14]

To understand *Hohfeld* abductions and their relation to *legal* abductions, we must distinguish explanatory *applications* of Hohfeld's system from Hohfeld's initial discovery of the explanation of legal relations that resulted in his system. The philosophical method Hohfeld used to arrive at (discover? invent?) his system is, I shall argue, akin to reasoning with what philosophers have come to call *reflective equilibrium*, a method of reasoning that is among the main methods of philosophical

[12] Schlag, *supra* note 9, at 187.

[13] In his thoroughly Hohfeldian glossary, Arthur Corbin defines 'operative facts' as: "Any fact the existence or occurrence of which will cause new legal relations between persons. A clear distinction should always be observed between the physical phenomena and the legal relations consequent thereon. The former are in the world of the senses, the latter are intellectual conceptions. Operative facts have also been described as 'investitive,' 'constitutive,' 'causal,' and 'dispositive.' The 'extinguishment' of a legal relation is necessarily the creation of a new one." *See* Arthur L. Corbin, *Legal Analysis and Terminology*, 29 YALE L.J. 163, 164 (1919). A note on my use of single-quotation marks. I shall follow two conventions, common in philosophical analysis of language, for referring to words and phrases. One is the convention of using single-quotation marks to name the word or phrase that appears between them, as, for example, 'word' is the name for word, 'Harvard' is the name of Harvard. Another is to use italics to name a word or phrase, as in *word* is the name of the word *word* (compare: *Hohfeld* is the name of Hohfeld). I also use double-quotation marks in the standard way, either directly to quote a text or to put "scare quotes" around a word or phrase to indicate that a text uses it. This is true of the double quotes around the phrase 'operative facts' in the text to this footnote. I also follow the standard convention of using single quotation marks *within* a quoted text surrounded by double-quotation marks. In a Hohfeldian spirit, precision matters, and I hope the use of these conventions will be clear in the context of the text.

[14] This basic point is in the Hohfeld literature with differing degrees of awareness, focus, and explanation. For one of the better-focused treatments, see, e.g., A. D. Cullison, A *Review of Hohfeld's Fundamental Legal Concepts*, 16 CLEV.-MARSHALL L. REV. 559, 563 (1967) ("a Hohfeldian duty to do something *arises when the positive law would make a person civilly liable for not doing it* … ") (emphasis added). This basic point is a central locus of my awareness, focus, and explanation in this chapter.

argument. I will try to show that, to arrive at his system, Hohfeld used a philosophical method, a type of philosophical abduction, that exhibits the basic structural features of analogical argument – they are *analogical* abductions. Moreover, analogical arguments offered in mathematics and logic rely on analogical abductions (when they are done "virtuously," in a way that I will explain) that have the same degree of conditional probability of the truth of the conclusion of the abductive argument, given the assumed truth of the argument's premises, that valid deductive arguments have. (That there are analogical arguments in these domains will come as a surprise to the many theorists of argument who maintain that analogical arguments are subsumable under the category of inductive arguments.) Hohfeld's analogical abduction also had that characteristic. In sum, I argue (explanatorily, abductively) that Hohfeld has fashioned an axiomatic system, as the result of analogical abduction, that can yield deductively valid inferences. To apply those axioms to specific, actual, or hypothetical cases is to do a *Hohfeld abduction*. My picture is analogous to the difference between, on the one hand, Lobachevsky explaining, abducing (creating? discovering?) the system of non-Euclidean geometry that results from rejecting Euclid's parallel postulate and, on the other hand, someone else, Mary, say, using the Lobachevskian axiom, coming to the system that Lobachevsky established, and applying it to make new theorems under his axiom. Lobachevsky is Hohfeld. We who use his system are Mary.

In this chapter, I offer two "meta-abductions." One, my explanatory argument about legal explanatory arguments (legal abductions), the other, my explanatory argument about Hohfeldian explanatory arguments (Hohfeld abductions). My enterprise thus exemplifies the quip of Yale Law School successor to Hohfeld's Southmayd Chair, my dear professor Arthur Allen Leff: "anything you can do, I can do meta."[15]

4.2 PLAN AND PROGRAM OF THIS CHAPTER

I proceed as follows. First, I introduce Hohfeld relations by presenting a contracts case that is rich with Hohfeld relations (as is every case). Then, adopting one standard interpretation (an *interpretive abduction*, as will be explained later) of the logic of these relations, I show how those relations are to be identified in that case. Next, I step back, as it were, and reflect on what these two examples (the case and analysis and its Hohfeldian analysis) are examples *of*, namely, abduction. It is here that I present sufficient details of the philosophical abduction of the nature of argument that I call the Logocratic Method to explain abduction and how it fits into a complete

[15] Arthur Allen Leff, *Unspeakable Ethics, Unnatural Law*, 1979 DUKE L.J. 1229, 1230 n.2 (1979) ("My colleague, Leon Lipson, once described a certain species of legal writing as, 'Anything you can do, I can do meta.' What follows is a pure instantiation of his category."). As is this one.

explanation of the nature of all arguments, including but not limited to abductive arguments. Folded into the presentation of the Logocratic Method are two concepts and methods central to analysis of Hohfeld. One is my account of the concept and structure of analogical argument, and of abduction, as (what I call) *modes of logical inference*, along with deduction and induction. The other is my account of the specific type of abduction that Hohfeld engages, a specific type of *philosophical* abduction, of which one finds several distinct types over the broad range of philosophers' works. I conclude by locating the specific type of philosophical abduction that Hohfeld engaged among other types of philosophical abduction, and then finally resolve my puzzle about why expert Hohfeldian professors tend not to teach Hohfeld in their doctrinal courses.

4.3 CASE STUDY FOR HOHFELDIAN (ABDUCTIVE) ANALYSIS: SUMMARY OF FACTS AND ARGUMENTS OF *WRIGHT V. NEWMAN*

I will anchor both my presentation of the Logocratic Method and my analysis of Hohfeld relations to the Georgia Supreme Court 1996 case *Wright v. Newman*.[16] In that case, Kim Newman sought to recover from Bruce Wright child support for her son. Wright and Newman had cohabited for some time but had never been married. Wright admitted that, as DNA testing indicated, he was the natural father of their daughter. But the DNA test also indicated that he was not the natural father of Newman's son. After supporting the boy for some time, Wright discontinued that support when his relationship with Newman ended. Newman brought an action for Wright to pay child support for Newman's son. The trial judge found in favor of Newman. In ordering Wright to pay support also for Newman's son, the judge referred to Wright's "actions in having himself listed on the child's birth certificate, giving the child his surname and establishing a parent-child relationship," actions which, in the judge's view, "allow[ed] the child to consider him his father and in so doing deterr[ed Newman] from seeking to establish the paternity of the child's natural father[,] thus denying the child an opportunity to establish a parent-child relationship with the natural father." On appeal to the Georgia Supreme Court, Wright challenged the trial judge's order requiring him to pay child support for Newman's son. Justice Carley, writing for the majority, affirmed the trial judge's award to Newman of Wright's payments for her son. There was a concurrence by Justice Sears and a lone dissent by Chief Justice Benham.

[16] 467 S.E.2d 533 (1996).

In his opinion for the majority, Justice Carley considered several possible legal explanations[17] of the relation between Newman and Wright according to which Wright would be legally obliged to pay support for the boy:

(1) Wright was the boy's natural father.
(2) Wright had formally adopted the boy.
(3) Wright had virtually adopted the boy.[18]

The justice concluded that in this case none of these three explanations explained the relation between Newman and Wright from a legal point of view. Wright was neither the natural nor the formally adoptive nor the virtually adoptive father of the boy. But Justice Carley considered two other possible explanations of the legal relation between Newman and Wright according to which Wright might be obliged to pay support for the boy – explanations that seem not to have been raised or litigated at the trial level:

(4) Wright had made a promise to pay for child support that was part of a bargained for exchange and met the requirement of a writing.
(5) Wright had made a promise to pay for child support that was enforceable under a reliance doctrine in the state's statutorily codified promissory estoppel law.

Justice Carley concluded that explanation (4) did not explain this case because "[t]here was no formal written contract whereby Wright agreed to support Newman's son."[19] However, the justice concluded that explanation (5) did explain the case from a legal point of view, both because state law on promissory estoppel[20] was available to explain the legal relation between Newman and

[17] Here and for some time in my analysis, I use the framework of legal abduction that I fully explicate later. Part of my goal in doing so is to invite the judgment that this way of explaining what judges do when applying rules to facts seems to represent and accord well with that familiar practice of legal analysis.

[18] "If Wright were the natural father of Newman's son, he would be legally obligated to provide support. OCGA § 19-7-2. Likewise, if Wright had formally adopted Newman's son, he would be legally obligated to provide support. OCGA § 19-8-19(a)(2). However, Wright is neither the natural nor the formally adoptive father of the child and 'the theory of "virtual adoption" is not applicable to a dispute as to who is legally responsible for the support of minor children.' *Ellison* v. *Thompson*, 240 Ga. 594, 596, 242 S.E.2d 95 (1978)." Wright, 467 S.E.2d at 534.

[19] "A number of jurisdictions have recognized that a legally enforceable obligation to provide child support can be "based upon parentage *or* contract" (emphasis supplied). *Albert* v. *Albert*, 415 So.2d 818, 819 (Fla.App.1982). *See also* Anno., 90 A.L.R.2d 583 (1963). Georgia is included among those jurisdictions. *Foltz* v. *Foltz*, 238 Ga. 193, 194, 232 S.E.2d 66 (1977). Accordingly, the issue for resolution is whether Wright can be held liable for child support for Newman's son under this state's contract law. There was no formal written contract whereby Wright agreed to support Newman's son." 467 S. E.2d at 534. Presumably the reference to the "formal written contract" reflects Justice Carley's legal explanation according to which the state's statute of frauds would require a promise of long-term support to be in writing in order to be enforceable.

[20] "[U]nder this state's contract law,[a] promise which the promisor should reasonably expect to induce action or forbearance on the part of the promisee or a third person and which does induce such action or forbearance is binding if injustice can be avoided only by enforcement of the promise. The remedy granted for breach may be limited as justice requires. OCGA § 13-3-44(a). This statute codifies the principle of promissory estoppel." 467 S.E.2d at 534. Georgia statute OCGA § 13-3-44(a) had codified the exact language of Restatement (Second) of Contracts § 90.

Wright *and* because the facts of the case, as found by the Supreme Court, permitted imposition of child support for the boy on Wright, even though this theory of the case was never argued below, which meant that the trial court did not find any fact explicitly under the criteria specified by the state's statutory promissory estoppel rule.

4.4 HOHFELDIAN PHILOSOPHICAL ABDUCTION OF *WRIGHT V. NEWMAN*

4.4.1 *The Enthymematic Nature of Hohfeld Jural Relations*

In the article that first presented it,[21] Hohfeld's system provides an *explanation of the jural relations* that obtain between (or among) persons who are subject to law within a legal system. In Hohfeld's system there are two sets of four relations that he styles "jural correlatives" (right-duty, privilege-no-right, power-liability, immunity-disability) and "jural opposites" (right-no-right, privilege-duty, power-disability, immunity-liability). There are many ways to characterize these relations both from a logical point of view (*logical abduction*) and from a *philosophical* (more specifically, jurisprudential) point of view. (These concepts of *abduction* and *point of view* are central to my Logocratic analysis of abduction, and I present them in Section 4.5.10.) One result of the Logocratic analysis of Hohfeld's system of jural relations is to reveal its *enthymematic* nature.

4.4.1.1 Simple Example of an Argument-Enthymeme and Rule-Enthymeme

The concept of the enthymeme is central to the Logocratic system of explanation of the nature of argument. In particular, the Logocratic Method is interested in the fact that arguments offered in natural language contexts (including the context of legal language use by judges and lawyers) are *enthymematic*. I offer more detailed analysis of this important concept in Section 4.5.4, but the basic idea is simple and familiar to theorists of argument. On the Logocratic conception of the concept of the enthymeme, an enthymeme is any rule (*rule-enthymeme*) or argument (*argument-enthymeme*) whose logical form is not explicit in its original mode of presentation. Suppose, for example, that Mom, a rule-making authority in the family, says to daughter Jane:

> (1) "On a weeknight, you can watch TV only when you've done all your homework, and you haven't tonight. No TV!"

Is there a rule in what Mom has said? Has she offered an argument based on that rule? An *argument* is a set of propositions some of which, premises, are or could be offered to support members of another set of propositions, conclusions. If (1) is an argument, what is the set of premises, and what is the set of conclusions? (Note that

[21] Hohfeld, *supra* note 2. He offered some useful supplementary explanations in Wesley N. Hohfeld, *Some Fundamental Conceptions as Applied in Legal Reasoning*, 23 YALE L.J. 16 (1917).

a set may have one member.) This is an *interpretive* decision. Further, if one does find in this speech act an *argument*, what is its *logical form* (see Section 4.5.3) – that is, is it (fairly represented as) a deductive, or inductive, or abductive, or analogical argument? And if, as a matter of interpretation, one decides that it has one of these logical forms, does it have those distinctive characteristics (distinctive of deduction, or of induction, or of abduction, or of analogy) that make it a strong argument of its kind? For example, if one interprets (1) as a deductive argument, does it have the *characteristic virtue* (see Section 4.5.6.3) of validity, namely, that in any possible set of circumstances in which all its premises are true, the conclusion is also true? These are questions that are central to the Logocratic explanation of argument, and I offer greater detail below.

For now, setting the stage for my specific point about Hohfeld (that Hohfeld jural relations are *enthymematic*), note that if one takes Mom's utterance in (1) to be an argument, it is an *argument-enthymeme*, that is, its logical form (its status as a deduction, or an induction, or an abduction, or an analogical argument) is not explicit in the mode of presentation of the utterance. We may give a fair formal representation of the argument-enthymeme, that is "argufy" it, by identifying ε_1 and ε_2 as the set of premises containing two elements, and h[22] as the singleton set comprising the conclusion:

ε_1	For all weeknights, if Jane has permission to watch TV then Jane has done her homework.
ε_2	On this weeknight, Jane has not done her homework.
h	On this weeknight, it is not the case that Jane has permission to watch TV.

Construed thus, her argument-enthymeme becomes an instantiation in predicate logic of *modus tollens* (the pattern of argument that corresponds to the conditional proposition function $(x)((Px \supset Qx) \wedge {\sim}Qx) \supset {\sim}Px)$. This argument, as interpreted and represented above, is both deductive and valid. Note that the first premise is a *rule* for the circumstances under which Jane may watch TV, so this "argufication" of the argument-enthymeme contains a "rulification" of a rule-enthymeme, namely, Mom's utterance: "On a weeknight, you may watch TV only when you've done all your homework."

4.4.1.2 The Enthymemicity of Hohfeld Propositions

Hohfeld's explanation of his jural relations is enthymematic in this way. Specifically, Hohfeld's system of jural relations, as presented (at first, and canonically) in his 1913 article "Some Fundamental Conceptions as Applied in Legal Reasoning,"[23] consists of a set of rule-enthymemes that one must rulify in order to use his system to explain the relations in any legal transaction or relation – such as I shall soon do with *Wright v. Newman*. It is indeed because of the enthymematic nature of Hohfeld jural

[22] The motivation for using 'ε_1', 'ε_2' and 'h' to number the premises and conclusion is discussed in Section 4.5.2.

[23] Hohfeld, *supra* note 2.

relations that one finds many different rulifications thereof in the Hohfeld literature. As has aptly been observed by a scholar very attentive to competing *logical* interpretations of the Hohfeld explanatory system,[24] Hohfeld was clearly trying to articulate a set of *logical relations*, and wanted to be understood thus. But he faced a challenge that faces any theorist who is offering a formal language that purports to track accurately a substantial part of the usages of non-formal natural language, namely, that the formal language regiments usage in a way that will almost certainly depart from natural usage in some ways.[25] And Hohfeld set himself an even more challenging variant of this task in that he sought to identify logical relations using only natural language, the same natural language of lawyers and judges whose problem of vagueness and ambiguity with regard to uses of the term 'right' was the central motivation for his project.[26] Compounding the interpretive challenge was his additional belief that the four basic terms that he used to disambiguate legal talk of rights were undefinable.[27]

24 Cullison, *supra* note 1, at 1221. Cullison points (*de re*, albeit not *de dicto* – 'point to' is an opaque verb here) to the enthymemicity of Hohfeld rule-enthymemes in this assertion: "Hohfeld's analytical system is built around eight 'fundamental legal conceptions,' four of which are normative terms-'right,' 'duty,' 'privilege,' and 'no-right.' According to Hohfeld's scheme of jural correlatives and jural opposites, various statements (normative statements, which we can call 'norms of law') using these four terms are logically interrelated. *Although students of Hohfeld have disagreed about many of the important details of his system*, it appears that he did have in mind a very specific and precise scheme of logical interrelations among these normative statements." Cullison, *supra* note 1, at 1211 (emphasis added). The enthymemicity of Hohfeld jural relations is also at least part of the explanation for Henry Smith's and Andrew Gold's observation that: "It is rare for something as precise and analytical as Wesley Hohfeld's system of legal relations to serve as a Rorschach blot." See Chapter 14.

25 J. L. Austin noted this issue in observing that: "Ordinary language breaks down in extraordinary cases. (In such cases, the cause of the breakdown is semantical.) Now, no doubt an *ideal* language would *not* break down, whatever happened. In doing physics, for example, where our language is tightened up in order to precisely describe complicated and unusual cases concisely, we *prepare linguistically for the worst*. In ordinary language we do not: *words fail us*. If we talk as though an ordinary must be like an ideal language, we shall misrepresent the facts." J. L. Austin, *The Meaning of a Word*, *in* Philosophical Papers 36 (J. Urmson & G. Warnock eds., 1961). But Austin's attempt to distinguish the language of physics (and presumably, other "hard" empirical sciences like biology and chemistry) on the ground that natural language, but not the language of hard science, could have vague terms (*see infra*, note 97), missed the explanatory power of the distinction between open texture and vagueness that Austin's Oxford colleague H. L. A. Hart started to explain more successfully. Terms in the hard-empirical sciences can also be both open-textured and vague.

26 "One of the greatest hindrances to the clear understanding, the incisive statement, and the true solution of legal problems frequently arises from the express or tacit assumption that all legal relations may be reduced to 'rights' and 'duties,' and that these latter categories are therefore adequate for the purpose of analyzing even the most complex legal interests, such as trusts, options, escrows, 'future' interests, corporate interests, etc ... As a matter of fact, however, the above-mentioned inadequacy and ambiguity of terms unfortunately reflect, all too often, corresponding paucity and confusion as regards actual legal conceptions." Hohfeld, *supra* note 2, at 28–29.

27 *Id.* at 30 ("The strictly fundamental legal relations are, after all, sui generis; and thus it is that attempts at formal definition are always unsatisfactory, if not altogether useless. Accordingly, the most promising line of procedure seems to consist in exhibiting all of the various relations in a scheme of 'opposites' and 'correlatives,' and then proceeding to exemplify their individual scope and application in concrete cases. An effort will be made to pursue this method."). Joseph Raz considers Hohfeld's

For simplicity, I here use a rulification of Hohfeld jural relations that is one of the most common interpretative choices for representing Hohfeld jural relations. On this rulification, in today's vocabulary of predicate logic, Hohfeld jural relations are triadic (three-place) relations.[28] The table below has two columns. The left column presents Hohfeld's *enthymematic* text from his 1913 article (enough of it to enable a rulification) in which he first articulated the jural relations. The table presents four of his eight jural relations, so-called "correlative" jural relations (or, more simply, the "correlatives"). This enthymematic text is completely in the "natural" language, meaning (in linguists' terms) non-mathematically or non-logically formalized language; Hohfeld's article preceded the development of the formal logical languages of predicate and deontic logic that logicians later developed. Again, it is a testament to Hohfeld's analytical acuity that his system scales up, or, more accurately, scales into formal logical languages that were developed long after his original – in both senses – work. Despite being "natural" in this sense, Hohfeld's language, like much legal language, is in another sense not "natural," in that it is stilted or formal or unusual. The right column of the table presents a "rulification" of Hohfeld's rule-enthymemes for the correlatives as a three-place relation, using the representation offered by John Finnis, an astute interpreter of the legal logic of Hohfeld relations.[29] Finnis' rulification of the Hohfeld correlatives uses the basic grammar of predicate logic (see Tables 4.1, 4.2, 4.3, and 4.4).

view that his basic terms were indefinable to be one of his four "particularly grave" mistakes, resulting from "a misconception of the nature and function of definitions. For Hohfeld himself defined 'privilege' in terms of 'no duty not to do', and immunity as the absence of liability." J. RAZ, THE CONCEPT OF A LEGAL SYSTEM 180 (2d ed. 1970).

28 A *monadic* predicate relates elements of sets to their sets (the relation of *membership in*), as in *Socrates is mortal*. A *dyadic* predicate relates two relata, such as in *Jack kissed Jill* and *Socrates is wiser than Euthyphro*. A *triadic* predicate relates three relata, as in (abstracting away from named individuals) *x introduced y to z*, *x extends from y to z*, *x gave y to z*, *x stole y from z*, *x hates y because of z*, *x is the sum of y and z*, and *x never got over the sight of y kicking z*. A *tetradic* predicate relates four relata, as in *x is further from y than z is from w*, *x entertained y while z was entertaining w*, *x introduced y to z at w's request*, and *when x times y is subtracted from z the result is w*.

29 *See* FINNIS, NATURAL LAW AND NATURAL RIGHTS, *supra* note 10, at 199 ("to assert a Hohfeldian right is to assert a three-term relation between one person, one act-description, and one other person"). As I say, this is a common representation of the logic of Hohfeld relations. For another example, see BRIAN BIX, JURISPRUDENCE: THEORY AND CONTEXT 128 (4th ed. 2006) ("Hohfeld argued that all rights-statements ('rights' here understood either narrowly, in their first sense, as claims correlative to another party's duty, or broadly, as involving any of the four legal concepts named) should be reducible to a three-variable proposition: A has a right against B for X (where A and B are people or institutions and X is an object or activity)." This logical interpretation (interpretive abduction of the logic of Hohfeld relations) is also found in the work of deontic logicians and logically oriented legal theorists. See, e.g., the pioneering paper by Alan Ross Anderson, *supra* note 11, at 233 ("Writers of the Hohfeldian school have stressed as central to their analysis of "legal relations," the view that such relations must be construed as two-termed relations between persons. '... in each case one plaintiff, one defendant, one issue; one privilege or one right is all that needs examination: the one relation between these two people.' ... But it is clear from the examples they discuss that the relations under consideration *are in fact three-termed at least*, namely, relations holding (say) among two litigants, and some state-of-affairs in dispute. When discussing examples, Hohfeld (and others) explicitly recognize the three-termed character of the relations in question ... ") (citation omitted, emphasis added).

TABLE 4.1 *Claim right is correlative to duty*

Hohfeld's enthymematic text[30]	Finnis' rulification
"In other words, if X has a right against Y that he shall stay off the former's land, the correlative (and equivalent) is that Y is under a duty toward X to stay off the place."[31]	A has a claim-right that B should Φ, if and only if B has a duty to A to Φ.

TABLE 4.2 *Liberty (privilege) is correlative to no-right*

Hohfeld's enthymematic text	Finnis' rulification
"The fundamental and important difference between a right (or claim) and a privilege, surely . . . is found in the fact that the correlative of the latter relation is a 'no-right,' there being no single term available to express the latter conception. Thus, the correlative of X's right that Y shall not enter on the land is Y's duty not to enter; but the correlative of X's privilege of entering himself is manifestly Y's 'no-right' that X shall not enter."[32] "The only correlative logically implied by the privileges or liberties in question are the 'no-rights' of 'third parties.' It would therefore be a *non-sequitur* to conclude from the mere existence of such liberties that "third parties" are under a *duty* not to interfere, etc."[33]	(i) B has a liberty (relative to A) *to* Φ, if and only if A has no claim-right ('a no-right') that B *should not* Φ. (ii) B has a liberty (relative to A) *not to* Φ, if and only if A has no claim-right ('a no-right') that B *should* Φ.[34]

30 I attempt to identify in the 1913 article, Hohfeld, *supra* note 2, some part of Hohfeld's original text that seems to be his assertion of the rule that comprises his statement of correlative relations. Is this a fair interpretive procedure? The whole of Hohfeld's text in the 1913 article contains not only assertions of the rule-enthymemes but also discursive illustrations of the application of those rules, as well as discussion of the use of the terms Hohfeld appropriates as the names of his jural relations in the discourse of scholars, judges, and lawyers. Thus, this article is similar to the Restatement of Contracts, which has both rules and illustrative discussions of the operations of those rules. In both Hohfeld's and the *Restatement* texts it is possible to isolate and identify the rule-enthymemes even though one gains additional information about how the text's author believes the rule is to be applied from the additional discussion. *See also* Anderson, *supra* note 11, at 233 ("When discussing examples, Hohfeld (and others) explicitly recognize the three-termed character of the relations in question: '. . . if X has a right against Y that he shall stay off the former's land, [then] Y is under a duty toward X that he stay off the place. X has the power to transfer his interest to Y . . .'") (quoting Hohfeld, *supra* note 2, at 32).

31 Hohfeld, *supra* note 2, at 32.

32 *Id.* at 33.

33 *Id.* at 36–37 (emphasis added).

34 As the table indicates, Finnis' rulification of the liberty-no-right correlatives distinguishes liberty *to do* (this is (i) in the table) from liberty *not to do* (this is (ii)).

TABLE 4.3 *Power is correlative to liability*

Hohfeld's enthymematic text	Finnis' rulification
"As indicated in the preliminary scheme of jural relations, a legal power (as distinguished, of course, from a mental or physical power) is the opposite of legal disability, and the correlative of legal liability. But what is the intrinsic nature of a legal power as such? Is it possible to analyze the conception represented by this constantly employed and very important term of legal discourse? Too close an analysis might seem metaphysical rather than useful; so that what is here presented is intended only as an approximate explanation sufficient for all practical purposes."[35]	A has a power (relative to B) to Φ, if and only if B has a liability to have his or her legal position changed by A's Φ-ing.[36]

4.4.2 *Warmup: A Hohfeldian Abduction of Mom's Rule*

The Hohfeldian abduction explaining Mom's TV rule in the example above (see Section 4.4.1.1) is as follows. If Mom has the authority to establish this rule as "law" within the family, then this rule says that Jane would have both a *claim-right* and a (distinct) *privilege* (as against each parent, it seems) to watch TV only if the alleged operative fact of her doing all her homework was true. Also, Mom has exercised her *power* to give Jane the *power* – a "meta-power"? – to change the "legal" relation between Jane and her parents from one in which Jane has neither the *claim right* nor

35 Hohfeld, *supra* note 2, at 44 (emphasis added). Note again Hohfeld's disclaimer of the possibility of precision. One might say (without churlishness?) that "too close an analysis" is *literally precisely* what is wanted for clear analysis of logical relations – in which case, of course, a precise analysis would not be "too close."

36 FINNIS, Natural Law and Natural Rights, *supra* note 10, at 199. Finnis here tries to fit Hohfeld's power-liability correlatives into the mold of a three-term relation. Here is another among abundant items of evidence of the enthymemicity of Hohfeld's natural-language description. Layman Allen offers an interpretation of the power-liability correlative pair that seems to compete with Finnis': "Hohfeld's treatment of 'power' is significantly different from the treatment of 'right' and 'privilege.' The latter pair of terms refer to three-term relationships, while 'power' is, in effect, stipulated to refer to a two-term relationship between (a) the changing of a legal relation and (b) the power-holder. To say that x has the (legal) power to create legal relation r is the same as to say that legal relation r does not exist now, that it is within the volitional control of x to do p, and that if x does p then legal relation r will be created." Layman E. Allen, *Formalizing Hohfeldian Analysis to Clarify the Multiple Senses of Legal Right*, 48 S. CAL. L. REV. 428, 435 (1974). In the terms of the Logocratic Method whose basics I'm still explaining, there is a *dialectical* competition of the *interpretive abductions* (specifically, the *rulifications*) of the Hohfeld rule-enthymemes for powers and liabilities. Further indication even in this brief example of options for the rulification of Hohfeld correlatives is found in Finnis' further discussion of the way in which "[l]awyers frequently talk about rights, not as three-term relations between two persons and an act of a certain type, but as two-term relations between persons and one subject-matter or (in a broad sense) thing: for example, someone's right to £10 under a contract, or to (a share in) a specified estate, or to the performing rights of an opera." FINNIS, NATURAL LAW AND NATURAL RIGHTS, *supra* note 10, at 201.

TABLE 4.4 *Immunity is correlative to disability*

Hohfeld's enthymematic text	Finnis' rulification
"[I]mmunity is the correlative of disability ('no-power'), and the opposite, or negation, of liability. Perhaps it will also be plain, from the preliminary outline and from the discussion down to this point, that a power bears the same general contrast to an immunity that a right does to a privilege. A right is one's affirmative claim against another, and a privilege is one's freedom from the right or claim of another. Similarly, a power is one's affirmative 'control' over a given legal relation as against another; whereas an immunity is one's freedom from the legal power or 'control' of another as regards some legal relation."[37]	B has an immunity (relative to A's Φ-ing), if and only if A has no power (i.e., a disability) to change B's legal position by Φ-ing.

the *privilege* (as against each parent) to watch TV to one in which Jane, by doing her homework, creates both of these Hohfeldian incidents.

4.4.3 *A Hohfeldian Abduction of Wright v. Newman*

In the case of *Wright v. Newman*, Hohfeld's system provides tools for an explanation of Hohfeldian legal relations between Newman (the mother) and Wright (the boyfriend), both before and after Wright made his promise to take care of the boy and before Newman relied on it in such a way as to make his promise legally enforceable under the Georgia promissory estoppel statute. I offer that explanation in this section.

4.4.3.1 Before Wright's Promise and (Perforce) before Newman's Reliance Thereon

In the Hohfeld explanatory scheme, before Wright's promise to take care of the boy (including financially) and Newman's reliance (as specified in the operative facts of the applicable Georgia statute),[38] Wright was *privileged not to pay* Newman for support of the boy, and, correlatively, Newman had a *no-right* to recover child support from him for the boy. Also, Wright was *privileged not to promise to pay support for the boy*, and correlatively, Newman had a *no-right* against him that he promise. Before Wright's promise and Newman's reliance, Newman was *disabled* from changing Wright's *privilege* of not paying support for the boy (for example, into

[37] Hohfeld, *supra* note 2, at 55.

[38] Regarding Hohfeld's useful concept of operative facts, see *supra* note 13.

a duty to pay), and, correlatively, Wright had an *immunity* to Newman's capacity to change that privilege into a duty.

4.4.3.2 After Wright's Promise and Newman's Reliance Thereon

Now consider the legal relations between Newman and Wright *after* Wright made the promise and *before* Newman relied on it in the way specified by the operative facts of the Georgia promissory estoppel statute. In the Hohfeld explanatory scheme, their legal relationship changes. In virtue of her capacity to go to court, Newman now had a *power* to change Wright's privilege not to pay support for the boy into a duty to pay support for the boy. From Wright's perspective, after he makes the promise to pay support for the boy, he is then under a *liability* of having his *privilege* of not paying support for the boy changed to a *duty* to pay.

Under the standard interpretation of the rules in the Hohfeld system, as evidenced in the table above by Finnis' interpretation of Hohfeld's rule-enthymemes, these Hohfeldian explanations seem straightforward. Much less straightforward, it turns out, is which of many *competing* interpretations of the Hohfeld enthymematic rules for his explanatory framework one ought to adopt. I return to this question later (see Section 4.6), but I now turn to presenting the basics of my own explanatory framework, the Logocratic Method, which is what I continue to use to explain the Hohfeld system as a type of abduction. Central to my project is the Logocratic conception of abduction in general, and, based on that conception, an articulation of *philosophical abduction* that I will use to identify the precise nature of Hohfeld's enterprise.

4.5 CONCEPTS AND PROCEDURES OF THE LOGOCRATIC METHOD (LOGOCRATIC ABDUCTION)

4.5.1 *The Term 'Logocratic'*

I construct the term 'Logocratic' from the Ancient Greek terms *λογος* [*logos*] meaning, among other things, 'argument,' and *κρατος* [*kratos*] meaning, among other things, 'strength.' (Compare this word to the word *democracy*, the "strength of the *demos*.")[39]

[39] The most complete recent statement of the Logocratic Method is found in Scott Brewer, *First Among Equals: Abduction in Legal Argument from a Logocratic Point of View*, in NEW ESSAYS ON THE NATURE OF LEGAL REASONING (Mark McBride & James Penner eds., 2022); J. WEINSTEIN ET AL., EVIDENCE: CASES AND MATERIALS 3–145 (10th ed. 2017). *See also* Scott Brewer, *Logocratic Method and the Analysis of Arguments in Evidence*, 10 L. PROBABILITY & RISK 175, 175–202 (2011); Scott Brewer, *Using Propositional Deductive Logic as an Aid to Teaching American Contract Law: The Logocratic Approach*, *in* LAW AND LOGIC: CONTEMPORARY ISSUES 97, 97–124 (Dieter Krimphove & Gabriel M. Lentner eds., 2017). For a very succinct account, see Scott Brewer, *HLS Thinks Big 2016*, YOUTUBE (July 5, 2016), www.youtube.com/watch?v=xkECmHYMJxA; Scott Brewer, *Harvard*

4.5.2 *Proposition, Sentence, Argument*

An *argument* is comprised of sets of propositions that stand in a particular binary relation. A proposition is an abstract entity to which sentences of natural languages correspond. The abstraction is best understood by noting that the same proposition can appear in different natural languages. When proposition P appears in language 1 as sentence 1 (e.g., English, such as, 'I should only believe in a God that would know how to dance.') and in language 2 as sentence 2 (e.g., German, such as 'Ich würde nur an einen Gott glauben, der zu tanzen verstünde.'), there is a translation of that one proposition into two languages. A sentence is the incarnation of an abstract proposition. Put another way, a sentence is a token of which the corresponding proposition is the type. Of course, we can identify any proposition only as it occurs in some natural language. In an important way, the proliferant (not infrequently competing) interpretations of Hohfeld relations by philosophers, jurisprudes, and logicians, involves trans-lating (etymologically, "carrying across") the natural language English, in which Hohfeld articulated his jural-relation rule-enthymemes, into the more precise language of deontic logic.[40]

Because an argument is composed of propositions, it is also an abstract entity, and, as with propositions, one argument can be translated into different languages (for example, 'Man is something that hath to be surpassed: and therefore shalt thou love thy virtues, – for thou wilt succumb by them' and 'Der Mensch ist Etwas, das überwunden werden muss: und darum sollst du deine Tugenden lieben, – denn du wirst an ihnen zu Grunde gehn' in English and German, respectively), and any given argument must appear in some natural language. We can mark the distinction between arguments, which are composed of propositions, and instantiations of arguments in some natural language, which are composed of sentences, as the difference between *argument types* and *argument tokens*, respectively.[41]

Lectures that Last 2015, YOUTUBE (June 23, 2015), www.youtube.com/watch?v=oPvwEsvtfso. Another recent succinct summary of the basic features is in Scott Brewer, *Agonophobia (Fear of Contest) in the Theory of Argument?: The Case of Gary Lawson's* Evidence of the Law, 97 B. U. L. REV. 2302 (2017).

40 See Cullison, *supra* note 1 and accompanying text.

41 I offer this footnote because I was raised, as it were, to take Quine seriously. It's beyond the scope of this chapter to discuss in greater detail the realist-seeming metaphysics that I adopt in recognizing a distinction between sentences (always concrete, appearing in some natural language) and propositions (always abstract, maintaining their identity even when appearing in different languages), which is also the distinction between types and tokens. As indicated above, I endorse a type-token distinction for both sentences (tokens) and propositions (types) as well as for argument-tokens (which are composed of sentences) and argument-types (which are composed of propositions). My endorsement of this type-token distinction reflects my acceptance of the idea that the same proposition or set of propositions (type) can appear as sentences (token) in different languages. I thus also endorse the idea that synonymy and translation are possible. I do believe that a more rigorously nominalist metaphysics would also allow me to explain the phenomena of argument that I now refer to using the ontology of argument-type/argument-token, proposition-type/sentence-token. This could be done, for example, along the lines of the "inscriptionalist" theory worked out by Israel Scheffler in BEYOND THE LETTER: A PHILOSOPHICAL INQUIRY INTO AMBIGUITY, VAGUENESS AND METAPHOR IN LANGUAGE (1979). For

As noted, an argument is comprised of sets of propositions that stand in a particular binary relation. One set of propositions of an argument is called *premises*. The other set of propositions is called *conclusions*. We may label the whole set of premise propositions 'E' and label each individual premise ε_1, ε_2, ε_3, ... ε_n. We may label the whole set of conclusion propositions 'H' and each individual conclusion h_1, h_2, h_3, ... h_n. (The use of these premise and conclusion names reflects and keeps before the Logocratic analyst the idea that, on the evidential conception of logic, premises of arguments are *evidence* for the conclusion as hypothesis – see Section 4.5.3 for more details.) We may identify the binary relation in an argument between the premises and conclusions as: *is claimed, or can be taken to claim, to provide support for*. That is, an argument is a relation between one set of propositions (premises) that are claimed to provide, or can be taken to claim to provide, support for the other set of propositions (conclusions). There are two ways we can describe the type of support that the set of premises E provides for the set of conclusions H in the relation *is claimed, or can be taken to claim, to provide support for*. We can say that the premises provide *inferential support* for the conclusion. This means that if the premises are true (or otherwise warranted), they provide support for *inferring the conclusion*. Another way to describe this support is that the premises provide *internal support* for the conclusion. This means that, on the assumption that the premises are true, we judge the conclusion to be true. (Although this is basically also a description of inferential support, the term 'internal' provides a useful way to characterize the difference between a *valid* argument, a deductive argument such that, in any possible world in which all the premises are true the conclusion must be true, and a *sound* argument, a valid argument whose premises are true in the actual world.)

Scheffler, the term 'inscriptionalist' "implies no theoretical contrast with nominalism; it simply calls attention to the favored status of tokens, and the exclusion of types, classes, meanings, forms, and attributes from our semantic apparatus." *Id.* at 8. In a non-inscriptionalist theory, such as what is often referred to as "Platonist" or "Realist," "Concepts, propositions, facts, and states-of-affairs may be introduced additionally, and related in diverse ways to the foregoing objects. The individuation of entities in this scheme, finally, rests at various points on presumed synonymies, analyticities, modal judgments, essences, counterfactual assertions, or intuitive descriptions of the supposed entities in question." Although Scheffler's inscriptionalism "takes for granted only the individual tokens and the individual things that may be denoted. Neither abstract entities associated with tokens nor those associated with denoted things, nor intensional intermediaries between tokens and things are, in short, to be employed as unanalyzed tools of semantic interpretation," he also recognizes – perhaps in good pragmatic, if not (but perhaps also) Pragmatist spirit – that, "[s]ince tokens and denoted things are assumed by any semantic scheme, inscriptionalism does not *add to* the entities commonly recognized; its interpretations are therefore ontologically acceptable to non-inscriptionalists, although the converse does not hold. Readers who do not share the inscriptionalistic assumptions of the present inquiry may therefore still find interest in its interpretations. They need not take its exclusions in any absolute sense, but only understand them hypothetically, as defining the methodological constraints of the study. They may, moreover, be assured that notions excluded by these constraints may be reintroduced at will by anyone who does not find them obscure." *Id.* at 9.

4.5.3 *Logical Form (Mode of Logical Inference): The Definition*

All arguments have what I call a *logical form* or (stipulatively synonymously) a *mode of logical inference*. I endorse an *evidential* conception of logic, according to which logic is the study of the *evidential relation* between the premises and conclusions of arguments.[42] Building on the evidential conception of logic, I conceive of an argument's premises as providing evidence for its conclusions, and I define an argument's *logical form* (*mode of logical inference*) as the *evidential relation* between the argument's premises and its conclusion. There are exactly four modes of logical inference: deduction, induction, abduction (also, synonymously, inference to the best explanation), and analogy. The premises of a deductive argument provide *deductive evidence* for its conclusion and, likewise, for the other three logic forms (*mutatis mutandis* – inductive evidence, abductive evidence, and analogical evidence).

4.5.4 *Arguments and Rules in Their Natural (Non-formal) Habitats: The Enthymeme, Rule-Enthymemes, and Argument-Enthymemes*

4.5.4.1 The Logocratic Conception of the Enthymeme (and Its Relevance to Analysis of Hohfeld Jural Relations)

I have already briefly introduced and deployed the concept of the enthymeme in order to present a set of closely related central claims of this chapter: (i) that Hohfeld jural relation axioms (so I shall understand them) are *rule-enthymemes*; (ii) that the interpreter of the logic of these axioms must "rulify" them, which means to give them a fair formal representation; (iii) that (like all texts, as *interpretanda* – where interpretation itself is a type of abduction) each enthymematic text underdetermines its interpretation;[43] these three features of Hohfeld axioms (iv) enable and occasion the divergence in interpretations of the logical structure of Hohfeld axioms that I have already briefly sampled. In the following sections, I return to the concept of the enthymeme, vital to both the Logocratic Method and my explanation of Hohfeld, to explain my conception of it compared to earlier conceptions.

The concept of the enthymeme has a long history, tracing its most important provenance to Aristotle's lecture notes, published as *The Rhetoric*.[44] Aristotle, the great discoverer (inventor) of syllogistic logical form (now represented in the

[42] I extend B. Skyrms, Choice & Chance 4 (1966) ("Logic is the study of the strength of the evidential link between the premises and conclusions of arguments.").

[43] For discussion of underdetermination in interpretation (in what is an early version of my developing Logocratic explanation of interpretation), see Scott Brewer, *Figuring the Law, Holism and Tropological Inference in Legal Interpretation*, 97 Yale L.J. 823, 837 (1988).

[44] A useful translation and guide is Aristotle, On Rhetoric: A Theory of Civic Discourse (G. Kennedy trans., 2007).

grammar of first-order predicate logic), treats the enthymeme as "a kind of syllogism" (Rhetoric, 1355a),[45] or as a "rhetorical syllogism" (Rhetoric, 1356b).[46] An Aristotelian enthymeme is also "derived from probabilities [*eikota*] and signs [*semeia*], so it is necessary that each of these be the same as each [of the truth values mentioned]; ... for a probability [*eikos*] is what happens for the most part, not in a simple sense, as some define it, but whatever, among things that can be other than they are, is so related to that in regard to which it is probable as a universal is related to a particular" (Rhetoric, 1357a–b[47]). In addition, for Aristotle, in an enthymeme the "major premises" of these enthymematic syllogisms are often commonly held generalizations (Rhetoric, 1357a).[48] Because the Aristotelian enthymeme, known as "rhetorical syllogism," relies on probabilistic premises that are generalizations from experience, these would be classed today not as deductive syllogisms but instead as instances of *defeasible modus ponens*.[49] It is this aspect of Aristotle's account of the enthymeme that yields the widely-used definition of an enthymeme as: "An argument in which one of the premises is not explicitly stated."[50]

This Aristotelian view that an enthymeme is an abbreviated, more easily accessible form of argument is central to the Logocratic development of the concept. The Logocratic conception of the enthymeme relies on the fact that in many contexts of argument, rules and arguments are presented without their logical form being explicit. Logocratic analysis (Logocratic abduction) is designed to handle a familiar, if not often recognized or theorized, problem in the logical evaluation of arguments that are composed of sentences and therefore encountered in natural languages: such arguments are *enthymematic*. Outside of specialized contexts of argument, such as in the practices in the professions of formal mathematics and logic, arguments are enthymematic. (Even in those professions, there is a question whether any argument

45 *Id.* at 33.

46 Aristotle, *supra* note 44, at 40.

47 *Id.* at 42.

48 *Id.* at 41–42 (footnotes omitted).

49 I discuss the basic concept of defeasible argument in Section 4.5.9. There is a rich growing literature on defeasible argument. One very interesting (technical) account is found in Henry Prakken, *Formalising Debates about Lawmaking Proposals as Practical Reasoning, in* Logic in the Theory and Practice of Lawmaking 301–21 (M. Araszkiewicz & K. Pleszka eds., 2015). Hohfeld axioms yield indefeasible deductive arguments.

50 *See* Simon Blackburn, The Oxford Dictionary of Philosophy (2d rev. ed. 2008), s.v. 'enthymeme.' *See also* Doug Walton, *The Three Bases for the Enthymeme: A Dialogical Theory*, 6 J. Appl. Logic 361, 362 (2008) ("According to analysis of enthymemes that will be put forward in this paper, an enthymeme is defined as an incomplete argument found in a text of discourse. More precisely, some components of the argument can be found as explicit premises or conclusions stated by its proponent, but some other statements need to be filled in as premises or conclusions before it can be determined precisely what the argument is. In many cases, the missing assumption is a premise ... On this definition, an argument has an explicit set of premises $\{P_1, P_2, \ldots P_n\}$ and an ultimate conclusion, C, that can, along with an implicit set of statements $\{Q_1, Q_2, \ldots Q_n\}$ be added to the explicit set to generate C by a chain of valid inferences.").

can ever avoid being enthymematic.[51]) Arguments offered by judges, lawyers, and other legal analysts are overwhelmingly enthymematic. And when those arguments prominently rely on legal rules, the legal rules are also enthymematic. A fundamental task of a Logocratic analyst is to identify rule-enthymemes and argument-enthymemes, and to "rulify" or "argufy" them (respectively), that is, to give a fair formal representation of the logical structure of the rule or the argument (in law, the arguments rely centrally on the legal rules).

We can be more precise regarding the ontology of rule and argument-enthymemes. Recall that a *sentence* is the incarnation of an abstract *proposition*. Generally, an enthymeme is a *sentence* or a *set of sentences* (the set may have one or more members) whose *logical structure* is not explicit. This is an extension of a traditional concept of "enthymeme," which was predicated only of arguments and was defined as an argument which was missing one of its *sentences* in its natural-language incarnate form – either one of the premises or one or more of the conclusions. Put another way, in Logocratic theory an enthymeme is a rule or argument whose logical form is not explicit in its original mode of presentation – its presentation in, for example, a judicial opinion, a lawyer's brief (which contains both argument-enthymemes and rule-enthymemes), a regulation, a statute, or a constitution (each of which contains rule-enthymemes). Two types of enthymeme are of special concern to the Logocratic Method: the *rule-enthymeme* and the *argument-enthymeme*.

4.5.4.2 Rule-Enthymeme and Argument-Enthymeme

A *rule-enthymeme* is a sentence (that is, a proposition incarnated in a natural language) whose propositional counterpart has a conditional structure and whose logical structure is not explicit from its original presentation in the natural language – that is, in its natural language presentation, as in a judge's opinion, lawyer's brief, statute, regulation. Note that most (but perhaps not all[52]) enthymemes occur in natural languages – indeed, it is to capture the metaphysics of enthymemes that the proposition-sentence distinction is particularly useful.[53] An *argument-enthymeme* is any argument (a

[51] Lewis Carroll's delightful essay *What the Tortoise Said to Achilles* may at least point in this direction. *See* Lewis Carroll, *What the Tortoise Said to Achilles*, 4 MIND 278 (1895). So may this perhaps apocryphal tale: While giving a lecture to colleagues demonstrating a proof, a mathematician wrote a line of the proof on the board, then wrote another line, and said to his audience in reference to the two lines on the board, "The reason for this step is obvious." An audience member objected. Flustered, the speaker left the stage and returned several minutes later with many pages of freshly scribbled notes in hand and said, "Yes it *is* obvious."

[52] *See supra* note 51.

[53] In this section, I map the ontology of type/token, proposition/sentence, argument type/argument-token, onto the Logocratic concepts of rule-enthymeme and argument-enthymeme. Regarding the realist-seeming ontology that I endorse here and in my discussion of the definition of 'argument,' see *supra* note 41 and accompanying text.

sentential argument is composed of sentences and is an incarnation of a propositional argument, which is composed of propositions) whose logical form is not explicit in its original mode of presentation, such as in a lawyer's brief or judge's opinion. As I will discuss below, *Wright v. Newman* provides illustrations of both rule-enthymemes and argument-enthymemes. I shall also argue that Hohfeld's system, as presented in the two articles explaining his system,[54] is enthymematic, calling for the same kind of interpretive procedure (namely, interpretive abduction) that the Logocratic analyst uses to interpret rule-enthymemes and argument-enthymemes.

4.5.4.3 Rulification of a Rule-Enthymeme

"Rulification" is the interpretive process (interpretive abduction[55]) in which the analyst gives a rule-enthymeme a fair formal representation that makes explicit the logical structure of that rule-enthymeme. Criteria for "fairness" in rulification include, chiefly, interpretation in accord with the *charitably judged intent of the rule-enthymeme promulgator.* To interpret according to the charitably judged intent of the rule-enthymeme promulgator requires that a rule-enthymeme be interpreted so as to make as intelligible as possible the fact that the rule-enthymeme promulgator promulgated that rule in the context in which he or she promulgated it. (This same norm also applies to the interpretation of argument-enthymemes, see Section 4.5.4.6.) On this view, sometimes a charitable interpretation will attribute some sort of error to the rule promulgator. That is, charitable interpretation does not presuppose the infallibility of the rule-promulgator. In some circumstances, what makes the rule-enthymeme most intelligible in the context in which the person uttered it is an interpretive explanation (interpretive abduction) according to which the rule was in some way logically incoherent.[56]

54 Both articles (cited *supra* note 2 and *supra* note 21) are also reprinted in WESLEY N. HOHFELD, FUNDAMENTAL LEGAL CONCEPTIONS AS APPLIED IN JUDICIAL REASONING AND OTHER LEGAL ESSAYS (Walter Wheeler Cook ed., 1919).

55 For another approach that correctly regards interpretation as a type of abduction but differs from the Logocratic account in its rival meta-abduction (abduction of the nature of abduction), see D. GABBAY & J. WOODS, THE REACH OF ABDUCTION: INSIGHT AND TRIAL (2005). In Chapter 9 ("Interpretation Abduction"), Gabbay and Woods correctly consider enthymeme resolution and principles of charity as components of interpretive abduction, but unlike the Logocratic account, theirs concludes that text interpretation is not intrinsically abductive, although some instances are.

56 American analytic philosophers of one-half century ago (such as Quine, Davidson, and Lewis) paid a good deal of attention to something they referred to as the "principle of charity" in either "radical translation" or "radical interpretation." The basic idea was that in some way, the very act of interpretation (or translation) required the interpreter to treat either the person being translated, or her text, as rationally intelligible. In *The Nature of Rationality*, Robert Nozick canvasses and critiques the main influential variants of this idea, such as *interpret or translate what the person says and does so as to make the person as rational as possible* (David Lewis, Richard Grandy, and Donald Davidson) and *interpret (and translate) so as to make what the person says and does as good as possible, as justified, principled, and correct as possible* (Ronald Dworkin). R. NOZICK, THE NATURE OF RATIONALITY 151–59 (1993). In accord with Nozick's trenchant critique, I believe that such theories tend to conflate the

Because rules have a conditional structure, it's worth making a quick observation about the interpretive options that could face a suitably situated rulifier of a rule-enthymeme. There are many different types of logical conditionals – including material conditionals (in propositional deductive logic), stochastic conditionals, strict conditionals, and causal conditionals – and a vitally important part of the skill of moving from enthymematic rules to their fair formal representation involves interpretive skill in deciding which type of conditional best fairly formally represents the rule-enthymeme. As a matter of interpretation, legal rule-enthymemes often can (and the rule-enthymeme in *Wright* can) be fairly formally represented with the material conditional in the grammar of propositional deductive logic.[57] In that system, one assigns propositional constants to the sentences that incarnate propositions in the rule-enthymeme. A proposition is any attribution of one or more predicates to a subject in a way that is capable of being true or false.

4.5.4.4 Rule-Enthymeme in *Wright*

In *Wright*, the central rule that the majority applied to resolve the dispute was a provision of the Georgia statute that had adopted verbatim the terms of

defense of or *advocacy* for a person or a text, on the one hand, with the *interpretation* of a person or a text. To interpret a text is to state that text's meaning in terms other than those of the text being interpreted (otherwise one repeats the text instead of interpreting it). *Interpretive norms* are always involved in guiding an interpretation, however reflectively aware an interpreter is of their operation. I first sketched this approach to explaining interpretation (in Logocratic terms, this is an abduction of interpretive abduction), in Brewer, *Figuring the Law*, *supra* note 43. The injunction to interpret charitably is such an interpretive norm. After his critique of the dominant versions of the principle of charity, Nozick endorses a version that I think works best for the Logocratic idea of giving rule and argument-enthymemes a *fair* formal representation, namely: "Translate the text 'p' so as to make as intelligible as possible the fact that in that context that person said 'p.'" Nozick, *id.* at 157. For rule and argument-enthymemes, on the Logocratic view, the rule or argument-enthymeme ought to be interpreted *to make as intelligible as possible the fact that in that context that person (or persons) promulgating the rule or making the argument promulgated it or made it.* This accords well with the Logocratic Method's deep reliance on pragmatics as core parts of its approach to the interpretation of rules and arguments. As Nozick explains regarding his "intelligibility" variant on the principle of charity: "It is this whole fact that is to be made intelligible, the fact that in that context that person said 'p.' [This principle] offers guidance about how to translate 'p,' and it also allows leeway to include what historians and anthropologists do in considering the historical and cultural context, as well as the person's aims and motives, his fears and superstitions." Nozick, *id.* at 157.

57 The choice to represent a natural language conditional as a material conditional, strict conditional, causal conditional, or some other type is also a matter of interpretive abduction, guided by the process of reflective adjustment first articulated by Nelson Goodman: "A rule [of inference] is amended if it yields an inference we are unwilling to accept; an inference is rejected if it violates a rule we are unwilling to amend." NELSON GOODMAN, FACT, FICTION, AND FORECAST 62 (4th ed. 1983). Some philosophers have noticed that this process of reflective adjustment is also a model for interpretation. *See, e.g.*, RONALD DWORKIN, LAW'S EMPIRE 90 (1986) ("constructive interpretations . . . try to show legal practice as a whole in its best light, to achieve equilibrium between legal practice as they find it and the best justification of that practice.").

Restatement (Second) of Contracts § 90(1). The relevant part of the rule-enthymeme, as it appears in the statute, the Georgia Code, is as follows:

> **§ 13-3-44. Promise reasonably inducing action or forbearance**
> (a) A promise which the promisor should reasonably expect to induce action or forbearance on the part of the promisee or a third person and which does induce such action or forbearance is binding if injustice can be avoided only by enforcement of the promise. The remedy granted for breach may be limited as justice requires.[58]

4.5.4.5 Rulification of the Rule-Enthymeme in *Wright*

The following are assignments of propositional constants to the sentence-tokens of the propositions that constitute the *Wright* rule-enthymeme. With one exception, each sentence appears in the statute explicitly, and one (proposition K below) is a statement that is clearly implicit in the statute:

Assignment of propositional constants to this rule-enthymeme:

P: There is a promise.

R: There is a promise which the promisor should reasonably expect to induce action or forbearance on the part of the promisee or a third person.

D: There is a promise which does induce such action or forbearance action or forbearance on the part of the promisee or a third person.

I: Injustice can be avoided only by enforcement of the promise.

K: A promise is binding.[59]

In the grammar of propositional deductive logic, the "rulified rule" – the fair formal representation – of the rule-enthymeme in *Wright* is (I present the same rulification in two grammars below):

Rulification (fair formal representation) 1 (slightly less symbolically formal)
If (P and R and D and I) then K[60]

Rulification 1' (slightly more symbolically formal)
$(P \wedge R \wedge D \wedge I) \supset K$[61]

[58] The statute also contains a section (b) that governs charitable subscriptions and marriage settlements, but the *Wright* court did not rely on that part of the statute.

[59] The Restatement (Second) of Contracts defines 'contract' as "a promise or a set of promises for the breach of which the law gives a remedy, or the performance of which the law in some way recognizes as a duty." Succinctly: a contract is a legally enforceable promise, that is, a contract is a legally "binding" promise.

[60] This representation stays close to natural language, albeit using the propositional constants, including a representation of the conditional as 'if . . . then'.

[61] This representation uses the "full monty" of symbolic representations, using '∧' for the conjunction truth-functional operator, '⊃' for the material implication truth-functional operator, and parentheses to express the precise logical structure of the rule-enthymeme in its rulified form.

This rule-enthymeme articulates four jointly sufficient and (under this rule[62]) individually necessary criteria, P, R, D, and I, required to warrant the conclusion K.[63]

4.5.4.6 Argument-Enthymeme and Argufication

As previously noted in Section 4.5.4.2, Logocratic theory focuses on two types of enthymeme: the rule-enthymeme and the argument-enthymeme. In Logocratic analysis, one "argufies" the argument-enthymeme. This means that one gives a fair formal representation of the sentences of the argument-enthymeme in a way that makes explicit: (i) the premises and conclusions of the argument-enthymeme; and (ii) the logical form of the argument-enthymeme – deduction, induction, abduction, or analogy.

62 Judges and lawyers routinely rely on the application of a rule of interpretive logic (in Logocratic terms, they act at the intersection of logical abduction and interpretive abduction) in context. Rodes and Pospesel refer to this as the "sole sufficient condition" rule. R. RODES & H. POSPESEL, PREMISES AND CONCLUSIONS 235–39 (1996). According to this rule, if p is a sufficient condition for q (i.e., if '$p \supset q$' is true) and p is, in context, the sole sufficient condition for q (that is, there is no proposition α other than p that makes the propositional function '$\alpha \supset q$' true), then p is also a necessary condition for q (i.e., '$q \supset p$' is true). In that context, p is necessary and sufficient for q. In propositional deductive logic, this is expressed by using the biconditional '$p \equiv q$'. This is the logical expression of a rule of interpretation that is perhaps more familiar to jurists as the rule *expressio unius est exclusio alterius*. It is a pervasive phenomenon of legal argument that a rule whose antecedent appears to provide only sufficient conditions for its consequent (in the Logocratic terms of interpretive abduction: that would be a plausible interpretation of the rule-enthymeme, which suggests only a uni-conditional and not a biconditional) actually, in context, provides the only way to arrive at the proposition stated in the rule's consequent, and in that context, the antecedent of the rule provides not only sufficient but also necessary conditions. For another application of this device of interpretive-cum-logical abduction, see Scott Brewer, *Exemplary Reasoning: Semantics, Pragmatics, and the Rational Force of Legal Argument By Analogy*, 109 HARV. L. REV. 923, 998 n.215 (1996).

63 The slightly varying but equivalent formulations in Rulification 1 and Rulification 1' represent only the first proposition of the statute § 13-3-44(a). There is also a second proposition (expressed by a sentence in the statute): "The remedy granted for breach may be limited as justice requires." I need not rulify this proposition for my main purposes in the text above, but to give an indication of the flexibility of the use of propositional deductive logic grammar to rulify legal rules, note that one can offer the following rulification (fair formal representation) of that second proposition as well. Where we assign these propositional constants–

J: Justice requires a limit on the remedy granted for breach.
L: There is a limit on the remedy granted for breach.

– we may rulify that proposition as

$J \supset L$ [If J then L].

Thus, rulification takes advantage of the rule of interpretive logic described in note 62 above and also shows how propositional deductive logic can, if carefully used, represent deontic operators like "may," "must," and "must not," without using the more complex resources of formal deontic logic. Note also that the surface grammar of this proposition is *not* conditional, whereas all rules are conditionals of one type or another. My rulification here relies on an interpretive abduction according to which the depth grammar reflected in the rulification is different from the surface grammar. This is an interpretive phenomenon not uncommon in moving from natural language rule-enthymemes to their rulified interpretations.

The basic norm that guides argufication, according to the Logocratic Method, is the norm of charity (articulated in Section 4.5.4.3) that guides the interpretive process of rulifying a rule-enthymeme. As applied to argument-enthymemes, the criteria for "fairness" in argufication include, chiefly, interpretation in accord with the *charitably judged intent of the argument-maker* (or, more simply, the arguer whose argument is being interpreted). The norm of interpreting according to the charitably judged intent of the arguer requires that an argument-enthymeme be interpreted so as to make as intelligible as possible the fact that the arguer made that argument in the context in which he or she made it.

Note that in a very common pattern of legal argument-enthymemes, a rule-enthymeme is used as the "major premise" of the legal argument-enthymeme. This observation provides an opportunity to address an important issue in the theory of legal argument and to indicate how the Logocratic Method addresses that issue. The term 'major premise' harks from Aristotelian syllogistic logic, now more commonly referred to as first-order predicate logic. Argument-enthymemes sometimes admit of "*enthymematic-ambiguity*," a semantic circumstance in which there is more than one plausible fair formal interpretive representation of the argument-enthymeme as interpretandum.[64] In such cases, the choice among the plausible interpretations is part of the process of interpretive-cum-logical abduction. This question arises both across logical forms and within logical forms. Here is an example of argument-enthymeme-ambiguity across two logical forms: deduction and induction. Should Argument 1 below be fairly formally represented as a valid deductive argument or, instead, as an *inductive specification* modeled by *defeasible modus ponens*, in which the major premise, ε_1, is itself the conclusion of a previously stated inductive generalization?[65]

Argument 1

ε_1	All men are mortal
ε_2	Socrates is a man
h	Socrates is mortal

We can also use Argument 1 to illustrate not only argument-enthymeme-ambiguity *within* the logical form of deduction but also across two distinct types of deduction. Suppose we chose to represent this argument in the grammar of propositional deductive logic. One representation might assign propositional constants, in the standard manner of propositional deductive logic, as follows:

M	All men are mortal
S	Socrates is a man
T	Socrates is mortal

[64] As noted above, an *interpretandum* is a *text to be interpreted*. The interpretandum in interpretive abduction is also the first premise, the *explanandum*, the *thing to be explained* by the interpretive abduction. *See* Brewer, *Figuring the Law*, *supra* note 43.

[65] See the discussion of inductive specification in Section 4.5.4.6.

On this representation we fail to capture what we surely believe is a valid argument (defined as an argument in which, whenever all the premises are true the conclusion must be true), for:

M
S
therefore
T

is not a deductively valid argument form. There is however a workaround for this that gives us the benefits of using the propositional deductive logic grammar[66] while also reflecting our intuitive sense that the argument is deductively valid. We may assign these propositional constants:

M: something is a man
S: something is mortal

Using them, the argument is:

ε_1 $M \supset S$
ε_2 M
h S

which is the familiar valid argument *modus ponens*. This workaround succeeds if, but only if, we keep in mind what we are doing in using such a representation. We judge "behind the scenes," as it were, that it is the individual named 'Socrates' that makes premise ε_2 true, although, unlike what we would do were we to use the grammar of predicate logic, we do not explicitly try to represent any individual, including Socrates. A similar kind of "workaround" also can be used to represent legal rule-enthymemes whose ambiguity crosses several types of deductive inference, including propositional and predicate (just illustrated) and deontic.[67]

4.5.4.7 Rulified Rule-Enthymeme in *Wright* for Comparison to Justice Carley's Rule-Enthymeme: Does His Rulification Fail the Statute?

I wish briefly to use the rulification of the rule-enthymeme in *Wright* as an example of the kind of "payoff" one can get from application of the Logocratic tools I have been describing. An important virtue of the Logocratic method, I believe, is that it

[66] Those benefits include a ready way to identify precisely the logical structure of a rule, so as to aid legal abduction in the way I illustrate with the *Wright* case. Propositional deductive logic is also a decidable system (a formal system in which there is an effective method for determining whether any given well-formed formula is a theorem) and an intuitively accessible visual representation of validity, in the form of truth tables using truth-functional operators.

[67] This is illustrated (briefly) *supra* note 63 and accompanying text.

can help disclose unclarities in rules and arguments that may be related to important questions of political and legal value.

In his opinion for the majority in *Wright*, Justice Carley quotes the rule-enthymeme in the Georgia statute noted above. He then applies that rule-enthymeme in the argument-enthymeme he offers to resolve the case, the conclusion of which is that, under the statute's promissory estoppel rule, Wright (the former boyfriend) is legally obliged to pay child support for the son of his former girlfriend Newman. When we compare the rule-enthymeme and our rulification of that rule-enthymeme to Justice Carley's own version of the rule-enthymeme, his rulification and his related argufied argument-enthymeme, an interesting result surfaces.

Let's remind ourselves of the assignments of propositional constants to the propositions that constitute the *Wright* rule-enthymeme, as specified above:

Rule-enthymeme in *Wright* (from a Georgia statute)
A promise which the promisor should reasonably expect to induce action or forbearance on the part of the promisee or a third person and which does induce such action or forbearance is binding if injustice can be avoided only by enforcement of the promise.

Rulification of this rule-enthymeme offered above (Section 4.5.4.5)

P: There is a promise.

R: There is a promise which the promisor should reasonably expect to induce action or forbearance on the part of the promisee or a third person.

D: There is a promise which does induce such action or forbearance action or forbearance on the part of the promisee or a third person.

I: Injustice can be avoided only by enforcement of the promise.

K: A promise is binding.

As I have said, with these propositional constants, the rulification of the *Wright* rule-enthymeme yields a rule that can serve as the major premise in the argufication of the *Wright* argument-enthymeme (see Section 4.5.4.3):

Rule 1
$(P \land R \land D \land I) \supset K$ *[(If P and R and D and I) then K]*

If a judge were to use this rulified rule-enthymeme as the major premise of an argument applying the statute to the facts of the case, he could offer a valid deductive argument only if he finds that each element of the antecedent of the rule is true on the facts of the case. Represented in symbolic grammar, he could argue:

ε_1 $(P \land R \land D \land I) \supset K$

ε2 P

ε3 R

ε4 D

$\varepsilon 5$ *I*

∴

K

Because, under this rule, these elements are jointly sufficient and individually necessary, he cannot reach the conclusion K, validly, unless he finds that each of the elements P, R, D, and I is true.

Now let's compare this rulified rule-enthymeme and the deductively valid argument it could yield to Justice Carley's argument. When we read Justice Carley's argument-enthymeme (the actual sentences that comprise the main steps of his argument), we may observe what seems to be *his* rulification of the statutory rule-enthymeme and note the argufied argument he offers on the basis of his rulification. At risk of dense complexity, I present all three together because we must ourselves discern Justice Carley's version of the rulified rule *from his application of the rule-enthymeme in his argument-enthymeme.* What emerges from this Logocratic analysis seems to me to be the serious question whether Justice Carley's rulification is actually a fair formal representation of the rule-enthymeme. Each sentence quoted in what follows is itself the conclusion of an argument that Justice Carley uses to support it. For conciseness, in the text here I quote only the conclusions, which, for the most part, clearly track the logical elements of the statutory rule (as I have rulified that rule, see above):

ε_1 "The evidence authorizes[68] the finding that Wright promised both Newman and her son that he would assume all of the obligations and responsibilities of fatherhood, including that of providing support."

Here it seems clear that Justice Carley thinks he is applying logical element P.

ε_2 "The evidence further authorizes the finding that Newman and her son relied upon Wright's promise to their detriment."

Here it seems fairly clear that Justice Carley thinks he's applying logical elements R and D. Note however that he does not stick to the literal requirements of the statute, and like many judges applying either *Restatement (Second) of Contracts* § 90 or its predecessor provision *Restatement (First) of Contracts* § 90,[69] the justice seems

[68] Justice Carley relies on but does not state explicitly an additional rule for the standard of review by an appellate court of a trial court result, the rule for sufficiency of evidence. This rule directs an appellate court to affirm findings by a trial judge (or trial judge plus jury) if there is sufficient evidence to support each material element of the claim, charge, or defense that was established in the court below. From a logical point of view, this rule provides a propositional function whose content we can describe in two ways, the second a slight generalization of the first:

Version 1: If there is sufficient evidence to support a jury finding that P, then P.
Version 2: If there is sufficient evidence that P, then P.

[69] The rule-enthymeme of Restatement (First) of Contracts § 90 provides: "A promise which the promisor should reasonably expect to induce action or forbearance of a definite and substantial character on the part of the promisee and which does induce such action or forbearance is binding if injustice can be avoided only by enforcement of the promise."

to rulify the statute he is interpreting in a way that combines elements R and D into one element S: there is "detrimental reliance." That is, in place of these elements of the statutory rule-enthymeme:

R: There is a promise which the promisor should reasonably expect to induce action or forbearance on the part of the promisee or a third person.
D: There is a promise which does induce such action or forbearance action or forbearance on the part of the promisee or a third person.

Justice Carley offers this single prong:

S: There is detrimental reliance.

This free rewriting of the statute is already noteworthy and presumptively problematic for the analyst who seeks precision in argument, but a more striking rewriting is to come in the justice's analysis:

ε_3 If, after 10 years of honoring his voluntary commitment, Wright were now allowed to evade the consequences of his promise, an injustice to Newman and her son would result.

This is a striking departure – and relaxation – of the literal requirements of element I of the statute. As one of the jointly sufficient and individually necessary conditions for enforcing a promise, it requires that it be the case that enforcement of the promise is the only way to avoid injustice. Note that this element of the statute (and *Restatement (Second) of Contracts* § 90) actually has two conceptually distinct components: one, that there is an injustice, the other, that the enforcement of the promise is *the only way to avoid the injustice*. Justice Carley states that "If, after 10 years of honoring his voluntary commitment, Wright were now allowed to evade the consequences of his promise, an injustice to Newman and her son would result." But he has, in effect, rewritten this statutory element from what I have labelled:

I: *injustice can be avoided only by enforcing the promise*

to the less demanding

T: *there is an injustice.*[70]

70 My main purpose here is not to argue the details of contract policy. I seek here only to show what kinds of questions this precision-oriented Logocratic tool can raise. Nevertheless, I observe that one might seek to defend Justice Carley's free rewriting of crucial elements of the statute by noting that the statute, and Restatement (Second) of Contracts § 90 from which the statute is taken verbatim, seems to have made the literal element of the rule too strong for what this *equitable* rule was intended to accomplish. The statute itself seems to have rushed to ameliorate this harshness with a qualification in a second rule: "The remedy granted for breach may be limited as justice requires." (This can, as noted above, be represented in non-deontic propositional deductive logic, see *supra* note 63.) This is at the very least in some tension with the rest of the provision, since by the time a judge has concluded that all of the jointly sufficient conditions (elements P, R, D, and I) for enforcement (element K) are true, she seems perforce to have concluded that there is no way to meet the requirements *of justice* other than by enforcing the promise. What, consistent with that conclusion already reached, could be a "limit that justice requires"?

With his rulification in place, Justice Carley reaches the conclusion of his argument:

h: Under the evidence, the duty to support which Wright voluntarily assumed 10 years ago remains enforceable under the contractual doctrine of promissory estoppel and the trial court's order which compels Wright to discharge that obligation must be affirmed.

Here it seems clear that Justice Carley thinks he's applying logical element K – and concluding that K is warranted because, under the rule (the rulified version), there is *deductive evidence*[71] for K, namely, the sufficient evidence for elements P, R, D (as subsumed in his rewrite of the literal rule in which R and D become absorbed into the single proposition 'S'), and I. Taking account of the slippages noted above in the *rule as stated* in the statute and the *rule as applied* by Justice Carley, he seems to offer an argument that is fairly formally reconstructed as follows:

4.5.4.8 Justice Carley's Argufied Argument

ε_1 $(P \wedge S \wedge T) \supset K$

ε_2 P

ε_3 S

ε_4 T

h K

This is a valid argument from premises ε_1 through ε_4 to conclusion h, with an application of the *modus ponens* inference rule.

4.5.5 *Legal Rules as Axioms*

The Logocratic Method treats what are often referred to as "major premises" in legal arguments as *axioms* of legal argument. An axiom is a "well-formed formula" that is stipulated as a premise for a proof of other well-formed formulas within a formal system. Axioms play a special role in deductive arguments, namely, *once they are chosen* they are unquestioned, and if there is for a reasoner a question of which axioms to adopt, that question is answered for the purposes of, and by the time for

[71] Here I have made the interpretive judgment in context that Justice Carley's argument-enthymeme should be argufied (fairly formally represented) in propositional deductive logic. It is also plausible (a step in what is at the intersection of logical and interpretive abduction) that we could reconstruct the argument-enthymeme as an application of defeasible *modus ponens*. For discussion of the contextual interpretive criteria I use, see Brewer, *Exemplary Reasoning*, *supra* note 62, at 989–1000.

the use of them in, an argument.[72] Within what we might call a "classical" – i.e., pre-*Modernist*[73] – understanding of the justification for choosing one rather than another axiom or set of axioms, axioms are chosen because they are "self-evidently" *true*.[74] But twentieth-century Modernist developments in logic demoted (or instead, elevated?) axioms from the status of self-evident truths to a string of symbols that serve as fixed points for making proofs in deductive systems.[75]

Treating legal rules as axioms in a deductive system is a type of philosophical abduction of the phenomena ("*explananda*") of the practices of legal argument. One need not represent legal arguments – argufy them – in a deductive system, and one of the surprisingly hot energies of twentieth-century jurisprudence, especially American Legal Realist jurisprudence, concerns itself with what I have referred to as the "Jurisprudence of Logical Form."[76] In the Logocratic terms I have been developing, this branch of jurisprudence focuses on the question of what is the best *argufication* in general of legal argument-enthymemes (the question of what I call 'structural enthymemicity').[77] For reasons I will not offer here, I make a deliberate

72 For this common understanding of the role of axioms in argument, see, e.g., S. HAACK, THE PHILOSOPHY OF LOGICS 243 (1978) (axiom A is a well-formed formula of language L if A *is laid down, its truth unquestioned, in the system* L); Peter Suber, *Legal Reasoning after the Postmodern Critique of Reason*, 3 LEGAL WRITING 21, 24–25 (1997).

73 See generally the deeply illuminating essay by David Luban, *Legal Modernism*, 84 MICH. L. REV. 1656 (1986); D. KENNEDY, A CRITIQUE OF ADJUDICATION: FIN DE SIECLE 1–20 (1997). In conversation, Duncan Kennedy argued that Hohfeld's system of jural relations is the most important text in legal modernism of the twentieth century. To similar effect are works on Hohfeld by Joseph Singer and Pierre Schlag, among many others.

74 *See, e.g.*, ALFRED TARSKI, INTRODUCTION TO LOGIC AND TO THE METHODOLOGY OF THE DEDUCTIVE SCIENCES 110 (4th ed. 1994) (some statements in a deductive theory "whose truth appears to us evident, are chosen for the so-called PRIMITIVE STATEMENTS or AXIOMS . . .; we accept them as true without establishing them in any way" (emphasis added)); M. KLINE, MATHEMATICS THE LOSS OF CERTAINTY 4 (1980) ("To achieve its marvelous and powerful results, mathematics relied upon a special method, namely, deductive proof from self-evident principles called axioms, the methodology we still learn, usually in high school geometry. Deductive reasoning, by its very nature, guarantees the truth of what is deduced if the axioms are truths. By utilizing this seemingly clear, infallible, and impeccable logic, mathematicians produced apparently indubitable and irrefutable conclusions. This feature of mathematics is still cited today. Whenever someone wants an example of certitude and exactness of reasoning, he appeals to mathematics."). Such a conception of mathematics as a system of axiomatic certainty animated Holmes' (confused and equivocal, see Scott Brewer, *On the Possibility of Necessity in Legal Argument: A Dilemma for Holmes and Dewey*, 34 J. MARSHALL L. REV. 9, 10–11 (2000)) argument that law is not "something different from what is decided by the courts of Massachusetts or England, that it is a system of reason, that it is a deduction from principles of ethics or admitted axioms or what not, which may or may not coincide with the decisions," and is instead – from the lawyer's point of view, at least, "the prophecies of what the courts will do in fact." Perhaps in his defense, we may note that Holmes used this Classical (pre-Modernist) conception of *mathematics* to help usher in a (philosophically irrigorous) legal Modernist conception of *law*.

75 *See* Suber, *supra* note 72, at 24–26; KLINE, *supra* note 74, chs. 4 and 5.

76 *See* Scott Brewer, *Traversing Holmes' Path toward a Jurisprudence of Logical Form*, *in* THE PATH OF THE LAW AND ITS INFLUENCE: THE LEGACY OF OLIVER WENDELL HOLMES 94 (S. Burton ed., 2000).

77 *See* Brewer, Exemplary Reasoning, *supra* note 62, at 985 ("*Structural and Practical Enthymemicity* . . . The theorist of informal (including legal) argument must reconstruct enthymematic arguments in order to explain, from a theoretical point of view, what logical form they have in general – deductive, inductive,

interpretive choice to model legal rules using a deductive system.[78] It is possible that Hohfeld did too. But while his system of jural relations can very usefully be presented as part of an axiomatic deductive system,[79] Hohfeld's axioms do not operate within legal argument directly – that is, they do not operate in legal abduction. Instead, they operate in his philosophical abduction *of* legal abduction. At least, that is how I abduce Hohfeld's system.

It's important to note two things that are needed for an axiomatic interpretation of legal argument to succeed. First, contrary to the Classical view of mathematics – that axioms need no justification because they are self-evidently true – which legal axioms properly apply for use by judges and lawyers to resolve a given case can be, and indeed routinely are, the subjects of justificatory arguments by judges and lawyers. Such arguments are interpretive abductions of the applicable rules. *Wright* illustrates the point well. The court offered an interpretation of Georgia's law, citing and quoting statutes and precedents, to discern that the promissory estoppel rule was available to explain, from a legal point of view, the transactions between Newman and Wright. Justice Carley's interpretive abduction made available the statutory promissory estoppel rule as a *plausible explanation* of the litigant's transactions. In the Modernist understanding of logic and mathematics one can also argue for one's axioms, not on the grounds that they are self-evidently true but rather on the ground that it can be useful to adopt those axioms, if only to advance an understanding of what kinds of deductive system can be built around a given axiom set. Such an exercise motivated, for example, the development of systems of geometry that adopted axioms that differed from those of Euclidean geometry.[80] (Speaking of his own interpretation of Hohfeld axioms, Layman Allen describes his instrumentalist approach as being "in the spirit in which Felix S. Cohen explored

analogical (exemplary), or abductive. That is, what is not perspicuous in the manner of presentation of an informal argument, and what therefore calls for theoretical explication, is its logical type (inductive, deductive, etc.). We may call this type of non-perspicuity 'structural enthymemicity'. The practical legal interpreter (the judge, the lawyer, etc.) must also engage in interpretive reconstruction of legal arguments, but from a point of view different from that of the theorist, and with different aims and criteria of success. The practical legal interpreter reconstructs judicial enthymemes in order to be guided in various ways (for example, to conform conduct to rules that may emerge from those arguments, or to apply rules to instant cases) by enthymematic legal arguments in particular circumstances. From the point of view of this practical interpreter, what is non-perspicuous in an argument (say, a precedential judicial opinion) is the guidance it provides in the case sub judice. I will refer to this kind of non-perspicuity as 'practical enthymemicity.'").

78 I offer pragmatics-based (not pragm*atist*) arguments for this interpretive choice in Brewer, *Exemplary Reasoning*, *supra* note 62, at 989–1003.

79 John Finnis has very cogently done so. *See* John Finnis, *Some Professorial Fallacies About Rights*, 4 ADEL. L. REV. 377, 378–81 (1971–1972) (interpreting Hohfeld's system into, and articulating "three axioms essential to the comprehension of Hohfeld's work").

80 See discussion in KLINE, *supra* note 75, ch. 4 ("The first debacle: the withering of truth"), esp. at 78 ("God decided that He would punish the Kantians and especially those egotistic, proud, and overconfident mathematicians. And He proceeded to encourage non-Euclidean geometry, a creation that devastated the achievements.").

such ideas . . . not asking, What does the term 'right' really mean? but rather, How is it most useful to define it?"[81])

It's also important to note that, for a deductive axiomatic explanation of the phenomena of legal argument to be plausible (this is part of my own philosophical abduction of the structural enthymemicity of legal argument), a legal analyst can arrive at deductively applicable axioms by empirical methods. This method of arriving at axioms is utterly routine in the physical sciences, in which induction and abduction on the basis of empirical data issue in propositions that are treated as axioms.[82] An anthropologist can discover the axioms and rules of inference that comprise the deductive system of a game in a given culture by empirical means – indeed, it is not clear that there is any other way to do so for anyone who learns the rules of a deductive system (leaving aside here questions of the cogency of Kant's concept of a *synthetic a priori*, which is not needed for this point). Savigny, for example, may have understood himself to be engaged in just such an explanatory project of legal rules.[83]

4.5.6 *From Enthymeme to Argument: Logocratic Method the Virtues and Vices of Arguments*

One of the most important features of the Logocratic Method is that it takes *virtue* seriously.

4.5.6.1 Arguing Virtue and Vice

In the Logocratic Method, once the argument-enthymeme has been argufied, the analyst moves to the next step, which is to assess the *virtues and vices* of the arguments, including strength and weakness as one type of virtue and vice, respectively. There is a counterpart analysis of the virtues and vices of rules as well: the virtue is discernible clarity of logical structure, the vice, a lack thereof. Once we have fairly formally represented an argument-enthymeme, we are in a position to ask a vital question about the argument thus represented: How *good* is it? We can be more precise about what we mean in characterizing an argument as "good" or "bad" by speaking of an argument's *virtues* or *vices*. When we have offered simple and clear definitions of those terms, we can ask, for example, of Justice Carley's argument in *Wright*: in what ways does it exhibit virtue, or fail to do so?

81 Allen, *supra* note 36, at 429 (quoting and citing Felix Cohen, *Transcendental Nonsense and the Functional Approach*, 35 COLUM. L. REV. 809, 824–29 (1935)).

82 There is a large literature on this topic. One toe-dip is available in Patrick Suppes, *The Axiomatic Method in the Empirical Sciences*, *in* PROCEEDINGS OF THE TARSKI SYMPOSIUM (PROCEEDINGS OF SYMPOSIA IN PURE MATHEMATICS) 465–79 (L. Henkin et al. eds., 1974).

83 See discussion in Brewer, *On the Possibility of Necessity*, *supra* note 75, at 44–45.

4.5.6.2 Virtue and the Kinds of Things That Can Be Virtuous

The Logocratic Method relies extensively on a conception of virtue, harking back to Aristotle's conception but also departing from it in significant ways. As I use the term, 'virtue' means *functional excellence*. The basic framework is found in Aristotle's conception of *arete* (Greek: ἀρετή), translated as 'virtue' or 'excellence'.[84] If some object x is an F then the virtue of x as an F is that characteristic of x that makes x a good F. Put concisely: an object x's virtue reflects its good performance of the function of Fs. For example, consider an object (x) that is a knife (F). The virtues of a knife are those features that make it a good knife, such as having an appropriately sharp blade – we say "appropriately" because, as one can see on quick reflection, the virtue of a butter knife differs from that of a steak knife in the degree of sharpness required for functional excellence.

Many and varied kinds of things can be "bearers" of virtue, that is, can properly be said to be virtuous (or not). Among this vast array of possibly virtuous (or vicious)[85] items are tools such as knives, hammers, and spoons; institutions, such as schools, universities, and the legal institutions that comprise the rule of law;[86] professionals, such as lawyers, doctors, judges, and professors; and arguments, which are the central focus of the Logocratic Method used to generate and evaluate evidentiary arguments. As we will see, there are various kinds of purpose one might have for arguments, and those purposes guide our judgments about what is virtuous, that is, what is functionally excellent in arguments.

I must emphasize that the sense of the concept of virtue that animates the Logocratic Method is not *moral* virtue, such as is familiar to Western culture as inheritor of moral traditions from Aristotle into Christianity into modern moral theories that are, even when

84 *See* ARISTOTLE, NICOMACHEAN ETHICS (Terence Irwin trans., 1999) (c. 350 B.C.E.).

85 From here on, unless otherwise noted, an ascription to an item of virtue should be understood to mean virtue or vice (the latter of which is a failure of virtue). Thus, for example, our discussion of the criteria for virtuous evidentiary argument is also perforce a discussion of the vices of evidentiary arguments. Virtue and vice are best understood as on a spectrum rather than a bivalent, yes-no, state, more virtuous and less vicious, or more vicious and less virtuous.

86 Joseph Raz provides a trenchant example of a conception of the *rule of law* as an instrument that has a specific virtue:

> Regarding the rule of law as the inherent or specific virtue of law is a result of an instrumental conception of law. The law is not just a fact of life. It is a form of social organization which should be used properly and for the proper ends. It is a tool in the hands of men differing from many others in being versatile and capable of being used for a large variety of proper purposes. As with some other tools, machines, and instruments a thing is not of the kind unless it has a least some ability to perform its function. A knife is not a knife unless it has some ability to cut. The law to be law must be capable of guiding behaviour, however inefficiently. Like other instruments, the law has a specific virtue which is being morally neutral as to the end to which the instrument is put. It is the virtue of efficiency; the virtue of an instrument as an instrument. For the law this virtue is the rule of law. Thus the rule of law is an inherent virtue of the law, but not a moral virtue as such.

Joseph Raz, *The Rule of Law and Its Virtue*, *in* THE AUTHORITY OF LAW: ESSAYS ON LAW AND MORALITY 210, 226 (2d ed. 2009).

secular, still significantly influenced by a dominating Judeo-Christian worldview. Rather, the type of virtue or vice that is central to the Logocratic Method and its theoretical framework is the *amoral* virtue of a knife. And a knife, virtuous or vicious, can be used for moral or immoral purposes. The conception of virtue as *amoral functional excellence* animates and organizes the Logocratic Method, in which the *bearers of virtue* of interest are *arguments* and *arguers*.[87] A central part of my task here is to offer the Logocratic explanation of two distinct purposes that arguers have, and to offer a way to evaluate arguments for their excellences or failures, their strengths or weaknesses, their virtues or vices.

4.5.6.3 Two Types of Logocratic Virtue: "Mode-Independent" and "Mode-Dependent"

Logocratic Method identifies two types of Logocratic virtue, "mode-independent" and "mode-dependent." The reference in these phrases to "mode" is to the "mode of logical inference" of an argument.

4.5.7 *Mode-Independent Logocratic Virtues*

Mode-independent virtues of arguments are those that an argument in any of the four modes can possess. These virtues are less important for our analysis of Hohfeld than are the mode-dependent virtues. I summarize them here so that the contrasting idea of mode-dependent virtues makes sense. (To make a Hohfeldian analogy: mode-dependent and mode-independent virtues are conceptual opposites.) Mode-independent virtues are independent of their mode of inference. These virtues of arguments are, more specifically, types of *strength* (virtue) or *weakness* (vice) understood as *instrumental efficacy for achieving one or another (or some combination) of two goals or purposes*. We refer to these two types of mode-independent strength (or weakness) as *internal-inferential* and *dialectical-rhetorical*.

4.5.7.1 Internal-Inferential Strength or Weakness

One mode-independent goal-purpose for arguments is use of them to infer conclusions from premises in such a way that the argument is *internally strong*, in the sense that *if* the premises of the argument are true, then they provide strong support for inferring the conclusion of the argument. One clear way to grasp the idea of internal-inferential strength is by reference to conditional probability. The measure of internal-inferential strength of an argument is the probability that the conclusion is true assuming that the premises are true. A valid deductive argument, for example,

[87] In this respect, the Logocratic abduction of tools of argument has the same amoral structure that Joseph Raz attributes to the rule of law as a tool. *Id.*

has the highest possible degree of internal-inferential strength, because in such an argument, by definition, on the assumption – the condition – that the premises are true, the conclusion must be true.

4.5.7.2 Dialectical-Rhetorical Strength or Weakness

A *dialectic* of arguments, as that term occurs in Logocratic theory, is a *contest* among arguments (and arguers). Recognizing that dialectical strength (or weakness) is a type of strength (or weakness) that is analytically distinct from internal-inferential strength allows Logocratic theory to make further distinctions among dialectical argument contests. There can be: *external contests among arguers and their arguments* as, for example, in the litigation in contest of prosecutor or plaintiff against a defendant, or in the contest on a multi-judge panel of majority and dissenting judges; *internal contests within an arguer*, as for example when a judge or lawyer debates the pros and cons of a legal argument, or when a philosopher does likewise with philosophical arguments – compare Socrates in Plato's dialogue in *The Apology*: "[T]he greatest good of man is daily to converse about virtue and all that concerning which you hear me *examining myself and others*, and ... the life which is unexamined is not worth living." (38A) (emphasis added); *formal contests of arguments (and arguers)*, guided by formal rules, as, for example, in litigation (rules of evidence and procedure may be very usefully understood as rules that guide the formal contest of litigants' and judges' arguments) or in various scholastic debate competitions; *informal contests of arguments (and arguers)*, guided by informal rules, as for example in Socrates' debates with his interlocutors in the Socratic *elenchos* (ἔλεγχος, 'cross-examination'). Note that Hohfeld abductions make a very important explanatory contribution to legal dialectical competitions of arguments, or potential arguments, between the agents and patients of Hohfeld relations.

Dialectical contest is one aspect of the dialectical-rhetorical **strength** of arguments. The other aspect is an argument's *rhetorical* strength (or weakness). Building on Aristotle's conception of rhetoric,[88] Logocratic Method defines *rhetoric* as the attempt by a source rhetor to persuade a target audience either to accept a proposition or set of propositions or to accept a different or additional set of premises as the inferential basis for a proposition or set of propositions that the audience already accepts. Legal arguers, including judges, lawyers, and law students (as well as arguers in many other settings) seek to offer arguments that are *persuasive* to one or more target audiences. Each of those target audiences serves as the referee of the contest of arguments, whether explicitly offered (as, for example, in litigation) or implicitly understood as a potential challenging argument (as, for example, when

[88] See ARISTOTLE, RHETORIC 7 (W. Rhys Roberts trans., 2010) ("Rhetoric may be defined as the faculty of observing in any given case the available means of persuasion ... [R]hetoric we look upon as the power of observing the means of persuasion on almost any subject presented to us; and that is why we say that, in its technical character, it is not concerned with any special or definite class of subjects.").

an arguer considers one argument in contrast to other arguments that contest some part of the argument – its premises, its conclusion, or the supposed inferential support of the premises for the conclusion). Indeed, according to Logocratic theory, inferential-internal virtue *is a type of dialectical-rhetorical virtue*. For even the identification of the degree of internal-inferential support that the premises of a given argument provide for its conclusion is always a matter of exercising *contestable* judgment, according to the actually or possibly contested epistemic authority of the dialectical-rhetorical referee of the argument. It is beyond the scope of this chapter to argue this point in detail, but one finds support for it in the existence of a metalogical theory such as *dialetheism*, according to which there are *true contradictions* (that is, that there are propositions *p* such that both *p* and *not-p* are true). The existence of such a metalogical theory illustrates and supports the Logocratic view that the assessment of the internal-inferential strength of a given deductively invalid argument by a dialetheist referee could differ from the assessment of the internal-inferential strength of that argument by a referee who accepts and deploys the law of non-contradiction (the proposition that there cannot be true contradictions).[89] Thus, even the judgment of the internal-inferential of an argument depends on *which* dialectical-rhetorical referee assesses it – is *persuaded* to accept it – in judging the argument against other actual or possible contesting arguments, and for this reason internal-inferential strength is a type of dialectical-rhetorical strength.

4.5.8 *Mode-Dependent Logocratic Virtues: The Four Modes of Logical Inference and Their Characteristic Virtues*

Recall that, as defined above, an argument's *mode of logical inference* (or, synonymously, its *logical form*) is *the evidential relation between the argument's premises*, which (for reasons offered in Section 4.5.2) we find it useful to abbreviate as ε_1, ε_2, ε_3 . . . and its *conclusion*, which we find it useful to abbreviate as h_1 (or h_2, h_3, h_4 . . . if there is more than one conclusion). Recall also that, in my account, there are four fundamental, irreducible modes of logical inference. They are distinguished from one another by the relation that obtains between the premises of the argument and its conclusion when the argument yields the most warranted inference (that is, "internally strong," as defined in Section 4.5.7.1) from premises to conclusion that it is logically capable of yielding.[90] All four modes of logical inference are found in

89 See Graham Priest, In Contradiction (expanded ed. 2006). I find additional strong support for this position in the argument practices of Pyrrhonian skepticism, whose pertinence to the issue of the possibility of true contradictions and their relevance to the assessment of arguments is cogently presented in Diego E. Machuca, *Pyrrhonism and the Law of Non-Contradiction*, *in* Pyrrhonism in Ancient, Modern, and Contemporary Philosophy 51–77 (Diego. E. Machuca ed., 2011).

90 We might say that the criteria of identity of each logical form is an ideal – something like a Platonic "Form." What distinguishes deductive, inductive, analogical, and inference to the best explanation arguments from each other are the *ideal forms* of those arguments.

legal arguments in general, in evidentiary legal arguments in particular, and indeed in arguments in every domain of argument. A clear understanding of the mode-specific virtues of an argument, that is, the characteristic virtues of a deductive, inductive, analogical, or abductive argument, is essential to the Logocratic Method as a type of philosophical abduction (explanation of the nature of argument) and to its application to assess the strengths or weaknesses of a particular argument.

Given the scope of this chapter, I will not try to specify the characteristic virtues of deduction other than to say that its virtue, the property it has when it is the best of its type, is validity. Nor will I try to summarize the characteristic virtues of induction here.[91] Recall from the Introduction that I have set out to show that the nature of Hohfeld's enterprise is philosophical abduction, that enterprise of a judge, lawyer, or other legal analyst who is trying to assess the applicability and consequences of a set of legal rules to a specific fact pattern, in a specific jurisdiction, is engaged in the project of *legal abduction*, and that Hohfeldian abductions are logically parasitic on legal abductions. To make these explanatory arguments, I offer pertinent details from the Logocratic account of analogical argument and abduction.

4.5.9 *Analogical Argument and Its Mode-Specific Virtue*

According to the Logocratic account,[92] an analogical argument involves a judgment that, because two or more items, the *source* (or sources) and the target (there is usually one) of the analogy[93] share some characteristics, they can be inferred to share an additional characteristic. Analogical argument always involves a step of abduction, *analogical abduction*, in which the reasoner discerns the pattern of similarity between the source and target *such that* possession of the characteristics that they share (shared characteristics) warrants the *inference* that they share an additional characteristic (the *inferred characteristic*). This pattern of reasoning requires identification of an *analogy-warranting rule*, whose antecedent states the shared characteristics and whose consequent states the inferred characteristic. Analogy cannot consist simply of pointing to shared characteristics and inferring from their

91 I offer a detailed account of analogy, and a brief account of deduction, induction, and abduction in Brewer, *Exemplary Reasoning*, *supra* note 62. I offer more detailed accounts of induction and analogy, and a detailed account of legal abduction, focusing on arguments under the aegis of evidence law, in chs. 1 and 2 of J. Weinstein et al., Evidence Cases and Materials (10th ed. 2017). For another summary of all four modes of logical inference, see Brewer, *Logocratic Method*, *supra* note 39, at 177–78.

92 My detailed Logocratic (or proto-Logocratic) explanation of analogical argument is found in Brewer, *Exemplary Reasoning*, *supra* note 62. A more recent treatment of one type of analogical argument (particularly pertinent to my analysis of Hohfeld) is Scott Brewer, *Indefeasible Analogical Argument*, *in* Analogy and Exemplary Reasoning in Legal Discourse 27 (H. Kaptein & B. van der Velden eds., 2018).

93 I distinguish analogical *assertions*, such as, "a steamboat is analogous to a hotel," from analogical arguments, which, like all arguments, involve the inference of conclusion proposition(s) from premise propositions. But for simplicity I will sometimes refer to analogical arguments as "analogies."

possession by source(s) and target that the inferred characteristic is present, because any two items share an indefinite number of characteristics. This is easily shown by, for example, any two items that are not moose: both are not identical to one moose, two moose, . . . ; and even for two items that are moose, take for instance, moose A and moose B, each is identical to itself or to one chair, two chairs, ... Thus, there must be an *analogy-warranting rationale* that serves to offer a justification for the analogy-warranting *rule*, a rule that explains why one may infer the presence of the inferred characteristic from possession of the shared characteristic. Argument by disanalogy has substantially the same structure, the change being that one argues that because source and target do not share a particular characteristic, or equivalently, that they have an unshared characteristic, one is *not* warranted in inferring that they share the inferred characteristic even when they possess shared characteristics that one might otherwise believe warrants the inference of the inferred characteristic.

H. L. A Hart offers a simple example of an analogical argument that is useful to illustrate the abstract pattern I have described:

> Two principal devices, at first sight very different from each other, have been used for the communication of . . . general standards of conduct in advance of the successive occasions on which they are to be applied. One of them makes a maximal and the other a minimal use of general classifying words. The first is typified by what we call legislation and the second by precedent. We can see the distinguishing features of these in the following simple non-legal cases. One father before going to church says to his son, "Every man and boy must take off his hat on entering a church." *Another, baring his head as he enters the church, says, "Look: this is the right way to behave on such occasions."*[94]

On the Logocratic explanation of analogical argument, in this example, the father invites the son to reason by *example* (the father's behavior) rather than by *edict* ("Every man and boy must take off his hat on entering a church"). The *argument-enthymeme* consists of the statement by the father in the context of offering what he intends to be behavior that is identifiable as the basis for the son's reconstructing the analogical argument in accord with the father's intent. One assumes a context in which both father and son are wearing hats. The *source* for the analogy is the father's behavior on entering the church. The *target* is the son's behavior on entering the church. The father invites the son to identify, as the *pertinent shared characteristic*, among the indefinite characteristics that they share (including that neither is one moose, two moose . . .), the removal of a hat. The *inferred characteristic* is taking off one's hat. The *analogy-warranting rule* is, *If one removes a hat then one is behaving as one should on entering a church*. The *analogy-warranting rationale*, or the most plausible for such an example, is the intent of the father, who is trying, as Hart points out, to govern the behavior of his son by example. One of the most powerful uses of

94 H. L. A. HART, THE CONCEPT OF LAW 122 (3d ed. 2012).

argument by analogy is its capacity to *convert examples* (sources) *into edicts* (analogy-warranting rules).

Two other features of analogy will be important for my upcoming discussion of the nature of Hohfeld abductions. One is that *the pattern of relevant similarity* must be discerned by a separate step of abduction within the analogical argument. What is *explained* in this step is the pattern of relevant similarity and difference, such that one is warranted in inferring that the inferred characteristic is present because the shared characteristics are present. The analogy-warranting rationale is what justifies the abduction of the analogy-warranting rule. In Hart's example above, the boy might plausibly abduce that it is removing one's hat that warrants the inference that one is behaving the right way on such occasions, and would reject the abduction that, for example, it is breathing – which both father and son were doing – that licensed such an inference. This step of abduction within the multi-step pattern of analogical argument will be central to my own explanation of Hohfeld abductions.

The other feature of analogy that will be important for my upcoming discussion of the nature of Hohfeld abductions is that some analogies take place in what I call *deduction-warranting contexts.* In these contexts, the analogy-warranting rule is applied to the target to yield the conclusion of the analogical argument *by means of yet another separate step in the overall analogical argument*, namely, deduction. If, again to use Hart's example above, the father is best taken as establishing the analogy-warranting rule as a true universal generalization, then the inference from *If one removes a hat then one is behaving as one should on entering a church*, and *I [the boy] am removing my hat* to *I am behaving as I should on entering a church* is a valid deductive inference. Note that this could be the best way for the boy to reason in accord with the principle of charity,[95] a central interpretive norm that guides analogical reasoners – the son, in this case – in making a fair formal representation of the argument-enthymeme. The son could reconstruct the father's analogical argument in this way even if the father would be unreasonable to assume that such rule was indefeasible (if the son had to wear a hat for urgent medical reasons, that would surely be a reasonable exception to the rule, *defeasing* the obligation for the son to remove his hat under those circumstances).

Some analogical arguments take place in what I call *defeasibility-warranting contexts.* Recall that, on our evidential conception of the discipline of logic endorsed by the Logocratic Method, logic studies the evidential relation between the argument's premises and its conclusion. An argument from premises to a conclusion is *defeasible* if and only if the argument is one in which it is possible that the addition of some premises to the argument's original premises can undermine the degree of evidential warrant that the original premises provide for the conclusion. Thus, for example, the mailman might, from several *sources* of pit bulls he's experienced to the *target* of a pit bull he anticipates experiencing,

95 See *supra* note 56 and accompanying text.

fashion an analogy-warranting rule, *If something is a pit bull then it's vicious* [or, more epistemically modestly, . . . *it's likely to be vicious*], and apply it to the next pit bull to conclude, as the final step of the analogical argument, that the next pit bull will be (or, is likely to be), vicious. In this defeasibility-warranting context the inference is not valid. It's an instance of *defeasible modus ponens*.

To grasp my explanation of Hohfeld abductions, it is important that one recognize the phenomenon of analogical arguments that are offered in *deduction-warranting contexts.*[96] The following is an example. Suppose that one is unsure about whether this is a valid inference: *My senses sometimes deceive me, therefore it's possible that they always deceive me.* One could reason by analogy in such a case to conclude that it is not a valid argument. One would have to *abduce* (analogical abduction) a *source* for this target and their shared and inferred characteristics in such a way as to answer the question. A creative element, but disciplined by some knowledge of the meta-logic of deductive systems, would be required to make such an analogical argument. (True genius and pioneer, Hohfeld seems to have had this kind of knowledge.) The source might be, for example, the inference: *Some paintings are forgeries, therefore it's possible that all paintings are forgeries.*[97] The shared characteristic is: *Is an inference of the logical form 'some X are Y, therefore it's possible that all X are Y'.* The inferred characteristic is, *Is an invalid argument.* The analogy-warranting rationale would involve and be licensed by norms of deductive logic, such as the principle: *If an argument has the logical form 'some X are Y, therefore it's possible that all X are Y', then the argument is invalid.* Crucially for my point about Hohfeld, and contrary to much literature about analogical argument, this kind of analogical argument (namely, in a deduction-warranting context), has *as much internal strength as a valid deductive argument.*

Some of the characteristic virtues of analogical argument are what we might call *Gricean virtues*, drawing on Grice's justly influential paper on conversational implicature.[98] Virtuous analogical arguers meet the requirements of what Grice calls the maxim of *manner*: Avoid obscurity of expression. For an analogical reasoner to meet this requirement includes being sufficiently clear about source, target, identified shared characteristic (or, for a dis-analogical argument, unshared characteristic), inferred characteristic, and analogy-warranting (or disanalogy-warranting rule).

As noted, a type of abduction is involved as one step in the multi-step process of analogical argument. To understand Hohfeld abductions, we should get in view the basics of abduction, to which I turn next.

96 I discuss this class of analogical arguments in Brewer, *Indefeasible Analogical Argument*, *supra* note 92.

97 I borrow the example from J. Rosenberg, The Practice of Philosophy 15–17 (1984). Rosenberg was illustrating logical form, not analogical argument. His is a lovely example of what is referred to as *refutation by logical analogy*.

98 H. P. Grice, *Logic and Conversation*, reprinted in many places, including H. P. Grice, Studies in the Way of Words 41 (1967).

4.5.10 *Abduction and Its Mode-Specific Virtue*

The mode of logical inference referred to as *abduction* is also referred to as *inference to the best explanation*. As the latter name suggests, the argument involves inference to an explanation of some fact or set of facts. In this argument, a statement of the phenomenon (or phenomena) to be explained and the putative explanation both appear as premises of the argument and the explanation that the reasoner settles on is the argument's conclusion. The Logocratic Method exemplifies one type of abduction, philosophical abduction. The scheme of Hohfeld relations also exemplifies philosophical abduction. The case *Wright v. Newman* exemplifies a distinct abductive type, perhaps the most common form of legal reasoning, which is the application of legal rules (or, more precisely, legal rule-enthymemes: see Section 4.5.4) to a statement of facts, which Logocratic analysis calls *legal abduction*. *Wright* also exemplifies another type of abduction, called *interpretive abduction*.

A central claim I offer in this chapter is that Hohfeld's philosophical abduction is logically distinct from and wholly reliant on legal abduction. And the point of view from which I self-reflectively make that claim is the *Logocratic point of view*, a point of view I adopt here also for the task of offering a philosophical abduction of the nature of argument. I proceed to explain (abduce) all of these categories and concepts of abduction.

4.5.10.1 The Terminology and Epistemology of Abduction

A successful meta-abduction – abduction *of* abduction – must have or rely on some cogent conception of the speech act of explanation. Central to the Logocratic account of abduction is an account of explanation as the application of a *point of view*, whose operation and identity criteria I explicate by reference to Larry Laudan's valuable model of scientific explanation, suitably generalized.

According to this account, explanations are always offered from and according to the criteria of a *point of view*.[99] The explanatory role of point of view is familiar to

[99] I developed this account of abduction in Scott Brewer, *Scientific Expert Testimony and Intellectual Due Process*, 107 YALE L.J. 1535 (1998). A recent development of the account is Brewer, *First Among Equals, supra* note 39. More recently I have come across the work of epistemologist and philosopher of science Ronald Giere, whose "perspectivist" account of scientific explanation seems to strongly resonate with my own "point of view"-based approach to explanation and thus to abduction. *See* R. GIERE, SCIENCE WITHOUT LAWS (1999); R. GIERE, SCIENTIFIC PERSPECTIVISM (2006); R. Giere, *Scientific Perspectivism, Behind the Stage Door*, 40 STUD. HIST. & PHIL. SCI. 221–23 (2009). In *Science Without Laws*, Giere offers a trenchant analogy that reflects the similarities and one important difference between my view and his (a difference that might be more stylistic than substantive, but I do not yet have a firm view about this). To illustrate the role in his abductive system of "models" of the world, a view that he calls 'perspectival realism', he offers the following analogy. A map is made by and for human beings. If well made, it is useful in enabling them to navigate. It must answer to particular local, contextual human needs. A map of Paris to be used by a tourist to navigate the *arrondissements* or to find a particular restaurant or museum will and should differ from a map used by military defenders or attackers of Paris concerned about the reach from or into Paris of artillery fire

philosophers and jurisprudes. Holmes uses the point of view of the "bad man" (that is, the *amoral* man) to explicate his prediction theory of law, a theory itself that must, for plausibility, be relativized to the point of view of a lawyer or citizen, instead of a judge. H. L. A. Hart made central to his Legal Positivist account of law the explanatory devices of "internal" and "external" attitudes – points of view – toward legal rules. Ronald Dworkin made central to his non-Legal-Positivist theory of law the "standpoint of political morality," from which, he argues, legal interpreters seek to put the legal materials they interpret in their "best light."

One might be said literally to have a point of view, that is, actually to occupy some position in space that gives one a particular visual vantage. On the forest floor, one might see only trees; from a point atop a mountain, one might see the forest, and not only the trees; from a bird's-eye view (say, from an airplane), one might see the shape of a lake; from an astronaut's-eye view, the shape of the earth. Expertise provides another type of point of view. An expert witness might tell a jury or judge what the facts are from the point of view of a biologist, a chemist, a ballistician, a psychiatrist, and so on. One might also identify an institutional or social point of view, the point of view of a particular type of actor in an institutional or other social setting – the point of view, for example, of a legislator, a judge, a lawyer, a citizen, a president, a "bad man," a parent, a child, a professor, a student. One might also identify an "enterprise" conception of point of view, and indeed the enterprise conception is, I suggest, the common

into or from adjacent countries. Maps are contextual and interest-relative and purpose-relative – there is no one "true" or ideal or universal map. And yet maps do also represent – or anyway purport to represent – the terrain that they map. There is something to which a map must answer. In Giere's analogy, maps provide *realist perspectives*:

> It is not stretching an analogy too far to say that the selection of scale and of features to be mapped determines the perspective from which a particular map represents the intended terrain. Photographs taken from different locations provide more literal examples of different perspectives on a terrain or a building. In any case, given a perspective in this sense, it is an empirical question whether a particular map successfully represents the intended terrain. If it does, we can reasonably claim a form of realism for the relationship between the map and the terrain mapped. I call this form of realism perspectival realism.
>
> Standard analyses of reference and truth suggest a metaphysics in which the domain of interest consists of discrete objects grouped into sets defined by necessary and sufficient conditions. Likewise, there is a metaphysics suggested by perspectival realism. Rather than thinking of the world as packaged into sets of objects sharing definite properties, perspectival realism presents it as highly complex and exhibiting many qualities that at least appear to vary continuously. One might then construct maps that depict this world from various perspectives. In such a world, even a fairly successful realistic science might well contain individual concepts and relationships inspired by various cultural interests. It is possible, therefore, that our currently accepted scientific theories embody cultural values and nevertheless possess many genuinely representational virtues.

See R. GIERE, SCIENCE WITHOUT LAWS 214–15 (1999) (footnotes omitted). I quite like the analogy, though I develop this point a bit differently, in a manner beholden to Nelson Goodman's "irrealism," see N. GOODMAN, WAYS OF WORLDMAKING (1978); Nietzsche's perspectivism, see F. NIETZSCHE, BEYOND GOOD AND EVIL (1886); F. NIETZSCHE, THE JOYFUL WISDOM (1882); and Pyrrhonian skeptical dialectic – on which, see *infra* note 103 and accompanying text.

thread that runs through all the notions of point of view mentioned above, both the more ordinary and the more reflectively philosophical. This point of view might even be understood as the point of view *of an enterprise*, an enterprise in which particular methods of analysis are chosen *both* to produce factual judgments and to serve specified cognitive goals. Examples of such enterprises include: systems of moral reasoning (on a cognitivist account of morality, at least, this yields the "moral point of view"); philosophical reasoning (the "philosophical point of view" – which, as in the case of Hohfeld, are sub-domain specific, such as a "logical point of view" and "metaphysical point of view," at the intersection of which lies Hohfeld's system of jural relations); systems of reasoning in support of business objectives (the "business point of view"); the "military point of view"; the "economic point of view"; "the religious point of view," and so on for many other enterprises.

In each use of the points of view noted above, *the concept of point of view is invoked to justify some claim,* either a claim about what we ought to believe (a theoretical claim) or how we ought to act (a practical claim). Each claim is thus implicitly a claim that a certain belief is justified, and that its justification comes in significant part from the method the epistemic "enterprise" uses to produce it. For example:

- "the lake is rectangular in shape": If you are justified in claiming that a lake is rectangular in shape, it is because you have a bird's eye (or some other reliable) point of view on it (or are reliably relying on someone who does).
- "defendant was present at the scene of a crime": A geneticist might be justified in believing, on the basis of "DNA fingerprint" evidence, that a defendant was present at the scene of a crime, because the geneticist has the appropriate expert point of view.
- "you ought not to sign that contract": Because she is a lawyer (or other legally trained person), and so has the lawyer's point of view, a person might be justified in her belief that her friend ought not sign some contract (given, of course, that she has sufficient information about the friend's interests and desires).
- "we ought to have a surge in troops": a military commander's claim that a particular bombing mission was the right thing to have done might be correct from a military point of view although highly questionable from either a legal or a moral point of view.

Note that simply identifying the general point of view of an enterprise does not by itself answer the following question: "What are the specific aims of the enterprise for abductive reasoners who recognize themselves as pursuing the same generic enterprise, but who often disagree about what are the proper specific aims of the enterprise?" Such disagreements are a principal source (but not the only source) of the differences among theories within an enterprise.

It is worth pausing to note also the different kinds of things we speech-actors do with explanatory speech acts, and how the enterprise-justificatory view of explanation reflects those things that abductive reasoners do. "How to do things" with the tool of abduction: explain *why* something is what it is, explain *how* something is what it is, by virtue of what, what genealogy, explain *what* something is. It is explanatory enterprises that enable explainers to do these things with explanations.

4.5.10.2 The Identity Criteria of a *Point of View*: Building on Larry Laudan's Three-Part Model of Scientific Explanation

Work by epistemologist and philosopher of science Larry Laudan helps build the Logocratic account of abduction. The Logocratic account is indebted to him for the way in which his tripartite coherentist model of scientific explanation helps give structure to the enterprise conception of point of view.[100] Generalized from the particular intellectual domain of science, Laudan's axiological model of scientific explanation helps us to explicate the role of viewpoint on the enterprise conception of explanation. The enterprise conception of a point of view posits that an intellectual enterprise that produces distinctive justificatory claims may be dissected into three separate components: *factual judgments*, the distinctive *methods* that the enterprise uses to generate those factual judgments, and the distinctive *cognitive aims* that the methods are chosen to advance and serve. One invokes a point of view to justify some claim. To serve this justificatory function, the point of view is assumed to be a reliable method of achieving the (explicit or implicit) aims of some explanatory enterprise. Because of the holistic, "reticulated" relation among aims, methods, and beliefs, we may understand claims about points of view to be claims about the axiological net that is associated with the point of view that a justificatory argument invokes.

Here are the basics of Laudan's three-level model of the means by which scientific consensus or dissensus is formed. Scientists issue judgments about the facts of their domains (biology, physics, etc.) at a *factual level*. At this level are all manner of judgments about what there is in the world, including theoretical and unobservable entities.

The factual judgments are issued by applications of *methods* at the *methodological level*. Scientists use methods both to generate factual judgments and to try to resolve factual disagreements when they exist. The idea is that a disagreement about a factual judgment might be resolved by agreeing to the results of an accurate application of a method, and then running the method in a way that both parties accept. The methodological level includes mechanical algorithms for sharing factual statements, but more often are "constraints or injunctions concerning the attributes we should seek or avoid." Examples of methodological rules are

[100] See generally L. LAUDAN, SCIENCE AND VALUES (1984).

"avoid ad-hoc explanations," "enable independent testability," "formulate testable and simple hypotheses," "prefer the results of double-blind to single-blind experiments," and "make sure to calibrate instrument *x* against standard *y*."

The *axiological level* is the level of aims or goals of science. Axiological rules are statements, often in the form of rules, of the cognitive aims of science, for example: a scientist ought to use methods for generating factual beliefs that achieve empirical accuracy, or that achieve coherence with the set of currently held theories and beliefs, or that produce the simplest theory among those theories that explain the data equally well, or that produce a predictively fertile theory, or that produce a theory that possesses a high degree of generality and breadth of scope. Although such cognitive norms are often vague,[101] and always open-textured, they are not so vague as to be without action-guiding or belief-guiding content. As with the tendency to resort to shared views about proper methods in order to resolve disagreements about factual judgments, so scientists sometimes seek to resolve disagreements about which methods to use by resorting to shared cognitive aims. For example, at a particular point in history, only "single-blind" experiments were used to generate judgments about the efficacy of medical therapies or medications, and there emerged "single-blind" vs. "double-blind" methodological camps. If it could be shown that double-blind experiments eliminated unconscious transmission of researchers' therapeutic expectations to the therapeutic subjects they were testing, medical scientists who dispute which of these methods to adopt might agree to the double-blind method if both camps agree that the double-blind method better helps to advance their shared cognitive aim (assuming they happened to share it and interpret the rule expressing the aim in substantially similar ways) of using methods for generating factual beliefs that achieve empirical accuracy.[102] This example also illustrates Laudan's coherentist "reticular" picture of scientific explanations. It is possible for judgments at the factual level to influence both the methods chosen (methodological level) and the aims chosen (axiological level); if a cognitive aim

101 A term is *vague*, relative to a given language user, at time t_1, with regard to a given potential object of application, if that language user has indecision about whether the term applies to the object, and that indecision cannot properly be attributed to lack of competence with the language. A term is *open-textured* when it is possible that it will be vague for some language user at some time t_2, with regard to some object of possible application, even though it is not vague for a given language user, at time t_1, with regard to a given potential object of application. This account of vagueness and open-texture is basically a friendly amendment to that offered by H. L. A. Hart, who brought these semantic concepts into legal, epistemological, and semantic theory – but not completely cogently – in The Concept of Law. *See* Hart, *supra* note 94, at ch. VII. To use Hart's example, in applying a municipal ordinance that makes it an infraction punishable by a fine to drive a "vehicle" into a public park, a judge may have no doubt that a Hummer, driven into the park for a cookout, is a "vehicle" for purposes of the ordinance, and thus for her at that time with regard to that object the term is not vague, even though "vehicle" might be vague, for that or another language user, at another time, with regard to a motorized wheelchair or a Segway.

102 Laudan, *supra* note 100, at 39.

seemed in fact to be unrealizable, for example, a scientific reasoner might well modify the aim to make it more realistic.

The enterprise conception of point of view, supplemented with Laudan's axiological model, allows us to offer an identity criterion for an individual point of view:

> The point of view of enterprise E consists of the factual judgments of E, produced by the methodological rules of E that are adopted to serve the axiological goals of E.

According to this criterion, there are a great many *logical species of abduction*. The list of these types is long and likely, in principle, to be unending. I here identify some of the domains of abduction that are of particular interest for both the Logocratic analysis of law and my analysis in this article of Hohfeld's philosophical abduction of legal relations: legal abduction (illustrated by Justice Carley's analysis in *Wright*), moral abduction, logical abduction, interpretive abduction, and philosophical abduction, including metaphysical abduction. We can also identify particular schools, "platforms," or systems that are within these domains, or cut across them. *Hohfeldian abduction* (explanation from a *Hohfeldian point of view*) consists of logical and metaphysical abduction (but *not* legal abduction) and *Logocratic abduction* (inference to the best Logocratic explanation).

Several enterprises can be brought to bear to explain a given phenomenon; for example, every legal dispute that involves a dispute about the legal explanation of facts will also involve factual explanations and sometimes (increasingly) will involve one or more domains of empirical science (e.g., genetics, ballistics, psychology). Crucially, different enterprises will offer different explanations of the same phenomena. Sometimes those explanations won't just differ, they will also disagree (note that explanations that disagree with one another are also inconsistent with each other). This is one of the principle sources of philosophical skepticism.[103] And the

[103] Here is a basic pattern of Pyrrhonian skeptical analysis, according to that paragon of skeptical subtlety, Sextus Empiricus, in OUTLINES OF PYRRHONISM. In general, where F and F* refer to appearances of propositional thought (e.g., moral or legal propositions) or of the senses (looks like, sounds like, tastes like, feels like, smells like):

(1) x appears F to those who have custom or law [or point of view] L,
(2) x appears F* to those who have custom or law [or point of view] L*,
(3) we seem to have no reason to prefer L to L*,
(4) we suspend judgment as to whether x really is F or F*.

Note that this skeptical argument is effective only if F and F* are in some way incompatible – for example, they are expressed as propositions that are inconsistent (cannot both be true) or contradictory (one is true if and only if the other is false). Consider, for example, biologist Stephen Jay Gould's claim that the points of view of religious and scientific explanation are *not* incompatible because the domains of religion and science are "non-overlapping magisteria." Stephen Jay Gould, *Nonoverlapping Magisteria*, 106 NAT. HIST. 16 (1997). This claim is very unconvincing because it misunderstands the range of claims that are included within the theories of the world offered by many of the best-known religions. Religious claims in central texts like the Bible are ontologically committed (see Quine, *On What There Is*, "to be is to be the value of a bound variable") to supernatural entities and forces, and contrary to what Gould seemed to believe, do not only

viewpoint-based account of explanation, and thus of abduction, that I develop here, is itself informed and inflected by skeptical concerns.[104]

4.5.11 *Logocratic Method as Philosophical Abduction of the Nature of Argument*

The Logocratic Method is a type of philosophical abduction. The target of its explanatory inferences are *arguments*: what they are and some of the typical *uses of arguments in context*. It owes some significant part of its theoretical basis to the domain of "pragmatics,"[105] as pioneered by J. L. Austin,[106] Paul Grice,[107] John Searle,[108] and Ludwig Wittgenstein.[109] In 1955, Oxford philosopher J. L. Austin delivered a set of lectures at Harvard that was soon published as a classic of contemporary philosophy, *How To Do Things With Words*. In that work, Austin offered a theory to show that we use words not only to *describe* things but, in a great variety of ways, also to *do* things – to perform actions (such as, in the right circumstances, naming something, getting married, or, for a judge, officially resolving a case with use of the phrase "so ordered"). Indeed, he rightly came to wonder whether all our uses of words are *doings*, including the "doing" of *describing*.[110]

promulgate moral rules and guides for living. Those ontological commitments are incompatible with those of the sciences of biology, chemistry, and physics. Thus, in terms of the Logocratic account of abduction, ontological and (more broadly) metaphysical claims from the *points of view* of many prominent religions, they not only differ from and contrast with but also *contest* with the points of view of physics, biology, chemistry. The central method of Pyrrhonian skepticism is to point to this kind of clash of points of view to establish (*it seems to me* – as asserted by a Pyrrhonian, is what we might call a "Pyrrhonian operator," functioning as a propositional attitude to be prepended by a good Pyrrhonian to every proposition she utters) the "*isostheneia*" (equal strength) of competing points of view, leading (it seems to the Pyrrhonian) the Pyrrhonian to a perplexity (*aporia*) about which point of view to adopt, and in turn leading (it seems to the Pyrrhonian) the Pyrrhonian to a "suspension" (*epoche*) of judgment about which point of view to adopt, leading (it seems to the Pyrrhonian) the Pyrrhonian to stick to how things appear to her, in turn leading (it seems to the Pyrrhonian) to a kind of meditative tranquility (*ataraxia*).

104 See *supra* note 103 and accompanying text.

105 The concept of pragmatics harks back to a tripartite distinction among syntax, semantics, and pragmatics, articulated in work by, among others, Mead and Carnap. *See* C. W. Morris, *Foundations of the Theory of Signs, in* 1 International Encyclopaedia of Unified Science Pt 2 (1938); R. Carnap, *Foundations of Logic and Mathematics, in* 1 International Encyclopaedia of Unified Science Pt 3 (1939).

106 *See, e.g.*, J. L. Austin, How To Do Things With Words (1962); J. L. Austin, *Performative Utterances, in* Philosophical Papers 233–52 (J. O. Urmson and G. J. Warnock eds., 1979); J. L. Austin, *Performative-Constative, in* Philosophy and Ordinary Language 22–54 (C. E. Caton ed., 1963).

107 *See* P. Grice, *Logic and Conversation, in* 3 Syntax and Semantics: Speech Arts 41–58 (P. Cole et al. eds., 1975).

108 *See, e.g.*, J. Searle, Speech Acts: An Essay in the Philosophy of Language (1969).

109 *See* L. Wittgenstein, Philosophical Investigations (E. Anscombe trans., 1953).

110 See J. L. Austin, *Performative-Constative, in* Philosophy and Ordinary Language 22 (C. E. Caton ed., 1963).

The Logocratic Method follows the core idea of Austin (and other philosophers) who find significant explanatory value in treating words, concepts, and arguments as *tools* for achieving certain tasks. It focuses closely on three types of tasks that people perform by means of arguments and on the two distinct types of virtue or vice of arguments – internal-inferential and dialectical-rhetorical – as measured by the degree of achievement of these tasks (see Section 4.5.7). Important twin emphases of the Logocratic Method are theoretical and practical. It offers a philosophical abduction of arguments including detailed analysis of three of their principal uses. It also provides a set of specific practices by means of which the Logocratic consumer can cultivate the capacity to evaluate his or her own and others' arguments, a skill that can serve well the interests of a citizen, lawyer, student, philosopher – indeed, anyone for whom arguments are valuable in some domain of life or reflection.

4.5.11.1 The Characteristic Virtues of Abduction

An account of the characteristic virtues of abduction closely tracks the enterprise conception of point of view as elaborated with the help of Laudan's axiological model. A virtuous abduction accurately deploys *methods* to issue the judgments that are characteristic of that point of view, and in turn, chooses methods that do a good job of serving the axiological aims. Because the contexts and domains of abductive argument vary so widely, it is not possible to say much that is specific about the virtues of an abductive argument apart from this. However, a deep research project is involved by practitioners of abduction in their respective fields concerning the elements of their respective points of view. They perforce consider and argue about (albeit not usually in these terms) what are and what *should be* the axiological goals, methods chosen to serve those goals, as well as about what are the judgments that issue from application of those methods. As Laudan's model makes clear, disagreement among abductive reasoners is possible regarding any of the reticulated judgment-method-goal triads that comprise a point of view. For example, a significant part of jurisprudence is concerned with such questions as: *What is the legal point of view? What should be the legal point of view?* and *What are or should be the forms of the judgments, methods, and aims of the legal point of view?* Hohfeld research (of the sort reflected in this volume) addresses these questions about the Hohfeldian point of view.

4.5.11.2 The Formal Structure of Abduction

There is wide variation in approaches to the explanation of abduction (which is itself a type of abduction, a meta-abduction – it's "abduction all the way down"). Some approaches are mostly discursive and offer relatively little in the way of formal logical grammar and apparatus.[111] Some are heavily formal.[112] One can explain (abduce!) the reason for this variation by noting the different purposes driving different theorists' meta-abductions. There has been, for example, considerable interest among abduction theorists in developing computational models of abduction that can serve the needs of artificial intelligence, and these theories need a computationally rich, ideally, even programmable, set of representations of the form of abduction. Others are epistemologists who have less need for formalism in their meta-abductions. My own Logocratic analysis is relatively light on formalism in its meta-abduction, but there is some, mainly to mark concisely exactly what, on the Logocratic view, happens at each step in an abductive argument. Part of this formal scheme reflects the Logocratic view that abduction is a type of conditional but it is neither a material conditional nor a strict conditional nor a causal conditional.[113]

The *conclusion* of an abductive inference is an *explanatory proposition*, Φ_n, sometimes referred to as an *explanans*, an "explaining thing."

The *premises* of an abductive inference consist of:

(i) a proposition that describes some event or phenomenon that the abductive reasoner believes stands in need of explanation (the *explanandum*)
(ii) one or more propositions to the effect that, *if* some specific explanatory hypothesis were in fact true or otherwise warranted, then the *explanandum* would be sufficiently explained for the reasoner's purposes; this we will refer to as the *sufficient explanation conditional*

As suggested by this phrase, this premise appears in the form of a logical conditional: *If* $\Phi \surd \rightarrow \Theta$ (read *If* Φ *were true [or, were otherwise warranted] that might sufficiently explain* Θ) in which the antecedent (Φ) is some specific explanatory hypothesis (the *explanans*) that the reasoner has "discovered" (for this reasoning process, creating a hitherto unstated hypothesis counts as a type of discovery as much as applying an already existing hypothesis) in the course of the abduction from some point of view, and the consequent (Θ) is the *explanandum* that is asserted in the first premise of the abduction.

Note that there can be several such explanantia (Φ_i), each of which can be represented as a separate premise in the abduction. In fact, at this stage of abductive inference, reasoners *tend to, but do not always,* pass the Φ_i through a "plausibility filter" – that is, each Φ_i tends to provide a plausible explanation of the *explanandum* – sufficiently plausible to warrant the effort of confirming or disconfirming the Φ_i. Both the criteria of plausibility and even the need for and degree of plausibility will vary greatly according to the point of view from which the explanation is offered (logical, legal, interpretative, religious, etc.). However, passing the considered Φ_i

111 A justly influential example is P. Lipton, Inference to the Best Explanation (2d ed. 2004).
112 Worthy examples are: A. Aliseda, Abductive Reasoning: Logical Investigations into Discovery and Explanation (2008); D. Gabbay & J. Wood, The Reach of Abduction (2005).
113 See *supra* note 57 and accompanying text.

through a plausibility filter is not a formal or invariant requirement at this step of abduction. Sometimes an abductive reasoner might actually seek to provide an *implausible* explanation and doing so might be *best* from the abductive arguer's *point of view*. This is true, for example, in some of the most celebrated legal abductions in American history, such as the one that attorney Thurgood Marshall offered in his argument for *Shelley v. Kramer*.[114] It is also true of many absurd (or even absurdist) explanations offered by characters in logically rich literary works, such as the works of Lewis Carroll (*Alice in Wonderland* and *Through the Looking Glass*) and Joseph Heller (*Catch-22*), and in some religious abductive texts whose explanations of phenomena expressly embrace absurdity, such as Kierkegaard's "leap of faith" and the maxim *credo quia absurdum*.[115] (Of course, a great deal more needs to be said about abductive plausibility than I can say here.[116])

(iii) a proposition asserting that, for some explanans Φ_n among all the Φ_i for which the sufficient explanation conditional is true, if Φ_n were true, Φ_n would explain Θ *better than* any other of the Φ_i for which the sufficient explanation conditional is true. The assertion of the proposition in this step is warranted when the reasoner has confirmed Φ_n and either disconfirmed each other Φ_i or determined that Φ_n is a better explanation than other still potentially plausible competitors. The result of this judgment is the abductive reasoner's assertion of a *best explanation conditional*. The best explanation conditional may be represented as, 'If $\Phi_n \surd\surd \rightarrow \Theta$', read as, "If Φ_n were true, then Φ_n would explain Θ better than any Φ_i where $\Phi_i \neq \Phi_n$." Note that in some argumentative settings abduction can be *inconclusive*, pending more data or more theory. In

[114] *Shelley* v. *Kramer*, 334 U.S. 1 (1948).

[115] Attributed by some to Tertullian. For discussion, see P. Harrison, *"I Believe Because it is Absurd": The Enlightenment Invention of Tertullian's Credo*, 86 Church Hist. 339 (2017).

[116] Here is one data point for the question of the judgment of plausibility in abduction:

> There is a marvelous story illustrating these points told by Freeman Dyson about a lecture given by Wolfgang Pauli outlining an unorthodox theory suggested by him and Heisenberg. In the discussion after the lecture, many of the younger scientists were sharply critical of Pauli, and at one point, Neils Bohr, who was also present, rose to speak. "We are all agreed," he said to Pauli, "that your theory is crazy. The question which divides us is whether it is crazy enough to have a chance of being correct. My own feeling is that it is not crazy enough." Dyson then comments: "The objection that they are not crazy enough applies to all the attempts which have so far been launched at a radically new theory of elementary particles. it applies especially to crackpots. Most of the crackpot papers which are submitted to The Physical Review are rejected, not because it is impossible to understand them, but because it is possible. Those which are impossible to understand are usually published. When the great innovation appears, it will almost certainly be in a muddled, incomplete, and confusing form. To the discoverer himself it will be only half-understood; to everybody else it will be a mystery. For any speculation which does not at first glance look crazy, there is no hope.

W. M. Brown, *The Economy of Peirce's Abduction*, 19 Transactions of the Charles S. Peirce Soc'y 397, 407–08 (1983).

the special domain of legal abduction, however, burdens of persuasion and burdens of production virtually always yield a selection of a single Φ_n.

4.5.11.2.1 GLOSSARY

'Θ'	STANDS FOR AN *explanandum*
'$\phi_1 \ldots \phi_N$'	STANDS FOR EXPLANATORY HYPOTHESES (ONE OR MORE *explanantia*)
'IF $\phi_I \surd \rightarrow \Theta$'	STANDS FOR A "SUFFICIENT EXPLANATION CONDITIONAL" "IF ϕ_N WERE TRUE, THAT WOULD (SUFFICIENTLY) EXPLAIN Θ"
'IF $\phi_N \surd\surd \rightarrow \Theta$'	STANDS FOR A "BEST EXPLANATION CONDITIONAL" "IF ϕ_N WERE TRUE, THEN ϕ_N WOULD EXPLAIN θ BETTER THAN ANY ϕ_I WHERE $\phi_I \neq \phi_N$"

4.5.11.2.2 SCHEMA

ε_1	Θ
ε_2	FOR EACH CANDIDATE ϕ_I, '$\phi_I \surd \rightarrow \Theta$' IS TRUE.
ε_3	FOR CANDIDATE ϕ_N, '$\phi_N \surd\surd \rightarrow \Theta$' IS TRUE.
THEREFORE	
H	ϕ_N

4.5.11.3 A Simple Example of Abduction: Why Do I Have a Pain in My Heel?

Suppose I am walking along and suddenly feel a pain in my heel. What might explain that? Groups of students to whom I have put this example over the years tend to come up with three or so plausible explanations. In the structure of abduction presented above, I represent their analysis as follows:

ε_1	Θ	*Explanandum:*	There is a pain in my heel.
ε_{2a}	If $\Phi_1 \surd \rightarrow \Theta$	*Sufficient explanation conditional$_1$:*	If it were the case that I have a pebble in my shoe, **that would explain** the fact that there is a pain in my heel.
ε_{2b}	If $\Phi_2 \surd \rightarrow \Theta$	*Sufficient explanation conditional$_2$:*	If it were the case that I have an overuse injury from too much walking, **that would explain** the fact that there is a pain in my heel.
ε_{2c}	If $\Phi_3 \surd \rightarrow \Theta$	*Sufficient explanation conditional$_3$:*	If it were the case that I stepped on a nail, **that would explain** the fact that there is a pain in my heel.

[The abductive reasoner works to confirm or disconfirm the hypotheses generated; suppose one confirms Φ_1 and disconfirms Φ_2 and Φ_3 by inspecting one's foot. This leads to ε_3:]

ε_3 $\Phi_1 \surd \surd \rightarrow \Theta$: No other explanation explains the pain in my heel as well as that there is a pebble in my shoe.

Therefore,

h Φ_1 *Explanans*: There is a pebble in my shoe.

4.5.11.4 Legal Abduction and the Role of Deduction within Legal Abduction

Abduction is extremely common, nay, ubiquitous, in legal analysis. Every time a legal analyst explains a set of facts from a legal point of view – are the facts of this transaction best explained as contract, or as tort, or as the crime of murder, or is the proffered evidence logically relevant, or conditionally relevant, or hearsay, or character evidence – that analyst uses the argument pattern of inference to the best *legal* explanation. And when the factfinder (judge alone, or judge plus jury) finds those facts that are material to a substantive law claim (which Hohfeld calls "operative facts"[117]), the factfinder uses inference to the best factual explanation.

There are ways in which one mode of logical inference can play a role *within* another, and legal abduction is one such instance. In legal abduction, the Logocratic analyst seeks to explain the facts of a given case (or hypothetical) by determining what legal rules might apply to the fact pattern, and then determining the outcome of the application of the rule to the fact pattern. In that process, according to the plausible philosophical explanation of legal argument that I favor and here advance, deduction operates *within* the overall legal abduction, as analogy and induction often also do.

Another way to describe this legal abduction is to say that the analyst *explains the fact pattern from a legal point of view*. Thus, for example, when Justice Carley in *Wright* reasoned his way to the best legal explanation (the legal abduction) of the transaction between Newman and Wright, he used *an application, by means of deduction*, of the statutory rule for promissory estoppel to determine that the best explanation of the litigant's transaction was that it was breach of contract. The explanatory speech act here answers the question: *What kind of event is this set of events, from a legal point of view?* The answer Justice Carley gave for the *Wright* majority was that it was breach of contract. In so doing, he used his application of the deductively applicable rule for logical relevance to conclude that, because the requirements of the rule were in fact satisfied by the facts of the case before him ('satisfied' here means that there was sufficient evidence for the fact, under the appropriate burden of persuasion), the best explanation of the operative facts between Wright and Newman was, from a legal point

117 See *supra* note 13.

of view, contractual liability of Wright to Newman. In effect, the justice reasoned that, because the requirements of the rule of promissory estoppel (which we identified as rule elements P, S, and T in his rulified rule '$P \wedge S \wedge T) \supset K$') were satisfied, an argument from that rule would be the best explanation of the litigant's transactions.

Note in this connection that some abductive inferences can be fairly represented as having as much force as valid deductive inferences. This we might call *non-ampliative abduction*, and in recognizing this type of abduction Logocratic theory departs sharply from other theories of abduction (meta-abductions), a great many of which treat abduction as ampliative, that is, defeasible. For a simple example of non-ampliative abduction, consider how one might explain how it is that a pawn in chess can appear on the same column as a pawn on the same "team" (color) in the course of legal play. The answer – that one pawn on that team "captured" an opposing piece directly or *en passant* – is an application of deductively applicable rules of chess. Other abductions have only as much force as the inductive specifications on which they rely. These are defeasible, ampliative abductions. Thus, in some abductions the premises provide *incorrigible, indefeasible evidence* for the truth of their conclusions (as in the chess explanation, and when abduction is used, as it indeed is, in mathematical and logical reasoning), and sometimes only probabilistic warrant (probability less than 1). Whether inferences to the best *legal* explanation, in which legal rules play such an important role (as we just observed), also have the force of deductively applicable rules is a nice and important jurisprudential question.[118]

Using the formal presentation of abduction offered above, Justice Carley's legal abduction looks like this. Here I return to the presentation of the justice's arguments that I offered in Section 4.3 before having presented the formal structure of abduction.

ε_1	Θ	*Explanandum*:	What is the legal significance, from a legal point of view, of *the facts that*: (i) Kim Newman and Bruce Wright had for a time cohabited, *but* (ii) were never married *and* (iii) together had a biological daughter *and* (iv) Wright was not the natural father of Newman's son *and* (v) Bruce Wright promised both Kim Newman and her son that Wright would assume all of the obligations and responsibilities of fatherhood, including that of providing support and this promise was evidenced by Wright's listing of

[118] For a discussion of relevant considerations on this issue, see Brewer, *On the Possibility of Necessity*, *supra* note 74.

			himself as the father on the child's birth certificate and giving the child his last name *and* (vi) after supporting the boy for some time, he discontinued that support when his relationship with Newman ended.[119]
ε_{2a}	If $\Phi_1 \surd \rightarrow \Theta$	*Sufficient explanation conditional*$_1$:	if Wright were the boy's *natural father*, that would explain their relationship, from a legal point of view: Wright would be obliged to pay child-support for the boy.
ε_{2b}	If $\Phi_2 \surd \rightarrow \Theta$	*Sufficient explanation conditional*$_2$:	if Wright had *formally adopted* the boy, that would explain their relationship, from a legal point of view: Wright would be obliged to pay child-support for the boy.
ε_{2c}	If $\Phi_3 \surd \rightarrow \Theta$	*Sufficient explanation conditional*$_3$:	if Wright had "*virtually adopted*" the boy that would explain their relationship, from a legal point of view: Wright would be obliged to pay child-support for the boy.
ε_{2d}	If $\Phi_4 \surd \rightarrow \Theta$	*Sufficient explanation conditional*$_4$:	if Wright had made a promise to pay child-support that was part of a bargained-for exchange and met the requirement of a writing, that would explain their relationship, from a legal point of view: Wright would be obliged to pay child-support for the boy.
ε_{2e}	If $\Phi_5 \surd \rightarrow \Theta$	*Sufficient explanation conditional*$_5$:	if Wright had made a promise to pay for child-support that was enforceable under a reliance doctrine in the state's statutorily codified promissory estoppel law, that would explain their relationship, from a legal point of view.

Justice Carley disconfirms ε_{2a} through ε_{2d} by inspecting the available evidence – including legal records and testimony – on marriage, DNA paternity, adoption, and written and oral promises.

Justice Carley confirms ε_{2e} by applying the criteria of the rule for the Georgia promissory estoppel provision to the facts of his case (under the sufficiency of the evidence operator rule: *If there is sufficient evidence that P, then P*; see discussion above note 70). The *criteria* of a rule, as I am using the term here, are the logical

[119] Note that a typical feature of abduction of any kind is that the abductive reasoner may reframe the statement of the *explanandum* as she gets new information about the item whose explanation she seeks. In other words, flexibility in the understanding and articulation of the explanandum is familiar in abduction, including legal abduction.

elements of the rule. The criteria of a rule are satisfied when, given the logical structure of the rule,[120] the antecedent of the rule is *true*.

Justice Carley reaches his conclusion that *not only* is sufficient explanation conditional$_5$ (namely, ε_{2e}: If $\Phi_5 \surd \rightarrow \Theta$: if Wright had made a promise to pay for child support that was enforceable under a reliance doctrine in the state's statutorily codified promissory estoppel law) true, *but also* that ε_3 is true, namely, that Φ_5 also figures in the best explanation conditional (ε_3 $\Phi_1 \surd \surd \rightarrow \Theta$: No other plausible explanation explains, from a legal point of view, the relevant facts of the relation between Wright and Newman (that is, Θ) as well as does Φ_5). Put another way, Justice Carley determines that there is sufficient evidence for each of the three jointly sufficient conditions in Rule 1 such that K is the result, under *modus ponens*.

This leads him to step ε_3:

ε_3	$\Phi_5 \surd \surd \rightarrow \Theta$:	if Wright had made a promise to pay for child-support that was enforceable under a reliance doctrine in the state's statutorily codified promissory estoppel law, that would *best explain* their relationship, from a legal point of view.

Therefore,

h	Φ_5	*Explanans*:	Wright made a promise to pay for child-support that was enforceable under a reliance doctrine in the state's statutorily codified promissory estoppel law.

4.5.12 *What Is Philosophical Abduction?*

As I have noted, both Hohfeld jural relation explanations and the Logocratic Method are a distinctive type of abduction – philosophical abduction. What is distinctive about philosophical abduction as a type of abduction? We may use the Laudan framework offered above to offer an explanation (an abduction) of philosophical abduction. There are many ways to offer philosophical explanations and I do not claim or seek to reflect them all in this discussion. Instead, I will discuss some of the more common types of philosophical abduction an understanding of which will explain the Logocratic Method and the Logocratic point of view as an instance of philosophical abduction.

120 For the elements of the rule, see Sections 4.5.4.4 and 4.5.4.5.

4.5.12.1 Factual Level of Philosophical Abduction

4.5.12.1.1 METAPHYSICAL JUDGMENTS IN PHILOSOPHICAL ABDUCTION First, what kinds of phenomena does philosophical abduction seek to explain? A great deal of philosophical abduction – including Hohfeld abductions – may be fairly characterized as seeking to offer metaphysical judgments, in this special sense: metaphysics is the conceptual analysis of the kinds of things that exist and the kinds of relations that obtain among them. So understood, the factual level of philosophical abduction is concerned with making judgments about the kinds of things that exist (known as the study of "ontology") – for example, are all existing things mental (the philosophical explanation called "idealism"), or instead are all existing things material (the philosophical explanation called "materialism"), or do both exist ("mind-body dualism").

4.5.12.1.2 SOME OF THE TYPES OF RELATIONS EXPLICATED IN PHILOSOPHICAL ABDUCTION The types of relations of interest to philosophical abduction include *causal relations*, *logical relations* (e.g., entailment, consequence), *meaning relations* (e.g., interpretation, text A is the meaning of text B), and *epistemic relations* (e.g., know that, believe that, justifiably believe that).[121] Also on this broad conception, metaphysics includes the conceptual analysis of values and value relations (including moral, prudential, aesthetic), and *justification relations* (including moral justification, prudential justification, epistemic justification, inferential justification). *Hohfeld jural relations* are a paradigm instance of the kinds of relations explicated in philosophical abduction.

4.5.12.2 Methodological Level of Philosophical Abduction

Any sustained treatment of the philosophy of philosophy is beyond the scope of this chapter. A discussion of one central and pervasive method (at least, on *one* abduction of philosophical abduction) will suffice to allow me to offer my abduction of Hohfeldian abduction. Among the most typical methods of philosophical abduction is *conceptual analysis*, which involves testing various framings of concepts and the rules or principles in which those concepts figure (such as rules or principles for *justice*, *truth*, *meaning*) with potential *counter-examples*.

121 On this broad conception, the domain of metaphysics includes *epistemology*. Epistemology is the study of particular epistemic relations between epistemic agents and the objects of their propositional attitudes, which include *knowing that, believing that, justifiably believing that, appearing that, being aware that, being perplexed that* (a result for some people, for example, undergoing Pyrrhonian or Socratic elenchos (*ἔλεγχος, cross-examination*)).

4.5.12.3 Axiological Level of Philosophical Abduction

It seems – and it is interesting to note – that many of the conceptual aims of science that Laudan identifies seem also to be aims of philosophical abduction, including: a philosophical abduction ought to achieve coherence with the set of currently held theories and beliefs; a philosophical abduction ought to produce the simplest theory among those theories that explain the data equally well; a philosophical abduction ought to produce the most elegant theory among those theories that explain the data equally well; a philosophical abduction ought to possess a high degree of generality and breadth of scope, and more controversially (or perhaps counter-intuitively), a philosopher ought to use methods for generating factual beliefs that achieve empirical accuracy.[122]

The axiological goal of the method of conceptual analysis mentioned in the previous section is, for some philosophers, the articulation of *all* the necessary and sufficient conditions for the concept. For other philosophers (especially those influenced by the later work of Wittgenstein), the goal might instead be to articulate a *partial* set of conditions, as mediated by "family resemblance" instead of entailment relations. Both the more ambitious and the less ambitious variants of conceptual explication involve explanations of concepts by *reflective equilibrium*.[123] This method of explicating concepts consists of forming an intuitively attractive rule or principle, challenging it with potential outcomes of the principle, such as possible counter-examples, and adjusting one's endorsement of either the rule or principle on the one hand, or the outcomes of the rule or principle, on the other, until one arrives at a supposed equilibrium point in the process. Importantly for my explanation of Hohfeld relations, reflective equilibrium itself can be modeled as a type of argument by

122 *See, e.g.*, Raymond Geuss, Outside Ethics 220 (2005) ("Socrates, however, 'dragged moralizing into science,' and Plato followed in his wake. Such moralizing, Nietzsche thought, was a result of weakness, of a deep-seated inability to bear looking the facts of the world in the face; it crippled Plato intellectually and prevented him from ever developing that most highly prized of Nietzschean traits: '*Tatsachen-Sinn*,' a 'sense for the facts,' that steely realism that is so abundantly evident on every page of Thucydides. Characters of whom Plato ethically disapproves, such as Thrasymachus or Callicles, are always shown in his dialogues to be confuted by Socrates. Vicious people, however, as we all know, do *not* always lose the argument. What Plato takes to be morally reprehensible behavior *must*, he thinks, finally be a form of irrationality that is self-defeating, and this puts such narrow limits to his ability to understand humans that it renders him unfit to be a serious guide to the world in which we live.").

123 See A. Appiah, Thinking It Through 378 (2003) ("What is at the root of the philosophical style is a desire to give a general and systematic account of our thought and experience, one that is developed critically, in the light of evidence and argument. You will remember that John Rawls used the notion of reflective equilibrium to describe the goal of philosophical thought. We start with an intuitive understanding of a problem, seeing it 'through a glass, darkly'; and from these intuitions we build a little theory. The theory sharpens and guides our intuitions, and we return to theorizing. As we move back and forth from intuition to theory, we approach, we hope, a reflective equilibrium where theory and intuition coincide. If the history of philosophy is anything to go by, one person's reflective equilibrium is another person's state of puzzlement.").

analogy.[124] In this process, one uses *analogical abduction* (see Section 4.5.9) to discover rule or principle. Suppose (to borrow an example from Plato's *Republic*), you find yourself convinced by reading some philosopher that the principle *It is always wrong to lie* is true. Then perhaps your "inner Socrates" confronts you with this hypothetical *example*: You have been asked by a friend to hold onto his hunting knife. He later comes to you expressing murderous rage about one of his rivals and asks to have his knife back. What should you do? Under pressure of this example, you might be led to modify the principle you endorse so that it instead reads: *It is always wrong to lie unless lying is required to save a human life.* Thus, you lie to your friend ("I don't have access to the knife right now, sorry"). Or you could accept the consequence of your principle, however uncomfortably, conclude that you ought to return the knife, and do so. The source for this analogical argument is the example that your inner Socrates has adduced. The target is your behavior in some circumstance, actual or imagined. Perhaps you have been placed in a circumstance in which lying seems called for, despite your awareness of your current commitment to a never-lie principle; or perhaps you are trying to do moral philosophy concerning the morality of lying and try to test the no-lie principle with examples; this method of counterexample is traceable to Plato's Socrates. Finding – *abducing* – a principle that sorts out what you regard as relevant examples, sources and targets, into an analogy-warranting rule suitably supported by an analogy-warranting rationale – is one of the most fundamental methods of philosophical analysis.

4.6 TWO TYPES OF HOHFELD JURAL-RELATIONS PHILOSOPHICAL ABDUCTIONS

Throughout this chapter I have spoken of *Hohfeldian abductions*. There are two distinct questions one might ask about the Hohfeld system.[125] One is, *given* the Hohfeld axioms (as rulified from the rule-enthymemes found in Hohfeld's 1913 and 1917 papers), how does one explain the Hohfeldian incidents that pertain to the various parties in a particular setting? I offered a few Hohfeldian abductions earlier in this chapter, namely, a simple example of a "family law" rule (see Section 4.4.2) and various time-slices of *Wright v. Newman* (see Section 4.4.3). I've tried to show that using the Logocratic model of abduction to explain a set of legal relations, transactions, or obligations from the Hohfeldian point of view is to offer factual judgments about which parties in a transaction have (or would have) which Hohfeldian incidents. And one of my central points is that these kinds of Hohfeldian abductions are logically parasitic on prior legal abductions of the sort that I offered regarding *Wright v. Newman*.

[124] See the discussion in Brewer, *Exemplary Reasoning*, *supra* note 62, at 927–28, 938–40, 962–63, 982, 1023–26.

[125] Thanks to Ted Sichelman for focusing me on this question.

A distinct question is how did Hohfeld himself, the man, the logician, first abduce the explanatory system that is comprised by the Hohfeld axioms? I can only suggest, not develop at any length, my answer to that question. Hohfeld discovered or invented (here I offer no realist or anti-realist view on which of these is the superior description) the axiomatic system that provides Hohfeld abductions by means of *analogical reasoning in a deduction-warranting context* (recall this idea explained in Section 4.5.9). Examining, as a philosophical anthropologist, the behavior of rights-talking by American and English judges, lawyers, and other legal analysts, he spotted a pattern that made intelligible sense of that talk. In his landmark article he tells us:

> Reverting, for example, to the subject powers, it might be difficult at first glance to discover any essential and fundamental *similarity* between conditional sales of personalty, escrow transactions, option agreements, agency relations, powers of appointment, etc. But if all these relations are reduced to their lowest generic terms, the conceptions of legal power and legal liability are seen to be dominantly, though not exclusively, applicable throughout the series. By such a process it becomes possible not only to discover *essential similarities and illuminating analogies* in the midst of what appears superficially to be infinite and hopeless variety, but also *to discern common principles of justice and policy underlying the various jural problems involved*. An indirect, yet very practical, consequence is that it frequently becomes feasible, by virtue of such analysis, to use as persuasive authorities judicial precedents that might otherwise seem altogether irrelevant. If this point be valid with respect to powers, it would seem to be equally so as regards all of the other basic conceptions of the law. In short, the deeper the analysis, the great become one's perception of fundamental unity and harmony in the law.[126]

I suggest that Hohfeld created (discovered) his system of axioms by using a familiar type of philosophical reasoning, reflective equilibrium, which is a type of analogical argument.[127] Hohfeld abduced his axioms, I suggest, by means of analogical abduction that constitutes reflective equilibrium. (See also the discussion of legal rules as axioms in Section 4.5.5.) Recall in this connection that what came to be called 'reflective equilibrium' by John Rawls had earlier been identified (as Rawls acknowledges) by his colleague Nelson Goodman, and that Goodman originally proposed that *rules of deductive and inductive inference* were arrived at by this process. In Goodman's terms: "A rule [of inference] is amended if it yields an inference we are unwilling to accept; an inference is rejected if it violates a rule we are unwilling to amend."[128]

We see one illustration of how this process may have worked in a fact I noticed early in this chapter, that Hohfeld axioms are enthymematic (see Section 4.4.1 and, specifically, Section 4.4.1.2). Legal Realist interpreters of Hohfeld, like Arthur Corbin, Hohfeld's close colleague and firm booster, present Hohfeld's relations in terms of a "Giant" – the government, in the form of judiciary – whose actions or inactions,

[126] Hohfeld, *supra* note 2, at 59 (emphasis added).

[127] See Sections 4.5.9, 4.5.12.3, note 57, and citations to Brewer, *Exemplary Reasoning*, *supra* note 124.

[128] GOODMAN, *supra* note 57, at 62.

assistances or inertias, they make a central part of the ontology of Hohfeld relations.[129] Thus, for example, Hohfeld *jural opposite* relations look like this, according to Corbin's "Giant" rulification of the Hohfeld rule-enthymemes (see Table 4.5):

TABLE 4.5 *Corbin's "giant" rulifications of Hohfeld opposites jural relations*

	Jural relation (a) and its opposite (b)	Hohfeld enthymeme[130]	Corbin rulification[131]
1a	Claim-right	A has a claim-right against B	"The concept that the giant ***will aid* A** by forcibly controlling B's conduct we express by saying that A has a RIGHT."
1b	No-right	A has a no-right against B	"If the giant ***will not [aid* A** by forcibly controlling B's conduct] A, [A] has NO RIGHT."
2a	Liberty (Privilege)	A has a privilege against B	"If [the giant] ***will not [aid* B** by using force to control A's conduct], and A is free from such constraint, this fact is expressed by saying that A has a PRIVILEGE."
2b	Duty	A has a duty to B	"If the giant ***will aid* B** by using force to control A's conduct, A has a DUTY."
3a	Power	A has a power against (?) B	"If ***A can, by his voluntary act, influence the giant's conduct with respect to B, whether to act or not to act, and whether presently or contingently***, A has a POWER."
3b	Disability	A has a disability with respect to (?) B	"If ***A cannot [by his voluntary act, influence the giant's conduct with respect to B, whether to act or not to act, and whether presently or contingently***], [A] has a DISABILITY."

129 See Corbin, *supra* note 3, at 227–28: "It is not meant by the foregoing that this is the only possible usage of the terms in question. It is believed to be the actual usage, and that it is of advantage to abide by it. According to this usage, there is no law and there can be no legal relations of any sort where there is no organized society. The fact that is essential is the existence of societal force; and the question that is of supreme interest is as to when and how that force will be applied. What will the community of citizens cause their agents to do. It is this multitude of busy little fellow citizens who constitute 'society' or 'the state' and it is their cumulative strength that constitutes the personified giant whose arm may be so powerful to aid or to destroy. In law, the ultimate question is, what will this giant do."

130 In referring here to "Hohfeld enthymemes," I am offering a concise version of the Hohfeld relation as he expressed it. For more detailed reference to the actual enthymematic text for the rule-enthymemes that first created and expressed Hohfeld relations in his 1913 paper, see Section 4.4.1.2 above.

131 Corbin, *supra* note 3, at 229 (emphases in the table are added).

4a	Immunity	A has an immunity to B	"If **B** ***cannot [by his voluntary act, influence the giant's conduct with respect to*** A], A has an IMMUNITY."
4b	Liability	A has a liability to B	"If **B** ***can, by his voluntary act, influence the giant's conduct with respect to*** A, A has a LIABILITY."

Many Critical Legal Studies scholars, self-proclaimed inheritors of Legal Realist understandings, also emphasize thc role of the State (Corbin's "Giant") in their rulification of Hohfeld rule-enthymemes.[132] From a *logical point of view* (this is *logical abduction*), such conceptions of Hohfeld relations seem to make of them *tetradic* (four-place) relations, rather than as triadic relations. (See Section 4.4.1.2 and especially *supra* note 28.) Is it possible to reason about which representation is a better, fairer formal representation, under a principle of interpretive charity?[133] Yes. By Goodman-style reflective equilibrium. This, for example, is exactly the process illustrated and instantiated by John Goldberg and Benjamin Zipursky in Chapter 12. Against the Corbin-style four-place-relation rulification of Hohfeld axioms, they argue that such rulifications are tantamount to conflating claim-rights with powers and

> propose to do exactly what Hohfeld warned legal analysts not to do: they link claim rights and powers *analytically* ... While it is thus a central feature of certain bodies of law, including tort and contract, that they link claim rights to powers, it is perfectly possible for a valid legal directive to generate a claim right and a duty even if the right-holder is not herself empowered to enforce it . . . .[134]

In Chapter 14 Henry Smith and Andrew Gold make a related point about the rulification of Hohfeld axioms, when they note what we might call the "flipability" of baseline assumptions about the State's posture toward norms. The Legal Realist-CLS view that "the state is everywhere," as Pierre Schlag puts the point in his chapter

132 *See, e.g.*, Singer, *supra* note 6, at 986–87 ("'Rights' are claims, *enforceable by state power*, that *others* act in a certain manner in relation to the rightholder; 'Privileges' are permissions to act in a certain manner without being liable for damages to others *and without others being able to summon state power to prevent those acts*; 'Powers' are *state-enforced abilities* to change legal entitlements held by oneself or others, and 'immunities' are security from having one's own entitlements changed by others.") (emphases added).

133 See the discussion of interpretive charity *supra* note 56 and accompanying text.

134 *See* Chapter 12 pp. 371, 373. In the first part of the quoted text they are referring to Hart's and Feinberg's interpretation of Hohfeldian rights, but their point applies also to such tetradic rulifications as are suggested by Corbin, Singer, and others in what Pierre Schlag calls the "critical strand" of Hohfeld scholarship. See Schlag, *supra* note 9, at 191.

for this volume,[135] seems to presume that the State has a ubiquitous intentional presence creating what is forbidden and permitted. Thus, for example, if some citizens organize butterfly racing competitions and no agent of the State knows anything about the competitions, the State is said to permit the event – the butterfly-racers are said to have a Hohfeldian privilege. Against this seeming presupposition of a Corbin-style tetradic Hohfeldian axiom according to which the State is one of the terms of the relation, Andrew Gold and Henry Smith argue that:

> [O]ne need not be a libertarian to appreciate that government action and inaction are not the same. The question can be framed as what to make the default: universal liberty displaced by other legal relations, or some other default, or no default at all. These may be extensionally equivalent in a static sense, but otherwise they are quite different . . . One could in theory achieve the same "result" by allowing everything and forbidding some things or forbidding everything but allowing somethings.[136]

My task here is to call attention to, not to resolve, this interpretive debate about how Hohfeld rule-enthymemes are best and most fairly formally represented (is it, in the example I have just been discussing, by three-place relations that do not explicitly reflect State action, or four-place relations that do?). I call attention to it because it seems a fair abductive speculation that Hohfeld conducted in his own interior thoughts the kind of reflective equilibrial debate rehearsed externally in the dialectical-rhetorical competitions of interpretative abductions I have just observed.

4.7 CONCLUSION: WHY DON'T HOHFELD-LOVING PROFESSORS TEACH HOHFELD TO DOCTRINAL STUDENTS?

Hohfeld abductions are best represented as parts of a deductive axiomatic system, and as such, are always indefeasible. But, as Hohfeld himself was aware (and as many commentators also point out), it is always empirical investigation that discloses *which* legal relations obtain in a given jurisdiction on a given legal topic. For this reason, one may conclude that Hohfeld abductions that rely on his original creation (discovery) of his axioms (which he arrived at by means of analogical abduction in reflective equilibrium) are parasitic on *legal abductions*, of the sort that Justice Carley does in *Wright*. One cannot explain which Hohfeld relations pertain to a given transaction until one performs a legal abduction. The Logocratic Method both explains and guides (or can guide) the process of legal abduction, and in that way, can serve and enable Hohfeld abductions.

Thus, the puzzle solved. A great deal of law professoring in doctrinal courses consists of, or anyway relies centrally on, the process that I have called, and exhibited (with the *Wright* case), legal abduction. One can stop here without going the step

[135] *See* Chapter 15.
[136] Chapter 14 p. 424.

further – as Hohfeld himself insisted on doing[137] – of adding Hohfeldian abduction to legal abduction. In an age of the baneful influence of the misbegotten idea that "the life of the law has not been logic," stopping short may often contribute to a kind of intellectual decadence in our legal culture.

Long live logic, long live Hohfeld!

137 See *supra* note 4 and accompanying text.

PART II

Hohfeld and Property

5

Property's Building Blocks: Hohfeld in Europe and Beyond

Anna di Robilant and Talha Syed[*]

5.1 INTRODUCTION

In the hundred years since Hohfeld published his two "Fundamental Legal Conceptions" articles, the "bundle-of-rights" view of property associated with his work has come to enjoy the status of conventional wisdom in American legal scholarship.[1] Seen as a corrective to lay conceptions and a predecessor "Blackstonian" view of property as the "sole and despotic dominion" of an "owner" over a thing,[2] the central insight of Hohfeldian analysis is standardly taken to be that property is not a single "thing" but rather a "bundle of rights" with respect to things and persons.[3] In recent years, however, this Hohfeldian view has

* Boston University School of Law and UC Berkeley School of Law, respectively. Talha Syed is the principal author of Sections 5.2 and 5.4 of this chapter and Anna di Robilant of Section 5.3. We wish to thank Saki Bailey, Yochai Benkler, Hanoch Dagan, Terry Fisher, Pierre Schlag, and, especially, Oren Bracha and Henry Smith for invaluable feedback on an earlier draft of this chapter.

1 *See* Gregory S. Alexander, Commodity and Propriety 319 (1997) ("No expression better captures the modern legal understanding of ownership than the metaphor of property as a 'bundle of rights.'"). As Professor Alexander points out, the "bundle of rights" phrase precedes Hohfeld, who in fact never used it. Nevertheless, it has become the conventional moniker for his analysis of property as "a complex aggregate of jural relations." *Id.* at 319, 322. For a review of leading legal scholars and casebooks adopting the bundle of rights picture, see Eric Claeys, *Is Property a Thing or a Bundle?*, 32 Seattle U. L. Rev. 617, 619–21 (2009). For a review of leading philosophical works doing the same, see J. E. Penner, *The "Bundle of Rights" Picture of Property*, 43 UCLA L. Rev. 711, 712–14 (1996).

2 William Blackstone, Commentaries on the Laws of England *2 (1979) (1765–69). It is standard to refer to this view as "Blackstonian" since, as Professors Alexander and Dagan suggest, even if Blackstone himself "did not intend that phrase to be taken literally," nevertheless, the "dictum ... has become an icon of property theory." Gregory S. Alexander & Hanoch Dagan, Properties of Property 100–01 (2012). For doubts that this was Blackstone's own considered view, see Carol M. Rose, *Canons of Property Talk, or, Blackstone's Anxiety*, 108 Yale L.J. 601 (1998); David Schorr, *How Blackstone Became a Blackstonian*, 10 Theor. Inq. L. 103 (2009). For doubts about the doubts, see Claeys, *supra* note 1, at 632–33. *See infra* note 24 and accompanying text.

3 *See* Alexander, *supra* note 1, at 319; Claeys, *supra* note 1, at 617, 619–21; Penner, *supra* note 1, at 711, 712–14; Bruce Ackerman, Private Property and the Constitution 26–29, 97–100 (1977); Stephen Munzer, A Theory of Property 15–31 (1990); Joseph Singer, Entitlement: The Paradoxes of

come under increasing attack by critics calling to replace the bundle-of-rights picture with a return to lay or neo-Blackstonian conceptions of property, as the "right to a thing," "thing-ownership," or, simply, "the law of things."[4] Yet what precisely is at stake in this dispute has remained somewhat nebulous. In the words of one critic, although all sides to the debate "agree that the thing versus ad hoc bundle contrast is significant, it is surprisingly difficult to specify what the contrast really means."[5] Do the critics of the bundle-of-rights view really mean to claim that property, as a legal concept, should be taken to refer to the "thing" or object itself, rather than to legal rights pertaining to it? Or, is it rather that the legal rights should be taken to pertain to a person-thing relation, rather than to one between persons? Or, is it that the rights at issue should be seen as one or a few rather than many? Or, if many, then necessarily as "unified" rather than disaggregated? Or, whether single or multiple, as "absolute" rather than "qualified"? And, finally, is the dispute – with respect to any or all of these questions – a matter of descriptive or normative or conceptual disagreement?

The crux of the problem, we suggest, is a fundamental mischaracterization of the Hohfeldian analysis of property – by both critics *and* defenders. The "bundle of rights" label obscures from view a distinct – and more fundamental – dimension of Hohfeldian analysis, namely that property is a social relation. And as, or more, important than getting right the precise content of each of these claims is understanding their *inter-connection*: the "social relations" claim is the fundamental platform of the analysis, generating in its turn the "bundle of rights" claim as a conclusion. Indeed, if a short moniker were wanted for Hohfeldian analysis, *much* preferable to the "bundle of rights" would be the *relational* conception of property.

PROPERTY 3–13 (2000). We hasten to add that a central thrust of our argument in Section 5.2 is that this standard understanding of the Hohfeldian conception given in the text is, in significant respects, misleading, if not simply flawed. *See generally* Section 5.2, especially *infra* notes 8, 15–17 and accompanying text.

4 *See* Penner, *supra* note 1, at 799 ("despite the bundle of rights picture of property, property truly is a right to things"); J. E. PENNER, THE IDEA OF PROPERTY IN LAW (1997) (advocating, in place of the bundle of rights picture, the view "that property is what the average citizen ... thinks it is: the right to a thing"); THOMAS W. MERRILL & HENRY E. SMITH, PROPERTY: PRINCIPLES AND POLICIES v, 1 (2007) (defending, in contrast to "an ad hoc 'bundle of rights'" view, a "traditional everyday view" of property as "a right to a thing good against the world"); Claeys, *supra* note 1, at 618, 631ff (advancing "a 'thing' or 'thing-ownership' conception of property" in opposition to "'the ad hoc bundle' conception"); Henry E. Smith, *Property as the Law of Things*, 125 HARV. L. REV. 1691 (2012) (arguing that "property is, after all, a law of things" contrary to the "conventional wisdom" that "property is a bundle of rights"). *See generally* Symposium, *Property: A Bundle of Rights?* 8 ECON J. WATCH 193 (2011). We use "neo-Blackstonian" here as an umbrella term to group those critics of the Hohfeldian conception, such as the foregoing, who propose to replace it with a "thing"-based alternative of some sort. We do so while noting, again, that there remains debate on the extent to which Blackstone himself subscribed to what is called the "Blackstonian" conception (*see supra* note 2 and accompanying text) and while also bearing in mind the need to attend to important differences among the critics themselves (*see infra* notes 15, 89–90 and accompanying text).

5 *See* Claeys, *supra* note 1, at 618.

Fully grasping this point, in turn, would fundamentally recast our understanding of the "bundle of rights" claim. It is *neither* merely a descriptive claim about how existing law, in fact, treats property rights *nor* a normative claim about how they should be treated, but rather a *conceptual claim* about the character of property analysis in any existing or potential legal system.

Finally, each of these components of Hohfeldian analysis – social relations and bundle of rights – is fundamentally distinct from a *third* set of points with which they are commonly fused, concerning the *dematerialization* of the objects and interests of property. It is the blurring of what are three distinct lines of analysis – what we may call *dephysicalization*, *disaggregation*, and *dematerialization* – that has led many to the conclusion that Hohfeldian analysis results in the "disintegration" of property, rendering it no longer a distinct concept or field of law; an outcome embraced by some (neo-Hohfeldians) and decried by others (neo-Blackstonians).

This conclusion, we believe, is both too hasty and imprecise. Imprecise because it fails to locate the contest between Hohfeldian and neo-Blackstonian conceptions of property as pivoting around not one, but at least two and perhaps three, points of contrast, tracking each of the central but distinct lines of Hohfeldian analysis: dephysicalization, disaggregation, and dematerialization. It is too hasty because the dephysicalization of property, as a social relation, poses no problems; and while disaggregation and dematerialization may indeed lead to troubling – if *very* distinct – forms of disintegration, the fault lies less with the specific content of Hohfeld's claims than with a failure, post-Hohfeld, to follow through on his underlying method and structure of analysis in a constructive fashion. And so the solution to disintegration, we urge, is *not* a "rethingification" of property but rather its "reintegration," to be achieved by carrying forward the method of Hohfeldian analysis in two constructive directions: (a) a *resource-specific* answer to the question of "what is property about?" and (b) an architectural analysis of the basic entitlements that serve as the *fundamental building blocks* of all property forms in answer to "what does property consist of?".

The aims of this chapter are threefold. First, we provide a novel distillation of the central insights and structure of the Hohfeldian analysis of property and use it to pinpoint the central fault lines of the contemporary debate in American property theory. Second, we set this analytical scheme in a comparative-historical context, drawing insights from European traditions of property analysis on the resource-specific character of property entitlements that further enrich and develop our scheme. Finally, drawing simultaneously on the tools of Hohfeldian analysis and the lessons of the American and European debates, we chart two constructive ways forward for the legal-institutional analysis of property, as social relations regarding resources.

This chapter is structured in four sections. Section 5.1 provides an introduction to, and overview of, the chapter. Section 5.2 sets out our distinct view of the fundamental components and structure of Hohfeldian analysis. Section 5.3 then examines what Hohfeld has to teach Europe and vice versa. Finally, Section 5.4 charts a way forward with two constructive lessons, each responding to one of the central perils of disintegration facing Hohfeldian analysis.

5.2 THE STRUCTURE OF HOHFELDIAN ANALYSIS

The Hohfeldian analysis of property consists, in our view, of two pairs of distinct but interrelated *conceptual* claims, each one leading to the next in a tightly integrated theoretical structure. Each discrete claim should on its own seem familiar, but this may prove rather misleading in two respects. First, our treatment of the exact content and implications of each point, even on its own, often differs from standard understandings among both defenders and critics of Hohfeldian analysis (as we indicate in the margins) – in ways that may at first seem subtle but ultimately have powerful implications.[6] Second, in any case, what merits special emphasis is our view of the *interconnection* of the claims, specifically of their order of conceptual priority and the distinct role played by each in the structure of the analysis.[7] The full-blown implications of the distinct content and structure of our analysis will only emerge at the end, when we deploy it to clarify the precise fault lines of the debate on "disintegration" and specify where, in our view, both defenders and critics of Hohfeldian analysis go awry in their understanding of the sources of the problem and potential ways forward.

5.2.1 *Property Is a Social Relation*

5.2.1.1 Social Relationality: A Relation Between Persons Regarding Things

The beginning of wisdom for Hohfeldian analysis, the foundational claim from which all others flow, is that property is – *always and only* – a social relation.[8] As Hohfeld went to great pains and length to emphasize at the outset of both his 1913 and 1917 articles, property as a legal concept refers *neither* to the thing that may be the ultimate object of legal entitlements *nor* to the relation of a person to the thing,

6 This applies even with respect to the pioneering understanding of the discrete claims to which we are most heavily indebted, that advanced by Professor Joseph Singer. *See infra* notes 8, 19 and accompanying text.

7 In this respect, the differences between the view we develop here and that advanced by Professor Singer may be somewhat greater. *See infra* notes 16, 17, 91 and accompanying text.

8 The singular content and centrality of this claim to Hohfeldian analysis merits emphasizing its distinction from formulations of the point that suggest that property is *both* a relation between a person and a thing *and* one between persons with respect to a thing. *See, e.g.*, SINGER, *supra* note 3, at 6, 10; Carol Rose, *Storytelling about Property*, 2 YALE J.L. & HUMAN. 37, 40 (1990). For further discussion, see *infra* note 20 and accompanying text.

but rather *solely* to the relation between persons regarding the thing.[9] In other words, to a social relation.[10]

As a legal institution, property always pertains to how two or more persons are related with respect to a resource: Can one use the resource without another's interference? Can one exclude another's use of it? Can one remain secure against another's removal of one's use and exclusion entitlements? And so forth.[11] There is no such thing as property on a desert island with one person.[12] Similarly, contrary to a misunderstanding persisting to the present, "possession" is simply not an entitlement of property: it denotes a relation between a person and a thing, not between persons regarding a thing (that relation is denoted by exclusion).[13]

The basic import of this claim is, of course, to guard against the false naturalization of normative social judgments, by checking against attempts to move straight

9 *See* Wesley N. Hohfeld, *Some Fundamental Legal Conceptions as Applied in Judicial Reasoning*, 23 YALE L.J. 16, 20–28 (1913) [hereinafter Hohfeld, *Some Fundamental Legal Conceptions*] (devoting eight pages "[a]t the very outset ... to emphasize the importance of differentiating purely legal relations from the physical and mental facts that call such relations into being"); *see* also Wesley N. Hohfeld, *Fundamental Legal Conceptions as Applied in Judicial Reasoning*, 26 YALE L.J. 710, 720–33 (1917) (devoting twelve pages to establish his first point, namely that "a right *in rem* is not a 'right against a thing'").

10 This is not to say that all interpersonal relations are, as such, properly considered "social," where that term is taken to impute a "public" rather than "private" character to such relations. However, the relations in question here are clearly "social" in the requisite sense, for at least two distinct reasons: (a) they are clearly "public" rather than "private," in the sense of obtaining between persons who may be perfect strangers, without any prior acquaintance; and (b) they are "public" in the sense of involving decisions by the state.

11 As Professor Schlag rightly emphasizes, it is *not* "so much that rights 'imply' or 'give rise' to duties," as it is that "to say that B has a duty toward A" is "exactly what it means to say that A has a right." *See* Pierre Schlag, *How To Do Things With Hohfeld*, 78 LAW & CONTEMP. PROBS. 185, 201 (2015).

12 There are, in fact, no legal rights at all in such a situation, but we leave that aside here.

13 *See, e.g.*, A. M. Honoré, *Ownership*, *in* OXFORD ESSAYS IN JURISPRUDENCE 107 (A. G. Guest ed., 1961) (referring to "the right to possess" as involving "exclusive physical control" over an object); JESSE DUKEMINIER ET AL., PROPERTY 81 n.2 (6th ed. 2006) (Property consists of "a number of disparate rights, a 'bundle' of them: the right to possess, the right to use, the right to exclude, the right to transfer."). Ours is not a terminological quibble. In other words, we recognize of course that in speaking of a "right to possess" one *might* have clearly in mind that this is not a matter of "control over" an "object" – i.e., a person-thing relation – but rather precisely about "exclusion of" a person – i.e., a person-person relation – and hence be making no conceptual error, only using words loosely. But to speak of a right to "exclusive physical control" over an object is surely to slide into the sorts of conceptual confusions and normative elisions that Hohfeld was at pains to dispel. And even more clearly: to list a "right to possess" as part of the "bundle" of property rights *alongside* rights "to use" and "to exclude" can only evince faulty conceptualization: robbed of its role as a hazy substitute for the more precise "right to exclude," the phrase "right to possess" can only plausibly be taken to mean the flawed notion of a "right of control" over/against a thing, or simply be empty of meaning (a third possibility – that it is serving as a substitute coverall term for the misleading "right to own" – is foreclosed by the fact that it is precisely "ownership" that is being unbundled by the enumerated rights). *See also* Burke Shartel, *Meanings of Possession*, 16 MINN. L. REV. 611 (1932) (seeking to disambiguate different legal usages of the term "possession" and focusing primarily on distinguishing between different aspects of person-thing relations and their legal consequences, while viewing its use to refer to person-person relations in property as tertiary and irretrievably confused). We thank Henry Smith for drawing our attention to this article.

from descriptions of physical facts and relations to substantive conclusions of "justice and policy."[14] We will elaborate on other powerful implications momentarily. Presently, however, the central point we wish to underline pertains not to the further implications of Hohfeld's central claim – that property is a social relation – standing on its own, but to the special status and role of this claim within Hohfeldian analysis, namely, its conceptual character and foundational role.[15] It is *not* a normative claim about how property rights *should* be shaped, but rather a positive claim about what property, as a legal concept and institution, simply *is*.[16] And it lies at the basis of the Hohfeldian analysis, being the platform upon which all subsequent claims are developed.[17]

5.2.1.2 Correlativity: The Competing-Interests Structure of the Social Relation

The social relations at issue in property are structured by correlative entitlement-disentitlement pairs, whereby an advantage for one person means a disadvantage for another. One cannot identify an entitlement or benefit for X without a correlative

14 *See* Hohfeld, *Some Fundamental Legal Conceptions*, *supra* note 9, at 36.

15 It is the conceptual character and foundational role of the social-relational claim that we are at pains to underline here. In other words, our argument is less concerned with what express *verbal* formulations are used by scholars when articulating the character of property rights, although some examples of formulations that are ambiguous in their formal recognition of the social-relational point are given *supra* in notes 6, 10, 13, and 14. Rather, our concern is with whether, as a *substantive* matter, the core lessons of the social-relational claim, its central thrust, and its powerful implications have been fully registered in property theory. Reasons for doubt on this score are given *supra* in notes 21–29 and accompanying text, where we also seek to bring out and drive home these lessons in a systematic way. This applies even more to the claim's foundational role in the overall architectonic of Hohfeldian analysis – the way it serves as a platform for all other claims – something also not fully appreciated by either defenders or critics of the Hohfeldian view, as we discuss in due course. Finally, however, even with respect to its purely verbal recognition, some scholars do seem expressly to reject the person-person conception of property rights in favor of a person-thing one and, indeed, take this as an important divide internal to the critics of the Hohfeldian conception. *See* Adam Mossoff, *The False Promise of the Right to Exclude*, 8 Econ J. Watch 255 (2011) ("Among scholars who reject the bundle conception of property, there have been two different and opposing positions. On the one hand, I and others have sought to recover the earlier concept of property that was buried by the realists, recognizing that it refers to a specific relationship between someone and something in the world. Thus, the right to property secures a use-right in, agenda-setting control over, or a sphere of liberty in using this thing . . . On the other hand, Tom Merrill and Henry Smith advance an alternative approach to recovering the right to property. They accept the legal realists' social conception of rights.") We thank Oren Bracha for this reference.

16 This is in contrast to those who treat the "social relations" claim as a purely normative position, e.g., Joseph Singer et al., Property Law: Rules, Policies, and Practices xlix–1 (2006), and ever more so to those who, in a reversal of conceptual priority, see it as building upon the bundle of rights claim rather than vice versa, *see* Claeys, *supra* note 1, at 620.

17 This is in contrast to treatments of the point that fuse it with the bundle of rights claim. *See, e.g.*, Hanoch Dagan, *Doctrinal Categories, Legal Realism and the Rule of Law*, 163 U. Pa. L. Rev. 1889, 1912 (2015). Or that treat it as simply one of a series of discrete points, and seemingly a secondary one at that, in comparison to the bundle of rights claim. *See* Singer, *supra* note 3, at 6.

disentitlement or burden on Y.[18] Thus, the social relations of property involve – *always and necessarily* – pairs of competing interests.[19]

Among the implications that follow from this pair of claims, three are central.

"*Absolute*" ownership is a misnomer, not just normatively contestable. It is commonplace among those following in Hohfeld's footsteps to inveigh against an "absolutist" Blackstonian conception of property on the grounds that it is either undesirable or not descriptive of our present arrangements – and hence that the entitlements of property ought to be "relative" or subject to varying limits. However, once we fully internalize the point that property is a social relation, with correlative/competing entitlements, then the claim that its entitlements *ought to be* "qualified" or "relative" is somewhat curious, since there is really no coherent sense to the notion of "unqualified" or "absolute" entitlements once we understand their relational/correlative character.[20] Once, that is, we fully internalize the social-relational character of property, it is simply either empty or unclear or incoherent to speak of "absolute" entitlements: the term either has no or only vague meaning or it means "unfettered," which would involve a case that no jurist has ever had in mind.[21] The point, then, is not really a normative, but rather an elemental, conceptual one. To challenge absolutist conceptions on normative grounds is to presuppose their analytical tenability, and to do that is to reinforce unilateral, person-thing, conceptions of property. The same is true for any discussion that emphasizes the "relative" character of property as being a somehow controversial or "modern" move.[22] The

[18] This point is a distinct further development of the preceding social-relational claim because of course not all social relations need be so structured around correlative claims/competing interests. For instance, the teacher-student relation is an institutionalized, or social, relation that does not have this inherently competing-claims structure.

[19] *See infra* note 95 and accompanying text, on the "Cook/Corbin puzzle" regarding whether or not the power-liability pair may (sometimes) be an exception to this.

[20] To underline this point as clearly as we can, we would go even further than Professor Singer's important statement that "[t]he recognition and exercise of a property right in one person *often* affects and *may* even conflict with the personal or property rights of others," by dropping his qualifiers. *See* SINGER ET AL., *supra* note 16, at x (emphasis added). This is related to our emphasis, *supra* note 8, on the distinction between our formulation that property is *always and only* a social relation and Professor Singer's formulation of property as *both* a relation between a person and a thing *and* one between persons with respect to a thing. *See* SINGER, *supra* note 3, at 6; SINGER ET AL., *supra* note 16, at x.

[21] For X to have unfettered entitlements against all persons with respect to a thing or good would mean not only (a) that others had no legitimate interests in that thing or good meriting legal protection, but also (b) that they had no legitimate interests in other things or goods meriting legal protection, the exercise of which may in some cases come into conflict with X's exercise of entitlements pertaining to their thing or good, and finally (c) that others also had no *other* legitimate interests – for instance, in their person – meriting legal protection, which may in some cases come into conflict with X's exercise of entitlements in their thing or good. The only actual imaginable case of "absolute" entitlements, then, is of a person living alone on an island – but in that case they have *no* property or, for that matter, *any other legal entitlements* since *all legal entitlements always and only* pertain to social relations.

[22] *See* Kenneth J. Vandevelde, *The New Property of the Nineteenth Century: The Development of the Modern Concept of Property*, 29 BUFF. L. REV. 325 (1979); ALEXANDER & DAGAN, *supra* note 2, at 255.

only modern thing about it is the explicit recognition of something that was always inescapable.[23]

This neatly resolves a long-standing puzzle of contemporary property scholarship: "Was Blackstone really a Blackstonian?" As a number of scholars including Carol Rose and Daniel Schorr have argued, in his detailed discussions of the contours of specific property rights Blackstone did not, in fact, hold to the "absolutism" for which his name has become a byword and his "sole and despotic dominion" a catch-phrase.[24] On the present analysis, not only is this unsurprising, it is hardly avoidable: since absolutism is simply a misnomer, conceptually not on the cards, it is hardly surprising that when he turned from abstract declarations to the concrete specifics of the system, Blackstone simply *had to* cast aside a view that, whatever its normative appeal, is simply conceptually untenable – namely, that property is a person-thing relation, conferring a set of rights that may be enjoyed absolutely – and to register, however implicitly, the unavoidable reality brought home by any detailed acquaintance with the specifics of property rights, namely that property is a social relation in which unfettered rights are simply a chimera.[25]

Property is *not* a form of "negative liberty." Both defenders and critics of traditional or Blackstonian conceptions often accept the premise that these conceptions constitute species of "negative liberty" – with defenders embracing that position and critics urging that in many circumstances we should normatively go beyond it.[26] But this, again, betrays a failure fully to internalize the relational character of property rights. Negative liberty means the "freedom from" or "absence of" coercive interference, either of the state or other private individuals. While positive liberty means the "freedom to" effectively pursue one's ends, via the "presence of" necessary means, including by way of positive state provision of resources or other assistance.[27] In the

23 As a striking illustration of this point, think of Roman property. Property scholars and historians long presented it as the most perfect example of "absolute property," and only in "modern" times have they admitted its relational and qualified nature. On the view that Roman property was absolute, see 2 PIETRO BONFANTE, CORSO DI DIRITTO ROMANO: LA PROPRIETÀ 327 (1968). For the modern view, see Eva Jakab, *Land, Law and Exploitation of Natural Resources: Property Rights in Ancient Rome, in* OWNERSHIP AND EXPLOITATION OF LAND AND NATURAL RESOURCES IN THE ROMAN WORLD (P. Erdkamp et al. eds., 2015).

24 *See* Rose, *supra* note 2; Schorr, *supra* note 2.

25 Does this mean, then, that the contrast between "Blackstonian" and "Hohfeldian" conceptions of property can simply evaporate like hot air? Not at all. What it *does* mean is that we have to be more precise in specifying what we might mean by "Blackstonian" in contrast to "Hohfeldian" views. A central aim of this chapter is to establish that this contrast is most usefully understood as operating along three possible axes, as discussed in Section 5.2.3.

26 *See* PENNER, *supra* note 4, at 50; Hanoch Dagan, *The Craft of Property*, 91 CALIF. L. REV. 1517, 1560 (2003).

27 To be more accurate, these are the common meanings attributed to the terms in contemporary political theory. But it bears noting that in the foundational modern discussion of the terms, Isaiah Berlin himself oscillates between this contrast and a fundamentally different one, in which "negative liberty" denotes the freedom to pursue one's own ends – via *both* the absence of coercive interference *and* the presence of positive means – while "positive liberty" denotes the freedom to ensure that one's ends be truly one's own, what might be better called self-determination, and also perhaps that one's

case of property, unless we hew merely to use-privileges – which no participant of this debate has in mind – then all other entitlements necessarily involve the intervention of the state to burden one person's negative liberty for the sake of enforcing another's entitlements. Moreover, such enforcement results, directly, in the deprivation of resources. And although the absence of resources is typically thought to be a deficit only in "positive" rather than "negative" liberty, the point is that such deficits in positive liberty may stem directly from state action and not, as is commonly thought, only from state *in*action.[28] The persistent assimilation of "the right to property" as among the species of "negative" rights/liberty is another telltale sign of the failure to fully absorb the relational character of property.

We hasten to add – to forestall a third misunderstanding – that the *conceptual* point that property is a social relation does not by itself settle any *normative* questions. In particular, it does not automatically issue in the normative claim that property must have a "social function" or serve the "social interest," where these are taken to mean a "public interest" in contrast to private ones.[29] Or, in a related vein, in the conclusion that we have somehow ruled out justifications for property entitlements based on "natural rights" arguments of, for instance, labor/desert, autonomy, or personhood. What the social-relational claim does do, however, is press upon such normative justifications the need for an explicit shift in frame: away from a unilateral focus on a given person and their activities and interests and toward forthrightly taking up the bilateral character of the question involving, as it always does, contending claims.[30]

It bears emphasis that to this point nothing has been said about property as a bundle of rights.

5.2.2 *Property Is a Bundle of Rights*

From the first two foundational claims, that property (a) is a social relation and (b) has a correlative/competing-interests structure, flow the next two claims, subsumable under the distinct heading of "property is a bundle of rights."

ends be "objectively" valuable. *See* Isaiah Berlin, *Two Concepts of Liberty*, *in* LIBERTY: INCORPORATING FOUR ESSAYS ON LIBERTY 166, 170–72 (Henry Hardy ed., 2d ed. 2002).

[28] Indeed, in what is commonly seen as the touchstone essay on this topic – and the one that serves as the source for Professor Penner's claim, *see supra* note 26 – Isaiah Berlin in fact recognized a version of this Hohfeldian/legal-realist point. Namely that, once we register the pervasive role of the state in structuring the "background conditions" of the private sphere, the realm of "negative liberty" infringements expands dramatically, which attenuates the conceptual and normative significance of the contrast between "freedom from" and "freedom to" to the point of replacing it with an alternative distinction, between a freedom of means and a freedom of ends, or freedom as voluntariness and effective agency versus freedom as self-determination. *See* Berlin, *supra* note 27, at 170–72.

[29] For examples of this blurring, see *infra* note 72 and accompanying text.

[30] For an illustrative example of the extent and depth of the difficulties that meeting this requirement can pose for natural rights arguments, in this case of a Lockean stripe, see G. A. Cohen, *Nozick on Appropriation*, I/150 NEW LEFT REV. 89 (1985).

5.2.2.1 Divisibility: Distinct Pairs of Competing Interests = Distinct Entitlements

Precisely because any given entitlement of property entails a disentitlement for someone else, and hence implicates competing interests, we must be careful not to conflate distinct pairs of competing interests under the cover of some single umbrella term (be it "property" or "right" or "ownership"). Thus: (a) it is one thing to protect Jill's interest in the use of a space by not conferring on Jack any entitlement to exclude Jill from accessing the space; (b) it is another thing entirely also to entitle Jill to prevent Jack from using the space as well, by conferring upon Jill the entitlement to exclude access; and (c) it is a third thing altogether to confer upon Jill the entitlement to prevent Jack from engaging in a noisy activity outside, in a neighboring space, that interferes with Jill's "quiet enjoyment" of the first space. Each of these cases implicates distinct kinds of competing interests. And so, the entitlements of property are best understood not as consisting of only one or a necessarily unified aggregate, but, rather, as a divisible "bundle."

This "divisibility" of ownership into discrete sets of entitlement-disentitlement pairs is of course the most familiar, indeed well-worn, theme of Hohfeldian analysis, going by the name of "disaggregation." Less well appreciated, however, is the difference between a formal versus a *purposive* approach to the drawing of Hohfeldian distinctions. Illustrative of the former is an example commonly used – across a century of Hohfeld reception – to convey the distinction between a privilege and a claim-right: the case of having merely an "exclusion-privilege" with respect to a piece of land, without an "exclusion-right" regarding the same.[31] Yet, conferral of an *exclusion*-privilege without the corresponding right, while certainly a formal possibility, is, we suggest, also *merely* a formal one, one having little sense or purpose in most real-world contexts we might be interested in. And the upshot of drawing up such formally possible, but practically inert, options is, we believe, a tendency for the meaning and point of Hohfeldian analysis to become lost in the mists of the ad hoc proliferation of logical variations without end.[32]

A purposive approach, by contrast, provides a controlling orientation to the elaboration of the distinctions, showing clearly their point by grounding them in real-world issues involving policy-relevant distinctions between competing interests.[33] Take, for example, the distinctions elucidated in the previous paragraph. Our first distinction, between a *use*-privilege and an *exclusion*-right, is of signal

[31] *See* Arthur Corbin, *Foreword*, *in* FUNDAMENTAL LEGAL CONCEPTIONS 8 (Walter Wheeler Cook ed., 1919); Schlag, *supra* note 11, at 185, 202–03.

[32] We should emphasize that neither Professors Corbin nor Schlag endorse such a formalistic approach to Hohfeld – indeed, both go to pains explicitly to underline the practical or policy significance of his analysis, which we build upon here. *See* Corbin, *supra* note 31, at xi; Schlag, *supra* note 11, at 189, 191–92. Our point, however, is that the use of examples such as exclusion-privilege versus exclusion-right to illustrate Hohfeldian distinctions partially undermines their own pioneering insistence on a practical or purposive, as opposed to a pure or formalist, approach to Hohfeldian analysis.

[33] This is one of two ways in which the view we are advancing here differs from the standard understanding of the Hohfeldian analysis of "the bundle of rights" as a "purely analytic" approach.

importance in the context of resources susceptible to nonrival uses. Meanwhile, the latter distinction, between a use-privilege and a use-*right* is, of course, central to the historical development of nuisance law,[34] in which context the latter claim – being applied to neighboring or conflicting uses – is, in fact, better understood as converting a use-privilege over one's own resource into a distinct *exclusion*-right, now over a neighbor's (use of their) resource. Purposively grounding the analysis of divisibility in this way provides, we believe, an important first safeguard against the slide of disaggregation into "disintegration."[35]

5.2.2.2 Variability: Distinct Contexts = Distinct Shapes for a Given Entitlement

An extension of the preceding point – one that merits being singled out – is that not only may the conferral of discrete entitlements upon distinct persons sensibly vary by purpose and context (divisibility), but so may the *shape of each discrete entitlement* – in terms of its existence (should it be conferred at all?), content (which activities should it cover?), holders (who and how many should enjoy it?), and enforcement (what remedy for its violation?). Highlighting this serves to guard against a tendency to take the content of the distinct entitlements as fixed, and thus to limit our understanding of the malleability of the bundle of rights to the subdivision and reshuffling of fixed sticks among different holders, as opposed to an understanding of malleability that includes the reshaping of the sticks themselves.

The content of these claims about the "disaggregation" – or divisibility and variability – of the entitlements of property is, again, the most familiar

On this view, Hohfeld's analysis is taken to be both "pure" in the sense of "formal," and "analytic" in the sense of "atomistic." By contrast, we take the method underlying Hohfeld's analysis to be *purposive* rather than "formal" – as discussed here – and *relational* in contrast to "atomistic," as discussed *infra* notes 91–94 and accompanying text.

34 *See, e.g.*, Robert Bone, *Normative Theory and Legal Doctrine in American Nuisance Law: 1850–1920*, 59 S. CAL. L. REV. 1101 (1986).

35 To be sure, simply grounding the analysis of divisibility in purposes is hardly an elixir against the perils of disintegration. Indeed, Professor Smith has argued that it is precisely purposivity run amuck that leads the "bundle of rights" approach to untenable ad-hocery. *See* Smith, *supra* note 4, at 1719–20. But, as we discuss below, Professor Smith's argument here runs together what for present purposes we seek to keep importantly distinct, namely, the case for conceptual parsimony in devising a theory of property versus the case for institutional parsimony in devising or evaluating real-world property arrangements. *See infra* notes 88–89 and accompanying text. Bearing that in mind, our argument here is simply that a purposive approach to the analysis of disaggregation – i.e., of divisibility and, discussed next, of variability – is an important *first* step to check against *conceptual* ad-hocery (not, to be sure, the last step, as we elaborate below). This leaves open, as a matter for further *substantive* inquiry, the question of "how much" divisibility we should actually countenance in real-world property architectures: that will no doubt depend on our sense of the balance of considerations such as the pursuit of substantive policy purposes versus administrability, information costs, and so forth, as these play out in the context of different sorts of resources (with the drawing of distinctions between resources being subject to a parallel set of conceptual and substantive considerations, as discussed in Section 5.4.1). Whatever the outcome of such specific substantive inquiries, we remain steadfast in our view that, as an analysis of property's general form, "divisibility" – as expounded here – is (along with variability, which is discussed next) the proper *conceptual* upshot of Hohfeldian "disaggregation" analysis.

component of Hohfeldian analysis, squarely falling within the "bundle of rights" rubric. What is less well recognized is an important point about their *status*. The "bundle of rights" claim is *not* merely a descriptive assertion about the shape existing legal arrangements take (i.e., that they often do unbundle or disaggregate "ownership") *nor* just a normative exhortation about what shape they should take. Rather, it is a *conclusion* drawn from the social-relational claim: once we register that each entitlement is a social relation involving a pair of competing interests, then we realize that distinct pairs of competing interests are at issue with distinct entitlements. Consequently, it would simply be a mistake of logic and practical reason – a flaw in the cogency of the reasoning that is covered up by its lack of transparency – to treat a decision on one pair of interests as the same as, or controlling, a decision on a distinct pair. In a word, then, the bundle of rights claim is *neither* a descriptive *nor* a normative claim regarding the specific content of existing or desirable legal arrangements; rather, it is a *conceptual* claim about what the analysis of property must involve in *any* legal system.

When, however, the claim of disaggregation is advanced in isolation of its underlying basis in the social-relational claim and in a manner delinked from its driving purpose – to ensure careful consideration of meaningful distinctions in interests – it threatens to spin out into an endless proliferation of formally possible (even if practically inert) entitlement options or devolve into a laundry-list taxonomy of the fine-grained details of various and sundry existing arrangements. To threaten, in a word, disintegration.

5.2.3 *Dereification ≠ "Disintegration"*

Does Hohfeldian analysis tend toward the disintegration of property – emptying it of any distinguishing features as a concept or field of law – as declaimed by some and decried by others?[36] In our view, it need not: with the foregoing understanding of its content and structure in place, Hohfeldian analysis both *can and should* avoid the fate of disintegrating property. But for it to do so requires, first, that we disentangle a series of intricate conceptual wrangles that frequently bedevil received understandings of the central dimensions of Hohfeldian analysis and of what is at stake in disintegration. Unpacking these is the task of the present section. Its upshot is the need to supplement Hohfeldian analysis with two constructive developments – absent in the original scheme but true to its spirit – which we sketch in Section 5.4.

[36] *See* Vandevelde, *supra* note 22; Thomas C. Grey, *The Disintegration of Property*, *in* XXII NOMOS: PROPERTY 69 (J. Roland Pennock & John W. Chapman eds., 1980); Penner, *supra* note 1; Smith, *supra* note 4.

5.2.3.1 Dereification = Dephysicalization + Disaggregation + Dematerialization

To the core components of Hohfeldian analysis just elucidated may be added a third pair of *distinct* points concerning the *dematerialization* of both the objects and the interests of property, as follows:

> *Social relations*: (a) property denotes neither a thing nor a relation between a person and a thing, but a relation between persons with respect to a thing; (b) the social relation consists of legal entitlement-disentitlement pairs that simultaneously benefit the interests of some and burden the interests of others with respect to the thing; and (c) *dematerialization of objects*: finally, the things themselves, that are the object of the social relations, need not be tangible but may take intangible form, such as with inventive practical ideas or creative forms of expression.
>
> *Bundle of Rights*: the entitlements of property are multiple, divisible, and variable: (a) not just a single one nor a necessarily unified package; (b) nor uniform or invariant in their discrete content; and (c) *dematerialization of interests*: the interests protected by the discrete entitlements need not be concretely "physical" like "consumptive use," but may take increasingly "abstract" form, such as expected monetary value.

Two points are fundamental to establish with respect to how dematerialization relates to the core components of Hohfeldian analysis. First, as a long line of scholars has emphasized, as a matter of historical development the practices and insights associated with dematerialization likely proved crucial catalysts for the crystallization of the core social-relations and bundle-of-rights claims.[37] They did so by helping to "*dereify*" thinking about property, by making plainly unavailable – in the case of intangible objects or very abstract interests – reliance on any physical attributes, relations, or activities as the sole basis of legal decisions.[38] However, and second, it must also be clearly borne in mind that, notwithstanding its historical stimulus, dematerialization is not only distinct from the relational and bundle claims but of secondary significance in the Hohfeldian scheme. Indeed, the order of conceptual

[37] *See* Vandevelde, *supra* note 22; Grey, *supra* note 36; Morton J. Horwitz, The Transformation of American Law, 1870–1960 (1992); Jane B. Baron, *Rescuing the Bundle-of-Rights Metaphor in Property Law*, 82 U. Cin. L. Rev. 57 (2014).

[38] Frederick Pollock's path-breaking treatment of these issues, which lies at the center of the historical process of dematerialization, is illustrative here. Pollock's argument that to be a "thing" in law, an object of property need not have any physical properties, has precisely the upshot of underlining that legal conceptualizations and decisions pertaining to such "things" must explicitly advert to underlying human interests and social purposes – *and that this also holds for physical things*, with the line of reasoning forced upon us with special clarity by dematerialization now reaching back also to apply to material objects. *See* Frederick Pollock, *What Is a Thing?*, 10 Law. Q. Rev. 318, 320 (1894) ("At this point it may be worth considering, at the risk of an apparent paradox, whether corporeal things are themselves so corporeal as we think at first. For a material object is really nothing to law, whatever it may be to science or philosophy, save as an occasion of use or enjoyment to man, or as an instrument in human acts"). We thank Henry Smith for urging the significance of Pollock's analysis in this connection. For reliance on Pollock's argument as a basis for the "rethingification" of the objects of property in a post-dematerialization world, see *infra* note 79 and accompanying text.

priority is the reverse of historical sequence: not only do the relational and bundle claims, once we have grasped them, not stand or fall with dematerialization, they are also more deeply secure, *conceptual*, claims. Dematerialization, by contrast, is more contingent in two respects: (a) its validity hinges upon specific historical developments in technology, culture, and economic practices; and (b) even today, we could *choose not to* consider various intangible objects and abstract interests as conceptually or normatively adjacent to tangible and physical ones for purposes of organizing fields of law or making substantive decisions. The relational and bundle claims, on the other hand, are bedrock.

Unfortunately, likely as a result of their historical intertwinement, the radically distinct character and content of these three dimensions of analysis have often been missed. Starting with Arthur Corbin at the onset of the reception of Hohfeld and continuing to the present, a persistent tendency for both defenders and critics of Hohfeldian analysis has been to blur these distinct lines of analysis: not only to conflate the dematerialization of interests with the dematerialization of objects but also, more fundamentally, to lump in both with the relational claim (often under cover of the umbrella term "dephysicalization") or even to lose sight of the relational claim altogether.[39] The problems created by such blurring are manifold: the fundamental content and character of the relational claim – as the platform for all Hohfeldian analysis – is lost from view, which deprives the disaggregation claim of its underlying basis, setting it loose as a free-floating claim of uncertain provenance or status. The result – once we add the way in which the dematerialization of the objects and interests of property is conflated with the "dephysicalization" of property which is the product of the relational claim[40] – is to render entirely opaque the precise bases for neo-Hohfeldian claims of "disintegration" and the specific targets of the neo-Blackstonians' critical fire.

In general, the distinctive power and components of Hohfeldian analysis, with its clear delineation of distinct lines of analysis, alongside their relations of conceptual priority – which form a tightly integrated and generative structure – are displaced by a hodgepodge of jumbled claims. As a result, scholars either herald or decry a hazy

39 In perhaps the leading discussion in this vein, Kenneth Vandevelde under the heading of the "dephysicalization" of property focuses exclusively on what we call here "dematerialization," which he then couples with disaggregation to form the two central insights of Hohfeldian analysis – with the crucially distinct, and more foundational, social-relational point dropped out of sight entirely. *See* Vandevelde, *supra* note 22, at 334–40, 360–62; *see also* Grey, *supra* note 36; HORWITZ, *supra* note 37, at 145–56. For other receptions blurring together the claims – and, crucially, burying the relational claim and its foundational status – see Arthur Corbin, *Taxation of Seats on the Stock Exchange*, 31 YALE L.J. 429 (1922); Penner, *supra* note 1; Stephen Munzer, A *Bundle Theorist Holds On to His Collection of Sticks*, 8 ECON J. WATCH 265 (2011); Henry E. Smith, *Property Is Not Just a Bundle of Rights*, 8 ECON J. WATCH 279 (2011); ALEXANDER & DAGAN, *supra* note 2; Baron, *supra* note 37.

40 We hasten to add that it is *our* use of these terms that is idiosyncratic. Standardly, "dephysicalization" is used as synonymous with what we prefer to give the distinct label of the "dematerialization" of the objects and interests of property. *See* Vandevelde, *supra* note 22, at 334–40, 360–62; HORWITZ, *supra* note 37, at 145–56. We prefer to reserve "dephysicalization" for the radically distinct, and more fundamental, idea of a relational rather than thing or person-thing conception of property.

"disintegration" whose distinct sources and perils become harder and harder to specify or repair.

Specifically, talk of a single contrast between "right to a thing" versus "bundle of rights" views[41] obscures (when it doesn't simply conflate) three distinct dimensions of the Hohfeldian view that neo-Blackstonian critics may mean to target and replace with a "rethingification" alternative: (a) the dephysicalization of property, meaning the account of property as a social relation; (b) the disaggregation of the entitlements of property into a divisible and variable set; or (c) the dematerialization of the objects and interests of property entitlements. A comprehensive exploration of which of these targets different critics have in mind – and of the cogency of their criticisms and merits of their proposed alternatives – lies beyond our present scope.[42] Here it suffices to emphasize that clarity about these distinct lines of analysis is simply the indispensable first step, both for specifying the precise concerns posed by disintegration and for developing constructive ways forward. In what follows, we focus on advancing our own views along these two fronts, while touching briefly in the margins on how these relate to *neo*-Hohfeldian disintegration views and the rethingification responses of neo-Blackstonian critics.[43]

5.2.3.2 Disintegration = Unmooring Dematerialization + Unspooling Disaggregation

To begin at the end, so to speak, the way out of disintegration starts by breaking down the question – "what is property?" – into two distinct lines of inquiry: (a) What is property *about*? That is, what differentiates property, as a concept or field, from other areas of law in terms of its distinctive subject matter? and (b) What does property *consist of*? That is, what are the central legal entitlements that can provide the organizing focal points for positive, normative, and institutional analysis of the field?[44]

41 *See, e.g.*, Claeys, *supra* note 1 at (speaking of "*the* [. . .] contrast" between "thing versus ad hoc bundle" views) (emphasis added).

42 One of us is presently engaged in such a comprehensive examination, as part of a fuller treatment of many of the topics addressed in more abbreviated form in this essay. Talha Syed, *The Architecture of Property* (draft manuscript on file with the authors).

43 *See infra* notes 44, 77, 79, 88–89 and accompanying text.

44 These are not, of course, the only ways to frame the inquiry. Indeed, part of our argument concerns the advantages of this particular framing – one that flows directly from our understanding of the structure and purpose of Hohfeld's own enterprise – over alternatives. As an illustrative contrast, consider Professor Grey's influential discussion of disintegration, framing the issue in terms of the following two questions: First, what does ownership consist of? Second, what can one have property rights "in"? *See* Grey, *supra* note 36, at 69–70. (A similar frame is adopted in Vandevelde, *supra* note 22.) From our vantage, this way of approaching the issues has two significant drawbacks. First, to consider the ownership question first – before, and in isolation of, the issue of "ownership of *what*" – is precisely to put the cart before the horse. On our – purposive – view of concept-formation, we cannot

With the questions so framed, does Hohfeldian analysis provide clear, nondisintegrative, answers? Yes and no. On the one hand, nothing in the social relations claim prevents us from offering a relatively clear answer to the first question: property is the field of law pertaining to "social relations with respect to things." Of course, this answer does face difficulties on a Hohfeldian view, but what is important to recognize is that these difficulties stem *not* from the social relations or "dephysicalization" claim, but rather from a set of further insights – those pertaining to the dematerialization of the objects and interest of property. These insights, by loosening property from the anchor of "things," threaten to unmoor the field, robbing it of any firm grounding in a distinctive subject matter. The task, then, is how to avoid this "unmooring" of the field, while retaining the core insight that property is, indeed, a field of social relations about . . . *what*? Our answer, developed in what follows, is neither *everything and hence nothing in particular* (disintegration), nor a reassertion of *things* (rethingification), but rather, *resources*.

Concerning the second question – of what entitlements does property consist? – here the difficulty with the core of Hohfeldian analysis is greater. Traveling under the heading of "disaggregation" are a pair of conceptual insights, regarding the divisibility and variability of entitlements, the import of which is unclear going forward. Are there any "core" or central entitlements to serve as focal points of analysis, or does disaggregation simply "unspool" into a laundry list of discrete entitlements, devolving into ad hoc analysis of piecemeal decisions taken up one at a time? This latter peril would seem to loom especially large where, as previously discussed, the analysis of entitlements is not grounded in any controlling purposes. And one possible grounding – that the entitlements pertain to "things" – is, again, made unavailable by dematerialization. The first step, then, in avoiding unspooling is to anchor the analysis of property's entitlements in an analysis of its distinctive subject matter, resources. A second step – equally necessary – is to structure the analysis of the entitlements themselves in a more conceptually integrated manner. We advance a way of doing so in Section 5.4.2 by developing a picture of property as consisting neither of *anything* (disintegration), nor of *one single thing* (a "core" or "essence"), but rather of an *architecture* of elemental entitlements, the *fundamental building blocks* of all property forms.

even begin to answer what ownership may, does, or should consist of unless we first have an idea of what property is *about* (and thus *what* may be "owned"). Second, to inquire into what one can have property rights "in" is a quite distinct matter from asking what property is about. The latter formulation directs our attention precisely to the task at hand: namely, to conceptualize an institution or field in light of some sense of our governing purposes, the cognitive and practical interests at stake. The former question, on the other hand, invites not only a purely descriptive inquiry into existing legal practices but also one that takes their surface terminology at conceptual face value – so that, whenever the term "property" is invoked by legal professionals, we simply accept that the relevant underlying concept is at play. This disables us, right at the outset, from developing any theoretically powerful conceptualizations.

5.3 AN AUTONOMOUS TRADITION OF PROPERTY ANALYTICS IN EUROPE: RESOURCE-SPECIFIC PROPERTY DISAGGREGATION

The revised Hohfeldian analytical scheme that we have just outlined highlights the contextual and, as we will develop, resource-specific character of property. Property, we argue, is a legal relation between persons with respect to "things" (resources), a relation structured by correlative legal entitlement-disentitlement pairs, in which the conferral and shape of any particular entitlement depend on context and purpose – more precisely, we will argue, on the distinct interests and values implicated by distinct kinds of *resources*. The focus on the "thing" was marginal to Hohfeld himself and intentionally dropped in neo-Hohfeldian dematerialization accounts, in which property became unmoored so as to no longer be anchored in *any*thing. But the resource-specific character of property was central to an autonomous tradition of property disaggregation developed in Continental Europe. It is to this tradition that we now turn, with the aim of retrieving its fundamental insights and illustrating the main stages in its development.

5.3.1 *The Roman "Law of Things" and the Contextualist Focus on Resources*

As is often the case when one seeks to understand Continental European property law, we have to start with Roman law.[45] Our search for the European Hohfelds takes us back to the late Republic, a time of great juristic creativity when the main features of Roman law as we know it today took shape.[46] Roman property has long struck the imagination not only of lawyers but also of historians, economists, and philosophers because of its allegedly "absolute," "individualistic," "unitary," and "extremely concentrated" nature.[47] This idea of Roman *dominium* being absolute and unitary is a pervasive one and its traces in the modern philosophical, economic, and legal literature on property are ubiquitous. But, as Italian Roman law scholar Vittorio Scialoja put it, it is a legend.[48] This legend was concocted by the "Romano-Bourgeois" jurists, liberal jurists in the

45 For a relatively recent discussion of the importance of grounding the study of European property law in its Roman and medieval past, see George L. Gretton, *Ownership and its Objects*, 71 Rabel J. Comp. & Int'l Priv. L. 802–51 (2007).

46 H. F. Jolowicz & Barry Nicholas, Historical Introduction to the Study of Roman Law 5 (3d ed. 2008).

47 A quick glance at Roman law textbooks reveals the ubiquitous presence of the idea that Roman property is absolute and unitary. *See* Jolowicz & Nicholas, *supra* note 46, at 140 (arguing that "[t]he Roman law of classical times is dominated by what is commonly called the absolute conception of ownership" defined as "the unrestricted right of control over a physical thing"); W. W. Buckland & Arnold D. McNair, Roman Law and Common Law 81–82 (2d ed. 2008) (arguing that the owner has very limited ability to parcel out to other individuals these three entitlements and that this limited ability makes property a "unitary" or "concentrated" right).

48 Vittorio Scialoja, Lezioni di Diritto Romano (1885) ("The Roman theory of property has inspired the strangest legends not only among the populace but also, sometimes, among the educated.").

nineteenth century who sought to construct a modern, individualistic property law for liberal, capitalist European nation states along the lines of Roman *dominium*. The truth is that Roman property law was less "absolute," "individualistic," and "unitary" than the Roman-Bourgeois jurists would have us believe.[49] Moreover, *dominium* was just one of the many forms of ownership available in Roman law. It was the supreme form of ownership, reserved to Roman citizens, exempt from taxation, and protected through the action known as *rei vindicatio*, which was a formal assertion of absolute title.[50] However, alongside *dominium* there existed a large menu of more limited and differently shaped forms of "ownership" that were largely "resource-specific," i.e., tailored to the specific characteristics of, and interests implicated by, different resources.

The contextual focus on resources is a critical feature of Roman property law that has attracted scant attention in contemporary property law literature. Roman jurists developed a highly sophisticated "law of things," i.e., a classification of the various types of *res* that can be the object of property rights. Roman law classified the various *res* according to their physical characteristics, the economic and social policy interests they involved, and the moral and cultural values they implicated. In modern property law, the most familiar and fundamental distinctions are those between real property and personal property, and between private property and public property. But these two sets of categories were marginal to the Roman law of things. For the Romans, the critical distinction was that between *res in commercio* and *res extra commercium*.[51] The former were things that could be the object of private property, while the latter were things that, because of the social, moral, or cultural values associated with them, could not be the object of private property and of market transactions. The *res extra commercium* were further divided in *res (extra commercium) divini iuris*, which could not be privately owned and exchanged because of their religious significance; and *res (extra commercium) humani iuris*, which were exempted from private property and commerce because they implicated important public interests. Among the things that were exempt from private property and market transactions because of the public interest they involved, the *res communes* were particularly important.[52] These were things like the sun, the air, the sea, and the shores, that were regarded as given to all as an essential, innate gift and hence as belonging not to the state but to the public, who had a temporary and limited, but legally protected, right to access and use. Another critical category was that of *res mancipi*, things that had critical socio-economic value, the transfer of

49 Eva Jakab, *Property Rights in Ancient Rome*, *in* Ownership and Exploitation of Land and Natural Resources in the Roman World 107 (P. Erdkamp et al. eds., 2015).

50 *See* Bonfante, *supra* note 23.

51 *See* Yan Thomas, *La valeur des choses. Le droit romain hors la religion*, 57 Annales, Histoire, Sciences Sociales 1431–62 (2002) (arguing that by classifying things into *res in commercio* and *res extra commercium*, the Romans marked off a separate realm, that of the sacred, the religious, and the public, which are seen as contiguous and very close to each other).

52 The list of *res communes* is in J. Inst. 2.2.1 (Peter Birks & Grant McLeod trans., 1987). On the debate on the nature and significance of the concept of *res communes*, see Bonfante, *supra* note 23, at 55.

which required specific, highly ritualized modalities capable of ensuring certainty and publicity in economic transactions.[53] Yet another distinction, largely opaque to us because of its roots in Stoic physics, was that between *res unitae* (single things, infused with one single breath of *pneuma*, the world soul), *res compositae* (composite things), and *universitates rerum* (totalities of things).

For each of these *res*, the owner's entitlements were shaped to reflect the special interests and values implicated by the resource. The characteristics of the resource determined: (a) which entitlements were conferred to the owner; (b) the scope of the owner's entitlements; and (c) whether these entitlements were exclusive or shared with others. This contextualist focus on resources meant that, alongside *dominium*, the supreme and full (even if never "absolute") form of ownership, Roman law allowed for a wide menu of more limited forms of ownership for specific resources that were critical for the Empire's economic, military, and political needs. For example, land situated in the provinces of the Empire was a critical resource for both economic and geopolitical reasons. Accordingly, property entitlements were split between the Roman state and private "owners" or users and shaped to achieve a variety of goals. The vast literature on the Roman province of Egypt gives us a good sense of what some of these goals and policies were. By recognizing "ownership" bundles with different scopes and shapes, the Roman state sought to balance two, largely conflicting, goals: (a) advancing the economic power and political influence of the Empire's landowning elite; and (b) securing significant and stable state revenues in the long term.[54] Another reason for the state to retain control over provincial lands was the role it played as an economic actor, deciding what crops would be planted and, for example, subsidizing the production of wheat by leasing farm land on favorable terms.[55] Another specially tailored form of ownership was ownership of "*ager publicus*," i.e., land for which the state retained title while granting private users entitlements that, with time, came to resemble "ownership." The content and scope of users' entitlements were shaped to encourage the establishment of large-scale commercial farming at a time when a Mediterranean market economy was developing.[56]

[53] PIETRO BONFANTE, RES MANCIPI E NEC MANCIPI (1888).

[54] *See* Dennis P. Kehoe, *Property Rights over Land and Economic Growth in the Roman Empire, in* OWNERSHIP AND EXPLOITATION OF LAND AND NATURAL RESOURCES IN THE ROMAN WORLD, *supra* note 23, at 89, 90–91; DENNIS P. KEHOE, LAW AND RURAL ECONOMY IN THE ROMAN EMPIRE (2007). On the political significance of the imperial agrarian land policy in Egypt, see ANDREW MONSON, FROM THE PTOLEMIES TO THE ROMANS: POLITICAL AND ECONOMIC CHANGE IN EGYPT (2012).

[55] *See* Kehoe, *supra* note 54, at 101.

[56] SASKIA ROSELAAR, PUBLIC LAND IN THE ROMAN REPUBLIC: A SOCIAL AND ECONOMIC HISTORY OF AGER *PUBLICUS* IN ITALY, 396–89 BC 3–4 (2010).

5.3.2 *The Medieval Concept of "Dominium Divisum"*

While these more limited forms of resource-specific property were central to Rome's social and economic life, they were never explicitly theorized or conceptualized. Roman legal thought was eminently practical and disinclined to offer abstract definitions.[57] Modern jurists have painstakingly searched for *the* definition of the concept of property in the Roman sources, but none of the many supposed definitions they found can be considered *the* definition. For a conceptualization of property able to accommodate these more limited forms of resource-specific ownership we have to wait for the fourteenth century, when the jurists known as the "Glossators" and the "Commentators" were busy developing a property law functionally suited to the socio-economic and political needs of their own world, medieval society, using Roman materials.[58] This task required conceptual creativity as well as pragmatic awareness of the problems and needs of the real, actual life of property law. It is to the creativity and pragmatism of one of the most prominent "Commentators," Bartolus of Saxoferrato (1313–57), that we owe *dominium divisum*, a new concept of property informed by two fundamental intuitions that today we associate with Hohfeld: (a) that property consists of analytically distinct entitlements; and (b) that each entitlement in the bundle is variable, i.e., that its very existence, scope, and the number of its holders can vary without property losing its "propertiness." The concept of *dominium divisum* describes a type of property in which the distinct entitlements that ownership comprises were split between two "owners," who have, respectively, "*dominium directum*" and "*dominium utile*." While, roughly, the former had formal title, the right to receive some form of rent, and the right to transfer title, and the latter had the right to use, to appropriate the revenue generated by the property, and the duty to pay rent, the specific shape and scope of the two owners' entitlements varied. In each of the property forms that Bartolus conceptualized as instances of *dominium divisum*, i.e., feudal tenure, *emphyteusis*, *superficies*, and long-term prescription (*longi temporis praescriptio*), the two owners' bundles were differently shaped and yet they were still "*dominium*," thereby emphasizing the malleability of property.[59]

57 Aldo Schiavone, The Invention of Law in the West 76–80 (2012); Fritz Schultz, History of Roman Legal Science 6–20 (1946); Bruce W. Frier, The Rise of the Roman Jurists 191 (1985).

58 Manlio Bellomo, The Common Legal Past of Europe (Lydia G. Cochrane trans., 1995).

59 André van der Walt & D. G. Kleyn, *Duplex Dominium: The History and Significance of the Concept of Divided Ownership*, *in* Essays on the History of Law 213–60 (D. P. Visser ed., 1989); Thomas Rufner, *The Roman Concept of Ownership and the Medieval Doctrine of Dominium Utile*, *in* The Creation of the Ius Commune: From Casus to Regula 127–42 (John W. Cairns & Paul J. du Plessis eds., 2010); Ennio Cortese, *Controversie medievali sul dominio utile: Bartolo e il quidam doctor de Aurelianis*, *in* Amicitiae Pignus, Studi in ricordo di Adriano Cavanna 613–35 (Antonio Padoa Schioppa et al. eds., 2003); Robert Feenstra, *Les origines du dominium utile chez les glossateurs (avec un appendice concernant l'opinion des ultramontani)*, *in* Fata Iuris Romani Etudes d'histoire du droit 215–59 (1974); Paolo Grossi, Le situazioni reali nell'esperienza giuridica medievale: Corso di storia del diritto 144–208 (1968).

Why Bartolus felt the need finally to formulate a concept of variable and divided ownership – the absence of which had not precluded the development of a sizable menu of forms of divided, resource-specific ownership in Roman times – is a fascinating question. The answer we suggest is that the structure and the daily lived experience of medieval society made medieval jurists uniquely aware of the fundamental insight in which any concept of variable and divided property is rooted, i.e., that property is a social relation, a relation between persons concerning a resource. Crafting a new concept of *dominium divisum*, consisting of analytically distinct entitlements – each of which can be variously shaped – requires abandoning any abstract notion that property is a thing or a physical relation between a person and a thing and realizing that property, always and inevitably, involves relations between persons. The Roman political and cultural imaginary, largely shaped by "classical" Roman law, obscured the web of social relations regarding resources; instead, it spotlighted the relation between two poles of power, strong private property, conceived in very abstract terms, and a well-developed central state.[60] The disintegration of the Roman state ushered in a feudal structure in which everyone, feudal lords, vassals, and serfs, was tied up in hierarchical relations regarding access to land. Feudalism forced medieval jurists to abandon abstractions and to realize that property was about hierarchies and complex webs of social relations.[61] Of course, it would be anachronistic to expect medieval jurists explicitly to crystallize their intuitions into an articulate conceptualization of property as a social relation. However, we should not, in avoiding the anachronism, also fail to see how, in retrospect, their development of the concept of *dominium divisum* was, indeed, rooted in glimmers of this realization.

Dominium divisum was the general conceptual category to describe the many feudal and nonfeudal property forms that involved a relation between a "superior" owner and an "inferior" owner regarding access to a parcel of land. In each of the many property forms that belonged to the larger category of *dominium divisum*, ownership entitlements were differently shaped so as to structure different types of relations between the two owners with regard to the land. In some forms, the relation between the two owners was social and political, with the superior owner entitled to receive homage, military aid, and to exercise a variety of jurisdictional rights and recreational privileges.[62] Other forms of *dominium divisum* were largely economic in character and resembled today's lease, with entitlements shaped to give the parties different degrees of control over the management and profits of the

60 Of course, our modern understanding of the Roman law is largely based on what generations of modern Roman law scholars regarded as "classical law," the layer of juristic writing they believed to be "original," see SCHIAVONE, *supra* note 57, at 26–28; FRIER, *supra* note 57, at 252–68.

61 *See* ELLEN M. WOOD, LIBERTY AND PROPERTY: A SOCIAL HISTORY OF WESTERN POLITICAL THOUGHT FROM RENAISSANCE TO ENLIGHTENMENT (2012).

62 For a detailed discussion of the many forms of *dominium divisum* in medieval and early modern France, see MARCEL GARAUD, LA RÉVOLUTION ET LA PROPRIÉTÉ FONCIÈRE 15–51 (1959).

land.[63] In other words, medieval jurists felt the need to develop the concept of *dominium divisum* when faced with the new reality of feudal society, in which people were immersed in a complex web of political, social, and economic relations with regards to land. The new concept of property as *dominium divisum* allowed the jurists to describe the new reality and to acknowledge and embrace their role as the technicians who shaped ownership entitlements to achieve a variety of political, social, and economic goals. Practically, articulating the new concept required overcoming a number of major conceptual difficulties, such as the Roman rule that explicitly rules out the possibility of two owners for the same thing.[64] However, Bartolus and his contemporaries were ready to bend and twist the Roman rules because the Roman abstraction of absolute *dominium* had lost its descriptive power. The new feudal world required a new property methodology that married the need for conceptual systematization with close sociological attention to the variety of relations between individuals regarding land.

5.3.3 *The Concept of Property as a Tree*

The Roman "law of things" and the concept of *dominium divisum* introduced into European property thought the awareness that property, rather than being a monolithic right, involves a number of distinct and limited entitlements, each of which may be shaped and divided to best promote the values and interests implicated by the different resources that are the object of property. *Dominium divisum* continued to be an accurate description of land ownership in Continental Europe throughout the early modern era. However, starting in the eighteenth century, as feudal property relations transformed and economic and political modernity started taking shape, *dominium divisum* and the focus on the resource

[63] This was the case for forms such as *emphyteusis* and *bail à rente*. *Id.* at 39, 122–24.

[64] The road toward *dominium divisum* was not a smooth one. The most significant obstacle was that, while in both feudal property and nonfeudal forms of split ownership there appeared to be two owners, the superior owner and the inferior owner, Roman law explicitly ruled out the possibility of two owners of the same thing. A passage of the Digest (Dig. 13.6.5.15) made it clear that "*duo non possunt habere dominium eiusdem rei in solidum*." What this rule meant is that there can very well be two or more co-owners of one thing, each owning a "share," but no two persons can own the entirety of the same thing at the same time. This raised a crucial question, clearly stated in a passage from the collection of Roman definitions known as *Excerpta Codicis Vaticani*: are the inferior parties in the relationship (the *emphyteuticarius*, the *superficiarius*, the *colonus*) actual owners or mere holders of *iura in re aliena*? Bartolus confidently declares that *both* are owners because there are two types of ownership, *dominium directum* and *dominium utile*. "A German doctor who yesterday held a class (*repetitio*) here," Bartolus explains, "reports that there is only one type of ownership. But there are two." Bartolus then proceeds to support his statement with Roman texts. The *lex possessores* (Code Just. 11.62.12), a late constitution included in Justinian's compilation, described the holders of a right of *emphyteusis* as "owners of the land" (*fundorum domini*). And yet, according to another text (Code Just. 4.66.1–2), Bartolus explains, someone else remains the owner vis-à-vis the lessor. If there are two owners, Bartolus concludes, then the types of ownership must be different, because the same ownership cannot belong to two persons as stated in the Digest (Dig. 13.6.5.15). *See* Rufner, *supra* note 59, at 131, 139–41.

lost both their descriptive usefulness and their appeal. By the eighteenth century, landholding relations throughout Europe had fundamentally transformed, with a gradual but steady shift in the socio-economic and legal status of "superior" and "inferior" "owners."[65] The bond between the "superior" owner and the land became increasingly tenuous while the bond between the "inferior" owner and the land grew stronger. One of the fundamental ideas of political and economic modernity was to transform medieval limited "inferior" ownership into full-blown ownership.[66] Jurists, economists, and philosophers embarked on the project of crafting "Roman-Bourgeois" property, a new concept of unitary and full property for modern, liberal, capitalist European nation states, modeled along the lines of Roman *dominium*. The jurists did the conceptual groundwork, while the economists developed a new political economy that praised the economic and civic-republican benefits of absolute property,[67] and political theorists proposed a new constitutional vision of equal citizenship based on the demarcation between absolute private property and public sovereignty.[68] At the dawn of the nineteenth century, absolute and unitary property was enshrined in the *Code Napoleon*.[69] And, in the decades between the bourgeois monarchy of Louis Philippe and the end of the nineteenth century, French jurists completed the work, interpreting the *Code*'s property in light of the mandates of liberal individualism, effectively transforming it into full-blown Roman-Bourgeois property.[70] Charles Bonaventure Marie Touiller, the author of one of the most influential "commentaries" on the *Code Napoleon*, captured the essence of Roman-Bourgeois property in one brief sentence that seems a direct refutation of any Hohfeldian insight: "property is the relation between a person and a thing irrespectively of all others."[71]

Roman-Bourgeois property was the dominant conceptualization of property throughout the nineteenth century. Classical liberal jurists and their social critics engaged in a close debate over its conceptual accuracy, its policy implications, and its moral foundations. Critics exposed the unrealistic assumptions behind Roman-Bourgeois property, sought to mitigate its most obvious distributive inequities, and questioned its moral foundations. However, they did not provide an alternative conceptualization of property. It is only in the first half of the twentieth century

65 See GARAUD, *supra* note 62, at 2.

66 *See* RAFE BLAUFARB, THE GREAT DEMARCATION: THE FRENCH REVOLUTION AND THE INVENTION OF MODERN PROPERTY 48–57 (2016). Of course, the other parallel transformation was the enclosure of common lands and the abolition of rights over communal lands. *See* JOHN MARKOFF, THE ABOLITION OF FEUDALISM: PEASANTS, LORDS AND LEGISLATORS IN THE FRENCH REVOLUTION 485 (1996).

67 JOHN SHLOVIN, THE POLITICAL ECONOMY OF VIRTUE: LUXURY, PATRIOTISM AND THE ORIGINS OF THE FRENCH REVOLUTION (2006).

68 *See* BLAUFARB, *supra* note 66, at 48–80.

69 ANDRE-JEAN ARNAUD, LES ORIGINES DOCTRINALES DU CODE CIVIL FRANÇAIS 179ff (1969).

70 Michel Vidal, *La propriété dans l'école de l'exégèse en France*, 5–6 QUADERNI FIORENTINI 7–40 (1976–77).

71 CHARLES BONAVENTURE MARIE TOUILLER, 3 LE DROIT CIVIL FRANÇAIS, SUIVANT L'ORDRE DU CODE NAPOLÉON 70 para. 84 (1811) .

that a new generation of French and Italian jurists developed a new conception of property that rested on some intuitions that had an affinity with the ideas underlying Hohfeld's approach. A recent and radical transformation in the actual life of property law, these jurists argued, demanded a new concept of property. The decades between 1850 and 1920 witnessed momentous economic, social, and political changes: the rapid industrialization of late-blooming economies such as France and Italy, the agrarian crisis of the 1880s, World War I, the crisis of liberalism, and the rise of Fascism. Under the pressure of these events, property was transformed, becoming more limited and "specialized" or "pluralistic." Special legislation limited the use rights and transfer rights of owners of things of historical and artistic interest, imposed duties on owners to improve and to cultivate their land, subjected owners of utilities or industries of critical importance for the national economy, such as textile or manufacturing, to duties and limits. Emergency legislation passed during World War I further limited the rights of owners of resources critical to national security and the inventory of resources subtracted from private property and held by the state in trust for the public was expanded to include water, forests, and mines. The protection of the owner's absolute rights was no longer the paramount concern and equal access to property and the public interest became part of the vocabulary of property. These changes in the legal regime of property were the catalysts that helped this new generation of jurists come to see the concept of property in a new light, revealing what more than a century of Roman-Bourgeois emphasis on the individual owner's absolute right had obscured: that property rights have significant effects on social relations among individuals regarding access and use of resources. Articulated in the guise of the "social function" of property, this new concept closely interwove the empirical observation of increasing social interdependence with a normative emphasis on the need for property to serve a "public interest."[72]

The two jurists who made the greatest contribution to the reconceptualization of property were the French Louis Josserand (1868–1941) and the Italian Salvatore Pugliatti (1903–76). The concept of property Josserand and Pugliatti developed sought to mediate between two conflicting impulses: disaggregating property into a plurality of resource-specific regimes, to reflect the changes they were witnessing in property law, and preserving a robust core for property rights in a Europe threatened

[72] In two respects, then, this process paralleled the one we described above concerning dematerialization: (a) just as dematerialization of the objects and interests of property proved a crucial historical stimulus to the conceptual crystallization, by Hohfeld, of property as a social relation, so increasing industrialization and socioeconomic interdependence catalyzed a conceptual focus, by Josserand and Pugliatti, toward property's "social function"; and (b) just as Hohfeld's social relations insight was often buried under a mass of dematerialization points (with which it was entangled), so here the conceptual aspect of property's "social function" was often directly assimilated to normative claims regarding the "public interest." Indeed, the conceptual claim of property *as a social relation* – as distinct from its empirical (property *affecting* social relations) and normative (property *serving* social interests) dimensions – seems not to have been explicitly recognized, or at least articulated, by the "social function" theorists.

by totalitarianism. In Pugliatti and Josserand's new conceptualization, property resembles a tree with a unitary trunk and many branches.[73]

The trunk is the essence of property, the core entitlement or entitlements necessary for a right over a thing to be property. For Josserand and Pugliatti, the trunk is the owner's right to control the use of the resource.[74] However, the theorists of the tree concept realized that protecting the owner's sphere of autonomous control was not enough and that a modern, liberal concept of property had to acknowledge that property also implicates the public interest. The rise of Fascism, they realized, was the consequence of liberals' insensibility to new ideas about the proper balance between individual rights and the interest of the collectivity. The tree concept jurists' solution was to argue that owners should exercise their use-control entitlements while remaining mindful of property's "social function."[75] The "social function" of property is part of the trunk of the tree. Property, Josserand and Pugliatti suggested, had always included social elements. At no point in history, not even in Roman law, was property absolute and the idea of a social interest, parallel to the interest of the individual owner, had always been there.

The problem with the notion of property's social function was that it was hopelessly indeterminate. Its content and the precise extent of the duties it imposed on owners were highly contested. The tree concept theorists' response to the indeterminacy of the social function was captured in the image of the branches of the tree. Josserand and Pugliatti drew inspiration from the Roman "law of things" and argued that the social function concept alludes to the multiple values and interests implicated by different resources. The branches of the property tree are the many resource-specific agglomerates of entitlements: agrarian property, family property, affordable urban residential property, entrepreneurial property, and intellectual property. The content of the social function of property is different for each of the branches. Because of the differences in its object, Josserand argued, "property takes on different shapes depending on the type of resource involved. Property is no longer uniform, rather it is multiform, infinitely diverse and varied. There is no longer one property but many properties subject each to its own specialized regime."[76] No longer "one" but "infinitely ... varied," property, it would seem, had again disintegrated.

73 Salvatore Pugliatti, La proprietà nel nuovo diritto 149 (Dott. A. Giuffrè ed., 1964).

74 The conceptualization of this "right" involved eliding precisely what Hohfeldian analysis would insist on keeping sharply distinct, namely interests in use protected by use-privileges versus interests in use protected by exclusion-rights.

75 *See* Pugliatti, *supra* note 73, at 281 (starting his discussion on the social function of property by saying that "the core of property is now open to transformations").

76 Louis Josserand, *Configuration du droit de propriété dans l'ordre juridique noveau*, *in* Mélanges juridiques dédiés à M. le Professeur Sugiyama 95, 100 (1940).

5.4 WHAT IS PROPERTY? TWO MODEST WAYS FORWARD

As we have seen, the specter of disintegration haunts both US and European debates on post-formalist conceptions of property, making clear the need for better answers to "what is property?" An initial step in the right direction, we have suggested, is to break that question down into two distinct parts: (a) what is property *about* – as a distinct concept or field of law?[77] and (b) what does property *consist of* – in terms of its central, identifying forms of legal entitlements? And answers to each of these can only be evaluated in light of our reasons for wanting an answer, in light of, that is, our sense of precisely what is wrong with the forms of disintegration corresponding to each question: unmooring dematerialization and unspooling disaggregation.

5.4.1 *What Is Property About? Resource-Specific Analysis of the Objects of Property*

On the disintegration view, the dematerialization of the objects and interests of property is taken to lead to the conclusion that since property rights need not relate to tangible "things," they can obtain in "anything and everything." But if property is about everything, then it is also about nothing in particular, emptying the field of any distinguishing features. And what's wrong with *that* is twofold. First, such an intellectual move disarms us in the face of real-world cognitive and institutional practices, where "property law" is still taught in law schools, understood as a field of legal scholarship, and where its concepts are regularly invoked in real-world legal disputes and policy decisions. If these practices really are about nothing in particular, then we should at least explain why their distinguishing boundaries nevertheless persist and, preferably, also offer some prescriptions for reforming our conceptualization and organization of fields and practices.

But, and second, in any case, these fields and practices are not about nothing in particular. Rather, as is made clear by both long-standing social practices and "external" social and political theory, they are about the legal regulation of resources. The anchoring of property in resources may well be the single most enduring theme in the history of European practices and theory around property law, as we showed in Section 5.3. And even today, no matter how loud the disintegration cry of "there's nothing (distinctive) there," historical, economic, and philosophical works continue to provide descriptive, explanatory, and normative accounts of "property." Why? Because there really is "something" there, something of distinct significance to humans in society. And that is how we structure social relations with respect to *resources*, to form persons and satisfy interests through the allocation, production, and distribution of "goods."

[77] For a discussion of the differences between this formulation and an alternative often used by both disintegration and neo-Blackstonian theorists (namely, "in what may one have property?"), see *supra* note 44.

By "resources" we do not mean simply some intuitive, straightforward, or pre-theoretical notion. Rather, we mean to invoke a notion requiring explicit conceptualization, one that can be made sense of only within *external* frames of positive (e.g., economic) and normative (e.g., political-philosophical) analysis, which lie to a considerable extent outside of law.[78] Frames of analysis for issues such as the static allocation and dynamic production of "goods-types" that vary in rivalry and excludability, or the constitutive effects of different goods on interests in freedom, personhood, or flourishing, or their strategic implications for values such as distributive justice or democracy. Although developing a full account of resources along these lines lies beyond our present scope, two important implications of having such a conception serve as the anchor for property merit emphasis here.

First, resources so conceived are not synonymous with "things." Not only may resources be immaterial, but not all material objects need be resources.[79] A signal

[78] Central to our point here, then, is to emphasize a contrast with more traditional "inside out" approaches, whereby the salient features of resources, if specified at all, are perceived through a glass darkly, through the filter of existing lay usages and legal doctrines. By contrast, we wish to underline the importance of starting "outside in," so as to conceive of resources, at least initially, independently of their existing legal-property treatment, by foregrounding, as the initial drivers of the analysis, a conceptualization of what resources and their distinctive features are that draws systematically on external frames of positive and normative analysis. For illustrative analyses along these lines, see Yochai Benkler, *Intellectual Property and the Organization of Information Production*, (Oct. 1999) (draft), http://www.benkler.org/Ipec99.pdf (final draft published at 22 INT'L REV. L. & ECON. 81 (2002)); Yochai Benkler, *Sharing Nicely: On Shareable Goods and the Emergence of Sharing as a Modality of Economic Production*, 114 YALE L.J. 273 (2004); BRETT FRISCHMANN, INFRASTRUCTURE: THE SOCIAL VALUE OF SHARED RESOURCES (2012); Lee Anne Fennell, *The Problem of Resource Access*, 126 HARV. L. REV. 1471 (2013). An alternative way forward beyond Blackstonian and disintegration views has been articulated in important recent work by Hanoch Dagan. *See* HANOCH DAGAN, PROPERTY: VALUES AND INSTITUTIONS (2011). Space limitations prevent us from exploring here possible points of convergence and contrast between Professor Dagan's value-centered approach and our resource-anchored view. The same is true for points of convergence and contrast between our emphasis on *external frames of analysis* of "*resources*" and, what we very much build on here, an emphasis on *external institutional regimes* to *private property* for governing resources, as advanced in an important line of (principally intellectual) property scholarship. *See, e.g.*, William W. Fisher, *Intellectual Property and Innovation: Theoretical, Empirical and Historical Perspectives* (2001), https://cyber.harvard.edu/people/tfisher/Innovation.pdf; Michael J. Madison et al., *Constructing Commons in the Cultural Environment*, 95 CORNELL L. REV. 657 (2010); Amy Kapczynski, *The Cost of Price: How and Why to Get Beyond IP Internalism*, 59 UCLA L. REV. 970 (2012).

[79] It may be objected, with respect to the first two points we have just made demarcating "resources" from "things" – namely, first, that resources as an object require explicit conceptualization, rather than simply registering a pre-theoretical perception or intuition of a pre-given (likely tangible) "thing," and, second, that resources so conceived need not be tangible at all – that these points may also be shared by those offering a revised account of "things," fit for a post-dematerialization world. Indeed, an important such account, by Frederick Pollock, serves as a touchstone for Professors Penner and Smith's views that, dematerialization notwithstanding, the objects of property remain "things." *See* PENNER, *supra* note 4, at 111; Henry E. Smith, *The Thing About Exclusion*, 3 BRIGHAM-KANNER PROP. RTS. CONF. J. 94, 117ff (2014). At the center of Pollock's account is the idea that a "thing," for purposes of legal analysis, is simply any individuated matter of discrete rights and duties. *See* Pollock, *supra* note 38, at 318 ("A thing is, in law, some possible matter of rights and duties conceived

example in this latter respect – of material objects that are not "resources" in the sense meant here – are the tangible insignia that are the subject of trademark protection. As a distinguished line of analysis has insisted from the origins of trademark law through to the present, there is a sharp distinction to be drawn between "misrepresentation" and "misappropriation" bases for "unfair competition," just as there is between "consumer confusion" and confusion-independent "dilution" claims in trademark.[80] Underlying these, we suggest, is a fundamental distinction to be drawn between treating commercial insignia as "communicative" vehicles, for the sake of regulating the integrity of market information for consumers, and treating them as "resources," for the sake of protecting firms' investments in goodwill.[81]

Second, once we start down this road – of anchoring property in a purposive analysis of what matters, requiring external positive and normative analysis of the object of significance rather than simply registering lay and legal usages – there is likely to be little reason to stop at "resources" as a crude monolith. Rather, we will likely need to break our analysis down into resource-specific units, as suggested by categories and

as a whole and apart from all others, just as, in the world of common experience, whatever can be separately perceived is a thing."). However illuminating in other respects Pollock's – quite brilliant – treatment of this topic may be, as the basis for an account of the objects of property, it faces a strong – we think insuperable – objection: so conceived, "things" are so general as to run precisely the risk that one may now have "property" in "*anything*." Thus, for instance, among the "things" in which we may have property-like rights, Pollock lists the "exclusive right to ferry passengers across a river for hire at a certain place." *See* Pollock, *supra* note 38, at 319. But this would seem precisely to usher in the disintegration of property as a distinct field of law, very much along the lines heralded by Professor Grey. *See* Grey, *supra* note 36. And, thus, to serve as an unpromising basis upon which to re-integrate, post-dematerialization, property as a distinct field of law.

Needless to say, this is far from the last word on different proposals and bases for the "rethingification" of the objects of property in a post-dematerialization world, including those that would simply reject dematerialization and insist on retaining a sharp distinction between "property" in tangible things as the heart of the field, with any legal rights in intangible things, such as those commonly referred to as "intellectual property," as lying outside the scope of "property" strictly speaking. Space limitations prevent us from undertaking here a fuller exploration of the potential points of difference or convergence between these two views – (a) of "things" as the objects of property; and (b) "resources" as the distinctive subject matter of property, as what it is about – and hence for present purposes we will limit ourselves to simply delineating the central outlines of our contrasting "resource" view. For a fuller exploration, see Syed, *supra* note 42.

80 On misrepresentation versus misappropriation in unfair competition law, see Felix Cohen, *Transcendental Nonsense and the Functional Approach*, 35 COLUM. L. REV. 809 (1935); Ralph S. Brown, Jr., *Advertising and the Public Interest: Legal Protection of Trade Symbols*, 57 YALE L.J. 1165 (1948); Richard Posner, *Misappropriation: A Dirge*, 40 HOUS. L. REV. 641 (2003). On consumer confusion versus confusion-independent "dilution" claims within trademark, see Glyn Lunney, *Trademark Monopolies*, 48 EMORY L.J. 367 (1999); Mark Lemley, *The Modern Lanham Act and the Death of Common Sense*, 108 YALE L.J. 1687 (1999).

81 Such a distinction would serve as the conceptual marker for drawing two sharp substantive lines in this area: First, *between* trademark and other regimes of "intellectual *property*" proper, such as copyright, patent, and trade secret protection. *See, e.g.*, Peter Menell & Suzanne Scotchmer, *Intellectual Property*, *in* 2 HANDBOOK OF LAW AND ECONOMICS 1474 (A. Mitchel Polinsky & Steven Shavell eds., 2007). Second, *within* trademark, between "consumer confusion" and "dilution" sources of concern. *See* Lunney, *supra* note 80; Lemley, *supra* note 80.

implications of positive and normative analysis. Consider three illustrations. First, as revealed by positive economic analysis of goods-types, the purpose, feasibility, and desirability both of conferring exclusionary rights over resources *and* of organizing their production on the basis of markets or commons or the state vary dramatically for private, common-pool, club, toll, and public goods. The virtual absence of such elementary analytics in our current property law curriculum is disconcerting.[82] Or, to take a second, more normative, frame of analysis: are there resources of such fundamental significance for self-determination or the development of personhood – housing being a prime candidate – that equitable access to them should be understood as imperative as a matter of "right" and not "merely" to promote social welfare or even general distributive justice?[83] If so, can such goods be classed into sufficiently coarse-grained units as to provide distinct foci of analysis from other, more "generic" resources subject merely to the imperatives of efficiency and distribution?[84] Or, to shift lenses

82 To speak of a "virtual absence" may be thought to overstate matters, but for purposes of underlining both the precise content of our point and our sense of its import, we think it worthwhile to state it somewhat starkly. It is not only that a review of leading property casebooks reveals, as Julie Cohen observes, that they "are organized almost entirely around the intricacies that attend land use and land transactions." Julie Cohen, *Property as Institutions for Resources: Lessons from and for IP*, 94 TEX. L. REV. 1, 6 (2014) (citing in support JESSE DUKEMINIER ET AL., PROPERTY xi–xxiv (8th ed. 2014); ERIC T. FREYFOGLE & BRADLEY C. KARKKAINEN, PROPERTY LAW: POWER, GOVERNANCES, AND THE COMMON GOOD vii–xv (2012); THOMAS W. MERRILL & HENRY E. SMITH, PROPERTY: PRINCIPLES AND POLICIES xix–xxx (2d ed. 2012); JOSEPH W. SINGER, PROPERTY LAW: RULES, POLICIES, AND PRACTICES xiii–xxviii (6th ed. 2014); JOHN G. SPRANKLING & RAYMOND R. COLLETTA, PROPERTY: A CONTEMPORARY APPROACH xi–xx (2d ed. 2012)). But it is also that, even with respect to land, there is little by way of external positive and normative analysis of it as a resource (indeed, as a set of distinct resources, as such external analysis would likely conclude). Moreover, the absence of such external analytics can be felt even in the one exceptional casebook, which explicitly seeks to remedy the "lack" of "theoretical and structural coherence" of the "traditional" property syllabus of "a disparate set of doctrinal areas loosely tied together by their relationship to land" – and does so by "address[ing] not only issues regard land, but also the many other resources, including natural resources and intellectual property, that are increasingly important in our society." *See* JOHN P. DWYER & PETER MENELL, PROPERTY LAW AND POLICY: A COMPARATIVE INSTITUTIONAL PERSPECTIVE v (1998). Here also, however, the distinctive positive and normative features of resources are not explicitly developed, but perceived primarily through the prism of existing legal doctrines and categories. *Id.* at xix–xxix. Indeed, telling in this respect is the reference to intangible resources as "intellectual property." Not because it necessarily portends the hazards of a bygone era, where the use of "property" to refer both to the good and potential rights regarding it would tend to smuggle normative conclusions into one's descriptive premises. But rather because use of the same label for two distinct notions is illustrative, we believe, of the lack of explicit conceptualization of the second notion, i.e., of the underlying goods protected by IP rights, as *resources* of, e.g., "information, knowledge and culture" or "expressive forms" and "functional ideas," which merit being expressly conceived and analyzed as such, independently of their existing legal treatment, and thus also require a distinctive label from the one appended to the legal rights.

83 *See, e.g.*, Nestor Davidson, *Property and Identity: Vulnerability and Identity in the Housing Crisis*, 47 HARV. C.R.-C.L. L. REV. 119 (2012); Tim Iglesias, *Our Pluralist Housing Ethics and the Struggle for Affordability*, 42 WAKE FOREST L. REV. 511 (2007).

84 For an example of another set of goods deemed amenable to analysis as a demarcated sub-domain on account of their distinctive normative salience, see Carolyn J. Frantz & Hanoch Dagan, *Properties of Marriage*, 104 COLUM. L. REV. 75 (2004).

again, do certain resources – say, financial assets – have such strategic social significance, impacting concentrations not only of wealth but also of power, as to merit special attention from the vantage of democratic commitments?[85] Analysis proceeding along such lines would, we suggest, remain sensitive to important "delineation cost" concerns raised against ad-hoc disaggregation, while simultaneously attending to similarly significant "uniformity costs" concerns in the other direction.[86]

5.4.2 *What Does Property Consist Of? Architectural Analysis of the Entitlements of Property*

On the disintegration view, the disaggregation of the entitlements of ownership is taken to result in the conclusion that since property rights need not take any one form – i.e., since the "right" of ownership is neither a single entitlement nor any necessarily unified package of entitlements – then property rights can take *any* form. And seemingly counseling in favor of this view is an argument from flexibility: "Well at least here," says the disintegrationist, "there can be no complaint. Once we accept that property law, policy, and theory is about the structuring of social relations regarding resources through legal entitlements, it can only be a boon to be maximally open-ended about the relevant entitlement options, no?"

No. The unspooling of disaggregation into an ad hoc laundry list of entitlements is not about analytic or institutional flexibility. Rather, it is a counsel of intellectual and programmatic disorientation. Real-world thinking and institutional design need focal points for normative and positive analysis. A telling illustration in this respect is the fact that virtually all philosophical treatments of property, no matter how much they initially genuflect to the "bundle of rights" view, revert precisely to some strong "ownership" model to provide a focal point, some possible legal content of entitlement, for purposes of positive, normative, and institutional analysis.[87] Thus, we agree here with the insistence of Professor Henry Smith that we need a theoretically powerful analysis of the "architecture" of property.[88] On our view, however, it should be one that does not prejudge

85 For an analysis of how agricultural land may have been such a strategically significant resource in an earlier phase of the American economy, with design choices in the configuration of property entitlements having fundamental implications for the construction of individual freedom, see Yochai Benkler, *Distributive Liberty: A Relational Model of Freedom, Coercion, and Property Law*, 107 Harv. L. Rev. 859 (1994).

86 For "delineation costs," see Smith, *supra* note 4, at 1698. For "uniformity costs," see Michael W. Carroll, *One for All: The Problem of Uniformity Cost in Intellectual Property Law*, 55 Am. U. L. Rev. 845 (2006).

87 *See, e.g.*, Jeremy Waldron, The Right to Private Property (1988). *See also* Singer, *supra* note 3, at 6ff (observing that the bundle of rights model has had little impact in displacing the "ownership" model even among legally sophisticated philosophical accounts).

88 *See* Smith, *supra* note 4, at 1692–97, 1700. We should note that, as discussed above and below, Professor Smith's discussion of the "why and how" of an "*architectural* or *modular* theory of property" combine what we wish here to keep separate, namely: theoretical reasons for conceptual parsimony (e.g., simplicity and generative power) and substantive reasons for institutional parsimony (e.g., transaction costs). *See supra* note 35, *infra* note 89 and accompanying text. It is with the former that

substantive questions of positive, normative, and institutional analysis regarding the existence, content, and conferral of entitlements in any specific setting. Rather, its role should be limited to providing the conceptual focal points for such substantive analysis.[89]

We offer such an account here, of the fundamental building blocks of *all* property analysis, consisting of four elemental entitlements: use-privilege, exclusion-right, expropriation-immunity, and transfer-power. Before elaborating on the *content* of these entitlements, a word about their *status* is in order: (a) they form a conceptually tightly integrated set, starting out from the most basic one, a use-privilege, to build out to the rest in a series of close conceptual steps of correlatives and opposites, primary and secondary entitlements, which, in turn, track core underlying interests in resources; (b) this results in a theoretically powerful, indeed, generative, architecture: yielding the four primitive building blocks for all property entitlement analysis, the ones necessary and sufficient for generating all possible permutations and combinations of property buildings; and (c) they are the *differentia specifica* of all property entitlements, distinguishing the field from other areas of law.

The most basic human interest in a resource is simply to "use" it in some direct and immediate way. It is the foundational interest upon which all others are built. Indeed, there are two distinct reasons why the use-privilege is the basic unit of analysis, the primitive building block for all the rest. One has been emphasized by both sides of the debate among neo-Blackstonians: namely, the "substantive" or "external" point that, simply as a matter of human interests, the primary interest in resources is not to exclude

we are concerned here, in our effort conceptually to specify the focal points for any substantive – i.e., positive, normative, and institutional – analysis of real-world property arrangements. We bracket here the latter, substantive issues, such as how to weigh, in evaluating and shaping such arrangements, considerations of administrative simplicity against fine-grained pursuit of social policy objectives.

89 Thus, our approach is less substantive and more conceptual than most alternatives to unspooled disaggregation that have been proposed by critics of the Hohfeldian view, which take the form of an "essence" or "core" of property. Many of these accounts base their views of a core entitlement or set of entitlements in a substantive normative conception of the central interests that ought to be protected by property rights as a general matter. *See, e.g.*, Penner, *supra* note 1, at 742ff; PENNER, *supra* note 4, at 71ff; Larissa Katz, *Exclusion and Exclusivity in Property Law*, 58 U. TORONTO L.J. 275 (2008); Claeys, *supra* note 1, at 631ff (defending a "core" or "essence" of "exclusive use," centered on normative considerations of autonomy). Or, alternatively, in substantive positive-cum-normative suppositions concerning the relative merits of facilitating market-based private ordering versus directly pursuing social policy objectives. *See* Thomas W. Merrill & Henry E. Smith, *Optimal Standardization in the Law of Property: The Numerus Clausus Principle*, 110 YALE L.J. 1 (2000) (arguing for a limited menu of property forms based on "information" and "frustration" cost concerns). By contrast, our aim is simply to specify, as a conceptual matter, the elemental building blocks that are the necessary and sufficient focal points for *any* substantive account of what matters in terms of the positive, normative, and institutional analysis of the design of property rights. Much closer to our focus on conceptual, over substantive, considerations is Professor Smith's more recent emphasis on formal criteria such as simplicity and generative power in devising and evaluating theories of property's architecture. *See* Smith, *supra* note 4, at 1694–95. In our view, however, Professor Smith's category of "delineation costs" straddles the divide between more formal and substantive criteria, in part being concerned with the theoretical costs of undue complexity, which involve the loss of conceptual simplicity and generative power, and in part with more substantive costs of such complexity, in terms of real-world "information costs" in administering property rights. *See* Smith, *supra* note 4, at 1698.

others but to use ourselves.[90] But there is also a tighter, more internal-conceptual reason: you simply cannot specify the content of (the concept of) Exclusion, without first already possessing the content of (the concept of) Use. But this is not so for Use. We cannot understand what it means for A to exclude B from Y unless we already possess some notion of "what" we are excluding regarding Y. But we can understand what it means for A to "use" Y without possessing any notion of "exclusion."

If A has the legal entitlement to use resource Y, this means of course that B has no entitlement to exclude A from Y. And so we arrive at our first entitlement-disentitlement pair:

(1) (a) Use-privilege of A
which correlates with
(b) no-right of Exclusion for B

What is our next step from here? For lawyers already familiar with various contingencies and options, any number of alternative next moves suggest themselves, including: What if B *did* have an exclusion-right? What if A had a use-right? What if A had an exclusion-right? While we could build out the analysis taking any of these steps, we suggest that, in fact, the most basic and obvious next step, conceptually, is simply to ask: Can B still have a Use-privilege over Y as well? That is, not to introduce any new concepts/entitlements or persons or resources, but simply to transfer an existing known entitlement over a known resource to a known person. The answer, of course,

90 Thus, even those advancing a "right to exclude" as the "core" or "essence" of property have typically recognized that, as a substantive normative matter, interests in use are prior to, indeed provide the basis for, those in exclusion. *See* Penner, *supra* note 1, at 743 ("[U]se justifies the right, while exclusion frames the practical essence of the right."); PENNER, *supra* note 4, at 71 ("[T]he right to property is a right to exclude others from things which is grounded by the interest we have in the use of things."); Thomas W. Merrill, *Property and the Right to Exclude*, 77 NEB. L. REV. 730, 731 (1998) ("[T]he right to exclude others is a necessary and sufficient condition of identifying the existence of property."); Thomas W. Merrill, *Property and the Right to Exclude II*, 3 BRIGHAM-KANNER PROP. RTS. CONF. J. 1, 3 (2014) (agreeing with PENNER, *supra* note 4, that interests in use are a precondition for the right to exclude, while maintaining that exclusion-entitlements, not use-entitlements, are the "defining feature" of property); Smith, *supra* note at 4, at 1693 ("There is no interest in exclusion per se. Instead, . . . the right to exclude . . . serve[s] the interest in use.") (For a dissenting view, arguing that exclusion stands on its own bottom, see Arthur Ripstein, *Possession and Use*, *in* PHILOSOPHICAL FOUNDATION OF PROPERTY LAW 156 (James Penner & Henry E. Smith eds., 2013).) Others, by contrast, insist that the normative priority of use-interests should result in the conceptual priority of use-entitlements, so that the core or essence of property is conceived in terms of "exclusive use" – i.e., a bundling together (or, less charitably, a muddling as one) of the distinct Hohfeldian entitlements of a use-privilege and exclusion-right (although with less than crystalline clarity on whether the core or essential use-entitlement is to be understood in terms of a "privilege" or a "right"). *See* Claeys, *supra* note 1, at 631ff; Katz, *supra* note 89. (We should note that Professor Smith has also underlined the incompleteness of "the right to exclude" as a "linchpin" or "core" for property law, and emphasized the need to supplement it with an account of "things" as the object of property. *See* Smith, *supra* note 79. From our vantage, however, that goes to a distinct issue, concerning not what property *consists of*, but rather what property *is about* – and our reasons for preferring, in that latter respect, "resources" over "things" are briefly given below. *See infra* note 79.)

is yes: alongside A's use-privilege, coexisting simultaneously with it, we may confer upon B the same use-privilege.

At this point, the next question virtually forces itself upon us: What would it mean for only one of them to have the use-privilege? Suppose the uses in question are rivalrous of the resource and we wish only to let either A or B use it. We would then need to confer upon one of them the *opposite* of what correlates with a use-privilege: i.e., not a no-right of exclusion but an exclusion-right. Which, in turn, correlates with a no-privilege to use, or a duty to refrain from using. This results in the following two pairs of entitlements:

(1) (a) Use-privilege of A which correlates with (b) no-right of Exclusion for B	which is the opposite of	(2) (a) Exclusion-right of B which correlates with (b) no-privilege to Use for A

It is worth dwelling for a moment on the conceptual interrelations between entitlements and how they unfold. We began with a concept of an entitlement and then moved to understand what its jural *correlative* was. At that point, we had no idea – or even the need for an idea – of something called its "opposite." The move to develop a concept of the opposite of an entitlement only happens at a subsequent stage of the analysis, when we go on either (a) to ask, as a formal matter, what if B did have what they do not have here? or (b) more substantively, to inquire into a distinct new interest (what if we needed to enable B not only to use but to prevent A from using?). This point, although seemingly elementary, is quite fundamental: the failure to appreciate the conceptual centrality and priority of correlatives *over* opposites is precisely to fail to grasp the relational method of Hohfeldian analysis.[91] Foregrounding, as is often done, jural "opposites" as central to the analysis[92] – rather than understanding them as *entirely* derivative of a correlative-then-distinct-interest structure of the analysis[93] – is precisely to invite

91 For important discussions of Hohfeldian analysis in a somewhat distinct "structuralist" vein, see Jack Balkin, *The Hohfeldian Approach to Law and Semiotics*, 44 U. MIAMI L. REV. 119 (1990); Duncan Kennedy, A *Semiotics of Legal Argument*, 42 SYRACUSE L. REV. 75 (1991). Our analysis here places greater emphasis than these authors on the purposive and concretely relational – as opposed to the self-contained and generally "structuralist" – character of Hohfeldian analysis, i.e., on grounding the relevant conceptual distinctions, between discrete entitlements, in substantive judgments concerning important differences in underlying interests-in-resources, and grounding the relevant conceptual inter-relations, between correlatives, in the underlying social relations they track.

92 *See, e.g.*, Duncan Kennedy & Frank Michelman, *Are Property and Contract Efficient?* 8 HOFSTRA L. REV. 711, 752–53, 759 (1980); Joseph Singer, *The Legal Rights Debate in Analytical Jurisprudence from Bentham to Hohfeld*, WIS. L. REV. 975, 986–87 (1982). We should note that the foregrounding of opposites in these pioneering articles runs against the grain of their animating aim in recovering Hohfeldian analysis – namely, to retrieve it from the sawdust of formal taxonomies – an aim that we share and are indebted to.

93 To underline the point as clearly as we can, in contrast to a long-standing tradition of foregrounding opposites such as "right/no-right" as the center of the analysis, in our view the central relations and contrasts of significance are privilege/no-right and privilege-right, with "right/no-right" simply having no real significance at all on its own. In other words, it is not only that jural correlatives such as privilege/no-right or right/duty are conceptually prior and the central drivers of the analysis, but also

the (on our view) misleading understanding of Hohfeldian analysis as "atomistic."[94]

Returning from method to substance, we now have before us the basic quartet of Hohfeldian entitlement-disentitlements concerning resources. This quartet pertains, of course, solely to "primary" entitlements-disentitlements, meaning here entitlements (that structure relations) pertaining directly to the object or resource itself. We now continue to the second quartet of "secondary" entitlements or entitlements about entitlements.

Suppose we have conferred upon A both a use-privilege and an exclusion-right relating to a house which is now their "home." What secondary entitlement might make sense as the next step? We suggest that it is immunity from the expropriation of their primary use and exclusion entitlements, to protect their interest in "security" in holding said entitlements regarding their home. What good is it to enjoy use and exclusion regarding one's home on Monday without any security that these entitlements cannot simply be "taken" on Tuesday by either a private person or the state? This brings us to our third entitlement-disentitlement pair:

(3) (a) Expropriation-immunity (of A)
which correlates with
(b) No-power/disability to transfer (of other private persons or state)

And, again, we face the ineluctable question: what if A did not have this entitlement or, at least, not against all parties? What if, for instance, we conferred upon A this entitlement only against private persons, but not against the state? We would then arrive at a fourth pair:

(4) (a) Transfer-power (of the state)
which correlates with
(b) Liability (vulnerability-to-loss) (of A)

An interesting feature of this analysis is that it resolves, at least for this pair, the puzzle raised long ago by Walter Wheeler Cook and Arthur Corbin as to whether a Hohfeldian "liability" or exposure of B, correlating with the transfer power of A, is really a "disadvantage" – since often B is the one in a position to receive the

that jural opposites are not even of secondary significance on their own: they are merely the connective tissue between two distinct pairs of jural correlatives, as shown in our basic quartet of primary entitlement-disentitlements above. The important relations or contrasts are: (a) first, the inter-relations between jural correlatives (privilege/no-right, right/duty); and (b) next, the distinctions between different pairs of correlatives (privilege versus right). Jural opposites such as right/no-right are of unclear import standing alone.

94 *See* Smith, *supra* note 39 (treating Hohfeldian analysis as "atomistic"); Schlag, *supra* note 11, at 218–33 (accepting the characterization of Hohfeldian analysis as atomistic, but defending it against some perils associated with atomism).

entitlement.[95] Here, however, the liability correlating to the state's transfer power is that of A, who is vulnerable to having their primary entitlements transferred away. This, clearly, is a disadvantage to, or burdening of, A's interests. Hence, at least for this correlative pair, the Cook–Corbin puzzle is solved.

This completes our analysis of the four fundamental building block entitlement-disentitlement pairs of property, those necessary and sufficient for generating all permutations and combinations of property structures – the *differentia specifica* of property as a legal form.[96]

5.5 CONCLUSION

Imagine a property law casebook organized around the interaction of two levels of analysis: (1) the "stuff of the world," as broken down into resource-specific categories conceived in terms of their (im)material characteristics, human interests, and social significance; and (2) the "building blocks of society" conceived in terms of the fundamental entitlement options necessary and sufficient for constructing all the legal architectures of social relations regarding resources. That such a curriculum is even now – a full century after Hohfeld – only a glimmer on the horizon is one measure of the distance by which this pioneer's thoughts outstripped his world. To honor his legacy would be to bridge that gap.

95 *See* Walter Wheeler Cook, *Introduction: Hohfeld's Contribution to the Science of Law*, *in* FUNDAMENTAL LEGAL CONCEPTIONS 8 (Walter Wheeler Cook ed., 1919); Arthur Corbin, *Legal Analysis and Terminology*, 29 YALE L.J. 163, 169 (1921).

96 To be sure, this is only the barest sketch both of the content of the elemental entitlements and of their architectural status. Regarding their content, what is important to underline is that our analysis does *not* provide any argument in favor of or against the existence, shape, or conferral of any of these entitlements, either singly or in their combined configuration, in any specific setting. That of course is the work of concrete legal analysis and institutional design, ideally sensitive to the distinct contexts and purposes implicated by different resources in terms of the positive, normative, and strategic concerns they raise. And it is indeed precisely our aim here *not* to prejudge such substantive analysis, but rather simply to furnish the indispensable focal points for organizing the inquiry. Regarding their architectural status, a further step of institutional analysis, not undertaken here, would be to specify not only how these elements may be used as fundamental building blocks in the configuration of all specific ensembles of property rights, but also how such ensembles may then usefully be conceived and labeled as belonging to larger families of, e.g., "private," versus "commons" versus "public" property regimes. Or, to move even further afield, to specify when an institutional regime for structuring the allocation, production, and distribution of resources may be said to leave "property" altogether (as it might be said, for instance, of "prize" system alternatives to patent rights). These are matters for another day. *See* Syed, *supra* note 42.

6

The *In Rem/In Personam* Distinction and Conceptual Partitioning for Persistence

Shyamkrishna Balganesh[*] *and Leo Katz*[**]

6.1 INTRODUCTION

In the second of his two famous articles, Hohfeld seeks to do for the *in rem/in personam* distinction what he did so persuasively in his first for the terminology of rights, claims, duties, privileges, powers, immunities, and disabilities, which was to identify their essence, and to thereby describe the "natural kind" (in more modern parlance) lurking beneath the thicket of confused juristic rhetoric.[1] The thesis in this second article, however, is a simpler and in some way more beguiling one than in his first. He claims that what the distinction between *in rem* and *in personam* jural relations comes down to is the contrast between what he calls "multital" and "paucital" relationships.[2]

The paradigmatic case of an *in personam* relationship is that of a contract between two parties. The paradigmatic case of an *in rem* relationship is that which the owner of a piece of land has to the rest of the world, through such property. The fundamental distinction between the two, as Hohfeld sees it, is that the *in personam* relationship is with a single party, whereas the property relationship is with a multiplicity of parties, albeit on identical terms with every one of them, i.e., a relationship consisting of the right to exclude each of them from the property. He calls this last relationship multital and the first one paucital. Multitality versus paucitality – that is what he thinks the *in rem/in personam* distinction comes to: Having a right against one person, or having a set of identical rights, typically of the right-to-exclude variety, against a group of persons.[3]

* Sol Goldman Professor of Law, Columbia Law School.

** Frank Carano Professor of Law, University of Pennsylvania Carey Law School.

1 *See* Wesley N. Hohfeld, *Some Fundamental Legal Conceptions as Applied in Judicial Reasoning*, 23 Yale L.J. 16 (1913).

2 *See* Wesley N. Hohfeld, *Fundamental Legal Conceptions as Applied in Judicial Reasoning*, 26 Yale L.J. 710, 712 (1917).

3 *Id.* at 718–20.

Numerosity, therefore, appears to be the primary distinguishing feature for Hohfeld. Yet, connected to this numerosity is an additional dimension: namely, the indefiniteness of the group on one side of the *in rem* relationship. While clearly a consequence of the numerosity, this indefiniteness introduces a qualitative aspect into the distinction, something that others have elaborated on since.[4]

While numerosity and indefiniteness are certainly typical of the distinction between contractual relations and those generated by property rights, we will argue that Hohfeld was perhaps a little too quick to suggest that this is all that there is analytically in the *in rem/in personam* distinction. In particular, our claim is that the *in rem/in personam* distinction is epiphenomenal of a more basic conceptual phenomenon that the distinction represents, best described as "persistence." In this Essay, we will argue that the contrast between multitality and paucitality as Hohfeld sets them out does not fully capture the conceptual roots of the *in rem/in personam* distinction. Instead, we show how the general idea of persistence, manifested in particular rights and relationships generates the *in rem/in personam* distinction, even though courts and scholars routinely treat the former distinction as caused by the latter. In so doing, we will argue that the idea of persistence is closely related to courts' efforts to engage, classify, and prioritize among different relationship sets, within different contexts. Persistence as a classificatory ideal is therefore closely related to the idea of conceptual sequencing, made prominent by Bruce Chapman some years ago.

We divide our argument into four sections. Section 6.2 sets out the idea of persistence, tracing it to the law's treatment of priorities in property contexts, and its efforts to partition the relationships differentially. Section 6.3 connects this prioritization produced by the ideal of persistence to the process of conceptual sequencing or partitioning. Section 6.4 then reveals how both persistence and partitioning are significantly more commonplace than is originally believed, and that the property/contract distinction that Hohfeld relied on is representative of the distinction, but hardly exhaustive of it. Finally, Section 6.5 offers some thoughts on how the law chooses between different perspectives while partitioning the inquiry.

6.2 THE SEARCH FOR PERSISTENCE

The first steps in the direction of the account that we propose to give were taken by Ben McFarlane in his treatise *The Structure of Property Law*.[5] McFarlane does two things that we think help considerably in understanding the phenomenon underlying the *in rem/in personam* distinction. He puts something at the center of property

[4] *Id.* at 718. Albert Kocourek was perhaps the earliest to explicitly identify the significance of the idea. *See* Albert Kocourek, *Rights In Rem*, 68 U. PA. L. REV. 332, 332–33 (1920). For a more recent elucidation, see Thomas W. Merrill & Henry E. Smith, *The Property/Contract Interface*, 101 COLUM. L. REV. 773, 783–86 (2001).

[5] BEN MCFARLANE, THE STRUCTURE OF PROPERTY LAW (2008).

law that usually is cast in a more supporting role, namely, the *triangular* nature of the most important property disputes.

His standard examples are like the following: "A has an account with Z Bank. A goes into bankruptcy. A's rights, including his bank account, therefore pass to C, A's trustee in bankruptcy. C is under a statutory duty to use A's rights, including A's bank account, to pay off A's creditors. However, B claims that, before going bankrupt, A declared a trust in B's favor, of A's bank account."[6]

In this hypothetical, B now has what McFarlane calls a "persistent right" against C, and the creditors that C represents.[7] This idea, that of a "persistent right," is in our view, key to understanding the *in rem/in personam* distinction. McFarlane goes to some length to define a persistent right as a "right against a right" and to distinguish it from a regular *in rem* relationship. Much of this is prompted by his effort to characterize the nature of the relationships that emerge in equity.[8]

While we adopt McFarlane's idea of persistent rights, our point is not to distinguish it from *in rem* rights. The concept of persistent rights, to us, captures the essence of why the law seeks to prioritize one set of relationships (or one right) over others in different triangular settings. Our point is therefore that what makes something a *persistent* right will vary by setting and that the persistent quality that the law is looking for in various contexts will be motivated by different normative considerations. Property rights all have this persistent quality by virtue of being tied to a tangible object, the *res*, which both mediates and anchors the relationship(s). In the hypothetical above, we could replace the trust in favor of B with a valid transfer in favor of B (of possession and title), to produce the same result. B's right is now seen as qualitatively different from C's. And so it is with the declaration of a trust too, which is seen to have a persistent quality as well, which causes the law to treat it as proprietary (*in rem*).

The persistent right is in contrast to a more symmetrical set of claims by the various parties competing for A's assets. The symmetrical and interchangeable nature of these claims gives them a distinctively nonpersistent quality, which we believe underlies the characterization as *in personam*. The notion/quality of persistence captures the distinction in an important way, insofar as it suggests that the normative basis for the right is impervious – in part or in whole – to the immediate interactions of the parties.

To be clear, we do not suggest that the notion of persistence has a verifiable epistemic component in all situations, nor that it is driven by a common normative goal. Our point is quite the opposite. It is that the idea of persistence is an aspirational ideal that the law attempts to realize in different settings where there

6 *Id.* at 12.

7 *Id.* at 23–27.

8 *See, e.g.*, Ben McFarlane, *Equity, Obligations, and Third Parties*, 2008 Sing. J. Legal Stud. 308 (2008); Simon Gardner, *"Persistent Rights" Appraised*, *in* 7 Modern Studies in Property Law 321 (Nicholas Hopkins ed., 2013).

are competing claims/rights, causing it to prioritize among them in different ways. In property law, it is ordained by the "thing" and representations of it, which explains why Hohfeld took property rights to be paradigmatic of *in rem* relationships.

But we think that this only goes so far, and that what the law is groping for, somewhat uncertainly, and not quite coherently under this notion that we describe as persistence, is something far more general than the thingness seen in the context of property. We further believe that this search for persistence is best captured by a neat idea introduced by Bruce Chapman, which is encapsulated in two pieces of vocabulary he introduces: "partitioning" and "conceptual sequencing," which we find useful to blend into "conceptual partitioning," to which we next turn.[9]

6.3 CONCEPTUAL PARTITIONING AS THE SEARCH FOR PERSISTENCE

Conceptual sequencing and the partitioning of a decision refers to a rational process that decision-makers – within the law and beyond – routinely use to avoid the problem of cycling among choices. It enables the decision-maker to prioritize between alternatives in sequenced pairs, thereby rendering the decision process rational and at the same time suggesting a partial solution to the problem of intransitivity.

Drawing on this idea, we argue that when presented with triangular relationships, courts have different ways to partition the choice so as to sequence the comparisons between competing rights. Of these, one method generally favors identifying one right/relationship as pivotal to the adjudication and then comparing that right/relationship to the others. This is in contrast to other methods of partitioning that do not accord such primacy to one right/relationship, but instead treat all the claims as being largely equivalent. We call the first approach "persistent partitioning" and the latter "symmetrical partitioning." Our claim is that in different areas of the law, the process of persistent partitioning produces results analogous to those generated by *in rem* rights when prioritized in property law.

To understand the idea of partitioning, we draw on the work of Bruce Chapman. Chapman's point of departure is an example first presented by Amartya Sen for a purpose different from the one to which Chapman puts it. Sen was interested in showing how an entirely rational person might nonetheless engage in what behavioral economists tend to regard as the essence of irrationality, namely an intransitive set of choices.[10] To this end, he asks us to imagine someone presented with a set of hypothetical dessert choices at a dinner party. Hypothetical choice number 1 is between a small apple (sA) and an orange (O). Let us suppose he would choose the

9 Bruce Chapman, *Law, Incommensurability, and Conceptually Sequenced Argument*, 146 U. Pa. L. Rev. 1487 (1998).

10 Amartya K. Sen, Collective Choice and Social Welfare (1970).

orange (O). Hypothetical choice number 2 is between an orange and a large apple (lA). Let us suppose he would choose the large apple.

Choice 1: O > sA
Choice 2: lA > O

Hypothetical choice number 3 is between the small apple (sA) and the large apple (lA). Now, if the chooser's choices were transitive, we would expect him to choose the large apple, since he has previously chosen the orange over the small apple, and the large apple over the orange. (We might possibly expect this to be because of size, with the orange positioned between the two apples.) But suppose we actually observe him choosing the small apple?

Choice 3: sA > lA (intransitive)

How do we make sense of this choice? Quite possibly, for the simple reason that he might feel that as a matter of etiquette he cannot choose the larger of the two apples. In this way, intransitivity can arise in a perfectly mundane way and without any seeming irrationality. So far Sen.

Chapman is interested in different aspects of this example (which we will present in a slightly different way than he does).[11] Suppose the chooser is presented with the choice between all three fruits. Which one should he choose – assuming that he has the same preferences as before and the same reluctance to violate etiquette? That will depend, as Chapman points out, on how the chooser "partitions" and "conceptually sequences" those choices, based on the incommensurable criteria of *size* and *etiquette*. Here is what Chapman means by that. Suppose the chooser first focuses on the small apple/big apple pair, and thereby on etiquette. He decides that as between them he is obligated to take the small apple. Having chosen the small apple over the large apple he next compares it to the orange. As between those two, he decides to take the orange because of its size, without any rule of etiquette standing in the way. Thus, he ends up taking the orange. That would be one way of going about it.

But there are others. He might for instance choose to partition off the small apple/orange pair first, and prioritize size first. As between those two, he prefers the orange. Next he compares that alternative to the large apple, which he prefers based on size and is able to choose because no rule of etiquette requires him to choose the orange over the large apple. Thus he ends up with the large apple.

He might also try a third way of partitioning the choice. He could first consider the large apple/orange combination. As between those, he would choose the large apple, given his preference for size. Next he compares the large apple to the small apple, and there he would feel compelled to choose the small apple, given his respect for etiquette. Thus he would end up with the small apple.

[11] For Chapman's account, see Chapman, *supra* note 9, at 1496–1500.

There are other possibilities. He might consider all three alternatives simultaneously. Looking at them together, he might decide that etiquette precludes his choosing the larger of two smaller fruits, and thus end up choosing the orange (which he prefers to the only apple he would feel entitled to take). He might also weigh the three possibilities in a more artificial fashion yet, noting that what was to be said in favor of the large apple is that he liked it best, but that what counted against it was the presence of the smaller apple and the rule of etiquette. He might note that what was to be said in favor of the orange was that in taking it he would not be offending any rule of etiquette and he liked it well enough, but what cut against it was that he would be giving up on his most preferred option, the large apple. Finally he might note that what was to be said in favor of the small apple was that he would not be breaking a rule of etiquette, but in that regard it was no better than the orange, and he liked oranges better than small apples. In this way, he might end up considering the large apple and the orange tied.

Whether or not you think this cycle is a genuine problem, the more interesting thing we want to focus on here is the way in which the decision will be shaped by the way that the decision-maker "conceptually partitions" his choices and prioritizes the criterion of decision-making. Another example of the same ilk, in some ways the most realistic, is the familiar case of circular priorities, which arises in all contexts in which acquired interests are subject to a recording requirement. The classic scenario is the following. A acquires some land from O, and fails to record it as he is supposed to. O next sells the same land to B, who actually has heard that O previously sold it to A, but somehow ignores that fact, and records his purchase. Finally, O sells the land yet a third time, this time to C, who pays no attention to the existence of B's recorded claim. Now a court has to decide between the three claimants. Once again, how we sequence and partition the choices will be determinative of the outcome.[12]

All of this will remind people of the famous voting paradox, and the similarities are certainly there and worth spelling out more fully.[13] Imagine there to be three candidates running for office. One third of the electorate puts candidate A first, candidate B second, and candidate C third. Another third of the electorate puts B first, C second, and A third. The last third of the electorate puts C first, A second, and B third. Who should prevail? The paradox arises because one might proceed to partition things as follows. First, we compare A and B. A would beat B by a two-thirds majority, therefore, it seems A should prevail as between the two. Second, we compare the winner A to C. In a contest between the two, two-thirds of the voters

12 For prior literature on circular priorities in property law, see 4 James Casner, American Law of Property § 17.33 (1977); Carville D. Benson, Jr., *Circuity of Lien: A Problem in Priorities*, 19 Minn. L. Rev. 139, 153 (1935); Albert Kocourek, *Note, Diversities De La Ley: A First-Rate Legal Puzzle – A Problem in Priorities*, 29 Ill. L. Rev. 952, 955 (1935). *See also* 2 Grant Gilmore, Security Interests In Personal Property 1020–46 (1965).

13 *See* Leo Katz, Why the Law Is So Perverse 93–106 (2011).

would vote for C. Therefore, C will be the winner. Suppose instead we had partitioned things so as to start by running B against C. Now B would win, by a two-thirds majority. Next, we pit A against B and A would prevail. Third, we could start by first pitting A against C, and the winner, C, against B, and in that way B would be the winner. Finally, we could consider all three candidates simultaneously and then it would seem that it is a tie as between all of them since each is ranked first by one third of the electorate, second by one third, and third by another third. Once again, partitioning and sequencing determine the outcome.

What does all of this have to do with *in rem/in personam*? Our simple point is that the distinction routinely arises in triangular property situations and, when it does, *the decision-maker's preference for the* in rem *is but representative of the impulse to partition the inquiry in a way that accords primacy to identifying the most persistent right.*[14]

Let us consider McFarlane's property example again:

> A has an account with Z Bank. A goes into bankruptcy. A's rights, including his bank account, therefore pass to C, A's trustee in bankruptcy. C is under a statutory duty to use A's rights, including A's bank account, to pay off A's creditors. However, B claims that, before going bankrupt, A declared a trust in B's favor, of A's bank account.

Let us now consider several different ways of partitioning this three-way constellation. One is to start with the pair of A and B. As between them, B prevails because A is holding the property in trust for him. As between C and B, C is asking B to give up something he owns for the benefit of some other people who happen to have unsatisfied claims against A, which does not sound like a compelling request. In this sequencing of the decision-making, the adjudication has clearly exhibited a preference for the persistent right (B's right) over the others. An alternative of course is to consider all claimants at once: A, B, and C. Here, B and C will seem in something of a tie as against A. Each has a claim against A, one of them is temporally prior to the other, but it is not clear why there is any magical significance to that. That is the symmetrical way of looking at things, which does not exhibit the

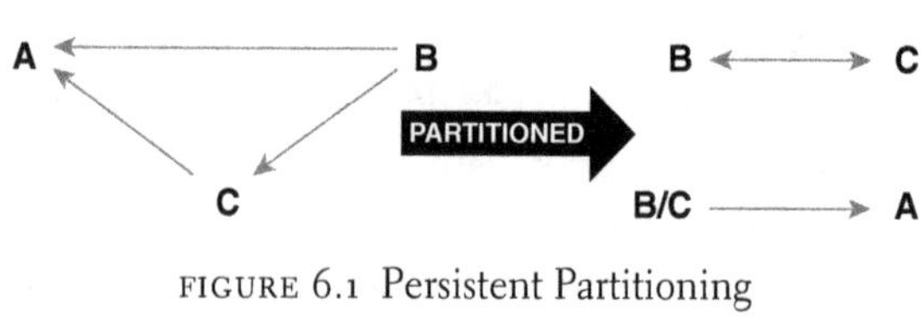

FIGURE 6.1 Persistent Partitioning

[14] For a contrasting argument on the law's use of the *in rem* strategy within property law, see BENITO ARRUÑADA, INSTITUTIONAL FOUNDATIONS OF IMPERSONAL EXCHANGE: THEORY AND POLICY OF CONTRACTUAL REGISTRIES 21–24 (2012). Arruñada's central argument is that property law forms the "institutional foundation for impersonal exchange" through its deployment of *in rem* rights in lieu of *in personam* ones. *Id.* at 24.

preference to persistence. We could try other ways of partitioning, but none of those in this particular case turn out to have much plausibility.

What this example illustrates is that, in different triangular settings, the law (or courts) have the option of partitioning the inquiry in different ways. One way of doing it accords primacy to the persistent right and prioritizes the identification of that right before comparing it with competing claims. The property example illustrates this. This approach might be best described as *persistent partitioning* or as partitioning for persistence.

The same problem however arises in many other legal contexts. In some of these, our claim is that the courts are grappling with the identification of a right that is seen as the most persistent, equivalent to the ownership interest in property cases. In others, they perhaps choose not to do so – for overriding considerations. The phenomenon is, therefore, a larger one, of which the distinction between *in rem/ in personam* in the property context is but a special case.[15]

6.4 PERSISTENT (AND NONPERSISTENT) PARTITIONING BEYOND PROPERTY

Looking beyond property law, where the law prioritizes the search for the persistent right (*in rem* right) over other nonpersistent claims, we see that largely identical patterns exist in a variety of other situations as well. As we shall see, in many contexts this is *not* how we (or the law) conceptualize the dispute or the matter in partitioning the inquiry. Our claim here is not that in these situations where the law can prioritize the persistent right over nonpersistent claims that it actually does so or should do so. Instead, our point is a simple one. Namely, that the law might so choose to if it were to be driven by normative considerations that suggest according primacy to the persistent right. In a variety of situations, the law simply does not seem to be driven in this manner and instead appears to be motivated by other considerations.

This may certainly suggest a strong preference for persistence within the context of property. But in revealing that the element of persistency is not ubiquitous to property, it suggests that property's *in rem* rights should not be taken to be exhaustive of the category.

Given that the idea of persistence, at its roots, represents the notion of a "right against a right" or of the law's accordance of normative superiority to one right over another, a question that might be asked is whether persistence itself embodies a (Hohfeldian) jural relation of a kind. And here, we fail to see an appropriate Hohfeldian analog, i.e., one that would encumber one claim-right by recognizing

[15] For a different account within property law, see James Stern, *The Essential Structure of Property Law*, 115 MICH. L. REV. 1167, 1183–85 (2017) (arguing that the principle of "mutual exclusivity" explains property law's accordance of primacy to one right in different contexts and its concomitant classification as a property right).

the normative (and conceptual) primacy of another. The idea of "defeasibility," developed by some scholars of rights and logic perhaps comes closest but it too remains an incomplete characterization of persistence.[16] Whereas defeasibility merely suggests that a nonpersistent right is capable of being defeated by a persistent one in various contexts, it says little about the nature of the encumbrances that the latter places on the former. In this sense, we therefore suggest that persistence is a somewhat *sui generis* characteristic and worthy of consideration on its own terms.

6.4.1 *Libel*

There is something paradoxical about libel that no one in general seems to pay much attention to and it has to do with the different ways in which the tort can be partitioned, depending on how one prioritizes the parties' relationships. The usual way we think about libel is this: there is a tortfeasor, the Libeler, who spreads lies about the Victim, which are received by the audience of the libel who then modify their conduct toward the Victim in ways that are disadvantageous to him. It seems straightforward that there should be liability for such harms just as there should be for other wrongful conduct that results in harm to someone.[17] But that is not the only way to look at the matter.

What is the alternative way of looking at the situation? To see it, let us consider a highly stylized case of libel. In due course we will see that despite being stylized it is, in fact, not as artificial or unrealistic or uncommon as it at first appears. Imagine two friends who like to email each other scandalous, salacious gossip about other people. Not infrequently they embellish what they have heard. They do not much care whether what they are sending each other is likely to be true or not. They want to be entertained and to be entertaining. Sometimes, they even make stuff up out of whole cloth, just to see if it will go over. They rarely correct anything they have sent. It is just not important to them, given their focus on entertainment.

Now, let us suppose that one such email message contains some extremely unflattering facts, which we need not bother to specify, about someone we will simply call Victim. The message is a total fabrication by one of the friends, whom we will call from here on out Defendant. The other friend we will call Friend. Well, Friend, the recipient of this unflattering information decides he does not want to do business any longer with someone who might have done what Defendant has told him Victim did. To be sure, he knows that Defendant might have made the whole thing up, but he just does not care. It is enough for him that it *might* be true. There are other firms offering the same service at the same price. He has no reason not to just switch to them. Victim learns of this and sues Defendant. At first, the matter

16 *See* Frederick Schauer, *On the Supposed Defeasibility of Legal Rules*, 51 Current Legal Probs. 223 (1998).

17 *See* Dan B. Dobbs et al., The Law of Torts § 519 (2d ed. 2015).

seems straightforward. Defendant did something that proximately caused injury to Victim. It seems totally intuitive that Defendant should be held liable. This is the ordinary way in which defamation law approaches the matter.

But that is not the only way to look at it. The fact is that the two friends have agreed to tell each other lies and are each perfectly willing to take action that may well be erroneous on the basis of those lies. What is more, Friend is completely within his rights to take his business elsewhere and not use Victim's services. He does not mind being deflected from Victim's doorstep by false information that Defendant has fed him. Therefore, what legitimate ground does Victim have for complaining?

It is worth noting that this is not as exotic an example as it seems. One suspects that the relationship most readers have with the *National Inquirer* or other tabloids is much like the relationship that Defendant and Friend have with each other: to be entertained regularly, albeit with fabrications on occasion. Readers of such publications understand that they are being fed information that will have only an intermittent connection with the truth (e.g., *The Onion*), but that as a result they are going to be a great deal more entertained and they like it that way. They also understand if they take any action on the basis of that information they may well be doing someone else an injustice, but that is their good right and they do not mind. Viewed in this way, it is not at all clear what right Victim should have to complain about anything and to seek any redress from Defendant.

What is more, the problem arises even in cases in which the audience to the libel did not so unequivocally consent to being deceived. In fact, let us suppose that Friend's arrangement with Defendant is one in which he expects him to tell the truth, or at least make a reasonable effort to do so, and Defendant is very much in breach of that expectation when he does not. Has the objection to holding him liable gone away? No, not really, or at least not entirely. Let us suppose that, upon discovering how upset Friend is with having been deflected from doing business with Victim, Defendant decides to compensate Friend for that loss and does that so generously that, in retrospect, Friend no longer minds having been lied to. In fact, he is happy to have received the money and to not have done business with Victim's firm, all things considered. What this leads one to is the conclusion that the only person who should legitimately claim damages in case of libel is the audience for the libel, not the victim of the action that the audience of the libel then takes.

Yet, that is not how we usually proceed. It is not the perspective on the matter that the law usually takes. For our purposes, it does not matter if one perspective is right or wrong or, indeed, the normative reasons for the law's own position. The thing we want to note prominently, however, is that what is being rejected, the competing perspective, is what we have described as persistent partitioning. Recall that what the primacy of the *in rem* right in property seems to do is to sort out the relationship between two parties and, having done so, then proceeds to evaluate the claims of the third party in light of that initial sorting out between the two parties. This "rebel" persistent perspective on libel would do the same thing. It would begin by sorting things out between the Defendant and Friend by identifying which of them has an interest that was affected by the falsity, and only after having done so decide on what claim the third party, the Victim, should have. In so doing, it prioritizes the reality that the most direct harm – from the falsehood – is sustained by the recipient of it. The causal perspective (the current or nonpersistent perspective) pretty much rejects this way of prioritizing things and proceeds, instead, in a manner more reminiscent of the *in personam* approach that looks at all claims simultaneously and symmetrically.

In this example (and in the others that follow), it might well be asked whether the distinction being drawn here is one between an *in rem* and an *in personam* perspective or, instead, whether they merely represent two *alternate* ways of characterizing a persistent approach. Indeed, what makes the libel law's current framework implausible as a persistent approach is its willingness to sequence the inquiry in a manner that accords primacy to Defendant's right over Victim's (both against Friend). Had that been the case – such that, for instance, Defendant's claim would functionally (or conceptually) address Victim's harm (say either through a sharing of the recovery or by precluding an action), it might be plausible to suggest that it too was a persistent approach. The fact that the law fails to even consider such primacy therefore renders it nonpersistent in our characterization.

6.4.2 *Products Liability*

This hidden persistent perspective can be found in other places. An interesting – and historically important – instance of it is seen in the creation of products liability in the early part of the twentieth century, wherein the doctrine of privity was jettisoned in favor of liability. Before Cardozo more or less inaugurated products liability with his opinion in *MacPherson v. Buick Motor Co.*,[18] the prevailing view of such cases had a distinctively *in rem* cast, i.e., in prioritizing the persistent right.

Consider the standard case in which the question arose. Manufacturer sold Retailer the defective product. He warranted it to have certain attributes (i.e., that it be nondefective), and he was prepared to be held liable for any way in which it fell short of that warranty. Sometimes of course he made no warranties, but sold it "as is." Next, Retailer sells the product to Consumer with whatever warranty Consumer insists on. The perspective that courts used to find the most natural for thinking about this case was to first sort out the claims between the Manufacturer and the Retailer, and then grant the Retailer whatever remedy he might be entitled to if the product he was sold turned out to have a problem, and next to sort out the claims the Consumer might have against the Retailer. To be sure, the Retailer's liability to the Consumer might have repercussions for the damages that Retailer could then claim from Manufacturer

[18] *MacPherson* v. *Buick Motor Co.*, 111 N.E. 1050 (N.Y. 1916).

(e.g., to avoid a double recovery), but the Consumer had no direct claim against the Manufacturer.

In the persistent perspective, the law is essentially prioritizing the bilateral relationship between Manufacturer and Retailer over the harm sustained by the Consumer. Something about that relationship – and the harm sustained by the Retailer from it (perhaps the breach of the promise that it entails?) – takes priority over the injury sustained by the Consumer. The alternative perspective chosen by Cardozo was the "causal" one also adopted in the libel cases, wherein the Consumer's claims against the Retailer and the Manufacturer were treated as symmetrical as a structural matter. Manufacturer did something that caused harm to the Consumer and should, therefore, have to pay for it.

It is easy to overlook just how plausible the persistent perspective in fact is. If we think of the Manufacturer's damage payments to the Retailer as essentially curing the wrong, then, as in the libel case, there simply is no wrongful conduct left on which to pin the Consumer's claim against him. To make the case against him, Consumer would need to be able to say that his harm eventuated from some sort of wrongful conduct, but Retailer having been compensated, there really is none. Note, how Cardozo's refusal to look at things this way (i.e., and find that Manufacturer owes a duty only to Retailer and not Consumer) conflicts with the perspective he takes in his famous *Palsgraf* opinion,[19] in which he insists that the only negligence victim entitled to damages was the one in relation to whom the duty-breaching conduct occurred and concludes that the plaintiff was owed no duty of care by the railroad company.[20] The persistent perspective is basically the relational perspective he considered imperative in that case.

6.4.3 *Intentional Interference with Contractual Relations*

Consider an ordinary case of intentionally induced contract breach. That is, promisor has entered into a contract with promisee. Along comes a third party who – with full knowledge of the existing contract between the promisor and promisee – persuades promisor to sell whatever he promised to promisee to him instead.[21] Should the aggrieved promisee now have a cause of action against the interfering third party? The debate about this question is what makes intentional interference with contractual

19 *See Palsgraf* v. *Long Island R.R. Co.*, 248 N.Y. 339, 345, 162 N.E. 99, 101 (1928).

20 Scholars argue that Cardozo's positions in *MacPherson* and *Buick* can be reconciled in so far as he was attempting to identify "relational" duties or care (rather than universal) ones in both cases. *See* John C. P. Goldberg & Benjamin C. Zipursky, *The Moral of MacPherson*, 146 U. Pa. L. Rev. 1733, 1813–14 (1998). Yet these scholars too conclude that he located a duty in one but not the other, and did so in the former because of prior precedent that enabled the finding. *Id.* at 1814. Our point here is not to dispute the analytical consistency of Cardozo's search for a relational duty. It is, instead, to note that his basis for finding it in one case – *Palsgraf* – reflects an adoption of the persistent approach and its prioritization of one relationship (the victim-package owner one) over the other (the victim-railroad company one).

21 Dobbs et al., *supra* note 17, at § 619.

relations such a controversial doctrine. The debate can be effectively recast as one about choice of partitions.

One way of proceeding would be to partition the inquiry by first sorting out the bilateral relationship between the promisor and promisee and then dealing with the third party's interference. This approach would track the *in rem* perspective. Such sorting out might involve having the promisor pay damages to the promisee, such that the promisee is no longer in a position to complain about being the victim of wrongful conduct and, thus, without any basis on which to launch a claim against the interfering third party. In this persistent perspective, the inquiry would be prioritizing the contractual relationship (and the obligations that it generates between the parties) over the weaker interest that either have against the third party. The nonpersistence perspective, i.e., resembling the *in personam* approach, would involve looking at all parties simultaneously, focusing on the causal connection between the third party's actions and the injury suffered by the promisee, and thus imposing liability on the third party.

Much of the decades-long controversy surrounding tortious interference with a contract can be explained as a product of the law's equivocation between these two perspectives in partitioning. Critics of the tort have long insisted that the contractual obligations generated by the triangular structure are qualitatively different from (and more important than) any that the third party might have, in effect adopting the persistent perspective. Supporters have demurred by arguing that, even if this were true, those obligations are not purely bilateral but, instead, extend to third parties as well. In so doing, these supporters have even, on occasion, invoked the logic of *in rem* obligations to note how the contract casts an obligation on everyone in the world to respect its existence. A modern resolution of the impasse, albeit a somewhat fragile one, has produced a somewhat modified tort wherein the law does identify an obligation in third parties, but only when third parties act using "improper means."[22]

6.5 THE CHOICE OF PARTITION

Therefore, we can see that, in different contexts, courts have the option of choosing between persistent partitioning and symmetrical partitioning of the inquiry. The former produces a framework that largely resembles the manner in which property law prioritizes *in rem* rights/relationships over *in personam* ones.

Thus far, we have said nothing about the motivations behind the law's (i.e., courts') choice of partition perspective which, as we have seen, makes a world of difference to the outcome in many areas. All that we note here is that the choice does not reflect a generalizable pattern, as such, and is most often influenced by the law's consideration of competing normative values in the substantive area (and individual case) and its decision to treat one (or one set) as persistent. The choice is, therefore, far from arbitrary.

[22] *Id.*

An additional complication is that a particular choice, while suitable to the resolution of a particular problem, may prove unpalatable when extended as a logical matter to cognate situations. Consider, for example, intentional interference with contractual relations. Many people support the doctrine by suggesting that we have the option to partition things in such a way as to regard a contractual claim as a form of property, which is enveloped by the right to exclude that the third party's interference violates.[23] The problem with this simple solution is that this way of partitioning things classifies as "property" something that for other purposes we would be extremely reluctant to treat in this manner. We do not so treat it for the purposes of the *numerus clausus*, or importantly we do not so treat it for purposes of the law of self-defense, or a variety of other legal doctrines in which classifying something as a "property" interest as opposed to a mere promissory or even lesser interest, or as a greater interest (such as the one we have in our bodily integrity) greatly matters. The law is therefore far more comfortable adopting the nonpersistent partitioning in products liability cases than it is for tortious interference, which continues to grapple with its analytical bases.

We also note that the choice of partition, while path dependent within a context, is nonetheless capable of being changed over time. And here, we conjecture that at least one variable that will be of consideration in such a shift will be the level of persistence seen (by the decision-maker) in one or more of the relationships under consideration. Again, we define the idea of persistence somewhat nebulously to cover situations where the relationship is externally influenced or mandated. When this occurs, we should not be surprised to see a change in the partitioning perspective adopted in different areas. For instance, should we move to a system (one day perhaps) when *all* contractual obligations have, as an additional prerequisite for their validity, a mandatory registration/recordation, we might indeed expect the law to become more willing to adopt what is right now the nonpersistent partitioning in dealing with tortious interference, since the mandatory registration (notice) would inject a new element of persistence into the equation. What this indelibly points to then, is that the notion of persistence itself may be contextual and changing.

6.6 CONCLUSION

In this Essay, we have sought to make two claims. The first is that the *in rem/in personam* distinction might indeed entail more than just the property/contract difference contained in the ideas of numerosity (of parties) and indefiniteness (of the parties' identities). Instead, we claim that the distinction derives from a focus on the idea of persistence, wherein one right, relationship, or obligation between parties acquires significantly greater salience than the others owing to factors external to the right, relationship or obligation itself. For property, this emanates

[23] *Id.* at §§ 622–30.

from the thing-ness of the owner-resource relationship, which was of course a confusion that Hohfeld's terminology itself sought to minimize.

Hohfeld examined the *in rem/in personam* distinction in isolation and in doing so likely overlooked the extent to which it interacts with and/or was reflective of other distinctions embedded in the analytical framework of law. Indeed, Hohfeld readily acknowledged this early on in his account, when he identified a variety of other "overspreading classifications" in the law, but "confined" himself to the *in rem/in personam* one "owing to limitations of space."[24] Of the other classifications that he identified by name, one in particular might have encompassed the idea of persistence if Hohfeld had developed it further: the distinction between "common" and "special" relations.[25] Had this been developed, perhaps Hohfeld too would have readily recognized that the distinctions were themselves interrelated and overlapping in some measure. Yet this is all speculation, given that Hohfeld's untimely death never enabled him to develop these promising ideas further. His account of the *in rem/in personam* therefore limited itself to the property/contract distinction. And here too, as others have pointed out,[26] Hohfeld's arguments underplayed the role of the *res* in mediating the human relationship at stake and in the process. We argue that this extends to the element of persistence as well.

Our second claim is that the element of persistence enters the fray as a variable in a variety of doctrinal areas that involve triangular relationships, even when it doesn't dominate. Whether it dominates or not, is effectively a question of the way in which the different triangular relationships are partitioned (and sequenced) for decision-making. In some areas, the element of persistence is effectively overridden by other competing normative considerations, while in others it exerts an influence that causes courts to modify the law in important ways. Either way, as we have shown, the element of persistence can influence the partitioning, and with it entire doctrinal areas.

In the end, our argument is hardly that Hohfeld was wrong in trying to distill the conceptual content of *in rem* and *in personam* obligations, or that his exercise was futile. Our point is simply that in focusing too narrowly on property and contract – rather than other areas (e.g., tort) or the interaction between them – Hohfeld might have missed an additional component of the distinction, and one that extends beyond property and contract.

While Hohfeld is to be lauded for curing a good deal of the confusion embedded in usage of these terms within the domains of property and contract, one wonders whether his insistence of identifying conceptual patterns *within* identified doctrinal domains imposed a constraint on his project that might have allowed its influence to reach even further than it has.

24 Hohfeld, *supra* note 2, at 712–13.

25 *Id.* at 712.

26 *See, e.g.*, James E. Penner, The Idea of Property in Law 27 (1997); Thomas W. Merrill & Henry E. Smith, *What Happened to Property in Law and Economics?* 111 Yale L.J. 357, 364 (2001).

7

Hohfeld and the Theory of *In Rem* Rights: An Attempted Mediation

Christopher M. Newman[*]

7.1 HOHFELD VERSUS PROPERTY?

Having cast Hohfeld as the progenitor of the "bundle of rights" theory, thinkers in the property strand either celebrate or disparage Hohfeld.[1]

I come neither to celebrate nor to disparage Hohfeld, but to parley with him. Perhaps it is worth exploring why the former courses are said to be on the table, depending upon one's preferred strand of property theory. After all, Hohfeld's project is presented as purely analytical. He does not purport to tell us what the substantive contents of the law should be, but merely to provide tools that permit unambiguous analytical description of a given positive landscape. There is no reason why a project thus conceived should necessarily be in tension with any particular substantive theory of property law.

For example, one may use Hohfeld's 1913 vocabulary[2] to identify various distinct jural relations that arise from ownership of a fee simple[3] without thereby implying anything about the social, material, or other circumstances under which it is desirable for all of those relations to be aggregated together in a single interest, when it should be permissible to sunder them, or what the consequences of doing so should be. As Henry Smith has put it, one can use Hohfeld without adopting any particular "theory of how our world works."[4] And Hohfeld is worth using, because – as Pierre Schlag points out – you can actually "do things" with him.[5] Hohfeld's list of jural relations really does, as advertised, permit clear discussion of issues that would otherwise be hopelessly

* I wish to thank Ted Sichelman, Henry Smith, John Goldberg, James Penner, Pierre Schlag, Lee Fennell, Timothy Mulvaney, and Patrick Goold for valuable input.

1 Pierre Schlag, *How to Do Things with Hohfeld*, 78 LAW & CONTEMP. PROBS. 185, 191 n.18 (2015).

2 Wesley N. Hohfeld, *Some Fundamental Legal Conceptions as Applied in Judicial Reasoning* 23 YALE L. J. 16 (1913) [hereinafter Hohfeld (1913)].

3 As he himself does at one point. *See* Wesley N. Hohfeld, *Fundamental Legal Conceptions as Applied in Judicial Reasoning*, 26 YALE L.J. 710, 746–47 (1917) [hereinafter Hohfeld (1917)].

4 Henry E. Smith, *Property as the Law of Things*, 125 HARV. L. REV. 1691, 1697 (2012).

5 Schlag, *supra* note 1.

confusing or cumbersome to express using only the term "right," or other doctrinal terms whose meaning has evolved over time.[6]

And yet, as Schlag also points out, it is by now commonplace to regard Hohfeld's work as having provided intellectual spadework for the so-called "bundle of rights" approach to property.[7] The "bundle of rights," too, can be understood in innocuous descriptive terms, as no more than a metaphorical label for the uncontroversial observation that the institution of ownership gives rise to various jural relations that – for some purposes – need to be teased out and identified distinctly. It takes on substantive implications only if one additionally insists that the legal concept of property has no content *apart from* this laundry list of jural relations. Thence, one might segue into such claims as: the traditional contents of the list are arbitrary, that any revised list furthering any revised set of social priorities is as worthy of the label "property" as any other, or that state actors can therefore make such revisions at will without running afoul of any constitutional protections afforded to "property."[8] These latter moves will obviously be unpalatable to someone who believes the institution of property to have more structural and functional coherence than that. But it ought to be obvious that whatever their merits, any assertion that those moves follow as logical implications of the initial analytic-descriptive one is every bit as fallacious as the arguments that Hohfeld was at pains to critique. The decomposition of title into a bundle of jural relations could just as easily cut the other way, leading to the conclusion that if property is just the list, *any* revision to the list is an expropriation.[9] In sum, Hohfeld's list of jural relations is not inherently at war with any higher level substantive *theory* of what property is, or should be, about.

Rather, it is in the 1917 follow-up article[10] – focusing on the phrases *in personam* and *in rem* – that Hohfeld seems to place himself in irreconcilable opposition to certain ways of thinking about property. He finds these terms so riddled with "linguistic contamination" that the only cure is to replace them with "paucital" and "multital," pristine terms he can define so as to avoid the "loose and misleading usages" to which he believes the

6 For example, my own interest in Hohfeld stems largely from work attempting to think through the nature of a "license," in order to disentangle the roles that contract and property doctrine play (and should play) in interpreting and enforcing copyright licenses. *See, e.g.*, Christopher M. Newman, *A License Is Not a "Contract Not To Sue": Disentangling Property and Contract in the Law of Copyright Licenses*, 98 IOWA L. REV. 1101 (2013). Hohfeld's terminology was very useful in this endeavor, making it easy to express such distinctions as that between: (1) a power that one has a duty not to exercise; and (2) a disability. Had Hohfeld's terminology not existed, I would have been obliged to construct something similar.

7 *See* Schlag, *supra* note 1, at 190; James E. Penner, *The "Bundle of Rights" Picture of Property*, 43 UCLA L. Rev. 711, 724 (1996).

8 *See* Schlag, *supra* note 1, at 190–91. For a good fleshing out of the overall debate, see Daniel B. Klein and John Robinson, *Property: A Bundle Of Rights? Prologue to the Property Symposium*, 8 ECON. J. WATCH 193 (2011).

9 *See* Richard A. Epstein, *Bundle-of-Rights Theory as a Bulwark Against Statist Conceptions of Private Property*, 8 ECON. J. WATCH 223 (2011).

10 Hohfeld (1917), *supra* note 3.

baggage-laden traditional terms have lent themselves.[11] The problem is that he includes among these "misleading usages" ways of speaking that reflect what some of us take to be key aspects of the way property – as well as private law more generally – functions. It would be one thing to observe that a pithy description of property like "right to a thing good against the world," while capturing something important and useful, will need more precise specification if one wishes to reason accurately about its implications in a given context. Such an approach would accord with the advice of Justice Franklin of the Arizona Supreme Court, whom Hohfeld quotes near the beginning of the 1917 article:

> In the development of the law it is seldom possible, or, when possible, seldom expedient, to discard established terms. ... Instead of rejecting convenient terms because they are ambiguous or not comprehensive, it is better to explain their meanings, or, in the language of old Hobbes, "to snuff them with distinctions and definitions," so as to give a better light.[12]

Yet, it is unclear to what extent Hohfeld himself actually embraces this advice. He is keen on the snuffing but he also seems to be keen on the rejecting. He wants his new term "multital" to replace *in rem* and his definition of this term to render obsolete any notion of *in rem* rights as anything but discrete rights against discrete parties that just happen to have lots of companions.[13] Read starkly, Hohfeld appears to insist that the traditional conception of an *in rem* right as one that is "good against the world,"[14] or one that is "availing against other persons generally"[15] is not merely a convenient term that may need clarification for some purposes, but a pernicious error needing extirpation. He seems to be saying, not: "Here, let me help you spell out more precisely what that means in practice," but rather: "That's just wrong. Stop saying that." This is the aspect of Hohfeld's work that has generated the most spirited pushback in property circles, most notably from James Penner.[16]

11 *Id.* at 716–17.

12 *Id.* at 713–14 (quoting *Hook* v. *Hoffman*, 16 Ariz. 540, 558 (1915)).

13 *Id.* at 745: "It is therefore to be hoped that, instead of continuing to be used to indicate the entire multiplicity of separate and independent rights, or claims, that a person may have against many others, the term right *in rem* may gradually come to be used to represent one, and only one, of this multiplicity of distinct rights. Whatever be the fate of the concept and term, right *in rem*, in this regard, it is surely of the utmost importance that the various possible analyses and meanings involved be carefully pondered and understood; and, in the meanwhile, the term 'multital'–free as it is from any previous hazy connotations–will without question serve definitely to indicate one, and one only, of such a multiplicity of rights as is now under consideration."

14 Thomas W. Merrill & Henry E. Smith, *What Happened to Property in Law and Economics?* 111 Yale L.J. 357 (2001).

15 Albert Kocourek, *Rights in Rem*, 68 U. Pa. L. Rev. 322, 322 (1919–1920) (quoting Austin, *Jurisprudence*).

16 Penner, *supra* note 7.

Hohfeld's attempt to purify the ways in which we think and talk about property has met with mixed success. Along with the "bundle of rights" depiction of property,[17] arguably his greatest success was in hammering home the first lesson he sought to impart in 1917, that "*A right in rem is not a right 'against a thing'.*"[18] This lesson became so engrained that sixty years later in *Shaffer v. Heitner*, Justice Thurgood Marshall could call into question the entire traditional doctrine of *in rem* jurisdiction with the passing observation that, whatever people may have thought at the time of *Pennoyer v. Neff*, "the overwhelming majority of commentators" had by then rejected the premise "that a proceeding 'against' property is not a proceeding against the owners of that property."[19]

On the other hand, judicial and academic discussions of property doctrine still make liberal use of terms that, from Hohfeld's perspective, are just as muddled as (indeed, part and parcel of) the notion that "*in rem*" means "against a thing." Two years after *Shaffer*, the Supreme Court spoke of "the right to exclude others" as "one of the most essential sticks in the bundle of rights that are commonly characterized as property,"[20] and while there is scholarly debate about the centrality of exclusion to property, there is no hesitation about use of the phrase "the right to exclude."[21] Yet this phrase is a flagrant violation of Hohfeldian syntax. First, a "right" is a claim that someone other than the right holder do something in fulfillment of a duty, yet all understand the holder of the "right to exclude" to be the one doing the excluding. The only Hohfeldian jural relations that can properly be used to describe the relationship between an actor and his own action are duty and privilege. The "right to exclude" is obviously not a duty, as all understand the property owner to be free to exclude or not. The term "right to exclude" could be interpreted as referring to a sort of privilege – the freedom to take actions physically impeding the access of others – but that is not what people mean by it. To accurately express what is meant by a "right to exclude" in Hohfeldian terms, one should say "a right that someone else shall not enter, coupled with the power to grant a privilege to do so."[22] But there is an additional problem: we persist in speaking of a *singular* "right to exclude others," whereas Hohfeld was adamant that you need a separate and distinct right for each of the excludees.[23] Indeed, this is the central contention of his 1917 article. Had the Hohfeldian revolution truly occurred, Thomas Merrill would have scrupulously entitled his famous article, "Property and the Aggregate of Rights That Others Shall Not Enter."[24]

17 As Schlag points out, Hohfeld never actually used this term. *See* Schlag, *supra* note 1, at 190 n.17.
18 Hohfeld (1917), *supra* note 3, at 720.
19 433 U.S. 186, 205–06 (1977).
20 *Kaiser Aetna* v. *United States*, 444 U.S. 164, 176 (1979).
21 *See, e.g.*, Thomas W. Merrill, *Property and the Right To Exclude*, 77 NEB. L. REV. 730 (1998).
22 The "right to exclude" is thus one of the composite relations about which Ted Sichelman writes in his contribution to this collection.
23 Hohfeld (1917), *supra* note 3, at 740–46.
24 Merrill, *supra* note 21.

Clearly, the legal world has failed to adopt this usage. This suggests that a term like "the right to exclude" has some value outweighing Hohfeld's fear that it will "blur and befog legal thought and argument."[25] The point of such terms is not to suppress or assume away analytic complexity, but to organize complexity into modules that are cognitively manageable, that tend to suggest desired results, and that reflect a theory of the overall system.[26] One suspects that, had he his druthers, Hohfeld would have banned analytically impure uses of the terms corresponding to his 1913 jural relations. This would not necessarily have ruled out a concept corresponding in meaning to our "right to exclude," but it would have obliged us to change the name, to call it something like an "exclusion interest." Of course, if Hohfeld had wanted his jural relations to have labels uncontaminated by sloppy traditional usage, he could have done what he did in 1917 and invented new words to serve as those labels. That he chose instead to take words already in common usage and attempt to purify them is telling.

What follows is written from the perspective of one who works within the strand of property theory from which disparagement of Hohfeld might be expected, but who actually finds much of Hohfeld extremely helpful. I am thus a person of overlapping kinships, who seeks to bring about the "peace in the feud."[27]

7.2 THE AMBIGUITY IN HOHFELDIAN PRECISION: HOW TO SPECIFY THE CONTENTS OF RIGHTS

The virtue of Hohfeld's 1913 vocabulary is its technical precision. Most colloquial – and even many technical – discussions of law tend (still) to use the term "right" indiscriminately to refer to any sort of legal entitlement that a party might invoke against others. This is not necessarily a problem – the term "right" used at this level of abstraction serves a useful communicative purpose. But once one moves beyond the basic concept of legal entitlement, the term quickly becomes ambiguous in ways that matter, particularly when one is trying to reason about the practical consequences of an asserted "right" for others who are expected to recognize it. A "right" to do something yourself is different from a "right" to have someone else do something for you. A "right" to do something without legal consequence is different from a "right" to do something without interference from other actors. A "right" to change your legal relation to someone is different from a "right" to be free from such changes. Hohfeld's 1913 terminology distinguishes between these relations, facilitating a more precise description of legal interests and what they imply.

And yet Hohfeld's terminology, precise though it is, remains inevitably tethered to an important form of ambiguity in application. The primary legal relations – right/

25 Hohfeld (1917), *supra* note 3, at 720.

26 *See* Henry E. Smith, *On the Economy of Concepts in Property*, 160 U. Pa. L. Rev. 2097 (2012).

27 *See* William Ian Miller, Bloodtaking and Peacemaking: Feud, Law and Society in Saga Iceland (1990).

duty, and their opposites no-right/privilege – have to be defined in terms of some identified action that is required of (or forbidden to) the duty-holder, or permitted to the privilege-holder. Ambiguity arises because there is a very wide range of levels of abstraction we can choose from in describing the enjoined action.

Consider a scenario where A and B enter into a contract in which B undertakes to personally protect A's family against foreseeable threats of infectious disease. Now suppose that a deer enters A's yard. B is contractually obliged to chase it away, to prevent it from leaving ticks in the family's environment. One way to express this is to say that under the circumstances, B has a "duty to chase deer out of A's yard." For some purposes, this is a perfectly useful way of describing B's legal obligation. For B himself, it provides the answer to the specific question as to what he should do in the moment. Should B fail to chase the deer away and later be sued, this will also be the way in which the legal question is framed: Did he have a duty to chase the deer away?

Note, however, that no legal authority prescribes a duty to B in these terms. He has a general duty to fulfill his contractual obligations, and his contract with A prescribes a more specific duty to protect the family from disease. That duty enjoins a class of unspecified actions on B, of which there is no *ex ante* enumeration to be found. B's job in the moment of decision, like the court's job in later judging his actions at that moment, is to decide whether the concrete action of chasing the deer falls within the defined class of actions prescribed by the duty. Unless and until that issue arises as a matter of practical importance, the question whether he is obliged to chase deer can be left uncontemplated and indeterminate. This gap in specification does not constitute any fatal deficiency in the definition of B's duty or his understanding of it. In this sense, we can say that deer chasing is *not* really constitutive of any duty of B's – rather, it is one of many possible contextual applications of a duty that is properly identified at a higher level of abstraction.

Note, too, that filling the gap between abstract description of duty and concrete action in the moment does not merely require deduction from the meanings of the abstract terms in which the relevant legal authority – here, the contract – is expressed. The question whether those terms apply to the action of chasing deer depends on contingent facts about the state of the world at the time. If the contract is entered into at time T1, and then later at time T2 Lyme disease is fully eradicated, the content of B's duty to A will no longer include "chasing deer out of the yard."

Now, as between these two ways of expressing the content of B's duty to A – namely, "protect A's family from disease" and "chase deer out of the yard" – is one superior to the other? The answer, of course, depends on what we are trying to accomplish. The more granular description has the virtue of concreteness. It allows us to compare the description of the duty to an actual course of action described in similarly granular terms, so that we can decide whether the latter constitutes compliance or breach. Indeed, much of the bread and butter of lawyering consists of taking descriptions of duties couched at a higher level of abstraction and seeking to translate them into statements at a lower one for precisely this purpose.

Yet it would be strange to assert that the more granular description of the duty is more accurate than the more abstract one, or that it provides a description of the jural relation that is adequate for all purposes. If, for example, we adhere to the description of B at T1 as having a "duty to chase deer out of A's yard," then we must conclude that at T2 this "duty" has been extinguished, despite the absence of any term in the contract purporting to make the parties' obligations variable or any exercise of any actor's power to alter jural relations. If we insist on identifying jural relations at this granular a level, we are left with a picture in which B is subject, not to a single persistent duty with many potential contextual applications, but to innumerable discrete duties that are constantly winking into and out of existence as the state of the world changes, for reasons whose logic is not discernible from any of their identifying descriptions. This level of focus simply does not distinguish between a duty that ceases because someone has exercised a power to waive it and one that ceases (perhaps only momentarily) because of a change in contingent investitive facts.

Then again, suppose that C, too, has a contract with A. C's contractual undertaking is to protect the plants in A's yard from being damaged. Thus when the deer arrives, C too is obliged to chase it away, lest it dine on the landscaping. Is the content of C's duty identical to B's? If we focus on the level of granular application, it seems that (apart from the identity of the duty holder) the answer is yes: each of them has a "duty to A to chase deer out of A's yard." Again, if our only need is for a static description of the state of jural relations pertaining to a very specific course of action,[28] this may be a perfectly serviceable one. But for other purposes it seems clear that this would be a misleading and inadequate description of the prevailing set of legal norms. The two putatively identical duties are derived from different principles and contingent on different facts. Only through coincidence do they require the same course of action. Drawing on the field of intensional logic, Henry Smith has discussed this phenomenon in terms of law having both *intensional* and *extensional* aspects: one can "attain the same set of real-world consequences by a variety of conceptual routes."[29] Of equal importance is that two intensions whose real-world consequences overlap in some circumstances may diverge in others.

The preceding observations are all fairly obvious to any lawyer. Yet Hohfeld's 1917 article has invited pushback because it can be read as insisting that this granular level is the only accurate one at which to describe jural relations. He asks us to consider the following case: A is owner of Blackacre. A enters into a contract with B in which B promises never to enter Whiteacre, which is owned by X. Hohfeld asserts that A's

[28] Of course, specificity remains relative. The phrase "chasing the deer" itself denotes a class of numerous possible physical motions that would have a given effect.

[29] *See* Henry E. Smith, *Emergent Property*, *in* Philosophical Foundations of Property Law 320, 321–31, 336–38 (James Penner & Henry E. Smith eds., 2013).

right that B not enter Blackacre and A's right that B not enter Whiteacre are, "*intrinsically considered*, of the same general character."[30] A's right against B as owner of Blackacre differs from A's contractual right against B concerning Whiteacre "only *extrinsically*, that is, in having many fundamentally similar, though distinct, rights as its 'companions.'"[31]

What are we to make of this, especially given that Hohfeld does not explain what he means by "intrinsically" or "general character"? James Penner takes Hohfeld to be asserting that the two rights are identical in nature, and articulates a cogent objection:

> In understanding a right, describing its place within a pre-existing normative framework as a right of property or a right arising from contract is important, if not essential. . . . It is not true that B's duties to A and to X are identical if it matters why they have those duties. . . . understanding a duty is not simply a matter of understanding what must be done, but is a matter of properly understanding the practical reason for doing so. . . . In short, it is more than a slight conceptual stretch to regard the content of B's duties as the same if we retain any memory of the fact that these duties could have arisen only within a pre-existing normative system which regulates the behavior of people according to a canonical and finite (though not immutable) list of protected interests, like interests arising under contract, or interests in property.[32]

I think Penner is quite right, though I also imagine Hohfeld might have said something along the following lines in response:

> The purpose of my analytic terminology is precisely to provide a set of terms that enables us to describe the practical meaning of legal entitlements without the contamination of any normative framework. Part of the confusion I am trying to dispel is that which tends to arise between the use of a term like "right" as a normative symbol and its use to describe a positive legal relationship having precise consequences within a given system. My analytical description of a set of jural relations does not purport to include all the information that would enable an actor within that system to "understand" the normative underpinnings that give rise to his jural relations or motivate him to act in accordance with them. The sort of description of rights you are talking about may be analogized to architecture, insofar as it is a normative theoretical discipline giving us reasons why our buildings should be configured in certain ways and explaining how their various features coalesce into a functional and harmonious whole. What I am doing is rather geometry, which provides precise tools for describing the actual dimensions and placement of structural elements, permitting us to discern whether the architect's more abstract ideas will prove to be coherent and non-contradictory when reduced to practice.

30 Hohfeld (1917), *supra* note 3, at 723 (emphasis in original).
31 *Id.* (emphasis in original).
32 Penner, *supra* note 7, at 728.

> Obviously I am aware that A's Blackacre right sounds in property whereas his Whiteacre right sounds in contract, and that this matters greatly in certain respects. None of those respects, however, is internal to the relationship I have defined as a "right," and each is fully capable of description in my terminology. From a positive perspective, exactly what difference does the property/contract distinction make with regard to the jural relations prevailing between A and B once they have already come into existence? Perhaps you are thinking of the fact that there are different doctrines concerning the circumstances under which B might be relieved of his respective duties not to enter, such as the doctrine of necessity (should he need to traverse Blackacre to flee a brigand) or a material breach of some obligation of A's under the Whiteacre contract. Those are liabilities that accompany the rights and can be defined as such; they are not intrinsic to the claim rights themselves. Or are you thinking of the different types of proceedings and remedies that A will have at his disposal in the event of B's breach of either duty? Those are secondary rights, which B has the power to confer on A through his breaching acts.[33] None of this affects the intrinsic content of the claim rights themselves. As for your concern that B needs to understand the normative framework underlying these jural relations in order be properly reconciled to compliance, that is simply a matter I do not purport to address. I deny, however, that such a normative framework is required in order to comprehend that the legal system regards him in each case as owing a duty to A to refrain from entry.

If this hypothetical rejoinder has force, it suggests that we can read Hohfeld more charitably than Penner does and assume that when he says two rights are, "intrinsically considered, of the same general character," he does not mean that the two legal relationships featuring these respective rights are identical in every important respect – that they would be experienced by the parties, or should be understood by doctrinalists, in exactly the same way. What does he mean then? To shield Hohfeld from Penner's attack, we must assume that by "intrinsically considered" he means, "paying attention solely to matters that are constitutive of the jural relation taken in isolation (which is to say, the identities of the right and duty holders and the nature of the enjoined action), and ignoring all other subsisting jural relations, however closely related." Hohfeld need not, and should not, be read as asserting that property and contract are theoretically or functionally superfluous categories; he is merely asserting that, when placed under his analytical microscope, they can be seen to be composed of different configurations of the same legal elements. Or to put it differently, Penner is interested in intensional terms because they tend to convey normative structure, whereas Hohfeld wishes to use extensional terms precisely because they do not.

[33] Hohfeld (1917), *supra* note 3, at 753.

7.3 HOHFELD'S TREATMENT OF *IN REM* RIGHTS

While Hohfeld may not deny the utility of a distinction between property and contract, he *does* deny emphatically the utility of describing property as concerned with rights "against a thing."[34] On this he is uncompromising:

> What is here insisted on, – i.e., that all rights *in rem* are against persons, – is not to be regarded merely as a matter of taste or preference for one out of several equally possible forms of statement or definition. Logical consistency seems to demand such a conception, and nothing less than that."[35]

The "logical consistency" Hohfeld is concerned to preserve is that of his own 1913 terminology, which is founded on bilateral jural relations as the irreducible atoms of which legal interests are made. Hohfeld does not consider whether a phrase like "right against [or to] a thing" might be a conceptual shorthand that serves a useful purpose in some contexts, or whether, properly construed, it might be reconcilable with his system. He treats the phrase as though it can only be taken literally, as though if it means anything, it must mean that Blackacre has duties to its owner for which it can be answerable at law. He writes as though lawyers and judges who use the phrase must have somehow failed to grasp that "[t]he purpose of law is to regulate the conduct of human beings, and all jural relations must therefore be predicated of human beings."[36] This is strange, and Hohfeld does not provide any cited examples of jurists whose imprecise definitions of *in rem* lead them to conclude that land or chattels may be held liable for harmful conduct.[37]

Hohfeld provides two versions of his own preferred understanding of rights *in rem*:

> A multital right, or claim (right *in rem*) is always *one* of a large *class of fundamentally similar* yet separate rights, actual and potential, residing in a *single* person (or single group of persons) but availing *respectively* against persons constituting a very large and indefinite class of people. . . .[38]
>
> A right *in rem*, correctly understood, is simply one of a large number of fundamentally similar rights residing in *one* person; and any one of such rights has as its correlative one, and only one, of a large number of general, or common duties – that is, fundamentally similar duties residing respectively in *many* different persons.[39]

As Albert Kocourek pointed out shortly after Hohfeld's death, this is far from adequate as a definition, in part because such terms as "large class," "fundamentally

34 *Id.* at 720–23.
35 *Id.* at 722–23.
36 *Id.* at 721.
37 As a matter of fact, such a conception was not always unknown to the law. *See* O. W. Holmes, The Common Law 24–30 (1881) (discussing deodand).
38 Hohfeld (1917), *supra* note 3, at 718 (emphasis in original).
39 *Id.* at 745 (emphasis in original).

similar," and "actual and potential" are of uncertain meaning.[40] More seriously, a definition should identify the essential attributes of some phenomenon that bring it within the scope of the concept being defined, and it is easy to show that Hohfeld's fails to do this:[41]

Suppose that A, the owner of Blackacre, grants (by means of a blanket public invitation) a nonexclusive license to enter Blackacre that extends to everyone in the world *except* C. This exercise of A's power means that B, D, and every other person in the world (apart from C) has now been relieved of her or his respective duty to A not to enter Blackacre and has instead been furnished with a privilege to do so. C alone remains under a duty not to enter. According to Hohfeld's definition, then, A's right that C not enter can no longer be *in rem*, for there is no longer any "very large and indefinite class of people" against whom A has fundamentally similar rights. The right must therefore now have become *in personam*, even though it did not arise that way, and A has only used her power directly to alter the jural relations between herself and others. The no-rights A now has with respect to everyone else, on the other hand, would appear to be *in rem*, for now there *is* a large and indefinite class of privilege holders.

The same result would obtain if, instead of issuing a blanket license, A were to go around granting licenses individually to each person she met. At first each of these licenses would clearly be *in personam*, while the duties of all the non-invitees would remain *in rem*. But at some point, once the group of licensees became sufficiently large, these designations would flip. Or perhaps not, for in one of his definitions Hohfeld says that the multital class is not only very large, but *indefinite* – and a very large class built up through individualized personal transactions would not be indefinite. Yet Hohfeld does not appear to put definitive weight on indefiniteness, focusing instead primarily on numerosity.

Perhaps the above hypothetical could explain why Hohfeld says in one place that an *in rem* right is one of a large class of fundamentally similar "actual *and potential*" rights residing in a single person. He could say that because A can revoke his invitation, his right against C still has as companions all the potential rights against others that could be reinstated at any moment. But absent some limiting explanation as to the type of potentiality intended, this would merely compound the problem that the definition permits one to construct an *in rem* right out of *in personam* ones, because now the mere potential existence of all those relations renders *every* right one *in rem*. Perhaps this flaw could be remedied by specifying more clearly what it means for rights to be "fundamentally similar," but it seems clear that in order to do so we would have to address the very matters that Penner criticizes Hohfeld for omitting.

40 Kocourek, *supra* note 15, at 332 ("[I]t may be doubted if he has made any advance in his definition of a right *in rem*.").

41 What follows is my own variation on an approach used by Kocourek (*id.* at 332–33).

In sum, Hohfeld does not really provide a *definition* of the concept of a right *in rem*, and probably should not even be read as purporting to. What he provides is merely a description of what *in rem* rights look like when placed under his analytical microscope and decomposed into individual bilateral relations. This extensional description gives us no help in determining whether a particular jural relation properly falls within the intension he has labeled "multital" or the one labeled "paucital." Nor does it aid us in understanding why the term *in rem* was ever thought a useful legal category.

Again, the charitable reading of Hohfeld is that these are not shortcomings of his approach but simply jobs he does not purport to do. It is difficult to give Hohfeld this charitable reading however, because he himself is so uncharitable to the customary turns of phrase – such as "right good against the world" – that *are* attempting to do those jobs. He structures the 1917 article around a list of six such usages, which he attacks as "loose and misleading."[42] Whereas I have just shielded Hohfeld from Penner's attack by pointing out that analytic description may differ from normative description, Hohfeld insists on assessing specimens of the latter against his standards for the former, inevitably finding them wanting.

7.4 THE NORMATIVE STRUCTURE OF THE *IN REM/IN PERSONAM* DISTINCTION

I will now provide a description of *in rem* rights that starts at the opposite end from Hohfeld's, taking my cue from Penner's statement that such rights are intelligible "only within a preexisting normative system which regulates the behavior of people according to a canonical and finite (though not immutable) list of protected interests."[43] Any such system faces two fundamental tasks. It must identify duties of restraint such that the costs of compliance borne by each individual are exceeded by the benefits expected from the universal compliance of others. And it must define and communicate those duties in a way that is cognitively manageable, so that the costs of recognizing them do not tip the balance against compliance. This means that any baseline duties with which we are expected to comply as routine default rules will have to be defined in fairly clear categorical terms that can be applied with fairly low levels of information.

The function of *in rem* norms is to enable people to structure their activities so as to avoid harmful interference with the activities of others, without needing to know anything about those others' goals and preferences. In order for an *in rem* norm to serve this function, both its applicability to a given interaction, and its substantive contents when applied, must be ascertainable by either party to the interaction without any need for personal communication or agreement between them. An *in*

42 Hohfeld (1917), *supra* note 3, at 720. Only the last two of these examples touch on matters sounding in categories other than primary rights. *Id.* at 752–53.

43 Penner, *supra* note 7, at 728.

rem jural relation is one that is understood to subsist as a general baseline matter between any two individuals, to the extent that they have not replaced it with some relation of their own choosing. *In personam* relations, by contrast, are ones whose applicability and contents depend on there having been some personal interaction between the parties.

The basic categories of primary *in rem* jural relations within the realm of private law can be characterized as follows:

- *Rights* (and correlative duties) designed to define certain baseline interests believed to be of foundational importance to every individual and to protect them against certain forms of harmful interference from the actions of others.
- *Privileges* (and correlative no-rights) designed to protect spheres of autonomous action (also believed to be of foundational importance to every individual), within which individuals are entitled to pursue interests not necessarily shared by everyone.
- *Powers* (and correlative liabilities) that enable individuals to alter the jural relations between them, replacing *pro tanto* the default contents of *in rem* relations with *in personam* relations whose contents are tailored to their specific needs.
- *Immunities* (and correlative disabilities) that impose limitations on the extent to which, and the means by which, individuals are empowered to alter the relations between them.

7.4.1 *Defining the Contents of* In Rem *Rights*

The definition of a duty (its syntax, if you will) always includes two basic elements:

(1) An identified object in which the right holder has a direct interest, or that is somehow bound up with the interest the right seeks to protect.

The paradigmatic examples are tangible objects, beginning with the right holder's person, moving thence to owned external objects such as chattels or expanses of land. But the object may also be an intangible, such as a reputation or a work of authorship.[44]

(2) Some identified relationship between the duty holder's action and that object.

Here there are three main strategies:

(a) The enjoined action is defined as some specified type of activity having the identified object as direct object (e.g., touching someone's person, entering someone's land, or distributing a copy of someone's copyrighted work).

[44] Or, to reference a few of Hohfeld's more quaint examples, the affection of a spouse (Hohfeld (1917), *supra* note 3, at 719) or chastity of a daughter (*id.* at 733).

(b) The enjoined action is defined not in terms of any specified activities directed at the object, but in terms of unspecified activities having some indirect consequential effect of specified nature on the object (e.g., foreseeably causing harm to person or property or creating a nuisance).
(c) The enjoined action is defined in terms of both specified forms of direct interaction and consequential effect (e.g., publishing falsehoods that harm someone's reputation or using a trademark in commerce so as to create likelihood of confusion).

The above syntax applies to all duties, whether *in rem* or *in personam*. When the right is *in rem*, however, its description omits any identification of a specific person at the other end of the relation. From the right holder's perspective, the right is addressed indiscriminately to whoever may encounter (be in a position to take some action having the specified relation to) the identified object. From the duty holder's perspective, the duty is owed to whoever may have an interest in such an object that he encounters. As Kocourek nicely puts it, "a right *in rem* is one of which the essential investitive facts do not serve directly to identify the person who owes the incident duty."[45] I would take this a step further, and say that a right *in rem* is one of which the essential investitive facts pertain solely to the relationship between the right holder and some identified thing, and the duty is defined solely in terms of the duty holder's actions with regard to that thing.

From the perspective of a duty holder, the way rights are defined makes it possible to determine whether a contemplated action violates a duty simply by looking out for objects of others' rights that are potentially affected by it (e.g., "Will walking down to the curb involve any sort of encounter with or likely effect on someone else's person or property?"). Only if such an object is identified is there any need to ask whether the contemplated action would have a proscribed relationship to it (e.g., "Will this bring me within the boundaries of someone else's property? Will it create a hazard foreseeably likely to harm someone else's person?"). The checklist of things that need to be considered is couched at a level of abstraction that makes the inquiry cognitively manageable.

A crucial aspect of this cognitive economy is that, from the perspective of a duty holder who wants only to avoid coming into violation of his *in rem* duties, information as to the actual identities of right holders is irrelevant to both the questions whether there is an applicable duty and what its contents are.[46] To be sure, the duty holder often has knowledge as to the identities of the relevant right holders, but he need not. The only information needed to fulfill the duty pertains to whether the intended activity will impinge on some object of rights. While it is part of the concept of an object of rights that there is some interested party behind it, that party's existence can be inferred without any knowledge as to its identity. When

45 Kocourek, *supra* note 15, at 335.
46 *See* J. E. Penner, The Idea of Property in Law 75 (1997).

I encounter an owned chattel, it is possible to identify it as such without knowing who owns it. When I engage in activities likely to pose a hazard of harm to others, it is possible to assess the hazard without knowing who the endangered parties will be.

7.4.2 In Personam *Relations as Exceptions to* In Rem *Relations*

It is only when the desire for some specific course of action that would violate baseline *in rem* duties is strong enough to warrant increased transaction costs that a duty holder needs to identify and communicate with relevant right holders concerning their actual preferences.[47] Thus, if I wish only to avoid violating duties, when I see a house not my own I need merely avoid it. I need not know who owns it or what their actual preferences might be with regard to who enters. Only if I wish to enter the house do I need to find out who owns it and communicate with them, and I know that if I enter, my freedom of action will thenceforth be governed by their preferences, which will determine the scope of the *in personam* privilege that permits me to be there.

A privilege created *in personam* is generally termed a license. A license permits one to engage in action that would otherwise be forbidden by an *in rem* duty. Again, there are two levels of abstraction at which we can imagine this. On the granular level, we might say that a license extinguishes a single right/duty relation ("do not enter my house") and replaces it with a granular privilege ("feel free to enter"). On the level of normative principle, *in personam* privileges provide specific contextual exceptions to persistent baseline norms. The general template of these exceptions is already understood to be inherent in the norm itself, because the power/liability relationship that permits owners to create license privileges is itself an *in rem* relation. In other words, though the shorthand way of describing the duty that follows from the "right to exclude" is "keep off," we all understand that it really means "keep off unless you have permission." When a license is granted, it merely adds informational content to this caveat. If there has been no personal interaction between me and the owner, then I know there is no permission, and so that term of the duty is not operative. In the absence of an *in personam* relation between us, I continue to be governed by the default content of the *in rem* norm. When there is an *in personam* relation, it does not displace the *in rem* norm entirely; rather, the *in rem* norm continues to govern except to the specific extent it is superseded by the *in personam* exception.[48]

A duty created *in personam* usually takes the form of a contract. On the granular level of analytical description, a contract extinguishes a specific privilege ("keep possession of my money") to replace it with a specific duty ("pay X $100"). On the level of normative structure, the general duty to fulfill one's contracts is *in rem*, but it

47 *Accord* Henry E. Smith, *The Language of Property*, 55 STAN. L. REV. 1105, 1138–57 (2003).

48 This is an example of the specific-over-general principle. *See* Henry E. Smith, *On the Economy of Concepts in Property*, 160 U. PA. L. REV. 2097, 2109–11, 2123 (2012).

has no operative content unless and until I engage in the *in personam* interactions that give rise to specific contractual duties. Just as the possibility of license is a latent term of the *in rem* duty to respect property, the possibility of contract is a latent term of the *in rem* privilege of personal liberty, to which content is added by actual agreements. The rules governing the ability to create binding contracts constitute a set of *in rem* power/liability relationships that govern everyone.

7.5 FINDING THE PEACE IN THE FEUD

I now wish to revisit a few of the "loose and misleading usages" Hohfeld attacks in the 1917 article, to see how far the understanding of *in rem* articulated above justifies their failure to disappear. We should expect the language of normative description to differ from that of analytical description in terms of its level of abstraction and focus, and we should expect each to contain information omitted from the other. The question is how best to let each level of description serve its own purpose without contradicting or creating misleading implications for the other.

7.5.1 "A *right* in rem *is not a right 'against a thing.'*"

Hohfeld deprecates as "laudable optimism" Justice Franklin's suggestion that the meaning of "*in rem*" can be illuminated by considering it in counter-distinction to the term "*in personam*."[49] Hohfeld thinks he knows where that leads: to a faulty "linguistic parallelism" according to which, since "*in personam*" means "against a person," "*in rem*" must mean "against a thing." Further, Hohfeld assumes that such a use of the preposition "against" must mean that the speaker is making (or leading others to make) one of two conceptual errors: either failure to appreciate that a right is inherently a claim "against" some duty holder, or belief that a "thing" can be a duty holder.

If my account of *in rem* rights is coherent, we can accept Hohfeld's insistence that such rights are "against people" – in that they enjoin particular duty-holding persons to act in certain ways – without accepting his insistence that it is merely misleading to think the distinction between "thing" and "person" sheds light on their nature. Hohfeld is quite right that the key feature of a primary duty described as "*in personam*" is not that it is "owed to a person"; *all* duties are owed to persons. Rather, what distinguishes an *in personam* duty is that it applies to the duty holder only as a result of some prior personal interaction with the person designated as right holder. In order to determine whether such a duty applies, and if so what its contents are, the putative duty holder has to focus on the specifics of his personal interactions with another person. Generally, any operative duty arising this way will be specific to a single right holder, having idiosyncratic contents that differ from those of other

49 Hohfeld (1917), *supra* note 3, at 720 (citing Hook v. Hoffman, 147 P. 722, 728 (Ariz. 1915)). *See also supra* note 12 and accompanying text.

duties owed to others. An *in personam* duty thus arises only "in person" and has some interaction with some identified person as its cognitive focal point. As Kocourek puts it, a right *in personam* is one of which the essential investitive facts serve directly to identify the person who owes the incident duty.[50] I would go a step further and say that not only do the investitive facts (i.e., those giving rise to the right) directly identify the duty holder, but that the substantive contents of the right can only be ascertained by reference to information generated through interactions with that person.

An *in rem* duty, on the other hand, arises without necessary reference to any identified person and always has some defined "thing" as its cognitive focal point. That there is no reference to any *identified* person does not mean, however, that the existence of a right holder is irrelevant. The categories of things to which *in rem* rights and duties attach are all defined in terms of their relationship to some right holder. To comply with property rights, for instance, I need not refrain from interacting with *all* things, but only *owned* things. Deciding whether a thing I encounter is owned will involve inference from social cues indicating the existence of someone currently intending to exercise ownership over it. Those cues, however, can all be gleaned from the characteristics of the thing itself, as well as its location and disposition.[51] Having identified the thing as owned, the duty holder need not know *who* the owner is in order to know the applicability or contents of the duty, which are defined in terms of the thing itself. The duty has standardized contents, such that any time a thing falling into the same broad category is implicated in the duty holder's actions, the nature of the enjoined actions will be defined in the same way. Information concerning the identity of the right holder is not needed to guide the duty holder's actions, and is therefore normatively inert.

Interpreted in this light, a locution like "right against a thing" (or, preferably to my ears, "right *to* a thing") seems less like woolly-headed befuddlement and more like functional economy of speech. While the preposition "against" is oppositional, has anyone who has used it actually meant that the thing itself was the duty holder? From the perspective of the right holder, the key point is that the entitlement is focused on the thing, not the identity of any particular person who might threaten the right holder's interest in it. If A detects someone within the confines of Blackacre, he need not know who it is to know his rights have been violated;[52] but his right concerning Whiteacre can be violated only if the entrant is B. Similarly, B need only recognize the "things" called Blackacre and Whiteacre as private property to know he is obliged by default to refrain from entry. He need only investigate the more information-intensive world of *in personam* norms (licenses and contracts) if he wishes to deviate from this default, in which case he will need to focus on his interactions with landowners and contracting parties.

50 Kocourek, *supra* note 15, at 335.

51 *See* Matt Corriel, *Up For Grabs: A Workable System for the Unilateral Acquisition of Chattels*, 161 U. Pa. L. Rev. 807 (2013).

52 The situation is more complicated if A has granted any licenses, in which case he still need not know who the entrant is, provided he knows it is not a licensee.

Thus, I would argue that a phrase taking the form "the right to X," where X is the object of an *in rem* right, is a perfectly serviceable description on the level of normative principle. Such a phrase does exactly what a conceptual label *should* do – it focuses on the key operative term of the relation that both identifies the nature of the right holder's protected interest and instructs the duty holder what to look for to avoid interfering with it.[53] This formulation omits any mention of the relevant duty holders, but that information is normatively inert, and the omission in no way implies that such duty holders do not exist.

7.5.2 "*A right* in rem *is not always one relating to a thing, i.e., a tangible object.*"

Hohfeld is correct that a right *in rem* does not necessarily relate to a *tangible* object.[54] Nevertheless, all rights *in rem* do relate to some identified thing (tangible or abstract) that is bound up with the interest the right seeks to protect, and function by enabling duty holders to understand their duties purely in terms of such objects and actions taken with respect to them.[55] So long as our notion of "thing" is broad enough to include both tangibles (human bodies, plots of land, chattels) and intangibles (reputations, works of authorship, other owned intangibles), the statement that a right *in rem* always relates to a thing is both accurate and useful.

It is important here to remember that the category of rights *in rem* is broader than that of property rights. For example, the right to bodily integrity vindicated by the tort of battery is an *in rem* right, because it has the human body as the focal point and imposes a uniform duty of noninterference not contingent on prior personal interactions. We generally do not, however, regard our bodies as property.[56] Similarly, the right against defamation is an *in rem* right having one's reputation as the conceptual focal point, even though we do not regard reputation as an object of property rights.

7.5.3 "*A single right* in rem *correlates with a duty resting on one person alone, not with many duties (or one duty) resting upon all the members of a very large and indefinite class of persons.*"

Hohfeld quotes the following passage from Frederick Pollock as an example of the kind of thinking he regards as perniciously muddled:

> Doubtless there are duties without any determinate rights corresponding to them: indeed, this is the case, in any view, with the negative duties which we owe to the

53 *See* Smith, *supra* note 4.

54 Hohfeld (1917), *supra* note 3, at 733.

55 For a more extensive discussion of this point, see Christopher Newman, *Using Things, Defining Property*, *in* PROPERTY THEORY 69 (James Penner & Michael Otsuka eds., 2018).

56 *See* PENNER, *supra* note 46, at 120–25 (discussing how the human body fails to satisfy the "separability thesis": that the property relation applies solely to things that are only contingently ours).

> community at large. For my duty not to damage other people's goods, for example, is one duty, not millions of separate duties owed to every one who has anything to be damaged, or in respect of every separate chattel of any value.[57]

I share Hohfeld's objection to the first sentence of this passage, which is not merely a normative statement omitting certain information, but one that directly contradicts a key analytic premise – the bilaterality of jural relations – without any normative payoff. When we speak of legal duties owed "to the community at large," we generally mean duties owed to each and every member of that community, each of whom has a corresponding right that could be violated by a breach of one of those duties.[58] Certainly, this is true of Pollock's example, the duty not to damage other people's goods. It is impossible to violate this duty without damaging some good to which some specific person had a right. Further, as discussed above, it is impossible to understand and comply with this duty without discerning which objects count as "other people's goods," a mental operation that necessarily (if implicitly) draws inferences as to the existence of some other person having such a right. It is true that one need not know *whose* property right is violated in order to recognize and comply with the duty, but nothing is gained in cognitive efficiency by going a step further and asserting that there is no corresponding right to be violated at all.

On the other hand, I would defend Pollock's insistence on conceiving of the duty not to damage other people's property as a singular rather than a set of millions. Hohfeld would say that I cannot have it both ways – if I agree that every legal duty corresponds to a right, it follows that I must have as many duties as there are property owners, unless I imagine that each single act of property violation implicates the entire class of property owners. Hohfeld is correct in this. Nevertheless, Pollock is correctly describing the manner in which duty holders cognitively experience their *in rem* duties. The duty to respect the goods of others is a single, intelligible principle with innumerable contextual applications. It would seem absurd to insist that people are merely confused any time they fail to conceive of it as a laundry list of millions of distinct duties corresponding to each property owner whose goods they might encounter, each owned good they might damage, and each action they might take that would result in such damage. To use a mathematical analogy, a function may be defined as an abstract way of describing an infinite set of data points. For the human being who as a practical matter will only ever need a small subset of those points, the function that lets her derive the locations of the ones she needs is the proper focus of her attention, not some hypothetical enumerated list identifying all of them.[59]

57 Hohfeld (1917), *supra* note 3, at 744 n.71.

58 There may also be duties owed to the community as a collective entity, such as the duty to pay taxes. In this case, it is the representative of the community – the state – that holds and may enforce the corresponding right. Moral theory may also posit so-called "imperfect duties" that do not correspond to rights, but that is a matter outside of positive legal analysis.

59 Smith, *supra* note 29, at 323: "No one thinks about the world in terms of every particular of a set: rather, a general concept allows one to grasp an important referential category: intensions are functions from the world to extensions."

Again, Hohfeld must surely have understood this obvious point, and yet he seems bent on denuding the legal vocabulary of terms that reflect the function rather than the list.[60]

Can we find a way of talking about *in rem* rights that does justice to both the intensional-normative and extensional-analytic perspectives? Here is an attempt at mediated settlement between Hohfeld and the theory of *in rem* rights developed above:

> The term "right *in rem*" denotes a relation between a right holder and a thing, that places the right holder in an identical right-duty relation pertaining to that thing with each person belonging to an open-ended class of duty holders. This class will generally include any person not sharing in the right holder's own relation to the thing (e.g., all "nonowners" of the thing are in the class, while co-owners of it are not). We say that the right holder has a (singular) "right to" the thing, which signifies that the substance of the duty imposed on each duty holder is identical and designed to protect the right holder's interest in the thing. We refer to this template duty as a (singular) "*in rem* duty." Nevertheless, the right-duty relation between the right holder and each duty holder is analytically distinct, and certain members of the class may have *in personam* relations (such as licenses) that modify the generally applicable contents of the *in rem* duty. Each of these distinct right-duty relations is termed a "multital" relation.

A few observations about my proposed settlement. It uses terms like "right" and "duty"[61] in conjunction with the modifier "*in rem*" to denote a complex interest that does not fit Hohfeld's concept of a distinct bilateral jural relation. This usage is akin to the "right to exclude" discussed earlier, or to the various compound relations discussed in Chapter 11. It reflects the understanding that from a normative perspective, an *in rem* relation is unitary – it governs relations pertaining to a single thing by means of a single cognizable template duty having uniform contents. On the other hand, my settlement honors Hohfeld's correct point that analytically this translates into a set of numerous distinct bilateral relations, as well as his request that we use the term "multital" to denote a single one of these.

Whether Hohfeld could have been persuaded to accept this settlement we cannot know. It is surely testament to the power of his analysis that, one hundred years after his death, I should feel compelled to offer it.

60 *Id.* at 324–30 (describing how Hohfeld paved the way for the "anti-conceptualist" program of the realists).

61 As illustrated in Section 7.4 above, I think all the other jural relations can occur as either *in rem* or *in personam* as well.

PART III

Hohfeld and Equity

8

Hohfeld's Equity

J. E. Penner[*]

8.1 INTRODUCTION

In 1913 Hohfeld published "The Relations Between Equity and Law" in the *Michigan Law Review*.[1] It is an odd sort of piece. In the first eight pages Hohfeld sets out his disagreement with Maitland, who held that the common law and equity are not (for the most part[2]) in conflict. Hohfeld claims that they are. The rest of the paper, some 25 pages, consists of the outline of his course on Equity, prepared for his students, with extensive "Supplemental Notes." In this paper I shall assess Hohfeld's claim that the rules of equity conflict with those of the common law, but also examine whether Hohfeld's general approach to equity reveals him to be an "equity purist" or an "equity pragmatist" (terms devised by Lionel Smith[3]). Equity purists hold that equity reflects a distinct form or mode of reasoning that resists assimilation to common law legal reasoning, reflecting some different understanding of justice, based perhaps on some idea of an individual's "conscience" being affected in a way that the common law disregards.[4] By contrast, equity pragmatists respect the historical division of labor that arose with the development of the "extraordinary" jurisdiction[5] of the Chancellor, but disagree that the rules of both equity and the common law answer to different standards of reasoning, justice, or morality. Besides

* Kwa Geok Choo Professor of Law, National University of Singapore. http://law.nus.edu.sg/about_us/faculty/staff/profileview.asp?UserID=lawjep. I thank the Yale workshop participants for their comments and suggestions. I owe especial thanks to Andrew Halpin and Henry Smith for their searching comments on this chapter. All remaining faults lie with me. I gratefully acknowledge the funding support of the National University of Singapore (WBS grant no. R-241–000-127–133).

1 Wesley N. Hohfeld, *The Relations Between Equity and Law*, 11 MICH. L. REV. 537 (1913).

2 *See infra* text accompanying note 19.

3 Lionel Smith, *Unravelling Proprietary Restitution*, 40 CAN. BUS. L.J. 317 (2004); Lionel D. Smith, *Book Review of Equitable Damages by Peter M. McDermott*; Equity: Issues and Trends *by Malcom Cope ed.*; Commercial Equity: Fiduciary Relationships *by John Glover*, 75 CAN. B. REV. 388 (1996).

4 Robert H. Rogers, *A Lesson In Equity*, 49 AM. L. REV. 510 (1915) argues (at 535) that, whilst the law is "approximate justice from the standpoint of social expediency," (at 536) equity embraces a notion of conscience which allows the courts to take part in "the development of our Christian civilization."

5 The term "extraordinary" refers to what is also called the "English" or equitable side of Chancery, that is what became the separate *court* of equity. The "ordinary" jurisdiction of the Chancery was that of

whatever historical interest there may be in Hohfeld's views on equity, his views are of particular interest today because of the recent revival of interest in equity as a distinct doctrinal phenomenon.[6]

The suggestion of this paper is that Hohfeld's treatment of the relations between equity and the law reveals more about his understanding of the way his "fundamental legal conceptions" framed in terms of his famous "jural relations"[7] interact in context than it does about any views Hohfeld might have had about the nature of justice as differently characterized or oriented in these two historic branches of English law. If anything, Hohfeld seems to believe that the origin of the Court of Chancery was a practical result of the deficiencies in the common law occasioned by the historical politics over the centuries in which the extraordinary jurisdiction of the chancellors arose. In that sense, Hohfeld might be regarded as an equity pragmatist. But, as far as I can see, Hohfeld only fleetingly explored the equity purist's claim that equity operated from a different perspective on morality or justice, so situating Hohfeld in the pragmatist camp is a tentative manoeuvre at best. For even if the origin of the Court of Chancery can be explained as a development of history which might not, as it happened, have occurred had things been different, it does not tell us whether the development of this jurisdiction *also* involved a particular self-conception on the part of chancellors and chancery lawyers which embraced a different attitude towards or reflection upon justice as administered under a systematic body of rules.

8.2 HOHFELD'S HISTORICAL TREATMENT OF EQUITY

Before proceeding, let me just mention one aspect of Hohfeld's characterization of equity that I am entirely in sympathy with. Hohfeld grounds his characterization of equitable doctrine in a fine-grained history, which takes up a significant part of his discussion,[8] and which I found, as someone who has taught the law of trusts for over 20 years, refreshingly informative. The overwhelming sense that one gets from these

preparing writs to initiate the legal process in the King's, i.e., the common law courts. Because the writs were in Latin, this ordinary jurisdiction or function of the Chancery was also called the "Latin side," as opposed to the "English side" of the Chancery, where the Chancellor's subpoenas and decrees were issued in English.

6 *See, e.g.*, Mark Leeming, *Equity: Ageless in the "Age of Statutes"*, 9 J. EQUITY 108 (2015); Leonard I. Rotman, *The "Fusion" of Law and Equity?: A Canadian Perspective on the Substantive, Jurisdictional, or Non-Fusion of Legal and Equitable Matters*, 2 CAN. J. COMP. & CONTEMP. L. 1 (2016); Henry E. Smith, *Why Fiduciary Law is Equitable*, *in* PHILOSOPHICAL FOUNDATIONS OF FIDUCIARY LAW (Andrew S. Gold & Paul B. Miller eds., 2014); Henry E. Smith, *Equity as Meta-Law*, 130 YALE L.J. 1050–287 (2021); Emily L. Sherwin, "Equity and the Modern Mind," Cornell Law School Research Paper No. 16-27, available at https://papers.ssrn.com/sol3/papers.cfm?abstract_id=2817803.

7 Wesley N. Hohfeld, *Some Fundamental Legal Conceptions As Applied In Judicial Reasoning*, 23 YALE L.J. 16 (1913); Wesley N. Hohfeld, *Fundamental Legal Conceptions As Applied In Judicial Reasoning*, 26 YALE L.J. 710 (1917).

8 Hohfeld, *supra* note 1, at 546–49 of the main text and supplemental notes 3–21, which take up over seven pages of fine print at 559–66.

passages is that Hohfeld understood the origin of equity to be *contingent* in the sense that the political structures of the time, and in particular the powers, or lack thereof, of the common law judges in relation to the executive, were the driving force behind the development of the extraordinary jurisdiction of the chancellor and the Court of Chancery. If that is right, this tends to frame Hohfeld as a pragmatist, if only because he did not think any particular "intellectual" development in terms of a different take on justice needed to be explored to explain this situation. Further evidence of Hohfeld's finding no such intellectual development is provided by his treating all legal jural relations as both legal and equitable jural relations, which we shall look at in detail below – if legal and equitable jural relations necessarily had different content because each framed a different take on justice, it is hard to see how they could be so easily treated as equally legal and equitable at the same time.

Moreover, Hohfeld's treatment of the maxims of equity is consonant with this view. Hohfeld said:[9]

> In the early development of equity the guiding ideas were "conscience," "good faith," "reason" and, more rarely, "equity."

After setting out the maxims, Hohfeld goes on to say:[10]

> The general principles and specific rules of equity are now for the most part defined by a large and well organized body of precedents, so that the above general ideas and maxims are, at the present time, of comparatively slight importance.[11]

I think this is right, and he might usefully have added that it would be difficult to frame any number of the maxims in terms of conscience, good faith, and so on, at least in a way that was distinctive of equity. To take but one example, it is difficult to find a moral precept which clearly distinguishes the idea underlying the equitable "clean hands" principle and the common law principle *ex turpi causa non oritur actio*.[12]

8.3 THE "JURISDICTIONS" OF EQUITY

As I have said, Hohfeld's stated purpose in the paper was to show that Maitland's view, that there was no conflict, or at least no thoroughgoing, systematic conflict, between equity and the common law, was wrong. Hohfeld's main way of attempting to show this turned on his distinction between the "concurrent" and "exclusive" jurisdictions of equity. According to Hohfeld, where equity acts within its

9 Hohfeld, *supra* note 1, at 549.

10 *Id.* at 550.

11 It is unclear whether Hohfeld's statement here implies that he believed that in equity's early days, prior to the "crystallization" of the maxims in a body of precedents, equity had a distinctive orientation to the resolution of the issues that came before it, as for example by focussing on the consciences of the parties.

12 *See, e.g.*, the discussion in *Tinsley* v. *Milligan* [1994] 1 AC 340.

concurrent jurisdiction with law, there is no conflict, because all the jural relations in this area of doctrine are both legal and equitable at the same time. For this reason, there can be no conflict between them. By contrast, where equity exercises its "exclusive" (sometimes called "original") jurisdiction, for example when it applies trusts law doctrine, or its "auxiliary jurisdiction," say where the Court of Chancery ordered a common law defendant to disclose documents to the plaintiff in the course of an action at law, the conflict between equity and the law is manifest, presumably ongoing, and only because of the rule that equity prevails over the common law can the law, as a whole, be seen to work. So the first thing that needs to be addressed is whether Hohfeld properly described and applied the idea that equity has different jurisdictions, and with respect, it appears that his views on this are both unorthodox and misguided in their own right.

Equity is conventionally said to have three jurisdictions, or areas of operation, each of which relates it to the common law: (1) equity's "exclusive" or "original" jurisdiction, where equity alone created law in an area; (2) its "concurrent" jurisdiction, where both it and the common law developed rules in relation to certain fact situations; and (3), its "auxiliary" jurisdiction, in which equity would assist plaintiffs at common law in pursuing their common law rights. Now this division is controversial and its utility has been criticized and, moreover, there is no general agreement about whether certain areas of equitable doctrine fit into (2) rather than (3), or indeed whether certain areas of doctrine originating in equity fit into any of these three categories.[13] Even so, it is submitted that these classifications do some analytic work in illuminating the relations between equity and the common law, and since Hohfeld relies upon one version of them, it is worth spending a little time on them.

The law of trusts is the most obvious example of equity's exclusive jurisdiction. The law of trusts was developed entirely by the Court of Chancery. The obvious sort of equitable intervention which exemplifies the auxiliary jurisdiction is an equitable order for disclosure or discovery of documents. In pursuance of her *common law* action against a defendant, a plaintiff could get a decree from the Court of Chancery requiring the defendant to make disclosure. Historically, that is, common law litigants were not afforded any right to disclosure under the procedures of the common law courts, but a common law litigant could get a decree from Chancery ordering the other party to disclose. (Nowadays, of course, this particular auxiliary power of equity has been superseded by statute-based codes of civil procedure.)

It is the concurrent jurisdiction and its relation to the auxiliary jurisdiction that is troublesome. It is troublesome because it can be taken in a narrow or broad sense, and in consequence the auxiliary jurisdiction must be taken to have a correspondingly wide or narrow ambit. Consider the power of a court of equity to award a decree of specific performance of a contract for the sale of land. On the

[13] *See* J. D. Heydon et al., Meagher, Gummow & Lehane's Equity: Doctrines & Remedies [1-90]–[1-110] (5th ed. 2015).

wide sense of the concurrent jurisdiction, this equitable power of the court of equity, and the correlative equitable remedy it provides, are part of the concurrent jurisdiction because both equity and the common law respond, though differently — at law only an award of damages is available — to the same wrong, a breach of contract.

By contrast, on the narrow reading, the concurrent jurisdiction is really quite restricted. It only concerns those areas of the law where the common law and equity each develop their own views of certain kinds of facts, and the appropriate remedies to provide, independently of each other. The two most clear examples are mistake in contract, and fraud. To consider just mistake, the common law doctrine of mistake in contract is quite narrow, finding a contract to be invalid only when there is a very basic mistake about the subject matter of the contract or the identity of the parties. Equity does not take such a restrictive view, allowing other kinds of mistakes to generate a remedy in certain circumstances. Thus although the jurisdiction is concurrent, the point about the concurrency is that both equity and the common law act *independently* of each other in analyzing the fact situation and providing remedies, and moreover, the particular facts in the fact situation to which each gives salience may differ. In other words, equity does not cede in such cases to the common law the decision about whether a mistake is operative so as to generate a remedy, and neither does the common law cede to equity what is relevant for the purposes of discerning a common law-relevant mistake. By contrast, in the case of a specifically enforceable contract, equity *does not* develop its own view about what amounts to a breach of contract in such a case — rather, it merely decides whether the common law remedy is an adequate remedy, and if not, assists the plaintiff in vindicating her *common law* rights under the contract by providing a better remedy of its own. In such a case equity cedes to the common law both the definition of the underlying substantive contractual right *and* the determination of whether the contract is breached.

It is submitted that the narrow reading of the concurrent jurisdiction is analytically superior. The basic reason why is that it allows us to maintain a proper distinction between the operation of the common law and equity, whereas the broad reading obscures it.

Let us consider again the case of equity's power to decree specific performance of a contract for the sale of land. It is hard to see the basis upon which it is analytically helpful to treat this as part of the concurrent jurisdiction, rather than the auxiliary jurisdiction. As I have just pointed out, in such a case equity cedes the question whether the parties are in breach to the common law. It is not the case that a breach of a common law contract is "a breach of contract in equity" — there are not separate "equitable principles" of breach of contract. Equity's only concern, and the only basis upon which the equitable jurisdiction is invoked, is that the common law remedies for breach of the contract *at common law* are inadequate. The same goes, for example, for invoking the jurisdiction of equity to seek an injunction in the case of a continuing trespass or nuisance. Equity does not develop its own principles of nuisance or trespass. It only seeks to determine whether its power to grant injunctions in such cases is warranted in light of the common law's response to the wrongs that *the common law* recognizes. Now, of course, in recognizing these wrongs as ones which justify equity's intervention, equity recognizes them *as wrongs;* but it does not follow from that that equity or the legal system as a whole turns them into *equitable* wrongs as well, any more than the fact that equity recognizes that the trustee of trust property has a legal title to that property turns that title into an *equitable* one. Indeed, if that were so the whole law of trusts would be undermined.

If this is right, then the fact that most of the interaction between equity and the common law falls within the ambit of equity's auxiliary jurisdiction is important. It shows equity saw itself to have no general jurisdiction to trench upon or reform the substantive common law, and this was always reflected in its own self-understanding of not having either the right or the power to change the common law.[14] Rather, it gave aid to common law litigants where the limitations of the common law would work injustice.

8.4 HOHFELD'S CHARACTERIZATION OF THE JURISDICTIONS OF EQUITY: THE CONCURRENT JURISDICTION

On the jurisdictions of equity, Hohfeld's position seems to be driven by his anti-Maitland "conflict" thesis. Hohfeld's extended statement of that thesis is as follows:[15]

> As against the proposition of these various scholars that there is no appreciable conflict between law and equity, the thesis of the present writer is this: while a large part of the rules of equity harmonize with the various rules of law, another large part of the rules of equity — more especially those relating to the so-called exclusive and auxiliary jurisdictions of equity — conflict with legal rules and, as a matter of substance, annul or negative the latter *pro tanto*. As just indicated, there is, it is believed, a very marked and constantly recurring conflict between equitable and legal rules relating to various jural relations; and whenever such conflict occurs, the equitable rule is, in the last analysis, paramount and determinative. Or, putting the matter in another way, the so-called legal rule in every such case has, *to that extent,* only an apparent validity and operation as a matter of *genuine* law. Though it may represent an important *stage of thought* in the solution of a given problem, and may also connote very important possibilities as to certain other, closely associated (and valid) jural relations, yet as regards the very relation in which it suffers direct competition with a rule of equity, such a conflicting rule of law is, *pro tanto*, of no greater force than an unconstitutional statute.[16]

[14] For a thorough examination of the way the common law courts sought to "police" the equitable jurisdiction of the various courts exercising an equitable jurisdiction in the period surrounding Lord Coke's quarrel with the Chancery in 1616, see Charles M. Gray, *The Boundaries of the Equitable Function*, 20 AM. J. LEGAL HIST. 192 (1976).

[15] Hohfeld, *supra* note 1, at 543–44 (emphasis in original, footnote omitted).

[16] At the end of this passage is footnote 10 (Hohfeld, *supra* note 1, at 544), which refers the reader to a later supplemental note, note 36 (*id.* at 570), in which Hohfeld analogizes the action of equity upon the

For Hohfeld, then, the auxiliary and exclusive jurisdictions are the site of conflict between equity and the common law, whilst the concurrent jurisdiction, as we shall see, is the jurisdiction where they are in harmony, because all substantive common law legal rights in this jurisdiction are at the same time substantive equitable rights. But to begin with, it is worth recording the unorthodoxy of this position. Rather than the auxiliary and exclusive jurisdictions being in conflict with equity, it is normally understood that where there is conflict this arises in the concurrent jurisdiction. As to the first two, the exclusive jurisdiction of equity is normally not regarded to be in conflict with the common law for the simple reason that the common law has nothing to say about the equitable norms in question and their application to any particular fact situation. To take the most clear examples, the law of trusts and the law governing fiduciaries are not regarded to be in conflict with the rules of common law for the simple reason that the common law does not recognize, or rather cognize, trusts or fiduciary relationships. As to the auxiliary jurisdiction, the whole point of this jurisdiction is that equity aims to give better rights to common law plaintiffs than the common law gives them itself. This is seen by equity as overcoming limitations of the common law, not *displacing* or overturning the common law. Hohfeld seems to think that *any* departure from common law doctrine amounts to a *repudiation* or *overruling* of the common law but, as we have already seen, this is not the way in which Chancery judges perceived their jurisdiction. Neither is it analytically sound. For example, a party to a contract for the sale of land need not seek a decree of specific performance if she is happy with an award of damages. That is, equity's willingness to make such a decree does not displace the common law remedy; it merely adds one of its own.[17]

Moving on to the concurrent jurisdiction, it is here, arguably, that genuine conflict can be found, because both equity and the common law take a look at a particular fact situation and based on their distinct views of justice will see different liabilities. We have already seen this in the case of mistake. But Hohfeld himself gives two excellent examples, in respect of one of which, Hohfeld points out that Maitland himself was willing to acknowledge a conflict between equity and the common law.[18]

At common law, a tenant for life would be liable to the remainderman for what was known as waste, that is, harming the land (including the buildings thereon) so as to give over to the remainderman an estate less valuable than that which the tenant for life received. Nevertheless, it was common for tenants for life to be granted their life interest "without impeachment for waste," thus relieving them of liability for, to use Hohfeld's example, cutting down some ornamental trees and selling the timber.

common law to the doctrine of implicit statutory repeal, i.e., repeal of an earlier statute by a later one with inconsistent provisions.

[17] Hohfeld's attitude here is doubtless related to his view that where equity does not intervene to alter the common law in respect of a certain set of common law rights and remedies, those rights and remedies are to be treated as rights and remedies both of the common law and of equity. *See infra* text accompanying note 20.

[18] *See id.* at 555 and supplemental note 36 at 570–71.

Despite this legal relief from liability for waste, equity developed its own doctrine of waste, equitable waste, such that whilst despite the fact that at common law a tenant for life who chopped down those trees was relieved of liability because of the "without impeachment for waste" provision in her grant, she would be liable for equitable waste, and could be subject to an injunction prior to chopping down the trees or an account of her profits from the sale of timber if she did.

The other pertinent example of conflict that Hohfeld raises is the case of a wife at common law making a loan contract with her husband.[19] At common law under the doctrine of "coverture," upon marrying a woman's private law legal personality more or less disappeared or merged with that of her husband. Thus there could be no legally valid common law relations between them. But if a woman made a loan of money from her separate equitable estate under a marriage settlement, equity would enforce the loan against the husband. Here, again, we seem to have a genuine case of conflict, equity overturning the common law to this limited extent, giving effect to a loan whose very legal possibility was denied at common law.

As we have seen,[20] Hohfeld's position on the nature of the different jurisdictions of equity seems to be driven by his anti-Maitland conflict thesis. In keeping with this thesis it seems to follow for him that where A has a substantive legal right, privilege, power or immunity, and there is no equitable doctrine which applies to alter or conflict with A's being in such a jural relation, such a jural relation is *ipso facto* also an equitable jural relation. In other words, where there is no conflict between the common law and equity, equity more or less absorbs the common law as part of itself.

Here is one of Hohfeld's examples of a "concurrent" right, that is a right which is both legal and equitable, that shows the flavor of his reasoning:[21]

> Example 11: If X has ownership and possession of certain land, and Y, a stranger, is about to walk across, X's right that Y should not commit this simple trespass and, correspondingly, the duty of Y not to do so are concurrently legal and equitable. In case of breach by Y, an action at law could be maintained by X; and equity would vindicate X's right by refusing an injunction sought by Y to restrain X from maintaining his vindicatory action at law; sometimes, by entertaining a bill for discovery in aid of X's action at law; sometimes, also, in case Y's act were being repeated from day to day, by granting an injunction.

On the conventional understanding of X's equitable right to the assistance of the court of equity, or at least on the characterization of the jurisdictions of equity I have set out above, this equitable assistance would fall under equity's auxiliary jurisdiction, for the equitable "action" in this example is equity's granting (or not granting) an injunction in aid of X's common law rights, or granting an order for discovery. But for Hohfeld, it seems, because equity and the common law are "on the same page" as

19 *See id.* at 555 and supplemental note 39 at 571.

20 *See supra* note 15 and accompanying text.

21 *See* Hohfeld, *supra* note 1, at 553.

it were, both supporting X's common law rights, such a right is both equitable and legal at the same time. To put this thought in another way, those areas of "equity-free" common law doctrine in which no such conflicts are found are what Hohfeld regards as equity's "concurrent" jurisdiction. Where equity does intervene in any way to affect the common law position we have a case of conflict, and this arises both in respect of equity's exclusive jurisdiction and its auxiliary jurisdiction, as we shall see.

Now, Hohfeld realizes perfectly well that this way of framing the concurrent jurisdiction can be challenged. Basically the idea is, why call these common law jural relations which remain uninfluenced by equity both "legal *and* equitable" jural relations? Why not just say they are "legal" relations? After all, they are only recognized at common law in the conventional understanding; they had their origin in the common law and all the doctrine realising them is exclusively common law doctrine. Why bring equity into their characterization at all? Hohfeld addresses this point in a long supplemental note.[22] As far as I can see, he has only one argument, though he illustrates it copiously.

This is the argument:[23]

> As regards both law and equity, all primary, or antecedent, relations and all secondary, or remedial, relations can, in general, be ascertained only by inference from the purely adjective juridical processes, that is, by inference from either affirmative or negative action regularly to be had from the particular courts from which a judgment or decree may be sought. As said by Maitland, in relation, more particularly, to the early law: "*De Natura Brevium*, Of the Nature of Writs, — such is the title of more than one well known text-book of our mediaeval law. Legal Remedies, Legal Procedure, these are the all-important topics for the student. These being mastered, a knowledge of substantive law will come of itself. Not the nature of rights, but the nature of writs must be his theme." . . .
>
> When a jural relation is such as to be recognized and vindicated only in equity, it is, according to general usage, called "exclusively equitable," — for instance, the right of a cestui against his trustee; and that usage seems justified by reason. Why, then, in aid of clear thinking, shouldn't all other jural relations be considered, by a precisely similar process of reasoning, "concurrently legal and equitable?"

With respect, this is not only a bad argument, but is also inconsistent with Hohfeld's own understanding of an individual jural relation.

It is a bad argument because it is not true that the substance of a right can only be understood, or even best understood, whether by "inference" or in some other way, from the adjectival or remedial consequences that flow from its breach. The considerations that determine whether one has such and such a duty are not the *same* considerations that determine what sort of response, such as the provision of a remedy, should be applied to someone who breaches that duty. I take it that this is

[22] *Id.* supplemental note 34, at 569–70.

[23] *Id.*

abundantly clear from the criminal law, but sticking with the civil law: it is the very same kind of duty that is breached when I fail to transfer the property in question under a contract of sale, whether it is a contract to transfer title to chattels or title to land, but only in the latter do we regard this as generally a case allowing the remedy of specific performance, and the orthodox justification for this is that damages in the latter case are inadequate because land is unique (location, location, location) whereas chattels (goods) typically are not, so that in the case of land one cannot just go out into the market and obtain a more or less perfect substitute. This is not to say that *no* information about the substantive right can be gleaned from the remedial responses to its breach. It is merely to say that it is not true that the two are epistemically transparent in the sense that knowing everything about the one will provide you with everything you need to know about the other. This is particularly evident if you happen to like the idea that equitable remedies are always discretionary. Just because the remedies are discretionary does not entail in any way that any discretion enters into the determination whether X holds the underlying substantive right or the determination that the right has been breached.

This strategy of Hohfeld's also seems to be fatally flawed on his own accounting of individual jural relations. Maybe it is anachronistic to attribute to him a couple of years before he published Fundamental Legal Conceptions I and II his thought that jural relations should only be "intrinsically" considered and not, as far as their identity was concerned, determined by whatever "extrinsic" relations they bore to other jural relations, including to whatever adjectival or remedial jural relations that would arise on the occasion of their breach.[24] But be that as it may, Hohfeld provides nothing here beyond his reference to Maitland to water down the views he later came to hold explicitly in order, in this paper, to bolster what is already a bad argument.

It is also important to note a possible contradiction in Hohfeld's thinking on this point in this very paper. It is clear from example 11 that equity's intervention to aid the common law litigant's ability to enforce such a right by, for example, ordering discovery in the litigation process, does not change matters as regards the substantive jural relation in question.[25] But, as we shall see below when we look at Hohfeld's characterization of equity's auxiliary jurisdiction,[26] the power of granting a decree for discovery *does*, according to Hohfeld, change matters as regards the plaintiff's secondary or adjectival jural relations. The equity judge's power of granting an order for discovery *conflicts*, Hohfeld maintains, with the common law judge's disability in being unable to make such an order. If that is so, it would seem that the same lesson could be applied to example 11 in so far as a substantive right is supposed to be reflective of its connection to adjectival jural relations: if the adjectival relation under which the common law court has a disability of granting an order of discovery

[24] *See* Hohfeld (1913), *supra* note 7, at 47, 59 n.100; Hohfeld (1917), *supra* note 7, at 723, 727.

[25] *See* Hohfeld, *supra* note 1, example 12 at 553.

[26] *See infra* text accompanying note 28.

conflicts with equity's power to do so, then the substantive right itself would seem to need to reflect this conflict. And if that is so, there are clear and thoroughgoing conflicts throughout Hohfeld's concurrent jurisdiction, ruling out the very basis for the classification as he presents it. There is nothing in Hohfeld's discussion which shows any awareness of this problem.[27]

Before leaving Hohfeld's flawed characterization of the "concurrent" jurisdiction, it is perhaps worthwhile considering whether Hohfeld's attitude here reflects a kind of "fusionist" thinking. The "fusion" of equity and the law is of course the idea that where both equitable and legal doctrine interact in a particular area, say in remedies for breach of contract, the historic origins of equity and the common law should cease to distinguish different rules of the operative law as "legal" and "equitable." The idea here would be that the law governing breach of contract is one law, the different aspects of which (the measure of damages, the question of remoteness, the availability of specific performance, and so on) should be just considered "legal," not divided up by their historical origins, and should be explained and assessed on the basis of principle, again not because the reasons given historically are to be divided by those reasons' first appearance in the decisions of common law or chancery judges. That is perfectly fine by me, and I would endorse it. But it does not seem to do any actual work when we are trying to determine the relations *between* law and equity, which requires us to keep the jurisdictions distinct for the purpose of the analysis at hand.

8.5 HOHFELD'S CHARACTERIZATION OF THE JURISDICTIONS OF EQUITY: THE "EXCLUSIVE" JURISDICTION

We can now move to Hohfeld's characterization of the exclusive and auxiliary jurisdictions, in so far as we can detect what he means by them. Let us consider some examples from each, reminding ourselves that, unlike the concurrent jurisdiction, these are areas of doctrine in which, according to Hohfeld, the common law and equity conflict. His examples are found under the rubric "The Conflict of Equity and Law," and he refers to all his examples as examples of "exclusive" jural relations, meaning "exclusively equitable"; so it may be the case that Hohfeld's one mention of "auxiliary" earlier in the text, as may be found in the quotation above,[28]

[27] In supplemental note 36 at 571, Hohfeld (*supra* note 1) recognizes that though a common law jural relation is substantively "repealed" by the existence of the opposite jural relation in equity, the common law jural relation is still effective in respect of some of the applications of certain adjectival jural relations connected with it. So, he says: "[E]ven though a legal primary right conflicts with an equitable 'no-right', it would be the duty of the common law judge to overrule a demurrer to a declaration setting forth such supposed legal right and its violation, and, ultimately, to render judgment for the plaintiff; and, of course, an execution sale based on such judgment would be valid. These independent (and valid) jural relations, though connoted by the original (invalid) legal right in question, must be carefully distinguished from the latter." It is very hard to square this thought both with the idea that the (invalid) legal right is reflective of its "connoted" adjectival jural relations, and his analogy with genuine equitable "repeal" of common law jural relations, discussed below. *See infra* text accompanying note 36.

[28] *See supra* note 15 and accompanying text.

may indicate that he felt that the auxiliary jurisdiction was part of, or for analytic purposes should be subsumed under, equity's exclusive jurisdiction. There is insufficient textual evidence to decide the matter one way or the other.

Here are several examples concerning trusts which conventionally would be regarded as being within equity's exclusive jurisdiction:

> Example 35:[29] If T holds Whiteacre in fee simple in trust for C in fee simple, C's equitable right *in personam* (i.e., special or "determinate" right) that T shall not cut down ornamental trees conflicts with C's legal "no-right"; and, correlatively, T's equitable duty not to cut down ornamental trees conflicts with his legal privilege of doing so.

> Example 51:[30] O, the owner of certain property may gratuitously declare himself trustee thereof for C. The power thus to create a trust is exclusively equitable; there is a legal disability to create such a trust. It may thus fairly be said that the rule of equity is in conflict with the rule of law.

And here are several examples which conventionally would be regarded as being within equity's auxiliary jurisdiction:

> Example 53:[31] If A on Jan. 1st contracts to convey realty to B on June 1st, and if B on June 1st performs all conditions precedent and concurrent, but A refuses and fails to convey the realty to B, B's ensuing equitable remedial right that A shall make specific reparation by actually conveying the realty to B conflicts with B's legal "no-right"; and, correlatively, A's equitable duty thus to make specific reparation conflicts with his legal privilege of not doing so. (That is, his only legal duty is to pay to B the difference between the market and the contract price of the realty.)

> Example 58:[32] If A sues B in a certain action at law, A's equitable right that B make written answers to interrogatories by A (such answers to be used in the pending action as "admissions" against B) conflicts with A's legal "no-right"; and, correlatively, B's equitable duty thus "to make discovery" conflicts with his legal privilege of not doing so.

> Example 60:[33] In any suit for an injunction, the power of the chancery judge to impose the "injunction obligation" on the defendant, and correlatively, the liability of the defendant to have such "injunction" obligation imposed on him are exclusively equitable – i.e., capable of recognition and vindication only in a court of equity. The chancery judge's equitable power conflicts with his legal disability, and the defendant's equitable liability conflicts with his legal immunity.

With respect, it is submitted that Hohfeld draws the wrong lessons from each of these examples, and this can be shown by comparing them with cases of genuine conflict between equity and the common law, the ones we have already noticed: mistake, waste, and the power of a wife to contract with her husband. Recall that in each of

29 Hohfeld, *supra* note 1, at 555.
30 *Id.* at 556.
31 *Id.*
32 *Id.*
33 *Id.* at 557.

these cases the common law and equity really do take different views of the fact situations in question. It is irrelevant to this point which jurisdiction of equity these examples are taken to belong to. The point is that, in contrast to these cases, no similar genuine conflict arises in the five examples just set out.

In example 35, the case of the trust, the example can be summarized by saying that at common law the trustee has no duty not to cut down the trees, but has a duty not to do so in equity, whereas C, the beneficiary, has no right at common law that the trustee not cut down the trees, but has a right in equity that he not do so. This would seem to be the form of Hohfeld's challenge to Maitland's view that equity and the common law do not conflict; that where a duty exists in equity but not in law, the two come into conflict. But this seems mistaken as a general analysis of jural relations.

Consider first a case wholly within the common law, the case of the formation of a contract of sale. Prior to entering into a contract of sale of my Picasso, I have no duty to transfer it, and I have the liberty to destroy it. After entering into a contract with X to do so, I do have a duty to transfer it to X, and whilst I am under an obligation not to transfer it to anyone but X nor destroy it, as regards everyone, including X, I still have the legal power to transfer it to Y or any other third party and the legal liberty to destroy it; exercising either this power or this liberty would, of course, be a breach of my contractual obligation to X, but having that obligation in no way eradicates my power to transfer my Picasso to anyone nor my liberty to destroy it. Now would we want to say that some of my common law jural relations following the entry into this contract are "in conflict" with my jural relations beforehand? For example, does my retaining the power to transfer, to transfer to anyone, including X of course, *conflict* with my obligation to transfer the Picasso to X? It would seem odd to say so; the only way I can fulfill my obligation to X is to exercise this power of transfer; the fact that it is a power to transfer to anyone does not generate a *conflict*, except in so far as exercising this power by transferring the Picasso to Y would be a breach of the obligation. But the mere possibility of a breach of duty does not generate a conflict; only a breach itself would, in the sense that now X and I have a dispute recognized at common law.

Now consider the case of the trust. Prior to undertaking the trust, the trustee has the legal liberty of cutting down the trees on Blackacre. By taking on the trust, whilst retaining the liberty at common law, he undertakes not to exercise this liberty, and will commit a breach of trust if he does so. By parity of reasoning with the contractual case, it is difficult to see that the undertaking of an obligation not to exercise a liberty one has and retains is fruitfully analyzed in terms of "conflict." Recall that Maitland's main anti-"conflict" point was that the trustee's retention of all of his common law rights, liberties, powers and so on that go with his title to the trust property is necessary for the trustee to provide the benefits of that property to the beneficiary under the terms of the trust, and on this point Maitland is absolutely right.[34] His continuing retention of all

[34] *See* J. E. Penner, *The (True) Nature of a Beneficiary's Equitable Proprietary Interest Under a Trust*, 27 CAN. J. L. & JURIS. 473 (2014).

these common law jural relations is not in conflict with his duty to the beneficiary; his retaining them is a prerequisite for his complying with the trust – it is only, for example, because he retains the power of title to the trust assets can he *fulfill* his duty to the beneficiary, say by distributing the trust assets to the beneficiary at the appropriate time under the terms of the trust.

In short then, both at common law and in equity, simply owing an obligation to someone else to exercise a power in a particular way does not reveal a conflict between the power and the obligation; the fulfillment of the latter depends upon the existence of the former. Moreover, if Hohfeld, or a Hohfeldian, wished to insist on treating these cases as cases of "conflict," then he or she would be required to find systematic conflicts throughout the law of obligations, not just in equity, but throughout the common law, as the Picasso example shows. And if that is so, there is nothing distinctive to be said here about the relations between equity and the common law. So Hohfeld, or the Hohfeldian, loses either way.

Example 51 reveals a different error. Why does having a power in equity to declare a trust conflict with the absence of such a power at common law? Compare again, a case purely within the common law. A person has a power under the common law of covenants to create a binding gratuitous promise by executing a deed, but no such power under the general common law of contract (i.e., that derived from the action of assumpsit): A has no power to undertake an obligation to B unless B provides some consideration in exchange. So the law of covenants (obligations under seal) provides a power to create binding, gratuitously-undertaken, obligations, which the general law of contract lacks. How is this a matter of conflict between the two? On this sort of reasoning *Hamlet* conflicts with *Romeo and Juliet* because *Hamlet* has characters that *Romeo and Juliet* lacks, and vice versa. The same lesson applies just as much to the case of a power to declare a trust. It is not true that the common law's *not* providing a power to declare a trust is the same thing as the common law's saying that there *should not* be a power to declare a trust. It is not like the case of waste, where both the common law and equity have spoken, and they disagree in what they say. The appropriate analytic perspective is not that of conflict, but that of a division of labor. This point deserves some emphasis. All bodies of law have within them departments which deal with different issues, and often address the same or similar fact situations differently as, for example, the law of covenants treats formal gratuitously undertaken obligations differently than does the general law of contract or, to take another example, when a certain act by the defendant gives rise to concurrent liability in tort and in contract. The law of contract is not in conflict with company law because one cannot create a legal personality by entering into a contract, or with the law of torts because you cannot create a legal personality by committing a trespass to the person. Rather, the law has different subject matters, and the law of trusts is no outlier in this respect just because it relates in a particular way to the common law of property, any more than the common law of security interests known as pledges is an outlier in virtue of the fact that it also relates to the common law of property in its own particular way. And once again, if this notion of conflict is sustained, then we can find examples of such conflicts throughout the common law itself, as the covenant/contract and concurrent liability in tort and contract examples show, so nothing distinctive about the relations between equity and the common law can be discerned. The same critique applies to examples 53, 58, and 60. In each of these cases Hohfeld finds that the existence of a jural relation in equity conflicts with its absence at common law, or the existence of the opposite jural relation at common law (right in equity, no-right at common law in 53, 58; equitable power/legal disability, equitable liability/legal immunity in 60). The framing of the judge's equitable power to award an injunction and his disability to do so at common law is a particularly disturbing example, since it seems any one judge is at conflict with himself in such a circumstance. But again, the conflict is illusory. A judge's power under a statute[35] to order an employer to reinstate an employee for "unfair" dismissal does not conflict with the judge's absence of such a power at common law, under which she can only give damages for "wrongful" dismissal. The statute just provides her with a power she lacks at common law.

8.6 THE ANALOGY WITH IMPLICIT STATUTORY REPEAL

As we have seen, in characterizing the "conflict of law and equity" Hohfeld said:[36]

> [A]s regards the very relation in which it suffers direct competition with a rule of equity, such a conflicting rule of law is, *pro tanto*, of no greater force than an unconstitutional statute.

The idea is elaborated in Supplemental Note 36.[37] Discussing again the example of waste, Hohfeld says:[38]

> Suppose that a statute of yesterday provided that a tenant "without impeachment" should be privileged to cut ornamental trees; and assume, further, that a statute of today were to declare that any tenant "without impeachment" should be under a duty not to cut ornamental trees. Would anyone hesitate to admit that the two statutes would be in conflict with each other, and that the first would be repealed by the second? A similar comparison with inconsistent statutes may be helpful in seeing the conflict of law and equity as regards the various other examples given in the text.

Now, this statutory repeal analogy presents Hohfeld with a conundrum – if the later statute genuinely repeals the former, the former now no longer forms part of the

35 E.g., section 94(1) of the Employment Rights Act 1996 (UK), which provides that an employee has the right not to be "unfairly" dismissed; sections 111 to 117 give employment tribunals a range of remedial powers, one of which is to order the employer to reinstate an employee who has been unfairly dismissed.

36 *See supra* note 15 and accompanying text.

37 *Id.* at 570–71.

38 *Id.* at 570.

law – it is abolished, in which case it is no longer a valid law that is in conflict with the later statute. If the analogy is taken seriously, then, it would seem that the "conflict thesis" fails. If, however, Hohfeld wants to maintain that there is an *ongoing* conflict between law and equity, then he must abandon the analogy of statutory repeal, and treat the resolution of each conflict, though predictable, only momentary when any individual judge, whilst admitting the conflict in the rules, resolves the conflict in favor of the equitable rule. As with the case whether a substantive jural relation is to be only "intrinsically" considered or must be taken to reflect or be connected to its adjectival jural relations, there is nothing in the text which indicates Hohfeld thought about this apparent inconsistency.

Nevertheless, in the final analysis, Hohfeld's "conflict" thesis appears to amount to the following two propositions:

(1) that the courts of equity can change the common law, but courts of common law cannot change equitable doctrine;
(2) the model of such change is to be analogized (how precisely it is impossible to tell) to the doctrine of implicit statutory repeal.

This is not so much a model of conflict as a model of legislation. Be that as it may, there is a further problem of treating the relations of common law and equity (outside Hohfeld's questionable "concurrent" jurisdiction) as one of legislation by the latter which implicitly repeals the former. It fails to appreciate two different kinds of legislation; legislation that genuinely overturns pre-existing law, and legislation that merely *adds to*, or rather *builds upon* the pre-existing law. This thought was foreshadowed by our discussion of the examples in the last part. Taking the case of waste once more, one can make the case that the equitable doctrine of waste really did implicitly repeal the common law doctrine. But, as in the case of a statute providing a judge with a power to reinstate an employee who has been unfairly dismissed, or the equitable power to declare a trust or a judge's equitable power to decree specific performance, the "legislation" involved does not implicitly *repeal* anything. It merely *adds* to the law, conferring powers that did not exist before.

One final point on this analogy.[39] Hohfeld may have been asserting, first, that equity is "second-order" law, in the sense that it does not exactly *repeal* the common law when it acts contrary to it, but that it *suspends* the common law so long as equity maintains its contrary view regarding a particular doctrine. It would be akin to a U.S. federal statute overriding state law in an area of joint legislative competence. If the federal statute were repealed, then the state law would "revive" in the sense of being fully operative again. Second, we might take his assertion to be that because equity is, in principle, unlimited in scope, it could potentially suspend any particular common law doctrine if it thought fit to do so, and so "conflict" is the right way to see the relation between law and equity: the *potential* for equitable intervention is

[39] I am grateful to Aditi Bagchi, John Harrison, and Henry Smith for suggestions on this point.

general and systematic. This may be a promising way of elaborating Hohfeld's thought, but if it does genuinely reflect his own views, it generates a problem for any modern system of precedent. Case law is developed all the time, and this notion of implicit suspension would presumably operate in any precedent case which departs from the pre-existing law, for example when a court overrules a long-standing precedent because it is felt to be out of keeping with modern notions of justice. The power of overruling is not restricted in modern legal systems to cases where recourse is made to "equitable" reasoning. But the same "putting in suspense" effect is thereby realised. If a later court overruled the overruling case, then the prior judge-made law would presumably revive. So, given modern judicial power and the doctrine of precedent, the "suspension" model of the analogy to statutory repeal would, again, not really identify a distinct equitable function. To find that, it seems to me, would require the identification of a *particular* second order function of equity, of the kind that Henry Smith pursues in his recent work, for example, that equity is a particular mode of decision-making that addresses opportunistic behavior within the extant rules of the system.[40] Nothing of that kind appears in this paper of Hohfeld's.

8.7 CONCLUSION

So where does all of this leave us? The paper is a matter of historical interest because it represents Hohfeld's first crack at analyzing legal doctrine by employing his scheme of fundamental legal conceptions, that is, by employing the eight jural relations that the scheme identifies. First attempts at anything are bound to be flawed in some respects, and we have noticed some inconsistencies and puzzles here. Unfortunately, Hohfeld's main thesis, that across a range of cases equity and the common law are in conflict, is not well supported by his arguments. Finally, to the extent that we can place Hohfeld on one side of the pragmatist/purist divide, it seems reasonable to say that he leans towards the former, but that there is insufficient textual support to say this with any real conviction.

[40] *See* Smith, *Equity as Meta-Law*, *supra* note 6.

9

The Essential Nature of Trusts and Other Equitable Interests: Two and a Half Cheers for Hohfeld

*Ben McFarlane**

9.1 INTRODUCTION

"From very early days down to the present time the essential nature of trusts and other equitable interests has formed a favorite subject for analysis and disputation."[1] Hohfeld's opening observation might have been written yesterday. Indeed, the liveliness of academic interest in the subject over the first two decades of this century[2] parallels that of the first two decades of the last:[3] Modern thinkers retain a "peculiar fascination"[4] for the subject. This chapter aims to show why, and how, Hohfeld's work is relevant to this contemporary debate; it also demonstrates why the subject is worth arguing about. In doing so, the chapter makes three main points. Each may also be important when considering the wider importance of Hohfeld's work.

First, whilst Hohfeld criticized the then prevailing academic analyses of the nature of trusts and equitable interests as "inadequate,"[5] he did not, of course, regard inquiry into the conceptual questions as redundant. Rather, Hohfeld emphasized the *practical* importance of the correct characterization of such rights, by showing

* Professor of English Law, University of Oxford and Fellow of St. John's College, Oxford. Formerly Professor of Law, University College London. I am grateful for the support of a British Academy/ Leverhulme Trust Small Research Grant and for comments received at the symposium, including those of Daniel Clarry, who kindly acted as a commentator.

1 Wesley N. Hohfeld, *Some Fundamental Legal Conceptions as Applied in Judicial Reasoning* 23 YALE L. J. 16 (1913).

2 For contributions to this debate, *see e.g.*, R. Nolan, *Equitable Property* 122 L.Q. REV. 232 (2006); L. Smith, *Trust and Patrimony*, 38 REVUE GÉNÉRALE DE DROIT 9 (2008); B. McFarlane & R. Stevens, *The Nature of Equitable Property*, 4 J. EQUITY 1 (2010); J. Penner, *The (True) Nature of a Beneficiary's Equitable Proprietary Interest Under a Trust*, 27 CAN. J. L. & JURIS. 473 (2014); P. Jaffey, *Explaining the Trust*, 131 L.Q. REV. 377 (2015); E. Zaccaria, *The Nature of the Beneficiary's Right Under a Trust: Proprietary Right, Purely Personal Right, or Right against a Right?* 135 L.Q. REV. 460 (2019).

3 *See, e.g.*, C. C. Langdell, *Classification of Rights and Wrongs*, 13 HARV. L. REV. 659 (1900); F. W. MAITLAND, LECTURES ON EQUITY (1909); A. W. Scott, *The Nature of the Rights of the "Cestui Que Trust"*, 17 COLUM. L. REV. 269 (1917); *and* H. F. Stone, *The Nature of the Rights of the "Cestui Que Trust"*, 17 COLUM. L. REV. 467 (1917).

4 Hohfeld, *supra* note 1, at 16.

5 *Id.* at 18.

how it might determine questions addressed by the courts.[6] By considering three such issues addressed relatively recently by courts in the United States, England, and Australia, this chapter demonstrates the continuing truth of Hohfeld's contention that: "the true analysis of trusts and other equitable interests is a matter that should appeal to even the most extreme pragmatists of the law."[7] This point is of wider significance: nowadays, it is often assumed that a careful analysis of doctrines employed by the courts is naïve, or even dangerous, as it takes the judges at their own words and can obscure important questions of policy or efficiency.[8] In this chapter, however, it will be seen that even the most practical issues (such as the information costs imposed on third parties by the recognition of particular rights) may depend on the precise nature of the relevant legal relations. Moreover, before one can properly evaluate the efficiency or otherwise of the current law, it is important to know not only the existing results, but also the means by which the law reaches those results.[9]

Second, whilst the academic debate as to the nature of trusts and other equitable interests is of course long-standing, this chapter will argue both that some advances have recently been made, and that such progress demonstrates the usefulness of some key parts of Hohfeld's analysis. This may be an example of a broader phenomenon – as shown by a number of the contributions to this volume,[10] an application of Hohfeld's scheme may assist in ensuring that, in any particular debate, the right questions are at least asked, and the opposing participants are really addressing the same questions. Indeed, like a cold but bracing shower, the technical nature of a Hohfeldian analysis may serve to take some of the muddling heat out of intemperate debates as to legal rights.

The third point includes a note of caution. Hohfeld regarded the then current debate as to the nature of trusts and other equitable interests as "inadequate" partly because:

> The tendency – and the fallacy – has been to treat the specific problem as if it were far less complex than it really is; and this commendable effort to treat as simple that which is really complex has, it is believed, furnished a serious obstacle to the clear understanding, the orderly statement, and the correct solution of legal problems. In

6 Two examples given by Hohfeld were London & SW Railway Co. v. *Gomm* (1882) 20 Ch D 562 (CA) and Re Nisbet and Potts Contract [1906] 1 Ch 386 (CA).

7 Hohfeld, *supra* note 1, at 18.

8 It is, however, significant that there are some more recent signs of a modified approach, which attaches greater value to doctrinal analysis: See, for example, the articles based on a symposium on *The New Doctrinalism* in 163 U. Pa. L. Rev. (2015) and The Oxford Handbook of the New Private Law (A. Gold et al. eds., 2021).

9 *See, e.g.*, H. Smith, *Property as the Law of Things*, 125 Harv. L. Rev. 1691 (2012); H. Smith, *The Persistence of System in Property Law*, 163 U. Pa. L. Rev. 2055 (2015); B. McFarlane, *Rights and Value: Means and Ends*, *in* The Restatement Third, Restitution and Unjust Enrichment: Critical and Comparative Essays 1 (C. Mitchell & W. Swadling eds., 2013).

10 *See, e.g.*, Chapters 3, 5, 6, 7, 11, 12, and 17.

> short, it is submitted that the right kind of simplicity can result only from more searching and more discriminating analysis.[11]

It will be seen that Hohfeld was correct in identifying certain views as too simplistic. In Section 9.3, for example, it will be shown that some recent judgments have fallen into the trap of assuming that, because a beneficial interest gives its holder many of the economic advantages of outright ownership, it must involve the same legal relations as such ownership. To regard the beneficiary of a trust as an owner to whom a bona fide purchaser defense may apply is to adopt a heuristic that is serviceable in many cases, but which may be dangerously misleading in others. This, again, reflects an important wider lesson of Hohfeld's work: the fact that two legal relations frequently operate in a similar way, or are just as often called by the same name, does not mean that those relations are necessarily identical.[12] Nonetheless, it may well be that some degree of simplification is necessary in order for laypeople,[13] lawyers and judges to make sense of legal ideas such as the trust and other equitable interests, and there is a risk that a strict adherence to Hohfeld's scheme may make it harder to explain the law comprehensibly.[14] More specifically, when considering equitable doctrines, it may be that Hohfeld's focus on atomized outcomes obscures an important and elegant aspect of the operation of equity as a secondary system:[15] its ability to function as means to control the exercise of primary legal rights. This, again, leads to a wider point: there is a risk (evidenced, by the adoption of at least some variants of the "bundle of rights" view of property) that, by leading to an extreme disaggregation of particular legal rights, Hohfeld's approach may obscure the very thing it aimed to reveal: how legal conceptions function in practice in judicial reasoning.

9.2 THE NATURE OF THE DEBATE

The conceptual aspect of the debate as to the "essential nature of trusts and other equitable interests" takes particular practical aspects of the operation of such

11 Hohfeld, *supra* note 1, at 19–20; *see also* B. McFarlane & A. Televantos, *Third Party Effects in Private Law: Form and Function*, *in* I OXFORD STUDIES IN PRIVATE LAW THEORY 107 (P. Miller & J. Oberdiek eds., 2021).

12 *See, e.g.*, Allen v. Flood (1898) AC 1 (HL) (appeal from Eng.) (discussing the distinction between a claim-right and a privilege); Hohfeld, *supra* note 1, at 36–37.

13 It is interesting to note that, in each of *Some Fundmental Legal Conceptions as Applied in Judicial Reasoning* 23 YALE L.J. 16, 20 (1913); and *The Relations Between Equity and Law* 23 MICH L.R 537, 540 (1912–1913), Hohfeld emphasized that law students were a key intended audience of his work.

14 It is worth noting that the complexity of the law of trusts is already such as to magnify the risk of judges falling into error. *See* J. Penner, *An Untheory of the Law of Trusts, or Some Notes Towards Understanding the Structure of Trusts Law Doctrine*, 63 CURRENT LEGAL PROBS. 653 (2010).

15 For discussion of equity's ability to prevent oppressive use of primary, common law rules, *see, e.g.*, H. Smith, *Property, Equity, and the Rule of Law*, *in* PRIVATE LAW AND THE RULE OF LAW 224 (L. Austin & D. Klimchuk eds., 2014); H. Smith, *Equity as Meta-Law*, 130 YALE L.J. 1050 (2021).

interests as given, and strives to find the most satisfactory explanation for those effects. For example, the position where T holds a bank account, now $100 in credit, on trust for B can be contrasted in various ways with the position where D, having borrowed money from P, now owes P $100.

First, B is protected in the event of T's insolvency: the bank account, as trust property, does not form part of the estate available for distribution to T's creditors. In contrast, P has no such protection, and, in D's insolvency, will have to accept whatever reduced sum is available as an unsecured creditor of D. Second, if T makes an unauthorized transfer of the bank account or its proceeds to a third party, C, then, if C still has that property or its traceable proceeds, and C cannot establish the defense of bona fide purchase for value, B will be able to make a claim against C, as well as against T. Such a claim can succeed even if, before the claim was made, C had no knowledge, or means of knowing, about the existence of the trust. In contrast, P has no such protection: if, for example, D were to choose to make a gift of $100 to C, rather than paying that $100 to P, P has no claim against C. Third, if T acquires new rights through an authorized or unauthorized use of the trust property, B can claim that those new rights are held subject to the terms of the initial trust in B's favor. In contrast, if D takes $100 and, rather than paying it to P, instead purchases shares that increase in value, P has no claim to the shares or the increased value.

Those well-established aspects of B's position suggest that the nature of at least some of B's rights differs in important ways from that of P's contractual right to be paid $100 by D. They suggest that B's rights may be seen as closer to those of O, a party with ownership of a physical thing, than to those of P against D. After all, if X steals O's car and goes into insolvency when retaining possession of it, the car will not be available for distribution to X's creditors; if X purports to sell the car to C then O will have a claim against C as well as against X.[16] In such a case, C will not be able to take advantage of any general bona fide purchase for value defense, and this has long been acknowledged as an important practical difference between B's rights and those of O. Nonetheless, as noted by Maitland, the features of B's interest under a trust have allowed it to be seen by some as "just ownership pure and simple, though it is subject to a peculiar, technical and not very intelligible rule in favour of bona fide purchasers."[17]

The conceptual puzzle arises because there are, however, some equally long-standing features of the trust (and of other equitable interests) that are shared with P's position, and distinguish B's position from that of O. Perhaps most obviously, the trust depends on the existence of a particular relationship between B and another

[16] *See, e.g., Farquharson Bros & Co. v. King & Co.* [1902] AC 325 at 329–30 (HL) (appeal taken from Eng.).

[17] F. Maitland, *Trust and Corporation*, 32 Grunhüt's Zeitschrift für das Privat- und Öffentliche Recht 167 (1904), *reprinted in* Maitland: State, Trust and Corporation 94 (D. Runciman & M. Ryan, eds., 2003).

party, T (the trustee), whose position is distinct from that of the rest of the world. It may be that the court assists B in finding a party to fill that role of trustee, but it is nonetheless true that such a special relationship must exist for the trust to take full effect.[18] This feature is reflected in the means by which a trust may come into existence. It is, for example, possible for a party to acquire certain property rights independently, as occurs, for example, when O takes possession, on his or her own behalf, of a physical thing. The acquisition of an equitable interest, in contrast, depends on finding a specific party who is under a duty to B. This also means that, in principle, the varied means by which one party can come under a duty to another (e.g., the conclusion of a contract; the commission of a wrong; an unjust enrichment) may also give rise to a trust or other equitable interest. When considering the acquisition of equitable interests, it is noteworthy that such interests can generally be acquired without the formality (such as the use of signed writing or registration) or overt acts (such as the transfer of possession) often required for the acquisition of legal interests in property. The flexibility of the trust is also apparent when considering the content of the rights of an individual beneficiary. The trust can be used as a means to divide the benefits of T's rights between many different people in many different ways, and the content of the rights of any individual beneficiary does not have to match that of a right on any closed list of interests. In other words, as is the case when considering the content of a purely contractual right of P against D, the *numerus clausus* principle does not apply to the content of an individual beneficiary's rights under a trust. Given the importance of that principle in protecting strangers from the information and notice costs imposed by legal property rights,[19] the distinction between legal and equitable property rights is thus clearly of practical, as well as conceptual, importance.

9.3 PRACTICAL CONSEQUENCES

Hohfeld noted that the correct analysis of the rights of a beneficiary, or holder of a different equitable interest, may be necessary to reach the "solution of many difficult and delicate problems in constitutional law and in the conflict of laws."[20] Modern demonstrations of the practical importance of analyzing equitable interests abound:[21] Three examples will be considered here.

18 *See, e.g.*, Smith, *supra* note 2, at 14 (pointing out that "[a]lthough a trust will not usually fail for the want of a trustee, there is no such thing as a common law trust without a trustee."). Smith refers to Lysaght [1966] Ch 191, 207 to demonstrate that an express trust will fail for want of a trustee "if the settlor made it clear that the identity of his or her chosen trustee(s) was essential to the trust" and that trustee refuses so to act.

19 *See, e.g.*, T. Merrill & H. Smith, *Optimal Standardization in the Law of Property: The* Numerus Clausus *Principle*, 110 YALE L.J. 1 (2000).

20 Hohfeld, *supra* note 1, at 18.

21 In relation to constitutional law, *see infra* Section 9.3.1. In relation to the conflict of laws, *see, e.g.*, *Akers* v. *Samba Fin. Grp.* [2017] AC 424 (SC); *Webb* v. *Webb* [1994] 3 WLR 801 (Ch) and [1991] 1 WLR 1410 (CA), discussed in S. Agnew & B. McFarlane, *The Nature of Trusts and the Conflict of Laws*, 137

9.3.1 *Example 1: Distinguishing the Enjoyment of the Benefit of a Right from the Holding of That Right*

Where T holds property on trust for B, it may be convenient, as a short-cut, to think of B as having the benefit of that property, or as being entitled to its value. Certainly, in many cases, that will be the practical outcome of the existence of the trust. Such a simplification, however, overlooks the specific legal relations between the relevant parties, and fails to distinguish properly between the rights of B against T, and the rights that T has against others; as a result, it can, in some cases, lead a judge astray.

In *Sprint Communications Co. v. APCC Services Inc.*,[22] for example, the U. S. Supreme Court considered whether the plaintiff aggregators, to whom payphone operators had assigned their statutory claims against carriers, had standing under Article III of the Constitution to pursue those claims. The defendants' argument was that, as the plaintiffs had promised (in return for payment of a fee) to remit all sums thus recovered to the payphone operators, no "injury in fact" would be suffered by the plaintiffs if their claim were denied. In rejecting that argument, the majority opinion considered the rights of a beneficiary under a trust, noting the well-established point that a trustee may bring a claim against a third party, even if the proceeds of that claim will benefit the beneficiaries and not the trustee. This demonstrates that a claim may be within "the traditional concern of the courts at Westminster"[23] even if the plaintiff will not retain the benefits of the claim. Such analysis also reveals a significant aspect of the operation of a trust: protection for the beneficiary against third parties may depend on the existence of the *trustee's* rights against third parties. More broadly, it demonstrates an important aspect of private law claim-rights: in general, a party with such a right may simply enforce it, and so does not need to establish 'standing' in the same way as a party seeking to enforce a limit on the power of a public authority that does not correlate to a claim-right.[24]

A Hohfeldian analysis (particularly apt, of course, when the very question asked is as to the nature of jural relations) is thus useful in exposing a difficulty in the minority position in *Sprint Communications*. That position was premised on the idea that the plaintiffs would suffer no "injury in fact" as, being under a duty to transfer any proceeds of the claim to the assignees, they had, in practice, no right to the benefit of the claim. The error here is to invoke an abstract sense of a right

L.Q. Rev. 405 (2021). In relation to determining the extent of statutory protection given to occupiers of land, *see, e.g.*, *R* v. *Tower Hamlets LBC*, Ex p von Goetz [1999] QB 1019 (CA).

22 *Sprint Commc'ns Co.* v. *APCC Services Inc.*, 554 U.S. 269 (2008).

23 To adopt the words of Justice Frankfurter interpreting the Article III judicial power in *Coleman* v. *Miller*, 307 U.S. 433, 460 (1939).

24 *See, e.g.*, R. Stevens, *Contractual Aspects of Debt Financing, in* Corporate Finance Law in the UK and EU 213 (A. Reisberg & D. Prentice eds., 2010). There may of course be circumstances in which a party who holds a right is unable to enforce it by means of an action: the expiry of a limitation period may, for example, have such an effect. For discussion of such unenforceable rights, *see, e.g.*, S. Smith, Rights, Wrongs and Injustices: The Structure of Remedial Law 64–65 (2019); *and* R. Stevens, *Defences, in* The Oxford Handbook of the New Private Law 529 (A. Gold et al. eds., 2021).

to a benefit, thus overlooking that a right must involve at least two parties. The plaintiffs *did* have a valid contractual right *against the defendant carriers*, correlating to the defendants' duty to pay the sums due; the existence of that right was not negated by the fact that the assignors also had a similar right against the plaintiffs, correlating to the plaintiffs' duty to pay the sums recovered from the defendants. The majority's invocation of the trust analogy was appropriate. If, for example, A holds a bank account, and then declares that she holds that account on trust for B, she retains the claim-right against the bank arising under her contract with the bank, even though she is now under a new duty to B in relation to that right. The declaration of trust does not remove A's initial right against the bank; on the contrary, that right is the very subject matter of the trust.

A nice example of this point, provided by English law, is the "charge-back." Where A has a bank account with B Bank, she can create an equitable charge over that account for the benefit of B Bank, by coming under a duty to hold that right as security for a debt owed to B Bank.[25] It had been thought that such a device, whilst common in practice, was conceptually dubious,[26] as, where A has a personal right against B, it is not possible to create a mortgage of that right in favor of B. The bar on a "mortgage-back," however, follows simply from the fact that a mortgage, strictly speaking, involves a transfer of a right, and an attempt by A to transfer to B a right correlating to B's duty to A operates instead as a release of B's duty to A. An equitable charge, in contrast, involves no transfer, but instead, like a trust, depends on A's retaining the right, and coming under a duty to B in relation to that right. B can thus benefit from the right (in this case A's bank account) without needing to hold that right.

In commercial practice, the opportunity to enter an aggregating or factoring arrangement such as that in *Sprint Communications*, or to create a charge-back in favor of a creditor, may be valuable to a company seeking to raise finance. Those opportunities would be lost, however, if judges, such as the minority in *Sprint Communications*, misunderstand the specific legal relations involved in such arrangements. The crucial point, also evident in a trust, is that the party that ultimately enjoys the practical benefit of a right need not be the holder of that right. As a corollary, it is of course possible, as in an aggregating arrangement, for a party to hold a right without ultimately enjoying its practical benefit. It is tempting to identify the ultimate beneficiary (the assignors in *Sprint Communications*; the lending bank in a charge-back; the beneficiary of a trust) with the right itself, but this may cause confusion as it overlooks the *means* by which that benefit is accessed. It is a two-stage rather than one-stage process: in a trust, for example, B does not directly hold the property, but rather has rights against T which then give B access to the benefit of T's rights in that property.

25 *See, e.g.*, Re BCCI (No. 8) [1998] AC 214 (HL) (appeal taken from Eng.), discussed in McFarlane & Stevens, *supra* note 2, at 25–26.

26 *See, e.g.*, Re Charge Card Services Ltd. (No. 2) [1987] Ch 150.

9.3.2 *Example 2: Distinguishing Between Two Different Sorts of Third Party*

The correct analysis of the trust and other equitable interests may be relevant not only to the interpretation of particular constitutional or statutory provisions, but also in determining directly the operation of equitable interests in contested areas. At this point, the debate is no longer about how best to explain accepted aspects of such interests, but is instead as to how those interests should operate. The answer given to such questions will, of course, feed back into the conceptual analysis. For example, the stance traditionally taken by the courts on two practical issues, to be examined here as Examples 2 and 3, undermines the common contention that the only significant difference between the position of a beneficiary and that of an unencumbered legal owner is the vulnerability of the former to the bona fide purchaser defense.

The first of these two further examples relates to the position of X, a party who intentionally or carelessly damages physical property where T's rights to that property are held by T on trust for B. In such a case, does B have a direct claim against X? It is convenient, as a short-cut, to think of B as having a right that is generally good against third parties, other than a bona fide purchaser for value: certainly that view holds true where B's claim is against C, a party to whom T has made an unauthorized distribution of trust property. That simplification, however, overlooks the specific legal relations between the relevant parties, and fails to distinguish properly between two different types of third parties: those, such as C, who receive the trust property or its traceable proceeds; and those such as X, who do not.

As noted in Section 9.2, it is of course clear that, where T makes an unauthorized disposal of the trust property to C, who is not a bona fide purchaser for value, the general position is that B can bring a direct claim against C: B can thus follow the trust property into the hands of C. As a result, it is tempting to think of B's right as simply being *in rem*,[27] in the sense of being prima facie binding on *all* third parties. However, the long-standing position throughout the common law world is that if X simply intentionally or carelessly damages the trust property, but acquires no right from T, then B has no direct claim against X.[28] B's protection in such a case depends on the rights of T, who can be compelled by B to bring a claim against X. This is no mere technicality: if, for example, T has consented to X's action, then T has no claim against X, and B's only recourse will be against T. Similarly, if B has suffered consequential economic loss as a result of B's particular activities, that loss will

[27] *See, e.g.*, *Akers* v. *Samba Fin. Grp.* [2017] AC 424 (SC) at [82] (Lord Sumption) ("An equitable interest possesses the essential hallmark of any right *in rem*, namely that it is good against third parties into whose hands the property or its traceable proceeds may have come, subject to the rules of equity for the protection of bona fide purchasers without notice"). It is to be noted that this definition of a right *in rem* is somewhat unusual, as it does not require the *in rem* right to bind strangers who simply interfere with the property.

[28] *See, e.g.*, The Lord Compton's Case (1587) 3 Leo 197; *Leigh and Sillavan Ltd.* v. *Aliakmon Shipping Co. Ltd.* ("The Aliakmon") [1986] AC 785 (HL) (appeal taken from Eng.); Restatement (Third) of Trusts (2003) §§ 107–08.

not be recoverable from X, as X is liable only for the loss in value of the property and for any reasonably foreseeable consequential loss suffered by T.[29] It was argued above that, where a trust of a debt is declared, the key legal relation of creditor and debtor does not change. Similarly, where a trust of ownership of a physical thing arises, the key legal relations between owner (now trustee) and the rest of the world do not change: strangers continue to owe a duty of noninterference with the physical thing to the owner (now trustee).[30]

This analysis is consistent, first, with the flexibility of the rules governing the acquisition and content of equitable interests: if B's acquisition of such an interest does *not* impose on strangers an additional strict duty, owed to B, of noninterference with the thing, an important justification for controls on the acquisition and content of legal interests (the need to lower information costs to third parties affected by such a duty)[31] does not apply. It is also consistent with the point that B does not have an abstract right to the benefit of the trust property, allowing a claim against any party who intentionally or carelessly reduces the value of that property: B's protection depends instead on T's rights. Indeed, this demonstrates an important aspect of the means by which equity can take advantage of its nature as a secondary system: rather than creating a whole new scheme of jural relations, in competition with those established at common law, it can instead impose duties that assume the existence of, and relate to, particular rights already held by a defendant. This is, finally, also consistent with Hohfeld's observation that the position at common law, even if supplemented by a different equitable rule, "may represent an important *stage of thought* in the solution of a given problem."[32]

It is therefore surprising that the English Court of Appeal, in *Shell UK Ltd. v. Total UK Ltd.*,[33] appeared to depart from the long-standing rule that a beneficiary of a trust has no direct claim against a stranger interfering with trust property. The case concerned the largest peace-time explosion in Britain: it occurred at the Buncefield oil storage terminal as a result, in part, of the carelessness of the defendant, X. The destruction and damage extended to fuel storage and pipeline facilities used by B. As a result, B suffered serious economic loss through its inability to supply fuel to its customers. B did not, however, have legal title to the land or facilities: that title was instead held by T (in fact, two service companies) on trust for four companies, of which B was one. Such was the structure chosen by the

[29] The position is different where X has expressly or impliedly assumed responsibility to B (as may occur where, for example, X, knowing of the trust, contracts with T to perform a service for the benefit of B. *See, e.g.*, *Chappell* v. *Somers & Blake* [2004] Ch 19).

[30] This point is discussed by P. Matthews, *The Compatibility of the Trust with the Civil Law Notion of Property*, *in* The Worlds of the Trust 313 (L. Smith ed., 2013).

[31] See Merrill & Smith, *supra* note 19.

[32] *See* Wesley N. Hohfeld, *The Relations Between Equity and Law*, 11 Mich. L.Rev. 537, 544 (1913) (emphasis in original).

[33] [2011] QB 86 (CA); *see also* the discussion of the decision in B. McFarlane, *Form and Substance in Equity*, *in* Form and Substance in the Law of Obligations 197, 203–06 (A. Robertson & J. Goudkamp eds., 2019).

companies when cooperating to establish the terminal. It was held at first instance that, as B had no legal ownership or possessory title to the property, the loss it had suffered as a result of the damage was purely economic loss, and so the general "exclusionary rule" applied, meaning that X was not liable for having carelessly caused such loss.[34]

The Court of Appeal, in contrast, allowed B's claim for substantial damages. Particular weight was placed on the ability of B to describe itself as an "equitable owner" of the damaged property, with the court holding that:

> [I]t is legalistic to deny a right to recovery by reference to the exclusionary rule. It is, after all, who is (along with [the other three beneficiaries]) the 'real' owner, the 'legal' owner being little more than a bare trustee of the pipelines.[35]

The court then went on to find that the recovery of purely economic loss could be permitted only if some special relationship of proximity can be established between claimant and defendant, and it held that: "[b]eneficial ownership of the damaged property goes well beyond contractual or non-contractual dependence on the damaged property and does indeed constitute a special relationship of the kind required."[36]

The reasoning of the Court of Appeal in *Shell UK* has been subject to widespread criticism,[37] chiefly as a result of its departure from the settled precedent[38] establishing that the existence of a trust does not impose additional direct duties of noninterference on strangers to the trust. Even on its own terms, however, the decision is hopelessly confused:[39] it evidences the dangers, adverted to by Hohfeld, of taking an overly simplified view of the trust. First, whilst it might be reasonable to regard B, as opposed to T, as the "real owner" when considering, for example, T's duties to use its rights for the benefit of B, that does not mean that B should be regarded as having the same complex aggregate of rights as an unencumbered owner of property: to do so is to confuse one particular jural relation (between B and T) with other jural relations (between B and strangers to the trust such as X). Second, whilst such rhetoric supports the view that B has a proprietary right in the trust property, the exclusionary

34 The first instance decision is reported as *Colour Quest Ltd.* v. *Total Downstream Ltd.* [2009] EWHC 540 (Comm).

35 [2011] QB 86 (CA) at [132].

36 *Id.* at [134].

37 *See, e.g.*, K. Low, *Equitable Title and Economic Loss*, 126 L.Q. Rev. 507 (2010); P. Turner, *Consequential Economic Loss and the Trust Beneficiary*, 69 Cambridge L.J. 445 (2010); J. Edelman, *Two Fundamental Questions for the Law of Trusts*, 129 L.Q. Rev. 66 (2013); W. Swadling, *In Defence of Formalism*, *in* Form and Substance in the Law of Obligations 95, 103–10 (A. Robertson & J. Goudkamp eds., 2019).

38 *See supra* note 28 and accompanying text.

39 *See also* B. McFarlane, *Avoiding Anarchy?* Common Law v. Equity *and* Maitland v. Hohfeld, *in* Equity and Law: Fusion and Fission 331 (P. Turner et al. eds., 2019). Note that the Supreme Court gave permission for an appeal against the Court of Appeal's decision in the *Shell* case, but the appeal was settled. Even if the defendant had succeeded on the point as to the negligence claim, B was also pursuing a claim against X based on public nuisance.

rule was seen by the Court of Appeal as prima facie applicable. This means that B's loss must have been regarded as purely economic, rather than as consequential on an interference with a property right of B: the unstated premise, then, is that X had *not* interfered with B's property. The court then regarded the case as falling within an exception to the exclusionary rule, as B's beneficial interest provided the required relationship of proximity. This involves a further error as to jural relations. The exception to the exclusionary rule depends on the existence of a special relationship of proximity between claimant and *defendant* (and so, in *Shell UK*, between B and X), not between the claimant and someone other than the defendant, such as T.

The Court of Appeal's reasoning in *Shell UK* is based on essentially the same error as that of the minority in the *Sprint Communications* case: it is motivated by a concern to ensure that an ability to bring a claim is linked to the suffering of actual loss.[40] Of course, it is very commonly the case that, where loss is suffered by a claimant as a result of X's actions, a claim arises: this occurs, for example, where X has carelessly damaged property owned by the claimant. The discussion in Section 9.3.1 showed, however, that it would be a mistake to assume that the suffering of such loss is a necessary condition for a claim to be made; it would equally be an error to regard such loss as a sufficient condition for a claim. This can be seen by considering Hohfeld's crucial distinction between a claim-right and a liberty, and his analysis of *Allen v. Flood*.[41] The plaintiff shipwrights in *Allen v. Flood* suffered loss when they were denied further work by the employer, but as they had no ongoing contract with the employer, their loss did not result from any denial of a claim-right: the employer was in any case free to choose not to give them further employment. In contemporary debates on the law of torts, Hohfeld's analysis has assumed great significance for supporters of a "right-based" view of the law of torts.[42]

The distinction between a claim-right and a liberty is also significant in property law, for example when considering the position of a licensee.[43] In *Hill v. Tupper*,[44] the owners of a canal gave the plaintiff an "exclusive" permission to hire boats out on the canal. X, who ran a public house on the bank of the canal, then also started to hire boats out, despite having no permission from the owners of the canal. The plaintiff wished to prevent X from doing so, and to claim damages for the loss caused

40 It could be argued that the Court of Appeal's decision rests on an underlying frustration with the exclusionary rule generally preventing the recovery of carelessly caused economic loss, and is motivated by policy concerns; the difficulty is that the judges, however, put forward a doctrinal basis for the decision, and so their reasoning must first be evaluated on those terms.

41 [1898] AC 1 (HL) (appeal from Eng.). See Chapter 11 for the note of caution that a judicial reference to a "liberty", such as that of Lord Lindley in *Quinn* v. *Leathem* [1901] AC 495 (HL) (appeal from Eng.), need not be a reference to a single Hohfeldian privilege.

42 *See, e.g.*, R. Stevens, *Torts and Rights* (2007).

43 *See* Wesley N. Hohfeld, *Faulty Analysis in Easement and License Cases*, 27 Yale L.J. 66 (1917).

44 (1863) 2 Hurl & C 121 (Exch.). *See also* B. McFarlane, *Keppell* v. *Bailey* (1834); *Hill* v. *Tupper* (1863): *The* Numerus Clausus *and the Common Law*, *in* Landmark Cases in Land Law 1 (N. Gravells ed., 2013).

to his business. X's action was clearly prohibited (as a tort against the owners of the canal) and also caused loss to the plaintiff, yet the claim was denied, on the basis that the plaintiff's license gave it only a personal right against the owners of the canal: the plaintiff had no proprietary interest in the canal and so had no claim against X. The denial of the claim might seem somewhat technical,[45] but it is motivated by the important practical concerns,[46] particularly as to controlling information costs to third parties, that underpin the *numerus clausus* rule.[47] As has traditionally been the case where X carelessly interferes with trust property, the mere fact that X has acted wrongfully and has caused loss to B does not suffice to give B a claim against X: the key point in the case of the trust is that the duty breached by X is a duty owed to T, not to B.

9.3.3 *Example 3: Distinguishing between the Retention of a Right and the Retention of a Benefit*

A parallel to the decision in *Shell UK Ltd. v. Total UK Ltd.*, showing the dangers of equating the position of a beneficiary of a trust with that of a holder of unencumbered legal title, can be found in the decision of the Court of Appeal of New South Wales,[48] later reversed by the High Court of Australia,[49] in *Farah Constructions Pty Ltd. v. Say-Dee Pty Ltd.* One of the errors identified by the High Court concerned the analysis of the position of C in our third example, where C is an innocent donee to whom T transfers the trust property in breach of trust.[50] If C acquires notice of the trust only at a point when C no longer has the trust property or its proceeds, is it possible for B to bring a claim against C based on C's retention of a benefit deriving from the receipt of the trust property?

In England[51] and Australia,[52] the well-established position is that there is no claim: a distinction is thus made between cases when C retains a specific right that can be identified as either the trust property or its traceable proceeds, and cases where C merely retains a benefit derived from having once held such a right. In *Farah*

45 *See, e.g.*, the quite different analysis of Bramwell B, dissenting, in *Stockport Waterworks Co.* v. *Potter* (1864) 3 H & C 300 (Exch.), where his Lordship argued that as the defendant, by polluting a river, had in any case committed a wrong against A, a riparian owner, the defendant could not complain about also being liable to compensate B, a non-riparian owner granted rights by A who had suffered loss as a result of the pollution. For an illuminating discussion of Bramwell's jurisprudence, *see* R. Epstein, *For a Bramwell Revival*, 28 AM. J. LEGAL HIST. 246 (1994).

46 *See, e.g.*, the judgment of Lord Brougham L.C. in *Keppell* v. *Bailey* (1834) 2 My & K 517.

47 See Merrill & Smith, *supra* note 19.

48 [2005] NSWCA 309 (Austl.).

49 (2007) 230 CLR 89 (Austl.).

50 The case itself involved a claimed breach of fiduciary duty, and the possible liability of a third party receiving property transferred in breach of such duty, but the Court of Appeal of New South Wales took the rule to be the same as applicable to the case of a breach of trust.

51 *BCCI* v. *Akindele* [2001] Ch 437 (CA).

52 *Farah Constr. Pty Ltd.* v. *Say-Dee Pty Ltd.*, (2007) 230 CLR 89 (Austl.).

Constructions, the New South Wales Court of Appeal had taken the view that, in the second set of cases, C may be subject to a constructive trust in favor of B, arising to reverse C's unjust enrichment at B's expense.[53] The court's adoption of that view rested on the fallacy that there was no longer any good reason to accord less protection to B than to O, an unencumbered owner of property. In a case where, for example, O mistakenly transfers a right to the defendant, it can be said that the defendant is enriched (and thus possibly unjustly enriched) at O's expense, as the right acquired by the defendant was formerly held by O. Where it arises, such liability in unjust enrichment helps to mitigate the effect on O of the rule that allows for the transfer of a right to be valid even where a mistake has been made.[54] In contrast, where T transfers trust property to C, it is clear that the rights acquired by C were formerly held by T: if, for example, the trust property consists of a chose in action against a debtor, it was T, rather than B, to whom the debtor owed the duty; if, for example, the trust property consists of a legal estate in land, it was T, rather than B, to whom strangers owed their duty of noninterference with the land. The vital Hohfeldian point, overlooked by the New South Wales Court of Appeal, is that the existence of a trust simply means that T is under a duty to B to use the trust property consistently with the terms of the trust; it does not mean that B has some sort of abstract, general right against the rest of the world to the value of the trust property.[55]

It is worth noting that, in relation to this example, the position in the United States is less clear. The Restatement (Third) of Restitution and Unjust Enrichment follows the First and Second Restatements of Trusts in assuming, without citation of authority, that even if acquiring knowledge of the trust only after disposing of the trust property and its proceeds, C, if she retains some benefit from the use of such property, will have no defense to B's personal restitutionary claim.[56] This is consistent with an analysis of the trust mentioned by Hohfeld:[57] that employed by James Barr Ames[58] when seeking to explain the restitutionary liability arising where, for

53 [2005] NSWCA 309 [233] (Austl.).

54 *See* B. McFarlane, *Equity and the Justification of Private Rights*, *in* JUSTIFYING PRIVATE RIGHTS 221 (S. Degeling et al. eds., 2021); B. McFarlane, *Unjust Enrichment, Rights and Value*, *in* RIGHTS IN PRIVATE LAW 581 (D. Nolan & A. Robertson eds., 2012); S. Smith, *A Duty to Make Restitution?* 26 CAN. J. L. & JURIS. 157 (2013).

55 *See* S. Agnew & B. McFarlane, *The Paradox of the Equitable Proprietary Claim*, *in* 10 MODERN STUDIES IN PROPERTY LAW 303 (B. McFarlane & S. Agnew eds., 2019). *See* J. Penner, *Value, Property, and Unjust Enrichment*, *in* PHILOSOPHICAL FOUNDATIONS OF THE LAW OF UNJUST ENRICHMENT (R. Chambers et al. eds., 2009) for a number of important general doubts about the utility of thinking of a party as having an abstract entitlement to value, as opposed to simply the ability to realise the exchange value of an asset.

56 Restatement (Third) of Restitution and Unjust Enrichment § 17, comment c, illustration 9 (2011). C's retention of an abstract enrichment prevents C's relying on the change of position defense set out in § 65.

57 Hohfeld, *supra* note 1, at 16.

58 J.B. Ames, *Purchaser for Value Without Notice*, 1 HARV L. REV. 1 (1887). For further discussion of the weakness of Ames' argument in this particular context, *see* McFarlane, *supra* note 39, at 343–45. For discussion of Ames' broader influence on the development in the United States of the law of restitution, *see* A. Kull, *James Barr Ames and the Early Modern History of Unjust Enrichment*, 25 OXFORD J. LEGAL STUD. 297 (2005).

example, a mistaken transfer of a right is made. It may seem puzzling that such liability can arise even though the transfer of the right is itself valid. Ames argued that an analogy with the receipt of trust property may assist: where T holds a right on trust for B and then transfers that right to C in breach of trust, the fact that C has indeed acquired the right is not inconsistent with holding that C, if her conscience is affected by knowledge of the trust, will come under a liability to B as a constructive trustee. One broad way of understanding that result would be to say that the transaction between T and C was effective to transfer a right from T to C, but that it did not transfer the *value* of that right from B to C. A similar analysis might then be said to apply to the mistaken transfer case: the imposition of liability on the defendant is not inconsistent with the finding that the right was indeed transferred, as it can be said that, as a result of the mistake of the claimant, the value of the right has not been validly transferred.

Such an argument, however, cannot meet the now familiar Hohfeldian objection: As a party's claim-rights are rights against another party that such a party act or not act in a particular way,[59] it makes little sense to talk of a transfer of value or, indeed, of a general right to value. This point is, again, of wider import: for example, when courts seek to explain the ability of a plaintiff to make a claim to traceable proceeds of an initial right, it is often said that the value of the initial right can be traced into such proceeds.[60] As Penner has forcefully argued,[61] however, it makes little sense to think of a holder of a right as also having a distinct or independent right to its value.[62] In the case of a trust, for example, B has no abstract right to the value of the trust property. Indeed, as against parties other than B, T has the same general privilege as an unencumbered owner to use the trust property for her own benefit: thus, if anyone has a broad 'right to the value' of the trust property, it is T rather than B. In order to deny a holder of a right the privilege, as against B, to use that right for her own benefit, it is necessary to find a specific reason why that party is under a duty to B: in the case of a trust or other equitable interest, that requires B to show that the conscience of the holder of the right has been affected, for example by agreeing to hold as trustee, or by acquiring knowledge of the initial trust.

59 *See, e.g.*, J. Finnis, *Some Professorial Fallacies about Rights*, 4 ADEL. L. REV. 377 (1972).

60 *See, e.g.*, *Foskett* v. *McKeown* [2001] 1 AC 102, 127 (HL) (appeal from Eng.) where Lord Millett refers to the choice of B either "to follow the original asset into the hands of the new owner or to trace its value into the new asset in the hands of the same owner." The facts of that case were very similar to those of *Homes* v. *Gilman*, 138 N.Y. 369, 34 N.E. 205 (1893).

61 Penner, *supra* note 55. Penner does not rely on Hohfeldian analysis in making his argument, but that argument is nonetheless perfectly consistent with, and can be supported by, such an analysis.

62 *See also* T. Cutts, *Tracing, Value and Transactions*, 79 MOD. L. REV. 381 (2016).

9.4 THE STATE OF THE DEBATE

9.4.1 *Progress*

Hohfeld linked the "inadequacy" of then current analyses of the trust and other equitable interests to a tendency to over-simplify the rights considered.[63] It can be argued that some recent progress in the perennial debate stems from the adoption of a more nuanced approach. For example, Nolan[64] carefully distinguished between the different types of right that compose B's complex aggregate of entitlements, pointing out correctly that not all of those rights are capable of binding a third party who receives the trust property,[65] thus illustrating the danger of an undifferentiated analyses of B's rights as proprietary. Nolan did claim, however, that B has some proprietary rights and that these "consist principally in the beneficiary's primary, negative right to exclude non-beneficiaries from the enjoyment of trust assets."[66] The danger of that view, however, is that, in a case such as Example 2, where a stranger carelessly damages trust property, it overlooks the indirect nature of B's protection, which depends on T's rights and so is unavailable, for example, where T consented to the interference.

Other more recent work on the nature of trusts and equitable interests can avoid those difficulties. It has been argued that some of the key features of equitable interests can best be explained as depending on one party (T) having a right and also being under a special sort of duty to the holder of the equitable interest (B): a duty that relates specifically to the particular right held by T.[67] On that view, some parts at least of B's rights under a trust are different from a right such as P's to be paid a sum of money by D. In the case of a simple debt, D's duty does not relate to any specific right held by D, and D can draw on any funds to make payment to P. Equally, some parts at least of B's rights differ from those of O, an owner of a physical thing, as the rest of the world owes B no prima facie duty of noninterference with any specific thing. If one adopts the conventional, but of course deeply un-Hohfeldian, practice of referring to P's right as a right against a person and O's right as a right against a thing, B's rights might then be said to include at least some "rights against rights": a term which is, of course, simply a shorthand for describing the content of at least some of T's duties to B.

63 Hohfeld, *supra* note 1, at 18–20.

64 Nolan, *supra* note 2.

65 So, for example, T may be under particular positive investment duties in relation to a trust fund: such duties will not bind C merely as a result of C's acquisition of the fund with knowledge of the trust.

66 Nolan, *supra* note 2, at 236.

67 *See, e.g.*, B. McFarlane, The Structure of Property Law (2008); Smith, *supra* note 2; McFarlane & Stevens, *supra* note 2. R. Chambers, An Introduction to Property Law in Australia 115 (2001) also stated that the property to which an equitable interest relates may be another right. Edelman, *supra* note 37 argues that the view that B's right is an "interest or encumbrance upon the rights held by the trustee" has a "distinguished lineage."

The "rights against rights" view can thus be seen as an attempt to capture two key parts of the definition of a trust provided in successive Restatements: the trust depends on T's being under a duty, but the duty is "with respect to property, subjecting the person by whom the property is held to equitable duties."[68] On this view, analyses of B's rights as either proprietary or personal may be too simplistic, not only in the sense of failing to distinguish between the different specific rights of B, but also in overlooking the possibility of a different type of right, which does not conform to the template of either a personal or a proprietary right. It is also no accident, on this view, that such rights are prominent in equity: where it operates as a gloss on the common law, for example, equity can impose duties the content of which can incorporate the rights already established at common law. If it is the case that legal proprietary interests have a modular character,[69] often using a physical thing as the organizing module, it can also be argued that, in relation to the trust, the trustee's rights constitute the module that regulates the operation of the trust and controls its effect on third parties.

Penner, whilst arguing that a proprietary characterization of at least some of B's rights can be defended,[70] has noted the value of emphasizing that B's rights *derive* from those of T, and has also made the important point that care must be taken in identifying the particular rights of T on which B's rights depend.[71] So, for example, where T holds a legal estate in land on trust for B then, as Penner points out, the rights of T correlating to strangers' duties not to interfere with the land are not the only (and, also, not the most practically significant) rights of T on which B's interest depends: what Penner refers to as the "powers of title" of T (e.g., the power to transfer the right) are also crucial to B, as T is under a duty to B in relation to the exercise of those powers.[72] This important point, as Penner argues, assists in explaining a component of B's rights: if T, acting in breach of trust, exchanges her rights to a car, held on trust for B, for ownership of a motorbike, T's rights to the motorbike derive from T's exercise of a power of title held for B, and there is a logic to finding that, as T was under a duty to use that power for B's benefit, B now has the power to claim that T in fact did so, and that T therefore now similarly holds her rights to the motorbike for B's benefit.[73] Whilst Penner does not make explicit reference to

[68] Restatement of Trusts § 2 (1930). See now Restatement (Third) of Trusts § 2 (2003), where "equitable duties" is replaced by "duties."

[69] Smith (2012), *supra* note 9.

[70] For other defenses of the proprietary characterization, see each of Jaffey and Zaccaria, *supra* note 2.

[71] Penner, *supra* note 2.

[72] *Id.* at 476.

[73] *See* B. McFarlane & R. Stevens, *What's Special about Equity? Rights against Rights*, *in* PHILOSOPHICAL FOUNDATIONS OF THE LAW OF EQUITY 191, 203–4 (D. Klimchuk et al. eds., 2020). In contrast, if O owns a car, which is then stolen by X and exchanged by X for Z's motorbike, the same analysis cannot apply: in acquiring from Z the right to the motorbike, X did not use any power held on trust for O. If, therefore, a constructive trust of X's right to the motorbike is to be imposed in O's favor in such a case (as suggested by Restatement (Third) of Restitution and Unjust Enrichment § 55, comment f, illustration 10 (2011)), a different explanation must be found for that trust.

Hohfeld in his analysis, he does draw on Nolan's work, which in turn refers, albeit briefly,[74] to the analysis in *Fundamental Legal Relations*. Certainly, it can be argued that, to the extent that more recent work has made progress in the age-old debate, such progress has depended on the nuanced analysis of the different components of a beneficiary's entitlements urged by Hohfeld over a century ago.

9.4.2 *A Note of Caution*

It is necessary to end with a note of caution. If, as suggested above, progress has recently been made, an important step in the right direction has been the general rejection, both judicially and amongst academics, of what Penner has called the "sausage meat" conception of equitable interests, according to which "an outright legal owner of property is regarded as having an equitable beneficial ownership which exists within the skin of his legal ownership."[75] In rejecting that view at the highest judicial level in England,[76] Lord Browne-Wilkinson stated that:

> A person solely entitled to the full beneficial ownership of money or property, both at law and in equity, does not enjoy an equitable interest in that property. The legal title carries with it all rights. Unless and until there is a separation of the legal and equitable estates, there is no separate equitable title.[77]

There is a danger, however, that Hohfeld's own analysis, by regarding law and equity as two separate systems each of which must provide an answer to any practical question posed, lends support to the contrary idea that O has distinct entitlements at each of law and equity. Indeed, in *The Relations Between Equity and Law*, in considering "concurrent rights and correlative concurrent duties," Hohfeld regards X, a stranger, as owing O, a party with an unencumbered legal estate in land, a concurrent legal *and equitable* duty not to damage trees on O's land; similarly, O's privilege against X to cut the trees down is seen as concurrently legal and equitable.[78] This strongly suggests that the complex of rights held by O against strangers gives O *both* a legal and an equitable proprietary interest.

In the supplemental notes to that article, Hohfeld does acknowledge the awkwardness of this analysis, noting that such jural relations are more usually styled "'exclusively legal' or simply 'legal'."[79] As always, there is a logical basis for Hohfeld's choice: X's duty not to interfere with O's trees is something that is recognized in

74 Nolan, *supra* note 2, at nn.18–20.

75 Penner, *supra* note 2, at 487–88.

76 *See* Brennan J. in the High Court of Australia in *DKLR Holding Co. (No. 2) Pty Ltd.* v. *Commissioner of Stamp Duties (NSW)* (1982) 149 CLR 431 (Austl.) ("[An] equitable interest is not carved out of a legal estate but impressed upon it").

77 *Westdeutsche Landesbank Girozentrale* v. *Islington LBC* [1996] AC 669 at 706 (HL) (appeal from Eng.).

78 Hohfeld, *supra* note 32, at 553, Examples 10 and 11.

79 *Id.* at 569 n.34.

equity by, for example, the possibility of an injunction being granted to prevent such action by X. The underlying assumption is that there is a practical question (is X under a duty to O not to cut down the trees?) and each of law and equity must provide an answer to that question. It is here, however, that the rigor of the Hohfeldian scheme, which focuses on ends, may obscure the crucial *means* by which equity operates when recognizing the trust and other equitable interests, and thus cause us to misunderstand this aspect of the relationship between common law and equity.

The key point, noted both before[80] and after[81] Hohfeld, is that equity did not seek to set up a competing and contrasting law of property which might parallel the common law scheme. Instead of reinventing the wheel, equity in fact adopted a more elegant, and in many ways simpler, approach. A trustee of land, for example, retains, as against all but the beneficiary (B), a complex aggregate of common law entitlements; equity, by recognizing that those rights are held subject to a core duty owed to B, gives B the practical benefit of those rights without needing to cut down the trustee's general rights against strangers. The extension of the trustee's core duty to third parties who hold the initial trust property, or its traceable proceeds, with the requisite knowledge of the initial trust, does not change B's core rights into rights that, like legal interests, impose a prima facie duty on the rest of the world. It rather allows B to show that there is a reason why a particular third party should come under a duty to B in relation to a specific right held by that third party. It also reflects the fact that, where a third party acquires trust property from the trustee, that party's entitlement depends on the trustee's exercise of what Penner calls a power of title: a power that, as part of the complex aggregate of rights constituting the trust property, the trustee held subject to a duty to B.[82]

9.5 CONCLUSION

There has not been space in this chapter for a full discussion of the ongoing debate as to the essential nature of trusts and other equitable interests. It has rather been argued that Hohfeldian rigor can be of great benefit to that debate and, indeed, in understanding private law rights more generally. First, it assists in understanding the practical operation of such interests and thus in avoiding the errors into which at

80 *See, e.g.*, C.C. Langdell, *Classification of Rights and Wrongs*, 13 HARV. L. REV. 659 (1900); F. W. MAITLAND, *LECTURES ON EQUITY* (1909). For discussion of the differences on this point between Maitland and Hohfeld, *see* McFarlane, *supra* note 39.

81 *See, e.g.*, J. HACKNEY, *UNDERSTANDING EQUITY AND TRUSTS* (1987).

82 I am grateful to Henry Smith for pointing out that a comparison can perhaps be drawn here with the account of fiduciary duties adopted by Miller. *See, e.g.*, P. Miller, *Dimensions of Fiduciary Loyalty*, *in* RESEARCH HANDBOOK ON FIDUCIARY LAW 180, 191 (D. Gordon Smith & A. Gold eds., 2018) ("Fiduciaries 'owe' the benefit of their judgment to another . . . precisely because their powers can best be understood normatively as a means belonging rightfully to the grantor, to be exercised for ends that he has specified (which ends may include creation of a beneficial interest and right in beneficiaries named by the grantor").

least some appellate judges have fallen when dealing with each of the three examples considered in this chapter. In particular, a Hohfeldian analysis emphasizes the crucial point that actual loss to the plaintiff is neither a necessary nor a sufficient condition for a successful private law claim. Second, such analysis underpins the progress that has recently been made in academic analyses of equitable interests, in particular by warning against the tempting, but inaccurate, idea that a holder of such an interest has a general right to the value of particular property. The crucial Hohfeldian point here is that all claim-rights are simply rights that another individual act, or not act, in a particular way.

So, two cheers for Hohfeld. Each of these two advances can be traced to his laudable determination not to over-simplify: a determination which merits another half-cheer. The concern, however, which must also be borne in mind when applying Hohfeld's approach in other areas of private law, is that the focus on results, on the practical linking of two parties and one activity, may obscure the particular ways in which the law as a whole, and in this case equity, achieves those results. The specific point in danger of being lost is that, in recognizing trusts and other equitable interests, equity built on, and did not compete with, common law rights. Equity's approach, whilst sophisticated, has the "right kind of simplicity"[83] as it did not require the reinvention of the proprietary wheel, but rather built on the existing system of rights, thus treating those common law rights as a "stage of thought." The broader point is that, by disaggregating particular jural relations, and in emphasizing ends rather than means, Hohfeld's approach contains some hints of the later excesses of legal realism, with its scant concern for debates such as that into the essential nature of trusts and other equitable interests: at large in Hohfeld's beautifully ordered formal garden are the seeds of the bramble bush.

[83] To adopt a term of Hohfeld's. *See* Hohfeld, *supra* note 1, at 20.

10

General and Particular Jural Relations

Emily Sherwin

10.1 INTRODUCTION

Hohfeld set out to precisify jural relations in a series of articles culminating in a book.[1] His basic scheme of rights, privileges, powers, and immunities and their correlatives and opposites is hard to dispute and helps bring clarity to law. The project, however, was not complete at the time of his death and leaves several important questions unanswered. One problem Hohfeld mentioned in his final article was the problem of "common (or general) and specific (or particular) relations." In this chapter, I will speculate about what he might have said about these subcategories of relations and what difficulties they might have raised for his overall scheme.

10.2 GENERAL RULES AND PARTICULAR CASES

Before turning to Hohfeld's picture of law, I will briefly summarize a problem that affects any mature system of law: The problem of general rules. For this purpose, the term "rules" refers to rules that are general in application and determinate enough to be understood in most cases. The rules under discussion in this chapter are also good rules, meaning rules that, if always followed, produce a better sum of results than individual actors otherwise would achieve by following their own best unregulated judgment about what to do in each case.[2] Of course, not all legal rules meet this test, but my discussion focuses on those that do.

[1] Wesley N. Hohfeld, *Some Fundamental Legal Conceptions as Applied in Judicial Reasoning*, 23 YALE L.J. 16 (1913) [hereinafter Hohfeld, *FLC 1*]; Wesley N. Hohfeld, *The Relations Between Law and Equity*, 11 MICH. L. REV. 537 (1913) [hereinafter Hohfeld, *Equity*]; Wesley N. Hohfeld, *Fundamental Legal Conceptions as Applied in Judicial Reasoning*, 26 YALE L.J. 710 (1917) [hereinafter Hohfeld, *FLC 2*]. An informal precis of topics to be covered appears in Hohfeld, *FLC 2* at 712.

[2] I leave open what counts as a good result. Joseph Raz, in his "service conception" of authority, proposes that rulemaking authority is justified to the extent that individual actors will better conform to reasons for action applicable to them if they follow the rules. *See* JOSEPH RAZ, THE MORALITY OF FREEDOM 129–31 (1986).

Rules, so defined, have significant value. Assuming that they are good rules, they reduce error when regularly followed. Most importantly, they reduce the type of error that results from lack of coordination. Actors can plan much more effectively if they know what other actors will do. There is no way to look into other peoples' minds, but when a rule has a reasonably clear meaning and is widely followed there is good reason to think that most people will do as it requires.

The problem of rules arises because all general, determinate rules, including good rules, will prescribe some results that are or appear to be wrong, all things considered. A general rule must be announced in advance of conduct, and so will cover some cases the rulemaker did not anticipate. Due to the imperfections of language, a rule that is determinate enough to govern conduct will also be overbroad, sweeping in cases to which the rule ought not apply. Nevertheless, if the rule is a good rule, the sum of outcomes will be best if individual actors follow the rule unreflectively. Not only is human reasoning imperfect, but a common form of cognitive bias makes salient facts appear more significant than background probabilities such as the long-term impact of a rule violation on the coordination value of the rule.[3] Consequently, individual actors exercising particularized judgment about whether to follow a rule will tend both to err and to err systematically against following the rule.

The result of this dilemma is a gap between the perspective of the rulemaking authority and those who must follow or apply the rules.[4] From the authority's point of view, it will appear that all those subject to the rule should follow it in all cases. From the point of view of an individual actor called on to follow the rule, it will sometimes be, or seem, clear that following the rule is a mistake. Judges are often rulemakers but, in their role as appliers of rules in individual cases, their perspective will resemble that of actors. Strict enforcement of the rule may appear to be at odds with the rule's purpose or simply unfair in the circumstances of the case. Accordingly, it may appear from this point of view that the best course of action is to follow the rule in all cases except this one.

The gap just described never completely closes. Particularistic decision-making does not close the gap because, as noted, human decision-makers are not omniscient and so cannot judge accurately when it is best to follow the rule. Rule-sensitive particularism, meaning particularistic decision-making that takes into account the effect of a rule violation on the rule's coordination value, fails to close the gap for the same reason.[5]

[3] *See generally* Judgment under Uncertainty: Heuristics and Biases 163 (Daniel Kahneman et al. eds., 1982); Heuristics and Biases: The Psychology of Intuitive Judgment (Daniel Kahneman et al. eds., 2002).

[4] Further discussion can be found in Larry Alexander & Emily Sherwin, The Rule of Rules: Morality, Rules, and the Dilemmas of Law 11–36 (2001); Joseph Raz, The Morality of Freedom 49–50 (1986); Frederick Schauer, Playing by the Rules: A Philosophical Examination of Rule-Based Decision-Making in Law and Life 1–121, 149–55 (1991).

[5] Frederick Schauer coined the term "rule-sensitive particularism." *See* Schauer, *supra* note 4, at 94–100; Frederick Schauer, *Rules and the Rule of Law*, 14 Harv. J.L. & Pub. Pol'y 645, 676 n.66 (1991). His own position, at least at the time, was "presumptive positivism," which adds a presumption in favor of rule-following to rule-sensitive particularism. *See* Schauer, *id.* at 691–94.

Sanctions do not close the gap because sanctions are imposed by judges who are likely to view strict enforcement as irrational and unjust.

10.3 EQUITY

Our legal system historically was divided between law and equity. Procedural merger ended the system of separate courts but did not eliminate judicial consciousness of distinctive doctrines, remedies, and principles traceable to the equity side of legal history. Although general and determinate rules can be found in both legal and equitable doctrine, one feature that is often associated with the equity doctrine is equity in the Aristotelian sense, meaning correction of the errors that sometimes result from strict application of rules.[6] Some commentators have characterized this softening of legal rules through equity as a supplemental function that does not bring equity into conflict with the law.[7] Others, including Hohfeld, have viewed it as an override. Either way, the effect is to alter the outcomes of legal rules when they appear too harsh.

The association between equity and correction of rules survived the merger. In post-merger law, the corrective function of equity is sometimes carried out directly, by means of indeterminate exceptions to rules. For example, courts may give relief against contractual forfeiture provisions in mortgage contracts when an accident or mistake makes enforcement unconscionable.[8] Equitable correction also may take the form of special, relatively indeterminate defenses to equitable remedies, such as unclean hands, disproportionate hardship, and unilateral mistake resulting in unconscionability. Equitable defenses theoretically do not affect the claimant's ability to obtain a legal damage remedy, but because damages often are inadequate to provide full relief, equitable defenses place significant limits on enforcement of claims.[9]

Equitable correction of the outcomes of rules does not eliminate the gap between the long-term benefits of enforcing determinate legal rules and the desire for just results in individual cases. Assuming the rule in question is a good rule in the sense described earlier, overall results will be best if judges refuse to engage in equitable correction and instead enforce the rules according to their terms. Moreover, in any

6 ARISTOTLE, NICOMACHEAN ETHICS ¶ 1138b25 (Terence Irwin ed. & trans., 1985) ("And this is the nature of what is decent – rectification of law in so far as the universality of law makes it deficient.").

7 For views on the relation between law and equity, *see, e.g.*, 3 WILLIAM BLACKSTONE, COMMENTARIES *430 (1769); Henry Home (Lord Kames), *Introduction*, *in* PRINCIPLES OF EQUITY vii (1760); F. W. MAITLAND, EQUITY, ALSO THE FORMS OF ACTION AT COMMON LAW: TWO COURSES OF LECTURES 2–11 (A. H. Chaytor & W. J. Whittaker eds., 1929); 1 JOSEPH STORY, COMMENTARIES ON EQUITY JURISPRUDENCE §§ 5, 8, 12, 13, 33 (4th ed. 1846).

8 *See, e.g.*, *Graf* v. *Hope Bldg. Corp.*, 171 N.E. 884 (N.Y. 1930) (Cardozo, C.J., dissenting) (discussed *infra* note 35).

9 For a full discussion of equitable defenses to contract claims and citation to many cases, see EDWARD YORIO, CONTRACT ENFORCEMENT: SPECIFIC PERFORMANCE AND INJUNCTIONS 73–126 (1989 & Supp. 2010).

legal system in which legal decisions are fully available to the public, corrective equity will tend over time to reduce the effectiveness of legal rules. Each instance of equitable correction undermines the apparent reliability of the applicable rule and so reduces the rule's capacity to coordinate future conduct. Thus, equitable correction in particular cases satisfies the desire to do justice when good rules produce bad results, but only at the cost of long-term harm to the value of rules.

At least for a time in our legal history, the relative obscurity of the equitable remedies and doctrines through which correction of general rules took place may have limited the harm done to rules. Judges typically characterize equity as supplemental to law and equitable remedies as extraordinary.[10] Further, even in a publicly accessible legal system, equity tends to remain obscure. Equitable remedies, the mechanisms by which they are enforced, and the special defenses that apply to them are relatively complex in comparison to the money remedies available at law. As long as equity remains in the background of the legal system, ordinary actors may continue to look to the rules for guidance.[11] As a result, equitable correction can enter in at the remedial stage without immediate impact on the coordination value of determinate rules.[12]

In the United States, one of the effects of American Legal Realism has been to de-emphasize the role of determinate rules in the legal system and to make explicit the more fact-specific principles traditionally applied in equity.[13] The Realists took the view that rules are neither effective nor desirable as guides to decision-making. They proposed, among other things, that "law" is not a set of established general rules but the outcome of judicial decision-making in response to the facts of particular cases and sound notions of social and economic policy.[14] The written law should either be

10 *Tower City Grain Co.* v. *Richmond*, 232 N.W.2d 61 (N.D. 1975) (denying specific performance of a contract for sale of grain). *See also* Story, *supra* note 7, at ch. I, §§ 12–13, 14–16; MAITLAND, *supra* note 7, at 19 (describing equity as a "collection of appendixes" to law).

11 For a discussion of the possibility that decision rules applied by judges may remain "acoustically separate" from the conduct rules that guide actors, see Meir Dan-Cohen, *Conduct Rules and Decision Rules: On Acoustic Separation in Criminal Law*, 97 HARV. L. REV. 625 (1984).

12 Henry Smith, in collaboration with John Goldberg and others, has depicted equity as performing a second-order function in the legal system, enabling judges to police transactions *ex post* for signs of opportunism without directly challenging rules of conduct. *See, e.g.*, John C. P. Goldberg & Henry E. Smith, *Wrongful Fusion*, *in* EQUITY AND LAW: FUSION OR FISSION? 309 (John C. P. Goldberg et al. eds., 2017); Henry E. Smith, *Why Fiduciary Law Is Equitable*, *in* PHILOSOPHICAL FOUNDATIONS OF FIDUCIARY LAW 261 (Andrew S. Gold & Paul B. Miller eds., 2014); Yuval Feldman & Henry E. Smith, *Behavioral Equity*, 170 J. INSTITUTIONAL & THEORETICAL ECON. 137 (2014); Henry E. Smith, *Equity as Meta-Law*, 130 YALE L.J. 1050 (2021).

13 For a similar argument focusing on procedural reforms following the advent of Realism, see Stephen N. Subrin, *How Equity Conquered Common Law: The Federal Rules of Civil Procedure in Historical Perspective*, 135 U. PA. L. REV. 909 (1987).

14 *See, e.g.*, JEROME FRANK, LAW AND THE MODERN MIND 276 (1930). *See also* KARL N. LLEWELLYN, THE BRAMBLE BUSH: SOME LECTURES ON THE LAW AND ITS STUDY 2–4 (1930) ("to my mind the main thing is seeing what officials do . . . and seeing that there is a certain regularity in their doing – a regularity which makes possible prediction").

reformulated in fact-specific terms or stated in the form of broad principles that prompt judges to assess in detail the situations that come before them. The hallmark of law and legal decision-making should be candor: courts should explain as clearly as possible the real grounds for their decisions. Realism, in other words, left no room for, and had no interest in maintaining, a covert system of equitable correction superimposed on determinate legal rules.

10.4 HOHFELD AND RULES

This quick summary of the problem of general and particular rules and the related problem of law and equity leads up to the questions I would pose to Hohfeld about jural relations. Hohfeld was aware of the emerging Realist movement, but at least on the face of things he does not appear to have been a rule skeptic. To the contrary, he presented jural relations as relations that can be identified, at least preliminarily, based on legal materials that precede particular interactions or judicial decisions. He was classifying relations that are regularly and predictably recognized by courts, not just after the fact but as a matter of abstract doctrine.[15]

Hohfeld's discussion of jural relations is filled with specific examples. His examples, however, are not drawn from the outcomes of particular disputes; instead they assume a background of rules governing property, contract, and tort, which he often described in if-then terms.[16] Although he frequently criticized judicial opinions and treatises, his quarrel was not with the authors' doctrinal assumptions but with their mischaracterization of the jural relations that result.

Hohfeld's treatment of operative and evidential facts provides further evidence that he was comfortable with fixed rules of law that predate disputes. One of the first points he made in discussing jural relations was that "purely legal relations" must be distinguished from "the physical and mental facts that call such relations into being."[17] Facts, in turn, are divided into "operative" facts and "evidential" facts. Operative facts are those that, "under the general rules that are applicable," establish or alter jural relations; evidential facts are those that tend to prove other facts.[18] Operative facts may be general, as when used to plead a cause of action, or they may be specific, as they appear in real life.[19] Either way, they presuppose a body of relatively fixed and determinate law that picks out certain facts as operative.

Hohfeld's attitude toward legal rules is also evident in his discussion of "multital" rights, a term he coined in hopes of dispelling the confusion surrounding rights *in rem*.[20]

15 To cite just one example, Hohfeld stated that an offer "*ipso facto* creates a legal relation" consisting of a power in the offeree and a liability in the offeror. *See* Hohfeld, *FLC 1*, *supra* note 1, at 51.

16 For example, conditional statements of law run throughout Hohfeld's shrimp salad hypothetical (borrowed from John Chipman Gray). *Id.* at 34–36.

17 *Id.* at 20.

18 *Id.* at 25.

19 *Id.*

20 *See* Hohfeld, *FCL 2*, *supra* note 1, at 718 (defining terms).

Multital rights are rights that belong to a large class of similar "actual and potential" rights. The term multital describes not only property rights, but also rights against tortious harm.[21] Each multital right is distinct, in the sense that it correlates to one person's duty not to transgress the right, and each violation results in a particular remedial right against the violator.[22] A particular violation of multital rights, however, leaves intact the set of unspecified multital rights the victim may have against other parties.[23] Thus, although multital rights are inert before they are individuated by a particular event, they presuppose a set of rules defining the conditions under which the corresponding duty is breached.

Finally, Hohfeld's discussion of equity implicitly assumes that there are rules of law with which equity may conflict.[24] As discussed in the next section, Hohfeld argued that equity overrides legal rules and thus eliminates their role in defining jural relations. I will suggest, however, that the extent and consequences of this equitable override are uncertain.

10.5 HOHFELD AND EQUITY

Hohfeld wrote his short article on the relation between law and equity partly in response to Frederick Maitland's argument that there is no conflict between law and equity.[25] Maitland suggested that equity simply supplements the law without direct contradiction: it upholds legal doctrine but improves it by softening its effect in hard cases.[26] Hohfeld argued, to the contrary, that a:

> [L]arge part of the rules of equity ... conflict with legal rules and, a matter of substance, annul or negative the latter *pro tanto* ... [Whenever] such conflict occurs, the equitable rule is ... paramount and determinative ... [T]he so-called legal rule ... has, *to that extent*, only an apparent validity and operation as a matter of *genuine* law. Though it may represent an important stage of thought in the solution of a given problem ... as regard the very relation in which it suffers direct

21 *Id.* at 733.

22 *Id.* at 740, 752.

23 *Id.* at 743.

24 *See* Hohfeld, *Equity*, *supra* note 1.

25 *See* Hohfeld, *Equity*, *supra* note 1. The body of the article is short; the attached appendix outlining and annotating Hohfeld's lectures on equity is not so short. Hohfeld was also responding to an address by Walter Wheeler Cook, in which Cook advocated full incorporation of equity doctrines into cognate areas of law. In this address, Cook cited Hohfeld's entry in the Stanford course catalog as a "typical, and in no respect whatever exceptional or peculiar" example of the current "belated and reactionary" treatment of equity as a separate system. *See* Walter Wheeler Cook, *The Place of Equity in Our Legal System*, 3 AM. L. SCH. REV. 173, 174 (1912). *See also* Hohfeld, *FLC* 2, at 712 n.6 (referring to Cook at a later point as his "friend and colleague").

26 *See* MAITLAND, *supra* note 7, at 18–19; *id.* at 19 ("[I]f the legislature had passed a short act saying 'Equity is hereby abolished,' we might still have got on fairly well, in some respects our law would have been barbarous, unjust, absurd, but still the great elementary rights ... would have been decently protected.")

competition with a rule of equity, the law is, *pro tanto*, of no greater force than an unconstitutional statute.[27]

Yet, the reasons Hohfeld gave for the equitable override of law are surprisingly technical. The synopsis for Hohfeld's Equity course, appended to the article, refers to certain substantive principles associated with equity, such as "conscience" and "good faith," and cites 11 standard equitable maxims expressing broad principles of justice.[28] But Hohfeld did not argue that these principles and maxims are substantively superior to the requirements and objectives of legal rules. Instead, he stated a general principle that a system of law can have only one set of jural relations; then he cited the equity courts' contempt power and King James' 1616 decision in favor of common injunctions to explain why, in cases of conflict, the prevailing set of relations must be the equitable set.[29]

Hohfeld also qualified his claim that equity overrides law by suggesting that the equitable override is "pro tanto" in several different ways. It is limited to the extent of overlap between legal and equitable doctrine, and it is also limited to particular instances of overlap. Apparently, then, the override affects only the jural relations between particular parties, and has no broader effect outside the context of a given interaction.[30] Legal rules are overridden as applied, not on their face.

10.6 A CLOSER LOOK AT THE EQUITABLE OVERRIDE OF LAW

Hohfeld divided the relations between law and equity into two main categories, those in which law and equity concurrently recognize a jural relation and those in which law and equity recognize conflicting jural relations.[31] He further divided each category into subcategories of primary relations, remedial relations, and adjective relations. Hohfeld provided numerous examples within each subcategory.

Despite the wealth of cases cited, however, Hohfeld's examples of conflict between law and equity are limited in that the equitable doctrines on which they rely are relatively stable and determinate. In one type of case, well-established equitable doctrines override legal rules in predictable ways. The equitable rights

[27] *See* Hohfeld, *Equity*, *supra* note 1, at 543–44 (emphasis in original). In later comments, Hohfeld acknowledged that equity traditionally used fictions to override the law functionally without directly contradicting it. Thus, for example, a trustee of real property, as legal owner of the property, has a legal privilege to cut trees, but an equitable duty to the trust beneficiary not to cut trees. Hohfeld insisted, however, that these fictions should be dropped and the equitable override acknowledged directly. *See* Hohfeld, *FLC* 2, *supra* note 1, supplemental note at 769–70 (we should "recognize this venerable fiction as such and see through it to ultimate jural realities").

[28] See Hohfeld, *Equity*, *supra* note 1, at synopsis III(I)(A), (B) at 549–50.

[29] *Id.* at synopsis IV(C).

[30] Referring to an equitable waste case, Hohfeld said that "[w]hen ... it is said that the legal rule is 'annulled' pro tanto ... this refers to the very jural relation under consideration and to that alone. It is meant simply that ... Y is under a duty not to cut ornamental trees." *Id.* at 571.

[31] Concurrent relations appear to be legal relations with which equity courts will not interfere by means of common injunction. *Id.* at 555 (example 23: contract).

of a trust beneficiary take priority over certain legal privileges of the trustee; or the established doctrine of equitable waste replaces a life tenant's duty with a privilege and the remainderman's right with a no-right.[32] In another type of case, a single set of primary legal relations is enforceable by legal and equitable remedies and choice of an equitable remedy overrides the secondary jural relations that otherwise would be available at law. In the case of a land sale contract, for example, the promisee's secondary equitable right to specific performance overrides the promisor's secondary legal privilege to pay rather than convey.[33] Thus, Hohfeld's main argument, that equity overrides law in cases of conflict, is illustrated by cases in which equity doctrines generate a predicable set of equitable relations.

Hohfeld's reliance on relatively determinate equitable doctrines to illustrate the dominance of equity avoids the problem of general rules and particular outcomes discussed at the beginning of this chapter. If equity is fairly concrete, then the primacy of equity means only that between two sets of pre-existing rules, the equitable set prevails unless jurisdictional limits exclude its operation. The jural relations that result remain general in form, and are later particularized only in the sense that particular parties come to stand in them from time to time.

Hohfeld's examples are also consistent with his conviction that over time, the accumulation of precedents has converted open-ended equitable principles into determinate equitable rules.[34] Nevertheless, modern courts apply a variety of relatively indeterminate doctrines, many of which can be traced to the equity side of the legal system, that continue to serve the corrective function traditionally associated with equity. When these doctrines come into play, the result is a conflict between legal rules that establish rights, privileges, powers, and immunities in relatively determinate form and more indeterminate standards of decision, usually equitable in origin, that alter the effect of the rules as applied. A full account of jural relations would have to explain what relations result when this type of conflict occurs. One reading of Hohfeld's reference to general and particular jural relations at the outset of his last article is that he intended eventually to address this question.

Several examples may help to illustrate the problem. First, suppose that B gives A a mortgage to secure payment of a construction loan. The mortgage provides for interest payments on certain dates and for acceleration of the principle debt if B fails to pay any installment of interest within twenty days after the due date. Through a series of errors, an employee of B sends A an interest check in the wrong amount while B is away. A rejects B's subsequent tender of the correct amount due, accelerates the loan, and sues to foreclose. The court denies foreclosure, stating that "a court

32 *Id.* at 555 (examples 34, 35).

33 *Id.* at 556 (example 53).

34 *See id.* at synopsis III(I)(C) at 550 ("The general principles and specific rules are now for the most part defined by a large and well organized body of precedents, so that the above general ideas and maxims are, at the present time, of comparatively slight importance"). At the same time, Hohfeld acknowledged that even when legal remedies are inadequate, equity may refuse a remedy based on "special impolicy or inexpediency." *Id.* at synopsis III(III)(B)(2) at 552.

of equity may intervene to prevent the creditor from taking an unconscionable advantage of the letter of his bargain."[35]

In this case legal rules (or more precisely, the established rules of equity governing mortgage agreements) gave A a power to accelerate and foreclose according to the terms of the mortgage and B a liability to acceleration and foreclosure. The court's decision, however, replaces A's power with a disability. It also gives B a power to reinstate the mortgage by paying the sum due.

Next suppose that A and B own adjoining beachfront properties improved with houses. B's house, built by a predecessor in title, encroaches on A's lot. When B bought his lot, neither B nor A was aware of the encroachment; the encroachment came to light much later when A surveyed his lot for unrelated reasons. A requests an injunction ordering B to remove the encroachment. To comply, B will need to destroy and rebuild his house. The court holds that A is entitled to damages for loss of value but denies an injunction, finding that an injunction in the circumstances would impose a disproportionate hardship on B and give A unwarranted bargaining power in subsequent negotiations.[36]

In this case, legal rules gave A a primary right that B must not enter A's land without permission and imposed on B a duty not to enter. Following the court's decision, B has a privilege to enter and soon, by adverse possession, will have a right against A and others that they must not enter. A will have no-right against B and soon will have no-right against others who enter the land. A has a secondary right to damages against B but no secondary right excluding B from the portion of land encroached. Meanwhile, damages are likely to be of little value because a small irregular amount of land has little market value.

In the next case, A, an actor, enters a contract with B to perform exclusively for B for an agreed period of time at a fixed salary. At the time, A is technically a minor, entitled by statute to repudiate contracts. While still a minor, A enters a contract with C for a higher salary. C does not know of A's prior agreement with B. When A turns 21, she repudiates her contract with B, intending to work for C. B then persuades C, by means of threats and payments, to break its contract with A. A sues B, asking for an injunction prohibiting B from interfering with her contractual relations with C.

The court agrees that A was entitled by statute to repudiate her contract with B, that B's subsequent conduct was tortious, and that A was entitled to damages against B. But it refuses to grant an injunction on the ground that, although A was not legally required to honor her contract with B, "she was under a moral obligation to abide by" the contract.[37] "One who comes into equity must come with clean hands, and her hands are not clean."[38]

35 This example is based on *Graf* v. *Hope Bldg. Corp.*, 171 N.E. 884 (N.Y. 1930). The court in this case declined to give relief, over Justice Cardozo's classic dissent.

36 This example is based on *Peters* v. *Archambault*, 278 N.E.2d 729 (Mass. 1972) (Tauro, C.H., dissenting).

37 This example is based on *Carmen* v. *Fox Film Corp.*, 269 F. 928 (2d Cir. 1920).

38 *Id.* at 931.

In this case, legal rules initially gave A a power to repudiate her contract with B and an immunity against enforcement of that contract. They also gave her a primary multital right against interference with her contract with C and placed a primary duty on B (and others) not to interfere. The court's equitable decision replaces A's primary right against interference by B with a secondary right to damages, leaving A with primary no-right against interference by B and B with a privilege to interfere.[39]

In the final example, A agrees to sell B a house. Evidence suggests that the price stated in the written contract of sale (which A did not read) is about half what A believed to be the price offered. Evidence also suggests that B committed no fraud and did not engage in other conduct that would support rescission under applicable legal rules. B sues for specific performance and A defends on the ground that he made a unilateral mistake about the price. The court denies specific performance but indicates that the contract remains valid and that B has a right to damages for the loss expectancy. The stated reason for the decision to deny equitable relief is that "[w]here the enforcement of a contract for sale of land would be harsh, oppressive, or manifestly unjust to one of the parties, specific performance will not be decreed."[40]

In this case, legal rules appeared to give B a primary legal right to performance of the contract and to place on A a primary duty to perform. B now has a secondary right to recover damages if A does not perform, and A has a legal duty to pay; but B has no right to performance and A has a privilege not to convey. The difference in jural relations is significant because damages may be of little value to B: A may have little money, B may want the particular land, and a jury's assessment of damages is likely to be low.

In each of these examples, judges relied on highly indeterminate equitable doctrines to make significant changes in the parties' jural relations as they appeared at the point of conduct. The question the examples raise is to what extent the particular equitable outcome decreed by a court supercedes general, rule-based jural relations. It may be that Hohfeld was content to show that his basic framework was capable of describing the relations in place at any point in time, without drawing any broad conclusions about how jural relations change at different stages in the legal process. Thus, for any question of law there might be a set of abstract jural relations prior to relevant conduct, a set of more concrete jural relations immediately following conduct, and a set of fully specified jural relations following a judicial decision. Hohfeld's table of relations, correlatives, and opposites seems quite capable of this descriptive task.

On the other hand, Hohfeld may have intended to develop a unified theory explaining how these different sets of jural relations interact over time within a legal system. Hohfeld took on a related task in his discussion of equity, concluding

39 At least, A has no primary right against this instance of interference.

40 This example is based on *Panco* v. *Rogers*, 87 A.2d 770 (N.J. Ch. 1952).

that, for mainly historical and procedural reasons, relations established by rules of equity supersede conflicting relations established by rules of law. The task becomes more difficult, however, when, as in the examples just given, the relations based on indeterminate decision rules appear to conflict with relations based on more determinate rules governing conduct.

10.7 CONCLUSION: WHAT WOULD HOHFELD DO?

In the example cases described above, one possible conclusion is that the only true jural relations between two parties are the relations likely to result from adjudication, taking into account any equitable adjustments the adjudicator might make to correct the outcomes prescribed by legal rules. In other words, the expected outcome of particularized decision-making supersedes what previously appeared to be the applicable rules of conduct. This conclusion is consistent with Hohfeld's assertions that there is room for only one set of jural relations in any legal system and that equity must prevail over law. If courts commonly invoke principles of equity to correct unjust results of rules, then the jural relations between A and B are defined by the final adjustment.

This result might be acceptable to a thoroughgoing Realist who equates law with the outcome of particular judicial decisions. I doubt, however, that it would have satisfied Hohfeld.[41] The examples Hohfeld relied on, his treatment of multital rights, and the distinction he drew between operative and evidentiary facts all suggest a significant role for general, forward-looking rules in the legal system. If the most fundamental legal relations are the products, rather than the starting points, of legal reasoning, then general rules fail to provide reliable guides to conduct or decision-making and thus have no meaningful function. Hohfeld maintained that jural relations recognized in equity displace conflicting jural relations recognized at law. Yet the equity doctrines on which Hohfeld relied in making this argument took the form of relatively fixed and determinate rules rather than licenses for discretionary decision-making. Thus, the priority he accorded to equity does not necessarily imply a Realist approach to law. Equitable correction in cases of the type described above is the product of highly indeterminate standards of decision applied to particular facts. It follows that the relations that appear to be in place when the parties interact are not reliable guides to conduct. An understanding of jural relations that eliminates or greatly reduces the role of general rules in defining jural relations is at odds with many of Hohfeld's examples, with his descriptions of pre-existing multital rights, and with the distinction he draws between operative and

[41] One way out, which might have appealed to Hohfeld, would be to press for significantly more rigid equitable rules of decision. The great advantage of traditional equitable principles, however, has been their capacity to reach unforeseen cases that cannot be captured in useful rules. Another possible way out is to press for a reduction in the scope of equity's mandate. *See, e.g.*, Smith, *Equity as Meta-Law*, *supra* note 12.

evidentiary facts. Nor does the Realist view of law as outcomes follow from Hohfeld's conclusion that jural relations recognized in equity displace conflicting jural relations recognized at law. The equity doctrines on which Hohfeld relied took the form of relatively fixed and determinate rules rather than licenses for discretionary decision-making.

Alternatively, Hohfeld might have concluded that the primary jural relations in place when parties interact continue to stand as general guides to conduct, but are subject to later adjustment at the time of decision by the set of secondary relations fashioned by a court. On this view, the jural relations of particular parties may change, but the change is *ex post* and affects only their remedial positions. The set of primary jural relations remains in place to govern conduct in advance of decision. In this way, the two sets of relations, one general and one particular, can coexist within a legal system.[42]

The difficulty with this second theory is that in a system in which adjudication is fully accessible to the public, parties have access to both primary and secondary jural relations at the time they first take action. Rational parties will take indeterminate decisional standards into account from the outset and will discount the set of primary jural relations as incompletely reliable. Consequently, the supposed primary jural relations will be less effective as a source of guidance and less useful as a basis for interpersonal coordination. Thus, if Hohfeld meant to say that there are two sets of jural relations, one operating *ex ante* and another operating *ex post*, his position is more moderate but may ultimately be unstable. In a fully public system of law, particular one that endorses Realist principles of transparency in legal decision-making, principles of equitable adjustment will bleed through and dilute the *ex ante* benefits of legal rules. The point is not that equity should be suppressed, but only that equity raises an intractable dilemma for law.

It appears, therefore, that Hohfeld ultimately would have confronted the basic problem of general rules and particular cases discussed at the beginning of this chapter. Nothing in his ingenious and enlightening system of jural relations provides a clear way out. One of the advantages of his system, however, is that it brings the problem to light and illustrates the difficulty of avoiding it.

42 Henry Smith defends the possibility of a separate, second-order role for equitable defenses in the legal system. *See* Smith, *Equity as Meta-Law*, *supra* note 12.

PART IV

Hohfeldian Complexities

11

Very Tight "Bundles of Sticks": Hohfeld's Complex Jural Relations

*Ted M. Sichelman**

11.1 INTRODUCTION

Wesley Hohfeld began his landmark 1913 article, *Some Fundamental Legal Conceptions as Applied in Judicial Reasoning,* by impugning existing analytical treatments of trusts, yet noticeably never fully explained his own view of trusts as a "complex aggregate" of "fundamental" relations.[1] In the last footnote to the article, Hohfeld stated that in his "next article . . . some attention will be given to the nature and analysis of complex legal interests, or aggregates of jural relations."[2] Unfortunately, as the editor of his collected works, Walter Wheeler Cook, explained in an annotated version of that footnote, "the 'next article' deals chiefly with rights, etc., *in personam* and rights, etc., *in rem*. The author's untimely death prevented the carrying out of the remainder of the plan."[3]

In this chapter, I undertake the beginnings of the "remainder of the plan" by proposing a set of Hohfeldian complex jural relations. For instance, a "common right" is defined as a Hohfeldian privilege to engage in some activity (e.g., walking down a sidewalk) coupled with a Hohfeldian right against (direct or indirect) interference with the activity (e.g., against assault and battery). A "common liberty" is the combination of a Hohfeldian privilege to do an action coupled with a Hohfeldian privilege not to do the action. A "constitutional right" is defined as an immunity against the State's attempt to restrict (or demand) actions otherwise

* Professor, University of San Diego School of Law. I especially thank Pierre Schlag for providing a detailed set of comments on an earlier draft. I also thank Larry Alexander, Donald Dripps, Lee Anne Fennell, David Frydrych, Andrew Gold, Andrew Halpin, John Harrison, Adam Hirsch, Leo Katz, Ben McFarlane, David McGowan, Michael Moore, James Penner, John Schlegel, Maimon Schwarzschild, Nikta Shahbaz, Sharmila Sohoni, Henry Smith, and Tom Smith, as well as participants at the Hohfeld Centennial Workshop held at Yale Law School and the Faculty Colloquium at the University of San Diego School of Law for their helpful comments and questions.

1 Wesley N. Hohfeld, *Some Fundamental Legal Conceptions as Applied in Judicial Reasoning*, 23 YALE L.J. 16 (1913) [hereinafter Hohfeld (1913)].

2 *Id.* at 59 n.100.

3 WESLEY N. HOHFELD, SOME FUNDAMENTAL LEGAL CONCEPTIONS AS APPLIED IN JUDICIAL REASONING 64 n.100 (1920) [hereinafter Hohfeld (1920)].

"protected" under the constitution; sometimes, coupled with a Hohfeldian remedial right against noninterference by State action with respect to any privileges to undertake such action (or not); sometimes, further coupled with a remedial immunity from the State's attempt to eliminate its duty of noninterference.

The complex relations are critical to the Hohfeldian program because, as Cook properly recognized, "nearly every situation upon analysis turns out to involve a more or less complex aggregate of all the different kinds of legal relations."[4] In this regard, while the precise construction of the complex Hohfeldian relations is surely of interest to legal theorists and jurists, as legal artificial intelligence has become increasingly prominent, properly categorizing these jural admixtures is of great practical concern to the growing digital economies leveraging legal "toolkits."[5]

Traditionally, legal realists have focused on how Hohfeld's eight "fundamental" legal relations ultimately constitute these complex aggregates of relations – like atoms constituting a molecule – in turn espousing a reductionist program. For example, Cook stated that "the usual analysis to which we have been accustomed has treated a very complex aggregate of legal relations as though it were a simple thing, a unit. The result is no more enlightening than it would be were a chemist to treat an extraordinarily complex chemical compound as if it were an element."[6] Such thinking evolved into the "bundle of sticks" picture of property and related realist approaches to law.

Yet, not all chemical molecules can be easily severed. Often, atoms can only be split with tremendous energy into protons, neutrons, and electrons. Like the quarks that are the "fundamental" building blocks of all matter, most legal relations are nearly always *very tightly* coupled with others, and rarely appear as singular, "naked" objects. Contrary to Cook's thesis, chemists often treat complex chemical compounds – and judges often treat complex legal relations – as "simple elements" for sound practical reasons.

As energy is to physical particles, information is to legal relations. In most instances, severing these tightly bound legal relations requires more information than is worth the candle. Drawing upon Henry Smith's work, the core jural relations that are regularly used in the law are often compact "modules" of complex Hohfeldian relations that serve to reduce the information costs involved in doing actual legal work. Indeed, I show that the usual criticisms by Hohfeld and others of so-called formalist reasoning that ostensibly conflates fundamental relations often no longer applies once it is understood that the reasoning concerns complex, rather than fundamental, relations. Thus, statements by scholars and jurists such as John

4 *Id.* at 9 n.9.

5 *See, e.g.*, Pieter Slootweg et al., *The Implementation of Hohfeldian Legal Concepts with Semantic Web Technologies*, *in* PROCEEDINGS OF AI4J – ARTIFICIAL INTELLIGENCE FOR JUSTICE, WORKSHOP AT THE 22ND EUROPEAN CONFERENCE ON ARTIFICIAL INTELLIGENCE (ECAI 2016) 65 (2013), www.ecai2016.org/content/uploads/2016/08/W2-ai4j-2016.pdf#page=69.

6 *Id.* at 15.

Chipman Gray and Lord Lindley that appear to be muddled, actually exhibit sophistication of language and reasoning when viewed through the lens of the complex relations. In turn, the realist view that Hohfeldian analysis necessarily leads to reductionist, disaggregated "bundles of rights" as the fundamental "unit" of legal analysis is not only misguided as a practical matter but mistaken as a theoretical one. Instead, I propose that the modular "thing" approach to reasoning about property and other legal concepts is not only consistent with – but indeed *identical* to – a "bundle" approach, at least one that properly takes account of the complex network of legal relations, actors, and actions that constitute "property" and other high-level legal concepts.

Section 11.2 of this chapter describes Hohfeld's brief treatment of the complex jural relations, as well as later scholars' discussion of them. In so doing, I explain that no scholar has yet to suggest even a rudimentary working set of mid-level, "molecular" relations that can be combined to form more complex legal modules, such as trusts, corporations, and the like. In Section 11.3, I propose several molecular complex relations, such as a "common right," "constitutional right," and "common liberty," and sketch how they may be combined to form more complex legal modules regularly used within the law. Section 11.4 discusses the implications of the molecular and complex relations for legal analysis and theory, and disputes the realist and post-realist views that legal concepts necessarily reduce to their constituent Hohfeldian atoms in all modes of legal analysis. Instead, I contended that although the "structure" of the law may ultimately reduce to Hohfeld's fundamental constituents, ordinary legal analysis in the run of everyday transactions and cases does not, in Hohfeld's words, "requi[re] . . . careful reasoning" employing the atomic relations.[7] I explain how this implication helps to bridge the divide – in the manner of Andrew Gold and Henry Smith's notion of "inclusive functionalism" and John Goldberg's "inclusive pragmatism"[8] – not only between treating property as a thing and as a disaggregated bundle but also between various modes of reasoning about the law.[9]

11.2 ADUMBRATING THE COMPLEX JURAL RELATIONS

Hohfeld left a number of clues as to what the complex relations might comprise. Additionally, several later scholars have addressed the notion. Yet, none of these efforts has been robust. In this section, I describe these attempts to construct the complex relations, including their strengths and shortcomings.

7 Hohfeld (1913), *supra* note 1, at 49.

8 *See* Andrew S. Gold & Henry E. Smith, *Sizing Up Private Law*, 70 U. Toronto L.J. 489 (2020); John C. P. Goldberg, *Introduction: Pragmatism and Private Law*, 125 Harv. L. Rev. 1640 (2012).

9 The cross-cutting nature of the complex relations is consistent with Hohfeld's reflection that his typology of atomic relations, properly employed, engender "one's perception of fundamental unity and harmony in the law," at least for what may be termed law's "structure." *See supra* note 7 and accompanying text.

11.2.1 *Hohfeld's Unfinished Work*

At many points in his work, Hohfeld refers to certain legal concepts as "complex aggregates" of the atomic jural relations. For instance, as to "property" – particularly, fee simple ownership – he asserts that "this legal concept can be broken down into "a complex aggregate of rights (or claims), privileges, powers, and immunities."[10] Hohfeld then proceeds to list many of the relations that compose fee simple ownership, such as "legal rights, or claims, that *others*, respectively, shall *not* enter on the land, that they shall not cause physical harm to the land, etc.," "an indefinite number of legal privileges of entering on the land, using the land, harming the land, etc.," and "the legal power to alienate his legal interest to another, i.e., to extinguish his complex aggregate of jural relations and create a new and similar aggregate in the other person."[11] Similarly, Hohfeld claimed that such notions as trusts, easements, corporations, and options are in actuality "complex aggregates" of more fundamental jural relations.[12]

Yet, other than for several real property concepts – fee simple ownership, easements, licenses, and rights of entry – Hohfeld did not make any notable attempt to delineate what these complex aggregates comprise.[13] Perhaps more importantly, Hohfeld's examples of complex aggregates of jural relations obscure more basic aggregates – such as Hohfeldian privileges coupled with duties of noninterference – that recur throughout the law and are used as intermediate-level relations to build more complex relations, such as fee simple ownership. To use an analogy, if the Hohfeldian fundamental relations are akin to quarks – one of the basic accepted building blocks of matter – his examples of complex relations are akin to molecules or even macro-molecules, which stand many layers up relative to other combinations of quarks, such as protons and neutrons. In sum, while Hohfeld's work adumbrates the complex relations, it does not sufficiently explicate them, nor does it propose lower-level complex relations that can be used regularly as building blocks within the law.

[10] Wesley N. Hohfeld, *Fundamental Legal Conceptions as Applied in Judicial Reasoning*, 26 Yale L.J. 710, 746–47 (1917) [hereinafter Hohfeld (1917)].

[11] *Id.*

[12] *See* Hohfeld (1913), *supra* note 1, at 28–29; Hohfeld (1917), *supra* note 10, at 767; Wesley N. Hohfeld, *The Relations between Equity and Law*, 11 Mich. L. Rev. 537 (1914) [hereinafter, Hohfeld, *Equity and Law*]; Wesley N. Hohfeld, *Faulty Analysis in Easement and License Cases*, 27 Yale L.J. 66, 70–71 (1917) [hereinafter, Hohfeld, *Faulty Analysis*]; Wesley N. Hohfeld, *Book Review*, 25 Yale L.J. 166, 170 (1915) (reviewing Charles Andrews Huston, The Enforcement of Decrees in Equity (1915)).

[13] To be certain, Hohfeld also described aggregates of similar relations across multiple legal actors in his attempt to disentangle *in personam* from *in rem* relations via his concepts of paucital and multital relations. *See* Hohfeld (1917), *supra* note 10. Additionally, Hohfeld analyzed how remedies couple to rights via powers of enforcement. *See* Hohfeld, *Equity and Law*, *supra* note 12. However, here I generally focus on *substantive* aggregates of the jural relations.

11.2.2 Other Scholarly Pursuits of the Complex Relations

Many scholars have discussed Hohfeld's notion of complex aggregates of legal relations in explaining the genesis of the "bundle of sticks" notion of property – namely, that property in the law is not a "thing" but rather a complex assortment of underlying legal relations between legal persons.[14] Yet, few scholars have attempted to expound the complex relations so as to more systematically explain and extend the concept.[15]

One important preliminary question addressed in the literature is, in the words of Gerald Postema, "What combinatorial principles account for familiar legal compounds?"[16] Again, using the analogy from physics, baryonic particles can only be composed of quarks of three different colors. Are there similar rules when combining fundamental legal relations – or are all combinations possible? Conversely, are there principles that *promote* common sets of complex relations? And so forth.

Matthew Kramer has examined one important restriction on combinations of fundamental legal relations.[17] Specifically, Hohfeld never addressed – at least explicitly – the question of whether one can simultaneously be subject to a duty to perform an action (call it A) and a duty to not perform A. This may seem odd given the precision of the Hohfeldian relations, but "careful analysis" (to use Hohfeld's words) shows that the logical connections among the Hohfeldian relations do not answer this critical question.

Specifically, a Hohfeldian duty to do A implies the absence of a Hohfeldian privilege *not* to do A and, conversely, a Hohfeldian duty *not* to do A implies the absence of a Hohfeldian privilege to do A. Yet, as Kramer rightly notes, nothing in the Hohfeldian scheme connects a duty to do A and a duty not to do A; in other words, both may as a logical matter occur simultaneously. Of course, such conflicting duties would imply that our legal actor would breach at least one of his obligations no matter what course of action is undertaken. As such, one immediate suggestion in combining the relations is to prevent aggregations that lead to such inconsistent obligations via a "consistency" condition. Standard deontic logic takes such a position.[18] On the other hand, Kramer describes an example in which a legal

14 *See, e.g.*, Pierre Schlag, *How to Do Things with Hohfeld*, 78 Law & Contemp. Probs. 185 (2015) [hereinafter Schlag, *Things with Hohfeld*]; Anna di Robilant, *Property: A Bundle of Sticks or A Tree?*, 66 Vand. L. Rev. 869 (2013); Henry E. Smith, *Property as the Law of Things*, 125 Harv. L. Rev. 1691 (2012); J. E. Penner, *The "Bundle of Rights" Picture of Property*, 43 UCLA L. Rev. 711, 724 (1996).

15 Penner has sketched how one might go about reconstructing "property" in this fashion, but ultimately finds such an approach wanting. *See* Penner, *supra* note 14.

16 Gerald Postema, Legal Philosophy in the Twentieth Century: The Common Law World 104 (2011).

17 Matthew Kramer, *Rights without Trimmings*, *in* A Debate Over Rights: Philosophical Enquiries (Matthew Kramer et al. eds., 1998).

18 *See, e.g.*, Ross Hilpinen & Paul McNamara, *Deontic Logic: A Historical Survey and Introduction*, *in* Handbook of Normative Systems 1, 26–27, 38 (Don Gabbay et al. eds., 2013).

person plausibly holds two conflicting duties – namely, one in which a legal actor agrees to mutually conflicting contractual obligations. (In what follows, I leave the necessity of such a consistency condition aside, as it does not impact the remaining discussion.)

Other scholars have addressed specific combinations of Hohfeldian fundamental relations in general terms. For instance, many scholars have recognized that Hohfeldian privileges are often coupled with various Hohfeldian rights vis-à-vis third parties against interference with the exercise of the privileges. For instance, Andrew Halpin has criticized the narrow notion of Hohfeldian privilege as unprotected by rights.[19] Instead, Halpin contended that privileges necessarily encompass a set of rights preventing interference with the underlying action associated with the privilege. On this basis, he states "a privilege may be further broken down into a set of protecting rights . . . on this ground, it can no longer be accepted as a fundamental conception." In its place, Halpin proposes the separate concepts of "fundamental" privilege and "reducible" privilege, with only the latter coupled to rights to noninterference. Yet, Halpin mistakenly criticizes Hohfeld for conflating the two notions. To be certain, Halpin does an admirable job in precisely formulating his "reducible privilege," and few other scholars have approached his level of theoretical granularity in delineating this complex relation.[20] Yet, neither Halpin nor other scholars have robustly analyzed the notion of "reducible" privilege in the context of judicial reasoning, or have identified the common terms used to refer to such an entitlement.

Some scholars have broadened Hohfeldian analysis of jural aggregates in specific areas of law. For instance, Ben McFarlane has extended Hohfeldian analysis in the field of real property.[21] Other scholars have addressed the application of Hohfeldian analysis to constitutional law, which involves aggregations of powers, immunities, and rights (and their correlatives). In this regard, Allen Thomas O'Rourke has recognized that, like the concept of property, a "constitutional right in the broader sense may also be called a bundle of relations, meaning a bundle of relations between an individual and the government that arise from a particular clause or value of the Constitution."[22] Yet, neither these nor other scholars attempt to clearly delineate a variety of low-level bundles of jural relations that may be used in a recurring fashion in legal analysis.

11.3 SOME PROPOSED "COMPACT" COMPLEX JURAL RELATIONS

In this section, I propose a set of distinct, "compact" complex relations that recur in the law. Although this set is clearly not exhaustive, as I contended in Section 11.4, it

[19] Andrew Halpin, Rights and Law, Analysis and Theory 38–43 (1997).

[20] One notable exception is Thomas D. Perry, *Reply in Defense of Hohfeld*, 37 Phil. Stud. 203 (1980).

[21] *See* Ben McFarlane, The Structure of Property Law (2008).

[22] *See* Allen Thomas O'Rourke, *Refuge from A Jurisprudence of Doubt: Hohfeldian Analysis of Constitutional Law*, 61 S.C. L. Rev. 141, 169 (2009).

can do substantial work in providing ready-made, very tightly coupled sets of relations that can be reused in legal analysis and adjudication without resort to their internal composition. Like protons and neutrons, one can build more complex legal "atoms" and "molecules" – such as the notions of property, trusts, corporations, and the like – by using these compact relations rather than the fundamental Hohfeldian relations, at least in substantial part.

11.3.1 *Common Rights and Protected Privileges*

Perhaps the greatest confusion regarding Hohfeld stems from his relatively narrow definition of a (claim) right. Specifically, a Hohfeldian right merely entails a duty on some other actor to perform (a positive right) or not perform (a negative right) some action. In this sense, a Hohfeldian right never provides its holder authority to engage in a particular action, but instead solely prevents others from engaging in a particular action (or, in some cases, demands that others engage in some particular action). As such, it is best termed a "strict right."[23] Conversely, a Hohfeldian privilege merely provides its holder the ability to engage in (or refrain from engaging in) some action without violating a duty, but does not impose any duties on third parties not to interfere with the action – in other words, a Hohfeldian privilege to do A does not imply a right to noninterference in the performance of A.

The narrowness of Hohfeldian privileges and rights is best illustrated by Hohfeld's "shrimp salad" hypothetical, derived from and criticizing an earlier hypothetical set forth by John Chipman Gray, a well-known property scholar of the late nineteenth and early twentieth centuries:

> A, B, C, and D, being the owners of the salad, might say to X: "Eat the salad, if you can; you have our license to do so, but we [do not] agree not to interfere with you." In such a case the privileges exist, so that if X succeeds in eating the salad, he has violated no rights of any of the parties. But it is equally clear that if A had succeeded in holding so fast to the dish that X [could not] eat the contents, no right of X would have been violated.[24]

If we assume that this hypothetical state of affairs truly provides X with no rights to noninterference, then X merely holds a "naked" or "strict" privilege to eat the salad in the sense that X's action violates no duties corresponding to potential "rights of any of the parties [A, B, C, and D]." Yet, in reality, most privileges are coupled with background tort, property, or other duties on the part of third parties not to interfere with the exercise of the privilege. Specifically, background private rights against assault, battery, false imprisonment, interference with contractual relations, trespass to chattels, conversion, trespass, nuisance, and so forth provide indirect protection to

[23] For a discussion of why "claim" is an inapt modifier of "right" in this context, at least in modern parlance, see *infra* Section 11.3.3. *See also* Chapter 12 (in this volume).

[24] *See* Hohfeld (1913), *supra* note 1, at 34–35.

a privilege holder that may effectively prevent interference with a Hohfeldian privilege.[25]

Indeed, even in the shrimp salad example, once the owners provided a "license" to X to eat it, A's subsequent "holding so fast to the dish" so "that X [could not] eat the contents" could very well constitute trespass to chattels, even in spite of the owners' disclaimer of noninterference.[26] Specifically, barring evidence that A, B, C, D, and X intended to construct a game,[27] a court may find that the owners' "license" to X to eat the salad was in effect a gift providing rightful possession of the salad to X. In this case, A's interference with X's ability to eat the salad would arguably constitute trespass to chattels, because it entails intentional interference with X's rightful possession of the salad that caused legally recognizable harm.[28]

Whatever the merits of a trespass to chattels argument in the specific hypothetical offered by Hohfeld, such reasoning seems certain to apply to the original example of Gray's that Hohfeld criticized as improperly blending the concepts of right and privilege:

> The eating of shrimp salad is an interest of mine, and, if I can pay for it, the law will protect that interest, and it is therefore a right of mine to eat shrimp salad which I have paid for, although I know that shrimp salad always gives me the colic.[29]

Here, the person eating the salad (let's assume it's Gray) in essence owns it, and there is no indication that the seller retained any privileges so as to potentially interfere with Gray's enjoyment of it. Thus, as Hohfeld rightly notes, this example involves two fundamental relations: first, Gray's privilege to eat the salad in the sense that it violates no duties; and second, Gray's right to noninterference in the eating of the

25 In some cases, the privilege holder may enjoy a direct right that is specifically tailored to prevent interference with a given action – for instance, a copyright owner's right to prevent copying by third parties directly protects the privilege of the owner to make copies. Additionally, duties imposed on third parties by criminal laws offer another layer of protection, though the relevant right is held by the State.

26 *See* Dobbs' Law of Torts, § 60. Moreover, as Halpin notes, whatever the result of the disclaimer, X's actions would still be protected by other tort rights, such as assault and battery – for instance, A arguably could not punch X in the nose to prevent him from eating the salad. *See* Halpin, *supra* note 19, at 37–42.

27 Games and sporting events are typical exceptions to the general rule that privileges are coupled with rights against interference, which is explicitly or implicitly waived by the players – though even in these instances, there remains a right against interference that extends beyond what is reasonable to achieve the purpose of the game. *See* Thomas McIntyre Cooley, A Treatise on the Law of Torts: Or the Wrongs Which Arise Independent of Contract 188 (2d ed. 1888) ("The exception to this general rule embraces only those cases in which that to which assent is given is [a] matter of indifference to public order, such as slight batteries in play or lawful games – such unimportant injuries as, even when they constitute technical wrongs, may well be overlooked and excused by the party injured, if not done of deliberate malice. But an injury, even in sport, would be an assault if it went beyond what was admissible in sports of the sort, and was intentional.").

28 *See* Restatement (Second) of Torts §§ 216–220; W. Page Keeton et al., Prosser and Keeton on the Law of Torts § 14 at 87 (5th ed. 1984).

29 John Chipman Gray, The Nature and Sources of Law 19–20 (1909).

salad. This right to noninterference derives from duties imposed by the tort of trespass to chattels (and, in the case of the seller, ordinary contract).[30]

Yet, while Hohfeld is correct in identifying these two relations as underlying Gray's explication, it seems inaccurate to impugn Gray's usage of the term "right" to refer to both relations in this instance. In other words, it is quite common for courts and others to use "right" to simultaneously refer to a Hohfeldian privilege to engage in some activity (e.g., walking down a sidewalk) coupled with one or more Hohfeldian rights against indirect (or direct) interference with the activity (e.g., against assault, battery, and false imprisonment).[31]

If we define such a complex relation as a "common right,"[32] Gray's explication and use of the term "right" is perfectly sensible as long as one is cognizant through context of the precise sense in which it is employed.[33] Of course, meaning is not always clear from context – this is especially so in the case of "right" because of its many meanings. Even a "common right" – that is, a Hohfeldian privilege coupled with a duty of noninterference – is often referred to as a "privilege." As such, it would ordinarily be preferable to use a more specific term, such as "common right" or "protected privilege" in order to avoid confusion. Nonetheless, in many cases, meaning is clear from context, so that even if the bare terms "right" or "liberty" are used, they do not introduce ambiguities.

11.3.2 *Common Liberties and Freedoms*

In a 1956 article, Glanville Williams argued that the term "liberty" is a more appropriate label for what Hohfeld categorized as "privilege."[34] Specifically,

30 Of course, rights that only indirectly protect a given privilege do not guarantee that the privilege is protected from interference by others. For instance, someone may dart in front of you to catch a subway train, lightly bumping you, causing you to miss it. Although the rude rider may interfere with your privilege to board the train as you please, this sort of behavior would not ordinarily be actionable in tort because it is not generally considered "harmful" or "offensive." *See* Restatement (Third) of Torts: Inten. Torts to Persons § 103 (2015). Such instances are truly ones of clashing privileges, and if a party is to be protected in the exercise of a privilege in these instances, courts must secure rights to noninterference via pure policy determinations. *See* Schlag, *Things with Hohfeld*, *supra* note 14, at 207–12. But it appears that in most situations of legal import, any privilege of concern is coupled to an indirect right to noninterference that is sufficiently robust to protect the privilege. *See* HALPIN, *supra* note 19, at 38–43.

31 *See* Manual Toscano, *"Shall Not Be Denied the Right to Use Their Own Language": A Hohfeldian Analysis of the Language of Rights*, *in* VARIETIES OF LIBERALISM: CONTEMPORARY CHALLENGES 223, 229 (Jan Harald Alnes & Manuel Toscano eds., 2014).

32 Here, I use "common" in the sense of "ordinary" or "typical" (as opposed to "strict" or "constitutional"), and not to refer to "rights common to the public," which was a phrase used in the context of public nuisance and other doctrines. *See* JOHN HAMILTON BAKER, AN INTRODUCTION TO ENGLISH LEGAL HISTORY 492–94 (3d ed. 1990). Indeed, what I term "common right" is, like most of the Hohfeldian senses of right, simply called a "right" when used by judges or in legal discourse more generally.

33 *See* Perry, *supra* note 20, at 204 (noting that if a "right" refers to a combination that includes a Hohfeldian privilege coupled to rights to noninterference, the inference of such duties from the use of the term "right" is not "fallacious").

34 Glanville Williams, *The Concept of Legal Liberty*, 56 COLUM. L. REV. 1129, 1131–35 (1956).

Williams contended that the term "privilege" typically connotes "exceptions to generally imposed duties," while the term "liberty" generally refers to "acts that are completely unregulated." Williams' view has been influential and many scholars now refer to Hohfeldian privileges as "liberties." Indeed, even Hohfeld stated that "[a] 'liberty' considered as a legal relation … must mean, if it have any definite content at all, precisely the same thing as *privilege*."[35]

Yet, the use of the term "liberty" to designate a Hohfeldian privilege can lead to the faulty view that a "liberty" in the Hohfeldian system represents a complete "absence of duty" with respect to an action, call it A.[36] In other words, on this (faulty) view, a Hohfeldian liberty (and, hence, privilege) consists of the absence of a duty to do A *and* the absence of a duty not to do A. In deontic logic, such a coupling of a positive and negative permission is known as an "option." When an agent holds an option, the agent is free (from a legal or moral standpoint) to engage in A *or* not to engage in A without repercussion.

This sort of complete freedom with respect to a given action is often referred to as "liberty" in political theory and judicial decisions. For example, Edmund Burke states that "the effect of liberty to individuals is … that they may do what they please."[37] Similarly, John Rawls espoused that "persons are at liberty to do something when they are free from certain constraints either to do it or not to do it."[38] In *Lenox v. Prout* (1818), the Supreme Court of the United States used the term "liberty" in an equivalent sense, finding that the holder of a promissory note "is at liberty to issue an execution or not, as he pleases, on the judgment against the maker."[39] In all of these circumstances, "liberty" refers not merely to a one-sided privilege to perform an action, but rather a two-sided privilege either to perform the action *or* not perform the action, at the actor's preference.

In contrast, in the Hohfeldian system, "privilege" is only one-sided (and, as noted earlier, does not imply a right against noninterference). In other words, a legal actor subject to a privilege to do A may simultaneously be subject to a duty to do A.[40] In this case, the actor has a privilege to do A but lacks a privilege not to do A. The one-sided nature of the Hohfeldian privilege demands not only a stricter conception of "liberty" as it is used in the Hohfeldian sense but also points to a broader notion of "liberty" as it is used more commonly.

Specifically, one can define a "strict" liberty as a mere Hohfeldian privilege (e.g., to do A *or* not to do A), and a "common" liberty as the coupling of a positive privilege

35 Hohfeld 1913, *supra* note 1, at 36.

36 *See* Heidi M. Hurd & Michael S. Moore, *The Hohfeldian Analysis of Rights*, 63 AM. J. JURIS. 295 (2018).

37 EDMUND BURKE, REFLECTIONS ON THE REVOLUTION IN FRANCE 9 (F. G. Selby et al. eds., 1924) (1790).

38 JOHN RAWLS, A THEORY OF JUSTICE 202–3 (1971). Indeed, Rawls's conception of liberty entailed not merely a two-sided Hohfeldian privilege but also a two-sided right against noninterference. *Id.*

39 16 U.S. 520, 525.

40 Indeed, in standard deontic logic, it is assumed that it is necessary to have permission to perform an action if one is under a duty to perform the action. *See supra*, note 18 and accompanying text.

(i.e., to do A) with a negative privilege (i.e., not to do A). Thus, a "common liberty" represents an aggregate of two fundamental Hohfeldian relations that is regularly used in legal analysis and adjudication. Recall that a "protected privilege" is defined as a privilege coupled with a right that others not interfere (directly or indirectly, as the case may be) with the exercise of the privilege. Thus, a "protected strict liberty" would entail merely duties of noninterference to the performance of some action, A (but not to the nonperformance of A), while a "protected common liberty" would entail duties of noninterference both to the performance of A and to the nonperformance of A.[41]

11.3.3 *Claims and "Empty" Rights*

Hohfeld averred that an effective synonym for his narrow conception of right is a "claim." Whatever the merits of that usage in the early twentieth century, "claim" today generally connotes the ability to bring a legal action for violation of a right. Thus, a modern "claim" is the coupling of two fundamental Hohfeldian relations – a duty (that is breached) and a contingent power (coupled to a contingent privilege) to bring an action for redress related to the breach that, in the event of a successful judgment, places remedial duties (e.g., of payment in damages) on the breaching party.[42] In this regard, not all rights are coupled with potential remedies. Rather, some rights are "empty" or "nugatory" in the sense that although they correlate with duties, they are wholly unenforceable.

In Hohfeldian parlance, empty rights are functionally equivalent to a person's holding a Hohfeldian right vis-à-vis some actor coupled with the actor's immunity from suit to enforce a breach of the right.[43] For instance, if the President of the United States is running late to the State of the Union address and decides to take the wheel of his car in order to "speed things up," the President will enjoy absolute immunity from any civil charges brought by a motorist for negligent injuries sustained by the President's speeding.[44] Thus, the injured party's right is nugatory because it cannot be enforced.

11.3.4 *Constitutional Rights*

In addition to the four senses of right noted by Hohfeld (right, privilege, power, and immunity) – as well as the notion of "common right" and "common liberty" offered earlier – there is yet another sense of "right" present in so-called constitutional rights. There are a number of possibilities in reducing a constitutional right to its

41 A protected common liberty is equivalent to Rawls' conception of liberty. *See supra*, note 38.

42 *See* Chapter 12.

43 One may distinguish nugatory rights preempted by effectively personal immunities that protect a small class of certain individuals from empty rights that provide no remedy whatsoever in the event of breach. In Hohfeldian terminology, the former would be paucital immunities and, the latter, multital immunities. *See* Hohfeld (1917), *supra* note 10.

44 *See Nixon* v. *Fitzgerald*, 457 U.S. 731, 762 (1982).

Hohfeldian equivalent. First, it may mean a Hohfeldian right of persons that the State not pass laws that impose duties to refrain from certain acts or to engage in certain acts.[45] In other words, the State might be placed under a Hohfeldian duty, for example, not to pass laws that prohibit the free exercise of religion, abridge the freedom of speech, and the like.[46] Second, it may mean an immunity of persons from the State's attempt to pass laws that attempt to impose such duties. Third, it may mean a privilege for persons to engage in certain actions, such as protected speech, keeping and bearing arms, and the like. This could be a naked privilege or a protected privilege, the latter comprising a duty on the part of the State not to interfere with the privilege. Finally, it may be an aggregation of these relations.

One could attempt to finely parse the actual words of the Constitution to determine the locus of a "constitutional right,"[47] but it is arguably more fruitful to focus on judicial interpretation of the Constitution, as the courts are the final arbiter of its meaning. In this regard, Supreme Court justices and constitutional scholars generally view constitutional rights as limitations on the power of Congress to enact laws that curtail certain behaviors. For instance, in *Texas v. Johnson*,[48] the Supreme Court held that Texas' law prohibiting flag desecration was inconsistent with the First Amendment as applied to the states. As Allen Thomas O'Rourke ably explains, such a holding was tantamount to finding that the First Amendment provided "Johnson [a Hohfeldian] immunity from Texas enacting certain laws rather than a [Hohfeldian privilege] to burn an American flag."[49] There was no privilege because although the attempt to impose a duty on Johnson via its anti-desecration statute was null and void, other laws, such as those against arson, could nonetheless prohibit such behavior. Of course, if such burning did not amount to arson, it would be privileged in the Hohfeldian sense, but only as a result of the maxim that "what is not expressly prohibited is allowed."[50] So, as a first step – and with the qualification

45 Although Hohfeld would have conceived of "the State" as a legal fiction, incapable of being subject to legal duties – because all relations are between natural persons in his scheme – as I have argued elsewhere, such a view is too constrained. *See* Ted Sichelman, *Reinvigorating the Public-Private Law Divide: A Hohfeldian Construction of the State*, NEW PRIVATE LAW (Oct. 19, 2015), http://blogs.harvard.edu/nplblog/2015/05/15/a-hohfeldian-take-on-the-public-private-law-divide/. Specifically, although entities such as governments and corporations are ultimately reducible to complex sets of relations among persons, it is feasible to suitably "modularize" these entities so as to speak of them as single legal actors, even within the Hohfeldian framework. *See id.*; Henry E. Smith, *Property as the Law of Things*, 125 HARV. L. REV. 1691 (2012).

46 *See generally* Frederick Schauer, *Hohfeld's First Amendment*, 76 GEO. WASH. L. REV. 914 (2008).

47 *See, e.g.*, H. Newcomb Morse, *Applying the Hohfeld System to Constitutional Analysis*, 9 WHITTIER L. REV. 639 (1988).

48 491 U.S. 397 (1989).

49 *See* Allen Thomas O'Rourke, *Refuge from A Jurisprudence of Doubt: Hohfeldian Analysis of Constitutional Law*, 61 S.C. L. REV. 141, 164 (2009).

50 *See* John Calvin Jeffries, Jr., *Legality, Vagueness, and the Construction of Penal Statutes*, 71 VA. L. REV. 189, 209 (1985). (" The underlying assumption must be that what is not expressly prohibited is allowed – that the individual is presumptively free to do as he or she pleases, and that in doubtful cases the burden of proof (so to speak) lies on the government.")

that some "constitutional rights" may be uniquely structured – it appears a constitutional right at least encompasses a disability on the part of the State in imposing certain restrictions on action that otherwise conflicts with constitutional dictates, which indirectly yields a privilege to engage in such action, but only so long as the action is not proscribed by other (constitutionally valid) laws.

Yet, such a view seems too limited, at least in the context of constitutional remedies. In addition to the State's disability to enact certain laws, the Constitution sometimes places the State under a remedial duty not to engage in actions that interfere with a person's exercise of a constitutionally "protected" (and otherwise lawful) privilege. In other situations, the State may be constitutionally mandated to affirmatively engage in certain remedial actions. For example, as in *Forsyth County v. The Nationalist Movement*,[51] a State's refusal to provide a permit for a political march on Main Street cannot always be remedied by resort to a Hohfeldian disability because, in this instance, the State is *withholding* executing its power to change a duty (not to march) into a privilege (to march).

In some instances, the withholding might violate a local or other "background" ordinance or statute ostensibly mandating the official to provide a permit consonant with constitutional dictates. In this instance, constitutional law would be of no import, because the aggrieved party could simply sue to have the background law enforced. In other instances, such as in *Forsyth County*, the official's withholding could be viewed as consistent – or least plausibly consistent – with the background law (and not violative of any other background law, such as tort or real property law). In these cases, the background law might be unconstitutional on its face, or at least as applied, and it would be necessary for the aggrieved party to vindicate its constitutional "rights" by forcing the State to undertake certain actions – at least assuming the aggrieved party did not simply flout the denial of the permit and march anyway (in which case the situation would be akin to that in the flag-burning case, i.e., one of governmental disability in enforcing the background law).

Specifically, if the aggrieved party desired to force the official to issue the permit prior to marching, it would be necessary for a court to constitutionally invalidate the background law – as a whole or as applied. Indeed, a court might then require that the official issue a permit, and even demand that background law be rewritten on a going-forward basis. (Judicially forced desegregation is another example of a remedy demanding that the State undertake some action.) In these instances, the remedy would necessitate a constitutional duty on the part of the State to undertake actions consistent with the bona fide exercise of a constitutionally protected privilege. More generally, these remedial constitutional duties could be positive or negative in tenor. Importantly, constitutionally mandated remedial duties do not simply arise from background law coming to the fore following the invalidation of a constitutionally infirm law, but are constitutionally mandated in

[51] 505 U.S. 123 (1992).

order to sufficiently protect a constitutional right. Related, the State would be disabled in any attempt to eliminate such a remedial duty imposed on it. Finally, to the extent that the State attempted to enforce any ostensible violation of background law in view of its failure to implement a constitutionally mandated remedy, any individual charged would be immune to such enforcement.

As such, a constitutional right – at least in many situations – comprises a complex set of underlying relations: (1) in nearly all instances, an immunity against the State's attempt via lawmaking, enforcement, or otherwise to restrict (or demand) particular actions otherwise "protected" under the constitution; (2) in some instances, a Hohfeldian remedial right against noninterference by State action, or possibly a right to positive action by the State, with respect to any residual privileges to engage in action not prohibited under other (constitutionally permissible) laws and not in conflict with constitutional dictates; and (3) in the event (2) applies, an immunity via State lawmaking or otherwise to any attempt to eliminate these remedial duties. Of course, any constitutional right could be extinguished, at least nominally,[52] by a suitable constitutional amendment – as such, the State retains a higher-order (contingent) power that may trump the lower-order immunities and duties comprising a constitutional right.

11.4 REDUCTIONISM, HOLISM, AND COMPLEXITY IN THE LAW

11.4.1 *Reasoning with the Complex Relations*

As my reevaluation of Gray's shrimp salad example illustrated, it is possible to reason with the individual terms representing complex Hohfeldian relations rather than the terminology of the fundamental relations. In other words, if one precisely refers to a complex set of fundamental relations via a specific term (e.g., "common right"), logical implications may follow from that reference even in the absence of reducing the complex relation to its constituent parts. For instance, when Gray referred to ownership of the salad and the common "right" to eat it that flowed from such ownership, this necessarily implied a duty on the part of others not to interfere with Gray's consuming the salad. Contrary to Hohfeld's claims, Gray did not commit a logical error, because his reference to "right" was to the complex "common right" rather than the Hohfeldian "strict right." Indeed, Gray referred to a complex relation in his usage of "right" not out of confusion, but arguably to economize on the number of words needed to express the underlying concepts when context made such usage clear.[53]

52 Some have argued that certain constitutional rights are implicit in the nature of a democracy, or follow from other principles, which if so, would place higher-order disabilities on State power to eliminate constitutional rights. *See* Philip A. Hamburger, *Natural Rights, Natural Law, and American Constitutions*, 102 YALE L.J. 907 (1993) (describing "natural rights" variants of such views).

53 Indeed, it is not even necessary that Gray fully understood the underlying concepts to properly use the term "right" in the context he did – rather, merely understanding what logically flows from such usage

A similar line of argument appears to rebut Hohfeld's oft-cited criticism of the 1901 British labor law case, *Quinn v. Leathem*,[54] which involved the propriety of a secondary boycott (i.e., of the customer) of the plaintiff, Leathem, a butcher. Hohfeld found the following language in the opinion problematic:

> The plaintiff had the ordinary rights of a British subject. He was at liberty to earn his living in his own way, provided he did not violate some special law prohibiting him from so doing, and provided he did not infringe the rights of other people. This liberty involved the liberty to deal with other persons who were willing to deal with him. This liberty is a right recognized by law; its correlative is the general duty of every one not to prevent the free exercise of this liberty except so far as his own liberty of action may justify him in so doing. But a person's liberty or right to deal with others is nugatory unless they are at liberty to deal with him if they choose to do so. Any interference with their liberty to deal with him affects him.[55]

Specifically, Hohfeld claimed that "a 'liberty' . . . must mean, if it have any definite content at all, precisely the same thing as privilege."[56] On this basis, Hohfeld found a logical or category error when Lord Lindley inferred a "duty of every one not to prevent the free exercise of this liberty." Rather, according to Hohfeld, "[w]hether there should be such concomitant rights (or claims) is ultimately a question of justice and policy; and it should be considered, as such, on its merits."[57]

Hohfeld's critique of *Quinn v. Leathem* has been an exemplar for many in the realist camp who claim that so-called formalist judges were surreptitiously importing policy into their opinions through the veneer of seemingly plausible, but ultimately illegitimate, reasoning. For instance, Pierre Schlag contended that "Lord Lindley seems to have speciously derived a right from a privilege . . . in the first part of the paragraph, Lord Lindley argues for the existence of a privilege, not a right. Then Lord Lindley moves illegitimately in the second part of the paragraph to the conclusion that Quinn has a duty not to interfere."[58]

To be fair, Schlag also notes that "[i]t is hard to be sure whether Lord Lindley has in fact made precisely this . . . mistake because Lord Lindley's language is so loose."[59] Yet, on another reading, Lord Lindley's language is neither loose nor misguided. Rather than using his terms to denote narrow, Hohfeldian "rights" and "liberties" – that is, "fundamental" legal conceptions – a seemingly more accurate reading is that Lord Lindley was referring to "common rights" and "protected

is sufficient. *See generally* Henry E. Smith, *On the Economy of Concepts in Property*, 160 U. Pa. L. Rev. 2097 (2012).

54 [1901] AC 495 (HL) (Lindley LJ).

55 *Id.* at 534.

56 Hohfeld (1913), *supra* note 1, at 36.

57 *Id.*

58 *See* Schlag, *Things with Hohfeld*, *supra* note 14, at 185.

59 *Id.*

liberties" – namely, *aggregates* of fundamental relations that include duties of noninterference.

To begin, Lord Lindley refers to the "ordinary rights" of a British subject, which in context most plausibly means: (i) a Hohfeldian privilege for the plaintiff Leathem to engage in action that does not affect the Hohfeldian rights of others (i.e., "except so far as his own liberty of action may justify him in so doing"); coupled with (ii) a duty on the part of third parties not to interfere with the exercise of such privilege by Leathem (again, within the scope of Leathem's actions that do not affect the Hohfeldian rights of others).[60] Such a connotation of "right" was quite common at the time of the decision. As Joseph Singer has explained, it was common under the "utilitarian theory [at the time] to assume that liberties should be accompanied by duties on others not to interfere with the permitted acts. Such duties [on this theory] promote the general welfare without harming anyone by guaranteeing each citizen full freedom to engage in acts that are of no legitimate concern to anyone else."[61]

Starting with the premise that Lord Lindley was referring to a complex aggregate of a Hohfeldian privilege and an associated set of Hohfeldian rights, his next statement follows directly: that the plaintiff had a *protected* "liberty" to earn his living (i.e., a protected Hohfeldian privilege) "provided he did not violate some special law prohibiting him from so doing, and provided he did not infringe the rights of other people." Such a *protected* liberty, in turn, implied a Hohfeldian right corresponding to "the general duty of every one not to prevent the free exercise of this liberty" within its proper bounds.

On these assumptions, Lord Lindley committed no logical error of wrongly deriving a right from a privilege, because he never began with the assumption that a mere, naked privilege was at issue, but instead a protected privilege, which necessarily included a right against interference. Of course, one could claim that Lord Lindley's starting premise of a common right was unjustified.[62] However, because such a common right was assumed as a normative matter to inhere in all British subjects, no justification in the opinion was required. Nor was such an assumption logically flawed – a privilege coupled with a duty of noninterference is perfectly viable, particularly when these relations apply only in so far as the privilege does not violate the rights of others. In this regard, it seems clear that Lord Lindley recognized that not all harms infringed others' rights. In *Allen v. Flood*, the House of Lords had not long before found that a defendant trade union official's informing an

60 *See* Perry, *supra* note 20 (suggesting that such a formulation of Lord Lindley's pronouncement is possible); Jonathan Crowe, *Explaining Natural Rights: Ontological Freedom and the Foundations of Political Discourse*, 4 N.Y.U. J. L. & Liberty 70, 97 (2009).

61 Joseph William Singer, *The Legal Rights Debate in Analytical Jurisprudence from Bentham to Hohfeld*, 1982 Wis. L. Rev. 975, 999 (1982). In this regard, Perry (*supra* note 20) misinterprets Lord Lindley's general language as adopting a "new tort" and wrongly infers that "there is substantial evidence that he was guilty of the fallacy as charged" by Hohfeld – rather, in accord with Singer, Lord Lindley was referring to a general principle regarding the "ordinary rights" of British subjects.

62 *See* Perry, *supra* note 20.

employer that union members would not work alongside plaintiff day laborers – which led to the plaintiffs' terminations by the employer – was not actionable because merely informing an employer of likely facts did not amount to "conspiracy, intimidation, coercion, or breach of contract."[63]

One could also claim that Lord Lindley overstated his argument when averring that "[a]ny interference with [Leathem's customers'] liberty to deal with [Leathem] affects him."[64] However, Hohfeld fails to quote the immediately following sentence, which states "[i]f such interference is justifiable in point of law, [Leathem] has no redress." Again, this qualification is entirely consistent with the notion that the Hohfeldian privilege of Leathem is limited in scope to the degree that Leathem's privilege and any associated rights only inhere to the extent that they do not affect the Hohfeldian rights of others.

The question then becomes whether the actions undertaken by the defendants were, as Lord Lindley stated, "justifiable in point of law." In other words, either the labor union or the business owner had a protected privilege with respect to their underlying actions, and whichever one had such an entitlement deserved judgment in its favor. Nonetheless, the realist might quip, "all you have shown is that the opinion boiled down to a conflict of protected – rather than naked – privileges. In Hohfeldian terms, determining who has the protected privilege remains a question of policy, morality, justice, or other interests that transcend the mere 'structural' Hohfeldian features of the case."

Yet, such a quip would be entirely correct. Contrary to Hohfeld's assertion, Lord Lindley determined later in the opinion, in several paragraphs of analysis, that the defendant's conduct was not justified as a *normative* matter. First, Lord Lindley recounted how the defendants' threat to strike Leathem's customer in the event Leathem did not fire his nonunion employees was determined by the jury to be "wrongful and malicious[.]" Second, Lord Lindley found that the defendants' conduct "was the more reprehensible" because Leathem had offered to pay for his nonunion employees to join the defendants' union. Third, unlike earlier cases, there was no dispute in this case between Leathem and his employees or his customer, or his customer and the employees. Relying upon this characterization of the facts, Lord Lindley distinguished the defendants' actions from direct strikes by workers – that is, simply refusing to work for an employer – which he considered lawful. For these and other reasons, he found that the action of the defendants amounted to a "form of coercion, intimidation, molestation, or annoyance ... very difficult to resist, [that] to say the least, requir[ed] justification." Finding no such justification, Lord Lindley held that the defendants' actions were unlawful – that is, not within their sphere of protected liberty, but instead infringed the rights of the plaintiff, Leathem, particularly because "immediate and intended" damage resulted.

63 [1901] AC 534.

64 *See* Isaac Husik, *Hohfeld's Jurisprudence*, 72 U. Pa. L. Rev. 263 (1924).

Although Lord Lindley arguably could have undertaken a more thorough investigation of the economic consequences of the defendants' actions – and there are clearly strong policy-based counter-arguments (indeed, the holding was arguably reversed by statute just five years later[65]) – his normative analysis is certainly as searching as many, if not most, judicial opinions today.[66]

In sum, a careful reading of the opinion shows that other than a few lines taken out of context, Lord Lindley neither made Hohfeldian category errors nor avoided difficult normative questions. The confusion in interpreting the opinion stems from the improper contention of Hohfeld and others that Lord Lindley began with two sets of "naked" Hohfeldian privileges – one on the part of the business owner, Leathem, and another on the part of the defendants – and thus, as a logical matter, wrongly inferred a duty binding the defendants not to interfere with Leathem's business. Rather, Lord Lindley began with two sets of protected liberties – complex Hohfeldian relations – and determined exactly where those liberties began and ended by resorting to normative claims. Based on a variety of arguments grounded in morality and policy, Lord Lindley found that the plaintiff was entitled to rights against interference. Although one may disagree with Lord Lindley's normative assertions, on the most plausible reading of the whole opinion, there is no room to disagree with him on logical grounds and little room to assert that he avoided difficult questions of policy.

Importantly, such a reading of *Quinn v. Leathem* shows that judicial reasoning can involve complex – rather than – fundamental relations in marshalling a sophisticated set of arguments. As I explore in the next section, in many modes of legal argumentation, it is arguably more economical to use a single term to denote complex aggregates of relations rather than unpacking each and every complex relation into its constituent parts. This is especially so when context makes the usage clear.

11.4.2 *The Hohfeldian "Bundle" Trope Reconsidered*

It is commonplace for scholars to assert that Hohfeld's notion of property as a "complex aggregate" of "multital" jural relations existing between persons – rather than between persons and things – played a major role in the development of the modern "bundle of sticks" notion of property.[67] Certainly, there is much credence to

65 *See* Trade Disputes Act of 1906. However, as the U.S. Supreme Court noted in *Truax* v. *Corrigan*, it was not entirely clear if the 1906 Act permitted secondary boycotts like the one at issue in *Quinn* v. *Leathem*. *See* Truax v. Corrigan, 257 U.S. 312, 360 (1921). ("It is probable that sections 1 and 3 of the act of 1906 make the secondary strike or boycott in the course of a trade dispute legal.")

66 In this regard, Perry wrongly states that Lord Lindley never addressed the normative question, claiming instead that Lord Lindley merely found liability by deriving a duty from a newly fashioned tort. *See* Perry, *supra* note 20.

67 *See, e.g.*, J. E. Penner, *The "Bundle of Rights" Picture of Property*, 43 UCLA L. REV. 711, 724 (1996); STEPHEN R. MUNZER, A THEORY OF PROPERTY 23 (1990).

such a view. Without laboring on the details – which have been ably recounted in many other forums – it suffices to say that Hohfeld succinctly stated "'[a] right in rem is not a right' against a thing."[68]

Yet, jumping from Hohfeld's view of property as a complex set of relations among legal persons to the "destruction" of property "as a thing" is too simplistic. Rather, like John Chipman Gray's usage of "ownership" and Lord Lindley's usage of "liberty," one can view "property as a thing" not merely as the improper use of an irreducible concept, but rather an altogether appropriate shorthand for the complex set of relations precisely described in the Hohfeldian system.

Such an approach draws upon Henry Smith's notion that "property as a thing" is a "modular" concept designed to reduce the information costs otherwise involved in delineating the full set of Hohfeldian entitlements inhering in property.[69] In Smith's view, the modularization of property via an exclusionary "boundary" serves to "hide" the large set of use and other entitlements that function behind the boundary, so that the exposed entitlements – which generally reside at or near the boundary (e.g., trespass) – are effectively isolated.[70] Because the hidden entitlements generally give rise to no claims (e.g., consider an "owner" of property cooking in her kitchen), while the exposed entitlements do (e.g., consider a trespasser), such a modularization is "efficient" in the sense of shearing off those Hohfeldian relations that tend not to be of interest in legal analysis. At the same time, such exclusionary modes leave a residuum of entitlements to governance modes (e.g., nuisance) that arise from actions conducted well outside the "thing" encircled by a given boundary.[71]

Yet, modularity need not involve the outright elimination of any Hohfeldian relations to achieve its purposes. Rather, like Gray's and Lord Lindley's analysis, one can begin with low-level "complex" relations – such as common rights and common liberties – and build up to mid-level and high-level sets of complex relations that exhibit sufficient structure that modules of interest "naturally" arise, perhaps "masking" but not eliminating nonmodular elements from the picture. In pending work with Henry Smith, we envision these structures as complex networks in which legal actors form "nodes" and the legal relations form "edges."[72] Using well-known mathematical techniques, one can "naturally" identify the modular elements within these Hohfeldian networks, which substantially reduces information costs in those legal situations in which elements substantially inside or outside the modular

68 Wesley N. Hohfeld, Fundamental Legal Conceptions as Applied in Judicial Reasoning and Other Legal Essays 74 (Walter W. Cook ed., 1923).

69 *See* Henry E. Smith, *Property as the Law of Things*, 125 Harv. L. Rev. 1691 (2012).

70 *Id. See also* Henry E. Smith, *Intellectual Property as Property: Delineating Entitlements in Information*, 116 Yale L.J. 1742, 1751–53 (2007).

71 *See* Henry E. Smith, *Exclusion and Property Rules in the Law of Nuisance*, 90 Va. L. Rev. 965, 1023–24 (2004).

72 Henry E. Smith & Ted Sichelman, Modeling Legal Modularity (working paper, 2022) (available upon request).

boundary can be disregarded. Nonetheless, these otherwise disregarded elements are always tracked and can be called to the fore in the event that the given law and facts necessitate as much.[73]

An analogy to physical "things" seems apt. A baseball is in a simple sense a "bundle" of particles, comprising a host of fundamental constituents behind the "boundary" of the ball interacting in complex ways to provide the ball its shape and structure. Typically, one need only analyze the interaction of another object (e.g., a bat) with the boundary of the ball but no more – indeed, a ball is often idealized as a point object with no dimensions. In other situations, it will be necessary to account for the internal aspects of the ball. And in even more complex situations, objects beyond the boundary of the ball (e.g., the air's movement, pressure, or temperature) will affect the ball, not only its trajectory but also its shape, and will need to be taken into account. Thus, the "ball" – to the extent we are concerned with all of the particles that affect "its" movement and shape – may reach far within and extend far beyond its boundary. Nonetheless, for most physical interactions with the ball, one can treat the ball as a modular object defined solely by its effectively stable boundary and its unchanging, global properties.

Like "property as a thing," treating "physical objects as a thing" serves to reduce the information costs in constructing appropriate theories about the world. At the same time, just as the "thingness" of a ball can be decomposed – at least in principle – into its constituent particles and their underlying physical relations – first inside, then outside, the boundary – property as a thing, at least in principle, can be similarly decomposed. As such, modularization and reductionism are not at odds. Property as a "complex aggregate" and as a "thing" ultimately refers to the one and the same set of complex relations.[74] Functionally, the "thing" approach merely serves to divide up the world into those relations that typically matter and those that don't for the usual legal problems. When the problems are *atypical* – resort must be made either to the functionally "hidden" relations inside the boundary or to the functionally "disregarded" relations beyond the boundary, but still only for those specific atypical relations that "matter."

Such equivalence of "thing" and "bundle" has further ramifications for the "bundle of rights" picture. Importantly, property as a thing – as a massive network of relations among many persons – has, like a baseball, an exceedingly "complex" nature that cannot be simply decomposed in an analytical sense. Of course, one can

73 Importantly, the ability to track the numerous relations in a given complex legal network does not solve the problem of indeterminacy in the network as to the specific Hohfeldian relations, actions, and actors that comprise it. In this regard, Hohfeld and most post-Hohfeldians assume a "classical" system of perfectly determined legal relations, but a more robust picture would account for the probabilistic nature of legal relations.

74 Although, as Gold and Smith contended, new properties may emerge in multi-party, multi-relation systems, the underlying structure of the system remains the same whether viewed as a bundled network of fundamental relations among multitudes of actors, or a "thing" modularized by boundaries. *See* Gold & Smith, *supra* note 8.

list the various "incidents" associated with property – as Hohfeld and Honoré have spelled out – but these incidents are merely the starting point for describing all the particular (in Gold and Smith's terms, "micro") relationships among the multitudes of individuals involved in a given piece of "macro" property.[75] Although Hohfeld's and Honoré's list of entitlements may appear at first glance as an undifferentiated "bundle of sticks" that can be easily unbundled and rearranged, this picture does not accurately portray property's complexity.[76] Rather, it is the millions of various jural relations relating to millions of different potential actions that are needed to describe the "thing." Just as it would take an enormous amount of energy to completely "unbundle" a baseball into its raw, "fundamental" particles, unbundling a particular piece of property often requires similar Herculean feats in terms of information. And just as we rejected J.J. Thomson's "plum pudding" model of the atom, in which particles sit in an undifferentiated "soup," we should reject the homogenizing "bundle of sticks" picture of property. At the same time, we should not lose sight of the fact that like a baseball, property can in principle be decomposed, keeping in mind that such reductionism does not threaten a holistic account of "property as a thing" properly conceived.[77]

11.5 CONCLUSION

Hohfeld's theory encompasses not merely fundamental, but also complex, jural relations. Although he was unable to expound upon the complex relations in any great detail, they arise "naturally" from the Hohfeldian framework, not merely at macro-level, but at a relatively low-level that reflects simple combinations of the fundamental relations. These low-level complex relations expose better understandings of standard legal language that Hohfeld and others have wrongly criticized as conflating the fundamental relations. Indeed, these uses of complex relations show that modularization through simple, legal "concepts" that represent more complex phenomena not only reduces the information costs needed to describe and analyze recurring legal phenomena, but do not necessarily remove fundamental relations "outside" of the module from their ambit.

75 *Id.*

76 *See* di Robilant, *supra* note 14.

77 Conversely, I do not view the practical difficulty – perhaps practical impossibility – in decomposing property as a complex relation into sets of fundamental relations as implying that "thingness" is the *only* sensible description of property and legal "objects" more generally. Rather, practical impossibility does not imply theoretical impossibility, and in my view, there is no plausible argument that the Hohfeldian typology cannot be used, at least in principle, to construct any macroscopic object in the law. Yet, again, such *structural* reductionism does not imply that all macroscopic "features" or "qualities" of legal objects are necessarily reducible to combinations of microscopic features or qualities.

12

Hohfeldian Analysis and the Separation of Rights and Powers

John C. P. Goldberg and Benjamin C. Zipursky[*]

12.1 INTRODUCTION

At the time he wrote, Wesley Hohfeld seemed to be of the view that long-standing conceptual confusions that had blocked progress in legal thought – particularly confusions about legal rights – would soon be put to rest. If so, rights have proved a tougher nut to crack than he expected. Indeed, the difficulty of providing an adequate account of rights has led many scholars, including scholars who share Hohfeld's aptitude and aspirations for analytic philosophy, to lose sight of a distinction central to his project, namely, the distinction between a *right* ("claim right") and a *power*. Or so we argue in Section 12.2. Worse, confusions over rights and powers, when combined with a particular understanding of what constitutes clear-eyed analysis of legal issues, have contributed to the now-familiar yet mistaken supposition that common law reasoning must (or should) take the form of instrumental reasoning. We outline this claim in Sections 12.3 and 12.4.

Ultimately, we suggest that Hohfeld's juristic legacy contains two profound ironies. His entirely sound insistence on the *analytic* separation of legal claim rights and legal powers has helped to obscure their deep *substantive* connection in certain bodies of law, especially tort and contract law. And his implicit acceptance of the idea that a commitment to conceptual clarity goes hand in hand with instrumentalism in legal analysis has indirectly led prominent courts – including, most famously, the California Supreme Court in landmark decisions such as *Rowland v. Christian*[1] – to misunderstand how rights, duties, and powers are linked within private law.

* Thanks for very helpful comments to our conference commentator Shyam Balganesh, to David Frydrych, Andrew Gold, Ted Sichelman, and Henry Smith, and to the participants in the Hohfeld centennial conference. Thanks also to Fordham University School of Law and to Harvard Law School for supporting our research. Remaining errors are ours.

1 441 P.2d 912 (1968).

12.2 RIGHTS AND CLAIMS

12.2.1 *Claim Rights, Privileges, Powers, and Immunities*

In Hohfeldian usage,[2] a legal *claim right* is the correlate of a legal duty. Thus, under a valid contract for the sale of a car between a seller and a buyer, the buyer in the first instance has a legal claim right that the seller transfer the car, and the seller owes a legal duty to the buyer to transfer the car.[3] Claim rights have as their jural opposite what Hohfeld termed "no-rights." Assuming that seller owns the car free and clear, and that, in accordance with the contract, title is transferred to buyer and no third party has a legally recognized interest in the car, the proper description of the relation of all other persons to the contractual arrangement between seller and buyer is that each has a "no-right." Neither seller nor buyer owes a legal obligation to any other person limiting either of them with respect to this transaction.

A central aspiration of Hohfeld's writings on fundamental legal conceptions was, of course, to distinguish claim rights from three other concepts that jurists sometimes use the word "right" to express. These are the concepts of *privilege*, *power*, and *immunity*. In Hohfeld's parlance, a legal privilege to undertake an action correlates with at least one other person (and sometimes each other person) having a no-right with respect to that action. To be under a duty, meanwhile, is the opposite of enjoying a privilege. For example, upon receiving title to, and possession of, the car from seller, buyer enjoys a privilege (or liberty) to use the car in certain ways, which means that he owes no legal duty to others to refrain from using the car in those ways, and that others have no right that he refrain from so using it.[4]

Like privileges, powers are not correlated with duties. The contract between seller and buyer, for example, generates in seller and buyer not only claim rights but also certain powers, including the power of each to obtain a remedy for breach of contract by filing a complaint in a court and proving its allegations. There is no

[2] Wesley N. Hohfeld, *Fundamental Legal Conceptions as Applied in Judicial Reasoning*, 26 YALE L.J. 710 (1917) [hereinafter *Fundamental Legal Conceptions*]; Wesley N. Hohfeld, *Some Fundamental Legal Conceptions as Applied in Judicial Reasoning*, 23 YALE L.J. 16 (1913) [hereinafter *Some Fundamental Legal Conceptions*].

[3] We use the qualifier "in the first instance" because of a possible ambiguity in Hohfeld's understanding of contractual rights and duties. *See infra* note 44 and accompanying text.

[4] Hohfeld suggested that the concept of a legal liberty is perhaps the "closest synonym" to the concept of a legal privilege. Hohfeld, *Some Fundamental Legal Conceptions*, *supra* note 2, at 41. However, it is doubtful that he regarded them as interchangeable, and in any event they are not. Both the statement that "X has a privilege to do A" and the statement that "X is at liberty to do A" entail that X has no duty to refrain from doing A. However, assertions of privileges are usually made against the background of a presumed duty to refrain from doing that which is deemed privileged. The same is not true of assertions of liberties. For example, lawyers speak of the privilege of self-defense against the background of rules forbidding a person from intentionally causing bodily injury to another. Likewise, lawyers speak of the attorney-client privilege against the backdrop of a rule requiring certain disclosures of information in court proceedings. They do not speak of the "liberty of self-defense" or the "attorney-client liberty."

legal duty correlative to this legal power: that seller or buyer can sue and potentially prevail on a breach-of-contract claim does not mean that merely by virtue of a breach, seller or buyer has a legal duty to bring suit or compensate the other for the breach. Instead, the correlate to this power is a legal liability. Thus, to say that contract law gives buyer a (conditional) power against seller for seller's breach of their contract is to say that, were seller to breach the contract, buyer – by choosing to bring suit and satisfying applicable procedural, evidentiary, and substantive requirements – would secure a court order imposing a new legal duty on the seller.[5]

Immunities, finally, are paired with yet another legal concept, in this case, a *disability*. Immunities are the opposite of liabilities, and disabilities are the opposite of powers. A person who has an immunity is not subject to the choice of another to change her legal position.

The phrase "claim right" helps to illuminate Hohfeld's point about the distinctiveness of what he deemed to be rights in their primary sense: that is, rights *qua* duty-correlates. To have a right (of this sort) is to have a *claim on* at least one other person: the person or persons who bear the duty that correlates to the right. By virtue of the contract between seller and buyer, buyer has a claim on seller that seller transfer the car to the buyer. By contrast, insofar as buyer, upon completion of the transaction, has (merely) a privilege or liberty to use the car, that privilege does not involve a claim on anyone else – no one else needs to adjust or limit her conduct in relation to buyer's exercise of that liberty.[6]

In *Fundamental Legal Conceptions* – the follow-on article to *Some Fundamental Legal Conceptions* – Hohfeld further distinguished between "paucital" rights (rights availing against a particular person or a defined group of persons) and "multital" rights (rights availing against each member of a large and indefinite class of persons). As part of his effort to dismantle the *in personam/in rem* distinction, he noted that many rights that have nothing to do with property, including, for example, rights against personal injury conferred by tort law, have the same quality that many have supposed to distinguish rights in relation to land. The right of a person that another not batter her is a *claim on each other person* that each refrain from touching her in certain ways. The same goes for various other tort rights recognized by the courts, including the rights against being confined, defamed, or defrauded.[7]

These examples suffice to illustrate what Hohfeld meant in equating *rights qua duty-correlates* with *claims*. To have such a right, on his view, is to have a *claim on* some other person (or persons) with respect to her (or their) otherwise unrestricted

[5] In Hohfeldian parlance, to be subject to a "liability" is not necessarily a bad thing. Someone named as a beneficiary in another's will is under a liability – i.e., is liable to receive assets per the terms of the will. The jural opposite of a power is a disability. To say that someone lacks a power to make a will is to say that she is under a legal disability with respect to that undertaking.

[6] While the buyer's liberty to use the car does not correspond to any duties owed to the buyer by others, various duties others do owe to the buyer – including the duty not to steal his car – help create the space within which the buyer can exercise his privileges.

[7] Hohfeld, *Fundamental Legal Conceptions*, *supra* note 2, at 719, 733–34.

freedom. To say that X has a (claim) right against Y is to say that X is entitled to Y's adjusting her conduct in relation to X. These required adjustments often correspond to 'negative' rights – that is, they often involve duty-bearers *refraining* from doing certain things (striking, defaming, etc.). However, Hohfeld's notion of claim rights applies also to 'affirmative' rights. A minor child has a legal right to support from a parent, which means that the child has a claim on the parent that the parent support her. The same idea is at work in those instances in which tort law recognizes a duty to protect or rescue. A customer who collapses while shopping in a store is entitled that the store administer first aid and call for medical assistance. Crucially, however, Hohfeld did *not* regard a person's *having a legal entitlement that others act in certain ways* as equivalent to that person actually possessing *a legal power to require that others so act.* Therein lies the core of the distinction between a legal claim right and a legal power.

12.2.2 *Claims and Claiming*

Philosophical analysis of rights long precedes Hohfeld's. Indeed, his preference for an unvarnished and nearly atomistic reduction of rights and related concepts is reminiscent of Bentham's. Here, however, we want to focus on what has followed Hohfeld in analytical jurisprudence, and we begin with Joel Feinberg's influential article *The Nature and Value of Rights.*[8]

Feinberg invited readers to imagine "Nowheresville," a place that differs from our world only in that its residents lack a notion of rights. This is not to say that it is a place without morality. Quite the opposite. Its residents are upstanding, decent, compassionate, and law-abiding. What, Feinberg asked, is the difference between our world, with rights, and Nowheresville, which lacks them? His answer, which owes an obvious debt to Hohfeld, is worth quoting at length:

> The most conspicuous difference ... between the Nowheresvillians and ourselves has something to do with the activity of *claiming*. Nowheresvillians, even when they are discriminated against invidiously, or left without the things they need, or otherwise badly treated, do not think to leap to their feet and make righteous demands against one another ... They have no notion of rights, so they do not have a notion of what is their due; hence they do not claim before they take. The conceptual linkage between personal rights and claiming has long been noticed by legal writers and is reflected in the standard usage in which "claim-rights" are distinguished from the mere liberties, immunities, and powers, also sometimes called "rights," with which they are easily confused. When a person has a legal claim-right to X, it must be the case (i) that he is at liberty with respect to X ... and also (ii) that his liberty is the ground of other people's *duties* to grant him X or not to interfere with him in respect to X. Thus, in the sense of claim-rights, it is true by definition that rights logically entail other people's duties ...

[8] Joel Feinberg, *The Nature and Value of Rights*, 4 J. VALUE INQUIRY 243 (1970).

> And yet, this is not quite an accurate account of the matter, for it fails to do justice to the way claim-rights are somehow prior to, or more basic than, the duties with which they are necessarily correlated. If Nip has a claim-right against Tuck, it is because of this fact that Tuck has a duty to Nip. It is only because something from Tuck is *due* Nip (directional element) that there is something Tuck *must do* (modal element). This is a relation, moreover, in which Tuck is bound and Nip is free. Nip not only *has* a right, but he can choose whether or not to exercise it, whether to claim it, whether to register complaints upon its infringement, even whether to release Tuck from his duty, and forget the whole thing.[9]

In Feinberg's view, for a person to have a claim right is not only for her to *be entitled to be treated* in a certain manner by another, and for that other to have a duty to treat her in that manner, it is also for her to be so situated as to be able to *demand* that the duty holder comply with the relevant duty.[10] This is a richer conception of claim right than Hohfeld's, precisely because it adds something to the idea of a normatively salient object of treatment that is owed. It adds the possession of an entitlement *to do something as against the duty-holder*, namely, to address a demand to him or her. For Feinberg, a claim right is not simply an entitlement to receive treatment of a certain kind (or be spared mistreatment). It is also an entitlement to demand that one be so treated.

Of similar vintage to Feinberg's article is H. L. A. Hart's work on the so-called "choice theory" of rights.[11] While Feinberg's focus was on moral rights, Hart's was on legal rights. (Hart, after all, aimed to build upon Bentham's theory of rights, and Bentham believed that rights terminology can only be supplied with referents if one is discussing legal rights.) Anticipating Hohfeld, Bentham had distinguished rights that were equivalent to no-obligations (permissive rights) from rights that were correlative to obligations. The former are virtually the same as Hohfeld's conception of privileges (liberties), while the latter are Hohfeldian claim rights. And Bentham also recognized that "right" sometimes connoted a legal power, although he did not necessarily offer this as a distinct meaning, so much as an accompaniment to certain other legal forms.

Hart's choice theory (like Feinberg's theory) was motivated in part by a perception that the simpler account offered by Bentham and others – an interest or "benefit" theory of claim rights – was inadequate[12] The interest theory supposes that having a right against some person is having an interest that warrants the imposition of a duty on another (or, quite similarly, that having a right is being the one for whose benefit the duty is imposed). It is a virtue of the interest theory that it captures a good

9 *Id.* at 249–50 (italics in original).

10 Stephen Darwall's writings on the second-personal nature of morality can be understood as deepening Feinberg's claiming-based account of claim rights. STEPHEN DARWALL, THE SECOND-PERSON STANDPOINT: MORALITY, RESPECT AND ACCOUNTABILITY (2006).

11 H. L. A. Hart, *Bentham on Legal Rights, in* OXFORD ESSAYS IN JURISPRUDENCE (SECOND SERIES) 171 (A. W. B. Simpson ed., 1973).

12 *Id.* at 183–96.

deal of rights talk. But it also suffers from some famous flaws. The most familiar concern third-party beneficiaries. It is quite common for legal systems to deny certain third-party beneficiaries of contracts the right to sue for breach and to deem the contractual obligee the only right-holder.[13] Yet the interest theory would suggest things should be otherwise. Similarly, a legislature that gives a new parent the right to six months' paid leave could conceivably craft such a law primarily for the benefit of newborns, not parents. Yet it is not a right of newborns but a right of parents.

Hart's complaints against Bentham's account included criticisms like these, as well as two others. First, and perhaps most importantly, Hart rejected the facile judgment that the concept of a claim right adds nothing to the idea of a relative duty: a duty owed to someone. From Hart's point of view, a successful account of a concept must show what work it performs. On this view, an account is defective if it renders the concept redundant with another concept, unless of course the aim of the account is to establish that the concept ought to be abandoned. Hart was not so confident. Secondly, Bentham's account struck Hart as theoretically inelegant, spawning multiple potentially unrelated uses of the term "right."

Hart aimed to put forward a parsimonious theory of rights that would solve all of these problems. That is what the choice theory purports to provide. A right to ride one's bicycle, for example, is a legal liberty or privilege, and it amounts to the law's permitting each to choose whether to ride a bicycle. A right of first refusal is also about choice; it is a power to enter into an enforceable legal contract on certain terms with another, if one chooses. A right against being punched is about choice too; one can choose to waive the right by consenting (as boxers do) or (sometimes) choose to obtain an injunction or a damages remedy against someone who punches. In this way, legal right *qua* liberty, legal right *qua* power, and legal right *qua* claim right could all be cast as devices that our legal system uses to protect a domain of individual choice.

There is a remarkable similarity between Feinberg's basic moves and those of Hart, even if Feinberg's relate in the first instance to moral rights and Hart's to legal rights. Both consider interest or benefit theories of claim rights to be inadequate and both purport to overcome these inadequacies by recognizing that the person whose claim right was invaded will typically be able to assert a right even as the claim right itself has been invaded. Strikingly, each is proposing to understand a claim right as something that is simultaneously an interest correlative to a duty and a kind of normative power. In so doing, Feinberg and Hart propose to do exactly what Hohfeld warned legal analysts not to do: they link claim rights and powers *analytically*.

Those familiar with the tort theory we have developed – civil recourse theory – might be surprised to find us fretting over Feinberg's and Hart's linkage of rights,

[13] A point emphasized by Hart in his critique of Bentham's theory of rights. *Id.* at 195.

duties, and powers. After all, civil recourse theory asserts that a right of action in tort is a legal power to have a court impose on the defendant a legal obligation to the plaintiff, typically an obligation to make a payment of some form.[14] We have argued that it is a crucially important fact about tort law that those who have been legally wronged by another – who have suffered an invasion of a claim right by a tortfeasor's breach of her correlative duty – are entitled to a legal power to obtain a remedy. We have also emphasized, as did Hart, that the obligee (and right holder) is nonaccidentally in a unique possession of this power: she is entitled to have this legal power because she is the person to whom the breached duty was owed. Finally, like Feinberg and unlike Bentham, we have maintained that this legal framework in an important sense captures the structure of moral rights. A person to whom a moral duty is owed and has been breached has special moral standing to demand ameliorative action of the wrongdoer; likewise, a person to whom a legal duty is owed and has been breached has special legal standing to demand ameliorative action of the party who breaches.

Notwithstanding this apparent affinity, we are entirely with Hohfeld on the importance of distinguishing different senses of "right" and on the existence of specifiable concepts that often stand alone as referents of the term "right." Indeed, it is *especially* important for our view that legal claim rights stand on their own as the correlative of relational (or relative) legal duties and that legal rights as powers are *not* built into the concept of a legal claim right. If they were, then it would be analytic rather than substantive to say that a person who has suffered the violation of a legal claim right is prima facie entitled to a legal power in relation to the right infringer. But this is not a tautologous statement. It is a substantive one, and one that does not always hold. Tort law is distinctive as a body of law in part because it embodies a substantive legal principle according to which those whose legal rights have been violated are entitled to demand certain kinds of remedial action from the violator.

The *ubi jus ibi remedium* principle ("where there's a right there's a remedy") is deeply entrenched in the Anglo-American legal system. It holds, roughly, that where there is a legal claim right, the holder of the right is entitled to a legal power to obtain a remedy as against a person violating the right (breaching the duty owed to her). The existence and precise content of this principle (including its exceptions) is in the first instance a matter of positive law. But it is this rule or principle that, in our legal system, connects legal claim rights and legal powers.

By virtue of substantive rules of state and federal law, each of us has various legal claim rights corresponding to relational legal duties (or relative legal duties, as Bentham called them). Both the rights and the duties – for they truly are correlates – are generated by relational legal directives (a subset of what Hart understood to be

14 *See* John C. P. Goldberg & Benjamin C. Zipursky, Recognizing Wrongs 82–146 (2020) (providing an in-depth account of the principle and defending it as a justifiable feature of liberal democratic legal regimes).

duty-imposing rules and Bentham viewed as a subset of positive commands or quasi-commands). These relational directives, whether embedded in judicial decisions or contained in statutes, identify a domain of legal actors and specify that each person in that domain is legally required to refrain from performing (or to perform) a certain kind of act on (or for) members of a range of potential victims (or beneficiaries). For example, contained within judicial decisions defining and applying the tort of battery is the recognition of a legal right enjoyed by each of us not to be subjected to intentional harmful or offensive touching by another, and a legal duty imposed on each of us to refrain from so touching others. When a claim right such as this is violated by a bearer of the correlative duty, the right-holder gains, by operation of the civil recourse principle, a legal power with respect to the duty-bearer. Likewise, judicial decisions that define the rights and duties of parties to a contract (such as the contract between the car buyer and seller imagined above) also typically recognize a power in each party to obtain a remedy in the form of court-ordered damages or injunctive relief (providing that an action is brought and procedural, evidentiary, and substantive requirements are satisfied).

While it is thus a central feature of certain bodies of law, including tort and contract, that they link claim rights to powers, it is perfectly possible for a valid legal directive to generate a claim right and a duty even if the right-holder is not herself empowered to enforce it (and this would be so even if one were to assume, controversially, that something cannot count as a legal duty without being enforceable). Preliminarily, we note one obvious reason for not providing a legal power to persons who appear to enjoy claim rights: in some cases, the appearance of claim rights and corresponding relational duties will turn out to be illusory.[15] However, even genuine legal claim rights can exist without corresponding powers. Consider a hypothetical state regulation applicable to insurance companies that issue liability insurance policies to car owners. It requires as follows: whenever a driver who is involved in an accident makes a successful claim for coverage from her insurer, and the driver's insurer in turn receives an offsetting payment from the insurer of another person involved in the accident, the driver's insurer must notify the driver of receipt of the payment. Given this law, it would be quite natural to describe insured drivers as having a legal right that the insurer inform them after it has recouped from another insurer the cost of coverage provided to the driver. It hardly follows that the insured driver has a legal power to demand notification, or to obtain a remedy from her insurer for its failure to provide this information. Nor does it follow that a driver can waive her right to this information. Yet if state regulators retain a power to fine

[15] Imagine a clerk employed by a metropolitan subway system to count each person who boards at a particular subway stop during the morning rush hour. The goal is to ensure that enough subway cars are provided to accommodate all persons traveling on that particular subway line at that time of day. A passenger who is not counted by the clerk would not be able to sue the clerk for violation of the clerk's duty to count her, but that is because (despite appearances) the legal directive under which the clerk is operating does not impose on the clerk a relational legal duty owed to the passenger, and (correlatively) does not generate a claim right for the passenger.

noncomplying insurers it would be perfectly standard and appropriate to assert that insurers have a "legal duty" to provide insureds with such information, and to describe the insureds as having a correlative "legal right."[16]

There are several motivations for our critical view, but the first and most obvious lies within law, and it is deeply connected with Hohfeld's project. We believe that the law is chock full of examples that are accurately described as involving claim rights but not powers, and in many cases, powers but not claim rights. Second, we believe that decoupling legal claim rights and legal powers at a definitional level allows for greater scrutiny of the normative foundation of the connection between the two. Third, once this normative foundation is laid bare – the idea of a right to recourse – the character of tort law and, more generally, the nature of the private law/public law distinction are illuminated.

Needless to say, Feinberg and Hart each developed their own account out of an understandable dissatisfaction with the interest or benefit theory of rights. There are many serious objections to the interest theory, and not just on anti-utilitarian grounds, redundancy grounds, or on the basis of third-party beneficiary puzzles. Nonetheless, as our prior work and that of others shows, even if those objections were found decisive, there is no reason to assume that a will theory like Feinberg's or a choice theory like Hart's is the only remaining option.[17] Our point here is not to put forward such a theory, only to indicate that the problems of interest theories do not undermine the soundness of Hohfeld's critique or of our neo-Hohfeldian critique, of Feinberg's and Hart's conflation of claim rights and powers.

12.3 HOHFELD, CRITIQUE, AND COMMON LAW

As we (and others before us) have noted, Hohfeld was in many respects an intellectual heir to Bentham, as well as Hobbes and Austin. Yet he did not share Bentham's disdain for the supposed idiocies of the common law, nor did he rail against the baleful sorceries of "Judge & Co." Indeed, although he made a living spotting putative flaws in judicial reasoning, he credited judges for exercising good judgment

16 For discussion of a comparable real cases, *see* GOLDBERG & ZIPURSKY, *supra* note 14, at 95–102. Although the discussion above concerns legal claim rights, Frances Kamm has suggested that moral claim rights can also be separated from powers and demands. *See* F. M. Kamm, *Rights*, *in* THE OXFORD HANDBOOK OF JURISPRUDENCE AND PHILOSOPHY OF LAW 477, 482 (Jules Coleman & Scott Shapiro eds., 2002).

17 A distinctive, directives-based theory of legal rights is set forth in Benjamin C. Zipursky, *Rights, Wrongs, and Recourse in the Law of Torts*, 51 VAND. L. REV. 1, 55–67 (1998) (offering a directives-based theory of legal rights). For the articulation of a directives-based theory of rights within a theory of torts, see John C. P. Goldberg & Benjamin C. Zipursky, *Rights and Responsibilities in the Law of Torts, in* RIGHTS AND PRIVATE LAW 251–74 (Andrew Robertson & Donal Nolan eds., 2012); GOLDBERG & ZIPURSKY, *supra* note 14, at 82–110. An alternative theory is set forth in Leif Wenar, *The Nature of Claim-Rights*, 123 ETHICS 202 (2013) (rejecting interest theories and will theories in favor of a role-based theory of rights).

in spite of the underdeveloped condition of legal science.[18] Hohfeld also appreciated the problems of legislation, and thus, for example, made a point of defending judges against criticisms properly directed at legislators.[19]

Still, there is an important sense in which Hohfeldian analysis sits uncomfortably with common law, or has a valence toward legislation and administration. In part, the awkwardness stems from Hohfeld's inclination to decompose complex legal concepts (such as "property"). A common lawyer, by contrast, typically will be inclined to suppose that such concepts – or at least those that have long been in service and that mesh well with ordinary nonlegal usage – may capture or provide something that would be lost upon decomposition.[20]

More broadly, Hohfeld appears to have been attracted to what might be described as a rationalistic or instrumentalist account of the relationship of conceptual analysis to other modes of legal analysis. It is no accident that he attributed "fundamental" status to concepts such as "right" and "power," and that he likened them to lowest common denominators in mathematics.[21] A legal system, he seemed to suppose, is assembled out of these building blocks. A further implication – though not one that Hohfeld ever seems to have stated explicitly – is that legal concepts are, in principle, available to be rearranged more or less de novo, based on instrumental considerations.

It is this aspect of Hohfeldian analysis that has understandably attracted scholars with a critical or deconstructive bent – especially those keen to identify instances in which courts have illicitly smuggled certain political values into law.[22] For example, in their view, once "property" is revealed to be a particular assemblage of rights, privileges, powers, and immunities, it ceases to qualify as the sort of thing that could count as a natural right, and instead is recognized as something that can be pulled apart and reassembled on different terms in light of lawmakers' goals. (The same goes for freedom of contract.) On this understanding of Hohfeld's larger project, the most significant practical payoff of conceptual analysis is not that it will help judges do a better job of deciding cases, though it will do that. More importantly, it stands to clear the decks for systematic, scientific law reform rooted in "solid grounds of public

[18] Wesley N. Hohfeld, *A Vital School of Jurisprudence and Law: Have American Universities Awakened to the Enlarged Opportunities and Responsibilities of the Present Day?*, Address to the Association of American Law Schools (December 1914), at 28 n.24.

[19] *Id.* at 2.

[20] A common lawyer might also be inclined to turn the tables on Hobbesian and Benthamite critics by suggesting that purported efforts at 'analytic' decomposition are just efforts to smuggle certain political values into law under the guise of 'neutral' analysis. (Wouldn't it be helpful for certain agendas if the concept of property turns out to be 'untenable' as a conceptual matter?)

[21] Hohfeld, *Some Fundamental Legal Conceptions*, *supra* note 2, at 58.

[22] Joseph Singer, in particular, has famously argued that Hohfeldian analysis exposes inescapable contradictions in liberal legalism. Joseph William Singer, *The Legal Rights Debate in Analytical Jurisprudence from Bentham to Hohfeld*, 1982 WIS. L. REV. 975 (1982). For a careful articulation of ways in which Hohfeldian conceptual analysis lends or does not lend itself to critical legal analysis, see Pierre Schlag, *How to Do Things with Hohfeld*, 78 LAW & CONTEMP. PROBS. 185 (2015).

welfare."[23] Such is the message of Hohfeld's famous AALS address on legal education, titled *A Vital School of Jurisprudence*.[24]

Hohfeld commenced his address by quoting approvingly Woodrow Wilson's description of the age:

> The transition we are witnessing is no equable transition of growth and normal alteration: no silent, unconscious unfolding of one age into another, its natural heir and successor. Society is looking itself over in our day from top to bottom; is making fresh and critical analysis of its very elements; is questioning its oldest practices as freely as its newest; scrutinizing every arrangement and motive of its life; ready to attempt nothing less than a radical reconstruction, which only frank and honest counsels and the forces of generous cooperation can hold back from becoming a revolution.[25]

Wilson's description, Hohfeld argued, was particularly apt with respect to law. As Roscoe Pound had observed, serious defects in the legal system, including the piecemeal approach of the common law and poorly drafted legislation, had generated a wave of criticism and had produced ill-considered reforms.[26] The question at hand was whether that clamor would foment a revolution or whether it could instead be channeled into less radical but still constructive measures.

Any hopes for systematic and rational reform rested on a fundamental revamping of legal education. Neither law professors nor the lawyers they trained were in a position intelligently to guide law reform, particularly given the focus in law schools on judicial decisions and the lack of attention to "the constructive science and art of legislation," which Hohfeld took to be, in his day, "the chief agency in the evolution of our legal system[.]"[27] Transformative change was required, both in personnel and curriculum. Cadres of well-trained academics would have to be hired to educate students systematically in three broad areas: legal systems generally, the Anglo-American legal system in particular, and the civic and cultural study of legal institutions. Each of these topics was itself vast. For example, to educate lawyers on the first of these required training in "historical," "comparative," "formal," "critical," "legislative," and "dynamic" jurisprudence.[28]

Historical jurisprudence would consist of the study of broad patterns in the rise, maturation, and decline of legal systems, as well as of the origin and development of particular legal rules. *Comparative* jurisprudence would focus particularly on civilian systems, for it was in them that the common lawyer was likely to find "radical

23 Hohfeld, *supra* note 18, at 10.

24 *Id.* For an illuminating discussion of the context of Hohfeld's address, see N. E. H. Hull, *Vital Schools of Jurisprudence: Roscoe Pound, Wesley Newcomb Hohfeld, and the Promotion of an Academic Jurisprudential Agenda, 1910–1919*, 45 J. Legal Educ. 235 (1995).

25 Hohfeld, *supra* note 18, at 1 (quoting Woodrow Wilson, *The Lawyer and the Community*, 1910 A.B.A Ann. Meeting Rep. 419, 420–21).

26 *Id.* at 1–2.

27 *Id.* at 4.

28 *Id.* at 8.

departures and superiorities in the treatment of whole departments of law,"[29] including guidance on what it would take "to secure the right kind of legislation."[30] *Formal* jurisprudence would involve not only the type of conceptual clarification for which Hohfeld would become known, but also restatements of law and revisions to extant legal categories. The hoped-for result was a "scientific terminology" that would minimize confusion and permit carefully drafted legislation. *Critical* jurisprudence, meanwhile, would involve systematically assessing the factual premises and causal efficacy of legal rules. *Legislative* jurisprudence would attend to issues ranging from drafting to parliamentary procedure to constitutional design. Finally, *functional* jurisprudence would involve empirical study to determine which institutional arrangements are most efficacious in addressing particular problems – for example, the circumstances in which it is best for a legislature, agency, court, or commission to address a given issue, when and whether it is better to have elected or appointed judges, etc.

We will not consider in depth the other two heads of legal education that Hohfeld identified as essential ("the Anglo-American legal system in particular," and "the civic and cultural study of legal institutions"), in part because he said less about them in his address. It is worth noting, however, two points he made in connection with them. The first is his expression of dismay over judicial resistance to the procedural improvements offered by the Field Code, and his hope that the lawyers of his day would be more receptive to legislation, uniform codes, and model laws. The second is his lamentation over the degree to which public opinion – the force that, at the end of the day, determines the fate of any legal system – was uninformed and hence had been the driving force behind foolish reforms (e.g., judicial recalls) and the installation of "inferior and ill-prepared men" as legislators, judges, and prosecutors.[31] Given public opinion's role as ultimate arbiter and engine of reform, the Hohfeldian program required a revamped scheme of legal education not merely for future lawyers, but for all future leaders. Thus, in his view, undergraduate programs had to offer basic (perhaps even mandatory) legal education.[32]

The picture that emerges from Hohfeld's address is mainly Benthamite in tone. In the same spirit as some of his more programmatic disciples, such as Felix Cohen, Hohfeld seemed to hope that if jurists could get past metaphor and fiction, gain command of basic terms, move beyond a narrow obsession with cases and doctrine, collect and analyze data, approach problems systematically rather than piecemeal, and attend to the natural and ethical sciences, the result would be real improvement in the functioning of law and legal institutions. Moreover, Hohfeld seemed to

[29] *Id.* at 12.

[30] *Id.* at 13. Following Maitland, Hohfeld held out German codes as models of legal rationalization. Through them, inherited German law "'has recently been passed through modern minds, has been debated, criticized, refined; and an endeavor has been made to present it as a single, coherent, homogenous whole.'" *Id.* at 15 (italics omitted).

[31] *Id.* at 55.

[32] *Id.* at 57–60.

suppose that comprehensive legislation would and should be the primary mechanism through which law reform would occur.

To be sure, Hohfeld's brand of rationalism left open the possibility that judges, once properly trained, could play a valuable role within the new and improved legal system. We see nothing in his corpus to suggest that he had a general objection to the legitimacy of judge-made law. It nonetheless seems erroneous to assert that he was agnostic on the proper place of the courts and judge-made law within a modern legal system. Precisely because of the high value he placed on rationality, comprehensiveness, and systematicity – qualities lacking in law made primarily by judges in the course of deciding particular disputes – Hohfeld's approach carried a valence toward legislatures, expert commissions, and agencies.[33] If all were to go well, there would be less for judges to do: the occasions for them to be lawmakers would diminish.[34] Indeed, he may have had in mind that, on occasions requiring lawmaking, judges might seek or recommend legislative action rather than making law themselves.

We noted above that Hohfeld conceived of his conceptual analysis as an effort to isolate law's building blocks. We now see that this conception meshes quite naturally with a particular way of approaching law; one that, in emphasizing the contingency and modularity of existing arrangements, invites those with rationalistic proclivities, including Hohfeld himself, to embrace a model of lawmaking that strongly favors systematic, comprehensive, functionally oriented law reform over the incremental teasing out of concepts and principles that tends to characterize the common law.

12.4 RIGHTS AND JUDICIAL REASONING

Sections 12.2 and 12.3 engaged different sides of Hohfeld's thought – its analytic and rational-reformer sides – and tried briefly to explain how they connect with one another. In this section, we aim to identify a potentially worrying consequence of their fusion.

We have seen that a Hohfeldian claim right is a legal configuration that connects the imposition of a relative or relational duty upon an actor and the conferral of an entitlement on another person that the actor constrain his actions as required by the duty.[35] Now let us ask what a judge should do in a case where the question is whether a plaintiff ought to prevail in a tort claim against a defendant, and where the

33 *Id.* at 13 (embracing the thought that his era was ripe for systematic and scientific lawmaking through legislation, though warning that, for this to happen, the right kind of legislation must be secured).

34 *Id.* at 25.

35 We are deliberately fudging here with the phrase "legal configuration" because it is not clear exactly what Hohfeld had in mind. It was likely not the Benthamite idea of a command or a quasi-command. Certainly, some post-Hartian positivists are comfortable speaking of a duty-imposing rule and depicting the rule as simultaneously conferring a right and imposing a duty. We have adopted roughly that sort of view in our own structural account of rights, and we see no reason to suppose that such a view is inconsistent with what Hohfeld had in mind.

difficulties do not lie in the facts of the case, but in determining who should prevail under existing rules. From a Hohfeldian point of view, we are asking whether, under the law, the plaintiff possesses a legal power to exact a legal remedy from the defendant – a question that is of course identical for Hohfeld to the question of whether the defendant has the correlative legal liability (to being placed under a legal obligation). Let us suppose that there is no obvious answer under the relevant precedents in the jurisdiction. How is a judge to decide?

Many post-Hohfeldian torts scholars have approached this question from within an instrumentalist and rule-utilitarian outlook. Their inclination is roughly as follows. In a hard case, a judge should consider the liability rule that would go along with the plaintiff prevailing and compare it to the liability rule that would go along with the defendant prevailing. The judge should determine what the consequences would be of each rule, and select whichever is better from a social-welfare perspective. A plaintiff-friendly liability rule would not necessarily follow from the fact that the plaintiff had a claim right against being treated as the defendant treated her, or that the defendant had a duty not to treat her in this manner. To suppose it did would be to fail to understand the distinction between claim rights and powers,[36] which is tantamount to a failure to understand the distinction between duties and liabilities. Conversely, the absence of a claim right on the part of the plaintiff as against the defendant would not count against the adoption of a plaintiff-friendly liability rule.

The clearest example of this way of thinking about tort law is the California Supreme Court's analysis of the duty of care in a line of negligence cases commencing with *Biakanja v. Irving*[37] and featuring *Rowland v. Christian*.[38] *Rowland* addressed the question of whether a social guest ("licensee") who had lacerated his hand on a cracked faucet handle in the defendant's apartment could recover on the ground that the defendant had carelessly failed to correct the condition or warn him of it. The court teed up the question this way: given that negligence law ordinarily empowers persons who suffer a physical injury to make an enforceable demand for compensation to a person whose careless conduct caused that injury, any plaintiff who comes to court prepared to prove that he suffered an injury because of a defendant's carelessness should enjoy this legal power unless the social disadvantages of conferring such a power outweigh the advantages. In turn, the court relied, as it had in previous cases, on a seven-factor balancing test to make the judgment about social advantages and disadvantages.

Unsurprisingly, the court concluded that there were not sufficient disadvantages associated with holding possessors liable for injuries to their guests caused by hidden and dangerous conditions. Somewhat more surprisingly, the court decided the case

36 We are not suggesting that Hart or Feinberg would have adopted either the "confused" view of the sort Hohfeld was criticizing or the instrumentalist view we attribute to the Hohfeldian.

37 *Biakanja* v. *Irving*, 320 P.2d 16 (Cal. 1958).

38 443 P.2d 561 (Cal. 1968).

by adopting a broad rule stating that any person injured by a landowner's unsafe premises in principle has the right to obtain compensation from the landowner if they prove carelessness causing harm, regardless of whether, for example, the person was trespassing on the premises at the time of the injury.

In some ways *Rowland* is a perfectly reasonable decision. It was nonetheless a transformative case in tort law and perhaps beyond. The conventional analysis of a premises liability claim prior to *Rowland* would have been something like the following. A possessor owes a duty to maintain safe premises for the benefit of those who are invited for commercial purposes. By contrast, the only duty owed to social guests is the less demanding duty to take care to alert them to hidden dangers on the premises (doctrinally referred to as "traps"). If a social guest were injured as a result of a possessor's failure to heed this duty, then the guest would have a power to sue the possessor for damages, but otherwise he would not, even if the host had been careless in failing to repair or correct the relevant condition. For example, (under the traditional rule), a hotel would owe its guests a duty to repair dangerous conditions, not just to warn guests of them when those conditions were invisible, while a social host was allowed to leave her guests to fend for themselves with respect to dangerous conditions, so long as the dangers were reasonably apparent.

The California Supreme Court clearly thought some sort of fallacy was involved in the traditional way of thinking about the duty element of the negligence tort in premises liability cases. On the traditional view, the analyst determines *whether a plaintiff such as Rowland had a right of action against a land possessor (like Christian) for the injury caused by the possessor's careless conduct* by conducting a liability-independent, matter-of-law assessment of *whether the plaintiff was among those to whom the land possessor had a duty to act carefully.* Rather than adapt or develop this framework, the Court in *Rowland* scrapped entirely the idea that the power to obtain damages, in tort, is predicated on the plaintiff having a claim right against the defendant, and the defendant owing a relational duty to the plaintiff. Indeed, it purported to find incomprehensible the conjunction, within the traditional view, of three ideas: (1) that an actor could owe a legal duty of reasonable care to members of one class of persons (invitees) and a less demanding duty to members of another (licensees); (2) that someone to whom the duty of reasonable care was *not* owed (a licensee) is not entitled to demand redress from such an actor, even if the actor carelessly injured him or her (yet did not breach the more specific, less demanding duty to warn of a hidden danger); and (3) the reason that such a plaintiff (licensee) is not entitled to demand redress is precisely that the actor did not owe him or her the duty of care alleged to have been breached. The Court thus rejected the idea that restrictions on rights-qua-powers *derive from* restrictions built into relational or relative duties of conduct. It did so because it rejected the idea that tort law contains rules that specify relational duties of conduct and corresponding rights. Instead, following the lead of Prosser and others, it deemed tort law's primary or substantive duties to be nonrelational – to be owed 'to the world.' On this conception, courts award damages not out of conformity with a substantive principle such as the *ubi jus* principle outlined in Section 12.2 (and discussed further below). Rather, damages are conceived instrumentally, as a means of furthering societal goals such as "compensation" and "deterrence." In making this jurisprudentially radical shift, the Court probably (and perhaps plausibly) supposed that it was being authentically Hohfeldian. After all, in aid of instrumental law reform, it was separating the issue of powers and liability (when can a tort plaintiff sue and recover damages from a defendant?) from the issue of claim right and duty (is the plaintiff among those who enjoy a right against being wrongfully injured in a certan manner by the defendant, which right corresponds to the defendant's duty to refrain from so injuring persons such as the plaintiff?).

We are not critics of the result in *Rowland v. Christian*, nor are we necessarily defenders of the traditional rule applicable to a social guest's negligence claims. We are, however, deeply skeptical of the grounds on which the court rejected the traditional rule. For while it is true, as Hohfeld explained (and Hart contested), that legal claim rights and legal powers are conceptually distinct, it hardly follows that there is *no* connection between them. Indeed, it is entirely cogent to maintain that – given a set of rules or norms or principles that are part and parcel of tort law – the absence of a legal claim right enjoyed by the plaintiff in relation to the defendant implies the absence of a legal power against that defendant. *The point is not that there is an analytical unity to these ideas, but instead that there are substantive rules, norms, or principles of the law that connect them.*

A core interpretive claim of our civil recourse theory is precisely that there is such a connection. Under the rules of our legal system, one is not entitled to pursue and prevail in a tort suit against another unless the other violated a legal duty owed to that person. We have elsewhere referred to this as a "substantive standing" rule, explained its reach and rationales, and identified where within different torts the rule is located.[39] (It is not without exceptions, although the exceptions overwhelmingly have resulted from legislative amendments to the common law.)[40] The substantive standing rule is best understood alongside its companion principle, *ubi jus ibi remedium*, which we take to mean precisely that *where there is a violation of a legal claim right, the person suffering the rights violation is entitled to a legal power as against the person who breached the correlative duty*. In a liberal legal system in which there is a strong default rule according to which one is not subject to the legal powers of others, liability to another can nonetheless be generated by one's having

39 *See, e.g.*, Zipursky, *supra* note 17 (identifying the substantive standing component in various torts).

40 The most notable exceptions are wrongful death statutes' conferral on surviving family members of the power to sue and recover for losses caused by conduct that was tortious as to their decedent but not tortious as to them. *See generally* John Fabian Witt, *From Loss of Services to Loss of Support: The Wrongful Death Statutes, the Origins of Modern Tort Law, and the Making of the Nineteenth-Century Family*, 25 Law & Soc. Inquiry 717 (2000).

violated another's claim right (this is the import of *ubi jus*), or, equivalently, by having breached a legal duty owed to another.

It is fair to ask whether we are really entitled to lay the mistakes of *Rowland v. Christian* at Hohfeld's feet. After all, he merely emphasizes that legal claim rights are not analytically connected to legal powers. So far as we are aware, he did not go further and deny the existence of any connections between them. In fact, his analytic distinction is part of what permits us to appreciate the true (substantive) nature of the principle that connects the two.

Our answer to the envisioned query is equivocal, but not empty. As we have suggested, Hohfeld was nearly a Benthamite and certainly quite instrumentalist in describing what the intelligent elaboration of the common law would involve. It is thus hard to see what else a Hohfeldian judge on the California Supreme Court would do when the question of land possessor's liability was presented. Note also that Hohfeld was sufficiently positivistic in spirit and in substance that it is hard to know what he could say about whether landowners *should* be deemed to owe legal duties of care to licensees, absent traps. Once the common law rule was being challenged, it is simply unclear what he would say about the rule other than to engage in policy analysis. With the analytical tie between claim rights and powers severed, an instrumentalist progressive like Hohfeld would seem to be left to start from powers rather than claim rights, and to ask what array of powers would serve or disserve social welfare.

In our view, *Rowland* is in many ways the ideal focal point for these questions of jurisprudence, because there was in fact an alternative way to decide the case (albeit one that would have had costs of its own). California's tort doctrine was not entirely clear at the time of *Rowland* as to whether possessors actually did owe licensees a duty to warn of hidden, dangerous conditions. The court could have accepted or rejected a rule of liability to licensees for injuries caused by "traps," and, if they had accepted it they could have remanded the case to allow a jury to determine whether the condition that resulted in Rowland's injury was a trap. Intolerant of such nuanced and seemingly archaic doctrinal distinctions, and worried about the increasing complexity of the law, the court rejected this option. But it also could have said – as many jurisdictions in the United States and other common law jurisdictions now do – that possessors' duties of care are owed to whomever is foreseeably and permissibly on their land.[41] It could have respected the relational quality of the duty element in negligence law and conceded the analytical distinction between invitees and licensees, while deciding as a substantive matter that landowners are duty bound to be vigilant of invitees' and licensees' well-being to exactly the same extent. Bridling at the whole conceptual framework, the Court instead simply said that there was a policy question to be decided about the best

[41] Restatement (Third) of Torts: Liability for Physical and Emotional Harm § 51, Reporters' Note, comment *a* (2010) (noting that "24 states have adopted a unitary standard of reasonable care to at least licensees and invitees").

liability rule, and duty questions as such were meaningless. As torts professors know, the blunderbuss quality of the decision ended up creating a huge and inviting target for tort reformers. After all, once the power to recover damages is detached from claim rights and corresponding duties, one enters a world in which a burglar can sue for injuries caused by an unsafe fire escape that he used to effect his escape from the premises he has just burgled.

Again, our point is *not* to establish that legal powers must be grounded in claim rights. It is quite clear that legislatures have the authority to grant rights of action to persons whose claim rights have not been violated.[42] Arguably, certain judge-made equitable doctrines likewise grant legal powers to persons whose legal rights have not been violated. Instead, we aim to show that the absence of such a connection at the analytical level does not necessarily lead to the conclusion that there is no connection at all.

Although they come at tort law (and private law more generally) from an approach that stands opposed to *Rowland*'s instrumentalism – indeed, precisely because they do so – many contemporary corrective justice theorists similarly seem disinclined to observe the distinction on which we are insisting between an analytic and a substantive linkage of legal claim rights and legal powers. For example, in his brilliant and largely successful effort to display the failure of instrumentalist tort theorists to capture the content of the common law of tort, Ernest Weinrib has argued that the right to recover from a tortfeasor is closely connected to the primary right that was violated – i.e., the power is closely connected to the claim right. Yet today, Weinrib, as well as Arthur Ripstein and John Gardner, have embraced versions of (or relatives of) the "continuity thesis," according to which the payment of compensation by a tortfeasor to a tort victim is analytically continuous with the performance of the underlying duty of conduct owed to the claim right holder.[43] Speaking generally, at a level that glosses over important differences among the works of these scholars, we would suggest that this move is a philosophical overreaction to the sins of *Rowland*; one that hamstrings corrective justice theorists in the opposite way.[44]

42 As previously noted (*supra* note 40), wrongful death statutes that grant surviving family members rights of action to recover for losses they suffer as a result of a tort committed against their decedents, not against them, provide a familiar example.

43 Ernest J. Weinrib, The Idea of Private Law 135 (1995); John Gardner, *What is Tort Law For? Part 1: The Place of Corrective Justice*, 30 Law & Phil. 1, 28–33 (2011); Arthur Ripstein, *As If It Had Never Happened*, 48 Wm. & Mary L. Rev. 1957, 1978–82 (2007).

44 *See, e.g.*, John C. P. Goldberg & Benjamin C. Zipursky, *Civil Recourse Revisited*, 39 Fla. St. U. L. Rev. 341, 362–69 (2011) (briefly addressing Weinrib's, Gardner's, and Ripstein's tort theories, respectively); *see also* Goldberg & Zipursky, *supra* note 14, at 158–68, 352–58. David Frydrych has pointed us to a passage that could be read to suggest that Hohfeld, while not necessarily embracing the continuity thesis, nevertheless adopted a conception of private-law liability-imposition that more closely resembles the corrective justice theories we are criticizing than it does our civil recourse theory.

12.5 CONCLUSION

Legal Realists and Critical Legal Studies scholars have praised Hohfeld for untangling confused concepts and thereby allowing lawyers, judges, and jurists to spot substantive normative commitments concealed as definitions. As progressive scholars have learned the hard way, however, one cannot suppose that the identification of a normative commitment buried within a legal concept or construct will suffice to undermine it. To take but one example, the domain of contemporary constitutional law and theory obviously includes prominent voices that self-consciously embrace concepts and constructs associated with classical liberalism.[45] Exposing false claims of definitional connection can only serve as a prelude to evaluating the substantive principles that, for better or worse, are doing the normative work.

As we see it, the connection between claim rights and legal powers in a body of law such as tort law is a happier illustration of the same point. Claim rights and legal

In a 1909 *Columbia Law Review* article, Hohfeld imagines a contract between A and X by which A will pay X for a delivery of coal on a certain date, which agreement X breaches by failing to deliver. Upon X's breach, he asserts, "a new legal relation – a secondary, or remedial, obligation – arises between A and X. The latter, as a consequence of the breach of his primary duty, is now under a remedial duty to make *non-specific* reparation, that is, a duty to pay to A damages amounting to the difference between the market and the contract price of the coal, say ten dollars; and, correspondingly, A has a remedial right . . . If X fails to act under his remedial duty, A has *ab initio* the power, by action in the courts, to institute a process of compulsion against X. At this point, we reach, as the correlative of the power of A, the liability of X. This liability is called contractual, for the reason that it resulted from a breach of a primary contractual duty." *See* Wesley N. Hohfeld, *Nature of Stockholders' Individual Liability for Corporation Debts*, 9 COLUM. L. REV. 285, 293–94 (1909). *See also* Wesley N. Hohfeld, *Equity and Law*, 11 MICH. L. REV. 537, 554–56 (1913) (offering the same example).

One could read this passage to suggest that, for Hohfeld, as for many corrective justice theorists, the holder of a claim right whose right is violated by the breach of its correlative duty now is owed a legal duty of repair by the breaching party. This would be in contrast to our "civil recourse" view, according to which a right holder, upon a rights violation, is granted by law a power to make and enforce a demand on the violator that corresponds to a liability in the rights violator.

Alternatively, one could read this passage as reflecting Hohfeld's adoption of a particular (and roughly Holmesian) understanding of the rights and duties generated by certain contracts, including contracts for the sale of goods. On this understanding, the right of the promisee (along with the correlative duty of the promisor) is disjunctive: the promisee has a right that the promisor perform or, failing performance, that the promisor pay the promisee an amount equal to the value of performance. In turn, Hohfeld's use of the terms "secondary" and "remedial" would not be construed to suggest that X, the breaching party, incurred a duty of repair immediately upon breach, but rather that X's singular, substantive contractual duty had two parts or stages: an initial obligation to perform and a secondary (i.e., contingent) obligation to pay in the event of nonperformance. Only after nonpayment would there be a complete breach of the contract, at which point A would have a legal power to demand damages from X and X would incur a liability to A.

The latter reading would render the passage compatible with our own views. Of course, in the end the validity of our insistence on a strict *analytic* separation of legal rights and powers stands apart from whether Hohfeld himself, in his account of legal remedies, actually observed this separation or intended to do so.

45 *See, e.g.*, RANDY E. BARNETT, RESTORING THE LOST CONSTITUTION: THE PRESUMPTION OF LIBERTY (2003).

powers, even though conceptually distinct, are substantively connected in tort law and in other branches of private law. A laudable and basic moral commitment of our system holds that a person whose legal rights against being wrongfully injured have been violated is entitled to demand redress from the violator. As tort law's long-standing linkage of rights and powers attests, the right-remedy principle is and has long been a core substantive commitment of our legal system. We would go badly astray if a proper Hohfeldian insistence on the analytic separation of claim rights and powers caused us to lose sight of this commitment.

13

Immunity Rules

John Harrison

13.1 INTRODUCTION

Analysis based on Hohfeld's analytical system shows that liability rules, as defined by Guido Calabresi and A. Douglas Melamed, are a false category. The concept combines two kinds of legal rules, each important in itself, but not alike in any important way. Accident law, in which the injurer pays compensation for the victim's harm and is subject to no stronger remedy, is the leading example of one kind of liability rule. Eminent domain, in which the government acquires interests in property without the owner's consent and pays compensation, is the other leading example. The two are analytically distinct. Compensatory liability is a particular combination of a primary legal position and a remedial rule: it is the combination in which a claim-right is enforced only with compensation. Eminent domain operates in a different analytical category. It is a power of the government to which private property owners are subject, and is an exception to the general principle that owners are immune from changes in their rights of ownership by the unilateral act of another person. Rules about duty and remedy are distinct from rules about power, both analytically and for practical purposes. An individual who is subject only to a compensatory remedy for violating another's property right does not have the practical equivalent of the power to expropriate that right that the government has. Nor are the two kinds of liability rule united by the function of facilitating mutually beneficial exchanges by substituting objectively determined compensation for market prices. The compensation requirement for negligence operates as a sanction and not a price, and so cannot be explained as setting a price when parties are not in a position to bargain. Neither can the compensation requirement for eminent domain be so explained, because it is not necessary to cause the government to act in the public interest. Although each of the two kinds of liability rule is significant, combining them in one concept produces confusion. One such confusion is to obscure the point that as between private people, the basic rule governing private rights is not liability in the analytical sense, but immunity.

Ever since Holmes posited the Bad Man, U.S. legal thinkers have seen the importance of connecting primary legal rules with rules governing remedies.[1] The Bad Man cares only about the law's consequences, and judicially administered remedies are a crucial part of those consequences. Because remedial consequences are so important, the category of duties that are enforced only through compensation of the injured party's loss is important. Liability for accidents caused by negligence is a central example.

Decades ago, Calabresi and Melamed posited a larger category that includes, but is not limited to, wrongs for which the only remedy is a monetary payment often measured by compensation to the victim.[2] Whenever one person's decision with a detrimental consequence for another person results only in an obligation to pay compensation determined by the government, the decision is said to be subject to a liability rule.[3] Their concept of liability rules includes both ordinary tort liability and the government's power of eminent domain when that power is accompanied with a requirement of just compensation.[4]

Legal duties that are enforced only with compensatory remedies are an important category. The identification of that combination of rule and remedy with powers of eminent domain, and their inclusion in a larger category of liability rules, is misconceived.[5] Section 13.2 of this chapter argues that the two leading examples of

[1] "If you want to know the law and nothing else, you must look at it as a bad man, who cares only for the material consequences which such knowledge enables him to predict, not as a good one, who finds his reasons for conduct, whether inside the law or outside of it, in the vaguer sanctions of conscience." Oliver Wendell Holmes, Jr., *The Path of the Law*, 10 HARV. L. REV. 457, 459 (1897).

[2] Guido Calabresi & A. Douglas Melamed, *Property Rules, Liability Rules, and Inalienability: One View of the Cathedral*, 85 HARV. L. REV. 1089 (1972).

[3] "Whenever someone may destroy the initial entitlement if he is willing to pay an objectively determined value for it, an entitlement is protected by a liability rule." *Id.* at 1092. My formulation in terms of detrimental consequences, which I believe to be identical in substance, is designed to avoid a metaphor that characterizes as destruction both a change in a physical object that renders it useless and a change in legal relations such as a transfer of title. The burden of this chapter is that physical changes and changes in legal relations are fundamentally different. The concept of destruction of an entitlement, with its two applications, manifests the error I criticize.

Judge Calabresi has recently emphasized that the category of liability rules includes all arrangements under which the only consequence of some conduct is an objectively determined payment. *See* Guido Calabresi, *A Broader View of the Cathedral: The Significance of the Liability Rule, Correcting a Misimpression*, 71 LAW & CONTEMP. PROBS. 1, 4 (2014). It is thus not confined to compensation as measured by harm to the victim and so includes, for example, punitive damages in tort when they are used to provide strong deterrence and not just market-mimicking internalization. *Id.* at 7–8. This chapter is concerned with the difference between remedies for violations of duties on one hand, and powers on the other. That distinction is of great analytical and practical importance, and by itself makes the concept of liability rule not useful. Judge Calabresi's observation demonstrates that even if confined to remedies, the concept would be very heterogeneous.

[4] *Id.* at 1106 (eminent domain is a liability rule); *id.* at 1108 (accident law is a liability rule).

[5] As suggested by Judge Calabresi's recent comments, *see supra* note 3, it is possible to define a category of rules that are only about the remedy for a harm, and that does not include powers like eminent domain, in which the only remedy is a monetary payment objectively determined by the government. That category would include compensatory remedies as well as sub- and supra-compensatory

liability rules, tort liability for accidents and public eminent domain, are not identical as a conceptual matter, because they fall into distinct analytical categories in Hohfeld's scheme. A primary right that is protected only by a duty of compensation is not, because only so protected, subject to expropriation by potential violators of the duty, because remedies and powers to change legal positions are different.

Section 13.3 argues that a party subject to only compensatory liability for harm to some interest does not have the practical equivalent of the government's power of eminent domain with respect to that interest. The owner of the interest retains other advantages, like the privilege of self-help, that enable the owner to enjoy ownership for practical purposes and not just in principle. Protection of the owner's interest with remedies stronger than compensation is an important part of ownership, but does not come close to defining it.[6]

Section 13.4 denies that liability rules have the common feature that the compensation requirement functions as a substitute for a price that would be paid in a voluntary exchange and thereby brings about internalization. Many liability rules that provide compensation cannot be justified on that ground. For example, the compensation requirements of negligence liability for accidents, and public eminent domain, do not have that justification. Liability rules, even those that call for payment measured by harm, are not united by an internalizing function.

The chapter's conclusion illustrates the importance of the difference between compensatory liability and powers of eminent domain by showing how the failure to make that distinction accounts for two of the difficulties that scholars have identified with the Calabresi and Melamed typology. It then discusses the centrality in private law of the absence of private powers of eminent domain, and the corresponding immunity of private legal advantages from unilateral alteration by other private people.

13.2 LIABILITY RULES, DUTIES, REMEDIES, AND POWERS

In the Calabresi and Melamed typology, an entitlement is protected by a liability rule when, if another private individual damages the entitlement without the holder's consent, the damager's responsibility is only to pay an amount objectively determined by the government.[7] Because of the government's power of eminent domain, private property rights are protected only by liability rules as against the

payments. Whether that version of the concept of liability rules would be useful is a question I will not address. My criticism is directed to the version proposed by Calabresi and Melamed, the breadth of which Judge Calabresi has recently emphasized, which includes compensatory remedies and eminent domain.

6 Shyam Balganesh has explored the distinction between a central primary advantage of property ownership, the right to exclude, and the remedies that enforce it, such as injunctions. Shyamkrishna Balganesh, *Demystifying the Right to Exclude: Of Property, Inviolability, and Automatic Injunctions*, 31 HARV. J.L. & PUB. POL'Y 593 (2008).

7 Calabresi & Melamed, *supra* note 2, at 1092.

government.[8] Eminent domain, Calabresi and Melamed explain, "is simply one of numerous instances in which society uses liability rules. Accidents is another."[9] In general, if one person damages another's person or property by accident, the injurer's only responsibility is to pay compensatory damages, calculated by the harm inflicted. Accidental harm frequently is not a crime and does not give rise to any supra-compensatory private remedy such as restitution of the injurer's gain. Much of the power of the Calabresi and Melamed conceptualization comes from integrating substantive and remedial law in this way; the tort of negligence is governed by a liability rule because it identifies a type of conduct—infliction of harm through the creation of an unreasonable risk—and the remedial consequence of that conduct—compensatory damages.[10]

Compensatory tort liability and eminent domain are quite distinct, however, when described with Hohfeld's concepts of analytical jurisprudence. Those concepts are illustrated by the various legal positions of a property owner. The owner of land has a privilege of entering on the land, while nonowners must avoid physical contact with it. In analytic terms, the owner has a liberty or privilege to enter, while nonowners have a duty not to enter.[11] That duty is said to correlate with the owner's claim-right to exclude others.[12]

Duties, claim-rights, and liberties as Hohfeld defined them are referred to as primary legal relations and govern conduct not directly connected with litigation.[13] Violations of duties generally lead to some judicial remedy, in which a court creates a remedial legal relation. Damages judgments, injunctions, and criminal

[8] In response to the question, why have liability rules, Calabresi and Melamed point to transactions costs. "Often the cost of establishing the value of an initial entitlement by negotiation is so great that even though a transfer of the entitlement would benefit all concerned, such a transfer will not occur. If a collective determination of the value were available instead, the beneficial transfer would quickly come about." *Id.* at 1106. They then explain, "Eminent domain is a good example." *Id.*

[9] *Id.* at 1108. Their explanation again rests on transactions costs. "If we were to give victims a property entitlement not to be accidentally injured we would have to require all who engage in activities that may injure individuals to negotiate with them before an accident, and to buy the right to knock off an arm or a leg. Such pre-accident negotiations would be extremely expensive, often prohibitively so. To have them would thus preclude many activities that might, in fact, be worth having." *Id.* at 1108–1109 (footnotes omitted).

[10] Calabresi and Melamed apparently used the word "liability" to emphasize the affinity between eminent domain and accident law, and not in the analytical sense.

[11] Wesley N. Hohfeld, *Some Fundamental Legal Conceptions as Applied in Judicial Reasoning*, 23 Yale L.J. 16 (1913). Hohfeld describes the owner's liberty or privilege to enter, and the nonowner's duty not to enter, which correlates with the owner's right that the nonowner not enter. *Id.* at 32.

[12] *Id.* at 30 (describing jural correlatives, like right and duty, and opposites, like duty and privilege).

[13] Wesley N. Hohfeld, *Fundamental Legal Conceptions as Applied in Judicial Reasoning*, 26 Yale L.J. 752 (1917) (distinguishing primary and secondary legal relations and including remedial relations as secondary). Hart and Sacks emphasized the difference between primary and remedial relations. Henry M. Hart, Jr. & Albert M. Sacks, The Legal Process: Basic Problems in the Making and Application of Law 129 (William N. Eskridge, Jr. & Phillip P. Frickey eds., 1994) (stressing "the importance of distinguishing sharply between primary positions in the sphere of self-applying regulation with remedial positions").

punishment are examples.[14] Calabresi and Melamed often formulate the difference between property rules and liability rules in terms of remedies, saying that potential violations of a property rule may be enjoined, whereas violations of a liability rule give rise to damages that are often set so as to compensate the victim's harm.[15] After their seminal article was published, other scholars developed the distinction between prices and sanctions.[16] A sanction is a remedy designed to keep the violation from happening, whereas a price is designed to cause the potential violator to internalize the harms of the conduct and decide whether to engage in it.[17] Criminal punishment is a central example of a sanction, and injunctions are readily regarded as threatening sanctions because they are enforced through criminal punishment for contempt of court.[18] Punitive civil damages are also sanctions precisely because they go beyond compensation and are designed to prevent harm.[19]

Some duties, like those imposed by criminal law, are backed by the threat of sanctions. Many intentional torts, like battery, are also crimes and so subject to more than compensatory remedies. Some duties, like the duty to take reasonable care, are enforced only by compensatory damages, and the claim-rights that correlate with those duties are protected only by compensatory liability.[20] That is one of the

14 According to Hart and Sacks, the breach of a primary private duty that is not enforced criminally usually gives rise to a remedial private duty. *Id.* at 137. That remedial duty, in turn, may be judicially enforced, for example by a decree that includes the initial remedial duty and adds to it. "Commonly, the judgment of a tribunal of authoritative application, if it is favorable to the complainant, will be accompanied by the settlement of an *adjudicated remedial duty* on the part of the defendant . . . If an adjudicated remedial duty is established, it may or may not be a duplicate of the primary duty or of the original unadjudicated remedial duty. A money judgment, for example, may require the payment of interest or punitive damages, and an equitable decree may contain an endless variety of implementing provisions." *Id.* at 138. Hart and Sacks thus regarded the obligation to pay damages as a private remedial duty.

15 Calabresi & Melamed, *supra* note 2, at 1116.

16 A leading account is Robert Cooter, *Prices and Sanctions*, 84 COLUM. L. REV. 1523 (1984).

17 Cooter defines a sanction as "a detriment imposed for doing what is forbidden" and a price as "money extracted for doing what is permitted." *Id.* at 1523. "Officials should create prices to compel decision-makers to take into account the external costs of their acts, whereas officials should impose sanctions to deter people from doing what is wrong." *Id.*

18 Explaining why crimes are frequently subject to sanctions and not prices, Cooter gives the example of premeditated murder, "a discontinuous act whose optimal frequency is zero," *Id.* at 1548. Violation of an injunction issued by a federal court is punishable as criminal contempt. 18 U.S.C. § 401.

19 Cooter, *supra* note 16, at 1543–44.

20 Described quite strictly, the law of negligence imposes a duty not to cause harm through lack of due care. Negligence without harm, which is quite common, does not give rise to liability. *Palsgraf* v. *Long Island R.R. Co.*, 248 N.Y. 339, 162 N.E. 99 (N.Y. 1928).

Describing accident law as creating a duty with a compensatory remedy for its violation will seem inaccurate to those for whom someone who negligently injures another and then promptly provides compensation has not committed any legal wrong at all, and so has breached no duty. It is standard usage, however, to say that the law of negligence imposes a duty to take due care, and not just a duty to compensate, *Palsgraf*, 248 N.Y. at 341 (plaintiff had a claim "to be protected against unintentional invasion by conduct involving in the thought of reasonable men an unreasonable hazard that such invasion would ensue"), and I will follow that formulation. For my purposes, the two formulations are equivalent. The important point as far as I am concerned is that some duties either have compensatory

arrangements Calabresi and Melamed call a liability rule. I will refer to that combination of duty and remedy as a pure duty of compensation. Other duties, and the claim-rights that correlate with them, are associated with remedies that may include, but go beyond, compensation. I will refer to supra-compensatory remedies as providing strong enforcement of duties and strong protection for claim-rights.

Property owners' advantages are not limited to their liberties and claim-rights. Owners can change their legal relations with others by a voluntary act that has legal consequences. The ability to do that is called a power. An owner has the power to transfer title to another.[21] An owner also has the power to bring about a more limited change in relations, for example by granting a license, which creates a privilege to engage in conduct that otherwise would violate the nonowner's duty not to enter.[22] Owners have the power to make grants that are limited in the advantages they entail, like easements, or in the time during which they operate, like life estates.

In general, only the owner has those powers to change the legal landscape. If someone else purports to grant an easement, the act will be ineffective. Others are said to have a disability (the opposite of a power) with respect to changing the owner's legal position.[23] Those disabilities, in turn, correlate with an immunity in the owner.[24] To the extent that only the owner can change a legal position, the owner's position is protected by immunity, or an immunity rule.[25]

The claim-right against negligent harm is itself protected by immunity, just as is the claim-right against intentional harm. Third parties may not unilaterally eliminate that right so as to exempt themselves from damages for negligence. That is why

damages as their exclusive remedy or simply are duties to make compensation under certain circumstances. Moreover, a duty of prompt compensation would be violated by delayed compensation. Failure to provide prompt compensation would itself give rise to a remedial right that the compensation be paid.

21 Hohfeld, *supra* note 11, at 45.

22 *Id.* at 44.

23 *Id.* at 55.

24 *Id.* Hohfeld summarized the owner's positions in his second article on the analytical categories. "Suppose, for example that A is fee-simple owner of Blackacre. His 'legal interest' or 'property' relating to that tangible object that we call *land* consists of a complex aggregate of rights (or claims), privileges, powers, and immunities." Hohfeld, *supra* note 13, at 746. Hohfeld elaborated on the last point: A the owner "has the immunity that no ordinary person can alienate A's legal interest or aggregate of jural relations to another person." *Id.* The words "ordinary person" almost certainly allude to the government's power of eminent domain.

25 Immunity and invalidity or legal nullity go together. "Power law, it will be seen increasingly, presents distinctive remedial problems. The characteristic sanction of an empowering arrangement is the *sanction of nullity*." Hart & Sacks, *supra* note 13, at 134. As they go on to explain, "The sanction of nullity is pervasive in the whole theory of American public law, although the point is not always appreciated." *Id.* at 154. Common terminology sometimes applies the same terms in discussing both duties and powers, and so an invalid will, for example, can be said to violate the law governing wills. The remedy, if it should be called that, for failure to comply with a rule about power is simply that nothing happens. The remedy of nullity frequently arises automatically. A court may have occasion to decide whether a purported jural act was valid or not, as when parties contest the validity of a will, but the will either was valid or was not. The court makes it so only in the Realist sense in which adjudication about primary positions creates, and does not just conclusively determine, legal relations.

waivers of liability for negligence require the consent of the potential plaintiff if they are to be valid.[26] Only with the right-holder's consent can the duty to take due care be modified. Others are disabled from bringing about that change on their own, and the owner is immune from their attempts to do so.

The government has a power that private people generally lack. Through eminent domain, it can acquire limited interests in private property, or full title, by its own unilateral act. The government thus can alter the primary legal positions of private people and itself. Just compensation, determined by a court if necessary, is due the owner, but that is the only consequence when private property is taken for public use.[27] With respect to the government, private owners do not have immunity protection for their legal advantages. In analytical terms, their position is one of liability: that position is liable to change by the unilateral act of someone else.

In limited circumstances, private parties are given a power like that of the government by which they may unilaterally alter the property rights of others. For example, some states allow "landlocked" owners to acquire an easement of access from a neighbor without the neighbor's consent and at a price determined by a court.[28] I will refer to such powers as private powers of eminent domain.

Private powers of eminent domain exist, but they differ from pure duties of compensation.[29] The rules governing changes in primary legal position are not the same as the rules governing primary duties and rights, nor those governing the remedies for violations of duties and invasions of rights, nor the combination of the two. Identifying those two kinds of rules by putting them in the category of liability rules is an analytical error.

In general, the ability of private people to engage in conduct that violates their duties and invades the rights of others does not bring with it a power to change primary legal relations. Torts usually lead to secondary or remedial rights to compensation, but leave primary rights intact. If one neighbor negligently scrapes

[26] Jurisdictions differ as to parties' capacity to waive liability for negligence, but waiver is often possible. *See, e.g., Jones* v. *Dressel*, 40 Colo. App. 459, 462 (Colo. App. 1978) (waiver of negligence liability in sky-diving valid and precludes recovery for simple negligence).

[27] *See, e.g., Hawaii Hous. Auth.* v. *Midkiff*, 467 U.S. 229 (1984) (approving use of eminent domain power to deal with oligopoly in residential housing).

[28] A landlocked owner is one whose property has no access to a road or other way, like a river. North Carolina is among the states that enable landlocked owners to institute a proceeding to obtain a private way over adjoining land and provide for compensation to the burdened owner as would result from an exercise of public eminent domain. N.C. Gen. Stat. § 136–69.

[29] Sometimes powers of eminent domain are used simply to transfer an interest from one person to another, as when the government acquires full title and thus all of the former owner's rights against third parties. Other uses of eminent domain must be described with more nuance. For example, if the government acquires an easement, it has not simply acquired advantages that the primary owner previously had. With the easement in place, the owner's liberty to use the property is limited, and the easement owner has a claim-right, because the owner may not permanently block the easement. Rather than being transferred, the owner's liberty has partly been replaced with a duty with a correlative claim-right. The general concept at work here is change in legal positions, which includes but is not limited to transfers.

another's fence with her car on Monday and then does so again on Wednesday, both are torts. The first injury did not alter the neighbor's right to be free from physical intrusion, though it may produce a remedial right to compensation if the neighbor brings suit.[30]

For the same reason, if one person wrongfully walks off with another's suitcase, the owner has been deprived of physical possession, but the person who took the suitcase has not exercised and did not have a power to change ownership or any of its incidents. The owner's right continues, and the owner is entitled both to restoration of possession and damages for any injury from not having the suitcase while it was missing.[31] As the damages entitlement reflects, the owner's interest was unchanged all the time the owner was out of possession.

Committing a tort does not change primary duties or rights. The distinction between a violation of the duty to avoid negligent injury and a change in that duty is illustrated by the collision damage waiver offered by car rental companies. Although potential accidental tortfeasors and potential victims often cannot identify one another in advance, sometimes they can. Car rental companies know that their customers may be negligent, as do the customers. Through a collision damage waiver, the rental company waives its right to be free from negligent injury by the customer, in return for a fee negotiated in advance.[32] The waiver changes primary legal relations. Committing the tort of negligence does not.

The government's power of eminent domain provides clear illustrations of the difference between powers to change primary relations on one hand and duties and the remedies that enforce them on the other. The United States (U.S.) government has extensive authority to acquire property and interests in property through eminent domain.[33] As a result, private property owners are not immune to alteration of their rights by the government, but rather are liable to have those rights altered through exercises of the government's power. Most of the time, though, the federal government leaves private rights intact, and its officials are bound by them as to both

30 That is why plaintiffs in nuisance cases frequently seek both damages for harm already inflicted and an injunction against the nuisance in the future. *See, e.g.*, *Woody* v. *Machin*, 380 N.W. 2d 727 (Iowa 1986) (plaintiffs in nuisance proceeding awarded injunction abating the nuisance and damages for harm already inflicted).

31 A plaintiff who has been deprived of possession of a chattel is generally entitled to both recovery of the chattel through some possessory remedy and damages for the dispossession. *See, e.g.*, *Roebuck Auto Sales, Inc.* v. *Wallace*, 301 S. 2d 546 (Ala. 1974) (car owner who was wrongfully deprived of possession entitled to both return of vehicle and damages).

32 "Renting a car creates a bailment between the leasing company (bailor) and the customer (bailee). Generally, a bailee is responsible for any injury to the bailed property. Thus, the customer would be responsible for any damage to the rented vehicle." *Chabrata* v. *Rent A Car System*, 192 Ill. App. 3d 1074, 1077 (1989) (citations omitted). "However, when the customer (bailee) selects the CDW, responsibility for damage to the car returns to the leasing company (bailor). This is a change in the contract of bailment. The parties to a contract may agree to any terms they choose as long as the agreement is not contrary to public policy." *Id.*

33 The historical development of that power is described in William Baude, *Rethinking the Federal Eminent Domain Power*, 122 YALE L.J. 1738 (2013).

intentional torts and accidents. Threatened trespass by officials may be enjoined as would be a trespass threatened by a private person.[34] Because the U.S. has waived sovereign immunity for many accidental torts by officials acting within the scope of their employment, compensatory recovery from the government under the Federal Tort Claims Act is routine.[35] The private owner's possessory interest is thus strongly protected against intentional trespass and protected with compensation against negligence, but is also subject to the government's power of eminent domain as to both interests.[36]

The distinction between rules about duty and rules about power, which Calabresi and Melamed elide, can be seen by looking closely at their use of imperatives. That use equivocates, because they use imperatives to describe legal arrangements that fall into distinct analytical categories. Calabresi and Melamed say that an entitlement is protected by a property rule when someone who wishes to remove the entitlement "must" buy it from the holder in a voluntary transaction.[37] Their concept of removing an entitlement includes physical acts that violate rights, like punching another person.[38] To say that one person may box with another only with permission, and that people may not box with one another without permission, is to say that if A hits B without permission, A's physical act violates B's right and is subject to a remedy, be it compensatory damages or criminal punishment. In speaking of

34 A leading example is *Youngstown Sheet & Tube Co. v. Sawyer*, 343 U.S. 579 (1952), in which private property owners used an injunctive proceeding against the Secretary of Commerce to enforce their property rights against threatened invasion by the Secretary, who had been directed by the President to seize the plaintiffs' steel mills. The Court pointed out that the US had not used its power to acquire the mills by eminent domain. *Id.* at 585–86.

35 "The United States shall be liable, respecting the provisions of this title relating to tort claims, in the same manner and to the same extent as a private individual under like circumstances." 28 U.S.C. § 2674.

36 Another way to describe the same arrangement is to say that the government generally respects private rights. It does so by usually requiring its officials to perform their functions in a way consistent with those rights. Officials are required to respect private rights when they are given no privilege to invade them, and are subject to the same limitations as a private person would be. So when a court enjoins officials from a trespass connected with their duties, it is carrying out the principle that the government respects private rights. The United States Court of Federal Claims does the same when it awards compensatory damages under the Federal Tort Claims Act.

37 "An entitlement is protected by a property rule to the extent that someone who wishes to remove the entitlement from its holder must buy it from him in a voluntary transaction in which the value of the entitlement is agreed upon by the seller." Calabresi & Melamed, *supra* note 2, at 1092. In similar fashion, they say that, "If we were to give victims a property entitlement not to be injured we would have to require all who engage in activities that may injure other individuals to negotiate with them before an accident, and to buy the right to knock off an arm or a leg." *Id.* at 1108. What would happen if someone did other than as required, and knocked off an arm or a leg without negotiating in advance? In that passage, the imperative apparently is used to mean that a sanction will be imposed on those who injure one another without first having obtained consent. People sometimes do what they must not do, and do not do what they are required to do.

38 "Yet a nuisance with sufficient public utility to avoid injunction has, in effect, the right to take property with compensation." Calabresi & Melamed, *id.* at 1107. The presence or absence of injunctive relief marks the difference between a property rule and a liability rule, but injunctions operate on physical acts like harm to a neighbor's property.

property rule protection, Calabresi and Melamed apparently mean that the remedy will be more than compensatory.[39] Imperatives regarding physical acts imply some kind of remedy because they refer to duties.

To say that title may be transferred only with consent is to use imperatives in a quite different way, the way appropriate to powers as opposed to duties. A deed executed by a nonowner is simply ineffective, because the result of lack of power is invalidity and nullity.[40] In this context, must not means cannot, rather than, will be subject to a remedy like punishment. One might say that, with respect to powers, the remedy is both automatic and perfectly effective. Unlike injunctions, nullity actually keeps the unlawful result from happening. Invalid deeds are invalid.

One of Calabresi and Melamed's examples of an inalienable interest shows the two ways in which imperatives can be used, one for duties, the other for powers. The vote, they note, "cannot be sold."[41] That statement has two implications, one respecting power, the other respecting duty. Voters have no power to transfer their vote, and attempts to do so are void. If A gives B a deed to A's vote and B appears at the polling place to cast it, no vote will be recorded.[42] The purported transfer will be ineffective and election officials will disregard it. The prohibition on vote selling also imposes duties concerning physical acts.[43] If B gives A $2 in return for A's promise to vote for C and A does so, A and B have committed a crime. Nevertheless, A's vote may well be counted (unless somehow it can be identified). In that situation, an act that violates a duty is nevertheless legally effective.

39 Calabresi and Melamed say that a party that creates a nuisance but is not enjoined is subject to a liability rule and not a property rule, Calabresi & Melamed, *id.*, and liability rule protection produces only payment of "an objectively determined value," *id.* at 1092. Property rules are enforced through injunctions, the violation of which is a crime subject to criminal punishment that is not measured by harm to the victim. Insofar as the category of liability rules includes supra-compensatory monetary payments designed to ensure compliance, which Judge Calabresi's recent writing suggests that it does, *supra* note 3, enforcement by injunction would be a liability rule if the only penalty for violating the injunction were a monetary fine. There is no reason to think that Calabresi and Melamed, or Calabresi today, would say that enforcement by injunction is ever a liability rule. When Calabresi and Melamed contrast liability rules with property rules, I will take them to categorically exclude enforcement by injunction from the concept of liability rules and to assume that the liability rules involved are those that measure objective value by compensation to the victim. That is in keeping with the standard understanding, according to which an interest is protected by a property rule when the remedy for invasion of the interest is strong enough to deter invasions, and is not just a requirement of compensation. *See, e.g.*, Henry E. Smith, *Exclusion and Property Rules in the Law of Nuisance*, 90 VA. L. REV. 965, 973 (2004).

40 "The characteristic sanction of an empowering arrangement is the *sanction of nullity*." *See* HART & SACKS, *supra* note 13, at 134 (emphasis in original).

41 Calabresi & Melamed, *supra* note 2, at 1102 n.29.

42 For example, in Virginia only qualified voters are allowed to vote, the voter must show a statutorily prescribed form of identification that shows that he is on the list of registered voters, and the voter's name is then checked off on the official list. Code of Virginia § 24.2–643. As a result, someone who is not the person whose name appears on the list is not allowed to cast a vote, without regard to whether that person has what purports to be a transfer from the qualified voter whose name does appear.

43 *See, e.g.*, 52 U.S.C. § 10307(c) (whoever "pays or offers to pay or accepts payment either for registration to vote or for voting" commits an offense).

Calabresi and Melamed's neglect of the distinction between duty and power creates a problem for their typology, which unless adjusted to take the distinction into account, produces different answers to the same question. As they state it, the typology thus leads to problematic classifications. They treat both protection by injunction and immunity from unconsented transfer as sufficient conditions for property rule protection.[44] Similarly, they treat both compensatory damages and powers of eminent domain as sufficient conditions for liability rule protection.[45] Their definitions are thus disjunctive and overlapping. As a result, the definitions will classify some configurations as both property rules and liability rules.

For example, a private property owner's right against intentional trespass by the government enjoys supra-compensatory remedial protection, including by injunction, but may be altered by the government unilaterally through eminent domain.[46] The owner's claim-right against the government is thus protected by a property rule and is protected by a liability rule, though Calabresi and Melamed contrast the two protections with one another.[47]

As Judge Calabresi would put it, there are in fact four boxes rather than two, so the Calabresi and Melamed typology, which has two categories, can consistently classify only two of them.[48] Where a claim-right is strongly protected and its holder is

44 "An entitlement is protected by a property rule to the extent that someone who wishes to remove the entitlement from its holder must buy it from him in a voluntary transaction in which the value of the entitlement is agreed upon by the seller." Calabresi & Melamed, *supra* note 2, at 1092. That passage describes immunity. They also give the situation in which the victim of a nuisance is entitled to an injunction as an example of a property rule. That passage describes a supra-compensatory remedy that they would classify as property rule protection. *Id.* at 1115–16.

45 "Whenever someone may destroy the initial entitlement if he is willing to pay an objectively determined value for it, an entitlement is protected by a liability rule." Calabresi & Melamed, *supra* note 2, at 1092. Destruction of an entitlement includes both physical destruction (*id.* at 1108: accident law as an example of a liability rule) and transfer through a power like that of eminent domain (*id.* at 1106–07: eminent domain as an example of a liability rule).

46 Most of the time, injunctions are enforced through criminal punishment, which is not liability rule protection even on the broadest understanding of liability rules.

47 The same is true as between private owners where one holds an option to acquire the other's title. Until that option is exercised, the option-holder has the duties all other nonowners have, some of which are strongly enforced.

Calabresi and Melamed say that entitlements may be mixed. "Taney's house may be protected by a property rule in situations where Marshall wishes to purchase it, by a liability rule where the government decides to take it by eminent domain, and by a rule of inalienability in situations where Taney is drunk or incompetent." *See* Calabresi & Melamed, *supra* note 2, at 1093. They do not, however, distinguish between physical intrusions and exercises of the power of eminent domain, categorizing them both as the destruction of the owner's entitlement. If the two are equated, then physical intrusions by the government and acquisition through eminent domain are the same invasion of the same interest by the same party. Under their categorization, one is governed by a property rule and one by a liability rule. The Hohfeldian categories provide a distinction that Calabresi and Melamed elide and the Hohfeldian categories, therefore, treat physical intrusion and eminent domain as two situations governed by different rules, rather than the same situation governed by different rules.

48 "Model making is useful because it spins out boxes. Then the question becomes, 'Are the boxes full, or are the boxes empty?' A model may point to something that is of no use at all. Making a model, the simplest model, like the one I used in the *Cathedral* article, says, 'Here is a box. Gee, that is

immune from transfer by another, the interest is unequivocally protected by a property rule. Where it is protected by a pure compensatory duty and is subject to unilateral transfer by someone else, it is unequivocally protected by a liability rule.[49] The typology classifies the other two combinations inconsistently. The owner's right against intentional injury as against the government is subject to a property rule because of the strong enforcement of the duty and a liability rule because of the power of eminent domain.[50] A private person's right against negligent injury as against other private parties is subject to a liability rule because of the purely compensatory enforcement of the duty and a property rule because the right is immune from unilateral transfer by another party. That is why liability for negligence can be eliminated only by a waiver by the potential victim, not unilaterally by the potential tortfeasor.[51] The rule governing liability for accidents, which for Calabresi and Melamed is a quintessential liability rule, is actually a combination of liability and property rules.[52]

Although strictly speaking the typology produces inconsistent answers, the better interpretation is that a claim-right is protected by a liability rule when either the correlative duty has a purely compensatory remedy, or the right is subject to a power of eminent domain, or both. The main innovation Calabresi and Melamed introduce is the identification of both compensatory damages and eminent domain as liability rules, so either one should be a sufficient condition for the category of liability rule to apply. With the categories so understood, property rules appear only when a duty is strongly enforced and the right-holder is immune from change by another. That is the situation of property rights against intentional invasions by

interesting, there is a box there. Is there anything in the real world that fills that box?'" Guido Calabresi, *Neologisms Revisited*, 64 MD. L. REV. 736, 752–53 (2005).

49 That combination is unusual but possible. For example, a government may acquire, through eminent domain, a permission to inflict accidental damage, the way a car rental customer who pays for the collision damage waiver does.

50 As noted above, the same arrangement can arise between private people, where one has an option that has not been exercised.

51 Waivers of liability for negligence, discussed above, illustrate the point. The analysis I offer here breaks the distinction between property rules and liability rules into two distinctions. One distinction concerns the strength of enforcement of the nonowner's duty. The other concerns the nonowner's power of eminent domain or disability, which corresponds to the owner's liability or immunity. The resulting four categories do not correspond to the four rules concerning nuisance that Calabresi and Melamed discuss. Calabresi & Melamed, *supra* note 2, at 1115–16. As explained below, their failure to distinguish between rules about remedies and rules about powers caused them to overlook entirely the kind of liability rule that corresponds to tort damages and to focus only on private powers of eminent domain.

52 All four combinations assume that the primary relation between the parties is one of duty and claim-right. If the relation is one of privilege and no-right, there are only two possibilities, because privileges as such cannot be protected by affirmative remedies. *See* Lee Anne Fennell, *Property and Half-Torts*, 116 YALE L.J. 1400, 1412 (2007). When the relation is one of privilege and no-right, the question concerning the holder of the privilege is whether some other person has a power to alter that position unilaterally.

private persons, and so deserves the name of property rule.[53] The other three arrangements are liability rules.

Violations of pure duties of compensation do not change primary legal relations, whereas exercises of the power of eminent domain do. In that respect, torts are not takings. Perhaps the two nevertheless are the same, because committing a tort does change remedial legal relations, making the tortfeasor liable for a remedy. Moreover, the argument in favor of identifying the two situations would go, the power of eminent domain may be exercised in as limited a way as the government wishes; eminent domain could be used to create a permission to engage in a single harmful act, like test-firing one round of artillery at a private person's barn. Committing a tort creates a remedial legal position that is limited to a particular wrongful act and so is an exercise of a power to change legal relations in a very specific and limited way, just as an exercise of the power of eminent domain can be.[54]

Despite that one point of similarity, the ability to commit a tort is not the same as the power of eminent domain. Whether such abilities should be classified as powers at all is doubtful. Joseph Raz would say that they should not be, because powers include only abilities to bring about legal changes by a choice that usually is directed solely to that change.[55] The decision to commit a tort, including by creating an unreasonable risk, is directed to the tortious conduct, even if it is also directed to the remedial consequence, which it may or may not be.

Power or not, that ability differs from eminent domain in three other important ways. First, although the power of eminent domain can be exercised as to very

[53] *See* Henry E. Smith, *Property and Property Rules*, 79 N.Y.U. L. REV. 1719 (2004) (explaining why property is protected by property rules).

[54] This way of thinking may explain how Professors Balkin and Ayres, for example, note the distinctions among duties, claim-rights, liberties, and no-rights, and powers, liabilities, immunities, and disabilities (*see* Ian Ayres & J. M. Balkin, *Legal Entitlements as Auctions: Property Rules, Liability Rules, and Beyond*, 106 YALE L.J. 703, 704–5 n.5 (1996)) and then elide the distinction by equating changes in physical possession with exercises of the power of eminent domain, calling both takings. *Id.* at 708.

[55] Joseph Raz, *Voluntary Obligations and Normative Powers*, 46 PROC. ARISTOTELIAN SOC'Y: SUPPLEMENTARY VOLUMES 59, 80–81 (1972). "Hohfeld's and most of the other explanations of a legal power are too sweeping. Not every voluntary act which effects a legal change is an exercise of a legal power. Every offence or civil wrong changes the legal situation. It usually makes, e.g., the offender liable to a sanction, and imposes on the wrong-doer an obligation to compensate. There are many other acts which effect a legal change but are not the exercise of legal powers." *Id.* at 80. In Raz's view: "An action is the exercise of a legal power only if one of the law's reasons for acknowledging that it effects a legal change is that it is of a type such that it is reasonable to expect that actions of that type will, if they are recognized to have certain legal consequences, standardly be performed only if the person concerned wants to secure these legal consequences." *Id.* at 81 (footnote omitted).

Hohfeld does say that a person who has volitional control of the creation of facts that bring about a legal relation has a power. *See* Hohfeld, *supra* note 11, at 44. As Raz indicates, that definition includes cases in which the actor's volition is not directed to a change in legal relations, or is not directed only to a change in legal relations. Hohfeld's formulation is classic and I have adopted it, along with its possible breadth. The examples Hohfeld gave in his 1913 article suggest that he had in mind the narrower version of the concept that Raz uses, but they are not conclusive on the point.

limited interests, it need not be and rarely is. That power may be used to acquire the entire bundle of ownership rights, and routinely is. A government that had to acquire permissions to use private property one otherwise-tortious action at a time would have nothing like the power of eminent domain.

Next, although tortfeasors create for themselves remedial obligations, they do not create any legal benefit for themselves the way the government does when it exercises eminent domain. A wrongdoer usually acquires some practical benefit, like physical control of someone else's chattel or the unlawful use of someone else's property as with nuisance, but that practical benefit is a legal wrong. If a change in physical control changed primary legal relations, replevin and other possessory remedies would not be available to owners, who would cease to be owners upon the commission of the wrongful act. As to the ability to engage in tortious conduct, committing a tort generally changes nothing about it.[56] When governments exercise eminent domain, by contrast, they acquire some legal advantage, not just the obligation to pay for it. Indeed, the compensation obligation is not of the essence for eminent domain; when the First Congress proposed the Fifth Amendment with its Takings Clause, a constitutional requirement of just compensation was the exception and not the rule in this country.[57]

56 The failure to distinguish between physical acts and legal changes is a major source of confusion here. When a nonowner acquires physical possession of someone else's chattel, the chattel has been taken in a physical sense, but not in the legal sense in which a government takes property through eminent domain; the government takes ownership, not just physical possession. Landes and Posner liken torts to takings on the grounds that a tort constitutes an expropriation or transfer of resources. William M. Landes & Richard A. Posner, The Economic Structure of Tort Law 30–31 (1987). Ian Ayres regards torts as takings, noting that "many (if not most) torts concern unintentional takings." Ian Ayres, Optional Law: The Structure of Legal Entitlements 140 (2006). In recent writing Judge Calabresi puts physical harms resulting from violations of duties, and changes in primary legal relations, in the same category, calling them shifting of entitlements. *See, e.g.*, Calabresi, *supra* note 3, at 4 (torts, criminal law, and contracts as entitlement shifting) and 10 (eminent domain as change in entitlements). It is true that, in general, torts that damage tangible assets limit the uses to which the owner, if there is one, can put the asset. Automobile accidents frequently make cars unfit to drive and so of less use to their owners, who may have to repair or replace them. One might say that when one of two incompatible uses of a physical object takes place, the capacity to use the object has been transferred from one potential user to another. That physical act, however, does not affect either party's primary rights regarding the asset in question, although it does create a remedial right in the owner. Ayres' concept of unintentional takings includes torts but not exercises of the power of eminent domain, which are always intentional.

More than a century ago, Hohfeld emphasized the distinction between legal relations and the physical and mental events that call them into being. He gave as an example the two senses in which a watch might be said to be transferred from one person to another. Physically handing over the watch is one thing, changing ownership is another. Hohfeld, *supra* note 11, at 20.

57 Dean Treanor has discussed in detail the development of constitutional requirements that just compensation accompany exercises of the eminent domain power in the early days after independence. William Michael Treanor, *The Original Understanding of the Takings Clause and the Political Process*, 95 Colum. L. Rev. 782 (1995). When the Fifth Amendment was proposed, only Massachusetts and Vermont had constitutional provisions requiring just compensation when property was taken through eminent domain. *Id.* at 789–91

Perhaps the most important difference is that the power of eminent domain, when accompanied by a compensation requirement, can be used to shift risk in a particular way. Governments pay as compensation the market value of the asset or interest they acquire as of the point at which eminent domain is exercised.[58] The government thus acquires certainty as to its obligation, and is no longer exposed to liability to pay more if the value of the asset increases; rather, the government becomes entitled to the benefit of such an increase (and is exposed to reduction in value now that it is the owner). If the government were to acquire through eminent domain the liberty to engage in an otherwise unlawful act, payment would be based on market value at the time of the acquisition. The government's permitted act then would become lawful, and the subsequent consequences of lawful acts do not give rise to damages liability.

Private torts do not work that way. Although the compensation obligation of a tortfeasor sometimes is fixed by market value at the time of the tort, it frequently is not. Principles of tort remedies routinely measure the harm to the victim, and hence the victim's compensatory recovery, in light of events that affect the victim's harm and occur subsequent to the injurer's act. That feature of the law of remedies reflects the distinction between a wrong and an act that was permitted thanks to the acquisition through private eminent domain of a license to engage in the harmful conduct.

Several examples illustrate the point. Damages to crops are measured as of the time of harvest, not the defendant's harmful conduct.[59] Unlike a government that uses eminent domain to acquire an easement to flood a field, for example, a private person who does so tortiously will bear the risk that the consequences will be worse than the reduction of market value at the time of the wrong. A wrongdoer who destroys or appropriates an asset with fluctuating value, like a precious metal, may be subject to one of a number of rules that measure the asset's value at some time after the wrong, so that the rightful owner will continue to enjoy possible increases in that value. In some jurisdictions, the injured party's recovery is measured by the highest price the market reaches between the time of the wrong and the time of trial.[60] Others use the so-called New York rule, which bases recovery on the highest market value between the time of the wrong and a reasonable time to access the market for a replacement.[61] A government that acquires a gold statue through eminent domain simply pays the market value at the time of expropriation, and is not exposed to any risk that the value and its liability will increase.

When a tortfeasor damages or destroys a business asset that can be repaired or replaced, the asset's owner is in general entitled to recover for profits lost during the

58 The measure of just compensation is "the market value of the property at the time of the taking contemporaneously paid in money." *Olson* v. *United States*, 292 U.S. 246, 255 (1934).

59 *See, e.g.*, *Decatur Cnty. Ag-Serv.* v. *Young*, 426 N.E. 2d 644 (Ind. 1981) (harm from reduction in crop yield resulting from negligent crop dusting measured by price at time of harvest).

60 Dan B. Dobbs, Law of Remedies: Damages-Equity-Restitution 549 (2d ed. 1993).

61 *Id.* at 549–550. A case applying the New York rule is *Roxas* v. *Marcos*, 969 P.2d 1209 (Haw. 1998), which involved wrongful seizure of a large quantity of gold bullion and a statute of the Buddha allegedly made of gold.

period the asset was unavailable.[62] Identifying lost profits requires a counter-factual reconstruction of the events that would have taken place had the asset been available; that reconstruction is based on actual events after the wrong.[63] Temporary deprivation of assets used for personal purposes can lead to compensation based on the way in which the owner would have used the asset, which again requires inquiry into events that would have taken place after the wrong.[64]

Wrongdoers thus frequently pay compensation based on events that take place after the wrong and that affect the victim's injury. Results like that reflect the normative relationship between primary and remedial positions. The law of remedies measures the victim's recovery with reference to the victim's rightful position, the position the victim would occupy if the wrong had never occurred. For example, if a property owner is temporarily deprived of the use of an asset, the owner's rightful position remains the situation in which the asset is still available. For that reason, compensatory damages are a remedy for a prohibited act, and not just a mandatory payment.

The government's power of eminent domain enables it to appropriate the future benefits and burdens of ownership for a currently fixed price, the way the holder of an option to purchase can. If the government acquires land for a park that then dramatically increases in value because it could be put to another purpose, the government may sell the land, use the proceeds to buy another tract for the park, and use the profits for other public purposes. It need not share the profits with the owner who was paid after an exercise of eminent domain.[65]

Whether and when private people should have a power that resembles the government's eminent domain authority is an important question of policy.[66] The

62 Dobbs, *supra* note 60, at 561.

63 For example, in *McMillan* v. *McMillan*, 713 S.E. 2d 920 (Ga. App. 2011), the Court of Appeals of Georgia rejected the argument that the lost profits from a misappropriated partnership opportunity were to be measured by "the value that a reasonable person would have assigned to the prospective business opportunity at the time of its loss." *Id.* at 922. Because a reasonable person could conclude that the actual revenue made from the opportunity "could be a fair approximation of the revenue [the plaintiff] would have earned," that revenue was "probative of the lost revenue and profits" of the plaintiff and so subject to discovery. *Id.* at 924.

64 In *Story* v. *Gateway Chevrolet, Inc.*, 47 Cal. Rptr. 267 (Cal. Ct. App. 1965), for example, the defendant wrongfully held the plaintiff's pleasure boat for 143 weeks. The court awarded the cost of renting a replacement for 143 weekends, on the grounds that the plaintiff generally used the boat only on weekends and so would have done so had it not been held by the defendant. *Id.* at 270.

65 A collision damage waiver is a similar transaction done voluntarily by private parties. When a car rental company waives its claim for negligence against one of its customers in return for a fixed fee, it eliminates a pure duty of compensation for negligence. Risk shifts as a result, which is why collision damage waivers are a form of insurance. If the customer has an accident, the rental company is worse off than it would have been under the rule of negligence, and in the absence of an accident the company is better off and the customer worse off, having paid to transfer a risk that did not eventuate. If the customer had a private power of eminent domain, and could prospectively eliminate the company's claim for negligence in return for a price set by the government, that too would shift risk and produce a result different from that under the rule of negligence.

66 An important defense of property rule protection for property, both in the sense of supra-compensatory remedies and immunity from change by other private persons, appears in Smith, *supra* note 53. Smith argues that property rule protection keeps potential "takers" from

equation of accident liability with eminent domain makes it harder to answer that question by providing a false analogy. Because accident law uses a pure duty of compensation, which is a combination of primary duty and remedy, that combination is, indeed, common in U.S. law. But, the prevalence of pure duties of compensation implies nothing about private powers of eminent domain, which are quite different. A tortfeasor, unlike the government or a private option holder, cannot cut the victim off from payments based on later events that affect the interest the tortfeasor invaded.

Calabresi and Melamed and their followers may lose sight of this point because there are situations in which the ability to commit a tort does resemble an option to acquire a limited permission in return for a price.[67] The similarity is strongest when the measure of damages is based only on market value at the time of the wrong, as it often is. The damages for wrongful destruction of an asset are usually measured by the asset's market value at the time it was destroyed.[68] In *Boomer* v. *Atlantic Cement Co.*,[69] which has become canonical in this context, the Atlantic Cement Company was given the option of acquiring a servitude that would allow it to emit dust. The price of the servitude was set at the reduction in the market value of the plaintiffs' property.[70] *Boomer* applied the standard remedial principles governing so-called permanent nuisances: a nuisance that is not expected to end without judicial intervention – and that the court decides not to enjoin – is remedied with permanent damages measured by reduction in market value.[71] The victim of a permanent

opportunistically expropriating the upside of investments made by entrepreneurs. "Property rules are most called for when an entrepreneurial owner, broadly defined, is good at gathering information cost-effectively but results are not verifiable (entrepreneur makes bets), but a potential taker is good at informationally free-riding on the entrepreneur." *Id.* at 1781. "The problem with liability rules is a simple one of opportunism in the face of uncertainty." *Id.* Takers, as Smith conceives them, would be other private people with a power of eminent domain, and therefore the ability to expropriate the benefits of an investment in return for a payment fixed by a court at the time of the taking and not tied to future increases in the asset's value. In general, governments have such options and private people do not, even though private people pay only compensatory damages when they negligently injure one another.

67 Although the ability to commit a tort sometimes resembles the ability to acquire a permission to commit that very tort (but no future wrong), it never resembles the ability to acquire ownership. Wrongdoers who take physical possession of the property of others are subject to possessory remedies like replevin and ejectment. *See, e.g.*, Code of Virginia §§ 8.01–114 (action of detinue to recover possession of personal property); *Id.* at §§ 8.01–131 (action of ejectment to recover possession of real property). The physical ability to commit a tort is at most the power to bring about a very small change in legal relations, if it is that.

68 Dobbs, *supra* note 60, at 545.

69 26 N.Y. 2d 219, 257 N.E. 2d 870 (N.Y. 1970).

70 26 N.Y. 2d at 228 (permanent damages, and accompanying servitude). The Court of Appeals did not say whether the interest Atlantic Cement might acquire would be a pure Hohfeldian privilege, or would include a claim-right limiting the owner of the burdened land's liberty to interfere with Atlantic Cement's intrusions.

71 *Severt* v. *Beckley Coals, Inc.*, 170 S.E. 2d 577 (W. Va. 1969), was very much like *Boomer*. The defendant's coal mine emitted dust that reduced the value of the plaintiff's residence. The plaintiffs

nuisance may bring only one action for all damages, past and anticipated.[72] A different rule applies, however, to so-called temporary nuisances. If the court does not know whether the nuisance will continue in the absence of legal intervention, the victim must sue from time to time as harm is inflicted.[73] Even in the law of nuisance, the decision not to grant an injunction does not always imply that the defendant has an option to purchase a permission at a price determined by the court. Moreover, courts or legislatures could moderate or eliminate the single-action rule, and allow victims of permanent nuisances too to sue for periodic damages.

While market value at the time of the wrong is often the measure of recovery, it often is not. Calabresi and Melamed do not say that potential tortfeasors have a private power of eminent domain when, but only when, the victim's compensation will be set by market value at the time of the wrong. They say that potential tortfeasors are in the same position as the government, which has the power of eminent domain. Whether or not the former is correct, the latter is not.[74]

sought an injunction, and temporary damages for the harm already inflicted, *id.* at 581–82, but the court concluded that the remedy at law was adequate, *id.* at 582, and that the nuisance was permanent not temporary, *id.* at 582. It therefore ordered permanent damages, measured by reduction in market value. *Id.* at 582–84. The court noted that a license to continue the injuring conduct comes with permanent damages. *Id.* at 582–83. The Court did not say whether the interest acquired under West Virginia law is a pure Hohfeldian privilege, or includes a claim-right in the holder. The West Virginia Supreme Court of Appeals has more recently indicated that *Severt* incorrectly withheld an injunction. *Burch* v. *Nedpower Mount Storm LLC*, 647 S.E. 2d 879, 894 (W. Va. 2007). *Burch* does not reject the principle that when an injunction is denied and permanent damages are awarded, the defendant obtains an interest that makes its future conduct lawful.

72 *Id.* at 582–83. *Accord*, *Magruder* v. *Virginia-Carolina Chem. Co.*, 91 S.E. 121 (Va. 1917) (if a nuisance is expected to continue indefinitely, and so is permanent, the victim has only one action for past and future damage).

73 *See, e.g.*, *Norfolk & W. Ry. Co.* v. *Allen*, 118 Va. 428, 87 S.E. 558 (1915). In that case, the defendant's railroad's pumping station periodically interfered with the plaintiff's mill. An unlawful use of a lawful structure creates a temporary but not a permanent nuisance and gives rise to periodic claims for damages. *Id.* at 559. "It is further plain, under the established facts, that this case belongs to the class where the plaintiff is allowed to maintain successive actions for the damages sustained from time to time." *Id.* Similar was *Virginian Ry. Co.* v. *Jefferies' Adm'r*, 66 S.E. 731 (Va. 1909). The railroad built an embankment that flooded the plaintiff's land but was not a permanent nuisance because future flooding could not be foreseen. *Id.* at 734. The appropriate damages remedy was periodic damages, rather than the single recovery required for permanent nuisances. *Id.*

74 Recognizing the distinction between the two sets of Hohfeldian categories – duties, claim-rights, privileges, and no-rights as contrasted with liabilities, powers, immunities, and disabilities – also makes possible a better understanding of the configurations Calabresi and Melamed address with their discussion of inalienability rules. Calabresi & Melamed, *supra* note 2, at 1092–93. Inalienability as they define it is a disability on the holder of a claim-right, who may not waive or eliminate it voluntarily, and may not transfer it in a consensual transaction with another person. They seem to assume that a right that is inalienable in that sense is therefore not subject to any power like that of eminent domain, but that conclusion does not follow. The right-holder's power or disability is distinct from the right-holder's liability or immunity: a minor who lacks the power to convey title may be subject to the power of eminent domain, and so may have both a disability and a liability. A basic typology of powers identifies three questions: whether the right-holder has a power unilaterally to alter the right, for example by abandoning property, whether the right-holder and some third parties have interlocking powers to produce a change by mutual consent, for example by a sale, and whether some

13.3 OWNERSHIP AND THE STRENGTH OF REMEDIES

Calabresi and Melamed's identification of pure compensatory duties with private powers of eminent domain might be defended on the grounds that it is accurate as a practical matter. Property owners certainly value strong protection of their claim-rights, and often prefer it to pure compensatory protection. Perhaps that is because strong enforcement is essential to true ownership, so that if only compensation is available, the person paying the compensation may as well be the owner. Without strong remedies, according to this reasoning, nonowners have what amounts to a power to expropriate and pay, because they can use others' property as they please as long as they compensate.[75]

Strong protection is very useful, but there is more to ownership than that, and being subject only to compensatory damages does not give nonowners the ability to exercise eminent domain. That is true with respect to torts that actually transfer possession and use of a resource to the tortfeasor and those that are of benefit to the tortfeasor but impose some harm on the owner, like backing into someone else's car.[76]

The most obvious candidate for practical identification of pure compensatory liability and a private power of eminent domain may seem to be dispossession of tangible personal property.[77] If driving away with someone else's car is not a crime and will not be enjoined or otherwise be subject to supra-compensatory remedies, one might think that the first person to do so can expropriate the car much as the government can. The cases remain practically different, however. First, the true owner may retain extensive privileges of self-help, and those privileges may include a permission to impose harm on the thief that otherwise would be unlawful. The owner may be privileged to invade the thief's premises and break doors and locks, or

third party has a power unilaterally to alter the right, for example by a government's exercise of eminent domain. As to a third party that lacks a power like that of eminent domain and so has disability, the right-holder has immunity; as to a third party with that power, the right-holder has liability.

75 My criticism here is directed at the identification, within the category of liability rules, of eminent domain and tort liability, which is compensatory. The fact that the category of liability rules may include noncompensatory monetary liability is not relevant to that criticism.

76 Kaplow and Shavell discuss the difference between invasions of the possessory interest and torts that impose externalities. Louis Kaplow & Steven Shavell, *Property Rules Versus Liability Rules: An Economic Analysis*, 109 HARV. L. REV. 713, 715–716 (1996). They point out that possessory interests are generally protected by property rules, *id.* at 716, apparently meaning both that interference with possession is subject to supra-compensatory remedies and that nonowners do not have private powers of eminent domain. The differences between externalities and changes in possession "ultimately depend on whether the victim's harm is independent of the injurer's benefit." *Id.* at 772. Someone who takes someone else's overcoat and wears it on a cold day violates the possessory right and has a gain strongly correlated with the owner's loss. Someone who negligently collides with another's fence imposes an externality and gets a benefit – not having to take the costly precaution of paying attention – that is not much correlated with the owner's loss.

77 Hohfeld speculated that at earlier stages of the common law's development, the physical act of dispossession actually brought about a change in legal relations, as it does not now. Hohfeld, *supra* note 13, at 755–56.

at least to break locks if the car is in a public place.[78] If the thief had acquired title, the former owner would have no privilege of self-help.

Next, even if the only affirmative remedy is compensatory damages, the thief will not be able to expropriate the owner's right to those damages. If a second thief obtains possession, damages for dispossession will continue to accrue to the owner.[79] Nor can the thief convey title, including the privilege of self-help and the right to compensation. Finally, in contrast to a government that exercises eminent domain, the thief may be subject to damages assessed *ex post*, which expose thieves to risks that owners do not bear.[80]

Matters are similar with respect to possession of real property, with an additional twist. Whatever the remedy for trespass is, owners may put up all the walls and locks

78 Most current problems involving self-help to recover chattels involve repossession by lenders, frequently of automobiles. Lenders are privileged to engage in conduct that otherwise would constitute trespass, such as entering the borrower's property, but not to engage in acts that breach the peace. For example, in *Chrysler Credit Corp.* v. *Koontz*, 661 N.E. 2d 1171 (Ill. Ct. App. 2000), agents of the secured lender entered the borrower's property to repossess an automobile, and the court concluded that they were privileged to do so and had not breached the peace. Interpreting Article 9 of the Uniform Commercial Code, enacted in Illinois, the court found that breach of the peace means conduct that incites or is likely to incite "immediate public turbulence," or "immediate loss of public order or tranquility." *Id.* at 1173. Entry onto the borrower's property, without more, is privileged and not a breach of the peace, the court concluded. *Id.* at 1174–75. In this context the word "privilege" is used in its analytical sense, in which it means that conduct is lawful, so that when entry is privileged the owner has no right that the repossessors not enter. The court in *Koontz* implied that any conduct not amounting to breach of the peace and reasonably necessary to obtain possession would be privileged. For example, it indicated that the problem with breaking into a locked garage would be that it might breach the peace, not that it otherwise would be unprivileged. *Id.*

The self-help privilege of an owner might be made substantially more extensive than the privilege currently granted by the Uniform Commercial Code, and almost certainly would be more extensive in a system that had no affirmative judicial proceedings, including criminal punishment and other supra-compensatory remedies, to secure possession. As courts recognize, judicial remedies are substitutes for self-help, designed to keep property owners from "taking matters into their own hands." *Cla-Mil East Holding Corp.* v. *Medallion Funding Corp.*, 846 N.E. 2d 431, 432 (N.Y. 2006) (by obtaining assistance of city marshal to repossess collateral, lender properly used official process and avoided dangers of self-help, as called for by public policy).

79 The superior relative title that one wrongdoer may acquire against a later wrongdoer does not affect the title of the true owner. More fundamental is that a jurisdiction's law can provide that liability for damages continues to accrue to the true owner despite wrongful dispossession and any further changes of possession. The possibility of that arrangement shows that limiting true owners to compensatory recovery is not equivalent to giving wrongful takers a power of eminent domain.

It is quite important to recognize that private powers of eminent domain are not the only alternative to strongly enforced duties. A physical taking need not bring about a transfer of title such as happens when the government takes title to property through eminent domain. If physical taking transferred title, replevin and similar possessory remedies would not be available to parties out of possession, but they are. *See, e.g., BankAmerica Hous. Serv.* v. *P.D.N. & Assoc.*, 977 P. 2d 396 (Ore. Ct. App. 1999) (replevin available to retake possession of manufactured structure, which remained subject to replevin despite attachment to a foundation).

80 The points about risks and self-help show that even if the only affirmative remedy is compensatory damages, the ability to acquire bare possession through a wrongful act is not the practical equivalent of the legal power of expropriation through eminent domain even for a limited time.

they like, and may be given privileges to use force to protect possession.[81] Damages may be assessed *ex post*, and so may take into account developments after the wrong that affect the victim's harm.[82] Nor do trespassers receive any compensation themselves for a later trespass, just as they are without the power to convey any interest. The twist is that real estate often can be possessed by several people at once, as when a family lives in one house. Owners' rights are *in rem*, meaning that the owner has essentially the same claim-right with respect to every nonowner.[83] Reducing the remedial protection for the possessory interest in real property would make all real estate somewhat like a commons with a user fee measured by actual injury *ex post*, as far as affirmative remedies are concerned. That change would not pick out any particular person who could take and pay and would then enjoy the *in rem* rights of an owner. Self-help could still be privileged. Being a commoner subject to compensatory damages for using the land, provided you can climb over a fence with barbed wire on top in order to do so, is not much like being the only person with the power to acquire title. The government's power of eminent domain would be held only by the government, even if the only affirmative remedy were compensation.

For externalities as opposed to changes in possession, the argument for identifying pure compensatory duties with private powers of eminent domain is that a potential injurer who faces only compensation has what amounts to a power to acquire a privilege to engage in the conduct that imposes the externality. As explained in Section 13.2, the power of eminent domain makes it possible to shift risk in a way that the physical capacity to engage in harmful conduct does not. Even tortfeasors who face only damages liability may have that liability determined on the basis of unpredictable events that occur after their decision that leads to the wrong. A government that acquires a license through eminent domain can also obtain certainty as to the amount it must pay. A wrongdoer cannot.[84]

Potential tortfeasors, even when subject only to a compensatory remedy, do not in effect hold options to acquire interests in other people's property.

81 Alabama law for instance, gives someone in lawful possession of premises a privilege to use force to prevent a criminal trespass, including under certain circumstances deadly force. ALA. CODE § 13A-3-25 (2015).

82 For example, if A enters on B's land and plants a crop of alfalfa that prevents B from planting soybeans, and the price of soybeans has increased dramatically by harvest time, A may be required to pay the price at that point. Had the government expropriated the land, even for one growing season, it would have paid the market price as of the time it exercised its power of eminent domain and would not have been exposed to that risk.

83 Hohfeld called such advantages "multital" as opposed to the "paucital" relations created, for example by contract, which are often called *in personam*. Hohfeld, *supra* note 13, at 718.

84 As discussed in Section 13.2, the interest a wrongdoer might be said to acquire by committing a tort is no larger than that particular wrongful act.

13.4 TRANSACTION COSTS AND INTERNALIZING CHARGES

The identification of pure compensatory duties with private powers of eminent domain is thus mistaken on both conceptual and practical grounds.

By itself, that is not to say that torts are not like takings. Two distinct legal arrangements may belong in the same category if they have common features that matter. Injunctions against trespass and the writ of replevin are different remedies, one equitable and one legal, but both provide strong protection for the possessory interest. Injunctions and replevin are specific as opposed to substitutionary relief. Specific relief is an important category, even though specific remedies are importantly different from one another.[85] Whether the category of liability rules that Calabresi and Melamed define is useful depends on whether its components resemble one another in significant ways. The question here is whether compensatory liability for accidents and eminent domain are substantially alike.

Calabresi and Melamed suggest that the compensation requirement found in many liability rules, and in particular in accident law and eminent domain, can substitute for the market price.[86] When transactions costs are low, the price system causes decision-makers to take into account the consequences of their actions for others as reflected by the prices they face, and thereby to internalize those consequences. Ordinary market prices are predicated on the requirement of consent: the price is the point at which the seller is prepared to give consent to a transfer. When transactions costs are high, by contrast, even mutually beneficial bargains might not be made. Liability rules can mimic the price system, presenting decision-makers with a charge measured by the harm they impose that causes them to internalize effects that would be externalities if there were no legal consequences for their decision.[87] Prices internalize and compensation substitutes for prices.

85 "The most fundamental remedial choice is between substitutionary and specific remedies." Douglas Laycock, The Death of the Irreparable Injury Rule 12 (1991). Replevin and injunctions to return property are not perfect substitutes for one another. The inadequacy of replevin, for example because the defendant has hidden the asset or the plaintiff is unable to post the bond for replevin, is a reason to grant an injunction. Dobbs, *supra* note 60, at 586–87.

86 "It is enough for our purposes to note that a very common reason, perhaps the most common one, for employing a liability rule rather than a property rule to protect an entitlement is that market valuation of the entitlement is deemed inefficient, that is, it is either unavailable or too expensive compared to a collective valuation." Calabresi & Melamed, *supra* note 2, at 1110. Judge Calabresi has recently expressed some regret that the concept of liability rules has become so strongly associated with one particular function of liability rules, which is to mimic market outcomes. As he notes, he and Melamed identified that function and so contributed to the trend he describes. Calabresi, *supra* note 3, at 12.

87 Kaplow and Shavell describe one of the classic instances in which pure duties of compensation can bring about internalization that the price system would not. When one party creates a nuisance-like harm to another, the parties cannot bargain, and the government can identify the harm to the victim but not the cost of prevention to the injurer, a requirement of compensation can harness the injurer's private information about prevention costs and bring about the optimal result. *See* Kaplow & Shavell, *supra* note 76, at 725.

According to this reasoning, the category of liability rules is useful because leading members of the category share a common rationale. When liability is measured by compensation, the compensation requirement performs the internalizing function that a market price performs when transactions are easy and consent is required. Liability rules that provide for compensation do not, however, generally share that feature. In several leading examples of liability rules that provide compensation, the compensation requirement does not bring about internalization as a price would.

Liability for accidents does not in general entail compensatory payments that function like prices. Although strict liability may well bring about internalization as prices do, negligence and not strict liability predominates in US accident law.[88] Negligence does give rise to purely compensatory liability, but that liability functions like a sanction and not a price. A sanction creates a strong incentive not to engage in some conduct described by the law. A price causes the party paying the price to decide on an appropriate course of action, taking the price into account. Under strict liability for accidents, potential injurers decide on the appropriate level of care. The legal rules tell them, not what conduct is appropriate, but only that they will pay for harm.[89] Negligence law, by contrast, describes appropriate conduct and creates an incentive always to engage in it and never to engage in inappropriate conduct. Compensatory liability for negligence is not designed to allow potential injurers to decide whether to take due care, provided they pay compensation. The point is to keep them from being negligent. Because negligence is defined as conduct that creates more harm than benefit, imposing compensatory liability will create an incentive always to take due care. That is not internalization. It is the operation of a sanction, not a price.[90]

Negligence liability for accidents functions as a sanction and not a price, and Coasean reasoning implies that it should. As Calabresi and Melamed indicate, sanctioning injurers for causing accidents likely would lead to inefficiently high levels of care and inefficiently low levels of accidental harm; the optimal number of accidents is not zero.[91] Strict compensatory liability would

88 Major areas of tort law "including highway accidents, most personal injury cases, and professional negligence, are governed by common-law negligence." *See* Richard A. Epstein, Torts 109 (1999).

89 *Id.* at 69–70 (strict liability is based on causation, without regard to the precautions the injurer takes).

90 *See* Cooter, *supra* note 16, at 1538–40. (Judge Calabresi seems not to see negligence liability this way. Fault, he says, is "an odd system that seems to say, once we conclude that you should not have acted as you did, we will not *penalize* you, but will, in effect, 'let you do it,' so long as you pay damages and thereby bear the costs of what you did." Calabresi, *supra* note 48, at 748.)

91 "If we were to give victims a property entitlement not to be accidentally injured, we would have to require all who engage in activities that may injure individuals to negotiate with them before an accident, and to buy the right to knock off an arm or a leg. Such pre-accident negotiations would be extremely expensive, often prohibitively so. To require them would thus preclude many activities that might, in fact, be worth having." *See* Calabresi & Melamed, *supra* note 2, at 1108–9 (footnotes omitted). In this passage, Calabresi and Melamed seem to mean by a property entitlement the kind of protection that property owners generally enjoy: strong enforcement of their claim-rights and immunity from unconsented changes in that combination of right and remedy.

be better than sanctions for accidental harm, because it would induce the optimal level of care, which is in the parties' interest *ex ante* because it is more efficient.[92] But while the optimal level of accidents is not zero, the optimal level of negligence is. Negligence is by definition inefficient, and the legal rules should not create incentives to choose some positive level of negligence in the way in which they should create incentives to cause some positive level of accidents.[93]

In similar fashion, the compensation requirement in public eminent domain is not justified on the grounds that compensation functions as a substitute for the price system. The compensatory payment for exercises of the power of eminent domain does not come from the private funds of officials.[94] When a court makes an award of compensation for a taking, one part of the government directs another part of the government to pay the government's money to a private person.[95] The payment does not have the effect on incentives that a payment by a private individual would have.

As a result, the compensation requirement is either unnecessary or ineffective if its goal is to internalize to the government the consequences of exercises of eminent domain. If official decision-makers are seeking to perform their functions according to law and in the public interest, they should be instructed to use the power of eminent domain only when some appropriate government body has determined that the public benefits of doing so exceed the private costs. They need not also be instructed to pay compensation. Just as many government agencies use cost-benefit analysis in making regulatory decisions, so they could use cost-benefit analysis in making eminent domain decisions.[96] For purposes of management accounting, the private costs of eminent domain might be charged to the budget account of the agency exercising the power, but if officials operate in the public interest, accurate accounting will be enough.

If government decision-makers are not performing their functions to the best of their ability, the compensation requirement will not encourage them to do so, because it does not operate on them personally. Nor is there much reason to think that the compensation requirement causes the electorate, considered as the officials' principals, to encourage officials to weigh costs and benefits properly. As Daryl Levinson has shown, the fact that a compensation requirement is borne by taxpayers does not mean that decisions that trigger compensation will be efficient. When the benefits of a taking are more concentrated than the taxes that pay for it, the beneficiaries may be able to form a coalition

92 EPSTEIN, *supra* note 88, at 93–95 (with simplifying assumptions, strict liability induces the optimal level of care).

93 Negligence is a failure to exercise reasonable care. Restatement (Second) of Torts § 282 (1965).

94 The Tucker Act grants the United States Court of Federal Claims jurisdiction over claims against the U.S. founded on the Constitution. *See* 28 U.S.C. § 1291.

95 Judgments against the US are paid from the federal treasury. *See* 31 U.S.C. § 1304.

96 Regarding the use of cost-benefit analysis in making regulatory decisions, see generally CASS R. SUNSTEIN, THE COST-BENEFIT STATE (2003).

in favor of that exercise of eminent domain, even though its full social costs exceed its benefits.[97]

Although the compensation requirement makes little or no contribution to efficiency in exercises of eminent domain, accompanying eminent domain with compensation does have advantages unrelated to internalization through just compensation. Courts are a reasonably neutral government body that can measure private costs and may well be able to do so better than the programmatic agencies that acquire private property for public use. Courts thus can provide information that bears on whether a taking is efficient. The requirement that compensation be paid, and not just calculated and used to measure private costs, itself is justified on distributional and not efficiency grounds. As the Supreme Court has explained, a function of the Takings Clause is to ensure that the burden of producing public benefits does not fall specifically and unfairly on a small number of property owners.[98]

Governments are not private people, and perhaps public eminent domain is an anomaly in the category of liability rules. Several leading examples of private eminent domain, however, also do not have internalization as the function of their compensation requirement. Perhaps the best-known example of private eminent domain arises in nuisance cases, when the court denies an injunction and instead awards permanent damages along with a license to continue the activity in question. If the doctrine were designed to provide internalizing substitutes for prices through the compensation requirement, injunctions would never be granted, and injurers would automatically have the option to acquire a servitude by paying permanent damages. That would leave the choice to the party paying the price, as the price system does.

In general, however, courts withhold injunctions in such cases, and instead award permanent damages along with a servitude, only when the burden of the injunction is substantially in excess of its benefit.[99] The requirement of serious disproportion means that many efficiency-enhancing nuisances will be enjoined. If the cost of

[97] Daryl J. Levinson, *Making Government Pay: Markets, Politics, and the Allocation of Constitutional Costs*, 67 U. CHI. L. REV. 345, 364–65 (2000). Judge Calabresi recently has discussed the possibility that compensation for exercises of eminent domain might not be measured by the victim's loss, but instead might be designedly greater or less than that loss. *See* Calabresi, *supra* note 3, at 10–11. Insofar as the point of such variation would be to influence government decision-makers, the problem that Levinson points out remains.

[98] "One of the principal purposes of the Takings Clause is 'to bar Government from forcing some people alone to bear public burdens which, in all fairness and justice, should be borne by the public as a whole.'" *Dolan* v. *City of Tigard*, 512 U.S. 372, 384 (1994) (quoting *Armstrong* v. *United States*, 364 U.S. 40, 49 (1960)).

[99] Douglas Laycock, *The Neglected Defense of Undue Hardship*, 4 J. TORT L. 2–7 (2011). As Professor Laycock explains, the decision of the New York Court of Appeals in *Boomer* v. *Atl. Cement Co.*, 257 N. E. 2d 870 (N.Y. 1970) is confused and confusing. The Court of Appeals in *Boomer*, he concludes, applied the standard rule of undue hardship only after incorrectly saying that earlier New York cases did not recognize it. Laycock at 7–8. *Boomer* was in fact no innovation at all. *Id.*

abatement by a polluter is only $1,000 more than the harm to the plaintiffs, the polluter is likely to be enjoined because the hardship is not disproportionate. The polluter will not be allowed to acquire a servitude by tendering permanent damages. That result does not mimic the price system, under which a buyer who values a good $1 more than the seller's asking price will buy it, with no requirement of a large gap between the parties' reservation prices. A doctrine designed to present decision-makers with the equivalent of market prices would not have the disproportion requirement, but the law of nuisance does.[100] The permanent damages that are sometimes awarded under it are not much like a price.[101]

The private power of eminent domain that is sometimes accorded an accidental encroacher fits the pattern of market-mimicking compensatory charges even less well. When one property owner has inadvertently built a structure on another's land, courts face the question whether to grant an injunction that will require the structure to be dismantled, or deny the injunction and impose permanent damages in return for an easement or the fee interest. Many US jurisdictions deny an injunction and instead award permanent damages with an accompanying interest for the encroacher, but only if the encroachment was

100 In a jurisdiction that follows the Restatement as to the substance of nuisance law, the question of undue hardship may well never arise, because if the benefits of the defendant's conduct exceed its costs, that conduct is reasonable and not a nuisance. *See* Restatement (Second) of Torts, §§ 822, 826 (1979) (nuisance is unreasonable harm, and reasonableness is determined by comparing gravity of the harm with the utility of the conduct that produces it). In jurisdictions that genuinely follow that approach, the court will weigh harm and utility for itself, and not seek to cause the defendant to do so by imposing a requirement of compensation. The Restatement gives courts flexibility in their conceptions of harm and utility. That flexibility allows courts to develop doctrines under which, if the defendant would bear an undue hardship from ceasing the activity in question, that activity is categorically not a nuisance.

101 Private necessity sometimes does feature a compensation requirement that brings about internalization. When the privilege of necessity is incomplete, the party in necessity must compensate the owner whose property is invaded for any damage. Epstein, *supra* note 88, at 63–64. As with undue hardship in the law of nuisance, the initial determination that necessity has arisen requires a substantial disparity between the benefit to the person in necessity and the owner whose property is burdened: necessity arises only to prevent serious harm in emergencies. *See* Restatement (Second) of Torts § 197 (1965) (privilege of necessity available to prevent "serious harm"); *id.*, cmt. a (the privilege arises in "an emergency"). Once necessity has been established, the compensation requirement gives the party in necessity an incentive to minimize any resulting harm to the property owner. *See* Epstein, *supra* note 88, at 64–65.

In both nuisance cases like *Boomer* and necessity cases, a substantial disparity between harm and benefit is required to authorize the so-called private taking, and that disparity is identified by the court. If the power of eminent domain is limited to powers that may be unilaterally exercised by the possessor without anyone else's permission, then nuisance cases like *Boomer* and necessity cases are not private eminent domain at all, because the private person is not authorized to act unilaterally but must have a court's approval. If cases like that are not private eminent domain, they do not involve liability rules within Calabresi and Melamed's definition. In that case they are not counter-examples to the claim that liability rules are justified because they allow internalization, not because they allow internalization, but because they are not about liability rules. If those standard examples are not liability rules, public eminent domain and accident liability are not parts of the larger category of liability rules, and their compensation requirements are not justified on grounds of internalization.

inadvertent.[102] Knowing encroachers are subject to injunctions.[103] As Laycock puts it, the undue hardship principle in this situation is a litigation doctrine but not a planning doctrine.[104] A party who plans to rely on it will not be allowed to rely on it. Internalizing charges, like strict tort liability, perform their market-mimicking function only *ex ante* and hence only insofar as they act on the incentives of parties who know about them.[105]

Compensation requirements sometimes can perform the efficiency-enhancing function of the requirement of consent in ordinary market transactions when barriers to transacting are high. They often perform no such function, however, as in negligence liability, public eminent domain, and central instances of private eminent domain. The inclusion of tort liability and eminent domain in a single category thus cannot be explained on the grounds that the compensation requirement substitutes for the price system in situations of high transaction costs. Strict liability for accidents does meet that description, but many other liability rules do not.

13.5 LIABILITY, PROPERTY, AND IMMUNITY

Calabresi and Melamed's category of liability rules can seem natural from a common perspective on legal rules. That perspective looks at the law as associating consequences with choices. Holmes' description of contract law, according to which it presents the promisor with the choice of performing or paying, takes that perspective.[106] The choice not to perform brings the consequence of damages. Adopting that perspective has two consequences of its own. First, primary obligations concerning conduct, like the obligation to perform a contract, are understood in terms of the remedies that enforce them. Second, because committing a wrong that leads to damages and exercising a power that has a price associated with it both entail an obligation to pay, those choices are seen as fundamentally similar. The category of liability rules, in which duties that have only compensatory remedies are equated with powers of eminent domain, follows from that perspective.

Reasoning backwards from consequences can provide valuable insights. Pure duties of compensation are an important concept, and creating them is an

102 Laycock, *supra* note 99, at 3–4.

103 *Id.*

104 Douglas Laycock, Modern American Remedies 412 (4th ed. 2010).

105 Some states allow landlocked owners to acquire an easement of access without consent and require compensation. *See supra* note 28 and accompanying text. Although the requirement that the acquiring party have no other access to a public road is not identical to a requirement that the benefit of the easement exceed the cost, it is a strong proxy for that situation. In that context, the compensation requirement resembles an internalizing charge only to a very limited extent.

106 "The duty to keep a contract at common law means a prediction that you must pay damages if you do not keep it – and nothing else." Holmes, *supra* note 1, at 462.

important tool of policy. But as Hart and Sacks said, it is also important to reason frontwards, going from the rules that produce consequences to the consequences.[107] In describing those rules, the analytical concepts distinguish between primary and remedial positions, and between rules about remedies and rules about power. By eliding both of those distinctions, I have argued, the category of liability rules as Calabresi and Melamed define it treats legal arrangements that are quite distinct as if they were identical. Violations of rights are not changes in rights. The distinction between remedies and powers captures a genuine distinction in the substance of legal rules.

Calabresi and Melamed's failure to distinguish duties and the associated remedies from powers explains two difficulties with their typology that have been identified in subsequent scholarship.[108] Before Calabresi and Melamed wrote, Frank Michelman had described three ways in which the substantive and remedial law together might treat a potential nuisance: The harm might be found not to be a nuisance, and so permitted. It might be found to be a nuisance that gives rise to compensatory damages that can be collected periodically as they accrue. It might be found to be a nuisance and enjoined, and so forbidden and subject to a strong remedy.[109]

107 Hart and Sacks criticized Hohfeld and Corbin for "seeming to suggest that the right and the right of action necessarily went together so that if there was no right of action there was no primary right in a genuine sense to begin with, and *vice versa*. Lots of people have tried to think backwards in this way. It is the essence of clear analysis to see that it *is* backwards, and instead to think frontwards." HART & SACKS, *supra* note 13, at 136. As they went on to say, "The purposes of law are not expressed in the sanctions which it is feasible or expedient to impose." *Id.*

108 Calabresi and Melamed create their four rules by asking two questions: Is the polluter's conduct forbidden – as they put it, which party has the entitlement? – and does the party who would lose in a proceeding to enjoin that conduct have a power to reverse the result with a one-time compensatory payment – as they put it, is the entitlement protected by a property rule or a liability rule? Calabresi & Melamed, *supra* note 2, at 1116–17. Under Rule 1, the polluter's conduct is prohibited and the polluter, who would lose, has no power to change that result. Under Rule 2, the polluter's conduct is prohibited, but the polluter, who would lose, does have a power to change that result. Under Rule 3, the polluter's conduct is permitted, and the neighbor, who would lose in a proceeding to enjoin the polluter, has no power to change the parties' primary relation. Under Rule 4, the neighbor would lose, but has a power to impose a duty on the polluter conditioned on a compensatory payment. Although the presumed remedy is an injunction, *id.*, the typology is not really concerned with remedies, but only with duties and their correlative claim-rights, and powers. (That is why the typology does not take into account the asymmetry between claim-rights combined with duties, which give rise to remedies, and privileges combined with no-rights, which do not.)

109 Frank Michelman, *Pollution as a Tort: A Non-Accidental Perspective on Calabresi's Costs*, 80 YALE L.J. 647, 670 (1971) (book review). Michelman was explicit that his third rule involved periodic damages, and explained that rule's advantage over one that would provide for a lump-sum payment of permanent damages, "a kind of private eminent domain." *Id.* at 671 n.44. The problem with permanent damages as opposed to periodic damages is that "After an award of 'permanent damages,' the polluter is subject to no further incentive to seek out improved abatement methods." *Id.*

With respect to duties, claim-rights, and remedies, Michelman was fundamentally correct in two respects. First, there are three possible combinations of primary and remedial relations, if remedies are divided between compensatory and supra-compensatory (prices and sanctions). The conduct at issue may be permitted, it may be forbidden and subject to a purely compensatory remedy, and it may be forbidden and subject to a supra-compensatory remedy.[110] Second, if powers are not in play, compensation generally will take the form of periodic damages where the defendant engages in ongoing conduct. Cases like *Boomer*, in which permanent damages are paid, also involve a change in primary legal relations like the servitude the Atlantic Cement Company received in return for its payment. They thus involve the exercise of powers, and are not limited to duties and remedies.

Calabresi and Melamed's four rules do not include periodic damages, as Michelman emphasized years later.[111] Their liability rules are powers to bring about a change unilaterally. In *Boomer*, the Atlantic Cement Company was forbidden from creating the nuisance and subject to injunctive enforcement of that duty, but was given a power to acquire the servitude. In *Spur Industries*, Spur Industries was permitted to cause the harm, but Del Webb was given a power to impose a duty, which could be enforced with an injunction.[112] All four of Calabresi and Melamed's rules thus involve only permissions or strongly enforced duties, combined with powers to move from one of those relations to the other. In *Boomer*, the starting point was prohibition, and the power was to move to permission. In *Spur Industries*, the starting point was permission, and the power was to move to prohibition. Calabresi and Melamed never considered a combination of prohibition and compensatory damages, even though that is how accident law works, and accident law is their paradigm of a liability rule.

When pointed out, this gap may seem astonishing, but it resulted from the failure to distinguish the law of remedies from the law of powers. Because Calabresi and Melamed put compensatory damages and eminent domain compensation in the same category, they did not see the important differences between them. Their list of rules is incomplete, and significantly so, because of the benefits of periodic damages.[113] Moreover, the dizzying possibilities introduced by rules about power, which can include powers to move from any position to any other, and both puts and calls, should not be allowed to

110 As Michelman later put it, his 1971 review presented a "threefold typology of right/remedy combinations." *See* Frank I. Michelman, *"There Have to Be Four"*, 64 MD. L. REV. 136, 138 (2005). (Some would say that in the second situation the conduct is permitted but the party who engages in it must pay a price. Although the distinction can reflect real normative differences, I am not concerned with them here and so for my purposes the question is purely terminological.)

111 *Id.* at 154 (stressing the importance of periodic as opposed to permanent damages).

112 *Spur Indus., Inc.* v. *Del Webb Dev. Co.*, 494 P. 2d 700 (Ariz. 1972) (allowing injunction on condition that plaintiff compensated defendant for relocation costs).

113 *See* Michelman, *supra* note 109, at 154.

obscure the underlying simplicity of the combinations of duties and remedies.[114]

[114] Michelman assembles a six-part typology by combining the three combinations of duty and remedy he identifies with another piece of Calabresian apparatus, the concept of liability (as opposed to a liability rule). *Id.* at 155. Calabresi had pointed out that when an accident takes place, someone will be liable for it in an important sense no matter what the legal rules provide. If they provide no recovery, the victim will be liable, in that the victim will bear the harm. If the injurer is required to pay the victim some compensatory amount, then the injurer will be liable. If the injurer always pays compensation, the injurer is strictly liable. If the victim never receives compensation, the victim is strictly liable. *Id.* at 148 (citing GUIDO CALABRESI, THE COST OF ACCIDENTS: A LEGAL AND ECONOMIC ANALYSIS 137 (1970)). Using that concept, Michelman pairs each of the three combinations of right and remedy with a rule under which that combination is in turn combined with a one-time payment that might be thought to shift the burden of the rule, just as compensation for an accident shifts the burden of the accident. Michelman, *supra* note 109, at 153. Doing this, Michelman explains, shows how it is possible to decouple the assignment of an entitlement from the assignment of liability. *Id.* at 149–50. The result in *Spur Industries*, for example, assigned the entitlement to Del Webb while also making Del Webb liable. A plaintiff who obtains an injunction with no payment obligation has the entitlement and is not liable.

Michelman's pairings of legal rule with compensatory payment, however, is much stranger than it may seem to be at first. Accidents and nuisances are events in the physical world that change that world for the worse. They create a harm that may be shifted through compensatory payments but that cannot be eliminated. To liken a legal rule to an accident or a nuisance implies that the rule represents a change from some previous arrangement, a change that makes someone worse off, and opens up the possibility of shifting that liability through a compensatory payment. If Michelman's rules that include a one-time compensatory payment are seen as the result of a private party's exercise of an option to move from another combination of duty and remedy to another, the compensatory payment makes sense. That is how *Boomer* and *Spur Industries* worked: the Atlantic Cement Company was subject to an injunction, but had the option to move to a permission through a one-time payment to the plaintiffs. Spur Industries was permitted to continue its activities, but Del Webb had the option to impose a prohibition on Spur Industries by making a one-time payment.

Michelman, however, explicitly does not choose between the option-based account of his three rules that include compensation and one according to which a court simply imposes that rule, along with the compensatory payment. *Id.* at 154–55 n.66. The latter possibility is very strange. Compensation makes sense when a change for the worse has occurred, relative to some preexisting standard. With an accident or a nuisance, the preexisting standard is the nonlegal world as it existed before the tort. With an option, it is the legal world as it stood before the option was exercised. But why would a court conclude that its determination of the legal relations between the parties can somehow constitute a harm, like a tort, that makes someone worse off and for which that party should be compensated? If the answer is that the court itself is changing the parties' legal relations and should compensate the loser, the question arises, why make a change that has a loser? The natural-seeming Coasean answer, that someone always loses because either conduct is forbidden and the potential actor loses, or harm is permitted and the victim loses, makes sense only if the legal rule is itself seen as a change, perhaps from the state of nature with no legal rules at all. The idea of winners and losers applies only when making a comparison. It applies easily to changes in the physical world, like accidents and nuisances. But with respect to legal rules, it makes sense only if some preexisting arrangement is specified. In an operating legal system, that preexisting arrangement is never a legal vacuum. Although courts may be said to make law, they always do so by changing it, if only by making it more clear. A court that is considering announcing a legal relation between the parties and accompanying that announcement with a compensatory payment obligation thus should address this question: if this is a legal change that imposes a harm that should be compensated, why make the change? That question may have a good answer, but it should not be ignored.

Analysis of this question is impeded by peculiarities of nuisance. In a nuisance case, it may seem that the court is choosing the legal relation between the parties in the first instance, and not changing it. Courts in nuisance cases may seem to make law wholly afresh, and to neither change legal relations

Other scholars have noted an oddity in Calabresi and Melamed's Rule 3, in which harmful activity is permitted and the injurer's "entitlement" is said to be protected by a property rule.[115] By that, Calabresi and Melamed apparently mainly meant that the victim has no power to change the injurer's position to a strongly-enforced duty not to engage in the conduct. The absence of that power distinguishes Rule 3 from Rule 4.[116] But because Calabresi and Melamed define property rules in terms of strong enforcement, and not just immunity, they create the impression that the injurer with no duty is somehow entitled to an injunction against the victim. That injunction would have to direct the victim not to interfere with the harm, for example through self-help.[117] As Henry Smith and Lee Fennell have both pointed out, to say that the injurer has a "right" to pollute is ambiguous with respect to the analytical categories.[118] That right could be a bare permission, or it could include a claim-right correlated with a duty in

nor enforce preexisting relations. Nuisance law often calls for balancing, *see supra* note 96 (balancing test in nuisance law), and so a court in a nuisance case may seem to be making law rather than applying it. Moreover, when a court grants an injunction against conduct that had not previously been subject to a supra-compensatory remedy, it really does change the parties' legal relations, from a pure duty of compensation to a strongly enforced duty. (The pure duty of compensation must have existed previously, or the conduct would not have been a nuisance at all.) But even in a nuisance case, there must have been some legal relation between the parties that the court identifies and does not simply make, as reflected by the need to decide whether the plaintiff is entitled to damages for harm already incurred. The ability of courts to make law, either wholesale through precedents or retail through remedies like injunctions, presupposes that later courts will follow the law, including the law created by prior courts. The *ex ante* effect of legal rules, including legal rules announced by judges, rests on potential parties' assumption that a later court will enforce the existing rule, and not just fabricate a new one, the content of which cannot be predicted.

115 "Rule three (no nuisance) is instead an entitlement to [the polluter] protected by a property rule, for only by buying [the polluter] out at [the polluter's] price can [the victim] end the pollution." Calabresi & Melamed, *supra* note 2, at 1116.

116 "Missing is a fourth rule representing an entitlement in [the polluter] to pollute, but an entitlement which is protected only by a liability rule. The fourth rule, really a kind of partial eminent domain coupled with a benefits tax, can be stated as follows: [the victim] may stop [the polluter] from polluting, but if he does so he must compensate [the polluter]." *Id.*

117 Jules Coleman and Jody Kraus adopt this reading in their important study of legal rights. "[I]f the court decides in favor of the polluter, it may protect its right to pollute by a property rule," which "enjoins *B* [the victim] from reducing *A*'s [the polluter's] pollution without first securing *A*'s consent." Jules L. Coleman & Jody Kraus, *Rethinking the Theory of Legal Rights*, 95 Yale L.J. 1335, 1338 (1986).

118 As Smith explains, if Rule 3 entails only a bare permission for the polluter, it is not symmetrical with Rule 1, under which the polluter has a duty that may be strongly enforced through an injunction. "True symmetry would require that the polluter have not merely a privilege to pollute – 'Taney may pollute at will' – but a *right* to do so, backed up by the possibility of an injunction. In the Hohfeldian scheme, a right (or claim) is an entitlement that corresponds to a duty in another: if the resident has right to be free of pollution, there is a corresponding duty in the polluter not to pollute." Henry E. Smith, *Self-Help and the Nature of Property*, 1 J.L. Econ. & Pol'y 69, 75 (2005). Smith explains the consequences of a claim-right to pollute. "Flipping things around, if the polluter has a similar entitlement, a right to pollute, then the resident has a *duty* to accept pollution and possibly a duty not to interfere with the passage of pollution from the factory onto her land . . . Such an entitlement does exist: it is called an easement." *Id.* A permission to pollute, by itself, is not an easement, and polluters whose conduct is allowed do not in general hold easements. They have bare privileges or liberties in the analytical sense, not claim-rights with correlative duties resting on the victim. Fennell makes the same point in the course of developing her concept of half-torts. Fennell, *supra* note 52, at 1412–16.

someone else. The most natural bearer of the correlative duty would be the victim, who would have a duty not to interfere with the imposition of the harm. That duty would bar self-help. Yet victims generally may engage in self-help that does not invade the polluter's property, even when the conduct causing the injury is permitted. So the injunction that Calabresi and Melamed imply should be available by calling Rule 3 a property rule is in fact not available.[119]

No such injunction is implied by saying that, under Rule 3, the victim has no power unilaterally to change the parties' legal relations, so the injurer is immune from any attempt by the victim to do so. Although a free-standing liberty cannot be affirmatively enforced by an injunction or any other remedy, like any legal position, it can be protected by immunity, and frequently is. Remedies and powers are different.

Reasoning frontwards by attending to the legal principles that lead to remedial consequences is valuable not only because it draws attention to the differences among those principles, like the difference between remedies and powers. It also illuminates the pattern those principles form when taken together. A property owner's possessory interest is protected in several ways. Damages remedies, supra-compensatory remedies like criminal punishment, and permission for self-help, including otherwise-unlawful self-help in the face of violations, all make the possessory interest more secure. So does the owner's general immunity from changes in ownership rights resulting from the unilateral juridical act of another private person.

Those protections form a pattern because they complement and do not simply substitute for one another. Supra-compensatory remedies, like the criminal penalties threatened by injunctions, differ in their effects from immunity. That is why the absence of the former, as when the only compensatory remedy is damages, does not imply the absence of the latter. Immunity as against other private people may be the most fundamental protection, because it is hardly ever absent. Although pure duties of compensation are common, private powers of eminent domain are rare. In the vast bulk of situations, primary private rights against physical invasions may be waived or altered by their holder, but are not subject to change by the unilateral act of another private person.

This chapter has focused on the concept of liability rules, not property rules. The perspective suggested here also has important implications for the configuration in which an interest is strongly protected and not subject to any private power of eminent domain, which Calabresi and Melamed unequivocally would label as

[119] The problem Smith and Fennell discuss concerns only duties, privileges, claim-rights, and no-rights, along with remedies, and does not itself involve powers or the other positions associated with changes in legal relations. Claim-rights can be protected by affirmative remedies, but bare privileges cannot be. As Fennell notes, "'privileges' are different from 'rights' in the Hohfeldian taxonomy, in that they cannot be coercively enforced by the state." *Id.* at 1407 n.22 (citing Hohfeld). It may seem strange that Calabresi and Melamed failed to see this asymmetry, which arises from the interaction between primary and remedial legal positions; much of their point was to integrate substantive law and the law of remedies. They failed to consider the two different kinds of primary rules, those that involve conduct and those that involve change in legal relations.

a property rule. The first implication is that one argument in favor of strong protection is erroneous: the claim that without it, nonowners would in effect have a power to expropriate similar to the government's power of eminent domain. As previously explained, that is not correct, because of other features of the owner's bundle of advantages.

The second implication is that the important variable for policy purposes is strength of protection and not immunity from private expropriation, because the latter is almost always present and so can be taken for granted. Private people cannot obtain collision damage waivers without consent any more than they can obtain permission to trespass without consent. Neither strongly-enforced duties nor pure compensatory duties may be altered without the consent of the right-holder. Immunity is not an important variable because it is not a variable; it is pervasive.

Calabresi and Melamed did not use the word "liability" in the sense it has in the analytical categories. If their equation of pure duties of compensation with private powers of eminent domain were correct, the word would be apt in both senses. That equation is not correct, however, because pure duties of compensation do not make private people liable to have their primary legal positions changed by other private people. The proper word to describe the status of private rights relative to private people is not liability, but immunity.

14

Scaling Up Legal Relations

Andrew S. Gold[*] *and Henry E. Smith*[**]

14.1 INTRODUCTION

It is rare for something as precise and analytical as Wesley Hohfeld's system of legal relations to serve as a Rorschach blot. For a century now, legal theorists have seen reflected in it their picture of a flat undifferentiated landscape of law – protean material for refashioning on policy grounds. This was not Hohfeld's vision and yet it is not wholly untrue to it either. Hohfeld believed, as did many others in his day, that greater clarity about basic legal concepts and clearing away ambiguities would make law transparent to policy and lead inexorably to improvement in the law.[1] The first step in clearing away the cobwebs was to ground the law in its micro foundations. This is where the trouble starts.

We argue that a great but ignored problem in legal theory is the relation of the micro to the macro.[2] How do structures that people can inhabit and process at the micro level scale up to the macro level of society? For example, do the doctrines of negligence and nuisance lead to overall efficiency, or might the relationships between activities and evasion of the legal standard prevent a modeled two-party interaction from relating in linear fashion to society as a whole? Many structures would not scale up very well: if any actor's relations with any other actor could depend on any action with respect to any aspect of

[*] Professor of Law, Brooklyn Law School. Email: andrew.gold@brooklaw.edu.

[**] Fessenden Professor of Law, Harvard Law School. Email: hesmith@law.harvard.edu. We would like to thank Shyam Balganesh, Charlie Donahue, Ted Sichelman, and the participants at the Yale Conference on Hohfeld for their helpful comments and questions. Liability for all errors is ours.

[1] Wesley N. Hohfeld, *A Vital School of Jurisprudence and Law: Have American Universities Awakened to the Enlarged Opportunities and Responsibilities of the Present Day?*, *in* WESLEY N. HOHFELD, FUNDAMENTAL LEGAL CONCEPTIONS AS APPLIED IN JUDICIAL REASONING AND OTHER LEGAL ESSAYS 332–84 (Walter Wheeler Cook ed., 1923). Compare N. E. H. Hull, *Vital Schools of Jurisprudence: Roscoe Pound, Wesley Newcomb Hohfeld, and the Promotion of an Academic Jurisprudential Agenda, 1910–1919*, 45 J. LEGAL EDUC. 235, 270 (1995) (arguing that Hohfeld's conceptualism was part of a reformist outlook) with G. Edward White, *The American Law Institute and the Triumph of Modernist Jurisprudence*, 15 LAW & HIST. REV. 30 (1997) (arguing that Hohfeld was not primarily reformist).

[2] Andrew S. Gold & Henry E. Smith, *Sizing Up Private Law*, 70 U. TORONTO L.J. 489 (2020).

a thing and no interdependencies are ruled out, we have a classic intractable problem.[3] How to solve this intractability is central to many fields, and there is no reason law should be exempt. In the real world, such problems are ever present, and it is ironically some version of traditional legal institutions and doctrines that, among other things, manages this complexity.[4] And as in other fields, law tames complexity through modularity: breaking the world of interactions into chunks within which interaction is intense but between which interaction is less intense.[5]

Hohfeld's tragic death prevented him from pushing his framework into areas that would have required him to face up to the problem of scaling up and complexity. Analyzing notions like ownership and corporations into basic legal relations availing between individuals (both in and out group) is an important first step, but, as we will see, doing so does not automatically answer normative questions. Nor does it furnish a practical way for actors to navigate the world or judges to assess situations that come before them. What we need is a law that will be simple enough for individuals on the ground to navigate and at the same time that will organize the complexity of their interaction on larger scales in a manageable fashion.

This chapter will first show, in Section 14.2, how Hohfeld's system is a particularly rigorous example of a theory that treats law as being flat and relatively unstructured. Section 14.3 will introduce the problem of delineation, which breaks some of the symmetry of a single-level system. Going beyond single-level systems, Section 14.4 will show what is needed to permit law to scale up from the micro to the macro. Doing so allows us to capture larger structures and emergent properties in the law, to explain and justify the kinds of adjustments needed in scaling up, and to better account for the dynamic quality of legal relations. Although we do not justify a return to older formalism, we show that frequently-made claims of logical error in the traditional use of legal concepts and the supposed arbitrariness of baselines are wrong or overblown. We conclude with some thoughts on why legal theory in Hohfeld's era and afterwards has tended to flatten the law and how the Hohfeldian system can help point the way forward.

3 *See, e.g.*, MELANIE MITCHELL, COMPLEXITY: A GUIDED TOUR (2009); J. A. SCOTT KELSO & DAVID A. ENGSTRØM, THE COMPLEMENTARY NATURE (2006). Some earlier legal writers saw the importance of potential intractability. *See, e.g.*, LON L. FULLER, LEGAL FICTIONS 103–09 (1967); Albert Kocourek, *Formal Relation between Law and Discretion*, 9 ILL. L. REV. 225, 238 (1914) ("While the combinations of persons, things, and facts are beyond computation, yet these computations are not such that they cannot be managed by the aid of legal science. The same multiplicity is found in the domain of nature, but yet the external sciences are able to bring order out of chaos.").

4 Gold & Smith, *supra* note 2; Brian Angelo Lee & Henry E. Smith, *The Nature of Coasean Property*, 59 INT'L REV. L. & ECON. 145 (2012).

5 Henry E. Smith, *Property as the Law of Things*, 125 HARV. L. REV. 1691 (2012); Henry E. Smith, *Modularity and Morality in the Law of Torts*, 4 J. TORT L. (2011), www.bepress.com/jtl/vol4/iss2/art5.

14.2 FLAT AND STRUCTURED LEGAL INSTITUTIONS

Hohfeld's system of legal relations inspired a strand of Legal Realism, which was apparent to the Realists themselves.[6] We argue that this version of Hohfeld's system shares many strengths and weaknesses with later legal thought because of a deeper feature: it flattens out the legal system, which leads to the problem of scaling.

Hohfeld's system aimed to break down legal structures and doctrines into their atomic parts, and these parts were meant to offer a complete description of the legal relations availing between any persons. To take an analogy from logic, the system was supposed to be not only sound (getting accurate results whenever it operated), it was also meant to be complete (being able to capture any result of the legal system).[7] If so, the pairs right and duty, privilege and no-right, power and liability, and immunity and disability should be able in combination to capture any jural relations.[8] And every legal position should instantiate exactly one of each pair: on one reading, it would be contradictory for one person to have a right and a no-right or a duty and a privilege over the same subject matter (usually an activity). That is, there is a law of the excluded middle for jural relations.[9] In sum, a concept like ownership would consist of a cluster of such complete relations.

Something similar is true of Hohfeld's less famous, though also influential reconstruction or replacement of the concept of an *in rem* right with multital rights.[10] The term "*in rem*" derives from "against a thing," and Hohfeld was not alone in arguing that legal relations exist between persons, not between persons and things.[11] Property rights like the right to exclude from Blackacre avail against persons with respect to things. Hohfeld went a step further and argued that every legal relation is bilateral. For Hohfeld, a right against the world (*in rem*) is really

6 *See, e.g.*, JOHN R. COMMONS, LEGAL FOUNDATIONS OF CAPITALISM (1924); Max Radin, *A Restatement of Hohfeld*, 51 HARV. L. REV. 1156 (1937); Arthur L. Corbin, *Jural Relations and Their Classification*, 30 YALE L.J. 226 (1920). The use by Commons also presaged the use of the bundle of rights in law and economics, itself an offshoot of Realism.

7 *See, e.g.*, HERBERT B. ENDERTON, A MATHEMATICAL INTRODUCTION TO LOGIC 131–46 (2d ed. 2001); RAYMOND M. SMULLYAN, A BEGINNER'S GUIDE TO MATHEMATICAL LOGIC 4–6, 91–92, 109–10, 156–57 (2014).

8 Wesley N. Hohfeld, *Some Fundamental Legal Conceptions as Applied in Judicial Reasoning*, 23 YALE L.J. 16 (1913), reprinted in WESLEY N. HOHFELD, FUNDAMENTAL LEGAL CONCEPTIONS AS APPLIED IN JUDICIAL REASONING AND OTHER LEGAL ESSAYS 23–64 (Walter Wheeler Cook ed., 1923).

9 This is not to deny the possibility of conflicting duties within the Hohfeldian system. *See* Matthew H. Kramer, *Rights Without Trimmings*, *in* A DEBATE OVER RIGHTS 18–19 (Matthew H. Kramer et al. eds., 1998) (recognizing the possibility of conflicting legal duties). *See also* Chapter 11 (indicating that the logical connections among Hohfeldian relations do not address the question of conflicting duties).

10 Wesley N. Hohfeld, *Fundamental Legal Conceptions as Applied in Judicial Reasoning*, 26 YALE L.J. 710 (1917), reprinted in WESLEY N. HOHFELD, FUNDAMENTAL LEGAL CONCEPTIONS AS APPLIED IN JUDICIAL REASONING AND OTHER LEGAL ESSAYS 65–114 (Walter Wheeler Cook ed., 1923).

11 *Id.* at 720–35. Hohfeld quotes Holmes and others with approval on this point and criticizes instances of judges and authors speaking of rights against things; the Realists adopted this view later. This idea had also gained some currency in Germany. *See* MARIETTA AUER, DER PRIVATRECHTLICHE DISKURS DER MODERNE 98, 122 (2014); Paul Oertmann, *Der Dinglichkeitsbegriff*, 36 JHERINGS JAHRBÜCHER FÜR DIE DOGMATIK DES HEUTIGEN RÖMISCHEN UND DEUTSCHEN PRIVATRECHTS 415–67 (1892).

a collection of rights against every member in society. What makes a right "*in rem*" is that many similar rights between the holder and many others are grouped together. A "multital" right is one of an aggregation of similar unital rights (each corresponding to one duty holder). What we know as an *in personam* right Hohfeld analyzed as a unital right. It can stand alone or as one of a collection of a few similar rights, which he called "paucital."

Structure beyond the aggregation of primary legal relations is accommodated with some ambivalence. As has often been noted, powers are second order: they take legal relations as inputs and give other legal relations as outputs. So an offer confers a power on the offeree who by accepting can create a duty in the offeror (and a right in herself against the offeror). The offeror makes himself liable to an acceptance that creates duties and rights. Likewise, ownership of land typically includes the power to sell but not the power to abandon.[12]

Beyond this, the clusters of Hohfeldian legal relations that correspond to traditional legal concepts exhibit relatively little structure. The scheme is about legal results. To use an analogy from the philosophy of language, Hohfeld's scheme is extensional.[13] In an extensional approach to language, meaning is identified with the denoted object: the word "apple" denotes the set of apples. There are well-known problems with such approaches: "Morning Star" and "Evening Star" can both refer to the planet Venus, but "John believes the Morning Star to be Venus" is not true under the same circumstances as "John believes the Evening Star to be Venus."[14] To capture this and similar phenomena, we need intensions: two words can denote the same thing but by different routes; the intension is a function from words to things. Thus, "Morning Star" and "Evening Star" can both denote Venus extensionally but differ in how they get there intensionally. In some contexts, there is also a difference in cognitive ease. "FDR" and "32nd President of the United States" are extensionally equivalent but intensionally different, and "32nd President of the United States" is much more difficult to process than "FDR."

Something similar is true of legal relations. Legal Realists, drawing inspiration from Hohfeld, did not disavow concepts, but they preferred narrow, shallow concepts that would be as close to the particulars of reality as possible.[15] (More moderate Realists like Llewellyn espoused a mild version of this position.) Narrow, shallow

[12] In the Hohfeldian framework the transferor extinguishes a set of legal relations (such as his rights and privileges and powers) and creates new ones in the transferee. Hohfeld, *supra* note 10, at 746. This does not capture the transfer of a right that persists in new hands: the transferee has the same right the transferor had. *See* James Penner, *On the Very Idea of Transmissible Rights*, *in* PHILOSOPHICAL FOUNDATIONS OF PROPERTY LAW 244–71 (James Penner & Henry E. Smith eds., 2014).

[13] Henry E. Smith, *Emergent Property*, *in* PHILOSOPHICAL FOUNDATIONS OF PROPERTY LAW 320–38 (James Penner & Henry E. Smith eds., 2014).

[14] *See* Gottlob Frege, *On* Sinn *and* Bedeutung *(1892)*, *in* THE FREGE READER 151, 156 (Michael Beaney ed., 1997).

[15] *See* Felix S. Cohen, *Transcendental Nonsense and the Functional Approach*, 35 COLUM. L. REV. 809, 820 (1935) ("In every field of law we should find peculiar concepts which are not defined either in terms of empirical fact or in terms of ethics but which are used to answer empirical and ethical

concepts are closer to extensions, and if close enough in the relevant ways, they forgo the advantages that a more "intensional" approach can bring with it. Take ownership again. If ownership is partly specified as a right to exclude others from a thing, then this protects many privileges of use (residential, agricultural, recreational, etc.).[16] Note that most of the time the privileges need not be enumerated. A privilege is "real," but it needs less delineation than do rights. And if protected, privileges unlike rights need not be spelled out.

Moreover, it is a Realist trope that regarding state intervention as different from nonintervention is a logical error and a cover for libertarianism or crypto-political formalism.[17] In a fashion reminiscent of Coase, every dispute is potentially symmetric.[18] This is true in some sense, but not all baselines are equally costly to delineate. We could give people rights to be free from competition, rights to bargain collectively, rights to roam over land and particularized rights to use property they need, and people can argue about whether the benefits of these or any policy exceed the costs. The rule-by-rule analysis characteristic of Realism and its offshoot law and economics is ill-suited to ask about systemic benefits and costs: how does this proposed change interact with other rights and legal relations involving the owner?

In an inclusive functionalism, one would put the system back in the picture.[19] Elsewhere we have argued that taking system effects seriously causes external-functional theories to grow closer to internal-interpretive theories based on morally grounded rights.[20] For legal relations, this systemic perspective highlights how not every possible policy inspired result is equally costly or fits equally easily into the larger picture. Take fencing in and fencing out. The law – and even more so the norms of cattle raising areas – tends towards fencing in more than a simple comparison of the value of cattle and crops would suggest.[21] Fencing in fits into norms of possession better and is therefore easier to communicate than fencing out. More

questions alike, and thus bar the way to intelligent investigation of social fact and social policy."); Karl N. Llewellyn, *Some Realism About Realism – Responding to Dean Pound*, 44 HARV. L. REV. 1222, 1223 (1931) ("[Those involved in the new movement] want law to deal, they themselves want to deal, with things, with people, with tangibles, with *definite* tangibles, and *observable* relations between definite tangibles – not with words alone; when law deals with words, they want the words to represent tangibles which can be got at beneath the words, and observable relations between those tangibles."); Corbin, *supra* note 6, at 227 n.2 (arguing that recognizing that jural relations are ultimately about individuals "sends to the scrap heap a deal of juristic nonsense about corporate 'entities' and rights of 'the state' and 'social interests' and other cherished fictions – cherished among ourselves as well as among our quondam friends in Prussia").

16 *See* Simon Douglas & Ben McFarlane, *Defining Property Rights*, *in* PHILOSOPHICAL FOUNDATIONS OF PROPERTY LAW 219 (James Penner & Henry E. Smith eds., 2014).

17 *See, e.g.*, Cohen, *supra* note 15; Corbin, *supra* note 6; Thomas C. Grey, *Langdell's Orthodoxy*, 45 U. PITT. L. REV. 1, 9 (1983); MORTON WHITE, SOCIAL THOUGHT IN AMERICA: THE REVOLT AGAINST FORMALISM 12–13 (1957) (1947).

18 R. H. Coase, *The Problem of Social Cost*, 3 J.L. & ECON. 1, 2–15 (1960); Thomas W. Merrill & Henry E. Smith, *What Happened to Property in Law and Economics?* 111 YALE L.J. 357, 391–94 (2001).

19 Gold & Smith, *supra* note 2.

20 *Id.*

21 Merrill & Smith, *supra* note 18, at 388–91.

generally, considerations of complexity and information cost will tend to increase the attractiveness of private law rules that track everyday morality, basic tort law being a systematic example.[22]

On a larger scale, one need not be a libertarian to appreciate that government action and inaction are not the same in all important respects. The question can be framed as what to make the default: universal liberty displaced by other legal relations, or some other default, or no default at all. These may be extensionally equivalent in a static sense, but otherwise they are quite different. According to a modern version of an old (English) joke:

> The jocular saying is that, in England, "everything which is not forbidden is allowed," while, in Germany, the opposite applies, so "everything which is not allowed is forbidden." This may be extended to France – "everything is allowed even if it is forbidden."[23]

One could in theory achieve the same "result" by allowing everything and forbidding some things or forbidding everything but allowing some things. Even putting aside the implications about political liberty, delineation costs are quite different under different regimes of legal relations. In some contexts, one would choose one or the other depending on whether more things – and new things – are to be treated as allowed or forbidden. So delineation cost may correlate with the general political tenor of the system.

On a smaller scale, something similar is true of *in rem* rights. Analyzing an *in rem* right as a collection of unital rights is to treat *in rem* as merely a scaled up version of the *in personam*. This implies that the difference is quantitative and not qualitative. Shortly after Hohfeld proposed his analysis of *in rem*, Albert Kocourek argued that it was indefiniteness rather than numerosity that captures *in rem*-ness.[24] He preferred to define an "*in rem*" right as a right whose investitive facts (those that give rise to the right) do not serve to directly identify the duty bearer. This is like the "indefiniteness" favored by Austin, who claimed about property that "indefiniteness is of the very essence of the right; and implies that the right . . . cannot be determined by exact and positive circumscription."[25] For Kocourek the indefiniteness of *in rem* is more like "not directly specified." Kocourek gave an example of a landowner A who gives each individual in society a license to come onto his property except for B, who remains under a duty to keep off.[26] According to Kocourek, B was still under an *in*

[22] Gold & Smith, *supra* note 2; Smith, *Modularity*, *supra* note 5.

[23] https://en.wikipedia.org/wiki/Everything_which_is_not_forbidden_is_allowed. In a similar vein of English humor is *Rex* v. *Haddock*, *"Is It a Free Country?," in* A. P. Herbert, Uncommon Law 24, 28 (1935) (in case of defendant having jumped off a bridge during a regatta "for fun," appellate judge, struggling to find an offense, announces that "[i]t cannot be too clearly understood that this is *not* a free country, and it will be an evil day for the legal profession when it is . . . *Prima facie* all actions are illegal").

[24] Albert Kocourek, *Rights in Rem*, 68 U. Pa. L. Rev. 322, 322 (1920).

[25] 2 J. Austin, Lectures on Jurisprudence 827 (4th ed. 1873).

[26] Kocourek, *supra* note 23, at 335.

rem duty even though it is (now) single, and so would presumably be unital on Hohfeld's scheme. Pre-realists like Corbin had a hard time seeing this: surely A knows who B is.[27] Yet Kocourek's thought experiment shows how Hohfeldian multital rights are not equivalent to *in rem* rights in an "intensional" sense.[28] Correspondingly, the two methods are not equivalent in terms of delineation cost. Setting up a right wholesale (against the world) communicated through the thing (the *res*) is highly economical compared to spelling out extensionally equivalent unital rights one by one. In Kocourek's fanciful example one would be doing something on that order if one gave licenses individually to everyone except B.

Where we see indefiniteness in property rights, this is often a sign of a shortcut in delineation.[29] This goes not only for *in rem* duty bearers but also the indefinite reservoir of non-specified privileges protected by a right. And we will see that, in general, lack of specification in rights is a way of cutting costs in a dynamic sense as well: delineation of rights is often not undertaken until it is necessary.

Returning to *in rem* rights, the relation between numerosity and indefiniteness also points to the importance of information costs. One can have rights (or other legal relations) that are numerous and definite (mass contracts) and few and indefinite (successors in interest).[30] Numerosity and indefiniteness tend to go together because, pairing them typically economizes on information cost: one can reach a large number by specifying relations in a manner that is indefinite ("all the world" being the most extreme example) and relatively standardized.[31] It appears that in the intermediate cases – where duty bearers are numerous but definite or few but indefinite – we get an intermediate level of standardization between the relatively free customizability of contract and the *numerus clausus* of *in rem* rights in property.[32]

We said that privileges need not be spelled out "most of the time," because when under a spotlight, owners sometimes do have more than a privilege of use. The law does not set out in advance all the possible rights. Nor is it common to confuse rights

[27] Corbin, *supra* note 6, at 226, 232 n.4.

[28] Indeed, for Kocourek these rights come in different flavors: they are qualitatively distinct. When a right's investitive facts directly identify the party who owes the correlative duty, the right is "polarized." When the duty bearer is not so identified, the right is "unpolarized." *See* Albert Kocourek, *Polarized and Unpolarized Legal Relations*, 9 Ky. L. Rev. 131, 131 (1921). Interestingly, he also recognized that this intensional difference reflects practical legal needs. *See id.* at 137.

[29] On Austinian indefiniteness, see *supra* note 25 and accompanying text.

[30] Thomas W. Merrill & Henry E. Smith, *The Property/Contract Interface*, 101 Colum. L. Rev. 773, 780–89 (2001).

[31] In a fit of neo-Hohfeldian terminology-mongering, Merrill and Smith designate as "compound-paucital" those rights with numerous definite duty bearers and "quasi-multital" those with few indefinite duty bearers. *Id.* at 786. The *numerus clausus* (closed number) of *in rem* rights fits in here as an example of standardizing rights when duty holders are both numerous and indefinite. Thomas W. Merrill & Henry E. Smith, *Optimal Standardization in the Law of Property: The* Numerus Clausus *Principle*, 110 Yale L.J. 1 (2000).

[32] Merrill & Smith, *supra* note 30, at 809–51.

with privileges or to derive the former from the latter, despite constant claims from Realists and their successors. Instead, the traditional method was to set out privileges-plus or presumptive rights.[33] A privilege-plus is the jural aggregate of a privilege combined with a right of noninterference. A presumptive right is a right that the law assumes as a starting point for legal analysis. This approach is central to property, as one of us has written:

> By defining a thing and using trespass as a basic mode of protection, many of the protected privileges of use can remain implicit. The very ambiguity that Hohfeld decried in using the term "right" to cover both true claims and privileges (liberties) may be seen as a byproduct of costly delineation. Property involves innumerable privileges of use; one can always specify the use more narrowly, as in use for parking cars, use for parking cars on Mondays, use for parking cars on Mondays between 2 and 3 p.m., use for parking Chevrolets on Mondays between 2 and 3 p.m., etc. But generally, leaving the use privileges implicit is sufficient. When a resource conflict becomes severe enough, the law will pick out a use and may regard that use as a subject of a right rather than a privilege. This tendency is most explicit in the case of easements, but it also occurs with nuisance. The "Hohfeldian" intensions – functions from states of the world to packages of entitlements – are usually more elaborate than the delineation of actual property interests. Relatedly, consider the residual claim: it too could be formed synthetically out of all the small pieces or sticks. Or we can define it as the right to an asset after all the other more specific claims have been carved out. Same extension, different intensions.[34]

Nuisance is a prime example. Realists were fond of mocking the vacuousness of the maxim *sic utere tuo ut alienum non laedas* as empty and question-begging: how can we know what is an injury without specifying what rights one has against injury?[35] The only way to do that, then, is to engage in honest policy analysis. This is mistaken. One can disagree with traditional nuisance law, but it rested on an analysis in which each of two landowners had presumptive rights to use that would then be reconciled when they came into conflict. Rules of thumb like the locality rule (and secondarily malice, hardship, and the like) would be used in this process, subject to a constraint that the packages of rights should be symmetric. In the natural rights tradition, revived in legal theory among Lockeans and Kantians, one would look for that structure of interlocking rights that would symmetrically maximize the freedom of the two parties.[36] Thus, making a certain level of noise benefits both parties, but an argument that one's idiosyncratic use is especially meritorious would not entitle one to impose

33 We focus primarily on presumptive rights in the discussion below. For helpful discussion of privileges-plus, see Chapter 11.

34 Henry E. Smith, *On the Economy of Concepts in Property*, 160 U. Pa. L. Rev. 2097, 2104 (2012).

35 Henry E. Smith, *Fusing the Equitable Function in Private Law*, *in* Private Law in the 21st Century 173, 190–91 (Kit Barker et al. eds., 2017).

36 *See, e.g.*, Eric R. Claeys, *Jefferson Meets Coase: Land-Use Torts, Law and Economics, and Natural Property Rights*, 85 Notre Dame L. Rev. 1379 (2009); Richard A. Epstein, *Nuisance Law: Corrective Justice and Its Utilitarian Constraints*, 8 J. Legal Stud. 49 (1979); J. E. Penner, *Nuisance and the*

a level of noise on a neighbor that would preclude normal expected use. Live-and-let-live for low-level disturbances is easy. Someone with a highly valuable use who tells the neighbors to put up with it based on a cost-benefit criterion might satisfy some policy-oriented balancing tests, but would flunk the supposedly vacuous traditional analysis.[37]

As we will touch on later, the traditional analysis in nuisance was grounded until the late nineteenth century in natural rights. As that grounding found fewer adherents, the structures could have been given a new grounding in something else, and they probably were treated as resting on an informal consequentialism. Hence the apparent woodenness of pre-Realist formalism that Hohfeld reacted against.

The traditional approach was not a process of deduction, nor was it some kind of circular exercise or logical error, as Hohfeld and the Realists were fond of claiming. Instead pre-Realist law was struggling with the breakdown in this older system, making it seem arbitrary. Natural rights thinking persisted without the deeper commitment to natural rights. Compounding the problem was the major event of the late nineteenth and early twentieth centuries: the fusion (or merger) of law and equity. The equitable structure of second-order reconciliation between conflicting rights could have been given a new foundation (in utilitarianism or Kantianism or something else), but the kind of super-fusion prevalent in the United States resulted, as we will see, in second-order equity being flattened into the first-order law.[38]

We do not have the space or the evidence to trace out the extent to which Hohfeld's orientation towards flattening the law caused later reductionism in American legal theory or was instead symptomatic of a larger trend in that direction. Perhaps it is some of both. We return to this bigger picture at the end of the chapter.

14.3 THE PROBLEM OF DELINEATION

The treatment of legal relations as atomistic presents only part of the picture we are interested in. There is a further concern: a collection of results is not the same as the system that produces them. Listing legal results would be far costlier than a legal theory employing more abstract concepts.[39] Along this spectrum Hohfeld's system as it stood in 1919 and the use made of it by the Realists are too close to being list-like.

Character of the Neighbourhood, 5 J. ENVTL. L. 1 (1993); Arthur Ripstein, *Tort Law in a Liberal State*, 1 J. TORT L. 26–28 (2007).

37 Restatement (Second) of Torts §§ 822, 826 (1965).

38 *See* Section 14.4.2; Smith, *supra* note 34. *See also* John C. P. Goldberg & Henry E. Smith, *Wrongful Fusion: Equity and Tort*, *in* EQUITY AND LAW: FUSION AND FISSION 309 (John C. P. Goldberg et al. eds., 2019).

39 One drawback to an approach that lists legal results is that it may overlook the manner in which a concept's usage in one legal setting has bearing on that concept's usage in another legal setting. For helpful discussion of this interconnectedness, see Jeremy Waldron, *"Transcendental Nonsense" and System in the Law*, 100 COLUM. L. REV. 16 (2000). As Waldron indicates, a range of legal terms of art (including "corporation," "legal personality," "jurisdiction," and "locus standi") alert us to these systemic relations. *See id.* at 23. *See also* Paul B. Miller & Andrew S. Gold, *The Corporation as*

Start with aggregates of legal relations. Are legal relations collections of Hohfeldian atoms? One could regard Hohfeld's system as a "complete" one in the sense that it specifies maximally. For every subject matter between every pair of actors it specifies the legal relations in terms of the responsiveness of the legal system, while assuming that action counts as much as inaction. This was a big plus for the Realists who wanted the set of legal relations to be as malleable as possible, and found it convenient to act as if baselines were completely arbitrary.[40]

There are several shortcuts over the enumeration of the "complete" set of legal relations. First, we can protect a wide range of largely unspecified privileges with one right. The right to exclude from land and rights of bodily integrity protect many activities otherwise covered by what Hohfeld would call privileges or liberties. As we will see, these privileges are sometimes singled out and strengthened, but economies of delineation are often achieved by leaving them implicit.

Second, many commentators have objected that "no-rights" in general and privileges in many contexts are not legal relations at all.[41] On this view, the law is silent on many questions, and it is otiose or misleading to say that it affords an actor a "no-right." And in many situations an actor may be said to be exercising a background privilege not addressed by law. Recall the witticism about legal systems above. To Hohfeld arguably, and the Realists much more clearly, the idea that a no-right is on an equal footing with a right was welcome. Likewise, the Realists ran with the notion that non-intervention leading to a privilege is just as much a policy decision as positing a duty: for the Realists, removing traditional baselines and preventing the privileging (!) of traditional results was an important step towards law reform.[42] At the least it was required for honesty and transparency in judging. This complete and pervasive view of law, that it is omnipresent and regulative of all of social reality, was also designed to remove what was seen as a thumb on the scale for classical liberalism.

Again, we need to draw a distinction between legal relations and the means by which they are achieved. It may well be that in some logical sense or in terms of legally relevant results we can say there are "no-rights." And sometimes the law even involves effort at delineating a privilege (as in licenses). Nevertheless, it is no accident that what Hohfeld would call no-rights and privileges reflect little or no

a Category in Private Law, *in* RESEARCH HANDBOOK ON PRIVATE LAW THEORIES 429 (Hanoch Dagan & Benjamin Zipursky eds., 2020) (discussing the corporation as a legal person).

40 Thomas C. Grey, *The Disintegration of Property*, *in* NOMOS XXII: PROPERTY 69, 81 (J. Roland Pennock & John W. Chapman eds., 1980).

41 Albert Kocourek, *The Hohfeld System of Fundamental Legal Concepts*, 15 ILL. L. REV. 24, 34–35 (1920); Albert Kocourek, *Non-Legal-Content Relations*, 4 ILL. L.Q. 233 (1921); Roscoe Pound, *Fifty Years of Jurisprudence*, 50 HARV. L. REV. 557, 573–74 (1937). Agreeing with Hohfeld are Walter Wheeler Cook, *The Associated Press Case*, 28 YALE L.J. 387, 391 (1919); George W. Goble, *Affirmative and Negative Legal Relations*, 4 ILL. L.Q. 94 (1921).

42 *See, e.g.*, Joseph William Singer, *The Legal Rights Debate in Analytical Jurisprudence from Bentham to Hohfeld*, 1982 WIS. L. REV. 975 (1982); Cass R. Sunstein, *Lochner's Legacy*, 87 COLUM. L. REV. 873 (1987).

effort at legal delineation. In a sense that mattered to Hohfeld, privileges and no-rights are as "real" as other legal relations and can be the result of an adjudication. This leaves out how easy it is to specify them in a liberal legal order. Just as in most situations there being a fire is more surprising than there being no fire leads us to make siren-sounding or light-on the signal for fire and siren-off or light-off the signal for no fire, it is no accident that privileges, no-rights and the like are often the "less delineated" case.[43]

A greater awareness of how legal systems operate calls into question whether each Hohfeldian incident really is equal in the relevant sense. Lon Fuller clearly recognized this in his discussion of legal fictions. As Fuller noted, some fictions, which he terms "neglective fictions," involve simplification of the phenomena at issue.[44] In these contexts, it is necessary to leave certain details out in order to efficiently work towards a given end. Thus, as Fuller explained: "In a field where conduct is determined by the interplay of a large number of factors, artificial abstraction is necessary. Progress cannot be made without the conscious disregard of minor factors."[45] Other simplifying fictions involve the use of classifications, methods for organizing thought.[46] Whether such fictions are worthwhile for legal purposes is then dependent on how they are used.

Simplifying fictions are not a problem in the right context, if used with an awareness of their limits. They may, however, lead us astray when misapplied. In Fuller's view, the initial adoption of the Hohfeldian system illustrates how such fictions can be counterproductive. As Fuller recognized:

> When the Hohfeldian system was first announced, it seemed to throw so much light on hitherto darkened corners of legal analysis, it offered so much hope for a rational and clear expression of legal relations, that we felt we had at last discovered the atomic system which lay at the heart of legal thought.[47]

The tendency, unfortunately, was to oversimplify how this atomic system fit together in practice – and this, for Fuller, is where a fiction entered the picture.

It is one thing to recognize the various Hohfeldian incidents as relevant legal concepts, and another thing to assume that they are all equal in stature. The

43 In other words, we pick the costlier-to-provide legal relation where Shannon entropy is higher and the cheaper signal (sometimes doing almost nothing) for where it is lower. C. E. Shannon, *A Mathematical Theory of Communication (Parts 1 & 2)*, 27 BELL SYS. TECH. J. 379 (1948); 27 BELL SYS. TECH. J. 623 (1948), reprinted as CLAUDE E. SHANNON & WARREN WEAVER, THE MATHEMATICAL THEORY OF COMMUNICATION (1949). *See also* Chapter 11.

44 *See* FULLER, *supra* note 3, at 107.

45 *See id.* at 106–07. *See also* JOHN DEWEY, THE QUEST FOR CERTAINTY 217 (1929) ("Artificial simplification or abstraction is a necessary precondition of securing ability to deal with affairs which are complex, in which there are many more variables and where strict isolation destroys the special characteristics of the subject matter.").

46 *See* FULLER, *supra* note 3, at 108–12.

47 *Id.* at 112.

Hohfeldian system was often adopted with the latter assumption firmly in place.[48] Thus, Fuller argued:

> It was assumed that the whole set of Hohfeldian relations must form a geometric figure, and that much knowledge could be gained merely by manipulating the table, by arranging the elements into "opposites," "correlatives," etc. It was some time before we realized that the four pillars of this system are, unfortunately for symmetry, of rather unequal height and importance, and that very little is to be gained through a mere manipulation of the tables of "jural relations."[49]

Without detracting from Hohfeld's system as an exercise in logic, the relations carry different practical import – in a fashion obscured by Hohfeld's Realist followers. For example, the "privilege-no right" relationship is not nearly as significant, in terms of the delineated system, as the "right-duty" relationship, and it is a fiction to assume otherwise.[50] A failure to recognize existing defaults among rights, privileges, powers, and immunities (and their correlatives) can produce a much more complex system.

Now consider *in rem* rights again. As we have seen, Kocourek objected to the Hohfeldian reduction of *in rem* rights to a collection of multital rights, on grounds similar to those involved in the basic legal relations. If anything, the contrast between deep and shallow concepts is clearer in the case of *in rem*-ness. Whether or not one accepts Kocourek's alternative to Hohfeld, it is worth pointing out the role that things play in *in rem* rights – and it is not purely etymological ("*res*" being Latin for "thing"). One can agree with Hohfeld that a legal relation always holds between persons, without downplaying the importance of things to the delineation of property rights. An *in rem* right can be easily broadcast to a large and indefinite set of duty bearers precisely because it is communicated through the thing.[51] In James Penner's famous parking lot example, the duty bearers need not know anything about the owners of the cars in order to know and comply with the duties to those owners with respect to the cars.[52] All they have to do is keep off the cars. Moreover, defining rights in terms of things allows for economizing on delineation costs along other dimensions: the right to exclude (trespass) is keyed to the thing, residual claims are defined in terms of the part of the thing remaining after specific claims have been delineated and so on.[53] None of this economy in delineation is captured by merely enumerating the legal relations that make up fee simple ownership of land, especially if conceived as a formless bundle.

48 Fuller contended this pattern of thought is common to classifications. *See* FULLER, *supra* note 3, at 112 ("[W]e tend to suppose that the members of a class are of equal importance, and that the interrelations between them must form a balanced, geometric pattern.").

49 *Id.*

50 *See* FULLER, *supra* note 3, at n.37 (discussing how "[t]he 'right-duty' pillar is a much more substantial and imposing monument than the 'privilege-no-right' pillar."). *See supra* note 39 and accompanying text.

51 J. E. PENNER, THE IDEA OF PROPERTY IN LAW 75 (1997); Smith, *Law of Things*, *supra* note 5, at 1702–08.

52 PENNER, *supra* note 51, at 75–76.

53 Smith, *Law of Things*, *supra* note 5, at 1710; Smith, *supra* note 34, at 2104.

Finally, it is easy to confuse a concern about delineation with empty formalism. Not all formalism is empty. If formalism is the (relative) invariance to context, it is a matter of degree.[54] Everyday language is replete with pronouns and indirect expressions leaving much information implied. Formal speech tends to spell things out, and artificial languages (computer languages, the language of first-order logic) are even less context-dependent. In the law, the issue is not whether or not to be formal but when and how much. The Hohfeldian scheme tends to suppress this question. On the one hand, it can be regarded as a species of conceptualism, and concepts, even very concrete ones, are somewhat invariant to context. The beauty of Hohfeld's system is that in vastly different contexts and at very different levels of grain (a privilege of agricultural use versus a privilege of growing beans in May), the relations involved will fall into the four pairs. On the other hand, the Hohfeldian scheme is maximally sensitive to context: as we have seen it can be interpreted as specifying the entire jural context even when it seems irrelevant and even when to some it does not seem jural or legal at all.

14.4 SCALING UP AND EMERGENT PROPERTIES OF THE LEGAL SYSTEM

Whether it was fully intended by Hohfeld or used that way by his later fans, the Hohfeld system tends to flatten the law and needs something more in order to be able to scale up properly. That is, we must ask how local structures combine and interact, and whether they produce desirable effects at the level of the larger system. If not, we need to ask what more is needed for proper scaling up. Interestingly and not entirely coincidentally, the aspects of the system related to the scaling up problem point back towards underappreciated aspects of traditional legal doctrine and reasoning.

14.4.1 *Modular Structures*

Managing complexity often involves accommodating it through modular structures. If a set of interactions can be partitioned such that interaction is intense within modules and less intense across interfaces, a system can achieve the benefits of complexity without many of the costs.[55] Cars are modular systems and are easier to design, make, service, and use because the component subsystems interact in stylized ways – for example the fuel injection and the brakes. Such systems are

54 *See* Francis Heylighen, *Advantages and Limitations of Formal Expression*, 4 FOUND. SCI. 25, 27, 49–53 (1999) (defining formalism in language); Henry E. Smith, *The Language of Property: Form, Context, and Audience*, 55 STAN. L. REV. 1105, 1112–13, 1135–36 (2003) (discussing "differential formalism," the concept that formalism is a matter of degree).

55 *See, e.g.*, 1 CARLISS Y. BALDWIN & KIM B. CLARK, DESIGN RULES: THE POWER OF MODULARITY 58–59, 236–37, 257 (2000); HERBERT A. SIMON, THE SCIENCES OF THE ARTIFICIAL 210 (2d ed. 1981).

more robust,[56] easier to understand, and afford a range of flexibility in evolution and innovation.

In private law, many of the basic structures of the law are simple at the local level and track very local and informationally undemanding kinds of morality. Interpretive theories make much of the bilateral quality of corrective justice on the one hand and the structure of tort law on the other.[57] Doctrines like foreseeability and the economic loss rule make the decision-making problem facing individual actors simpler than a more all-things-considered standard.[58] And property keys off things which themselves lend a modular structure to the law: information is partially hidden at the boundary of the legal thing.[59]

At the same time, these structures generalize and scale up in part because of their simplicity. As we argue elsewhere, there is implicit in interpretive theories a criterion of simplicity.[60] Such theories seek to explain private law doctrine in light of its morality, coherence, and transparency – among other aspects – with the aim of capturing legal concepts from the perspective of legal actors. In doing so, such theories offer insights into legal concepts that functional theorists can use. The moral concepts that interpretive theories pick up on are characteristically simple, accessible, and well-suited for scaling up. These features both make structures possible for participants to use and allow the pieces of the system to generalize and fit together.[61]

From a functional point of view, local simplicity through modularity matters in order to ensure that models scale up properly. Regarding societal interaction as the summing up of pairwise interactions with associated (dis)utility ignores the possibility that properties will emerge in the aggregate.[62] We need an inclusive functionalism that also captures functional aspects of the law that work more systemically.[63] It requires more than the Hohfeldian atoms. We turn now to legal devices targeted at this problem of scaling up.

14.4.2 *Second-Order Adjustments*

Scaling up well does not happen automatically. In the first place, people are bound to disagree as to how well local forms of morality scale up, without more, to the level of society. Libertarians are likely to be optimistic that liability for force and fraud on

56 Or even antifragile, meaning that they become stronger in response to stress. *See* Nassim Nicholas Taleb, Antifragile: Things That Gain from Disorder (2012).

57 *See, e.g.*, Jules Coleman, The Practice of Principle 13–24 (2001) (discussing tort law's bilateralism); Ernest J. Weinrib, The Idea of Private Law 1–55 (1995) (same).

58 Smith, *Law of Torts*, *supra* note 5.

59 Smith, *Law of Things*, *supra* note 5, at 1702–08.

60 Gold & Smith, *supra* note 2.

61 *Id.*

62 *Id.* at 494–96.

63 *Id.* at 494–505.

the individual level will be close to the last word as we scale up.[64] Others will want to see adjustment for distributive justice introduced at the society level, and some will see these values as extending all the way to the local level.[65] And the libertarian view that the public is the aggregate of the private does not capture how public structures and doctrines may not be reducible to the sum of what is true of individuals.[66] Consider navigation servitudes: do they have content beyond what would be allowable individually for a large group of individuals?[67] Most would say so.

There is another sense in which we need something more than autopilot as we scale up in private law from the micro to the macro. There is no guarantee that structures are stable as we scale up, and they may require reconciliation for other reasons. Here is where equity comes in.

The problem is again a problem of the limits of flat approaches. The Hohfeldian framework does allow for second-order law in providing for powers.[68] A person with a power can change one legal relation into another. The power operates at a meta-level. With a broadening of focus, we could say that courts and legislatures exercise powers. Allowing for the possibility of such legal powers is different from recognizing when they are in operation.

One power that Hohfeld's own analysis flattens is the equity power. One of us has argued that the equitable function, loosely associated historically with equity courts, is meta-law: it is law about law.[69] Equity intervenes when law fails on account of its

64 For a frank and thoughtful take on this from a libertarian point of view, see David Friedman, *A Positive Account of Property Rights*, 11 SOC. PHIL. & POL'Y 1 (1994).

65 Realist skepticism about private law and the public-private distinction is usually accompanied by a view that all law is public law. *See, e.g.*, Leon Green, *Tort Law Public Law in Disguise*, 38 TEX. L. REV. 1 (1959).

66 There is a concern here with the fallacy of composition. *See* JON ELSTER, LOGIC AND SOCIETY 97–106 (1978) (discussing such fallacies in social science settings). Under this fallacy, one assumes that a whole has the features of its parts.

67 Compare Richard A. Epstein, *Rediscovering The Classical Liberal Constitution: A Reply To Professor Hovenkamp*, 101 IOWA L. REV. 55, 88 (2015) ("The moment public law is untethered from private law, it becomes a wild card in the hands of the judges that wipes aside everything that stands in its path, which is how the Supreme Court behaved when it insisted that the 'paramount' navigation servitude under the Commerce Clause swept everything aside.") and Richard A. Epstein, *Playing by Different Rules? Property Rights in Land and Water, in* PROPERTY IN LAND AND OTHER RESOURCES 317, 345–47 (Daniel H. Cole & Elinor Ostrom eds., 2012) with Henry E. Smith, *Commentary, in* PROPERTY IN LAND AND OTHER RESOURCES 317, 345–47 (Daniel H. Cole & Elinor Ostrom eds., 2012) ("It is true that in some sense, the public is the composite of individuals, but to argue that public rights should share the qualities of private rights is to commit the fallacy of composition. More empirically, the types of network effects associated with some types of public property, including the navigation servitude discussed in Epstein's chapter, may call for devices that are not simply the sum of private easements."); *id.* at 364 ("[S]ome problems are so inherently public that the hypothetical aggregation of private rights and duties does not fully explain or justify the public aspect of property law. The public is not just quantitatively but sometimes also qualitatively different from the private.").

68 Hohfeld, *supra* note 8, at 55. *See also* Chapter 13.

69 Henry E. Smith, *Equity as Meta-Law*, 130 YALE L.J. 1050 (2021); Henry E. Smith, *The Equitable Dimension of Contract*, 45 SUFFOLK L. REV. 897, 906 (2012).

generality, as in Aristotle's formulation,[70] and this is partly a matter of scaling up. Why does law fail and when does it call for a higher-order solution? Problems that are variable and uncertain – including opportunism, conflicting rights, and dense interactions between large numbers of parties – can call for the cost and uncertainty of setting up and running a higher-order component of the law, when it solves those problems sufficiently better than more elaborate first-order law.

Consider the problem of opportunism. Opportunism can cause law to fail to generalize – to scale up – properly. One way that law achieves simplicity is to use average information. Thus, liability rules calling for damages could be set at average harm, and in expectation actors would have correct incentives (putting risk aversion aside). In general, law and economics depends greatly on the idea that damages are correct in expectation – that the average of the harm across states of the world, i.e., its expected value – is equal to the expected value of liability, without the need for harm and liability to match up exactly in all states of the world.[71] On this approach, if liability is equal to expected harm, then ex ante, when actors are making decisions, they will face a correct set of incentives. The problem is that actors can manipulate such a system – which is why we see so many qualifications of it. Thus, imagine that all property were indeed protected by an average-harm liability rule rather than property rules that would force potential takers to get owners' consent. The takers would seek out property that is likely to be undervalued by the official doing the valuation, so the background domain over which the average is taken would change.[72] One way to counter this is to make use of injunctions, and to police behavior by both sides using equitable doctrines like good faith, disproportionate hardship, and unclean hands.

One function of equity is to counter opportunism.[73] And opportunism, going traditionally under the label "constructive fraud," often calls for second-order intervention. Because the opportunist is taking a holistic view of the legal system and finding its weak point, it may be easier to intervene selectively into the law rather than trying to fortify the law from within. This allows the law and equity to specialize: law is general and relatively simple, and equity is targeted and relatively complex with contextual detail.

Hohfeld's analysis of equity is famously bottom-line oriented. To Hohfeld, law and equity conflict because in many situations the law without equity would give one result and the law with equity would give another.[74] This is salient in trusts where it is often said that there is a legal owner and an

70 Aristotle, The Nicomachean Ethics 133 (J. L. Ackrill & J. O. Urmson eds., trans. David Ross, rev. ed., 1980).

71 Daniel R. Ortiz, *Neoactuarialism: Comment on Kaplow (1)*, 23 J. Legal Stud. 403, 403–06 (1994).

72 Henry E. Smith, *Property and Property Rules*, 79 N.Y.U. L. Rev. 1719, 1774–85 (2004).

73 Smith, *supra* note 34; Smith, *Equity as Meta-Law*, *supra* note 69.

74 Wesley N. Hohfeld, *The Relations Between Equity and Law*, 11 Mich. L. Rev. 537, 557 (1913) ("Since, in every sovereign state, there must, in the last analysis, be but a single system of *genuine law*, since the various rules and principles of that system must be consistent with one another, and since accordingly,

equitable owner.[75] Equity leads to different results than the law (legal versus equitable estates). Often contrasted with Hohfeld is Maitland who thought that equity may not have had any theme but it did not contradict the law; it supplemented the law and presupposed it.[76] In this sense Maitland saw equity as second order, although he did not put it this way and did not see equity as serving a definable function. If equity is aimed at problems like opportunism, Hohfeld is right if one looks only at results, but Maitland is correct that the two do not conflict at the same level: they inhabit different levels. It is this structure that allows the law to scale up without the distortions of the opportunists or the elaborate first-order measures that might be needed to defeat them.

14.4.3 *Dynamic Potential*

Combining modularity and the second-order gives new perspective on some old Hohfeldian analysis. The Hohfeldian system has to accommodate dynamic aspects and once it is so adjusted, certain Hohfeldian problems tend to dissolve.

The history of air rights illustrates the benefits of dynamic specification of rights. The traditional *ad coelum* principle provided that landowners owned to the heavens above and the depths below.[77] This is a simple and low-cost delineation method for defining the legal thing one can own. With the advent of airplane overflights, there was much discussion of what to do.[78] Taken literally, the *ad coelum* principle would allow surface landowners to obtain damages and sometimes even injunctions (for repeated and threatened flights) against operators of airplanes no matter how high they flew. With airplanes this was clearly undesirable and negotiations would be unfeasible in many cases, but the fear was that declaring a navigation servitude in the air could be a taking requiring compensation. The method hit on by the courts to avoid this result was to declare that the owner never did own the airspace, and perhaps *ad coelum* had never been the law.[79] The latter, however, can be considered "a piece of rhetorical excess."[80]

all *genuine* jural relations must be consistent with one another, two conflicting rules, the one 'legal' and the other 'equitable,' cannot be valid at the same moment in time: one must be valid and determinative to the exclusion of the other."). On Hohfeld's approach to equity, see Chapter 8 and Chapter 10. For a different take on how equity is meta-law, see Ben McFarlane & Robert Stevens, *What's Special About Equity? Laws About Laws*, *in* Philosophical Foundations of the Law of Equity 191 (Dennis Klimchuk et al. eds., 2020).

75 For a Hohfeldian account that does not require dual ownership of assets, see, Chapter 9.

76 F. W. Maitland, Equity: A Course of Lectures 17 (A. H. Chaytor & W. J. Whittaker eds., 1936).

77 The maxim is *cujus est solum, ejus est usque ad coelum et ad inferos* ("one who owns the soil owns also to the sky and to the depths").

78 *See, e.g.*, Stuart Banner, Who Owns the Sky?: The Struggle to Control Airspace from the Wright Brothers On (2008); Eric R. Claeys, *On the Use and Abuse of Overflight Column Doctrine*, 2 Brigham-Kanner Prop. Rts. Conf. J. 61 (2013).

79 *United States* v. *Causby*, 328 U.S. 256, 260 (1946) (discussing how high-altitude flights do not violate landowners' rights under *ad coelum* doctrine); *Hinman* v. *Pacific Air Transport*, 84 F.2d 755 (9th Cir. 1936).

80 Thomas W. Merrill & Henry E. Smith, Property: Principles and Policies 259 (3d ed. 2017).

Why? Because the *ad coelum* principle still holds, for subsurface trespass as in mining and even caves, although hydraulic fracturing raises a new issue.[81] Airspace owners do at least have better right to use it and thereby acquire it than others, but airplanes can traverse airspace without trespass and its strict liability. (Airplane overflights can still be subject to tort suit but only by alleging and proving actual harm, as in nuisance.[82]) The *ad coelum* principle never did spell out the owners' rights one by one (whatever that would mean), in a post-Hohfeldian bundle-of-rights fashion. If it did, one might regard this as a stick being taken from the owner and given to the public (or airlines), or one might deny the owner ever had the overflight stick at all. Delineation cost points in another direction. The *ad coelum* principle expressed in highly approximate fashion that the owner was the presumptive owner of airspace. When the need for precision arrived, the idea that *ad coelum* peters out into an option to acquire and gives way to a navigation servitude is less a matter of taking than (re-)specification. Even the notion of navigation can be regarded as latent and easily specified when the need arises: if human transporters required small tunnels to open for a microsecond deep underground, one might expect the right to block them to give way.[83] Of course, one has to worry that the government will "respecify" away all sorts of rights, and one purpose of the takings doctrine is to address this (admittedly difficult) problem of setting limits on re-specification.[84]

The advent of major innovations like airplane flight is rare, but presumptive rights requiring further specification are widely important in the law on an ongoing basis.

81 *Edwards* v. *Sims*, 24 S.W.2d 619 (Ky. 1929) (applying *ad coelum* doctrine to caves). These issues are presented in a stark way in fracking cases. *See, e.g.*, *Briggs* v. *Sw. Energy Prod. Co.*, 224 A.3d 334 (Pa. 2020) (indicating that traditional trespass principles based on physical intrusion apply in the context of hydraulic fracturing); *Coastal Oil & Gas Corp.* v. *Garza Energy Trust*, 268 S.W.3d 1 (Tex. 2008) (declining to hold fracking to be a trespass by means of injected fluids and proppants); Troy A. Rule, *Property Rights and Modern Energy*, 20 Geo. Mason L. Rev. 803, 827–28 (2013) (discussing unsettled state of law on *ad coelum* and landowner protections in fracking situations).

82 Nuisance requires a showing of harm, and some courts apply a version of trespass requiring harm to airplane overflights, which amounts to something similar. *Brown* v. *United States*, 73 F.3d 1100, 1103–04 (Fed. Cir. 1996) (reversing grant of summary judgment in case of military overflights because of genuine issue about substantial interference with owner's recreational use of land); Hinman, 74 F.2d at 755.

83 In fact, while the phenomena differ, indefiniteness is relevant to both the smaller scale (yet still mid-level) concerns of Kocourek and the larger scale concerns raised by airplane overflights. Greater specification can be provided if and when it becomes necessary. *Cf.* Kocourek, *supra* note 28, at 137 ("There is no practical need of knowing who these various persons are until the moment when they tender goods for transportation. At that moment polarized legal relations come into existence."). While Kocourek implicitly allows for the possibility of further specification, note that his understanding nonetheless takes legal concepts seriously. *See* Kocourek, *supra* note 3, at 238 ("A system of legal conceptions can no more be crystallized than the facts on which it operates; but there is an important [...] difference between subordinating conceptions to reality and emphasizing reality to the point of excluding the conceptual process altogether.").

84 The ease of re-specification may also hinge on how loosely interconnected the legal system is. On this question, see Andrew S. Gold & Henry E. Smith, *Restatements and the Common Law*, *in* American Law Institute Centennial History (forthcoming); Henry E. Smith, *Systems Theory: Emergent Private Law*, *in* The Oxford Handbook of The New Private Law 143, 145–51 (Andrew S. Gold et al. eds., 2020).

Indeed, the traditional method of reconciling conflicting rights partakes of this dynamic character. As we have seen, the law of nuisance traditionally recognized that conflicting presumptive rights would have to be reconciled when they came into conflict.

Let us return to one of Hohfeld's most famous examples, which was a hit with the Realists and their successors. Hohfeld thought that traditionally judges and jurists made the logical mistake of deriving rights from privileges. Thus, in Hohfeld's famous critique of *Quinn v. Leathem*,[85] the court per Lord Lindley supposedly derived from the liberty to do business a claim-right against union organizers who were trying to dissuade customers from dealing with him. Couldn't one derive the right to collectively press demands from the privilege to organize?[86] Yes and no. The common law of unfair competition had by that time developed an elaborate set of rules of thumb along the lines of the style of analysis in nuisance discussed above (and sometimes under the rubric of nuisance). This baseline favored competition and disfavored combinations, and was the precursor for antitrust law. As society developed a more pro-union stance, this baseline was changed, sometimes through legislation; notice that antitrust law required statutory and judicial exceptions for unions from its ban on combinations in restraint of trade.[87] The results in the "privilege-to-right" cases are not logical errors, but the product of reconciling conflicting rights on a set of (perhaps too narrow) rules of thumb.[88] They can and have been altered over time, especially though legislation, and conceivably more pro-union courts could have innovated along the lines of the airplane overflight cases. Even there, though, courts were neither writing on a blank slate nor engaging in logical deduction. Rather, the baselines have a dynamic potential but one that sometimes needs pushing along. The Hohfeldian atomic view, without more, obscures the dynamic aspect of the baselines and makes them appear more brittle and arbitrary than they are.

14.5 CONCLUSION

Hohfeld's system pursues the atomic approach to law, and the Realists and their successors do so with a vengeance. Because of the breakdown of the natural rights paradigm, the fusion of law and equity, and the rise of Legal Realism, the seeds he

85 [1901] AC 495 at 503 (HL).

86 For an excellent exposition of this problem, see Pierre Schlag, *How to Do Things with Hohfeld*, 78 Law & Contemp. Probs. 185, 208–12 (2015). For an argument that *Quinn* v. *Leathem* involved the "adjustment of [the plaintiff's and defendants'] respective liberties" and the "protection against unjustified interference" with legal liberty that rests ultimately on "our ideas of justice and policy," see Isaac Husik, *Hohfeld's Jurisprudence*, 72 U. Pa. L. Rev. 263, 270 (1924).

87 See Sections 6 and 20 of the Clayton Act (codified at 15 U.S.C. § 17 (1994) and 29 U.S.C. § 52); and sections 4, 5, and 13 of the Norris-La Guardia Act (codified at 29 U.S.C. §§ 104-05, 113); *Connell Constr. Co.* v. *Plumbers & Steamfitters Local Union No. 100*, 421 U.S. 616, 622–23 (1975).

88 For an analysis in terms of protected privileges, see Chapter 11.

planted grew and perhaps flourished in directions he never intended. The result is a general preference for legal concepts that are close to particulars.

And yet for a variety of reasons, relatively concrete, atomized concepts and a flat, unstructured picture of the legal system have their limits. Actual legal delineation, from the things of property law, to coarse-grained duties in torts, to *in rem* rights, are shortcuts over fully articulated legal relations, even if the two approaches are extensionally equivalent. Some of the traditional structures of the law and the baselines – such as distinctions between privileges and rights and symmetric clusters of rights in nuisance – help tame potentially runaway complexity. In general, managing the complexity of the law allows for locally simple structures to produce relatively predictable complex results at the societal level. While there will always be disagreement as to how much intervention to undertake in the name of considerations like distributive justice, the problem of linking local interactions with societal efficiency, fairness, and justice will require structure beyond the Hohfeldian atomic stratum.

Hohfeld's rigorous atomic approach to the law is a useful thought experiment that points to the importance of system effects and the modular structures and higher-order devices like equity that they call for. By the light of Hohfeld we can appreciate better the need for the micro world of legal relations to scale up.

PART V

Hohfeld and Society

15

Hohfeldian Analysis, Liberalism, and Adjudication (Some Tensions)

Pierre Schlag[*]

15.1 INTRODUCTION

In one sense, Hohfeld's 1913 article on fundamental legal conceptions has been a stunning success.[1] In the history of twentieth-century legal thought, it has played a significant role in shaping legal realism, law and economics, critical legal studies, analytical jurisprudence, and property theory. Today, more than a century later, it has opened areas of inquiry and lines of analytical advent that remain powerful and productive.

But the article has not been in all ways, or in all precincts, successful. Certainly, the Hohfeldian platform of jural correlatives and jural opposites has not met with widespread adoption among judges. Nor among most legal academics, either.

There are, of course, some obvious and very quick responses as to why this might be. For one thing, perhaps Hohfeld got *it* wrong. Or perhaps other legal thinkers got *it* better. Or perhaps Hohfeld's platform was too exigent. Or perhaps it was not necessary in many instances. Or perhaps Hohfeld's platform was occasionally stretched too far – enlisted to perform work it was not designed to do (and thus could not do very well).[2]

Let's hold these kinds of responses in abeyance.

Instead, consider the possibility that Hohfeldian analysis and its lessons are in fundamental ways in tension with the law of the liberal democratic state and its form of adjudication. This is not an argument against the use of Hohfeldian analysis. And in no way do I want to be taken as suggesting that somehow liberalism or liberal forms of adjudication are not amenable to Hohfeldian analysis. Nor am I suggesting

* University Distinguished Professor and Byron R. White Professor of Law, University of Colorado. I am grateful to David Frydrych, John Goldberg, Jack Schlegel, and Henry Smith for comments and criticisms.

1 Wesley N. Hohfeld, *Some Fundamental Legal Conceptions as Applied in Judicial Reasoning*, 23 YALE L.J. 16 (1913) [hereinafter Hohfeld (1913)]. The sequel is Wesley N. Hohfeld, *Fundamental Legal Conceptions as Applied in Judicial Reasoning*, 26 YALE L.J. 710 (1917) [hereinafter Hohfeld (1917)].

2 For elaboration, *see* Pierre Schlag, *How to Do Things with Hohfeld*, 78 LAW & CONTEMP. PROBS. 185 (2015). *See also* Chapter 7.

that there is something *intrinsically* or *especially* illiberal or anti-liberal to the Hohfeldian platform. Rather, the Hohfeldian platform reveals challenges for both liberalism and its forms of adjudication. I think there is nothing particularly sinister nor surprising about this. Liberalism, like other types of political-legal regimes, is normatively engaged and thus emphasizes certain problematics and concerns while occluding others. The Hofheldian platform, given its substantive and normative indifference, is often well poised to reveal such occlusions – and not just with regard to liberalism, but across a wide array of different political-legal regimes.

As I view the matter here, it is precisely because Hohfeld's approach is in tension with and does not fit swimmingly with received liberal institutional commitments and understandings, that his approach turns out to be richly rewarding in its intellectual promise for analyzing liberal law. That is to say, the Hohfeldian approach exercises an *estrangement function* that enables us to recognize aspects of liberal law that might otherwise be overlooked.[3] I am, therefore, not taking issue with the arguments made by some critics of Hohfeld: that his analysis does not scale up or down very well (yes) or that his atomism is substantively untethered (yes) or that his scheme is partial and incomplete (again, yes).[4] Instead, I am trying to show that we can, by changing our perspective, see those shortfalls as having their upsides.

15.2 HOHFELD'S PLATFORM

Hohfeld, by his own account, set out to clarify the uses of basic legal conceptions in case law and legal scholarship – notions such as rights, immunities, duties, and the like. His effort was less an attempt to elucidate the conceptions of others than to expose their confusions and to establish his own taxonomy – what I call Hohfeld's "platform."[5] Hohfeld was interested in setting forth a set of different possible legal relations which he saw instanced, albeit often in muddled form, in case law and legal scholarship.

Hohfeld's general strategy was to describe these basic legal conceptions as *relations of legal form* – that is to say, stripped so far as possible of *substantive content*. This attempt to isolate legal conceptions into pure relations of form is what gives his approach its austere, formalist, almost mathematical aura. Indeed, Hohfeld himself

3 Pierre Schlag, *The Knowledge Bubble: Something Amiss in Expertopia*, *in* CHRIS TOMLINS & JUSTIN DESAUTELS-STEIN, CONTEMPORARY LEGAL THOUGHT (2017). Obviously too little *fit* and that too becomes a problem.

4 See the formally parallel, but substantively different, arguments by Jeanne L. Schroeder, *Chix Nix Bundle-O-Stix: A Feminist Critique of the Disaggregation of Property*, 93 MICH. L. REV. 239, 243 (1994). *See also* JEANNE SCHROEDER , THE VESTAL AND THE FASCES: HEGEL, LACAN, PROPERTY AND THE FEMININE (1998); James Penner, *The "Bundle of Rights" Picture of Property*, 43 UCLA L. REV. 711, 714 (1996); Henry E. Smith, *Property as the Law of Things*, 125 HARV. L. REV. 1691 (2012); Henry E. Smith, *On the Economy of Concepts in Property*, 160 U. PA. L. REV. 2097 (2012).

5 This section borrows nearly *verbatim* from Schlag, *supra* note 2, at 189.

likened his jural relations to "lowest common denominators" and claimed for them both universality and irreducibility.[6]

How then, is Hohfeld's platform to be understood as *relations of legal form*? Perhaps the easiest response here is to turn directly to the platform. Hohfeld described four kinds of entitlements (rights, privileges, powers, and immunities) and four kinds of disablements (duty, no-right, liability, and disability). For each entitlement there is always a unique and distinct correlative disablement and *vice versa*. Thus, for every right in A, there must be a correlative duty in B. For every privilege in A, there must be a correlative ... (and so on and so forth). The correlatives thus form four distinct dyads of legal relations.

Hohfeld explicitly declined to provide any specific definitions for his eight conceptions. They are *sui generis*. Instead, he accords meaning to these conceptions by articulating their relations, by demonstrating their instantiation in case law and legal scholarship, and by showing how they can be used to reveal sloppy thinking and faulty analyses. Three kinds of relations are crucial:

(1) Each conception has its *unique correlative*. (Each conception is another way of stating its correlative.)
(2) Each conception has its *unique opposite*. (It would be nonsense to accord opposites to the same party for the same act.)
(3) Each conception is *never any of the others*. (Each conception is distinct; though, of course, they can be aggregated in a variety of ways into some greater whole as *jural composites* – for instance, the fee simple, the corporation, the ... and so on.)

Table 15.1 sets out Hohfeld's jural correlatives and jural opposites:

Notice that Hohfeld's jurisprudence of form is very different from the ways in which judges talk about rights, duties, powers, etc. Why is that? The short answer is that he is an academic analyst and they are judges: Hohfeld is interested in analyzing

TABLE 15.1 *Hohfeld's jural correlatives and jural opposites*

jural correlatives	jural opposites
Right←→Duty	Right/No-Right
Privilege←→No-Right	Privilege/Duty
Power←→Liability	Power/Disability
Immunity←→Disability	Immunity/Liability

6 Hohfeld (1913), *supra* note 1, at 58–59.

the law in ways that seem to him analytically correct (he has students to teach and articles to write),[7] while they are interested in an endeavor which is, as will be seen below, both broader and narrower.

15.3 THE PLATFORM AND THE JUDICIAL OPINION

The judicial endeavor of writing opinions goes far beyond performing legal analysis. Judges must be concerned with other functions, including application, decision, legitimation, and realization. These functions are in some ways symbiotic. But they are also antagonistic or reciprocally interfering. The judicial opinion is the rhetorical artifact where analysis, application, decision, legitimation, and realization are all melded together in ways that, from the perspective of the detached academic analyst, can often seem suspect, sloppy and sophistic. The academic can afford to be such a harsh critic because he has no institutional or professional obligation that would call for compromising analysis. He is thus free to criticize law for any and all analytical failings. The judge, on the other hand, believes that she must get the analysis right, but not so right as to overly compromise the other functions of the opinion (application, decision, legitimation, and realization).

The tension between Hohfeldian analysis and judicial discourse becomes apparent when we recognize that the judicial opinion conflates the reciprocally interfering functions – to wit, analysis, application, decision, legitimation and realization. And the conflation occurs, as will be seen, not just at the *paragraph* or the *sentence* level, but at the level of the *legal concept* itself. From this perspective, it becomes easy to understand the judicial resistance to Hohfeld. In some sense, judicial discourse – the semantics and grammar of judicial discourse – resists Hohfeldian translation because the former has other concerns besides analytical probity. Application, decision, legitimation, and realization require not just clear concepts, but *concepts on a mission*, in fact, *various missions*. Truth, precision, clarity, and exactitude are all intellectual qualities of analysis (and are generally highly valued in academic circles). However they are not the only or even the principal virtues sought or enabled by judicial discourse.[8] Of course, as a caveat, the great many legal academics who join pre-critically with judicial discourse (for both good and/or bad reasons) will be rehearsing the same compromised discourse.

Judges have to apply the law. It is thus not surprising, even if it is not analytically entirely satisfying (it is not) that judges would have developed a vocabulary in which legal concepts (e.g., employee, corporation, state) equivocate between the order of the world and the order of law. The legal realists – think here of Felix Cohen or

7 *See* Chapter 18.

8 To be clear about my orientation: I favor much greater decoupling between judicial discourse and legal academic thought than we have at present. For elaboration, see, Pierre Schlag, *Spam Jurisprudence, Air Law, and the Rank Anxiety of Nothing Happening (A Report on the State of the Art)*, 97 GEO L.J. 803 (2009).

Arthur Corbin and before them Hohfeld himself – took the judges to task for this.[9] And rather ferociously so. But imagine how much easier it is to apply the law to the facts, if one has at hand a concept (e.g., contract) that refers at once, within a single term, to *the law* that specifies *which facts* must be evidenced. Legal concepts as developed and used in judicial discourse thus partake of *systematicity* (the order of normative and conceptual coherence of law) and *reference* (specification of real world events). The fusion of the two is at once functional (sounds good) and an equivocation (not so great). Analysis may be compromised, but law application is facilitated.

Judges must decide. Judges have dockets, limited time, and a responsibility to decide (even if the dispute is intractable and the decisional options are ghastly).[10] It follows that analytical probity and analytical scruples are not necessarily an unqualified advantage here. One should not be surprised that judges develop a discourse with grammar and semantics that has a fair amount of give – the kind of give that allows for the production of both determinacy or indeterminacy as the occasion may warrant.

Judges must legitimate and realize their decisions. Decisions must be legitimated to many parties: perhaps the immediately higher court if there is one, the lower courts if there are any, the lawyers, the parties, other legal officials, the press, and any other parties affected. Already, this gives us significant audience differentiation in terms of intellectual and political capacities – thus complicating the task of communication. Decisions must also be realized. Law is particularly ambitious in this regard. Consider that while a philosophy professor needs to realize (make real) her lessons in the student's mind, a judge must somehow inscribe her decision through lawful means into the social, economic, and perhaps even cultural order. Not all analytically perfected concepts will be attuned to this latter mission. The concepts must accommodate the social practices of those to be subjected to law[11] or deploy coercion and enticements to induce compliance.

Meir Dan Cohen's famous article on acoustic separation suggests there is a tension here.[12] A judicial opinion must set down a *legal regime* capable of being rendered intelligible not only to the *cognoscenti* (lawyers, judges, other legal officials), but derivatively to the uninitiated as well (juries, officials, enforcers, citizens,

9 Schlag, *supra* note 2, at 192–200.

10 Apparently, Article 4 of the Napoleonic Code subjects the judge "who refuses to judge, on the pretense of silence, obscurity, or *insufficiency of the law*" to be prosecuted on "the charge of denial of justice." *See* Georgio Agamben, State of Exception 31 (2008) (emphasis added).

11 *See* Robert Cover, *The Supreme Court, 1982 Term – Foreword – Nomos and Narrative*, 97 Harv. L. Rev. 4, 18 (1983).

12 Meir Dan Cohen, *Decision Rules and Conduct Rules: On Acoustic Separation in Criminal Law*, 97 Harv. L. Rev. 625 (1983). One might also liken the problem to the logic of discovery and the logic of justification. The judicial opinion (consonant with the rule of law in one sense/and in one sense not) fuses the two together.

persons). This last requirement is something of a vexation because even as accessibility for the uninitiated is required, it is also the case that the opinion must perform an intelligent legal analysis that is not captive to the brute unfiltered beliefs of common sense, mass culture or corporate manipulation.

This yields a tension. On the one hand, while popular concepts may on occasion be perspicuous, intelligent, and precise, frequently they will not be. The epistemic record of common sense or more accurately at this point, mass culture, is hardly an unqualified epistemic triumph. And currently, as if to prove postmodern thought precocious in its insights, we are coming close to treating "alternative facts" as an aspect of the normal, if not one of its primary registers.

Intelligent legal analysis would thus seem to require some deviation from the semantics and grammar of common sense and mass culture. If law is to be rational and sensible, then it must have some sort of conceptual vocabulary and structure through which it can articulate issues and problems saliently and perspicuously. But, at the same time, if law goes too far in this direction, it will develop a language that is basically incomprehensible to anyone other than the *cognoscenti* and the initiated. Unless the context happens to be one with lawyer-savvy clients (e.g., corporate tax law), this will make it difficult for law to realize itself – to impress itself upon social and economic practices.[13]

One might think that it ought to be possible to accomplish both in a judicial opinion – in other words, that it ought to be possible to engage in *intelligent legal analysis* and yet provide *sound legal regime-setting* as well. One would think that the two could re-enforce each other. In some sense, that is so. But the existence of symbiosis does not preclude a simultaneous opposition. There is a tension here and it is wrought of the fact that judicial opinions have a *unitary legal discourse* used for both regime-setting and legal analysis.[14] There is a fusion of discourse. And this fusion masks an internal tension: What is necessary to render an opinion intelligible and legitimate to the public may well be at odds with what is necessary to perform an intelligent legal analysis.[15]

[13] Andrew Gold and Henry Smith have made a similar point in arguing about the importance of modularity in negotiating complexity:

> At the root of the complexity problem in both private law and theories about it is a fundamental tradeoff between accuracy and manageability. According to what is sometimes referred to as Bonini's Paradox, as scientific theories more accurately reflect the phenomena they cover they become less understandable – and as they become simpler they become less accurate as a representation of reality. Or as the poet-philosopher Paul Valéry captured this point even earlier, "Everything simple is false. Everything which is complex is unusable."

Andrew Gold & Henry Smith, *Sizing up Private Law*, available at SSRN: https://ssrn.com/abstract=2821354 August 10, 2016) (footnotes omitted).

[14] *Cf.* Edward Rubin, *The Practice and Discourse of Legal Scholarship*, 86 MICH. L. REV. 1835 (1988).

[15] *See* Cohen, *supra* note 12. In some sense, the rule of law requires this fusion. Certainly, the idea that lawyers and judges have a secret code would offend the rule of law. And yet, in some sense, don't they, don't we?

The truly important thing here is to recognize in a way analogous to Robert Cover's famous argument about law as "bonded with violence" that all the functions of the judicial opinion (analysis, decision, application, legitimation, realization) shape and leave their marks on the legal concept itself.[16] Judicial discourse is, from an analytical standpoint, a compromised discourse – all the way down to the level of the legal concept, down to the level of the single sign.

Hohfeld's platform, as I see it, is dedicated to analysis. Where the judicial opinion is concerned, the best analysis may well be called upon to sacrifice for the sake of discharging these other functions. Over time, *that sacrifice* repeated often enough (the rule of precedent or the rule of cut and paste) becomes inscribed in both the grammar and the semantics of law.

By contrast, the work of the legal academic – legal scholarship and law teaching – does not have to hew to the same demands. A work of legal scholarship does not require mimicking or joining with judicial discourse. On the contrary, in its most intellectually serious incarnations, it requires a certain reflective distancing from judicial discourse.[17] Hohfeld's 1913 article is clearly of this type. His platform assists legal analysis and diagnoses commonplace errors in reasoning. Apart from those contributions, the article offers virtually nothing in the way of guidance for how to apply the law to facts and cases, nor how to decide cases, and still less how to legitimate and realize those decisions. The platform is constructed so far as I can tell with absolutely no regard for and no pretense to aid in these other functions. The austere formal minimalism is its chief virtue and main limitation.[18]

One thing is clear: If as I am suggesting those other judicial functions play a crucial role in shaping the semantics and grammar of law as it is articulated in judicial discourse, then it is no surprise that there would be some tension between that law and the analytical probity of Hohfeld's platform. It would also be no surprise if judges and those great many academics who pre-critically embrace judicial discourse decided not to spend too much time on Hohfeldian analysis.[19]

15.4 DOUBLE-ENTRY BOOKKEEPING FOR LAW

In the Hohfeldian world, each entitlement granted means a disablement in someone else (and vice versa). This is the "double-entry" bookkeeping of the Hohfeldian

16 Robert Cover, *Violence and the Word*, 95 YALE L.J. 1601 (1986).

17 Schlag, *supra* note 3.

18 Arthur L. Corbin, *Jural Relations and Their Classification*, 30 YALE L.J. 226, 237–38 (1921) (on the limits of legal analysis).

19 One might also embrace judicial discourse in ways that are not pre-critical (but on the contrary conscious of the discourse's intellectual shortfalls). My guess, and it is no more than that, is that this does not happen often. But it could happen for both opportunistic careerist reasons and/or moral-political commitments.

platform.[20] Hohfeld did not invent the double-entry bookkeeping for law, but he did offer us an extremely elegant, irreducible, and ostensibly universal set of relations of form arranged into correlatives as well as opposites.[21]

Prior to Hohfeld, it had been understood that entitlements such as rights imply the imposition of duties (and vice versa).[22] Hohfeld, by presenting his conceptions as relations of form, was able to push things one step further. He was able to show that entitlements in person A are the same as the correlative disablements in person B. Karl Llewellyn perhaps put it best:

> There is a person on *each* end, always. A has a right that B shall do something, I repeat, when, should B fail to do it, A can get the court to make trouble for B. But the right has B on the other end. *The right is indeed the duty*, a duty seen other end to. *The relation is identical; the only difference is in the point of observation.*[23]

Hohfeldian double-entry bookkeeping means that legal analysis cannot escape the recognition that an entitlement in one person is a disablement in another. Accordingly, what Hohfeld does with his platform is establish a legal world that is relentlessly conflictual. To be sure, there may be gains from trade or improvements in total welfare achieved by tinkering with legal entitlements and disablements. The parties may, in an economic sense, both be made better off through alterations in the forced exchanges wrought by law. Cooperation is thus also very much an aspect of this world. But it will always be the case that any incremental enhancement of a legal entitlement in A means *at the formal level*, an incremental enhancement of the correlative legal disablement in B. The balance need not be zero-sum *in value* to the parties (that depends *inter alia* on their tastes, preferences, the measure, and the metric), but the law of double-entry remains inviolable at the formal level.[24] As Duncan Kennedy and Frank Michelman aptly put it: "The books are double-entry and they have to balance."[25]

This, of course, is at odds with much of the discourse of our judicial opinions and legal scholarship which is full of asymmetrical language that speaks triumphantly of correcting wrongs or of protecting liberty – with sometimes only a dim recognition (if any) that there are always two sides to the legal ledger. This tendency could be ascribed to rhetorical excess or to efforts at legitimation and realization – which would send us back to the previous section. On occasion, it will result in an egregious failure of judgment, due to the slighting of the stakes, concerns, and arguments raised by one side or the other.[26]

20 Duncan Kennedy & Frank Michelman, *Are Property and Contract Efficient?* 8 Hofstra L. Rev. 711, 760 (1980).
21 *See* Chapter 3.
22 *See* Chapter 17.
23 Karl Llewellyn, The Bramble Bush: On Our Law and Its Study 85 (2008).
24 Kennedy & Michelman, *supra* note 20, at 760.
25 *Id.*
26 *Korematsu* v. *United States*, 323 U.S. 214 (1944).

There is, however, another sense in which adjudication can be seen as giving rise to a deeper asymmetry in doctrinal discourse. This latter asymmetry can be seen as arguably at odds with the spirit of Hohfeldian double-entry bookkeeping.

By way of introducing this asymmetry, consider that cases brought to adjudication are often cast in a *perpetrator – victim* frame.[27] Indeed, the very idea of a "cause of action" enables the plaintiff to present herself as a *victim* of some harm caused by the defendant, the alleged *perpetrator*. Over time, this perpetrator-victim frame has helped yield among other things a *bifurcated doctrinal discourse* that offers judges various sets of doctrines and principles aimed at identifying whether they have before them an "eligible victim" or a "responsible perpetrator" and to do so by examining only one side of the perpetrator-victim dyad.

Notice that *bifurcated doctrinal discourse* hardly occupies or exhausts the doctrinal field. Indeed, some doctrines and principles are not bifurcated in this way, but might be called *relational* in the sense that the court looks at the parties and their actions interactively. For instance, causal tests used to link or sever relations between defendant's conduct and plaintiff's harm are often relational in this way. Balancing tests, for instance, that compare interests advanced or hindered by both plaintiff and defendant are *relational* in just this way as well. Academics, with their penchant for analytical probity tend to be more receptive to *relational doctrinal discourse* than judges.[28]

Because relational doctrinal discourse is easily compatible with double-entry Hohfeldian bookkeeping, we will say nothing more about it.

Rather, it is *bifurcated doctrinal discourse* that is *arguably* at odds with double-entry bookkeeping. Doctrines and principles can be deemed bifurcated (as opposed to holistic) to the degree that determinations about the eligibility of the victim and

[27] This is an adaptation and slight modification of the perpetrator – victim dyad developed by Alan David Freeman, *Legitimizing Racial Discrimination Through Antidiscrimination Law: A Critical Review of Supreme Court Doctrine*, 62 MINN. L. REV. 1049 (1978). Lee Anne Fennell, in more recent work, develops a parallel idea showing how torts decouple risk creation concerns (a perpetrator-focus) from harm outcome concerns (a victim-focus). Lee Anne Fennell, *Property and Half Torts*, 116 YALE L. J. 1400 (2007). Similarly, Henry Smith's elaboration of modularity as a crucial organizing principle of law is consonant with this account of bifurcation. Henry E. Smith, *Modularity in Contracts: Boilerplate and Information Flow*, 104 MICH. L. REV. 1175 (2006).

[28] In torts, for instance, Guido Calabresi's cheapest cost avoider approach or George Fletcher's neo-Kantian paradigm of reciprocity are clearly relational forms of analysis (even as they can yield bifurcated doctrine). Guido Calabresi & Jon T. Hirschoff, *Toward a Test for Strict Liability in Torts*, 81 YALE L.J. 1055 (1972); GUIDO CALABRESI, THE COSTS OF ACCIDENTS (1970); George Fletcher, *Fairness and Utility in Tort Theory*, 85 HARV. L. REV. 537 (1972). I suspect that one of the reasons academics are drawn to the relational is that, relative to judges, who cannot afford to lose faith in the positive law, legal academics have lost some (much?) of their faith in the structural integrity of doctrinal categories. The latter are often implicitly experienced and understood as not sufficiently robust to contain or delimit the push and pull of economic, political, social, and cultural forces. On the latter, *see* Schlag, *supra* note 3 (explaining various conundrums associated with the law's micro/macro relations). But even as faith in the structural integrity of doctrines has been lost, the inertial force of habit entrenched in such forms as the casebook, the law review article and the faculty workshop endures.

the responsibility of the perpetrator can be made independently of each other – that is to say, by examining only one side of the perpetrator–victim dyad. When bifurcated doctrinal discourse is available, the court will approach the case asymmetrically – asking for instance, "is there any reason why this victim should *not* recover?" If so, then "case dismissed." Or conversely the court will ask, for instance, "is there any reason why this perpetrator should *not* have to remedy?" If so, then "case dismissed."

As a theoretical matter, there could also be bifurcated doctrine on the plaintiff's side – that is to say, the plaintiff is automatically entitled to recover. While US law exhibits arguments and considerations steeped in this direction, it is difficult to find pure actualized examples of this phenomenon. The idea would be that plaintiff ought to recover regardless of whether defendant ought to be held responsible. The two formulae would go as follows. The victim perspective: the plaintiff is entitled to recover simply because he or she is deserving. From the perpetrator perspective: the plaintiff is entitled to recover simply because the defendant ought to be held responsible. Because these possibilities (bifurcated doctrine on the plaintiff's side) seem hypothetical, we will put these possibilities aside.

Here I offer with some hedging examples of doctrines which in their classic instantiations, seem to be bifurcated:[29]

Victim Perspective: No defendant responsibility because . . .

Non-cognizable harm
De Minimis harm
Dirty hands
Not real party in interest
Non-person
Volenti non fit injuria
Etc.

Perpetrator Perspective: No defendant responsibility because . . .

No requisite mental state
No actus reus
Incapacity
Non-person
No remedy
Etc.

29 Some caution and hedging are necessary here. Even when it seems that legal doctrines announce themselves as clearly bifurcated (e.g., *mens rea*) or clearly relational (e.g., comparative negligence), there is often a trace of alterity within. Hence, even bifurcated doctrines sometimes require examination of the other party's conduct (consider the evaluation of *mens rea* in the context of the other party's alleged provocation) and even relational doctrines will have threshold floors and ceilings (even comparative negligence in torts requires threshold findings of negligence and causation). Nonetheless, the distinction between bifurcated and relational is useful even in the presence of some degree of hybridity. None of this should take away from the main point which is that one can often rather easily tell when a judicial opinion is deploying doctrine in a bifurcated or relational manner.

Much more so than legal scholars, the courts are receptive to bifurcated doctrinal discourse. Part of the reason is that bifurcated doctrinal discourse enables early disposition of cases (e.g., JMOL) through the examination of a discrete set of decisive *nonrelational* facts. (Early disposition is nearly always an important consideration for judges). Bifurcated doctrinal discourse enables judges to say: "This plaintiff cannot possibly recover, so we don't even have to examine defendant's conduct"; or "Defendant is not obligated to remedy, so we don't even need to examine plaintiff's harm."

So how is this bifurcated doctrinal discourse at odds with Hohfeldian analysis if at all?[30] The answer is that bifurcated doctrinal discourse (for good or bad reasons) *arguably* cuts Hohfeldian double-entry analysis short.[31] That is to say, bifurcated doctrinal discourse allows consideration of only one side of the perpetrator-victim dyad. The court need not decide that the plaintiff has (or has not) been harmed if it finds that the defendant is not responsible for redress. Likewise, the court need not decide that the defendant is (or is not) responsible if the plaintiff has not been legally harmed. In this way, bifurcated doctrinal discourse reprieves the court from examining the legal claims, concerns, and arguments on both sides of the legal ledger.

Deciding whether and when this short-circuiting is warranted can be a tough problem. There are good reasons for adjudication to develop and follow bifurcated doctrinal discourse. For one thing, it seems to be intrinsic to the common law idea of following precedent (treating like cases alike and not having to reinvent the wheel). For another, it allows disposition of a case early in the litigation process. For yet a third, bifurcated doctrinal discourse may well strengthen the semantic meaningfulness of syntactical redundancy (as enacted in stare decisis) so as to promote coordination among otherwise decentralized decision-makers (i.e., courts).[32] And if one adds here that litigation has become a business and that lawyers may at times be all too willing to bring lawsuits for self-gain (an agency-principal problem) or to promote the client's leverage over others (strike suits) then bifurcation becomes an important judicial tool for controlling lawyers. Of course, here one does have to pay attention to the converse argument – to wit, that bifurcation perforce prevents the development of factual records and legal arguments that would allow new and deserving claims to be pressed forward in compelling ways. Moreover, bifurcated

30 Note, not surprisingly, that it is also arguably at odds with Coase's methodological causal agnosticism (the reciprocity of the harm). Ronald Coase, *The Problem of Social Cost*, 3 J.L. & ECON. 1 (1960).

31 This is a claim about Hohfeldian analysis – the form of analysis that Hohfeld's platform makes possible. It is not a claim about Hohfeld's jurisprudential views. On the latter, my guess is that Hohfeld would have felt fine with bifurcated doctrinal analysis on some, perhaps many, occasions. Indeed, I have great difficulties imagining Hohfeld (or indeed anyone) insisting that judges perform a full double-entry analysis in each and every case. The challenge lies in deciding when it is called for and when it is not. For a useful discussion, see Francis Heylighen, *Advantages and Limitations of Formal Expression*, 4 FOUND. SCI. 25, 27, 49–53 (1999).

32 *See* Martin Shapiro, *Towards a Theory of Stare Decisis*, 1 J. LEGAL STUD. 125, 132–34 (1972).

doctrine in the form of prophylactic rules, safe-havens, presumptions, and more, can obviate the need for complex factual analysis. So there are counter-arguments and these are hardly trivial.

Still another compelling reason for asymmetry in adjudication is a variant of Occam's Razor. Sometimes it seems easier to approach a question from the "entitlements side," letting the disablements fall where they may. At other times, it seems to be easier to approach a question from the "disablement side," letting the entitlements land where they will. We have many subjects of law that seem to be entitlement-focused while other areas seem disablement-focused. And the associated argument sets are aligned accordingly (i.e., heavily on the disablement side or heavily on the entitlement side). Hohfeld's platform is symmetrical and double-entry. But, what we (in all our social situatedness) find to be morally, politically, and economically-significant arguments need not be. Sometimes our concern is primarily with restraining the perpetrator. At other times, it may well be with helping victims. Of course, our predilections in this regard might well be wrong and Hohfeldian analysis would then serve as a welcome corrective.

Of course, Hohfeld's 1913 article hardly requires us to embrace symmetrical analysis by examining both sides of the legal ledger (rights *and* duties, privileges *and* no-rights) in each and every case. So certainly, bifurcated doctrine is not *logically inconsistent* with Hohfeldian analysis. At the same time, however, it would be difficult to read the 1913 article as an unabashed celebration of rule-following or a paean to precedent.[33] Hohfeld clearly wanted more analysis, not less. The problem he perceived and discussed was not the failure to interpret rules, precedents, or doctrines faithfully or accurately. The 1913 article is not a treatise on how to read legal authority. On the contrary, the problem he perceived and discussed was a failure to perform sound analysis in virtue of a flawed legal discourse that, in its confusions and conflations, short-circuited that analysis.

I do not wish to make too much of this point, however, for even if this observation about Hohfeld's main concern is right (I think it is) it still does not tell us (nor did Hohfeld tell us) where the line should be drawn. That is to say, we are still left with the question: When is it appropriate for judges to simply follow authority, a precedent, a rule and when instead should judges engage in double-entry Hohfeldian analysis? On that issue, Hohfeld seems to have left us to our own devices.

This is to say that the question does not goes away. On the contrary, as Joe Singer rightly points out in his contribution to this volume, this is a question that will sometimes pose itself for the judge: Is the present case an easy one "covered" by a rule, a precedent, a doctrine, or is the case instead a hard one that warrants Hohfeldian analysis in terms of "justice and policy?"[34] Jurisprudentially speaking, Hohfeld's 1913 article leaves us on our own to decide that question. Understandably,

33 It would not be difficult, of course, to read Hohfeld as taking all that for granted and in need of no defense.

34 *See* Chapter 17.

Hohfeld's failure to resolve this question in any theoretically cogent way (it seems he did not try to address the issue) has not met with much success elsewhere either. There are things to be said for sure (a future heuristics for judges?), but the question, "Do I follow the rule here or do I decompose the legal regimes and analyze the situation anew?" does not seem answerable by reference to any compelling overarching theory. In my view, that sort of action-question (what do I decide here?) seems to be a question of intellectual repertoire and facility as well as aesthetic, moral and political inclination. It is not a question susceptible to resolution by ordinary philosophical means for the simple reason that the philosophical itself – far from transcending the *aesthetic rifts* which undergird others: authority or analysis? formalism or function? stasis or dynamism? – is in fact anchored in, shaped by, and grounded on these very same aesthetic rifts.[35]

In short, as I view it, this is not a fundamental philosophical question susceptible to resolution by philosophical means. It is, in the first instance, *an aesthetic problem* – inscribed in the aesthetics of American law. It is the great tension between two competing aesthetics of twentieth century on which the great legal thinkers (Hart, Dworkin, and company) have all foundered one after the other pursuing a futile effort to surmount, tame, or circumvent an aesthetic rift by mere philosophical means. They succeeded only in reproducing it.

All this being said, my take is that judges generally do not do anything close to enough by way of double-entry Hohfeldian analysis. Why not? Well – it's their discourse. That discourse is not generally double-entry or relational, but rather bifurcated. Bifurcation, as mentioned, cuts down on decision costs and, when viewed in isolation, that is a plus. But it does have certain negative effects. One of them is that, with summary disposition, some cases never develop a record sufficient to render novel claims plausible, let alone compelling. To put it bluntly, sometimes the courts never learn. The press doesn't report. There are no opinions issued. The nonexistent opinions never make it into the law school casebooks. And the net result in the end, is that no one in law talks about [...] and the citizenry never hears about [...].

15.5 PRIVILEGE – NO-RIGHT AND HOHFELD'S RESIDUUM

One of the important contributions of Hohfeldian analysis was his affirmation of the distinction between the right-duty relation and the privilege-no-right relation. In Hohfeld's world, a right is never a privilege (and vice versa). A right in person A for Hohfeld is always a duty for some person *B* to do (or not do) X. A privilege in person A by contrast means that person *B* has a no-right to keep A from doing or not doing X. Technically, this means that *B* has, as a formal matter, no judicial recourse to keep

[35] For elaboration, *see* Pierre Schlag, *The Aesthetics of American Law*, 115 HARV. L. REV. 1047, 1075–80 (2002).

A from doing or not doing X. (Note that *B* might still be able to exercise his other rights in the juridical entourage (if any) to burden or hinder A from doing or not doing X.)

Among several important implications of this sharp distinction between rights and privileges was Hohfeld's recognition that the latter is a "real legal relation."[36] Hohfeld notes in his article that the privilege-no-right relation often goes unrecognized as a "real legal relation." Hohfeld ascribes this oversight to the fallacious tradition of viewing law "as consisting of 'commands,' or imperative rules." Hohfeld will have none of it: "A rule of law that permits is just as real as a rule that forbids . . ."

To make his case, Hohfeld introduces the privilege-no-right relation with some highly conventional examples. Hence, he notes the libel law's recognition of "privileged communications" as well as "the privilege against self-incrimination."[37] These are both instances where A is under some duty to B, but A has some recognized *specified* privilege that *claws back* on that duty. The privilege "defines out" from a broader duty, a discrete and articulated privilege enjoyed by A.[38] This is the sort of privilege encountered in the doctrinal law of torts, evidence, constitutional law, and so on. With these examples, Hohfeld is not offering anything terribly novel (other than his usual insistence on the *relational character* of the privilege-no-right relation and its sharp distinction from the right-duty relation). This all seems pretty straightforward and uncontroversial.

More interesting is Hohfeld's suggestion that the idea of privilege has a much "wider significance and utility as a matter of judicial usage." As an example of the "wider significance" and usage of the privilege, Hohfeld writes of the unspecified privileges of "a trader in *a free country*, in all matters not contrary to law, to regulate his own mode of carrying them [all matters] according to his own discretion and choice."[39] I will call these "unspecified privileges" as their scope or content has not yet been *concretely articulated* by a court or some other official legal institution.[40] Other thinkers sometimes refer to these as "liberties." Unlike the examples of the specified privileges we encountered immediately above, an unspecified privilege is not an explicit clawing back of an explicitly specified duty. Instead, it is as if background and foreground have been inverted. We now see the background between traders as unspecified privilege-no-right with whatever right-duty relations the traders might have to each other (e.g., don't commit fraud) as claw-backs from the unspecified background of trader privileges vis-à-vis each other.

36 The historical and jurisprudential importance of this insight was elaborated comprehensively by Joseph Singer. Joseph William Singer, *The Legal Rights Debate in Analytical Jurisprudence from Bentham to Hohfeld*, 1982 Wis. L. Rev. 975.

37 Hohfeld (1913), *supra* note 1, at 40.

38 For elaboration, *see* Fred Schauer, *Categories and the First Amendment: A Play in Three Acts*, 34 Vand. L. Rev. 265, 280–81 (1981) (conceptualizing "defining in" and "defining out").

39 Hohfeld (1913), *supra* note 1, at 41 (emphasis added).

40 It is understood that the distinction between "specified" and "unspecified" here operates on a spectrum running from concrete to general and is thus a question of more or less.

But, if these privilege-no-right relations are not specified, and if they are as extensive as Hohfeld claims them to be, then where do these trading privileges come from? And how is it that Hohfeld can be so confident that law does provide such a broad range of privileges? The key to the answer is to be found in the conjunction of: (1) the claimed exhaustiveness of Hohfeld's platform; and (2) his qualification that he is speaking of trade "*in a free country*."

Exhaustiveness first. The free country second.

Recall that Hohfeld's platform is not merely irreducible and universal, but also exhaustive. As Arthur Jacobson put it, Hohfeld's legal world is full – there are no "empty corners."[41] In the Hohfeldian legal world, relations between parties must always fall within some combination of the four jural correlatives. It is axiomatic that if we are sure a specific legal relation between A and B is *not* one of three Hohfeldian correlative relations, it must perforce be the fourth. This is a feature of the Hohfeldian scheme that has been noticed by a number of writers. Frank Michelman and Duncan Kennedy previously invoked it in connection with their announcement of the "law of the conservation of exposures."[42]

Now for the "free country" aspect. If Hohfeld is able to talk so casually about a broad array of privileges of "a trader in all matters not contrary to law, to regulate his own mode of carrying them according to his own discretion and choice,"[43] it is precisely because Hohfeld is writing about legal relations in a "*free country*" – or as I want to call it, a liberal democratic state (in the conventional nineteenth century sense of a sharp split between state and civil society). A liberal democratic state in this sense would be the kind of state that enacts limited government, democratic governance limited by rule of law, constitutional limitations (written or unwritten), protection of individual rights, and associated notions. Now, Hohfeld did not in fact tell us that this is what he meant by "free country," but the above seem like fair and noncontroversial inference. Indeed, with few exceptions throughout the article, Hohfeld is writing about the law of the United Kingdom, Australia, the United States – all of which, in the late nineteenth century, could be fairly described as liberal democratic states.[44]

How then can it be presumed that in liberal democratic states, the general default rule for entitlements and disablements that are not specified are privilege-no-right regimes?

Let's begin by thinking about how we might answer the question with regard to *any* legal regime. We might with any legal regime (monarchical, despotic, primitive etc.) encounter situations where we cannot tell what legal relations are in place because they are unspecified. This is what I want to call "*Hohfeld's residuum*," – that

[41] Arthur Jacobson, *Hegel's Legal Plenum*, 10 Cardozo L. Rev. 877, 882 (1988).

[42] As they put it, "entitlement abhors a vacuum." Michelman & Kennedy, *supra* note 20, at 760.

[43] *Id.*

[44] Hohfeld also did not specify whether "these privileges of traders" might be attended by immunities (vis-à-vis the government) or powers in the government to alter these privileges. But put that aside.

set of legal relations between persons or parties that have not yet been *fully and concretely specified* by any authorized official legal speaker, but that could well be.[45]

Why would this happen? There are a number of general theoretical reasons that can be identified: because . . .

(1) the state is immature and thus little positive law has in fact been declared by official bodies (there are still many gaps remaining and the residuum is large);
(2) the state is over-mature and the accrued positive law has become a nest of conflicting requirements making prediction insecure; or
(3) the state finds it neither useful nor necessary to fully specify all legal relations because generalized principles suffice to inform persons and legal officials.

What is a lawyer, a judge or an academic to do when confronted with Hohfeld's residuum?

One thing would be to say that the legal relations are unspecified and let it go at that. In some circumstances, that choice might be appropriate. It may be that the available legal materials are insufficient or too conflicted to enable any confident inference as to the precise character of the Hohfeldian relations contemplated. It may be that there is no need to specify the relations – either because it is too obvious for words, because specifications could lead to unwanted negative implications, because it is just totally unclear, or because of other reasons.

Another thing to do would be to recognize that in many cases, we can simply look to the higher-order general legal norms that organize the state. I am suggesting here that in any (non-failed) legal regime, there are such higher-order norms, and that these norms are – in their generality – more or less identifiable, that they are more or less conflicted, that they in fact do perform actual conceptual, political, and legal work in giving shape and filling gaps among lower-order norms, and that they delineate the scope or range of "legitimate" legal and political contestation.[46] Please note that this is not some coy appeal to a closet grundnorm or mystical master rule of recognition in the Kelsen/Hart tradition. I expect that the difference will emerge starkly in the discussion that follows.

In liberal democratic states, those higher-order general norms can be described as commitments to the separation of state and civil society, limited government, democratic governance subject to the rule of law, protection of individual rights, and the like. These are the higher-order organizational defaults in the liberal democratic state. They are permissive defaults in the sense that there can be departures through *lawful* legislative, judicial, or administrative procedures. In this last regard, it is important to recall that the idea of democratic governance (also fundamental to the liberal democratic state) gives rise to power-liability

[45] Hohfeld's residuum is a somewhat ironic expression because in the Hohfeld's legal world – a full one – there is none.

[46] A legal regime whose higher-order norms are in practice vigorously conflicted or wholly unidentifiable will not long stay legal (or a regime.) *See* AGAMBEN, *supra* note 10, at 8.

relations to change the default unspecified privilege-no-right relations. At the same time, the unspecified privilege-no-right relations are also often attended by immunity–disability relations tied to constitutionalism, rule of law, etc. that prevent modification of these privileges.[47]

The liberal democratic state is thus committed to leaving a broad realm of civil society as one that is as a matter of law *largely (not entirely) exempt* from any legal relations other than privilege-no-right. These privilege-no-right relations need not be specified because they are routinely inferred from the broad juridical commitments of the liberal democratic state. That is to say, we do not need an official legal body to *specifically identify or recognize* a privilege for these unspecified privileges to arise. They arise in the liberal state as a function of general legal norms. Sometimes these norms are enshrined in the authoritative written positive law of the state (i.e., written constitutions) and sometimes not:

(1) Constitutional limited government/Separation of state and civil society.
(2) Rule of law commitments/Generality of Norms.
(3) Individual rights/Sovereignty of the individual liberal subject/Dignity of persons.

Constitutional limited government. Putting aside the considerable complications posed by federalism, separation of powers, and the administrative state, the idea here is that only those "constitutional powers" that have been accorded to the federal and state governments and not otherwise clawed back (e.g., by rights) can be exercised by their agencies of those governments (e.g., legislatures, etc.). It follows that whatever is not traceable to self-executing constitutional authorization or to authorized enactments pursuant to the constitution or the state constitutions takes the form of privileges held by whatever constitutional "persons" are cognizable within the liberal ontology. **Rule of law commitments** also contribute to creating the privilege-no-right regime as the default jural relation in liberal legal regimes. The reason is that if the law-giver is "silent" on a given jural relation, then the idea that an agency of legal officialdom can retroactively, without notice or without publicity, impose some disablement is supposed to be out of the question. So, where we encounter something which on first impression looks like legal silence, unless there is some discrete local principle or norm to suggest otherwise, this legal silence means privilege-no-right regimes. **Individual rights** which correspond to and indeed are the juridical expression of the liberal commitment to the sovereignty of the individual liberal subject and the dignity of persons are in very large part rights against state interference with activities occurring in civil society. The imposition of duties and disabilities on the state not to interfere are designed as corroborative protections for the privileges of citizens vis-à-vis each other and vis–à-vis the state.[48]

47 *See* Chapter 11.
48 This is a rough approximation subject to many discrete qualifications (e.g., state of exception) and local complexities (e.g., internal institutional dispersion of the state as in federalism and separation of

Notice, of course, that our confidence in the idea of a broad residuum of privilege-no-rights resting in traders or other persons might well be in the end wrong. It could well turn out that when a court finally does come around to consider whether the law provides a particular privilege, the court decides, "No it doesn't." It might be that we have mistaken the identity of the higher-order norms or that they are more conflicted or incoherent than we initially believed. It could turn out that the paramount higher-order norm is "the state of exception."[49] It may be, in short, that our mistake was to pay too much attention to thinkers like Hayek and Rawls and not enough to thinkers like Schmitt and Agamben.

This is all possible, but it does not affect my analysis. If the state we happen to be dealing with has both rule of law and the state of exception as higher-order norms in equipoise, then in that state, the inference that unspecified legal relations are privilege-no-rights is no longer a safe bet. (This is why in dealing with any legal system, we jurists and legal scholars cannot just deal with its legitimation myths, but must instead try to *ascertain as coldly as possible something a bit more complex – namely its actual organizing principles.*)

But now we turn to a different question: How is Hohfeld's insistence that the privilege-no-right relation is a real legal relation in tension with the law of the liberal democratic state? Consider several points of tension.

15.5.1 *The Conflation of the Horizontal and Vertical Dimensions: Is Law Everywhere?*

The liberal democratic state is by design and by law a limited state – which is to say that it entrenches through both law and politics a deep division between state and civil society. While both "spheres" are subject to law (the rule of law) and politics (democracy), the state's power over and within the state and civil society are quite different. The state itself, as its name announces, is subject to the norms and practices of both democracy as well as the rule of law. When the state regulates civil society, it must in its actions and enactments observe both of those two commitments. Now comes the crucial point: Those persons and groups within civil society need not observe those commitments with regard to each other.

powers). And crucially, this is only what happens with regard to the residuum so long as the relations in the residuum remain unspecified. It is important to recall here that aspects of this residuum could be, at any point, specified through *lawful* legislative, judicial, or administrative procedure and could be specified as something other than privilege-no-right. Indeed, it is important to recall that the idea of democratic governance (also fundamental to the liberal democratic state) gives rise to power-liability relations to change the unspecified privilege-no-right relations. These power-liability relations are caught within a familiar dialectic with certain immunity-disability relations implicit in the rule of law. In the United States, the conflict reaches a kind of conventionally anaesthetized apotheosis in constitutional law under the names "the problem of judicial review," "the counter-majoritarian difficulty," and "the inter-temporal difficulty." When the conflict gets really serious (i.e., an inter-branch impasse), it is called a "constitutional crisis."

49 AGAMBEN, *supra* note 10, at 2–6.

Moreover, the state is importantly restricted in its capacity to impose such norms on those persons and groups. There is thus within the liberalism an effort to institute and follow a fundamental distinction between state relations vis-à-vis individual and groups (sometimes called "*the vertical dimension*") and the relations of individuals and groups vis-à-vis other such individuals and groups (sometimes called "*the horizontal dimension*").

The Hohfeldian insistence that privilege-no-right regimes are "real legal relations" puts this distinction between the horizontal and the vertical dimensions in question. The reason is that once unspecified privileges become "real legal relations" there is no longer in social or economic interaction a purely private sphere of action. Every unspecified privilege in a liberal democratic state becomes, absent contrary authorities described above, a legal permission in A to do X and a denial in B of judicial recourse to stop A from doing X.

Law is thus, in *a formal sense* everywhere we have social or economic relations in a liberal democratic state. Whether *that law is effectual* everywhere, and whether we should *care legally speaking* – are very different questions. Often the answer will be a very confident, "No." Often the answer will be, "Let the parties interfere with each other if they wish – we give them legal permission."

Even so, it is important to recognize what Hohfeldian analysis has just caused us to lose. Things were much easier for jurists and legal scholars in the liberal democratic state when law was not everywhere in social and economic relations. After Hohfeld it becomes much harder to view social and economic relations in the liberal democratic state as somehow "outside" of law or law's ambit. When the privilege-no-right relation is treated as a real legal relation, that move is no longer credible, and drawing a distinction or a set of distinctions between the horizontal dimension and vertical dimension, or between civil society and the state, becomes an overtly political, economic, and moral question calling for justification. In American constitutional law, this challenge arises in paradigmatic form in "state action doctrine," which, not surprisingly, is a locus of incoherence unbound.[50]

From our standpoint, what we need to register here is that the Hohfeldian platform is corrosive of the liberal insistence on the cogency and existence of an entrenched distinction between the vertical and the horizontal dimension. If we are constantly being presented with hybrid cases that present both horizontal and vertical dimensions (as indeed Hohfeldian analysis seems to suggest) then asking the question, "Is this relation horizontal or is it vertical?" seems unlikely to produce salient answers. Another way to state the point is that liberalism would very much like for law not to be everywhere while Hohfeld's analysis seems to lead us to the opposite realization.

Now, a caveat: It is important not to make too much of the idea that law is everywhere. That is true as a formal matter – at least where social and economic

50 Gary Peller, *Privilege*, 104 GEO. L.J. 883 (2016).

interaction is concerned. What does matter analytically (we will turn to this below) is not so much the presence or absence of law, but rather law's effectuality very broadly conceived.

But before we leave the formal plane, it must be emphasized that it is important for both the partisans and the critics of liberalism to recognize this last point. For one thing, it does run against an important liberal strategy for protecting the freedom of the sovereign individual subject. What strategy is that? It is . . .

15.5.2 *The Law-Free Zones*

Throughout the twentieth century, and despite the efforts of Hohfeld and his followers, liberalism has had a recurrent tendency to treat certain matters as sometimes "outside of law," even if from a Hohfeldian perspective, they are not. Among those matters that are *sometimes* treated as "outside of law" are the market, competition, the family, privacy, autonomy, free will, choice, or consent. These are treated in judicial discourse as if they were somehow *not* themselves legal constructs and also immune somehow (how?) to the regulatory effects and implications of law.

These domains are sometimes legally cast as "outside of law" because of liberalism's commitment to protect the sovereignty of the liberal individual subject and its supporting political-legal scaffolding. The principal liberal strategy for recognizing and realizing (making real) this commitment lies in defining and delineating "spheres," "realms," "zones," "sectors," "areas," "regions," and "enclaves," – in short, "spaces" *that are outside the law* and that accordingly should not be subjected to legal regulation. We have here the kind of spatialization that I have elsewhere described as "the grid aesthetic."[51] Liberal jurisprudence, certainly in the nineteenth century, even today remains marked with references to such spatialized determinations of protection: "private *sectors*," "*zones* of privacy," "*realms* of personal choice," "*areas* of liberty," "*regions* of discretion," "*spheres* of public discourse," "*enclaves* of private life," and "*spaces* of globalization." These in turn are defined and demarcated by "borders," "boundaries," "lines," or "distinctions" so that their scope, limits, bounds, can be delineated, and mapped.

From a Hohfeldian perspective, the treatment of a privilege-no-right relation as a law-free zone is an *analytical* error. But from the strictly political perspective of liberalism, it is not an error at all. On the contrary, the spatialization strategy is tied up with the fundamental political liberal project of protecting the freedom of the sovereign individual legal subject.[52] Indeed, if we are trying to establish for the

[51] Schlag, *supra* note 35, at 1055–70.

[52] Viewed historically, the spatialization of entitlements and disablement is entrenched. Arguably, the implicit source domain for this model – and here history reaches out to rule us from the grave – is that of the master exercising will and dominion over his (real) property. Duncan Kennedy, *Understanding Legal Consciousness, Toward an Understanding of Legal Consciousness; The Case of Classical Legal Thought in America, 1850–1940*, 3 RES. L. & SOC. 3, 7 (1980); Jennifer Nedelsky, *Law, Boundaries and the Bounded Self*, 30 REPRESENTATIONS 162–89 (1990); Pierre Schlag, *Rights in the Postmodern*

sovereign individual subject some legal entitlement that allows for the exercise of unconditioned will, choice, self-determination, autonomy or the like, then creating a law-free zone is an obvious way to do it.[53] The form is a perfect fit. Within the "bounds," of "the space" established, *a crucial determination*, it is the sovereign individual liberal subject who determines the content of the freedom. He rules unencumbered over his domain (or at least that's the idealized image). I do not wish to suggest that spatialization is the only aesthetic strategy available to liberal legalism. Hence, objectification is also clearly a key player. And, of course, both are often wrapped up in each other: the aesthetic of spaces and spatialization is swathed with the aesthetic of objects and objectification.[54] But as we are talking about law-free zones, it is spatialization, territorialization, boundaries, and the like that are most saliently implicated here.

The key thing is to recognize that spatialization (and the law-free zones) remain a crucial *realization strategy* for liberal legalism – one that has the distinct advantage of being already largely *realized*. This is in great part why partisans of liberal legalism are extremely unlikely to give up lightly on spatialization (there is a lot at stake *in this aesthetic*).

15.5.3 *The Effectuality of the Privilege-No-Right Relation*

One of things that the recognition of privilege-no-right as a "real legal relation" accomplishes is to transform all those ostensibly law-free zones, all those supposedly empty spaces, into legal relations that can be analyzed. This is an opening largely unexploited by Hohfeld himself, but his platform indicated the various paths forward. And if one turns to the subsequent history – in particular to the work of Corbin, Cohen, Cook, Commons, Hale, Coase, Singer, and Kennedy – one starts to see how Hohfeldian analysis might be used vis-à-vis privilege-no-right relations.

Of course, simply because law is everywhere in a formal sense, doesn't mean that it is everywhere effectual in ways that matter. *Presence* should not be confused with *effectuality* or *significance*. Much of the time, the law has not all that much effect on relations or interactions relative to other coordination systems (morality, technology, architecture, etc.), or to other factors of production (capital, skill, labor, talent, knowledge, etc.). It is hard to tell because identifying *the relative contributions* of these coordination systems and factors of production in any given context is itself an extremely difficult task. Even apart from having to do the work *in context* (the mere thought of doing that already hurts!) consider the thorny questions we encounter up front, "How will we differentiate each production factor or coordination system from

Condition, *in* LEGAL RIGHTS: HISTORICAL AND PHILOSOPHICAL PERSPECTIVES 263, 277–80 (Austin Sarat & Thomas R. Kearns eds., 1996).

53 Kennedy, *supra* note 52; Schlag, *supra* note 52, at 270–75.

54 Schlag, *supra* note 35, at 1055–70 (2002) (the "grid" aesthetic).

the others? What baseline will we use? What rates of substitutability? Hell, what substitutability? What measure and what metric do we use?

Nonetheless, the notion that we should look into the matter is evident. Indeed, if as Gary Becker claimed long ago, the criminal law can be seen as a pricing system (yes, it can if you want) then so can the moral, the religious, the cultural codes, along with whatever guilt and shame complexes they yield in the subject populations.[55] If one of these can be seen as a pricing system, then arguably they should all be seen in principle as pricing systems, and each ought to be seen as potentially re-enforcing and interfering with the others. Notice that this would greatly complicate, though also greatly improve, the work of economic analysis of law.

How and in what circumstances then is the privilege-no-right relation effectual? Can we say anything about that at least? Yes. It is effectual in several ways of which I will mention only three here.

A Privilege is not Nothing. A privilege, in Hohfeldian terms, is a negation of duty of the opposite tenor. *A* can thus in exchange for some payment from *B* surrender a privilege to *B* and assume a duty to *B*. *A*, of course, has a huge number of privileges that are of no interest to *B* or *C* or *D* or indeed to anyone including A himself. But that is of no moment here.[56] What does matter is that some of *A's* privileges might have some surrender value sometimes to someone else.[57] And here, of course, it is important to understand that *A's* privileges can interfere socioeconomically with the exercise of *B's* privileges and vice versa. Social and economic life is full of such examples of conflicting privilege-no-right relations – that is to say, relations where I am privileged to do X and you are privileged to do Y (which, frankly, interferes with my doing X). And then there are all those reciprocally conflicting privileges where doing Y interferes with X and doing X also interferes with Y.[58]

Entourage Matters. Building on the foregoing, privilege-no-rights are relations where parties can press other entitlements and disablements into effect. I have a privilege to sell my labor in exchange for a salary. The value of my privilege (what I can get from an employer) depends upon what other entitlements I have. Can I start a secondary boycott or engage in a sit-down strike or am I under a duty (prohibition of secondary boycotts, trespass laws) not to do so? It matters. The value of a privilege-no-right relation depends upon the entourage of other entitlements – disablements that can be called into play. The most obvious example – one routinely mentioned in the Hohfeldian literature is *A's* privilege to do X (no-right in *B*)

[55] Gary S. Becker, *Crime and Punishment: An Economic Approach*, 76 J. Pol. Econ. 169 (1968).

[56] Here I am keen on advancing a distinction between *legal* and *effectual/significant*. Against some commentators, I want to argue that state permissions are legal and that the absence of a *formal and specific* legal declaration ought not to suggest otherwise. At the same time and against another group of commentators, I want to suggest that simply because a privilege is legal in the foregoing sense does not mean that it is effectual/significant: it does not mean *ipso facto*, that we have reason to care about it in our analyses.

[57] For elaboration, *see* Schlag, *supra* note 2, at 212–15.

[58] *Id.*

combined with a "corroborating right" in A that *B* not interfere in some way with A's doing X. From here, it is easy to see that the relevant legal relations are almost always more complicated and diverse than this – that for any given privilege to do (or not do) X there is a rich entourage of other entitlement-disablement relations that affect the socioeconomic capacity of A to do (or not do) X. Criminal law, tort law, statutory and regulatory law are always in the entourage helping to enable or disable the parties from pressing the advantages of their privileges. Both transactional lawyers and litigators know this with a vengeance as they try to "corner" or "box in" their opposition (and occasionally allies and third parties).

The Textured Effect of Law. Perhaps it is legal training and the focus on discrete legal texts (the judicial opinion, the contract) or perhaps it is the interstitiality of contacts between lawyers and clients, but legal professionals of all kinds *tend to see law in punctuated terms.* That is to say, they register law as something that occurs in discrete texts, publications, fora, filings, motions, rulings, holdings, closings, dispositions, and so on. These are the *punctuations of law.* It is in these kinds of formalized artifacts and events that law supposedly happens and is registered (i.e., noticed and analyzed). But life and law, while often experienced as punctuated in exactly these ways, *also* dispenses effects in more continuous ways with ebbs and flows of effectuality. Indeed, the law that happens at the punctuated points where lawyers are often present is continually being worked and reworked *before and after* by the parties as they generate and apply this law to and on each other. Sometimes knowingly, sometimes not. Sometimes correctly and sometimes not. I do not want to understate the importance of legal punctuation which is most often performed by this or that agent of legal officialdom through highly formalized settings and artifacts. In this regard, notice that the last decided punctuations of law (including any future expected punctuations of law) continue to exercise their hold in any given human relation – orienting and shaping interaction and behavior in the meantime. But to focus solely on the legal punctuations yields a misapprehension of law.[59] Law doesn't happen merely at the points of legal punctuation – even if we law-types have both a professional and now, given the internet, a thoroughly journalistic tendency to focus just on those. To illustrate and exemplify my point about law before and after punctuation, I quote here a passage from Arthur Leff recounting fictional conversations between two businessmen:

1. BUYER: Hello, Morris? Those widgets you sent us. They're breaking every minute. You want me to pay for such junk?

SELLER: Look, if your men don't know how to use widgets right, what do you want from me? They're just what you ordered, Grade A-2 stainless steel widgets.

[59] This is an important and recurrent theme in the work of cultural studies in law. *See, e.g.*, Naomi Mezey, *Approaches to the Cultural Study of Law: Law as Culture*, 13 YALE J.L. & HUMAN. 35 (2001).

BUYER: Stainless steel they're not. Swiss cheese maybe, orange-crate wood, but not steel.

SELLER: Look, Kevin, maybe we've been having a little quality control problem – just temporary. Do the best you can and we'll make it up next time.

BUYER: OK, but don't forget. The noise of popping widgets my partner doesn't have to hear.

2. SELLER: Hello, Kevin? So what's with our last bill?

BUYER: My bookkeeper's been sick.

SELLER: Uh huh. Your hand cramps when you pick up a pen?

BUYER: Soon, Morris.

SELLER: How soon? Tomorrow?

BUYER: Come on, Morris; did I make such a stink when you were shipping out those cardboard widgets?

SELLER: OK, OK. Maybe I'll give you a couple of weeks more. You're not *really* in trouble are you?

BUYER: Absolutely not. I got plenty of orders. Go check with some of the other guys.

SELLER: Don't worry. I already did. OK, take a couple of weeks. Give my get-wells to your bookkeeper.

BUYER: Hah![60]

Arthur Leff concludes this dialogue by noting that it would be sheer folly to characterize these conversations as being either coercive or cooperative. For Leff, they were quite clearly both. Yes! I would add a parallel observation: It also would be sheer folly to analyze these conversations as either business or legal. They are quite clearly both. And yet, these conversations are the sorts of things that we, legal professionals, simply do not recognize, think about, or analyze as law. In fact, this sort of exchange between merchants *is* to law (for legal scholars) as the firm *used to be* a while ago to the market (for economists). What the firm used to be (pre-Coase) was a black hole, the missing link, an unmentionable. Ironically, we law professors have been really good at picking up on what economists *now* say about the firm – that it is a governance mechanism, that it is hugely important. What do we law-types have to say about merchant conversations *qua* law? "Oh that's not really law . . ."

Ah, but it is.

To recognize in all these ways that the privilege-no-right relation is effectual in social and economic life (somewhere between 0–100 percent) yields a perhaps unexpected implication. All of a sudden, those law-free zones that are now cognizable as privilege-no-right relations have become *subject to legal analysis* in terms of their social, economic, and political effects and implications. This is auspicious – there is much work to be done![61]

60 Arthur Leff, *Injury, Ignorance and Spite: The Dynamics of Coercive Collection*, 80 YALE L.J. 1, 25 (1970).

61 Or conversely, this is ghastly-dreadful.

Hohfeld thus invites the kind of analysis that subsequently developed along the lines of legal realism, law and economics, and critical legal studies. This latter sort of analysis pressed hard and seriously leads us intellectually to consider all legal relations – discounting or setting aside only those that are not effectual.[62]

It would be an untenable exaggeration to credit (or to blame) Hohfeld for all that the realist, law and economics, and critical legal studies scholars have wrought with his platform and his insights, let alone what I have said here. But the fashioning of privilege-no-right as a "real legal relation" (emphasis on real, legal, and relation) opened the door. One can see then why jurists and scholars committed to liberalism and its judicial discourse might resist Hohfeldian analysis. The latter can easily lead to the kind of analyses that are in some ways antithetical to the juridical commitments of the liberal democratic state.[63] Now to be sure, Hohfeldian analysis does not compel us to go there. But to say it again, it opens the door. And once the door is open and one can see what lies beyond, it's hard to look away, let alone shut the door.

15.6 CONCLUSION

Frankly, there can be none. At least not if what I have said makes sense. I could summarize, of course, but let's pass on that. My overarching aim was to highlight some productive tensions between Hohfeldian analysis on the one hand, and liberalism on the other. If I have done my job, then the tensions remain.

Tension, as I indicated earlier, is a designedly vague term. I have highlighted what I think are the sources and loci of these tensions. It is, of course, possible to undertake preclusive conceptual steps to avoid these tensions and render the encounter between Hohfeldian analysis and liberal law seamless.

But, I prefer not to – for two simple reasons. First, if one is interested in doing things with Hohfeld, the aim is to enable us to do or think – where it leads so to speak. Second, all of what I have been saying here is already happening. The kind of thinking (economic, political, normative, social) that Hohfeld's platform enables reveals that we have already traveled considerable distance down paths that place the liberal understanding and its judicial discourse in question. It may well be, of course, that both champions as well as critics of the liberal democratic state cannot or will not give up situating their work within or against the legitimating myths of liberalism.

In part, this is why the ethos and the aesthetics of the liberal democratic state remain center stage – at least in American law and legal thought. We are still – legal

62 In other words, it is lack of effectuality/significance (not lack of legality) that leads these various forms of thought to treat some legal relations as relatively unimportant. Ted Sichelman's and Henry Smith's views on the importance of modularity in legal regimes are, I think, consonant with this observation. See Chapter 11.

63 Peller, *supra* note 50.

champions and legal critics alike – writing as if we are still playing out the great dramas of the liberal democratic state. That is not good.

We need to move on. And yet as we do, it seems odd, a bit humbling, but also interesting to consider that Hohfeld, a legal thinker who peaked in 1913, can still provoke useful analysis and insights today. And this is to say nothing about legal regimes that have arisen in the wake of liberal democracy. To be sure, in the US, the liberal democratic state and its law are still on the scene, even if mostly honored in the breach. Those breaches are instanced in the advent of the administered state, the neoliberal state and the dissociative state. But that is a book for another day.

16

The Contingent Politics of Legal Formalism

Aditi Bagchi[*]

16.1 INTRODUCTION

Wesley Hohfeld deconstructed legal concepts to reveal unjustified assumptions about their structure. It is thus unfair or inevitable – probably both – that he be charged with analogous errors of his own. My worries about Hohfeld's classic text, *Fundamental Legal Conceptions as Applied in Judicial Reasoning*, are of just the sort that Hohfeld had himself, albeit with other targets in mind.

I will argue that Hohfeld's scheme has latent political implications that render the scheme less than hospitable to a more egalitarian private law structure. The aim here is not to defend an alternative regime, or even elaborate on it in detail; indeed, it may be ultimately undesirable once specified. But it is hard even to bring such an egalitarian scheme into view through the analytic lenses offered by Hohfeld, and that is itself a problem for his account.

Hohfeld appears to have targeted a different set of assumptions about legal concepts that disadvantaged the already disadvantaged. He made at least two fundamental contributions to legal discourse along these lines. First, he deconstructed property rights, disaggregating them such that holding certain entitlements over property no longer implied a full range of other entitlements.[1] Similarly, he distinguished rights from privileges, allowing that sometimes a so-called right to engage in a conduct is actually a mere privilege to engage in conduct, unaccompanied by any entitlement that others not undermine its value.[2] This point effectively

* Many thanks to conference organizers and editors for the invitation to participate in this volume; thanks also to other conference participants for their illumination of Hohfeld and his legacy; and special thanks to Guido Calabresi for his comments on this chapter.

1 Wesley N. Hohfeld, *Fundamental Legal Conceptions as Applied in Judicial Reasoning*, 23 YALE L.J. 16–59 (1913). He is for this reason associated with the "bundle of sticks" view of property, though he did not use that metaphor.

2 Pierre Schlag, *How to Do Things With Hohfeld*, 78 LAW & CONTEMP. PROBS. 185, 211 (2015) ("slippage from privileges to rights will tend to favor entrenched legal interests ... Because it is those already recognized legal interests or socioeconomically powerful interests that are likely to be featured as the frame, framework, baseline, or starting point for analysis"). *See also* Gary Peller, *Privilege*, 104 GEO. L.J. 883, 885 (2016).

helped to stop (analytically) a slide from privileges to rights, an inadvertent expansion of entitlements for the already entitled.

My immediate point is that even as Hohfeld deconstructs some analytic choices and reveals their contingency, he reifies other choices that are equally contingent. The broader point is that such simultaneous deconstruction-reification is unavoidable. Any reordering of a conceptual scheme to clear away the bramble will put the bramble somewhere else. And when attention eventually shifts to that latter location in the scheme, there will be clearing work to do all over again.

I observe three features of his scheme that undermine the intelligibility, and even more so the plausibility, of alternative private law orders. Each stems from hyper-individuation within the Hohfeldian scheme, or its treatment of a single legal relation between two individuals as the consistent unit of analysis. First, Hohfeld does not recognize any lateral references in his scheme of entitlements. A lateral reference would incorporate into our understanding of a legal relation some reference to another legal relation, whether between the same individuals; one of those individuals and another person, or; other individuals, none of whom is a party to the primary legal relation being described. In Hohfeld's account, rights, privileges, powers, and immunities are borne by individuals and are assigned no justificatory role; they are freestanding, as if they stand in only a logical rather than a normative relation to duties, "no-rights," liabilities, and disabilities. The result is that the content of entitlements between two people never depends conceptually on what other people's entitlements are.

Second, the correlative structure of rights and duties in Hohfeld's framework denies imperfect legal rights. He is committed famously to the idea that rights and duties run bilaterally, albeit between numerous pairs. By contrast, most private rights plausibly derivative from distributive injustice are imperfect.

Finally, Hohfeld's scheme lends itself to the idea that fully specified rights will rarely conflict. Properly sorted, all entitlements can be rearranged into the boxes he offers. He does not encourage us to expect anything will be left out; that the legal scheme might fail to recognize one type of entitlement by virtue of having committed itself to having recognized another; and that such a failure could be a cause for system regret.

16.2 LATERAL REFERENCES

Hohfeld does not purport to offer an exhaustive catalogue of the attributes an entitlement might have. Entitlements are defined only "logically" in relation to their corresponding burdens. Thus, rights or privileges of the Hohfeldian sort might be found in either a legal order in which everyone presumptively has the same legal rights and privileges or one in which they do not.

There is a literal sense in which people never have identical entitlements. Even if our resources were exactly the same, you would be entitled to one apple and I would be entitled to a different apple. But equality talk about rights gets off the ground because we can recognize some equivalence to our entitlements to our respective apples, and also because we can appreciate that a right to a unique apple in a situation where everyone has their own is very different from a unique right to the only apple. Hohfeld's scheme does not distinguish between entitlements that are general, like the right not to be assaulted, and ones that are (relatively) exceptional, like intellectual property. By conceiving of these rights as formally similar, his account invites us to expect that they will operate similarly. By contrast, a conceptual catalogue that distinguished among them would encourage disparate treatment, for example, with respect to their robustness and defeasibility.

Still more distant from the Hohfeldian picture are distinctions based on value. Just as it does not enter his picture that the contours of an entitlement will turn in part on the value of the entitlement to the right-holder as compared to the negative value of the corresponding burden, it does not matter whether defining the boundaries of the right one way affects the availability or value of a comparable entitlement for others. Although myriad lateral references are relevant to how we define entitlements, at least two features seem central. First, we can distinguish, on the one hand, between rights that are more general – in that they are held and valued more equally by all subjects of the legal regime – and on the other hand, rights that are special – in that they are allocated to relatively few legal subjects.

Second, rights differ in the extent to which their associated costs are borne by similar rights-holders or instead by non-rights-holders. That is, some rights are limited in the way that John Rawls describes under his first principle: political liberties are as expansive as possible given equal liberties for all. Other rights, such as the rights and privileges attendant to various forms of private property, impose burdens as much, if not largely on, people who do not have similar entitlements.

One might argue that the difference between general and special rights, and the distribution of costs associated with a right, are relevant only to the political choices that Hohfeld sets aside. These features, the argument would go, do not inhere in the logic of rights but pertain to the choice of whether to recognize a particular right or privilege. Certainly, a person's entitlements can be characterized without reference to how they compare to those of others. But such a limited characterization is, if not false, at least misleading for being incomplete. Both of the lateral dimensions above can just as well be framed as features of rights rather than merely considerations relevant to their merits.

Defenders of Hohfeld would be right that the particular incompleteness of his account that I am flagging here – namely, the absence of lateral references in the characterization of entitlements – follows from Hohfeld's apparent effort to avoid infusing his conceptual scheme with normativity. Moreover, this studied avoidance of normativity may have successfully exposed the normativity in conservative propositions about rights. But this normative blank distorts the picture of entitlements because entitlements are claims that are made by individuals at the expense of others, and whether a right or privilege applies in a given case is also a decision about whether to recognize it under the circumstances. The judgment need not be lawless – it is not fully determined even with lateral features of the entitlement duly noted. But without lateral reference, it is not possible even to apply precedent correctly, because like cases will not be distinguishable from those importantly dissimilar in their distributive implications.

The hollowness of a conceptual scheme drained of normativity is an objection that has been raised before with respect to Hohfeld's correlativity thesis. Scholars like Joseph Raz and Andrei Marmor (admittedly writing about rights as such, and not just legal rights) have observed that defining rights and duties as logical counterparts obscures their normative relation. A right is better characterized as a ground of duty; Hohfeld's picture implies false symmetry.[3]

Just as agnosticism about the normative relation between rights and duties may mislead us about their relationship, the failure to incorporate lateral references into the characterization of entitlements puts out of the picture a range of matters essential to practical and legal reasoning about entitlements. Hohfeld offers us a conceptual scheme that is supposed to enable us to think systematically and clearly about rights. Of course, he is not invoking rights in the "manifesto-style" and is concerned with legal validity rather than justification.[4] But as H. L. A. Hart observed, "the ways of thinking about rights common among serious critics of the law and social theorists must be accommodated."[5] Answering the question of whether a right exists on certain facts under existing law requires that we specify the right properly, and its lateral features are among those we would use to recognize it. A conceptual scheme cannot help us think clearly if it willfully ignores considerations central to the category of thought it aims to organize. Hohfeld failed to incorporate lateral references that ought to figure in systematic thinking about rights.

16.3 IMPERFECT RIGHTS

A similar limitation in Hohfeld's scheme lies in his failure to allow for imperfect rights and duties. Hohfeld's correlativity thesis implies that private rights are held by individuals against individuals.[6] His picture is, in this respect, consistent with that of Hart, who proposed that "[t]he idea [of private law] is that of one individual being given by the law exclusive control, more or less extensive, over another person's duty so that in the area of conduct covered by that duty the individual who has the right is a small-scale sovereign to whom the duty is owed."[7] In the case of an imperfect right,

3 Joseph Raz, *On the Nature of Rights*, 93 MIND 194, 199 (1984); Andrei Marmor, *On the Limits of Rights*, 16 LAW & PHIL. 1, 3 (1997).

4 *Cf.* JOEL FEINBERG, SOCIAL PHILOSOPHY 67 (1973).

5 H. L. A. Hart, *Legal Rights*, *in* ESSAYS ON BENTHAM 192 (1982).

6 *See* JOSEPH RAZ, THE CONCEPT OF A LEGAL SYSTEM 179 (1967) (rejecting Hohfeld's claim that a right is a relation between no more than two persons).

7 Hart, *supra* note 5, at 183.

by contrast, there is no single person with a corresponding duty to the right-holder; and in the case of an imperfect duty, there is no single right-holder with an enforceable claim against the person subject to the imperfect duty. The status of imperfect rights and duties in Hohfeld's conceptual scheme is politically significant because any private rights and duties derivative from principles of distributive justice are likely to take that form.[8] That is, we may each have an imperfect right to our fair share of social resources, and an imperfect duty to take no more than our fair share. Alternatively, those who in fact end up with less than their fair share may have an imperfect right of repair against those who benefit from the unjust scheme, while the latter are subject to an imperfect duty of repair. None of these rights and duties finds footing in the Hohfeldian scheme.

There are two ways to rebut this challenge to Hohfeld. One could observe that Hohfeld's scheme is easily compatible with rights held against the state, which is tasked with meeting the imperfect duties of citizens. One can also argue that imperfect rights as such have no legal status. Both of these arguments explain not only why Hohfeld's account resonates with contemporary legal theorists but also why its plausibility depends on contingent facts about law and legal discourse today.

The first defensive argument presents the state as agent for private individuals subject to imperfect duties. Those individuals may have perfect duties to the state to pay taxes or otherwise support state activity. Individuals with imperfect rights against other private individuals, in turn, are granted perfect rights against the state as to tax advantages or benefits. Matthew Kramer implies that the Hohfeldian scheme can thus accommodate imperfect rights and duties. The essential step, in his view, is to appreciate that:

> The power to seek enforcement does not necessarily lie within the discretion of the person who has the claim. So long as a claim is duly enforceable, its status as a genuine Hohfeldian claim is unaffected by the precise location of the power to seek enforcement; that power may be held by the claim-holder, or it may be held by someone acting as a fiduciary on behalf of the claim-holder, or it may be held by a governmental agency.[9]

This translation of imperfect rights and duties to perfect duties to and against the state is familiar because, to the extent imperfect rights and duties are realized, it is indeed through the state as intermediary. However, this articulation of rights fails to link a claimant's right against a state with any private imperfect duties that the state executes on other private parties' behalf. Formally stating the duty as between private persons and the state disconnects the ultimate bearers of rights and duties – at least on one view of the political morality of distribution and private law. Moreover, for

[8] These are not the only imperfect rights and duties that the scheme does not accommodate. *See* Feinberg, *supra* note 4, at 63 ("Many duties of obedience imposed by legal rules are not 'owed' to other persons, but rather to some wholly impersonal authority like 'the law' or a painted stop sign.").

[9] Matthew Kramer, *Rights without Trimmings*, *in* A Debate over Rights 9 (Matthew H. Kramer et al. eds., 1998).

those who regard current distributions as unjust, the state is failing in its role as intermediary. On this view, even if the state could theoretically serve as an intermediary that renders the notion of imperfect rights and duties unnecessary, its inadequate service in that regard results in either *residual* or *remedial* imperfect rights and duties that run directly among citizens.

The disconnect between bearers of imperfect rights and duties could be unproblematic for an account of *legal* concepts if there is no direct linkage between private imperfect duties and rights in law.[10] And, of course, not everyone agrees on the existence of residual imperfect rights and duties under conditions of distributive injustice. It might be that these objections to Hohfeld's conceptual scheme have not been lodged because so few scholars take seriously the claim that these imperfect rights exist and have legal form.

But there is reasonable disagreement about both the state of the law and the moral duties of citizens under distributive injustice – disagreement that an ostensibly neutral conceptual scheme should not preempt. One can plausibly argue that a variety of legal entitlements are delimited in consideration of imperfect rights that they occasionally abut. I have argued elsewhere that the doctrine of unconscionability serves this function in contract.[11] On this view, imperfect rights manifest in law even if they are not directly actionable. They are legal rights in the sense that they help define "ultimate" entitlements in specific cases, even if they are not freestanding and generate only excuses and defenses rather than affirmative claims. Similarly, imperfect legal duties show up in the restricted form that conflicting perfect rights and duties take. We can make sense of some limitations to simple property rights or contractual entitlements by reference to imperfect duties that attenuate the claims of those rights-holders against individual duty-bearers, even if the latter are only members of a set to whom the relevant imperfect duty is owed.

Whether one sees the law in this way will depend on one's conception of distributive justice and one's theory about how it operates on a legal order. Today, private law scholars do not pay a lot of attention to problems of distributive justice – oddly enough, not as a matter of neglect but as a matter of principle.[12] That dominant perspective in legal discourse today cannot be legitimately incorporated

[10] That is a common position. *See, e.g.*, FEINBERG, *supra* note 4, at 63 ("When we leave legal contexts to consider moral obligations and other extralegal duties, a greater variety of legal duties without correlative rights present themselves.").

[11] Aditi Bagchi, *Distributive Injustice and Private Law*, 60 HASTINGS L.J. 105 (2008).

[12] *See, e.g.*, Louis Kaplow & Steven Shavell, *Why the Legal System is Less Efficient than the Income Tax in Redistributing Income*, 23 J. LEGAL STUD. 667, 677 (1994) (arguing that because legal rules designed to redistribute income produce the distortions resulting from the redistribution itself as well as inefficiencies in the activities regulated by the legal rules, it is "appropriate for economic analysis of legal rules to focus on efficiency and to ignore the distribution of income in offering normative judgments"); MICHAEL TREBILCOCK, THE LIMITS OF FREEDOM OF CONTRACT 97–101 (1993); A. MITCHELL POLINSKY, AN INTRODUCTION TO LAW AND ECONOMICS 124–27 (2d ed. 1989). *See, e.g.*, Arthur Ripstein, *Private Order and Public Justice*, 92 VA. L. REV. 1391, 1395 (2006) ("Both tort and property protect what people happen to have, without any thought about how they got it or what they

into a conceptual scheme of legal entitlements any more than the once-dominant perspectives Hohfeld set out to overturn when he wrote.

16.4 NORMALIZED CONFLICT AND SYSTEM REGRET

My final complaint is about another feature of entitlements, conceived as a set, that is also missing in Hohfeld's account. Hohfeld does not take seriously the possibility of conflict among entitlements. This is not to say that he does not, strictly speaking, allow for conflicting legal norms. Matthew Kramer expressly argues that "a person can be under conflicting duties" in the Hohfeldian scheme.[13] However, these conflicts can be reconciled within the scheme, primarily through compensation that recognizes whichever duty is failed.[14]

More generally, Hohfeld's account is geared toward diffusing such conflict within the legal system. Conceptual formalism only delivers on its promise of clarity and determinacy if there are no basic inconsistencies in the system of entitlements that it describes. Adequate specification of entitlements might make apparent conflict go away. At worst, appeal to exogenous political considerations can be made to revise entitlements as necessary. Hohfeld does not entertain the possibility of *persistent* conflict of the sort that a legal system can never rid itself of entirely. In fact, the aim of conceptual *order* seems hostile to recognizing that kind of conflict.

The debate about internal conflict in law is sometimes framed as a matter of conceptual possibility. On the one hand, we have the argument that law must supply some way to identify applicable norms and to resolve conflict so that judges can deliver judgments in specific cases.[15] On the other hand, we have the argument that law is an imperfect human enterprise, the product of conflict, and carried on by actors with "many different wills and imaginations, interests and visions."[16]

should have from a moral point of view. The law attends to the form of the transaction or holding, rather than the needs or interests of the parties to it."); Stephen Perry, *On the Relationship between Corrective and Distributive Justice*, *in* OXFORD ESSAYS ON JURISPRUDENCE 237, 247 (Jeremy Horder ed., 2000) (corrective justice is "an independent moral principle that operates within the context of distributive justice, but not as part of it"); Peter Benson, *The Basis of Corrective Justice and its Relation to Distributive Justice*, 77 IOWA L. REV. 515, 607 (1992) ("The justification of abstract right and of its principles of acquisition does not depend in the least on the prior satisfaction of any distributive requirements of background justice."); ERNEST WEINRIB, THE IDEA OF PRIVATE LAW 80 (1995) ("As an autonomous form of justice, corrective justice operates on entitlements without addressing the justice of the underlying distribution.").

13 Kramer, *supra* note 9, at 18. *See also* Nigel Simmonds, *The Analytical Foundations of Justice*, 54 CAMBRIDGE L.J. 306, 337 (1995) ("The Hohfeldian analysis of rights . . . allows for practical conflicts between rights.").

14 Kramer, *supra* note 9, at 19.

15 *See* FEINBERG, *supra* note 4, at 72 ("A legal system cannot very well countenance conflicting specific rights.").

16 *See* ROBERTO UNGER, WHAT SHOULD LEGAL ANALYSIS BECOME? 65 (1996). *See also* Stephen Munzer, *Validity and Legal Conflicts*, 82 YALE L.J. 1140, 1174 (1973) ("the mistake [of a view of law as tidy and formal] lies in the . . . failure to appreciate that law is the result of human behavior").

My critique here differs from the usual argument for the possibility that legal rules conflict because the argument here is not ultimately conceptual. Nor is it epistemic; it does not aim to show that internal conflict is the most likely to accurately describe legal systems as a matter of freestanding truth. I am addressing the related but somewhat different question of whether it is a good idea to think of law as internally conflicting. That question is overtly normative, and the answer here is affirmative.

Conceptualism aims for analytic clarity. But, at least in law, this is more than an aesthetic preference; we hope it will produce more consistent, determinate answers to legal questions. We hope it will offer practical guidance without resorting to first order values on which we disagree.[17] But such consistency and determinacy are also a cost. The ideal of analytic clarity can be politically regressive where concepts have normative underpinnings that are contested and unstable.

Where people disagree about what legal norms should be, accommodating conflict is a more egalitarian alternative to definitive settlement because the latter entails a "total win" by the more powerful group, whose interpretation of the law is henceforth equivalent to the law itself. If the application of a legal norm is not entirely predictable, it motivates groups to push for their favored interpretation of it. Each mobilized group will win some and lose some.[18] Inconsistency across legal judgments or even legal rules undermines rule of law on the margin, but consistent failure to give credence to the interpretations advanced by major social groups undermines legitimacy too. Moreover, exaggerating the determinacy of existing rules by obfuscating deep disagreement about the principles that motivate rules and guide their extension undermines transparency, another rule of law value.

Legal evolution is driven by push at the margins. Courts will rarely undertake a deliberate rearrangement of legal categories; they will rarely characterize an anomalous case as anomalous. But without engaging in meta-talk, judges might gradually render a legal norm, or even a legal concept, outdated. The erosion of a concept – like that of privity – opens up new kinds of claims that were previously conceptually incoherent. Once the justifications for individual decisions are aggregated and recognized as a shift, it will have been legal progress.

Expecting conflict within the law may be even more valuable when evolution is slow and evolution in a particular direction is improbable. In these cases, managing conflict internally does not enable progress but it may lay the groundwork for a kind of *system regret*. When an apparent conflict between two rules is resolved in favor of one, there is a risk of devaluing the "losing" party's interests. Especially when the conflict is not a literal conflict of rule but a tension between the principles underlying legal rules, the failure to act on a background principle consistently over time

[17] Jeremy Waldron, *"Transcendental Nonsense" and System in the Law*, 100 COLUM. L. REV. 16, 25 (2000) (defending technical legal language and concepts that "accommodate policy initiatives inspired by different moralities, ideologies, and programs, while resisting theoretical identification with any one of them").

[18] *Cf.* Heather Gerken, *Dissenting by Deciding*, 57 STAN. L. REV. 1745 (2005).

risks being read as a total rejection of it, rather than a consistent privileging of a rival principle. For example, there are reasons to permit access to the private property of others that are consistently rejected in favor of the reasons for recognizing a more robust conception of private property. And there are reasons to protect individuals from exploitive bargains that are consistently rejected in favor of reasons to permit relative freedom of contract. In neither case is there a true conflict of legal rules. But there is a tension between commitments embodied in law: principles of free competition may favor less restrictive property rights, and principles against unjust enrichment (broadly construed) may cut against enforcement of an exploitive agreement. Those principles do not show up at all in the Hohfeldian scheme. If we take his scheme to be partial, it offers no guidance about how these background principles should figure into legal reasoning. If we attempt to shoehorn them into legal rules that he can recognize, they are either implausible or undesirable. The great temptation is to simply set aside those complicating principles and focus on applying the logic of legal rules that Hohfeld would recognize.

If we do that, those "losing" principles will not just fail to express in hard legal rules, they also will do less work in softening the "winning" legal norms. The rejected reasons may go off screen, which is a loss, because "recognition that a given party possess a right of any sort … is morally significant to that party, since it involves according that party respect."[19] The residual value of recognizing conflict is apparent in the duty to compensate even in cases where one is entitled to trespass by necessity.[20] Even if we can fine-tune legal rules to account for remedial duties in the case of first-order apparent conflict, recognizing conflict, or sustaining system regret, keeps defeated interests afloat within the legal system so that they might find representation on the margins, where recognized rules do not deliver a clear result.

Nothing in Hohfeld's conceptual scheme precludes conflict among legal rules, and he has nothing to say about defeated principles. But the quest for conceptual clarity promotes precision and determinacy to the detriment of those whose favored interpretations of rules are inconsistent with the prevailing account. A profession more open to conceptual confusion might prove more open to the evolution of legal norms. A discourse that normalizes conflict within law might be likely to recognize the force of losing reasons, and to give the interests behind those reasons more weight.

16.5 CONCLUSION

The irony of these worries about the implications of Hohfeld's conceptual scheme for egalitarian theories of private law is that Hohfeld himself was pushing back on

[19] *See* Christopher Wellman, *On Conflicts between Rights*, 14 LAW & PHIL. 271, 294–95 (1995).

[20] *Cf.* Judith Jarvis Thomson's view that specificationism view of non-conflict cannot account for duty to compensate. *See* JUDITH JARVIS THOMSON, SELF-DEFENSE AND RIGHTS 41 (1976). *See also* Simmonds, *supra* note 13, at 339.

assumptions about what followed from the content of legal concepts. By specifying forms more precisely, he narrowed entitlements that seemed to be granted in expansive bundles.[21]

There are three ways to describe his strategy. On one reading, Hohfeld set out to correct conceptual confusion by deciphering the logic of legal concepts. On a different reading, Hohfeld thought that the way some people were thinking about rights was not the best way to think about them. He facilitated his normative point by way of a neutral conceptual scheme that revealed latent normativity in the ostensibly neutral legal reasoning of others.[22] On still another reading, Hohfeld offered a conceptual scheme that he knew to be (inevitably) ideologically charged but which he regarded as preferable to others.[23]

I doubt that *Fundamental Legal Conceptions*, standing alone, reveals which of these is the best historical reading, though I have written here tacitly assuming the second, compromise reading. It seems unlikely that Hohfeld regarded his conceptual scheme as ideologically loaded; it would make mysterious those points at which he expressly reserves political questions.[24] The first reading, which reduces his critique to a logical one, is more plausible. For example, Hohfeld uses *Quinn v. Leathem* to show the conflation of rights and privileges, and he suggests that Lord Lindley mistakenly infers a right from a privilege.[25] It is not necessary for him to impute such conceptual confusion though. It seems plausible that Lord Lindley wants to recognize not only a privilege but also a right against at least a particular kind of interference. Hohfeld and many readers today will reject his conclusion, but it seems ungenerous to explain the agreement by way of attributing conceptual confusion to the basically conservative opposition. Conceptual confusion is rarely the best explanation for a poor judgment. It is, in turn, a less charitable reading of

21 *See* Joseph W. Singer, *The Legal Rights Debate in Analytical Jurisprudence from Bentham to Hohfeld*, 1982 Wis. L. Rev. 975, 1050 (1982) ("Hohfeld's concept of opposites was ideologically designed to demonstrate that to the extent individuals have freedom of action, others have no security.").

22 *Id.* at 1053 ("Hohfeld is properly understood as a participant in the anti-conceptualist revolt, even though some participants in the Hohfeldian debate thought he was a neo-conceptualist. Hohfeld demonstrated that any supposed connection between liberties and duties did not result from logical necessity."). Schlag, *supra* note 2, at 191, describes legal realists and critical theorists who regard Hohfeld "as having provided an analytical framework that reveals tendentious legal reasoning flaws and that exposes the inexorably practical, moral, policy, and political aspects of law."

23 I take this to be Jack Balkin's reading. *See* Jack Balkin, *The Hohfeldian Approach to Law and Semiotics*, 44 U. Miami L. Rev. 1119, 1123 (1990) ("It follows from Hohfeld's work that what constitutes a legally protected interest is arbitrary, and is not defined by the nature of things."). *See also* Schlag, *supra* note 2, at 199 ("some degree of concept-packing may . . . be unavoidable. The important point to recognize here is that before we can get to policy, principle, or value-based reasoning . . . the legal concepts and the conceptual architecture we deploy have already been invested with political and normative content.").

24 Hohfeld, *supra* note 1, at 36 ("Whether there should be such concomitant rights (or claims) is ultimately a question of justice and policy: and it should be considered, as such, on its merits.").

25 *Id.* at 36–37.

Hohfeld to characterize his objection to Lindley's argument as one rooted in logic alone. We would thus arrive at the second, moderate view of Hohfeld's ambitions.

There is, even then, enough apparent faith in the logic of legal concepts to give one pause. Even if Hohfeld set out to expose normativity in the way people used the language of rights, it is not clear that he viewed such ideology as inevitable. My observations about the limitations of Hohfeld's scheme might go to show, if not that ideology is inevitable, that it at least hovers over Hohfeld's own scheme. Others have shown the many benefits from Hohfeld's clear thinking about rights. My aim has been to highlight a few of its potential costs.

17

Religious Liberty and Public Accommodations: What Would Hohfeld Say?

*Joseph William Singer**

17.1 INTRODUCTION

Advances in civil rights ignite backlashes, and the triumph of same-sex marriage is no exception. *Obergefell*[1] begot *Elane Photography*,[2] *Sweet Cakes by Melissa*,[3] Timber Creek Bed and Breakfast,[4] *Liberty Ridge Farm*,[5] *Masterpiece Cakeshop*,[6] and Kim Davis.[7] Same-sex couples acquired the right to marry and to have those marriages respected by the state and federal governments. In response, some owners of public accommodations claim that their right to "religious liberty" gives them the right to deny same-sex couples access to goods and services such as wedding cakes, flowers, photography, wedding venues, inns, and hotels. These clashes involve claims of freedom on both sides – the freedom to marry, the freedom to exercise one's religion, the freedom to control one's own property, the freedom to make

* © 2022 Joseph William Singer. Bussey Professor of Law, Harvard Law School. Thanks and affection go to Martha Minow, Mira Singer, Hanoch Dagan, Isaac Saidel-Goley, and Chris Odinet.

1 *Obergefell* v. *Hodges*, 135 S.Ct. 2584 (2015).

2 *Elane Photography, LLC* v. *Willock*, 309 P.3d 53 (N.M. 2013).

3 Matter of Klein, dba Sweetcakes by Melissa, 2015 WL 4503460 (Or. Div. of Fin. & Corp. Sec. 2015); Michael McLaughlin, *Oregon Bakery Must Pay for Refusing to Make Wedding Cake for Lesbian Couple*, HUFFPOST QUEER VOICES (Feb. 2, 2016), http://www.huffingtonpost.com/2015/07/02/sweet-cakes-by-melissa-fined-same-sex-wedding_n_7718540.html.

4 *Wathen* v. *Walder Vacuflo, Inc.*, Charge No. 2011 SP 2488, 2011 SP 2489 (Ill. Human Rights Comm'n 2015), http://www.aclu-il.org/wp-content/uploads/2015/09/Wathen-liability-determination.pdf; Vikki Ortiz Healy, *Ruling sides with same-sex couple turned away by bed-and-breakfast*, CHICAGO TRIBUNE (Sept. 17, 2015), http://www.chicagotribune.com/news/local/politics/ct-lgbt-business-services-decision-met-20150917-story.html.

5 *Gifford* v. *McCarthy*, 23 N.Y.S.3d 422 (N.Y. App. Div. 2016); Zack Ford, *New York Wedding Venue Loses Appeal to Refuse Serving Same-Sex Couples*, THINKPROGRESS (Jan. 15, 2016), http://thinkprogress.org/lgbt/2016/01/15/3739998/liberty-ridge-appeal/.

6 Masterpiece Cakeshop v. Colo. Civ. Rights Comm'n, 138 S.Ct. 1719 (2018) (a state can protect store customers from sexual orientation discrimination, but not if it shows hostility to religion). *See also* Klein, dba Sweetcakes by Melissa v. Or. Bureau of Labor & Indus., 2022 WSL 221046 (Or. Ct. App. 2022) (Oregon bakery violated state public accommodation law by refusing to make a wedding cake for a same-sex couple).

7 Steve Benen, *Kentucky's Kim Davis jailed, held in contempt*, MSNBC (Sept. 3, 2015), http://www.msnbc.com/rachel-maddow-show/kentuckys-kim-davis-jailed-held-contempt.

contracts. They also involve a clash of rights – the right to marry, the right to exclude nonowners from one's property, the right *not* to make contracts, the right to enter the marketplace without exclusion because of invidious discrimination. What makes freedoms different from rights? The question turns out to matter quite a lot.

The problem is not only how to resolve these conflicts but also how to *conceptualize* them. When we talk about religious liberty, are we all talking about the same thing? That is where Wesley Hohfeld's analysis is helpful.[8] Hohfeld's vocabulary helps us see that some of the claims being made in this area unwittingly (or wittingly?) simplify complex choices.[9] In particular, we sometimes lump two separate claims together, assuming that protection of one type of legal entitlement entails protection of another. For example, a claim to "liberty" may include not only a claim to be free to do as one likes but also a right to control the behavior of other people. But the latter claim cannot be purely a matter of liberty; a right to control the behavior of another obviously *limits* the liberty (freedom of action) of the person whose behavior is being controlled. If liberty claims also entail duties on others, then liberty is being promoted by (selective) limits on liberty. Understanding this is crucial to deciding whether claims of religious liberty legitimately entail duties as well as freedoms.

Hohfeld did lawyers a great favor by insisting that we distinguish between entitlements of "privilege" and entitlements of "right."[10] Debates about the role of religious liberty in the context of public accommodations would benefit from a clear understanding of this distinction. Does "religious liberty" justify exemptions from the obligation to serve the public without discrimination? This normative question will be easier to address if we distinguish various meanings of "liberty." What would Hohfeld say about this?

17.2 CONCEPTUALIZATION

The issue of same-sex marriage is controversial and politically charged. To address it through analysis of concepts may seem to miss the point; the topic of conceptualization may seem old-fashioned and technical. It may even seem formalistic, reducing distributive and normative questions to matters of technical analysis that effectively immunize the status quo from consideration of whether it is just or unjust. Yet, analysis of concepts is helpful both analytically and normatively. It is particularly helpful in situations like this because both sides in the debate have been talking past each other. By framing concepts in particular ways, each side has assumed that their

8 Wesley N. Hohfeld, *Some Fundamental Legal Conceptions as Applied in Judicial Reasoning*, 23 Yale L.J. 16 (1913) [hereinafter Hohfeld (1913)]; Wesley N. Hohfeld, *Fundamental Legal Conceptions as Applied in Judicial Reasoning*, 26 Yale L.J. 710 (1917) [hereinafter Hohfeld (1917)].

9 Hohfeld (1913), *supra* note 8, at 19 ("the tendency – and the fallacy – has been to treat the specific problem as if it were far less complex than it really is").

10 *Id.* at 30–44.

position is stronger than it really is. They often assume or suggest that invocation of liberty is sufficient to justify placing duties on others. This rhetorical device allows them to negate competing claims without normative arguments. Getting the concepts right will reveal that each side's argument has several steps; normative persuasion is needed *at each step in the analysis*. Understanding this will enable each side to better support its position. It may even reveal surprising areas of agreement while clarifying where the disagreements actually lie.

The first conceptual problem is that both sides in this debate have sometimes conceptualized their claimed freedoms as *self-regarding acts*. If I want to marry another man, what business is that of yours? How does it affect you in any way? Conversely, if I want to exercise my religious liberty to deny support to same-sex couples, how does that interfere with your freedom to marry? Go ahead and get married; just leave me out of it. But if these claims are wrong – if liberties are not merely self-regarding but affect the interests of others – then failing to understand those effects undermines one's claim.

The second conceptual problem is that, even when they admit that their claims affect others, both sides in this debate have often assumed that legal rights are unitary, absolute within their spheres, and preemptive of competing claims. They treat rights as trumps. Reasoning in this way tends to insulate the claimant from a need to consider the claims of the other side. If a claim concerns oneself alone, there is no need to consider the harms experienced by the other side or to explain why those harms do not deserve legal protection. Conceptualizing rights as self-regarding and as trumps means that no reasons need be given for why one set of rights should prevail over the other. Considerations of justice and policy obviously enter the conversation but they are truncated and one-sided.

If a case is disputed by well-meaning people, that is a pretty clear indication that the legal claims at issue are not merely self-regarding. It may be the case that, after consideration, we decide that a harm does not deserve legal protection and that the conduct is therefore, *in that sense*, self-regarding. But we cannot reach that conclusion if we are blind to the effects the conduct has and the claims that others make that have been harmed. Nor can we persuade others that a legal entitlement does not affect them when they are standing before us explaining as clearly as they can how it *does* affect them. We need a normative argument about why one claim should yield to the other rather than a mere negation of the pain being expressed by the other side.

The same thing is true about the idea of rights as trumps. In hard cases, both parties may have legitimate liberties and legitimate rights. Legal entitlements are almost never absolute; often they can be appropriately exercised in one social context but not another. I am free to choose my friends as I wish and to invite whomever I like to my dinner party, but I may not choose customers to my restaurant on the basis of race. I am free to worship as I please in my synagogue, but I am not free to refuse to hire someone as an employee in my hotel because they are not

Jewish. Treating rights as relationships and as limited by the rights of others illuminates the full range of interests at stake rather than creating conceptual barriers to perceiving them. In contrast, assuming rights are trumps prompts us to stop listening to competing claims – claims we might well accept in a different social context. Legitimate justification requires acknowledging competing claims while limiting their appropriate application.

The third conceptual problem is that both sides frame their claims in *shifting terms* – sometimes they focus on freedom or liberty, sometimes they focus on rights. This matters because rights normally entail duties on others while liberties exist in the absence of duties. Read that sentence again: rights entail duties on others while liberties exist in the absence of duty. Rights are defined by the duties they impose on others; my right to bodily security means you have a duty not to punch me. Liberties are defined by an *absence* of duty; my freedom to act in self-defense means I have no duty not to hurt you if I punch you to stop you from punching me. Rights grant me the power to call on the state to control your conduct, limiting your freedom of action. Liberties grant me the freedom to act in certain ways and to be free from any claims by others that the state should limit my freedom of action; others have no right to stop me from exercising my liberty. Because of this difference, reasoning from liberties to rights jumps a chasm without a bridge. Champions of religious liberty, for example, seem to assume that the free exercise of religion and the freedom to control one's own land include the power to exclude others as one wishes, as well as the freedom to say and do whatever one likes on one's own land. Champions of same-sex marriage sometimes assume that the freedom to marry includes the right to act on that freedom without interference from others and that means immunity from suffering consequences for exercising the right to marry such as exclusion from the marketplace. One side or the other may be right as a normative matter, but arguments for freedoms are not sufficient to support imposing duties on others; *new* arguments are needed to explain why one side's liberties justify constraints on the liberty of others. Those arguments must be *normative* in nature; they cannot flow as a matter of deductive logic from the existence of the liberties. They must be based, as Hohfeld told us, on considerations of "justice and policy."[11]

Wesley Hohfeld taught us three major lessons and those lessons correspond to the three conceptual shortcuts I have identified. First, Hohfeld taught us to see all legal rights as "jural relations."[12] It had long been understood that rights and duties were correlative.[13] My right to bodily security means you have a duty not to assault me or to batter me. What had not been appreciated is the way that liberties and privileges are relationships. My freedom of speech may harm your reputation but, as long as I speak the truth, the first amendment (generally) protects my freedom to talk about

[11] Hohfeld (1913), *supra* note 8, at 36.

[12] *Id.* at 19.

[13] Joseph William Singer, *The Legal Rights Debate in Analytical Jurisprudence from Bentham to Hohfeld*, 1982 Wis. L. Rev. 975.

you in a manner that may cause others to think badly of you. Hohfeld called those relationships "privilege/no-right" relations.[14] He dramatized the vulnerability that others suffer when you exercise your freedom of action. Understanding religious liberty as a relationship helps us understand the ways in which liberty claims affect the interests of others, and thus are not merely petitions to be "left alone."

Hohfeld argued, second, that rights are often not unitary trumps. The fact that one is an owner of property does not mean that one wins the case; if that were true, property casebooks like my own would be pretty short. Those books are long because the person conventionally deemed "the owner" often loses disputes about property rights. Hohfeld emphasized that a property owner has a *bundle of rights*. He did not argue that this bundle of rights could be disentangled however one wants or that any combination of rights would work as well as any other. He did argue that property rights *can be* and *often are* disentangled. Our legal system often allows owners to disentangle rights from the core bundle and sometimes the law requires owners to do so.[15] Property rights are thus complex rather than unitary. Finding that someone is an "owner" does not mean that that person wins the lawsuit. If a plausible claim can be made that a right belongs to someone other than the conventional "owner," then we need to consider who *should* own the entitlement in question. Hohfeld taught us that doing this was not an exercise of legal logic; rather, defining property rights requires consideration of "justice and policy."[16]

Third, Hohfeld emphasized like no other person ever had that liberties are sometimes not protected by corroborative rights and duties. My freedom to build a gas station on a corner in my town does not mean I have the right to stop you from building a competing gas station right across the street. My freedom is not necessarily protected by a legal rule placing a duty on you not to interfere with my exercise of my freedom. You have the same liberty as I to set up a business. My freedom to practice my religion does not mean that you are not free to attempt to convert me. The separability of liberties and duties means that we cannot reason from a liberty in one person to a duty on others without making arguments of justice and policy. The mere invocation of a legal right or liberty does not settle the matter. There may be liberties on both sides. To appreciate the significance of these three Hohfeldian insights, consider current debates about religious liberty and public accommodations.

14 Hohfeld (1913), *supra* note 8, at 30, 32–44.

15 Hohfeld (1917), *supra* note 8, at 747 ("It is important, in order to have an adequate analytical view of property, to see all these various elements in the aggregate. It is equally important, for many reasons, that the different classes of jural relations should not be loosely confused with one another. A's privileges, e.g., are strikingly independent of his rights or claims against any given person, and either might exist without the other.").

16 Hohfeld (1913), *supra* note 8, at 36.

17.3 PROPERTY AS A BUNDLE OF RIGHTS

Two people enter a florist shop seeking flowers for their wedding ceremony. The shop owner sees that they are two men and refuses to sell them flowers because of her religious objections to the marriage of two men. They approach a hotel seeking to use its facilities as a venue for their wedding, the party afterwards, and a suite for their first night together as a married couple along with rooms for their guests. The hotel refuses to accommodate them, claiming religious liberty. What property rights are implicated in these conflicts?

One view is that only one of the parties has property rights: the owners of the shop or the hotel. They claim the shop or hotel as their property and that ownership claim entails a bundle of rights including the right to exclude nonowners, the freedom to build on the property and use it for business purposes, the power to sell goods or services, and immunity from being forced to enter a contract against the owner's will. On this view, owners have not only the right to exclude at will but the power to waive their right to exclude and to do so on a selective basis. Owners also own their own labor and under the thirteenth amendment have no duty to work for anyone else who claims their services against their will. Ownership rights so conceived correlate with a certain view of "freedom of contract" – the liberty to enter enforceable agreements and the liberty to refuse to enter such agreements.

We can call this the *ownership* or *absolutist* conception of property. It not only views "ownership" as a complete bundle of rights but views those rights as trumps to any competing claims by "nonowners." If this picture of property rights is accurate, owners are lords of their own castles. If you are in my house, you follow my rules. In this picture, store patrons have no property rights in the shop; they are "nonowners" who seek a right to use someone else's property and to compel someone else's labor. It is true that the legal system does sometimes grant nonowners rights of access to property owned by another. But if the ownership conception is accepted as the norm, such instances represent *intrusions* on property rights or *limitations* of them; property rights are being *sacrificed* to promote overriding social interests. Such cases represent takings of property from A and transfer of them to B. As such, they bear a heavy burden of justification.

Hohfeld both built and undermined this conception of property. He built it because he identified the individual rights that go along with "ownership." Rather than merely talking about "property rights," he disaggregated those rights into privileges, rights, powers, and immunities.[17] Privileges are freedoms to engage in activity. Rights entail duties on others to act so as to protect one's own interests. Powers are freedoms to alter legal rights held by oneself or others. Immunities are protections from loss or alteration of one's rights without one's consent. Further, Hohfeld led us to understand that owners have rights and privileges of many kinds. They have the freedom to enter their land, to build on it, and to use it for various

[17] Hohfeld (1913), *supra* note 8, at 30.

purposes. They have the right to exclude others, the right to stop neighbors from harming their property, and the right to quiet enjoyment. By identifying the component legal rights associated with ownership, Hohfeld turned property from a unitary conception of lordship or ownership to one of a complex bundle of entitlements.

Importantly, Hohfeld not only articulated the bundle conception; he undermined it. Ownership, according to Hohfeld, may entail a bundle of rights but only considerations of "justice and policy" can tell us what bundles of rights "owners" should have in different social contexts. In other words, the bundle of rights can be disaggregated – both by the owner and by the courts and legislatures. If a property owner possesses a bundle of rights, then it is logically possible for the legal system to assign some of those rights to one person and some of them to someone else. There may be reasons of "justice and policy" to bundle the rights together, *but there may also be reasons to unbundle them.*

If a conflict arises over a particular property claim (such as the right to buy flowers from a florist shop or to rent a hotel room the night of one's wedding), one cannot solve the conflict merely by asking "who is the owner?" If a claim can plausibly be made that a nonowner has not only the right to enter property of another but a power to force the store owner to enter a contractual relationship, then the land owner must respond to that claim with competing arguments of "justice and policy."[18] Merely stating that one is the "owner" is insufficient.

How can we tell whether a claim of access to another's land merits a response based on justice and policy rather than merely a recitation of "property rights" or "ownership"? That is both an easy and a hard question to answer. It is easy because the answer is that a claim is valid when a case is hard. It is a hard question to answer because there is no simple way to determine when a case is "hard." The only answer that works, according to Hohfeld, is one that is itself based on "justice and policy." If one is able to make a plausible claim that exclusion from another's land is unjust or has harmful social consequences, then, by definition, one has identified a hard case. A plausible claim is simply one that someone in our legal culture would take seriously. And that obviously changes over time as we can see from recent rulings finding that sexual orientation discrimination is a form of sex discrimination, a claim that would not have been accepted by most courts until recently.[19] According to

[18] Hohfeld (1913), *supra* note 8, at 35–38.

[19] *Videckis* v. *Pepperdine Univ.*, 2015 WL 8916764, at *5 (C.D. Cal. 2015); *Baldwin* v. *Foxx*, EEOC Appeal No. 0120133080, Agency No. 2012-24738-FAA-03, at *7 (2015), https://www.eeoc.gov/decisions/0120133080.pdf. *See e.g., Boutillier* v. *Hartford Pub. Sch.*, 2014 WL 4794527 (D. Conn. 2014) (denying an employer's motion to dismiss a Title VII sex discrimination claim alleging employment discrimination on the basis of sexual orientation); *Hall* v. *BNSF Ry. Co.*, 2014 WL 4719007 (W.D. Wash. 2014) (denying an employer's motion to dismiss a Title VII sex discrimination claim challenging the employer's policy of providing health insurance coverage for employees' legally married opposite-sex – but not same-sex – spouses); *Terveer* v. *Billington*, 2014 WL 1280301 (D.D.C. 2014) (denying an employer's motion to dismiss a Title VII sex discrimination claim alleging sexual orientation discrimination based on sex role stereotyping); *Koren* v. *Ohio Bell Tel. Co.*, 2012 WL 3484825 (N.D. Ohio 2012) (denying an employer's motion to dismiss a Title VII sex discrimination claim alleging

Hohfeld, deciding such cases depends on "justice and policy" rather than the inherent logic of property rights or claims of "ownership" that are divorced from normative considerations.

Further, Hohfeld criticized the idea that all property is the same. Public accommodations, he noted, are under a historic legal obligation to serve the public:[20]

> Thus, for example, a travelling member of the public has the legal power, by making proper application and sufficient tender, to impose a duty on the innkeeper to receive him as a guest. For breach of the duty thus created an action would of course lie. It would therefore seem that the innkeeper is, to some extent, like one who had given an option to every travelling member of the public. He differs, as regards net legal effect, only because he can extinguish his present liabilities and the correlative powers of the travelling members of the public by going out of business. Yet, on the other hand, his liabilities are more onerous than that of an ordinary contractual offerer, for he cannot extinguish his liabilities by any simple performance akin to revocation of offer.[21]

Owners of private homes have the right to exclude nonowners, but owners who devote their property to public accommodation purposes have waived part of their right to exclude. More than that, patrons not only have the privilege to enter the public accommodation but a power to compel the owner to serve them by providing services or goods. *The bundle of rights associated with the typical home is different from the bundle of rights associated with a public accommodation.*

When we ask why a hotel claims the right to exclude a same-sex couple, the answer "because I'm the owner" is nonresponsive. From a property law standpoint – from a Hohfeldian standpoint – that answer only leads to another question: "The owner *of what?*" Answering that question requires a judgment about the bundle of rights that is appropriate in the social context at hand. Because public accommodations owners have duties to serve the public, invocation of "property rights" is insufficient – as is invocation of "religious liberty." There may be both religious liberties and property rights on both sides. Rather than asking why an owner should be forced to serve nonowners, we could just as easily ask why owners of public accommodation should be entitled to selectively ignore their obligations to serve the public.

Most people assume that innkeepers and common carriers have a duty to serve the public but that all other owners have the right to exclude anyone they wish unless civil rights statutes limit their powers. I have explained elsewhere that this "rule" was invented after the Civil War to promote racial discrimination.[22] Prior to that, any

sexual orientation discrimination based on sex role stereotyping and reasoning that sexual orientation discrimination "is a claim of discrimination because of sex.").

20 Hohfeld (1913), *supra* note 8, at 52.

21 *Id.*

22 Joseph William Singer, *No Right to Exclude: Public Accommodations and Private Property*, 90 Nw. U. L. Rev. 1283 (1996).

owners who held themselves out as ready to serve the public had a moral (and legal) obligation to do so.[23] In 1982, New Jersey reverted to the traditional rule, giving all members of the public a right of reasonable access to all public accommodations of any sort.[24]

Recent debate has been confused on this point. Sometimes people assume that owners can exclude nonowners unless a statute limits that right; if that is true, then the absence of a statute prohibiting sexual orientation discrimination means that hotels may refuse service to same-sex couples. Sometimes, however, people assume that public accommodations like hotels do have a duty to serve the public – hence the need for a "religious liberty" bill granting owners the "freedom" to refuse service to same-sex couples. Hohfeld helps us analyze the problem by enabling us to isolate the particular entitlements we are fighting about. Do owners of public accommodations have the right to exclude same-sex couples and/or immunity from being required to sell them goods or services? Or, on the contrary, do such couples have the privilege to enter public accommodations and the power to demand service from the owner? The answer to these questions must come from considerations of "justice and policy," not a recitation of "property rights" nor naked claims of "ownership" or "liberty."

17.4 LIBERTIES AS RELATIONSHIPS

Before Hohfeld, it was clear that rights and duties entailed legal and social relationships. The owner's right to exclude means that nonowners have a duty to stay off the land unless the owner waives her right to exclude. Indeed, Hohfeld argued that the relationship between rights and duties was so tight that they were "correlatives" of each other. If we are interested in "jural relations," as Hohfeld saw it, then "rights" are nothing but the relational consequence of "duties." If I have a duty, then there are certain acts that I must do or not do *in relation to another person or persons*. The duty is not free-floating; it is a duty *toward the right-holder* who has the power either to enforce the duty or to waive her power to enforce it. A homeowner has the right to exclude me from her home; that means I have a duty to stay off her property unless she consents to my entry. And if I violate my duty, she may hale me into court to answer for the tort. This much is well-known.

What was not well-known or understood before Hohfeld is that legal liberties have a similar relational structure.[25] If I am legally free to paint my house purple, then my neighbor has no right to stop me from painting my house purple, no matter how much she hates the color. She has no power to go into court to get the state to stop me from exercising my liberty. If she does, the court will dismiss her complaint; she has

23 *Id.* at 1303–48. *Cf.* Hohfeld (1913), *supra* note 8, at 52 (explaining Bruce Wyman's theory of "public callings" as owners who were "holding out" to the public as open for business).

24 *Uston* v. *Resorts Int'l Hotel, Inc.*, 445 A.2d 370 (N.J. 1982).

25 Hohfeld (1913), *supra* note 8, at 33 (arguing that privileges entail "relations").

"no right" to stop me from exercising my "privilege" to paint my house purple. The plaintiff in such a case may have no legally-protected interests *but she is, nonetheless, aggrieved.* To the extent my liberties have effects on others that they find objectionable, they are vulnerable to harm. More importantly, the harm is lawful. *It is not the case that legal liberties entail only self-regarding acts.* We cannot reason directly from a claimed harm to a legal right to prevent the harm; rather, we need a reason to believe that the arguments of justice and policy in favor of protecting people from the harm outweigh the arguments in favor of enabling the exercise of the liberty that may result in the harm.

Recent debates about "religious liberty" have ignored this fundamental point. Claims of religious liberty suggest that florists and innkeepers just want to be left alone to exercise their liberty. Let gay men get married; just don't shove it in my face. Go where you are wanted; leave me out of it. The converse is also true. We sometimes hear the argument that if you are a man who is against same-sex marriage, then, fine, just don't marry a man. Do what you want but leave me alone. But this way of thinking about the problem obscures basic realities.

First, both sides affirm liberties that the other side experiences as causing harm or an affront to human dignity. And both sides sometimes refuse to acknowledge the damage that the other side claims to suffer. But harm we have, or at least, the experience of harm. The fact that the free exercise clause allows pastors to tell gay kids sitting in the pews that they are destined for Hell does not mean that those kids do not suffer psychological harm from the exercise of this liberty. Nor can one escape the fact that the recognition of same-sex marriage by the state causes many people to experience loss and disruption. To the extent that one side or the other is entitled to exercise their liberties, others will be affected. And to the extent that they have no right to stop the protected activity, they are (in their own terms) vulnerable to harm.

Persuasion is more likely to occur if we make clear to others that we have heard their pain, that we can acknowledge the effects of the liberties we claim. At the same time, it is important to remember that *acknowledging* the experience of harm does not mean *legitimizing* it. One function of moral and legal reasoning is to explain why some harms are legally (and morally) cognizable while others are not. You may oppose interracial marriage and view it as contrary to God's plan. Our constitutional system allows you to affirm that view in writing and to preach it from the pulpit. But that does not mean that your view can be enshrined in law. We now understand that position to deny both equal protection of law and religious liberty. One cannot reason from the mere claim of harm to a claim to legal protection from that harm. *Hohfeld taught us that the very nature of a "privilege" or legal liberty is that others affected by it have "no right" to stop it.*

Hohfeld reminded us that liberties may exist on both sides. It is astonishing the extent to which it has been assumed that LGBTQ people have no religious beliefs, practices, or commitments. For many of them, the freedom to marry someone you love is grounded precisely in religious commitments and values. That means that we face a clash of religious liberties. Public accommodation owners cannot assert religious liberty as a trump; *the patrons are asserting it as well.* To the extent that a person has a legal "liberty," others have "no rights." In the public accommodations context, neither side is actually being asked to be "left alone." Their claims affect others. Moreover, neither side is merely seeking "liberty." Each side hopes to impose duties on others which Hohfeld tells us limit the liberty of others. To adjudicate *that* conflict requires arguments of justice and policy to interpret the scope and meaning of religious liberty in this social context.

17.5 LIBERTIES WITHOUT RIGHTS

I have argued that religious liberty is often not self-regarding in nature. Exercises of such liberties may affect others. But the problem of public accommodations is of another order altogether. Religious liberty claims usually do not merely mean that one is free to oppose same-sex marriage or preach against it; they mean that owners are free to deny service to same-sex couples. Refusal of service by an owner of a public accommodation is *not* an exercise of liberty; it is an exercise of a Hohfeldian *right* and a Hohfeldian *immunity* – the right to exclude and immunity from being forced to deal with the customer against the owner's will. The right corresponds to a duty – a duty to stay off the property; the immunity corresponds to a "disability" – the disability to demand and receive service. That makes the claim of religious liberty even further from a self-regarding act than we may have thought. The religious liberty claimant seeks, not only the freedom to believe as she wishes and to live her life as she wishes, but *the right to limit the freedom of others.*

Hohfeld was especially critical of the idea that a legal liberty is invariably coupled with a legal right.[26] My privilege to open a gas station does not entail a right to stop you from exercising a similar privilege. My religious liberty does not mean that you do not have your own liberty, religious or nonreligious. Nor does it necessarily mean that I have a right to exclude you from a business I have opened to the general public. Whether my religious liberty should be coupled with a right to exclude is a question of "justice and policy" not legal logic.[27]

A claim of religious liberty does not merely concern the claimant alone if it is coupled with a right to deny service to others. The converse, of course, is also true. If public accommodations law requires owners to serve same-sex couples, then owners are liable to be forced to provide such services despite their religious objections. If

26 Hohfeld (1913), *supra* note 8, at 34 (explaining how conflicting privileges may exist without corroborating rights). *See also* Hohfeld (1917), *supra* note 8, at 747 ("[T]he property owner's rights, or claims, should be sharply differentiated from his privileges.").

27 Hohfeld (1913), *supra* note 8, at 36 ("[A]privilege or liberty . . . might very conceivably exist without any peculiar concomitant rights . . . as regards certain kinds of interference. Whether there should be such concomitant rights (or claims) is ultimately a question of justice and policy.").

same-sex couples have a power to obtain goods and services, then owners of public accommodations are obligated to provide such services. The question, Hohfeld tells us, is not whether we are for or against religious liberty. The question is whether that liberty should be coupled with rights, powers, or immunities that place obligations or vulnerabilities on others. In the case of public accommodations, we have no choice but to place an obligation or vulnerability on someone. We are not in a situation where one side or the other is actually asking "just to be left alone." Either the patron has the power to compel the owner to provide service or the owner has the right to exclude the patron and immunity from contracting against his will. Either way, one side's liberty claim is coupled with a claim to limit the liberty of someone else.

Religious liberty so conceived requires normative justification. The owner's claim of religious liberty does not necessarily entail a right to exclude patrons who do not share the owner's religious beliefs and practices. The customer's religious liberty does not necessarily entail a power to force the owner to provide services without regard to sexual orientation or religion. Hohfeld emphasized that liberties (what he called "privileges") are distinct from "rights" (or claims) and that one could one have type of legal entitlement without the other. Determining which liberty (if any) should be accompanied by a right (such as a right to exclude or a right to enter) required considerations of "justice and policy" rather than deductive logic. Just as the sentence "because I'm the owner" is an insufficient reason to solve a hard case, the sentence "because I have religious liberty" is similarly indeterminate. There are religious liberties on both sides and, as Hohfeld emphasized, there are often good reasons to confer liberties uncoupled with rights of protection from interference.

17.6 JUSTICE AND POLICY

The real issue is not whether we are for or against "religious liberty," but whether same-sex couples have a right to enter the marketplace on the same terms as everyone else. That question, Hohfeld tells us, cannot be answered merely by reference to "property rights," or "ownership," or "religious liberty." Rather, it is a question of "justice and policy." If we think about the issue this way, it becomes clear that we have addressed it before.

When the civil rights laws were passed in the 1960s we made a collective democratic choice to make public accommodations, employment, and housing open to the public without regard to race or religion or national origin. Since then we have added other forms of prohibited discrimination, including discrimination directed against women, children, and persons with disabilities. In recent times, such protection has begun to be extended to LGBTQ persons. Whenever we have enacted and enforced civil rights statutes, rights of access to the marketplace have prevailed over any competing claims of religious liberty. We have done this for several reasons, all of which apply to same-sex couples.

First, there are religious liberty claims on both sides. In the 1960s, racial segregation was justified by biblical references and sincere religious beliefs.[28] Those who believed that blacks and whites should not eat in the same place or sleep on the same beds coexisted in a world with others whose religious beliefs told them the precise opposite – that we are all created in the image of God and that all human beings are created equal. We are not talking about a clash between religious liberty and equality; we are talking about a clash of religious liberties. The same is true in the context of same-sex marriage. The first amendment grants both sides the freedom to believe what they like about same-sex marriage and to promote it or oppose it, to sanctify it or to ban it, to attend marriage ceremonies or boycott them.

But the clash of religious liberties is not really the issue. In reality, we confront, *not* a clash of liberties, but a clash of *rights* and *powers*. Owners who want to refuse service to same-sex couples claim a right to exclude them from their stores and immunity from being required to provide them goods and services. Same-sex marriage adherents claim a right to enter the store and the power to purchase goods and services on the same terms as others. We answered this question in the context of race by ensuring that people can enter public accommodations without discrimination on the basis of race. We did that for very good reasons.

You are free to worship as you please and to preach against homosexuality in the pulpit, but that does not mean that you are equally free to do so if you are a waiter in a restaurant when talking to a customer. You are free to limit church members to those who profess your faith but you are not free to refuse to rent an apartment to someone of a different religion. Religious liberty is relative to *place*. If it were otherwise, then restaurant and hotel owners in the South that opposed racial integration would have been free to continue excluding African American customers after passage of the Civil Rights Act of 1964. If that were the case, we might still have segregation in the South in public accommodations.

After it abolished apartheid, South Africa confronted a situation where roughly ten percent of the people owned ninety percent of the land, and the division was a racial one. If owners were free to exclude nonowners for religious reasons, then apartheid would have continued through the mechanism of the law of private property.[29] Public accommodations, housing, and employment could still have been segregated with no law requiring segregation. To abolish apartheid, public accommodation laws were needed to ensure that anyone could obtain access to the

[28] Shannon Gilreath & Arley Ward, *Same-Sex Marriage, Religious Accommodation, and the Race Analogy*, Wake Forest Univ. Legal Studies Paper No. 2748565. Available at SSRN: http://ssrn.com/abstract=2748565 or http://dx.doi.org/10.2139/ssrn.2748565 (Mar. 16, 2016); Louise Melling, *Religious Refusals to Public Accommodations Laws: Four Reasons to Say No*, 38 Harv. J. L. & Gender 177, 182–84 (2015). *See Newman* v. *Piggie Park Enter., Inc.*, 377 F.2d 433, 438 (4th Cir. 1967) (Winter, J., concurring), *aff'd and modified on other grounds*, 390 U.S. 400 (1968) (rejecting religious claims to exemption from public accommodations law).

[29] Joseph William Singer, *Property and Equality: Public Accommodations and the Constitution in South Africa and the United States*, 12 S. Afr. J. Pub. L. 53 (1997).

market and to property without regard to race. That is why the Supreme Court has interpreted "the right to make contracts" and the "right to purchase property" in the Civil Rights Act of 1866 as imposing duties on public accommodations to provide goods and services without regard to race.[30]

We have already addressed the question of whether religious beliefs justify allowing owners of public accommodations to engage in invidious discrimination that helps perpetuate a caste society. The answer is no. The place for exercising such liberties is elsewhere – in the church, in the pulpit, and in other private organizations that do not serve the public.

The same is true for sexual orientation. Exclusion from a public accommodation is not a self-regarding act. One who is excluded from a place open to the general public suffers impacts of a serious and harmful nature. Not only must one go elsewhere for service, but one must also suffer the humiliation of being treated as a pariah, as a member of a subordinate caste, as unfit for human company or the associations of honest folk. Refusing service is not merely an exercise of "religious liberty"; it is an attack on the customer, marking her as inferior, tainted, evil. In our society, owners of public accommodations are not entitled to treat their customers this way, at least when they are distinguishing among customers based on qualities that have been historically associated with systemic disempowerment.

The problem cannot be solved by asking the customer to "just go someplace else."[31] If many owners share exclusionary instincts, and if one lives in a small, homogeneous town, the effect of exclusion is enormous. To obtain service – to be treated with dignity – one may have to leave town. Even if other places are available, religious exemptions would shape the social world in a manner that balkanizes it. For the excluded minority group, the world would be a checkerboard with free and unfree places. Venturing into the world would require a guide like the *Negro Travelers' Green Book* used by African Americans traveling in the South in the 1940s and 1950s with lists of places they would be welcome.[32] In such a world, those in the privileged class have full access to the world of the market. They do not need to plan their lives by determining which stores, restaurants, professional offices, or hotels will let them in. But for the despised minority, living in such a world requires defensive measures. As singer Audra McDonald tells us, religious exemptions mean that same-sex

30 42 U.S.C. §1981; *Runyon* v. *McCrary*, 427 U.S. 160 (1976); Alfred Mayer Co., 392 U.S. 409, 443 (1968).

31 For an example of this view, see Andrew M. Koppelman, *Gay Rights, Religious Accommodations, and the Purposes of Antidiscrimination Law*, 88 S. Cal. L. Rev. 619 (2015).

32 Joseph William Singer, *We Don't Serve Your Kind Here: Public Accommodations and the Mark of Sodom*, 95 B.U. L. Rev. 929, 935 (2015). *See* Kent Greenfield, *Hobby Lobby and the Return of the "Negro Travelers' GreenBook,"* AM. PROSPECT (Mar. 26, 2014), https://prospect.org/article/hobby-lobby-and-returnnegro-travelers-green-book, archived at http://perma.cc/LE6K-JZ2N; Randall Kennedy, *The Civil Rights Act's Unsung Victory*, Harper's Mag. (June 2014) at 35.

couples will have to "call ahead" to see if they are welcome – a vulnerability not faced by the privileged class.[33]

Access to the marketplace and to property ownership are central rights that enable us to exercise our freedoms. That is why we have passed civil rights laws that grant access to public accommodations, employment, housing, and government services without regard to factors that we have come to believe are irrelevant to those spheres of social and economic and political life. If one has religious objections to interracial marriage, and if one believes that one's soul is imperiled by renting a hotel room to such a couple, then don't go into the hotel business. If one believes that Jews are destined for hell and that they should not be encouraged in any way, and one believes that selling a cake for the wedding reception is equivalent to performing the ceremony, then don't go into the bakery business. And if one is religiously opposed to same-sex marriage, then you are free not to marry someone of the same sex or attend a same-sex wedding; you are free to preach against same-sex marriage, to exclude parishioners from your church that promote same-sex relationships, and to write books condemning same-sex marriage. But you are not free to open a business that holds itself out as open to the public and then refuses service to patrons who hold different religious beliefs.

Public accommodations are open to the public because we should not have to call ahead to see if we are welcome. Properties open to the public must serve customers regardless of their sexual orientation because a dollar in the hands of a gay man should be worth the same as a dollar in the hands of straight man.[34] Our system protects "religious liberty" but that means the religious liberty of the customer as well as the store owner. It does not mean that one has the right to open a business to the general public and then selectively deny service to those who do not share one's religious views or practices. If that were the case, then we should delete the word "religion" from the 1964 Public Accommodations Act.[35] But no one advocating for religious liberty has suggested we do this. A Christian who was refused service in a restaurant or hotel because of her beliefs would be likely to feel offended and demand service, and under current law would have a right to demand service. But if discrimination on the basis of religion is prohibited, then the prohibition must go both ways. A store owner cannot demand that she be given service regardless of her religion while claiming a religious right to deny service to customers because of the customers' religious practices.

Of course we could interpret religious liberty to include the right to discriminate on the basis of religion. But choosing between a right to exclude or a right to receive service cannot be decided by reference to abstract concepts like "religious liberty" or

33 Joseph William Singer, *Should We Call Ahead? Property, Democracy, & the Rule of Law*, 4 Brigham-Kanner Prop. Conference J. 1 (2016); Singer, *supra* note 32.

34 *Cf. Jones* v. *Alfred Mayer Co.*, 392 U.S. 409, 443 (1968) (Congress has the power "to assure that a dollar in the hands of Negro will purchase the same thing as a dollar in the hands of a white man").

35 42 U.S.C. §2000a.

"property rights." Rather, it requires an exercise in world-making, and that means normative judgment. As Hohfeld taught us, it requires considerations of "justice and policy." Will we continue to oppress LGBTQ people and deny them the right to be treated with dignity in daily life or will we extend equal concern and respect to all persons regardless of their sexual orientation or gender identity? Will we require same-sex couples to call ahead to see if they are welcome? Or will we grant them the same freedom of access to markets that others take for granted? Invocations of religious liberty divert our attention from conceptualizing the issue in this way and they can distract us from asking *whose* religious liberty we are protecting. Importantly, liberty claims obscure the conflict of rights that public accommodation law addresses. Hohfeld taught us to disentangle liberties and rights and to see the complexities under the surface of property rights and property law. He taught us to focus on what matters. For these things, we owe him our thanks.

18

Wesley Newcomb Hohfeld: On the Difficulty of Becoming a Law Professor

John Henry Schlegel[*]

Anyone who spends a large amount of time with newly appointed, untenured colleagues – presumably because one's older colleagues are just not all that interesting any more – will recognize that acquiring a professional identity, in the sense of being comfortable putting on a suit, tying a tie, and keeping shoes shined, is both a matter of imitating the behavior of others and fitting that behavior into an existing self. Part of this activity is intellectual: what I do in terms of reading and writing; part is social: where I am and what I teach there; and part is mixed: what other people are reading, writing, being, and teaching. An individual's professional identity is a complex interaction of these three. However, for someone starting out in law teaching in the earliest years of the twentieth century, as did Wesley Newcomb Hohfeld, acquiring an identity was more difficult than it is today. Academic lawyers then were still busy creating such an identity out of the social and intellectual positions in which they found themselves and from which they, as existing selves, could only limitedly escape.

However, there were possible alternatives. The identity of a full-time teacher/scholar/practitioner, as opposed to that of a part-time practitioner/teacher of the

* UB Distinguished Professor and Floyd H. and Hilda Hurst Faculty Scholar, University at Buffalo School of Law, University at Buffalo. This chapter is for: Dan Ernst, who kept telling me that I was right, that there was a story in the Pound–Hohfeld letters; Ted Sichelman, who provided the occasion to tell it; the late Erica Chadbourn, whose knowledge of the materials in Special Collections at the Harvard Law Library pointed me to Hohfeld and Pound letters I would otherwise never have found; and Daniel Brantes Ferreira, who carefully transcribed all of Hohfeld's letters to Pound that Mario G. Lozano had not previously transcribed in his book LE FONTI DI "CONCETTI GUIRIDICI FONDAMENTALI" DI WESLEY N. HOHFELD (1976). Daniel's work was important for his book, ENSINO JURÍDICO E TEORIA DO DIREITO NOS EUA. A DUPLA FACETA DO REALISMO JURÍDICO NORTE-AMERICANO (2012). A faculty seminar at Buffalo helped with revision, as did my separately channeling of Janet and Rick. Avi helped. Thanks Fred, as always.

After I had finished my presentation draft of this chapter, I discovered that another version of this story was published while I was paying attention to nothing but community, economy, and law. N. E. H. Hull, *Vital Schools of Jurisprudence: Roscoe Pound, Wesley Newcomb Hohfeld and the Promotion of an Academic Jurisprudence Agenda, 1910–1919*, 45 J. LEGAL EDUC. 239 (1995). I tell this story quite differently than does Natalie. Still, I wish especially to thank her for providing me with a standard of research to live up to and a needed check on my own thinking.

mid-nineteenth century, was, I suppose, still viable in some schools were the practitioner's specialty sufficiently lucrative, though such an identity was implausible for a young, new teacher. The identity of a missionary bringing Langdellian legal science and its case method of instruction to the empty expanse West of the Appalachians might have been hard for a Westerner, such as Hohfeld, to embrace, though others surely did. Perhaps, one might have built an identity around having fully mastered a field of law as evidenced by a treatise or casebook. However, available fields were rapidly disappearing. In the wake of previous activity directed toward producing such monuments to the mastery of a field of law, the job of patiently chronicling modest changes in case law remained, though it was not a wholly attractive vision of a life's work. Other alternative identities, whatever they might have been, are no longer obvious. So, if Hohfeld wanted to forge a new one he might have had to act pretty much on his own, in many ways the opposite of forming a professional identity which, by definition, requires a social network of similar individuals. The existence of these alternatives and complexities suggest that to understand Hohfeld's academic life requires that one understand the world of law teaching before World War I as it, and he too, was forming an academic identity.

The American University was created between 1870 and 1910. Part of that invention was the proliferation of law schools across the land. They were not big deals, in fact, they were quite small, often financially independent of their college or university, which is to say anything but integrated into the fabric of the parent. They attracted the children of middle- or upper-middle-class parents anxious for the credential, even though it often did not replace apprenticeship as the minimum qualification to take the bar, a fact that made it clear that the bar was more than a little dubious of the relevance and value of such training, except where the faculty, almost exclusively part-time, was effectively a part of the local bar.

The full-time faculty gravitated toward the American Bar Association's Section on Legal Education, a group that desired to raise standards for admission to practice in order to exclude immigrants and others from the lower classes from the bar. Many academics shared this objective and, at the same time, independently supported raised standards as part of an attempt to become more a part of the university by building a disciplinary identity. In those days, creating such an identity was a relatively simple activity, in theory at least. "In each field a small group of scholars . . . began by staking out part of the intellectual world as its 'turf,' adopting a particular way of looking at that turf, a method as it were, and moving to cut out the 'amateurs' who formerly had a claim to that turf. Finally, they justified those activities by pointing to the 'mission' of that discipline."[1]

[1] John Henry Schlegel, *Between the Harvard Founders and the American Legal Realists: The Professionalization of the American Law Professor*, 35 J. Legal Educ. 311, 314 (1985).

Such professionalization was a common objective of the middle classes in the late nineteenth and early twentieth centuries.[2] In law, it pretty much started at Harvard where the turf was almost exclusively private law, the method was case analysis, in class and out, and the amateurs were the part-time teachers elsewhere.[3] However, creating a discipline is an easier task than keeping it going, especially where there is no Ph.D. degree that would distinguish teachers in a field from both present and future practitioners. Acculturating new teachers to Harvard's disciplinary norms was not easy. Harvard's faculty urged those of its students, and others who thought Langdell's reforms sensible, to spread the word as missionaries teaching at various law schools throughout the country, though primarily in the Midwest, the Great Plains, and the West Coast.[4] These individuals provided mutual disciplinary support by appealing to the "mission" of the law school – requiring an undergraduate degree for entrance to law school and three years of attendance taught primarily by full-time teachers using casebooks, not texts – and to the "vocation" of the law professor – a scholarly career focused on the analysis and scientific (meaning rationally ordered) presentation of legal doctrine, a combination of justification and boundary maintenance.[5] Contact with former teachers and friendly contemporaries also engaged in what might be seen as "colonial service,"[6] reinforced these activities as well as shared the implicit promise that good work would lead to being called to older, better schools, with larger salaries, located to the East.[7]

In the years after our (un)Civil War, there was an obvious topic for the scholarship implied by the law teacher's vocation. The slow adoption of code pleading meant that legal doctrine could no longer be organized by hanging it on the appropriate writ. So, some other scheme of organization was necessary. The Harvard curriculum – starting with contracts, torts, property, and crimes, followed by the "what-have-you" leftovers of the common law – created, what came to be seen, as the appropriate organization. Each "branch" of the law was first organized in casebooks and only later in treatises, the most famous of which were Williston's *Contracts* and Wigmore's *Evidence*.[8] But, by sometime after the turn of the century, when it became obvious that there was room for more than one set of teaching materials, that treatise creation was a job fit only for those people not easily bored, and that the basic job of organization was complete, some new central task was needed to be found in order for the scholarly vocation to secure significant

[2] *Id.*

[3] *Id.* "Elsewhere" because John Chipman Gray and James B. Thayer, the very models of the part-time teacher, as well as important scholars, were Harvard Faculty members.

[4] ROBERT STEVENS, LAW SCHOOL: LEGAL EDUCATION IN AMERICA FROM THE 1850S TO THE 1980S 60–61 (1983); JOHN HENRY SCHLEGEL, AMERICAN LEGAL REALISM AND EMPIRICAL SOCIAL SCIENCE 25–26 (1995). This understanding of such teachers as "missionaries" seems to have first been articulated by Harvard's President, Charles W. Elliot.

[5] SCHLEGEL, *supra* note 4, at 27.

[6] *Id.* at 26–27.

[7] *Id.* at 26.

[8] *Id.* at 27.

credibility within the growing university.[9] It was into this world that Hohfeld placed himself, with all his strengths, particularly the structural clarity of his mind – and weaknesses, particularly his obsession with detail, pugnaciousness, and social awkwardness – when he decided to become a law professor. First, however, he had to become a lawyer.

Hohfeld seems not to have taken to legal education at Harvard.[10] Perhaps it was a matter of living away from home for the first time in his life, as all previous education was in easy commuting distance from his birthplace in Oakland, California or the family residence in San Francisco.[11] Or, it may have been finally encountering a school where there were lots more very bright students in the class than he had experienced even at Berkeley where he was an undergraduate. However, it seems unlikely that the intellectual work at Austin Hall was too hard. After all, he had finished first in his class in grammar school, high school, and college. Rather, it is more likely that the nature of the work stoked a discomfort that had him giving up on the *Harvard Law Review* after a while[12] and, instead, working for John Chipman Gray, the great property scholar, in his law office, Ropes & Gray.[13]

Why this is so can be seen from a peculiar list of Hohfeld's likes and dislikes among the Harvard faculty. He was more attracted to Thayer than Ames, found Beale's thought so bad that it "did more harm than good,"[14] and refused to attend Bruce Wyman's classes in Public Utility Regulation.[15] Corbin asserted that Hohfeld had acquired and read Austin's "The Province of Jurisprudence Determined" while in college and annotated it extensively thereafter.[16] Anyone attracted to such a book at that early age would surely have had little patience for Ames' teleological historicism, Beale's completely disordered analytics, or Wyman's mixture of economics, business, and regulation, much less public law.[17] The pale versions of such varieties of reasoning produced by classmates on the *Review*[18] would have been annoying when compared to the patient case law analysis of Thayer and Gray, both successful

9 John Henry Schlegel, *Searching for Archimedes: Legal Education, Legal Scholarship and Liberal Ideology*, 34 J. LEGAL EDUC. 103, 107 (1984).

10 It is hard to reason from an absence, but it seems to me important that after Pound moved to Harvard, Hohfeld never sends his greetings to, or comments directly about, anyone other than Mrs. Pound, though many of the faculty members he knew as a student were still teaching there.

11 George W. Goble, *Wesley Newcomb Hohfeld*, *in* 9 DICTIONARY OF AMERICAN BIOGRAPHY 124, 124–25 (1932).

12 Edward Hohfeld (elder brother), Untitled Biography of Wesley Newcomb Hohfeld (June 5, 1930) (on file with the Hohfeld Family Papers); Letter from Arthur Corbin to E. V. Rostow (Aug. 10, 1957) (on file with the Hohfeld Family Papers) ("Quit" the Review).

13 Edward Hohfeld, *id.*

14 Corbin, *supra* note 12.

15 *Id.*

16 *Id.* This book can be found in Yale's Sterling Law Library.

17 It would be wonderful to know what he thought of Williston, whom he called "Sammy."

18 A good example would be: Note, *Priority of Railroad Receivers' Certificates over Existing Mortgages*, 16 HARV. L. REV. 53 (1902), in the first issue of the Review in Hohfeld's second year at Harvard, an

practitioners, for whom such careful reasoning was part of day-to-day practice. There is something very attractive about this degree of intellectual independence in a law student.

After graduating from Harvard Law School in 1904, Hohfeld worked for a year at Morrison & Cope, one of the many early incarnations of the firm later known as Morrison Forester.[19] Morrison & Cope was significantly larger than its name implied, in part because it represented Crocker National Bank and other important San Francisco businesses. Hohfeld was one of many young lawyers at the firm.[20] Significantly, he had a chance to work with Morrison on a case concerning a stockholder's liability for the debts of an insolvent California corporation under a peculiar California state constitutional provision, and corresponding legislation, that held a stockholder of an insolvent corporation liable for its debts in an amount equal to that stockholder's proportional equity in the corporation.[21] Morrison is said to have liked Hohfeld's work on this case enough to try to get him to stay in practice, rather than leave to teach, by offering the promise of becoming a partner quite soon.[22] However, from early in his brief time in practice, he seems to have had his eyes on a teaching career. At least, by the fall of 1904, he had already secured a general letter of recommendation from a member of the Classics Department at Berkeley.[23]

There is no evidence that might show whether Hohfeld tried to get a job teaching law at either Berkeley or Hastings, but it is clear that getting one in Stanford's "Law Department," as the place was then called, was no big deal. In the 1890s, it had started as an undergraduate program that, like the rest of the University, was poorly funded.[24] In 1900, when the University's finances had been modestly improved, the Law Department announced a program under which a student could earn both a B.A.

incredible mixture of assertions based on first principles completely divorced from the details of the relevant securities and statutes.

19 According to Edward Hohfeld, Wesley's elder brother and later a partner at Morrison, Wesley apparently secured his position on the recommendation of one of his former teachers who was Alexander F. Morrison's sister. Edward Hohfeld, *supra* note 12.

20 *Id.*

21 *Id.*

22 *Id.*

23 Letter from Edward B. Clapp to Wesley N. Hohfeld (Dec. 19, 1904) (on file with the Hohfeld Family Papers).

24 Marion Rice Kirkwood & William B. Owens, A Brief History of the Stanford Law School: 1893–1946 2–3 (1961). The reason for the school's poverty is complicated. It was scheduled to open in 1893, the same year that Leland Stanford, Sr. died. *Id.* at 3. Instead of his leaving a great estate to endow the University, Sanford's death coincided with the great Panic of that year which slashed the value of his estate. In addition, for two years the estate was tied up in litigation with the United States government over an unpaid debt of Stanford's great creation, the Central Pacific Railroad. *Id.* at 4–5. Interestingly, in part, the litigation was about the applicability of the same provision of California law that Hohfeld had worked on at Morrison. *United States* v. *Stanford*, 69 Fed. 25 (1895) (N.D. Cal.). The United States lost. *See United States* v. *Stanford*, 70 Fed. 346 (1895) (9th Cir.); *affd. United States* v. *Stanford*, 161 U.S. 412 (1896). However, the decline in the value of the estate, which in any case paid current income to Mrs. Stanford, and the difficulty of realizing on its illiquid assets, kept the University reliant

and LL.B in six years.[25] That program was, in effect, when Hohfeld started teaching in fall 1905.[26] He was a part of a small faculty with only one experienced teacher, Nathan Abbott, who left a year later.[27]

Following his appointment, Hohfeld made orderly progress up the academic ranks – instructor, assistant professor, associate professor – until, after five years, he became a full professor.[28] His scholarship consisted of the first two installments of a series of four articles totaling 135 pages of the *Columbia Law Review* on California corporations and the Conflict of Laws, articles that echoed the work he had done while working for Morrison.[29] Then, like all new full professors,[30] Hohfeld faced the question of what to do next? What does it mean to be a professor? How might I enact that role?

Enacting the role of law professor posed a difficult problem for Hohfeld. To begin with, he was a Westerner, not the Easterner envisioned by the notion of a missionary moving West to spread Langdell's word. He may have been trained at Harvard, but he was about a half generation younger than many of the missionaries sent West and, in any case, his heroes were not Ames and the men who followed the path that Langdell and Ames had mapped out.[31] Rather, his heroes were Gray and Thayer who had resisted Langdell's innovations for quite a long while.[32] But in some sense, though not fitting the missionary model under which legal academic life professionalized, it was difficult for Hohfeld to ignore it. He would have to create a cognate model that he could feel comfortable in.

on Mrs. Stanford's annual gifts from that income, since the university did not, and legally could not, charge tuition to California residents. KIRKWOOD & OWENS, *id.* at 2. To add to the financial mess, there were horrid problems under California Law with the terms of the Stanford Trust that required legislative action to fix. *Id.* at 13–14.

25 *Id.* at 14–15. The student would take half of the first year's work in law as a Junior in the undergraduate program and the balance as a Senior, and the final two years as a full-time law student – in total requiring three years of study for the law degree.

26 *Id.* at 18.

27 *Id.* at 18. 1905–1906 was not a particularly auspicious year for Hohfeld to have joined the University. In spring, the Great San Francisco earthquake caused an early end to classes as it wreaked significant destruction of the campus. *Id.* at 19–20. Equally important, only the current income of the estate could be used for repairs; thus this disaster returned the University to short rations for faculty and staff, though soon the Department's finances improved a bit when legislation permitted it to charge an annual fee of $25 per year for students taking courses for the LL.B. *Id.* at 22.

28 *Id.* at 18, 21–23.

29 Wesley N. Hohfeld, *Nature of Stockholders' Individual Liability for Corporation Debts*, 9 COLUM. L. REV. 285 (1909); Wesley N. Hohfeld, *The Individual Liability of Stockholders and the Conflict of Laws*, 9 COLUM. L. REV. 492 (1909); Wesley N. Hohfeld, *The Individual Liability of Stockholders and the Conflict of Laws*, 10 COLUM. L. REV. 283 (1910); Wesley N. Hohfeld, *The Individual Liability of Stockholders and the Conflict of Laws*, 10 COLUM. L. REV. 520 (1910).

30 At this time no one would confuse becoming a full professor at Stanford with securing tenure as that school was still suffering from the furor over the dismissal of the economist, E. A. Ross, for his public opposition to Japanese immigration.

31 SCHLEGEL, *supra* note 4, at 25–26.

32 BRUCE A. KIMBALL, THE INCEPTION OF MODERN PROFESSIONAL EDUCATION: C. C. LANGDELL, 1826–1906 259–60, 326–27 (2009).

The easiest part of that job of creation was the intellectual piece. Hohfeld already was, and probably always had been, interested in analytic jurisprudence. What that name that might mean in his hands would change from understanding the proper relationship of pieces of the corpus of law, the task he set himself in the corporations pieces,[33] through understanding the proper relationship of law's larger organizing concepts,[34] and eventually to understanding the proper relationship between law's most foundational concepts.[35] In so doing, he was participating in the work that tied Langdell, Holmes of *The Common Law*,[36] Thayer, and Gray together at the same time that he was driving far beyond their level of abstraction, as well as the degree of criticism of judicial and academic understanding that they had allowed themselves. This was his métier, what – in our more hard-bitten moments – we today call his "brand."

The social aspects of identity formation were much more difficult for Hohfeld to negotiate. Part of the reason was that it was hard for most full-time law teachers to build a social network in these years. Theirs was a tiny world – the first *Association of American Law Schools* (AALS) *Directory of Law Teachers*, published more than ten years later,[37] was all of fifty pages of ten-point type. In addition, it was a dispersed world and not an easily navigated one. Few people attended AALS meetings, in part because of the time and expense of rail travel made necessary by that organization's choice to pair its meetings with the peregrinations of the regular meetings of the American Bar Association's Section on Legal Education, a choice partly indicative of the concern about expense.[38] And the multitude of conferences and seminars for visiting firemen that are ubiquitous today was unknown. Summer or sabbatical teaching jobs were thus good ways to meet people, though even they surely required help from a better-known colleague or a favored law school professor turned mentor and took time away from writing, the other way of gaining attention, given that the number of law reviews was radically smaller than is the case today. Self-promotion via email, blogs, or SSRN was not yet possible.

Hohfeld had made his first step in the direction of building a model of what the social role of a law professor might be – learning what other people were doing and where – when, in the summer of 1908, he taught suretyship and trusts in the summer session at the University of Chicago's Law School.[39] Teaching there was one way of

33 Hohfeld, *supra* note 29.

34 Wesley N. Hohfeld, *The Relations Between Equity and Law*, 11 MICH. L. REV. 537 (1913).

35 Wesley N. Hohfeld, *Some Fundamental Legal Conceptions as Applied in Judicial Reasoning*, 23 YALE L.J. 16 (1913).

36 OLIVER WENDELL HOLMES, JR., THE COMMON LAW (1881).

37 ASSOCIATION OF AMERICAN LAW SCHOOLS (AALS), DIRECTORY OF TEACHERS AT MEMBER SCHOOLS (1923).

38 The rest was a concerted campaign to build support for increasing the number of years of college required for admission to law school, for the lengthening of the number of years required for graduation and limiting the ability to attend law school part-time. Schlegel, *supra* note 9, at 107–08.

39 Letter from Wesley N. Hohfeld to Roscoe Pound (Jan. 22, 1914) (on file with the Roscoe Pound Papers, Harvard Law School) [hereinafter RPP]. That law school's founding dean had been Joseph Beale, on

getting known, especially since it provided an outstanding occasion for faculty socialization.[40] Still, the mystery is really how Hohfeld managed to get invited, as at that point in time he had published nothing and had attended no AALS meetings.[41]

The most likely intermediary was Frederic Campbell Woodard who had come to Stanford from Northwestern in 1907 and had just been appointed its Dean.[42] He, too, was teaching at Chicago that summer.[43] Both Nathan Abbott – who had hired Hohfeld before he left for Columbia and knew Chicago's dean – and James Parker Hall – from the years they both taught at Stanford – may have helped too as, for some reason or other, Hohfeld thought of Abbott as a supporter of him and his work.[44] At Chicago that summer, Hohfeld met two other people who later figure in his life: Henry M. Bates – at the time, a faculty member at Michigan and soon to be dean there[45] – and Roscoe Pound – most recently, dean at Nebraska and then a faculty member at Northwestern.[46]

Two years later, Hohfeld again taught at Chicago's summer school, though two different courses: equity and evidence.[47] This time he taught with Clarke Whittier who had previously taught at Stanford and left for Chicago with Hall.[48] More importantly, Roscoe Pound was again teaching there.[49] The previous year he had moved from Northwestern to Chicago and was about to move again, this time to Harvard.[50] By the end of summer in 1910, it is clear that Hohfeld and Pound had become real friends, for it is at this time that their correspondence begins.[51] At the

loan from Harvard. Beale's successor was James Parker Hall, a refugee from Stanford. FRANK L. ELLSWORTH, LAW ON THE MIDWAY: THE FOUNDING OF THE UNIVERSITY OF CHICAGO LAW SCHOOL (1977). There is a wonderful annotated photo of the Chicago's summer school faculty in 1908 in the Hohfeld Family Papers

40 SCHLEGEL, *supra* note 4, at 40; Letter from Wesley N. Hohfeld to Roscoe Pound (Oct. 4, 1915) (on file with the RPP).

41 In his entire career, he only attended two: 1913 and 1914.

42 KIRKWOOD & OWENS, *supra* note 24, at 19–20.

43 Postcard from Wesley N. Hohfeld to Edward Hohfeld (Aug. 8, 1908) (on file with the Hohfeld Family Papers) is a picture of the summer session faculty that year.

44 Letters from Wesley N. Hohfeld to Roscoe Pound (Dec. 26, 1910), (Jan. 15, 1911), (May 22, 1913), (June 2, 1913) (on file with the RPP).

45 The University of Michigan Law School website provides a brief biography: https://www.law.umich.edu/historyandtraditions/faculty/Faculty_Lists/Alpha_Faculty/Pages/HenryMBates.aspx.

46 There are three books about Pound: PAUL SAYER, THE LIFE OF ROSCOE POUND (1948); DAVID WIGDOR, ROSCOE POUND PHILOSOPHER OF LAW (1977); N. E. H. HULL, ROSCOE POUND & KARL LLEWELLYN: SEARCHING FOR AN AMERICAN JURISPRUDENCE (1997).

47 *Notes and Personals*, 2 AM. L. SCH. REV. 479, 490 (1910).

48 KIRKWOOD & OWENS, *supra* note 24, at 9, 17.

49 Notes and Personals, *supra* note 47.

50 Letter from Wesley N. Hohfeld to Roscoe Pound (Jan. 22, 1914) (on file with the RPP).

51 Though their correspondence begins in 1910, there are no Pound replies to Hohfeld's letters until spring of 1915. Pound apparently kept incoming correspondence in files and outgoing in letter books; some of the latter were lost in a flood in the basement of the law buildings, just as was the case with some of the incoming correspondence. It is less clear what happened to Hohfeld's copies of Pound's

same time, their age difference, nearly ten years, made the relationship feel more than a bit like mentor/mentee.

It is quite likely that Hohfeld relied on these difficult-to-establish networks for placing his early publications, especially because Stanford did not then have a law review and so his early pieces had to be published elsewhere. The four pieces on California Corporation Law and the Conflict of Laws, published in the *Columbia Law Review*, two in the spring of 1909 and two more in the spring of 1910,[52] which were Hohfeld's major academic work before his sabbatical, likely appeared in that law review with Abbott's help. Law student editors could not have picked them out for their relevance to New York law. And Hohfeld's "The Relations between Equity and Law,"[53] his reply to Walter Wheeler Cook's paper on that topic,[54] likely appeared in the *Michigan Law Review* because Henry M. Bates, by then dean at Michigan, became acquainted with Hohfeld at Chicago's summer school in 1908 and the two men had stayed in touch.[55]

At the same time, these networks could make difficult the creation of a comfortable social understanding of what it was to be a law professor since, even at this early time, such an understanding was quite obviously a matter of where one was teaching and what one was being paid. At the time that Hohfeld returned to Chicago, he also took some private employment back at the Morrison firm[56] helping with an appeal in a fight over the estate of Claus Spreckels who had dominated West Coast beet sugar production and refining, as well as Hawaiian cane sugar production and refining.[57] While it is unlikely that Hohfeld seriously considered returning to practice, it is pretty clear that he was unsatisfied with the salary he was being paid at Stanford. After all, teaching summer school was already a common way for law professors to augment their salaries. Hohfeld's surviving correspondence with Roscoe Pound makes this clear as well.[58]

Salaries at Stanford and elsewhere were a regular topic on Hohfeld's side of his correspondence with Pound, though Pound's seldom discussed the question. It is not clear what was the root of Hohfeld's concern, for it would be hard to say that, in

letters. Presumably, they were to be found in Hohfeld's office at the time of his death, fell into Cook's possession, and were then lost or largely discarded, as seems to have happened to Cook's own papers.

52 Hohfeld, *supra* note 29.

53 Hohfeld, *supra* note 34.

54 Walter Wheeler Cook, *The Place of Equity in Our Legal System*, 3 AM. L. SCH. REV. 173 (1912).

55 Letter from Wesley N. Hohfeld to Roscoe Pound (May 20, 1913) (on file with the RPP).

56 Edward Hohfeld, *supra* note 12. It is not clear how Hohfeld came to be asked to help with this case. It is possible that his elder brother, Edward, a later graduate from Harvard Law School, was instrumental. He had just joined the firm in which he would soon be a partner and later a name partner.

57 Uwe Spiekermann, *Claus Spreckels: Robber Baron and Sugar King*, *in* 2 IMMIGRANT ENTREPRENEURSHIP: GERMAN-AMERICAN BUSINESS BIOGRAPHIES, 1720 TO THE PRESENT (William J. Hausman ed., 1916). The case was *In re* Spreckels' Estate, 123 Pac. Rep. 371 (1912) and the Morrison firm's clients lost. An argument made on remand, again with Hohfeld's participation, lost below and on appeal. In re Spreckels' Estate, 133 Pac. Rep. 289 (1913). *See also* letters from Wesley N. Hohfeld to Roscoe Pound (Dec. 26, 1910), (Apr. 19, 1911), (Oct. 23, 1913) (on file with the RPP).

58 *See* Letter from Wesley N. Hohfeld to Roscoe Pound (Jan. 15, 1911) (on file with the RPP).

any real sense, he was woefully underpaid at Stanford, whatever he might have thought to be the case.[59] For example, by the time that Hohfeld was made a full professor, Walter Wheeler Cook, who had been teaching four years longer than Hohfeld, was paid $3,000 at the University of Wisconsin,[60] an amount I believe that was Hohfeld's salary that year; at least it was close to it. Underhill Moore, who had started teaching two years later than Hohfeld and also taught at Wisconsin, was paid only $2,500 that year.[61] Surely the University of Wisconsin Law School was not a shabbier place than Stanford. And in the next three, and maybe four, years, Moore, who had stayed at Wisconsin after Cook left for Chicago, received only small, regular salary increases.[62]

Now, when Hohfeld became a full professor and taught for the second time at Chicago's summer session, he did not know Cook well and may have not known Moore at all, much less their salaries. However, for him, the relevant question seems to have been not whether his salary was comparable to that of other people at the same stage of their career, but rather whether it was the salary he felt that he deserved, and not deserved in relation to the work he had published, which, as noted above, was limited to his four long pieces about California Corporation Law and the Conflict of Laws, but in relation to his understanding of the quality of his thought. And Hohfeld thought highly about the quality of his thought; he was not a humble person, as his letters make clear and Arthur Corbin, his colleague at Yale, agreed.[63]

It would not be surprising if, after two summer sessions where he could compare the quality of his thought with that of others not at Stanford, and maybe taste Chicago's salary scale which was far beyond that of Sanford, Kansas (where Moore had taught),[64] Missouri (where Cook had taught),[65] and Wisconsin (where both were teaching), Hohfeld felt that he deserved to be at a school where he would be better paid. After all, Clarke Whittier whom Hohfeld got to know when teaching summer school in 1910, and whose work Hohfeld did not think much of,[66] was far better paid than he was, as can be seen from the fact that when Moore moved from Wisconsin to Chicago his salary rose from $3,500 to $5,500.[67] Such a disparity was surely galling to Hohfeld and likely made worse when, while on sabbatical from Stanford,[68] he taught evidence at Chicago in the fall quarter of 1911 and experienced

59 Inflation was modest during the years from 1905 to 1915. Thereafter, it rose rapidly with wartime price increases.

60 The equivalent of about $72,000 in 2015 dollars. *See* Cook Employment Records: 1906–1910 (on file with the University of Wisconsin Archives).

61 *See* Moore Employment Records: 1908–1915 (on file with the University of Wisconsin Archives).

62 *Id.*

63 Corbin, *supra* note 12.

64 Schlegel, *supra* note 4, at 30, 36, 38.

65 Letter from Walter W. Cook to President R. H. Jesse (June 4, 1904) (on file with the University of Missouri Archives).

66 Letter from Wesley N. Hohfeld to Roscoe Pound (Sept. 24, 1912) (on file with the RPP).

67 Schlegel, *supra* note 4, at 39 n.96.

68 Letter from Wesley N. Hohfeld to Roscoe Pound (Aug. 18, 1911) (on file with the RPP).

Whittier's disdain at Hohfeld's use of the "Fundamental Legal Conceptions" paper in his course there.[69]

Hohfeld's correspondence with Pound discloses other things than the younger man's concerns about his salary. There is a certain formality to many of Hohfeld's letters that frequently close with a wish to be remembered to Mrs. Pound.[70] From time to time, this formality is replaced by a kind of flattery that edges toward, but never really reaches, fawning, but clearly is evidence of sycophancy, as when Hohfeld is seeking missing reprints from Pound so as to complete his first to be bound volume of "Pounds Essays."[71] But much of this correspondence consists of a topic that academics know and love – academic gossip.

The gossip would be perfectly familiar to anyone who knew the names of early twentieth-century law professors, a topic more obscure than baseball trivia – who is, or might be, teaching full-time or at summer school somewhere or other;[72] who might be moving from one school to another and so opening up a vacancy, occasionally described by salary rather than subject matter;[73] or what schools might be doing "important things."[74] Surprisingly little was about who published what and where; such academic rivalry does not come until later. Only two names deserve to be remembered: Albert M. Kales, a full-time faculty member at Northwestern with a small, but elite, trusts practice and several texts and casebooks (one, coauthored with John Chipman Gray) on property topics,[75] and Walter Bingham, a Stanford colleague of whom Hohfeld made fun for an early legal realist-like piece, "What Is the Law?"[76] that contained echoes of Holmes' "Path of the Law"[77] and foreshadowed social science research topics of later, and more prominent, American Legal Realists.[78]

But gossip was not the only important part of informal relationships like that between Hohfeld and Pound. Pound kept trying to salve Hohfeld's unhappiness over

[69] Letter from Wesley N. Hohfeld to Roscoe Pound (Sept. 24, 1912) (on file with the RPP).

[70] Letters from Wesley N. Hohfeld to Roscoe Pound (Oct. 30, 1910), (Dec. 26, 1910), (Jan. 15, 1911), (Aug. 18, 1911) (on file with the RPP). The last of these letters makes clear that Hohfeld frequently had been a guest at Pound's home in Chicago while he was teaching the second time at the University of Chicago Law School's summer session.

[71] Letters from Wesley N. Hohfeld to Roscoe Pound (Mar. 15, 1912), (Feb. 25, 1913) (on file with the RPP).

[72] Letters from Wesley N. Hohfeld to Roscoe Pound (Jan. 19, 1911), (May 22, 1913), (July 15, 1913), (July 28, 1913) (on file with the RPP).

[73] Letters from Wesley N. Hohfeld to Roscoe Pound (Dec. 20, 1910), (Aug. 18, 1911), (May 22, 1913) (on file with the RPP).

[74] Letter from Wesley N. Hohfeld to Roscoe Pound (Sept. 24, 1912) (on file with the RPP).

[75] Letters from Wesley N. Hohfeld to Roscoe Pound (Oct. 30, 1910), (Dec. 26, 1910), (Oct. 18, 1910), (Oct. 28, 1912) (on file with the RPP).

[76] Walter Bingham, *What Is the Law?* 11 MICH. L. REV. 1 (1912). This piece was soon followed by Walter Bingham, *The Nature of Legal Rights and Duties*, 12 MICH. L. REV. 1 (1913). Two subsequent pieces defended these articles. The fun is to be found in Letter from Wesley N. Hohfeld to Roscoe Pound (Feb. 25, 1913) (on file with the RPP).

[77] Oliver Wendell Holmes, Jr., *The Path of the Law*, 10 HARV. L. REV. 456 (1897).

[78] SCHLEGEL, *supra* note 4.

his salary and prospects with assurances that soon a better spot would come.[79] He even attempted to secure a broader stage for Hohfeld to show off his talents by inviting him to speak at the AALS annual meeting in 1912, the year that Pound was President of that organization.[80] However, Hohfeld turned down the opportunity, pleading that doing so would interrupt a planned trip to Europe as part of his sabbatical, a trip that included stops in Paris, Munich, and London.[81] Instead, he suggested that Walter Wheeler Cook, a friend he made while teaching evidence at Chicago earlier in that sabbatical in 1911, speak in his place.[82]

Pound had known Cook from when both men taught in the Law School of the University of Nebraska,[83] so Pound's willingness to make such a substitution is understandable. What is difficult to understand is Hohfeld's relationship with Cook; the two men were a bit odd as academic friends. Both suffered from an excess of *amour proper*, not often a good basis on which to build a friendship, however much they shared similar concerns. Tellingly, after Cook made it to the big time with his move to Chicago in 1910, he too became very concerned with his salary.[84] The two men might also be seen as academic rivals. Hohfeld suggested that Cook speak in his place at the AALS because he believed that Cook too was devoted to analytic jurisprudence[85] – though there was little evidence of this fact in the scholarship Cook had produced before he met Hohfeld[86] – and because Cook shared Hohfeld's positions on the relationship between equity and law.[87] However, Cook's speech used Hohfeld's syllabus as an example of what not to teach[88] and his position on law and equity was different enough that Hohfeld felt that he needed to reply in print, and somewhat testily.[89]

Still, networks were not the only way that connections were made. Blame fool luck was then, as now, an operative principle in such matters. Hohfeld's article, "Some Fundamental Legal Conceptions as Applied in Judicial Reasoning,"[90] came to appear in the *Yale Law Journal*, at that time hardly a journal of the first rank at a school that itself was hardly of the first rank,[91] in just such a way. Curiously, Hohfeld submitted the piece at a time when he was contemplating sending it to Harvard or Columbia.[92] This fact, if it is such, suggests that it is also possible that

79 Letters from Wesley N. Hohfeld to Roscoe Pound (June 2, 1913), (July 15, 1913) (on file with the RPP).
80 Letter from Wesley N. Hohfeld to Roscoe Pound (Mar. 15, 1912) (on file with the RPP).
81 The fee he received for his work for Morrison possibly financed this trip.
82 Letter from Wesley N. Hohfeld to Roscoe Pound (Mar. 15, 1912) (on file with the RPP).
83 Schlegel, *supra* note 4, at 28.
84 *Id.* at 39–40.
85 Letter from Wesley N. Hohfeld to Roscoe Pound (Mar. 15, 1912) (on file with the RPP).
86 Schlegel, *supra* note 4, at 30–35.
87 Letter from Wesley N. Hohfeld to Roscoe Pound (Mar. 15, 1912) (on file with the RPP).
88 Cook, *supra* note 54.
89 Hohfeld, *supra* note 34.
90 Hohfeld, *supra* note 35.
91 Schlegel, *supra* note 4, at 50.
92 Letters from Wesley N. Hohfeld to Roscoe Pound (Oct. 10, 1913), (Oct. 23, 1913) (on file with the RPP).

Hohfeld was attempting to bring himself to the Yale faculty's notice, as it was rumored to have a faculty vacancy that needed filling.[93] Still, it was anything but inevitable that Arthur Corbin would be asked to read the piece and like it, so that the rest could be, as they say, "history" with Hohfeld's move to Yale.[94] The odd thing about that history is that it almost did not happen. Hohfeld turned down Yale's offer of a professorship once and that fact tells us much about his professional identity too.

By the fall of 1913, Hohfeld had secured a salary of $4,000 at Stanford.[95] The following spring, seemingly *a propos* of nothing in particular, Hohfeld told Pound five things: his dean and colleague, Frederic C. Woodward turned down an offer from Yale the previous year; Yale announced that it had adopted the case method; Hohfeld had received a nibble about his availability from Bates at Michigan; Michigan needed to up its salary scale if he were to leave Stanford where he would "naturally prefer to remain"; and his wish to feel "definitely settled," if he were to change location in the next few years.[96] He also asked Pound to be on the lookout if a position should come to his attention.[97] A bit of ambivalence here, no?

Less than a month later, Hohfeld informed Pound that he had received, but turned down, an offer of $4,500 from Fordham because he "didn't think it the best thing to join a Catholic institution, even though … the faculty is made up of all classes of Christians" and that he had several years earlier turned down an offer from Illinois, but had been told that the school was again looking at him. In a backhanded way, he also made it clear that he wished to join Abbott at Columbia.[98] "Definitely settled" seems to have been accompanied by certain preferences, articulated only when forced to confront them.

When Fordham renewed its offer, it appeared that the chance to build a practice such as Kales had was quite attractive to Hohfeld.[99] Still, he asked Pound for assistance in making up his mind as he had done before.[100] Pound's answer was the same, "No," and Hohfeld dutifully replied.[101] However, when Fordham dangled the possibility of $5,500, Hohfeld admitted that if he were going to leave California, it would be to New York City, or at least the Atlantic Coast, because of the "intellectual, social and humanizing influences and advantages" there.[102] It is unlikely that the assertion of Stanford's President that he would push for a salary increase to $4,500 for the next year and $5,000

93 Letter from Wesley N. Hohfeld to Roscoe Pound (July 15, 1913) (on file with the RPP).

94 Corbin, *supra* note 12, tells the story this way, but others have too, among them. SCHLEGEL, *supra* note 4, at 51.

95 Letter from Wesley N. Hohfeld to Roscoe Pound (June 2, 1913) (on file with the RPP).

96 Letter from Wesley N. Hohfeld to Roscoe Pound (May 22, 1913) (on file with the RPP).

97 *Id.*

98 Letter from Wesley N. Hohfeld to Roscoe Pound (June 2, 1913) (on file with the RPP).

99 Letter from Wesley N. Hohfeld to Roscoe Pound (Oct. 23, 1913) (on file with the RPP).

100 *Id.*

101 Letter from Wesley N. Hohfeld to Roscoe Pound (June 2, 1913) (on file with the RPP).

102 Letter from Wesley N. Hohfeld to Roscoe Pound (Nov. 24, 1913) (on file with the RPP).

thereafter was irrelevant to the decision.[103] Ambivalence again raises its head, maybe this time with a side order of covetousness.

It is about this time that Hohfeld sent "Some Fundamental Legal Conceptions" to the *Yale Law Journal*. Hohfeld appears to have started thinking about the ideas in that manuscript while he was working on the four pieces on California Corporation Law and the Conflict of Laws, for there are two different references to such relations in the pieces and the later is closer to his final structure.[104] He had fully worked out these relationships before the final manuscript was submitted to Yale because he spoke of his Stanford students as understanding them.[105] Also, the famous diagram of the conceptions and their relationships was included in the material he had written at Stanford for his students in the trusts course; this material was the greatest portion of his article on "Equity and Law" that was published just before "Some Fundamental Legal Conceptions."[106] The completed manuscript found its way from the Journal's editors to Corbin[107] and, thereafter, the usual story of how Hohfeld came to Yale quickly ends. But not really.

When the piece was about to appear, Hohfeld sheepishly told Pound that it was solicited, which may or may not be true.[108] More importantly, over the preceding months, Hohfeld had been talking up Yale indirectly[109] and he had both indicated that he felt that Yale was the place that was most likely to have a vacancy and noted that one faculty member there was leaving to become a judge and that the school's Dean, Henry Wade Rogers, had been appointed to the Second Circuit Court of Appeals.[110]

Soon, Yale came through with a $4,500 offer.[111] Pound clearly told Hohfeld to take it, but Stanford had already matched and Hohfeld said "No."[112] Yale came back with $5,000; all Stanford could do was to promise to match that sum within a year.[113] Again, Hohfeld said "No."[114] His reasons were strange, but telling. He explained that he could be "more useful" at Stanford; the teaching load there was slightly lower; he would need to learn some new courses, if he came to Yale; and he would "need for

103 *Id.*

104 Wesley N. Hohfeld, *Nature of Stockholders' Individual Liability for Corporation Debts*, 9 COLUM. L. REV. 285, 319 (1909) ("all corporate transactions can be adequately understood and stated in terms of rights, powers, liberties, duties, liabilities, disabilities, etc."); Wesley N. Hohfeld, *The Individual Liability of Stockholders and the Conflict of Laws*, 10 COLUM. L. REV. 520 (1910) ("persons having certain powers and disabilities, rights and 'no-rights,' privileges and duties, non-liabilities and liabilities").

105 Letter from Wesley N. Hohfeld to Roscoe Pound (Mar. 15, 1915) (on file with the RPP).

106 Hohfeld, *supra* note 34, at 546–71. The diagram is at 569.

107 Corbin, *supra* note 12.

108 Letter from Wesley N. Hohfeld to Roscoe Pound (Oct. 23, 1913) (on file with the RPP).

109 *Id.* See also Letter from Wesley N. Hohfeld to Roscoe Pound (July 15, 1913) (on file with the RPP).

110 Letter from Wesley N. Hohfeld to Roscoe Pound (Oct. 23, 1913) (on file with the RPP).

111 Letter from Wesley N. Hohfeld to Roscoe Pound (Apr. 4, 1914) (on file with the RPP).

112 *Id.*

113 *Id.*

114 *Id.*

adjustment to . . . new social surroundings," the last two of which reasons would take time away from writing.[115] However, he admitted that "had there been sufficient compensatory advantage ... as regards salary," the matter would have been different.[116] Is this about money or California Dreamin'?

Pound pushed again for Hohfeld to change his mind.[117] Yale was willing to bargain over courses and a deal was sealed.[118] When it came time for Hohfeld to tell Pound why he had such difficulty settling on Yale, Hohfeld's explanation pretty much ignored salary and admitted:

> I was born in . . . [California], and I have lived here all my life, – save for the few years at Harvard during my student days. My relatives are all in the city of San Francisco, including my parents, who, of course, are well advanced in years. Then, too, many business interests and professional opportunities and prospects have had to be considered. Finally, life here at Stanford – though somewhat "pastoral" and isolated – has great charm, and the loyal backing of Dean Woodward, President Banner and the members of the department made it almost ungrateful to leave.

It is not clear what was going on here either.[119]

Hohfeld's reference to the "loyal backing of . . . the members of the department" is quite strange for he almost never talked about his colleagues at Stanford, other than Abbott, who had left; Bingham, whom he made fun of;[120] Clarke Whittier, another person who had left the school and whose work he disliked;[121] and Woodward, then the Dean at Stanford, whom Hohfeld was afraid disliked him because he had favored a different person for the deanship.[122] Moreover, Hohfeld had baldly stated that he had more friends at Berkeley than at Stanford.[123]

All of which is not to say that California is not part of the story. The understanding that good scholarship would allow/entitle Langdellian missionaries scattered throughout the Midwest and West to secure better jobs with higher salaries back East was an important aspect of what made up a law professor's identity, even if

115 *Id.*

116 *Id.*

117 Letter from Wesley N. Hohfeld to Roscoe Pound (July 12, 1914) (on file with the RPP). Interestingly, when Cook later moved from Chicago, a Harvard clone, that from the beginning had "arrived," to Yale, a less fancy school that was only "up and coming," Pound expressed surprise at Cook's choice. Letter from Roscoe Pound to Walter Wheeler Cook (May 27, 1916) (on file with the RPP). One senses in Pound's actions, especially when later he ignored Hohfeld's "Fundamental Legal Conceptions" when writing a piece on the organization of law for the American Law Institute – *see* R. Pound, *Classification of Law*, 37 HARV. L. REV. 933 (1924) – expressed a rather fine-grained understanding of who belonged where and why. On this understanding Cook, a colleague at Nebraska, was at least a step above Hohfeld in the intellectual/social pecking order; Hohfeld thus belonged at Yale, which in Pound's eyes was a step above Fordham.

118 Letter from Wesley N. Hohfeld to Roscoe Pound (July 12, 1914) (on file with the RPP).

119 Letter from Wesley N. Hohfeld to Roscoe Pound (July 12, 1914) (on file with the RPP).

120 Letter from Wesley N. Hohfeld to Roscoe Pound (Feb. 25, 1913) (on file with the RPP).

121 Letter from Wesley N. Hohfeld to Roscoe Pound (Sept. 24, 1912) (on file with the RPP).

122 Letter from Wesley N. Hohfeld to Roscoe Pound (Oct. 17, 1915) (on file with the RPP).

123 Letter from Wesley N. Hohfeld to Roscoe Pound (Aug. 18, 1911) (on file with the RPP).

Hohfeld was not really such a missionary. He was sure that the quality of his mind, if not the volume of his scholarship, entitled him to just such a move and for him, the "Fundamental Legal Conceptions" was clear evidence of this fact. So, in a real sense, he had begun to think of himself as properly in the market back east. If he couldn't get to Columbia with Abbott where he belonged, the real question was where he should go. That the choice was between Fordham and Yale was, of course, accidental, but that it was a choice was not.

Corbin's observation about his colleague from the perspective of nearly forty years is helpful here. He remembered Hohfeld's "manner (except to a close friend) to be cold"; he was impatient "with what he regarded as incompetence" and "often gave offense, both socially and intellectually."[124] He was, at times, "so 'frank' in his criticisms that it was painful to his associates who were present."[125] He was, as one might say today, a bit of a jerk and so, taken together, these observations suggest why his social surroundings were generally family, people for whom "Oh, that's just Wesley," was a way of smoothing over behavior that they, and he, had been unsuccessful in controlling. In other circumstances, loneliness would be his lot in life. For Hohfeld, New York City, with its many cultural diversions, was far more attractive than the overgrown college town that he thought New Haven to be. On this understanding, money, which kept floating back and forth in all of these events, may have been important, but it was also a handy excuse for not making the move that he might have feared would destroy the world that provided the support he needed, and significantly, the support he had lacked at Harvard, as evidenced by his preference to work for Gray, rather than continuing to work on the *Law Review*.

After moving to Yale, Hohfeld settled in quite quickly, far more quickly than might have been expected given his hesitancy in moving there.[126] Indeed, one might say that, for the first time, he acted as if he felt himself to have become a real law professor by moving east. Some of his larger salary was spent on opera tickets in New York City and Victrola records for enjoyment at home.[127] More to the point, he solicited articles for the *Yale Law Journal* from people such as Pound[128] and Justice Holmes,[129] the former of whom was implausible and the latter, impossible. And he began to look for individuals who might join the faculty at Yale.[130] His first success was Cook[131] who repaid the favor by immediately producing several pieces of

124 Corbin, *supra* note 12.

125 *Id.*

126 Letter from Wesley N. Hohfeld to Roscoe Pound (Dec. 13, 1914) (on file with the RPP).

127 Letters from Wesley N. Hohfeld to Roscoe Pound (Dec. 13, 1914), (Jan. 7, 1915), (Apr. 4, 1915) (on file with the RPP); Letter from Wesley N. Hohfeld to Edward Hohfeld (Feb. 14, 1915) (on file with the Hohfeld Family Papers).

128 Letter from Wesley N. Hohfeld to Roscoe Pound (Aug. 4, 1914) (on file with the RPP).

129 Letter from Wesley N. Hohfeld to Oliver Wendell Holmes, Jr. (Nov. 7, 1914) (on file with the Oliver Wendell Holmes, Jr. Papers, Harvard Law Library).

130 Letter from Wesley N. Hohfeld to Roscoe Pound (June 6, 1915) (on file with the RPP).

131 Letters from Roscoe Pound to Wesley N. Hohfeld (June 10, 1916), (July 17, 1916) (on file with the RPP).

scholarship that directly used the "Fundamental Legal Conceptions,"[132] while relishing the fact that he was paid as much as the Dean.[133] As for personal connections within the faculty, at first, Corbin and his wife seem to have been it and Corbin suggests that, though only five years older than Hohfeld, he acted as a cross between a brother and a father in those early years at Yale.[134]

Most of Hohfeld's time was, however, spent preparing and teaching classes, several of which he had never taught before.[135] This was a doubly difficult job because all of his courses were for second- and third-year students and he insisted that the students use the schema of concepts as identified and defined in the "Fundamental Legal Conceptions." Though at the outset Hohfeld found the students to be "cordial and cooperative,"[136] ultimately some balked, especially the third-year students in Trusts, almost all of whom subscribed to a petition to the University's President demanding that Hohfeld be sent back to Stanford, apparently since they were convinced that he was going to flunk them because they could not master the conceptual system.[137] The President apparently told Hohfeld to be kinder to the students; Corbin explained to the President the famous terms of Hohfeld's contracts with Stanford and Yale; later that day Corbin spent a good deal of time walking with Hohfeld who was obsessing in anguish over the entire event.[138]

Interestingly, immediately after leaving the President's office, Hohfeld wired Stanford to tell the school that he was not coming back.[139] Why he did this is not difficult to understand. His choice to stay showed both how much he believed in his system and how much earlier letters from his former Stanford students, affirming the usefulness of that system to them now that they were in practice,[140] supported his belief that, ultimately, his Yale students would understand as well.

As he gained greater security in his teaching, Hohfeld turned his attention to what was then seen as law school administration.[141] It took two years after Henry Wade Rogers had been appointed to the Second Circuit Court of Appeals, for the University to convince him to announce his retirement.[142] Soon after that announcement, the Law School began searching for a new dean, as well as a search for a new faculty member. Though a majority of the faculty wanted to select a former member of the faculty, Ralph W. Gifford, who had recently decamped for Columbia, Corbin

132 SCHLEGEL, *supra* note 4, at 53–56.

133 Corbin, *supra* note 12.

134 Corbin, *supra* note 12; Letter from Wesley N. Hohfeld to Roscoe Pound (Mar. 15, 1915) (on file with the RPP).

135 Letter from Wesley N. Hohfeld to Roscoe Pound (Mar. 15, 1915) (on file with the RPP).

136 Letter from Wesley N. Hohfeld to Roscoe Pound (Dec. 13, 1914) (on file with the RPP).

137 Corbin, *supra* note 12.

138 *Id.*

139 Letter from Wesley N. Hohfeld to Roscoe Pound (Mar. 15, 1915) (on file with the RPP).

140 *Id.*

141 Letters from Wesley N. Hohfeld to Roscoe Pound (July 17, 1916), (Aug. 16, 1917) (on file with the RPP).

142 LAURA KALMAN, LEGAL REALISM AT YALE 99 (1986).

and Hohfeld were opposed and, with the help of the University's President, blocked that appointment.[143] Instead, the Law School chose Thomas W. Swan, a Chicago practitioner and Yale College graduate, who had been Editor-in-Chief of the *Harvard Law Review* during the period of Hohfeld's "affiliation," whatever that might have been, with that publication, and the candidate of Corbin and Hohfeld.[144] The new faculty member was Walter Wheeler Cook.[145] Cook teamed up with Corbin and Hohfeld to add four new colleagues, including two who became long-serving faculty members, Edwin Borchard[146] and Ernest Lorenzen,[147] and one Edmund M. Morgan, Jr. who, after ten years, departed for Harvard.[148]

Involvement in all of this administration seems not to have kept Hohfeld from writing. During his time at Yale, he published two articles – "Fundamental Legal Conceptions as Applied in Judicial Reasoning"[149] and "Faulty Analysis in Easements and License Cases,"[150] the latter of which Hohfeld considered to be the first part of a third piece for a proposed book on the "Fundamental Legal Conceptions."[151] More interesting for understanding Hohfeld was his single book review, that of a book by a former colleague at Stanford, Charles A. Huston, written as a Harvard S.J.D. thesis under the direction of Roscoe Pound and entitled "The Enforcement of Decrees in Equity."[152] This was, of course, the territory covered by Hohfeld in his "The Law and Equity" piece.[153] Curiously, the review began with a long encomium to the series, Harvard Studies in Jurisprudence, of which this book was the first volume, and Pound, the series editor.[154] Next came a long description of the text and finally, after a statement of a "hearty agreement with the author's main position,"[155] an equally long disquisition of the imperfections in Huston's terminology.[156]

A fourth piece was "A Vital School of Jurisprudence and Law,"[157] Hohfeld's grand attempt to add to the literature on the vocation of the law professor, and so a possible articulation of a professional identity. That literature began with Thayer and was

143 Corbin, *supra* note 12.
144 *Id.*
145 *Id.*
146 Charles E. Clark, *Edwin Borchard*, 60 YALE L.J. 1071 (1951).
147 Arthur L. Corbin, *Ernest Gustav Lorenzen*, 60 YALE L.J. 579 (1951).
148 KALMAN, *supra* note 142, at 54.
149 26 YALE L.J. 710 (1917).
150 27 YALE L.J. 66 (1917).
151 Letter from Wesley N. Hohfeld to Roscoe Pound (June 9, 1918) (on file with the RPP).
152 CHARLES ANDREWS HUSTON, THE ENFORCEMENT OF DECREES IN EQUITY (1915); Letter from Roscoe Pound to Wesley N. Hohfeld (June 11, 1915) (on file with the RPP).
153 Hohfeld, *supra* note 34.
154 Wesley N. Hohfeld, *Book Review*, 25 YALE L.J. 166 (1915).
155 *Id.* at 168.
156 *Id.* at 168–70.
157 Wesley N. Hohfeld, A *Vital School of Jurisprudence and Law: Have American Universities Awakened to the Enlarged Opportunities and Responsibility of the Present Day?*, 14 HANDBOOK ASS'N AM. L. SCH. 76 (1914).

continued by Ames.[158] Hohfeld presented his ideas at the 1914 AALS meeting in Chicago, a speaking engagement likely to have been secured on invitation from Bates and Pound who were members of the Executive Committee that year.[159] Incomprehensibly, Hohfeld chose to read the entirety of this very long paper to the multitudes assembled after dinner. The result was, as Corbin put it: "His audience became so restless and inattentive that it was *painful.*"[160]

The piece was a grand plan for a law school consisting of six different scholarly activities – analytic, historical, critical, legislative, functional, and empirical – directed at three different audiences – students who intended to practice law, students who expected to be active citizens but not to practice law, and students who expected to be law professors.[161] It was supposed to be published in the *American Law School Review*, the then equivalent of the *Journal of Legal Education*, as had been previous speeches at the Annual Meeting, but for some unknown reason this was not the case and instead it appeared in the Association's "Proceedings" and so was largely lost to law teachers.[162] However, his colleagues at Yale took the piece to heart and so it permeated a fundraising document that was part of a pre-World War I campaign to increase the Law School's endowment by proposing to turn Yale Law School into the "Yale School of Law and Jurisprudence."[163] As had Hohfeld's piece, the document envisioned offering programs of "professional education," "civic and cultural education" for "non-professional college men," and "scientific and constructive" instruction for "jurists broadly trained for service in many fields of useful and far reaching activity," all of whom would study "law and its evolution, historically, comparatively, analytically and critically, with the purpose of directing its development in the future, improving its administration and perfecting its methods of legislation."[164] Exactly why two of Hohfeld's categories – systematic and legislative jurisprudence – were obscured, is unclear, but in any case, one might say that Hohfeld's ideas had taken over the Law School, given that Corbin asserted that the entire faculty soon adopted the system set forth in the "Fundamental Legal Conceptions."[165]

158 James Bradley Thayer, *The Teaching of English Law at Universities*, 9 HARV. L. REV. 169 (1895); James Barr Ames, *The Vocation of the Law Professor*, 48 U. PA. L. REV. 129 (1900).

159 Hohfeld was to have been on the program with Eugen Ehrlich, a great sociologist of law, who was trapped in Europe, unable to obtain a visa because of the outbreak of World War I. Ehrlich's paper was presented, in paraphrase, by William Herbert Page as *Professor Ehrlich's Czernowitz Seminar of Living Law*, 14 HANDBOOK ASS'N AM. L. SCH. 46 (1914).

160 Corbin, *supra* note 12.

161 This piece is my favorite of Hohfeld's works for its capaciousness of vision. Just think how different law schools would be if every graduate needed to attend to all six varieties of jurisprudence.

162 The presidential address by Joseph Beale, *The Necessity for a Study of the Legal System*, 14 HANDBOOK ASS'N AM. L. SCH. 31 (1914), made it clear why Hohfeld disliked Beale's classes. It is the work of a flabby, but well-meaning, mind.

163 YALE ALUMNI WEEKLY (Mar. 23, 1917) (supp.).

164 SCHLEGEL, *supra* note 4, at 51–52.

165 Corbin, *supra* note 12.

While Corbin and Cook provided much of the social relations that Hohfeld had need of in New Haven, trips to see family and friends in California continued. At first, they took up all summer, but soon they shared time with Summer School teaching at Michigan or just writing.[166] Pound's correspondence with Hohfeld continued, but one has the sense that, after becoming Dean at Harvard in 1916, Pound had less time for such an activity.[167] Still, even that lesser amount tells a lot about what it was to become a law professor, or at least for Hohfeld to do so.

Pound continued to provide counsel, such as urging "practical idealism" in plans at Yale,[168] offering assurance such as knowledge that Woodward did not hold it against Hohfeld that he had supported another candidate for Stanford's deanship[169] or disclosing that the failure of the AALS to quickly publish the "Vital School" piece was not about hostility to Hohfeld, but about some obscure negotiation with the American Bar Association.[170] Pound also complained that Yale was trying to do too many different things,[171] asserted that Columbia was weak because its faculty engaged in too much private practice,[172] thought that its new dean, Harlan Fisk Stone, was moving that school in the right direction,[173] and urged Hohfeld to agree to teach summer school at Michigan because it was important to help Bates move that school to become a modern one.[174] In all of this there is a sense that by coming East to Yale, Hohfeld had earned a right to be somewhat in the know.

Not wholly surprisingly, Hohfeld's end of the correspondence changed little. The flattery directed at Pound continued.[175] Hohfeld complained that the Yale trustees favored the appointment of Yale men,[176] but crowed about his new office,[177] plans for salary increases at Yale,[178] a bequest to the Law School,[179] and his appointment to a named professorship.[180] It is also clear that he was really happier at Yale than at Stanford, as can be seen from comments about Corbin,[181] Cook,[182] Borchard,[183] and

166 Letters from Wesley N. Hohfeld to Roscoe Pound (July 17, 1915), (Sept. 19, 1915), (July 17, 1916) (Aug. 16, 1917) (on file with the RPP).

167 Letter from Roscoe Pound to Wesley N. Hohfeld (Nov. 24, 1916) (on file with the RPP).

168 Letter from Wesley N. Hohfeld to Roscoe Pound (Aug. 4, 1914) (on file with the RPP).

169 Letter from Wesley N. Hohfeld to Roscoe Pound (Oct. 17, 1915) (on file with the RPP).

170 Letters from Roscoe Pound to Wesley N. Hohfeld (Feb. 4, 1915), (Oct. 22, 1915); Letter from Wesley N. Hohfeld to Roscoe Pound (Nov. 24, 1915) (on file with the RPP).

171 Letter from Roscoe Pound to Wesley N. Hohfeld (Feb. 4, 1915) (on file with the RPP).

172 Letter from Roscoe Pound to Wesley N. Hohfeld (July 18, 1916) (on file with the RPP).

173 *Id.*

174 Letter from Roscoe Pound to Wesley N. Hohfeld (Oct. 22, 1915) (on file with the RPP).

175 Letters from Wesley N. Hohfeld to Roscoe Pound (Oct. 17, 1915), (Nov. 6, 1915), (July 17, 1916), (May 20, 1917), (Dec. 3, 1917) (on file with the RPP).

176 Letter from Wesley N. Hohfeld to Roscoe Pound (July 15, 1915) (on file with the RPP).

177 Letters from Wesley N. Hohfeld to Roscoe Pound (Jan. 7, 1915), (Jan. 15, 1915) (on file with the RPP).

178 Letters from Wesley N. Hohfeld to Roscoe Pound (Mar. 15, 1915), (May 20, 1917) (on file with the RPP).

179 Letter from Wesley N. Hohfeld to Roscoe Pound (Nov. 24, 1915) (on file with the RPP).

180 Letter from Wesley N. Hohfeld to Roscoe Pound (June 10, 1915) (on file with the RPP).

181 Letter from Wesley N. Hohfeld to Roscoe Pound (Mar. 15, 1915) (on file with the RPP).

182 Letter from Wesley N. Hohfeld to Roscoe Pound (July 17, 1916) (on file with the RPP).

183 Letter from Wesley N. Hohfeld to Roscoe Pound (Dec. 3, 1917) (on file with the RPP).

Lorenzen,[184] and just a bit more outward looking from comments about Huston[185] and Kales.[186] But there were still cultural limits to his openness.

Hohfeld used an article in the *Yale Law Journal* by Nathan Isaacs, then a professor at the Cincinnati Law School, that began with a discussion about why Pound's assertion that Maine's argument about the move from status to contract did not apply to the United States,[187] to attempt to lure Pound to place a reply in that Journal.[188] Pound brushed off both the solicitation and the article.[189] However, a subsequent piece by Isaacs in the *Harvard Law Review*[190] provided an occasion for Hohfeld again to criticize Isaacs' work.[191] In reply, Pound complained about the quality of Isaac's thought but observed that nevertheless his work should be encouraged because there were so few scholars working in jurisprudence.[192] When Pound inquired about what Isaacs was like,[193] Hohfeld answered that Isaacs' "racial features are very strongly defined."[194]

And then after only three-and-a-half years of teaching at Yale, and before the spring semester of 1918 was to begin, Hohfeld developed a problem with a tooth,[195] most likely bacterial, that led to a streptococcal infection of the

184 *Id.*

185 Letter from Wesley N. Hohfeld to Roscoe Pound (June 10, 1915) (on file with the RPP).

186 Letter from Wesley N. Hohfeld to Roscoe Pound (July 17, 1916) (on file with the RPP).

187 Nathan Isaacs, *Standardizing Contracts*, 27 Yale L.J. 46 (1917).

188 Letter from Wesley N. Hohfeld to Roscoe Pound (Dec. 3, 1917) (on file with the RPP).

189 Letter from Roscoe Pound to Wesley N. Hohfeld (Dec. 8, 1917) (on file with the RPP).

190 Nathan Isaacs, *Schools of Jurisprudence*, 31 Harv. L. Rev. 373 (1918).

191 Letter from Wesley N. Hohfeld to Roscoe Pound (Jan. 21, 1918) (on file with the RPP).

192 Letter from Roscoe Pound to Wesley N. Hohfeld (Jan. 28, 1918) (on file with the RPP).

193 *Id.*

194 Letter from Wesley N. Hohfeld to Roscoe Pound (Apr. 10, 1918) (on file with the RPP). The casual anti-Semitism that is implied by this comment is ubiquitous in Christian social life in these, as well as many earlier and later, years. It could be far more virulent. Fred Konefsky has told me of conversations he and Morty Horwitz had with Harvard Law Librarian, Morris Cohen, at the time when Cohen was editing for publication letters written by Austin Wakeman Scott, long-time Harvard Law Professor, to his parents, as part of a tribute to Scott on his ninetieth birthday. These letters were replete with anti-Semitic remarks. Cohen solved this delicate problem by focusing on the passages about Scott's "studies at the Law School," a choice that took the risk of giving "a somewhat misleading impression of concern only with the law and the Law School." Austin Wakeman Scott, Letters from a Law Student to His Family, 1906–1908, unnumbered introductory page (1974). The original letters are presumably in Scott's papers housed in Special Collections at the Harvard Law Library.

Isaacs' later studied with Pound at Harvard and Pound tried to hire him for that Law School's faculty. Harvard's President, A. Lawrence Lowell, a notorious anti-Semite, refused to acquiesce in the appointment. However, within two years Isaacs was the first Professor of Business Law in Harvard's new Business School. Either the question of who taught in the Business School was unimportant to Lowell or that School's Dean was more persuasive than Pound. *See* Samuel Flaks, *Law, Religion and Pluralism: The Thought and Experiences of Nathan Isaacs (1886–1941)*, 29 Touro L. Rev., 307, 311–13 (2013).

195 Letter from Wesley N. Hohfeld to Roscoe Pound (Apr. 10, 1918) (on file with the RPP). Interestingly Hohfeld's brother attributes the infection to a cold that Hohfeld acquired as a result of the chilly temperature of his office at the Law School, itself a result of coal rationing brought on by the American entry into World War I. *See* Edward Hohfeld, *supra* note 12.

lining of his heart (endocarditis),[196] this at a time when the antibiotics now used to treat this condition were unknown. His mother and brother[197] moved him from a New Haven Hospital to one in New York City where a specialist in this condition practiced.[198] Hohfeld asserted that he was getting better and, in the summer, insisted that he be moved to California to complete his recovery.[199] There he died on October 21, 1918, apparently of kidney failure, a not implausible result of the kind of treatments then administered to fight bacterial infections. He was thirty-nine years old.

Cook loudly lamented Hohfeld's death and publically proclaimed that he would memorialize his passing.[200] However, less than a year after that event, Cook left Yale for Columbia, then three years later returned to Yale where he began to trumpet the ideas of John Dewey, that most "un-Hohfeldian" of thinkers.[201] Hohfeld seems to have understood his fundamental legal relations as a way of more clearly understanding legal doctrine and disciplining legal thought. Dewey, on the other hand, could not have cared less about the clarity of legal doctrine and ignored considerations of discipline in its use. The whole point of his thought was the idea that in law, as in everything else, people reasoned in order to decide something, to deal with some trouble, and that in such circumstances they did not look for rules to govern the case or instance at hand, but for solutions to dispose of the matter to be decided, to fix the trouble. In doing so, people adjusted both the rule they intended to apply and the facts that they chose to draw from the welter of events until the two fit appropriately.

Hohfeld would have thrown up his hands at such an understanding of law that implicitly doubted that there was any such thing as fundamental legal relations. So the job of promoting Hohfeld's analytic system fell to Corbin and Karl Llewellyn, a student of both men.[202] Perhaps that was for the best. Though Cook and Hohfeld shared a serious interest in the Conflict of Laws,[203] that interest may have been all

196 Edward Hohfeld, *supra* note 12.

197 *Id.* It is also interesting that in this biography and in none of Hohfeld's letters is there any reference to Hohfeld's father, though he outlived his son by about 10 months. The three-line death notice of Hohfeld's father in the San Francisco Chronicle mentions neither spouse nor children.

198 Letter from Wesley N. Hohfeld to Roscoe Pound (Apr. 10, 1918) (on file with the RPP).

199 Letter from Wesley N. Hohfeld to Roscoe Pound (June 9, 1918) (on file with the RPP).

200 Letter from Walter Wheeler Cook to Roscoe Pound (Nov. 6, 1918) (on file with the RPP). The resulting piece was Walter Wheeler Cook, *Hohfeld's Contributions to the Science of Law*, 28 YALE L.J. (1919).

201 SCHLEGEL, *supra* note 4, at 59–62.

202 Arthur L. Corbin, *Terminology and Classification in Fundamental Jural Relations*, 4 AM. L. SCH. REV. 607 (1921). Corbin also published a companion piece explaining and applying Hohfeld's terminology for the benefit of law students. *See* Arthur L. Corbin, *Legal Analysis and Terminology*, 29 YALE LJ. 163 (1920). Llewellyn taught Hohfeld's terminology to the students in his course on "Elements of the Law" at both Columbia and Chicago, a practice his third wife, Soia Mentschikoff continued when she taught the course at Chicago.

203 WILLIAM TWINING, KARL LLEWELLYN AND THE REALIST MOVEMENT 416 n.55 (1973) tells a little story designed to show how important Hohfeld's work was to Llewellyn. It is about how after Hohfeld's death Llewellyn decided to steal Hohfeld's notes on the Conflict of Laws and his annotated copy of

they shared, except for a certain wish to conflate salary with professional achievement. This shared misconception can be seen in Cook's later peregrinations where he would regularly brag that he was the highest paid law professor in the country,[204] but always insisted that the reason for his moves was not salary, but rather a search for the place where the most progress in legal education was going to be made.[205] So, the two men's friendship may best be understood as having been built on Hohfeld's need for disciples and Cook's need for fresh ideas, a marriage of convenience formed in a world in which it was hard to build a network.

It is always sad when a good scholar, finally at the point of being able to put it all together, fades and dies, the intellectual project unfinished and, in this case, a possible different understanding of what a law professor's identity might be never completely enacted. This seems to be especially true of Hohfeld, however much his project misunderstands the practice of law, an activity that thrives, indeed depends, on the ambiguity of its concepts and relations, not on the clarity he sought to bring to it. Still, one wonders whether Hohfeld just might have died happier than he would have had he lived longer. He was not a person naturally comfortable in the world. Indeed, given Corbin's description of Hohfeld's behavior, it is fair to say that he was socially maladroit. And the fun Hohfeld made of the work of Bingham's scholarship[206] suggests that he would have been mighty unhappy if such a hypothetical future had unfolded pretty much as it did.

After all, analytic jurisprudence assumed that judicial decision-making was mostly founded in doctrine and that what both judges and lawyers needed to know was how to regularize the judicial action of applying doctrine, how to avoid the misuse of the Fundamental Legal Conceptions. This is precisely the task that Cook undertook in the years around the time of Hohfeld's death,[207] and a large portion of what Cook did for the rest of his life when writing on the Conflict of Laws.[208] But the Realist project that conventionally is taken to have started with Holmes' "Path of the Law" did not assume that judicial decision-making was mostly founded in doctrine and so spoke less to judges and more toward lawyers trying to understand all of the various factors that played a part in judicial, as well as their own, decision-making.

Story's treatise on the subject in order to keep Cook from stealing Hohfeld's ideas. Whether this story is true or not, Llewellyn's unsigned obituary of Hohfeld, makes clear the importance of Hohfeld's work to one of his students. *See* Karl N. Llewellyn, *Wesley Newcomb Hohfeld – Teacher*, 28 YALE L.J. 795 (1919).

204 SCHLEGEL, *supra* note 4, at 53.

205 *Id.* Hohfeld's death, in 1918, at least avoided the possibility of his playing a similar game of hopscotch between jobs as he too sought a higher salary, especially if Cook had bested him at the game.

206 *See supra* note 76 and accompanying text.

207 *See, e.g.*, Walter Wheeler Cook, *The Privileges of Labor Unions in the Struggle for Life*, 27 YALE L.J. 779 (1918); Walter Wheeler Cook, *Boycotts of "Non-Union Materials,"* 27 YALE L.J. 539 (1918); Walter Wheeler Cook, *The Injunction in the Railroad Strike*, 32 YALE L.J. 166 (1922); Walter Wheeler Cook, *Hohfeld's Contributions to the Science of Law*, 28 YALE L.J. 721, 721 (1919).

208 This material is collected in WALTER WHEELER COOK, THE LOGICAL AND LEGAL BASIS OF THE CONFLICT OF LAWS (1942).

For scholars such as Cook, Corbin, and Llewellyn, Hohfeld's categories identified some of the ways that the doctrinal system worked, but mostly they isolated occasions for their puzzling out why judges made the decisions that they did. Hohfeld probably understood the need for such work – after all, he made a place for it in his "Vital School of Jurisprudence and Law" as "functional or dynamic jurisprudence" – but he surely would have been unhappy when a "co-equal" branch of jurisprudence began to take over the law school world to the detriment of his analytical enterprise, especially when the results of that takeover combined a weak version of analytics that goes by the name of critique, a weak version of Realism's emphasis on social context, and a weak version of normative argument to produce the mess we call legal scholarship these days.

Index

CPSIA information can be obtained
at www.ICGtesting.com
Printed in the USA
LVHW050747260723
753383LV00006B/337

9 781107 1928